The BOOK of KNOWLEDGE

THE BOOK OF KNOWLEDGE ANNUAL
1949

The Western Hemisphere

This Book of Knowledge Annual has for a keynote The Western Hemisphere. To be sure, we report the year's events around the globe; but when we come to North and South America we speak also of the governments, the resources, the people, architecture and folklore and other special topics of particular interest. The Western Hemisphere is carrying a heavy responsibility for the world's welfare. Let us learn all we can about our task and ourselves, for knowledge lightens loads.

E. V. McLoughlin, *Editor-in-Chief*

Twenty-one flags stand side by side. Ninth International Conference of American States, Bogotá, Colombia.

WIDE WORLD

THE
BOOK OF KNOWLEDGE
ANNUAL
1949

EDITOR: E. V. McLOUGHLIN

THE GROLIER SOCIETY

NEW YORK • TORONTO

Table of Contents

Editorial Staff

E. V. McLOUGHLIN	EDITOR-IN-CHIEF
KATHARINE LANDON FUGUET	MANAGING EDITOR
LOUISE McDOWELL	INTERNATIONAL EDITOR
LAWRENCE M. LEVIN	ASSOCIATE EDITOR
HELEN HYNSON MERRICK	ASSOCIATE AND COPY EDITOR
JOHN E. SCANLAN	ASSOCIATE EDITOR
MARIAN LOCKWOOD	SCIENCE EDITOR
LEONARD POWER	EDUCATIONAL CONSULTANT
CHARLES CLAY	CONSULTANT FOR CANADA

ART

GLADYS D. CLEWELL	ART DIRECTOR
GLORIA MARIE GRAY	MAKE-UP EDITOR
NAN E. ALLENSWORTH	ARTIST AND ASSISTANT IN MAKE-UP
CATHERINE O'DEA	PICTURE RESEARCH EDITOR
HELEN D. SABBATINO	PICTURE RESEARCH EDITOR

PRODUCTION

HELEN RIEHL HITCHCOCK	PRODUCTION EDITOR
GEORGE MAHLSTEDT	PRODUCTION MANAGER
BRUCE GENTRY	ASSISTANT PRODUCTION MANAGER

Contributors

MARTHA F. ALLEN, A.M. *Camp Fire Girls*
National Director, Camp Fire Girls, Inc.; formerly, Supervisor of Community Relations on the Greenhills Project, Cincinnati, Ohio.

SIR EDWARD V. APPLETON, G.B.E., K.C.B., D.Sc., F.R.S. *Ultrasonics*
Permanent Secretary, Department of Scientific and Industrial Research, Great Britain. He was awarded the Nobel Prize for physics in 1947, in recognition of his great fundamental work, without which world radio-communications would not be as we now know them. Sir Edward is the discoverer of the Appleton Layer.

DAVID W. ARMSTRONG, M.A. *Boys' Clubs of America*
Executive Director, Boys' Clubs of America; writer on subjects of boy guidance and the prevention of juvenile delinquency.

MARGUERITE ASPINWALL *The Forty-niners*
Writer for young people; pen name often used, Marjorie Maxwell. Among her books: The Wind from Spain; Where Is Sylvia?; The Desert Calling; and (by Marjorie Maxwell) Lost Treasure Trail. Also a free-lance writer and editor.

MARIUS BARBEAU *Wandering Myths*
Anthropologist and Folklorist for the Canadian Government, National Museum of Canada; Associate Editor, The Journal of American Folklore; Rhodes Scholar for Quebec, University of Oxford; author of Folk Songs of French Canada; The Kingdom of Saguenay; Quebec, Where Ancient France Lingers, and many other books.

FRANK A. BEACH, M.S., Ph.D. *Monkey Business*
Professor of Psychology, Yale University; author: Hormones and Behavior.

CARLETON BEALS, M.A. *Peru*
Author and lecturer; associated with educational and newspaper work in many countries, particularly in Latin America; Among his many books: The Coming Struggle for Latin America; Dawn Over the Amazon; Lands of the Dawning Morrow: the Awakening from Rio Grande to Cape Horn.

MAY LAMBERTON BECKER *Books of the Year for Boys and Girls*
Editor of Books for Young People and of Reader's Guide for the New York Herald Tribune Weekly Book Review; author and editor. Recent anthology: Home Book of Laughter.

MEYER BERGER *Is There a Story in It?*
Well-known for his colorful reporting for the New York Times; contributor to leading national magazines; author of The Eight Million (stories about New York); and Men of Maryknoll.

MARY F. BISHOP, B.A. *Girl Guides*
Commissioner of Publications, Canadian Council, Girl Guides Association.

SPRUILLE BRADEN, Ph.B., LL.D., D.Eng. *Central American Picture*
Assistant Secretary of State, 1945-47, and United States Representative, with the rank of ambassador, on the Governing Board of the Pan-American Union; Ambassador to Argentina, 1945; Ambassador to Cuba, 1942-45; Ambassador to Colombia, 1939-1942; Honorary Fellow of the University of Buenos Aires, Argentina, 1938. Among his decorations and awards are medals from several South American and Central American countries, and from the United States Government.

LOUIS BROMFIELD, B.A., Litt.D. *Restoring the Land's Lost Riches*
Distinguished American novelist, writer on agriculture, economics, music and many other subjects. The wide range of Mr. Bromfield's achievements is indicated by the honors and awards he has received. A member of the Legion of Honor, he received the Croix de Guerre for his services in World War I. His novel, Early Autumn, won the Pulitzer Prize. Among his non-fiction works are Pleasant Valley; and Malabar Farm.

FRANK BUTLER *Plain of Olympia—1948*
Sports columnist of the London Daily Express. Mr. Butler has been to America several times to report Joe Louis fights and has been in most parts of Europe covering big sporting events.

JAMES LIPPITT CLARK, D.Sc. *Expedition from Nairobi*
Director of Preparation and Installation of the American Museum of Natural History; a distinguished sculptor of animals; avocations: writing, hunting and big-game photography; author of Trails of the Hunted; leader of the museum's 1948 Central African Expedition, which he tells us about in his article in this volume.

LLOYD CLARKE *Australia during the Year*
Deputy Director, Australian News and Information Bureau, New York; contributor to magazines in Australia, England and the United States.

CHARLES CLAY, A.B. *Canada—A Record of the Year; Helicopters in Canada*
Novelist and free-lance journalist; Director, Canadian Research and Editorial Institute. His books include Fur Trade Apprentice; Phantom Fur Thieves; Young Voyageur; Muskrat Man.

MORRILL CODY, A.B. *Paraguay*
Chief, American Republics Branch, Public Affairs Program Staff, Department of State; author and contributor to many magazines. During the past seven years, Mr. Cody has been in Latin America as Cultural Attaché of the United States Embassy in Asunción, Paraguay; Buenos Aires, Argentina; and Mexico City.

JAMES G. CONZELMAN, M.Sc. *Professional Sports*
Vice-President and Coach, Chicago Cardinals Football Club. A contributor to The Saturday Evening Post and Cosmopolitan Magazine.

LEE S. CRANDALL *Pets: Our Friends from the Wild*
General Curator, New York Zoological Park. Author of Paradise Quest, and Pets and How to Care for Them.

C. H. CURRAN, D.Sc., M.A., B.S.A. *Insects in Flight*
Curator, Department of Insects and Spiders, American Museum of Natural History. Author of Insects of the Pacific World; Families and Genera of North American Diptera.

MAC V. EDDS, Jr., Ph.D. *Discoveries in Biology and Medicine*
Assistant Professor of Biology, Brown University.

H. R. EKINS *Asia: Tempest in the East*
Director, The Citizens Foundation, Syracuse, New York; author of China Fights for Her Life. For a number of years he was foreign correspondent and editor with the United Press in Asia.

WAYNE M. FAUNCE, Sc.B. *Bimini—Scientists' Paradise*
Vice-Director and Executive Secretary, The American Museum of Natural History; Fellow of the New York Academy of Sciences.

BOB FELLER *Pitching Thrills*
Member, Cleveland Indians Baseball Club, which he joined at the age of seventeen; author of How to Pitch, and Strikeout Story.

E. S. FERGUSON, Ph.B.   *The Middle East during the Year*
Head, Research Department, E. F. Hutton and Company; formerly
Deputy Administrator General of the Finances for Iran.

RICHARD FINNIE   *Pipeline in Arabia; The Northwest Territories*
After specializing in exploring and filming northern Canada, where he was
born, Mr. Finnie turned to the Middle East; in 1947-48 he was official
historian of the Trans-Arabian Pipe Line Project; writer and lecturer;
author of Lure of the North; Canada Moves North; Canol.

KATHARINE LANDON FUGUET, A.B.   *Lighthouses; The Story of*
Staff Editor, The Book of Knowledge.   *Harry S. Truman*

RALPH FULGHUM, B.S.A.   *A 4-H Club Member Lives Here*
Assistant Chief, Division of Extension Information, Extension Service,
United States Department of Agriculture; formerly in charge of informa-
tion for Soil Conservation Service in seven southeastern states.

RALPH HANCOCK   *Mexico Today*
Author, editor, lecturer, authority on Latin America; among his books are
Opportunities in Latin America; The Rainbow Republics; Our Southern
Neighbors; America's Southern Neighbors; The Magic Land: Mexico.

EARL PARKER HANSON   *Colonization: New Worlds in the Americas*
Editor-in-Chief of the New World Guides to the Latin American Republics; author of New Worlds Emerging, scheduled for publication in the
spring of 1949; Research Professor of Geography, University of Delaware.

HALLDÓR HERMANNSSON, Ph.D.   *Iceland: Island of Frost and Fire*
Professor Emeritus of the Scandinavian Languages and Literatures, Cornell University; Curator of the Fiske Icelandic Collection at Cornell, the
largest Icelandic library in America. A native of Iceland, Dr. Hermannsson
has written more than thirty volumes on Icelandic subjects.

JOHN TASKER HOWARD, A.M.   *Musical Events*
Composer of songs, choral music, orchestral and other works. His books
include Our American Music; The World's Great Operas; This Modern
Music; and he has written many articles on musical subjects.

FRANK LEUER KELLER, Ph.D.   *What Happened in South America*
Assistant Professor of Latin American Geography, Rutgers University;
now engaged in geographic research on the Andes. During the war, Lieutenant Colonel and Assistant Military Attaché, La Paz, Bolivia; also
Chief, Central American Section, Military Intelligence Service.

FRANCIS PARKINSON KEYES, Litt.D.   *Happy Experiences of a*
                                              Doll Collector
Mrs. Keyes, whose many books are widely read, has done a great deal of
traveling in far places, where she found many of the dolls in her famous
collection. Author, poet, editor, magazine writer; her novels include Honor
Bright; Fielding's Folly; The River Road; Came a Cavalier; and (published in 1948) Dinner at Antoine's.

DAVID A. KEYS, Ph.D., D.Sc., F.R.S.C.   *Atomic Energy: Servant of Industry*
Vice-President (Scientific) of the National Research Council, Canada.

ALEXANDER LACEY, A.M., Ph.D.   *Newfoundland: Villages by the Sea*
Professor of French, Victoria College, Toronto; author of Basic Written
French, and of Pixérecourt and the French Romantic Drama.

LAWRENCE M. LEVIN, Ph.D.   *Governments of the Western Hemisphere;*
                          The United States; The Year in Europe
Author and translator; Managing Editor, The Book of Science; Assistant
Editor, The Book of Knowledge.

WILLY LEY *Aviation Advances; Guided Missiles*
Research Engineer, Washington Institute of Technology, Inc.; author of Rockets and Space Travel, fifth printing, 1948.

ILSE LICHTENSTADTER, Ph.D., D. Phil. Oxon. *Palestine*
Associate Professor of Arabic and Islamic Culture at the Asia Institute, New York City; author of books and articles on Arabic literature, history and folklore, and of minority and other problems in Islam.

TRYGVE LIE, LL.D. *The United Nations and World Welfare*
Secretary-General of the United Nations. Born in Oslo, Norway; graduate of Oslo University Law School.

MARIAN LOCKWOOD *Robert E. Peary, Explorer*
Science writer and lecturer; Associate Editor, The Book of Science; Managing Editor, The Story of Our Time; formerly Associate and Acting Curator of the Hayden Planetarium.

WILLEM J. LUYTEN, Ph.D. *Astronomy during the Year*
Professor of Astronomy, University of Minnesota; author of The Pageant of the Stars; has observed eclipses in Mexico, Lapland and Russia, and has observed at Cordoba, Argentina.

ROY K. MARSHALL, Ph.D. *Astronomy: Star Families*
Director, Fels Planetarium of the Franklin Institute; Science Editor of the Philadelphia Evening Bulletin; at present, producer and performer of a sponsored series of television broadcasts, NBC, on The Nature of Things, devoted to elementary science.

E. C. McDOWELL, E.E., M.E. *Industry's Seven-League Boots*
Consulting engineer, writer and contributor to The Encyclopedia Americana, The Book of Knowledge and other publications.

LOUISE McDOWELL *Place Names; Toronto*
Staff Editor, The Book of Knowledge.

HELEN HYNSON MERRICK *Gold Yarn and Sackcloth; Events of the Year*
Staff and Copy Editor, The Book of Knowledge; Associate and Copy Editor, The Book of Knowledge Annual; Associate Editor, The Story of Our Time.

ALFRED METRAUX, Ph.D. *Indians of South America; The Guianas*
Consultant sociologist, UNESCO, Paris; in charge of the UNESCO project in fundamental education in Haiti; founder of the Institute of Ethnology of the University of Tucuman, in the Argentine, and formerly its director; author of The Ethnology of Easter Island, and La civilisation matérielle des tribus Tupi-Guarani.

CLAIRE H. NEIKIND, B.A., M.S. *The Union of South Africa*
Free-lance journalist; contributor to leading magazines including The New Republic, Collier's and Coronet. Winner of Pulitzer Traveling Scholarship from Columbia University.

JOHN J. O'NEILL *Protein, the Builder*
Science Editor, The New York Herald Tribune; popularizer and interpreter of scientific research.

SAMUEL RALPH POWERS *Physics Advances*
Professor of Natural Sciences and Head of Department of Teaching of Natural Science, Teachers College, Columbia University.

ERWIN RAISZ, Ph.D. *Maps and New Inventions*
Lecturer in Cartography, Institute of Geographical Exploration, Harvard University; author of Atlas of Global Geography; General Cartography; Atlas of Cuba (in publication).

xi

ARTHUR F. RAPER, Ph.D. *Co-author, Deep South*
Social Scientist, Bureau of Agricultural Economics, Washington, D. C.; author of Tenants of the Almighty; co-author of Sharecroppers All.

MARTHA J. RAPER, A.B. *Co-author, Deep South*
A graduate of Randolph-Macon Woman's College, Mrs. Raper writes that she is a lover of the South, especially the rural and the Negro South.

CONSTANCE MORGAN RITTENHOUSE *Girl Scouts*
National Director, Girl Scouts of the United States of America; advocate of the citizenship training program in Girl Scouting.

HUBBELL ROBINSON, Jr., A.B. *Radio and Television Programming*
Vice-President and Director of Programs, Columbia Broadcasting System. During recent years he has been in charge of the production of such radio shows as Burns and Allen; Aldrich Family; and March of Time.

NORMAN ROCKWELL *Career as an Illustrator*
One of the best-known illustrators in the world and one of the best-loved. Painter of magazine covers and illustrations. Among his most famous works are the four paintings known as The Four Freedoms.

FINN RONNE, Commander, U.S.N.R., M.E. *Antarctic Adventure*
Leader of the Ronne Antarctic Research Expedition, 1946-1948; lecturer, author and consultant; holder of two Congressional medals; author of Antarctic Conquest, and a contributor to periodicals and reference books.

MELVIN ROSENBAUM *Furnace in the Earth*
Science writer and editor; formerly Associate Editor of The Book of Science and of The Story of Our Time.

GEORGE H. SAUER *T or Single Wing?*
Head Football Coach, United States Naval Academy; formerly Head Coach, Kansas University, where he led his squad to the co-championship of the Big Six two straight years and received an invitation to the Orange Bowl New Year's Day 1948.

JOHN E. SCANLAN *Automobiles; Fuel: More Power to You!*
Associate Editor, The Book of Knowledge Annual.

VINCENT J. SCHAEFER, D.Sc. *Spelunking*
Research Chemist, The General Electric Company; active in weather research concerned with cloud-seeding and the natural development of storms. Hobbies: mountain-climbing, skiing and exploring caves.

ARTHUR A. SCHUCK *Boy Scouts of America*
Chief Scout Executive, Boy Scouts of America; active in Scouting for more than thirty-five years, both as a volunteer and as a professional leader; co-author, Financing Social Work.

DOROTHY SHAVER, LL.D. *Careers in a Great Store*
President of Lord & Taylor.

R. H. SIMPSON, M.S. *Looking Down on a Hurricane!*
Official in Charge, U. S. Weather Bureau, Honolulu, T. H. Mr. Simpson has been a teacher of meteorology at the University of Chicago; Hurricane Forecaster at Miami, Florida; and Special Assistant to the Assistant Chief of the Bureau at Washington. He is now in charge of all Weather Bureau projects in the Pacific area.

MAJOR GENERAL D. C. SPRY, C.B.E., D.S.O. *Boy Scouts of Canada*
Chief Executive Commissioner of the Canadian General Council of the Boy Scouts Association. The youngest Major General in the British Commonwealth, he was appointed Vice-Chief of the General Staff of the Canadian Army in 1946, resigning to become head of the Boy Scouts.

IRENE M. SPRY, M.A. CANTAB., M.A. BRYN MAWR. *Inland Waterways*
Mrs. Spry has taught in the Department of Political Science and Economics of the University of Toronto.

VILHJALMUR STEFANSSON, Ph.D., LL.D., L.H.D. *Greenland*
Arctic explorer, whose contributions to scientific knowledge have won him many honors; author and editor. Among his many books are Greenland; Iceland, the First American Republic; Arctic Manual.

ROY STRYKER, A.B. *Careers in Industrial Photography*
Director of the Photographic Division of the Standard Oil Company of New Jersey.

WILLIAM H. TAYLOR *Break Out Your Mains'l!*
Associate Editor of Yachting, and contributor to Holiday, Sport, and various sailing magazines. Mr. Taylor was formerly a newspaper reporter and feature writer. He received the Pulitzer Prize for reporting for 1934.

ROBERT L. THOMPSON, Ed.D. *Leathercraft*
Assistant Professor of Education, School of Education, New York University. Dr. Thompson's special field of interest is interpreting our technological society to children through shop and craft activities. He is the author of Leathercraft, and co-author of Home Mechanic's Handbook, and Home Crafts Handbook.

ROGER VERNAM, illustrator *Place Names*
Author and illustrator of Drawing People for Fun; illustrator of Eight Little Indians; Monkey Shines; White Buffalo, and other books.

LEO WALDMAN, B.S. *Sports Review*
A former newspaper sports reporter, he has been writing about sports events for the last seventeen years. His article in this Book of Knowledge Annual, courtesy of A. G. Spalding and Brothers, Inc.

GERALD WENDT, Ph.D. *Chemistry during the Year*
Editorial Director, Science Illustrated. Formerly professor at the University of Chicago and Dean at the Pennsylvania State College.

CARL E. WIDEBERG, B.S., C.E. *Long Distance, Please!*
General Traffic Manager, Long Lines Department, American Telephone & Telegraph Company. Mr. Wideberg is a graduate of Alabama Polytechnic Institute and served in the U. S. Army in World War I.

FRANK ZAIC *A Model Airplane*
Editor-Publisher: Model Aeronautic Publications. He is the author of Model Aeronautics Year Books, and Model Glider Design.

The Editors gratefully acknowledge assistance and advice received from:

WILLIAM C. ACKERMAN, Columbia Broadcasting System
HARRY AMTMANN, A. G. Spalding & Brothers, Inc.
JEAN CHRISTGAU, Information Division, French Embassy
H. T. COLEMAN, Canadian Pacific Railway
MARGUERITE COONEY, The Grace Line
HELEN CORNTHWAITE, British Information Services
MARION GREENWOOD, Canadian Government Information Services
DOUGLAS HOUCHENS, Netherlands Information Bureau
REA LUBAR, Lord & Taylor
MRS. LAWRENCE MAXWELL, Public Information Division, Girl Scouts of America
FRANCES ORKIN, United Nations Press Information Bureau
ELLIOT M. SANGER, Promotion Department, New York Times
MARION SECUNDA, Camp Fire Girls
RITA STOCK, Australian News and Information Service
ANN McCUTCHEON, Standard Oil Company of New Jersey
RICHMOND B. WILLIAMS, American Telephone and Telegraph Company

RESTORING THE LAND'S

AGRICULTURE today is an immensely complex business and profession. It includes the growing of vegetables for people to eat, the cultivation of vast seas of wheat, the feeding and breeding of enormous herds of beef and dairy cattle, sheep, hogs, chickens and other animals and birds that provide food high in vitamin content, besides the growing of flax, corn, cotton, soybeans and other crops to be made into clothes, furniture and a world of other articles.

The good farmer has to know about more things than does any other man in our modern society. He has to be something of a chemist, a botanist, a biologist, a veterinarian, a mechanic. Above all he has to have an instinct and an immense knowledge about soil, weather, animals and plants. The good farmer, in our time, is part business man,

LOST RICHES

By Louis Bromfield
Agricultural Expert and Novelist

part scientist and part specialist in the fields to which he is devoting his time, his money and his energy.

Food has been the first concern of man since the beginning of time. The cave-man spent the greater part of his existence hunting and killing in order to eat. The primitive shepherds and their families lived off the herds of sheep and goats they tended, and were clothed by them as well. Even their tents were woven from the fleece or hair of their flocks. Later on, as great cities grew up, food became the cause of wars and revolutions. Food and the land on which to grow it are still among the chief causes of war in our modern world.

The growth of knowledge and skills in agriculture, over the long centuries since the first cave-man scratched the soil with a stick, has been slow and arduous. The cultivation

The seventeenth-century farmer plowed and cultivated his fields without the help of machinery.

Old and new ways of threshing grain. Primitive methods are still used by farmers in the Orient.

of the earth varies greatly according to soil, climate and even social customs. Some farms scattered over the world are plagued by drought, and can not be made to produce crops regularly unless water is brought by irrigation to the thirsty ground. Other farms, in wet climates, are plagued by too much rainfall, and must develop ways of carrying off the excess water quickly, before it drowns out the crops and livestock. Vast areas, such as are found in parts of Canada and Siberia, are adapted—generally speaking—only to wheat production because of the long, cold winters and short summers. Some lands that are short of rainfall, but grow grass rich in minerals, are valuable only for grazing be-

cause there is no means of bringing water to them. Even in a single one of the forty-eight states, climates, soils and conditions may vary so greatly that several different kinds of agriculture can be carried on in a comparatively small area.

The basic principles of irrigation and of drainage were worked out centuries ago by civilized and agricultural peoples. The fantastic and complex terraces of Java and the Philippines and Japan, where rice is grown in pools of water on steep mountain sides, represents the magnificent engineering skill of peoples who lived as long as two thousand years ago. On the other side of the world, in the Andes, the Incas also developed a system of terraces for the purpose of growing food crops on the steep mountain slopes without the washing away of the soil. The idea of drainage by ditching to draw off surplus water is just as old. The ancient Egyptians used wheels equipped with buckets to raise water from the Nile to irrigate their fields. Rich as the soil was, without water it would have produced nothing.

Many of Our Modern Farming Methods Were Known in Ancient Times

Ancient man knew all of these things—indeed, he invented them—but such primitive ditches and terraces are a long way removed from the immense dams, drainage and flood-control systems that have been developed and built in our own day. The huge Grand Coulee Dam in the northwestern United States, the great "barrages" of India and Egypt, the vast flood-control projects of the Tennessee Valley—all have been developed largely to help agriculture and to make it possible to raise more and more food.

Far removed, too, from the crude plows, hoes and carts of an earlier agriculture, is our magnificent modern farm machinery. The use of machinery on farms has increased production, cut labor costs and done away with drudgery. It has brought about the quick and efficient cultivation of fields and the rapid and economical harvesting of food. By comparison with the past, modern agriculture is not only a profession, but also a great industry—perhaps the most important one existing in the world today. In such countries as the United States and Canada, more than 50 per cent of the people get their incomes from the growing and processing of food, or from the manufacture and distribution of farm machinery, of gas, oil, steel fencing, rubber tires and so on, which are employed in agriculture.

Primitive Farmers Knew Nothing of Soil Chemistry

Primitive man and the men of earlier civilizations knew much that we know today about agriculture. In some times and places they developed fairly efficient systems of agriculture. They knew little, however, of the complex processes that take place in soils that are rich and highly productive. The farmers of the past would adopt a certain method because it worked and produced considerable yields of food. They did not, how-

ever, understand the rules of physics, of chemistry, of biochemistry and all the other sciences in agriculture, which produce abundant and therefore cheap food. They knew that certain practices worked, but they did not know how or why they worked.

It is probable that more has been discovered in the past generation about the actual workings of the soil, of animal husbandry and many other branches of agriculture, than in all the world's history. We have discovered the reasons *why* the agricultural practices of earlier tribes, nations and civilizations were sound. We have even discovered that many traditional sayings and practices embedded in ancient folklore were not superstitions but had—and have—an actual basis in science. These discoveries are of importance, since they have made it possible to convert poor or wornout farm lands into productive lands, and so raise more food for a half-starving world. We have even learned how to produce good crops in areas where there is not enough rainfall and not enough water to make irrigation possible.

Improved Ways of Farming Bring Life Back to the Dust Bowl

The best example of the good practices developed by modern agriculture is the checking of the Dust Bowl in the great plains of the United States and Canada. The Dust Bowl was one of the great tragedies of recent years in North America. In this vast grazing and wheat-growing region, during a dry period in the 1930's, millions of acres of good topsoil began being blown away. Across the continent and far out into the Atlantic Ocean this soil was carried in the form of dust. Within the Dust Bowl itself, the dust was so thick that daytime was as dark as night, and lights were kept burning around the clock in the farm houses and towns. In certain areas whole farms of great value literally blew away, and the farm families were forced to abandon them and go elsewhere to live. The losses in farm lands and food production totaled many hundred millions of dollars.

The Dust Bowl storms, we now know, were neither natural nor inevitable. They were the result of bad and wasteful agricultural methods, and of the overgrazing of livestock. Overgrazing kills the covering sods that hold the soil in place.

Grim necessity brought about a revolution in agricultural methods. Under the old methods that caused the dust storms, the straw left from the wheat was not returned to the earth, but was burned. The soil was turned over by the conventional moldboard plow and left unanchored by any organic material, such as roots, straw or even weeds. It had no protection from the strong winds and the hot sun of the Great Plains region. The result was that much of the scant rainfall ran off to form gullies instead of sinking into the soil. What rainfall the earth did drink up in these semi-arid regions was quickly evaporated by wind and sun, causing poor crop yields and, eventually, storms of dust.

Straw, Roots and Trash Protect Soil from Wind and Water

Today, in the same areas, the straw is no longer burned. It is incorporated in the soil by discing, or by the use of the new implement which rips up the earth without turning it over. In this way the straw, roots and other rubbish are left on the surface to bind the soil, mulch it against evaporation by wind and sun and break the velocity of the hot winds. Trash of this sort, left on the surface of the vast wheat fields, can make a sixty-mile-an-hour wind slow down to eight miles an hour on the ground. Mixing the straw, weeds and trash *into* the upper layer of the soil also leaves it open and loose, so that it can receive and absorb practically 100 per cent of the scanty rainfall, just as a sponge absorbs water. It also tends to slow evaporation both by wind and sun, so that today an eleven-inch rainfall can benefit the crops as much as a fifteen-inch rainfall under the old methods and conditions.

Since this revolution in agricultural methods there have been no dust storms and no crop failures in the Great Plains region. Since 1940 there have been only bumper crops, year after year, where, in the past, the three-year record was likely to be one good crop, one half-crop and one complete failure. There are, however, still greedy cattle and sheep men who overgraze, and during this era of high prices there are some wheat producers who are not sound or permanent agriculturists at all, but greedy, careless soil-gamblers. They are looked upon with contempt by the sound farmers, who call them Suitcase Farmers.

Although the Dust Bowl storms in the past were a great menace, not only to the region itself, but also to the country as a whole, there was, and still is, a much greater problem. This is the erosion of the soil, not by wind, but by water, and this problem affects the agriculture of the whole country.

It can be said with truth that no nation in the world has ever wasted and destroyed its vast natural resources so rapidly as has the United States. Within the space of a century and a half, ignorance, poor agricultural

This arrangement of buckets, called a shadoof, was used to water the fields in ancient Egypt.

methods and greed have destroyed most of the forests and one quarter of the good agricultural land of the nation. Another 50 per cent of the land has been very seriously damaged. Its low production per acre costs hundreds of millions of dollars each year in high prices for food and in taxes to support the agriculture of these areas. Greedy farming which takes everything out of the soil and puts nothing back is partly to blame, but the real demon of destruction has been the wasting away of the valuable topsoil which is the foundation of fertility.

Dr. Hugh Bennett, of the United States Soil Conservation Service, estimates that the topsoil that is lost each year from the surface of the once fabulously rich United States would fill a train of coal cars encircling the earth four times at the equator. To put it in another way, the topsoil of a forty-acre farm flows down the Mississippi past a given point every minute of the day. Such a rate of destruction can only mean disaster for the nation in terms of taxes, high prices and, eventually, of food itself. The periodical famines of Asia have been largely caused by the same process of destruction, although in Asia the rate of destruction has been much less rapid

United States and Canada—among them China, India, Palestine, South Africa, Australia and Venezuela. All of these nations have asked for and been given aid by the experts of the United States Soil Conservation Service.

Terracing means that long, flat terraces, or shelves, are constructed upon level lines, one above the other, on long sloping hillsides.

Grand Coulee Dam, which has been called the biggest man-made thing on earth, will eventually provide irrigation for more than a million acres of fertile, but dry, farmland.

than in the United States.

During the past century, however, a new system—or combination of systems—of agriculture has been worked out which is especially suited to American climates and soils. In this system one of the chief objectives has been to stop the terrible destruction of productive land through erosion by wind and water.

Both the Canadian and American governments have taken steps to restore and maintain the threatened land. Among the methods which have been adopted are the terracing of sloping land, contour agriculture, strip cropping, and the increased use of grass farming. Not all readers may know what these terms mean. They are of tremendous importance, because these methods are of value to many other nations besides the

These tend to check and hold runoff water, and prevent the tragic and destructive gullying that has ruined millions of acres of good farm land by carrying the soil down the streams and rivers into the ocean.

Contour agriculture means the plowing and planting of row crops, such as corn and cotton, around the hills and slopes instead of up and down them. This means that very nearly every row is on the level, so that the rain remains where it falls and sinks into the ground instead of running rapidly down the slope, carving out gullies.

Strip cropping is a system of planting hillsides with first a strip of open row crops, then a strip of grass, then another strip of crops, and so on. When this is done, any water or topsoil that tends to run off the crop strips is captured and absorbed by the sod of the grass strips. In this way it remains on the farm itself, instead of being washed off and carried off down the water courses into the sea.

Grass farming means more and more production of food by means of high-quality, high-yielding grass and legume forage—various kinds of clover, alfalfa, soybeans, etc. When a farm, however hilly, is covered with heavy grass sod, no erosion and very little water loss can take place. The stems and roots of the grass soak up the water and anchor the soil. Also it is possible by grass farming to produce a greater abundance of high-protein foods, such as livestock and dairy products, at a lower cost to the public and with much less labor.

Where the Rainfall Is Too Heavy the Land Must Be Drained

A great deal of progress has recently been made in areas where the rainfall is too heavy at certain seasons. Such areas include the states of the Deep South and the Texas coast of the Gulf of Mexico. There, in order to maintain any agriculture at all, or any really profitable cattle-grazing, it is necessary to drain the excess water rapidly off the land. In Florida, especially in the Everglades section, the heavy black soils are made up mostly of nitrogen, carbon and water, and do not contain nearly enough of the minerals that are especially necessary to health and vigor in plants, animals and people. By adding to these soils the minerals which they lack, the farmers have been able to build up a highly productive and profitable agriculture, combining the raising of vegetables and grazing of cattle.

The science of hydroponics has been the object of much research for some years. This deals with a specialized form of agriculture by which plants are grown in water which has been saturated with a combination of the minerals necessary for healthy growth. Up to the present, however, hydroponics has not been able to offer any really practical contribution toward increasing the desperately short supply of food in the world. For one thing, it is a costly operation.

In modern agriculture, more and more attention is being paid to growing food which is high in quality of mineral and vitamin nutrition, as well as in quantity. The medical profession has come to recognize the truth of the saying, "we are what we eat." Plants,

animals and people that grow up on wornout or poor soils become likewise deficient in health and vigor. In the case of people, intelligence, ambition and capability are apt to be handicapped by these deficiencies in the food they eat and the soil on which it grows. This knowledge, together with the understanding of the principles of what makes good, productive and living soil, marks the most notable advance that agriculture has made in many centuries.

It Is Not Too Late to Restore the Wornout Soil

Lately there have been published many books and articles of a more or less sensational nature, which paint pictures of despair with regard to food and the future of the world. While the food situation is undeniably serious, it is by no means so black as painted by certain authors. The scientific advances made in the field of agriculture have made it possible today to restore vast areas of land which were once thought to be worn out. They have also made it possible to improve land that was poor to begin with. If the farmers take full advantage of this increased knowledge, and practice better agriculture, the areas under cultivation in the United States alone could easily produce from three to five times as much food as is now being raised on the same areas.

The Position of the Farmer Today Is More Important Than Ever

Besides the great scientific advances, the profession of agriculture has benefited in other ways. Machinery has done away with the age-old drudgery of farming. Larger incomes have been achieved, not through high prices, but through sound and scientific production. Moreover, the profession of farmer, or livestock man or horticulturist has become not only better paid, but also greater in dignity. As one writer has put it, the place of the yacht and the Newport palace built by the rich man has in our time been taken by big, well-managed farms and fine herds of registered cattle. Farming has in many ways become fashionable. Today agriculture offers the young person as fine opportunities as any other profession, both in the sense of distinction as well as in the economic return for his brains and his energy. Never in the history of the world has the farmer held a position of greater importance than he does today.

ANTARCTIC ADVENTURE

THE STORY OF THE RONNE ANTARCTIC RESEARCH EXPEDITION

By COMMANDER FINN RONNE

WE set out for Antarctica from Beaumont, Texas, and sailed southward for 7,000 miles. Our ship, the Port of Beaumont, was a 1,200-ton, Diesel-driven vessel with a sturdy wooden hull. During the war, when the Navy used her as an ocean-going tug, she had carried a crew of about 60 men. Our full expedition consisted of 21 men and 2 women. For our 15-month adventure we took along 42 Husky dogs, 3 airplanes, 2 snowmobiles and many tons of other equipment and supplies.

Most of us were anything but trained seamen. Scientists, pilots, mechanics, photographers and the doctor had to stand wheelwatch (steering the ship) and engine-room watch when the ship was steaming to and from the Antarctic. They were on duty 4 hours and free 8 hours, on duty 4 hours and free 8 hours, and so on. In the hours off duty they usually had deck work to do and also had to take care of 42 hungry Huskies.

Our voyage took us down to the Panama

Mrs. Finn Ronne and a member of the expedition standing in front of the frozen-in vessel.

Canal and through it, and along the west coast of South America to Punta Arenas, Chile, which is the southernmost city in the world. From there we sailed across dangerous, uncharted waters to Antarctica. It was January 25, 1947 when we left Texas, and March 12 when we reached our main base in Marguerite Bay, Palmer Peninsula.

As we approached our goal we encountered the fields of pack ice which are ever present in Antarctic waters, and the iron-shod bow of the Port of Beaumont forced a path through. In this rugged, mountainous country great crevasse-filled glaciers flow slowly down the mountain passes to the sea. From time to time, huge chunks that we call icebergs break off into the water and drift aimlessly away. Other tremendous icebergs, almost as flat as the top of a table, break off from the edges of the shelf ice that forms along the shore and stretches out into the water. Some of these shelf-ice and glacier-formed bergs are as wide as a city block and as large as a ten-story office building. When we passed near one, we could see the wonderfully intricate arches carved in the floating ice by the constant wash and pounding of rough seas. It was an unforgettable sight.

We drew in to Marguerite Bay in the full splendor of a typical Antarctic sunset. The high, partly snow-covered mountains surrounding the bay were bathed in glowing color. The rose, green and dark purple radiance of the setting sun danced over water, snow and ice. We felt that this awe-inspiring scene was surely the eighth wonder of the world. I had been to Antarctica twice before and so I was among the few members of the expedition who realized the many dangers that lurked behind this unbelievable beauty.

We made our main base on Stonington Island in Marguerite Bay, and anchored our ship about a third of a mile away, not far from a glacier two hundred feet high. The Port of Beaumont was the first motor vessel ever to be intentionally frozen in, in Antarctic waters, and it was with mixed feelings that we watched the ice forming around her. Except by radio, we would have no more contact with the civilized world for a year! The ship's machinery and deck gear had been prepared for the long freeze-in, and soon we were able to ski over the ice between the ship and our base. By this time we had made the camp buildings ready and moved most of the supplies and equipment ashore.

Penguins gather around to inspect and discuss the strange creatures who have invaded their land.

ALL PHOTOS IN THIS ARTICLE, RONNE ANTARCTIC RESEARCH EXPEDITION

Now our scientists began to set up their delicate recording instruments in the Science Building or in small, specially constructed shacks. During the following year they carried on investigations in geology, meteorology, seismology, solar radiation, and made atmospheric refraction measurements, cosmic-ray recordings, and magnetic and tidal observations.

The Antarctic winter night occurs while it is summer in the Northern Hemisphere. It is a time of twilight and darkness, and with it came our most wretched weather and strongest windstorms. We did most of our work indoors, making plans and preparations for the field season that would begin on the return of the sun. For entertainment we had a well-stocked library and we enjoyed motion pictures three times a week in our Penguin Theater.

On cold, clear nights there was moonlight skiing on the glacier near camp, under stars as numerous and brilliant as any I have ever seen. The mountains surrounding our base were spectacularly beautiful, and the silence was broken only by the howls of our Huskies in the distance. Such occasions, rare though they were, are among our most outstanding memories of Antarctica.

In September, with the Rising of the Sun, Spring Comes to Antarctica

In September, with the coming of spring and the gradual return of the sun, field operations began. At one time or another almost everyone on the expedition had some field experience.

We had two sledge parties with their teams of Huskies. One party was purely geological. It was out in the field for three and a half months and obtained much valuable data and a large collection of geological specimens. The other dog-team party was geographical. It surveyed the unknown territory over which our planes took aerial photographs. With three teams of nine dogs each to carry food and necessary equipment, this party covered almost twelve hundred miles on skis and was able to push two hundred miles farther south in this sector than human foot had ever trod before.

Our flying program was governed by the weather, which, in fact, was so important to us that men camped in tents on the icy surfaces miles away from the main base in order to maintain two separate weather stations.

The members of the expedition found plenty of opportunities to catch up on their mending.

We had a twin-engine Beechcraft, a single engine Norseman and a small Stinson L-5. They flew a total of 346 hours in the air, which is a good bit more than any other Antarctic expedition had been able to fly. A total of about 250,000 square miles was seen for the first time, and many thousands of aerial photographs were taken for use later in making maps. The last major coastline in the world was discovered; and we were able to prove that the Antarctic is one continent instead of being divided by a frozen body of water, as some had believed possible.

When our chief explorations were over and everyone was back safe at the main base, the men used to sit around the dinner table in the evening and swap stories about events that had happened while they were in the field. The most dramatic incident of the entire expedition, however, did not take place on any of the long field trips with the dog-teams or on any of the flights in the planes. It occurred during the long winter night, just nine miles away from our base.

In the dark, bitter cold of July, I took a dog-team party up to Mile High Plateau, seventeen miles east of our camp, to establish a weather station. On the way, I reviewed instructions to the men in the method of traveling on skis through crevasse-filled terrain. We also went over the safety precautions that must be observed at all times.

We reached the top and established the camp. Then, for five days, we were marooned

EXPEDITION MEMBERS	SPECIAL DUTY ON SHIP

COMDR. FINN RONNE, U.S.N.R., *Expedition Leader*
MRS. FINN RONNE, *Recorder*
COMDR. ISAAC SCHLOSSBACH, U.S.N. (Ret.), *Second in Command
and Skipper of Ship*....................................Bridge
DR. ROBERT L. NICHOLS, *Geologist and Senior Scientist*....................Steering ship
H. C. PETERSON, *Physicist*....................................Steering ship
ANDREW A. THOMPSON, *Geophysicist*....................................Engine room
WILLIAM LATADY, *Aerial Photographer*....................................Engine room
CAPTAIN JAMES W. LASSITER, *Pilot,* on active duty from U. S.
Air Force with expedition....................................Steering ship
LIEUTENANT CHARLES J. ADAMS, *Pilot,* on active duty from
U. S. Air Force with expedition....................................2nd Asst. Engineer
HARRY DARLINGTON, *Aviation Pilot,* and MRS. HARRY DARLINGTON........Steering ship
JAMES B. ROBERTSON, *Aviation Mechanic*....................................Engine room
CHARLES HASSAGE, *Ship's Chief Engineer*....................................Chief Engineer
C. O. FISKE, *Climatologist*....................................Engine room
WALTER SMITH, *Ship's Mate, Navigator and Trail Man*....................Bridge
NELSON MCCLARY, *Ship's Mate*....................................Bridge
LAWRENCE KELSEY, *Radio Operator*....................................Radio
DR. DONALD MCLEAN, *Medical Officer*....................................Steering ship
CHIEF COMMISSARY STEWARD SIGMUND GUTENKO, U.S.N.,
on furlough with expedition....................................Galley
ROBERT H. T. DODSON, *Assistant Geologist and Surveyor*....................Steering ship
E. A. WOOD, *Ship's Engineer*....................................1st Asst. Engineer
ARTHUR OWEN, *Boy Scout and Trail Man*....................................Steering ship
JORGE DI GEORGIO, *Mess Cook*....................................Mess hall

in our tents and sleeping-bags while winds raged up to ninety miles an hour. It was all we could do to crawl out on our hands and knees to feed the dogs and see that they were free from drift. When the winds abated we left two men to man the weather station for a time, and the rest of us went back to base.

A few days later, the two men decided to abandon camp and return to base. As they were making their way down, several rules of safety that absolutely must be observed when traveling in the Antarctic were unfortunately overlooked. As a result, one of the men fell through the snow bridge of a crevasse and plunged headlong into its icy depths.

Racing against Time and Polar Cold to Save a Comrade's Life

All his companion could do was to get aid from base, nine miles away. For hours, a party from base made the best speed it could with dog-teams and sleds in an endeavor to reach the trapped man before it was too late. I am afraid those of us who had had much experience in the polar regions feared the worst. My mind was filled with the many things that could have happened to the man since the accident had taken place. The crevasse could have been bottomless; the surface temperatures of fifty-five degrees below freezing could have made existence impossible. It was so cold that a member of the rescue party had one of his toes severely frostbitten and a number of the others suffered from frostbite on their faces.

One of the men in the rescue party was lowered slowly down that unforgettable crevasse for 110 feet. Then, to our immense relief, he yelled that the victim was still alive. In utter darkness, for twelve hours, the man had been wedged face downward, with his arms and legs pinned so that movement of any kind was impossible.

It took four men pulling on ropes and tackle to break him free. He was talking as he came to the surface, and the doctor's examination gave us the good news that, although he had scratches on his face and arms, he had broken no bones. He was frostbitten on the left hand and on both sides of his face and he was treated immediately for shock and exposure. Within two weeks the rescued man was walking around the bunkhouse, deeply moved that his life had been spared. It was a truly miraculous escape.

The Antarctic is dangerous country. One false step is all that is needed to bring home this very serious fact. The greatest enemy of any expedition—one that can not always be overcome—is the inexperience of its personnel. We had several narrow escapes which were glaring examples to all and which none of us are likely to forget. The Antarctic can not be treated lightly. Knowledge of its mysteries can be won only through patience, over a long period of time and by observing every possible safety precaution at all times.

Why is Antarctica so little known? Well, for one thing, man first set foot on its shores only about fifty years ago. Comparatively speaking, only a handful of explorers have ever wintered there. It is not only the most isolated continent on this earth but also the coldest and bleakest—so barren that it is impossible to live off the land. Indeed, so far as we know, no natives have ever lived there. About two thirds of Antarctica has never been seen by human eyes! For this very reason, it has a tremendous appeal for explorers who are interested in helping to uncover some of its many mysteries.

As our year drew to a close, we began looking forward to leaving our friends the seals and penguins. Green shores and civilized lands would be a welcome sight. During January and February, 1948, the men began to reload the Port of Beaumont. Bay ice still surrounded her, and we timed the loading so that we could make use of the ice in getting the heavy equipment aboard. The engineers put the ship's machinery in good operating condition again and on February 21 we departed from our base in Marguerite Bay.

Following Magellan's Stormy Path around Cape Horn

We were rounding Cape Horn on the first leg of our return journey when a very heavy storm blew up. The waves were forty feet high and the ship rolled as much as fifty-two degrees. We took green seas over the bow and for five days no meals could be served on board. It was one of our most miserable experiences. Almost everyone found it difficult to get any rest and we were thankful when, at last, we sailed into calm waters.

I know I speak for all when I say that one of the most thrilling sights of the entire fifteen months was our first glimpse of the Statue of Liberty in New York Harbor, April 15, 1948.

Beacon Street's graceful façades reflect Boston's tradition of dignity and culture.

ARCHITECTURE

Beauty in
WOOD, BRICK AND STONE

A French Canadian house on the Ile d'Orleans.

Stately Stanton Hall, at Natchez, Mississippi.

The historic Billop House on Staten Island.

A modern Spanish-style house in California.

Canada and the United States, in domestic architecture as in the other arts of life, are truly the heirs of all countries and all ages. Spain and France, England and the Netherlands, even ancient Greece and Rome, have contributed to the many and varied designs of the houses that Americans and Canadians live in. On these pages you will see the snowy columns of the Greek Revival style in the old South; the bright tiles and creamy plaster of the modern adaptation of the Spanish houses of California; the quaint cottages that the French built long ago in Canada, remembering the homes in Brittany and Normandy which they had left forever. Of course, the climate and the conditions of life in the different regions of our broad continent bring about changes in the various styles. Altogether our homes form a colorful and charming pageant, as varied as the people who dwell in them.

27

The courtyard of a house in old **New Orleans**.

An Old-World scene in the city of Quebec.

A Charleston house with its side galleries.

A very old Spanish adobe house in Santa Fe.

ASIA

Tempest in the East

By H. R. EKINS
AUTHOR OF *China Fights for Her Life*

China today—refugees gather dry leaves for home fires, while soldiers fight Communist troops.

I HOPE that the readers of this edition of THE BOOK OF KNOWLEDGE ANNUAL will forgive me if I start this article on a personal note. It seems to me that human relationships, and the understanding that can grow out of them, are more important now than they have been at any time in the whole story of mankind.

I have had very great difficulty in writing about Asia this year, and I will tell you why. For many years I lived among the people of China, the Philippines, Japan and India, and very often, I went visiting in Korea, Malaya and Indonesia. In all of those lands I have old and good friends, and it hurts to try to write about them when so many unpleasant things are happening to them. I have started the article this way because I want you to understand that I think of Asia as *people*. What happens to the people—when there is a struggle for power or a struggle between ideas—is what matters.

Throughout 1948, more and more of us in the United States and Canada came to understand that there is a basic struggle going on in the world. The struggle is between the idea of freedom for individuals and nations, and the opposite idea—that people do not matter, except to be servants of an all-powerful state. The struggle has been marked on one side by Soviet Russian activity to extend communist rule or influence, and on the other side by activity to protect the right of people to select their own form of government freely and without interference. Many of us have been aware of this struggle as it has been fought out in Europe. However, not enough of us have realized how widely it has spread in Asia. More than half of the people of the world live in Asia, and ideas sponsored by Russian communism have been making very great gains there. The vast area of

29

central Asia, including Chinese Turkestan or Sinkiang, is already behind the Iron Curtain.

The struggle for and against Russian communism in Asia was so great during the year that it overshadowed nearly everything else. The effort of the people of Asia to improve their standard of living and the desire of these people to work out a solution to their national problems were seriously affected by the work of communist agents. These agents were determined—with disturbing success, too—to make the spread of the Kremlin's influence come first in Asia. As the year drew to a close, the British Government said in official papers—and through its spokesmen in the United Nations—that the turmoil in Asia generally has been the work of Russian agents or their Fifth Columns. The Government said that these people have made it their business to oppose, often by force, any system of freedom as we know it.

The struggle throughout the world has been called the "cold war." In Asia, though, it has been a "hot war," with long and bitter fighting, especially in China. It has brought widespread human misery at a time when we had hoped people would be recovering from the ravages of World War II.

China Loses Manchuria to Communist Armies

These things happened in Asia in 1948: The recognized government of China lost the rich and well-populated Northeastern Provinces (they are better known as Manchuria) to Chinese Communist armies. In addition, there was far-flung fighting south of the Great Wall. It was on such a scale that China had to spend most of her money on military needs and suffered wild inflation of her currency. I will return to China with more detail, later.

Meanwhile, let us remember the words of John Hay, who was the United States Secretary of State from 1898 to 1905. He said that "the world's peace rests with China, and whoever understands China . . . holds the key to world politics during the next five centuries."

Korea was divided into South Korea and North Korea at the end of World War II. South Korea was occupied by American soldiers and was administered by a government appointed by the United Nations. North Korea was occupied by Russia, and was so completely controlled that the Russians were

able to announce that their troops would be withdrawn by January 1, 1949. As the year ended, however, Communists who had managed to join the constabulary in South Korea were able to start an armed rebellion in the southern zone.

Burma Breaks Away from the Commonwealth of Nations

After achieving independence from the British Crown, Burma broke away from the Commonwealth of Nations, formerly called the British Commonwealth of Nations. The word "British" was dropped officially in October 1948—a fact which is important to emphasize here because it shows progress toward the ideal of nations associated together for the common good. Other nations in the Commonwealth—such as the United Kingdom, South Africa, Canada and so on —hope to bring Burma back into the fold. However, the success of that hope rests on the result of the world-wide struggle between democracy and totalitarianism.

The new dominions of India and Pakistan survived their first year of independence, and they are making progress in the solution of some of their important problems. The death of Mohandas K. Gandhi did not cause so much trouble as might have been expected. Gandhi had been a leader in India's long journey to nationhood, and his death at the hands of an assassin threatened more quarrels and strife. Wise statesmanship, however, prevented widespread disorders and provided one of the brighter spots in the 1948 story of Asia.

Pakistan survived the death of her "George Washington," Mohammed Ali Jinnah, who was the first governor-general of the new Dominion. Both India and Pakistan settled some of their territorial differences, and large numbers of Hindus and Moslems were resettled from one dominion to the other.

Both India and Pakistan, however, remain as pawns in the chess game of world politics —the cold war. As the year ended, Britain was trying hard to prevent the Dominion of India from proclaiming itself a republic. As a republic, India might come under the domination of Communists. Advocates of human freedom, however, hope to keep India and Pakistan within the group of freedom-loving nations.

The efforts of Communists to create disorder also were seen in the Philippines, Malaya, Indonesia and French Indo-China during the year. In the Philippines, they worked through a group of discontented people called the Hukbalahaps. Native communist forces in Malaya, Indonesia and French Indo-China terrorized the population and waged irregular (guerrilla) warfare.

It must be admitted that French rule in Indo-China and Netherlands rule in Indonesia caused discontent among the people of those countries. The people often were unjustly treated; much of the wealth created by the workers was sent to Europe and kept there. Communist Fifth Columns in Indo-China and Indonesia found these conditions favorable to their program, which was to spread communist influence, and to strike at America's program to restore Europe through the European Recovery Program (Marshall Plan). For example, as the Communists encouraged military activity by the Viet Nam revolutionary party in Indo-China, they increased the drain on the resources of France. As a result, the economic recovery of France was hindered. The economic re-

covery of the Netherlands suffered because of the troubles in Indonesia, where Communists blocked every effort to peacefully settle her dispute with Holland. Communism has wanted no settlements except on its own terms. It has found that it could strike at the Marshall Plan in the jungles of Malaya, Indo-China and Indonesia just as well as it could in the factories of Italy.

That is the broad picture of the major events in Asia during 1948.

Now let us go back and take a closer look at China during the year. It was inevitable that, after thirty-six years of revolution and wars, China would have domestic problems of real importance—even without the Russian attempt to impose communist rule on the country. In August, with inflation out of control, China tried a major economic reform. The Government discarded the worthless paper currency, which had gone down in value until 11,000,000 Chinese dollars were worth only *one* American dollar. Huge bales of paper money were sold to paper mills for less than old newspapers would sell in this country. Then the Chinese Gov-

Gandhi's death brought a government pledge by Prime Minister Nehru to prevent more violence.

ernment inaugurated a gold standard, and set the rate of exchange at one Chinese gold yuan (dollar) for four American dollars. We still do not know whether this attempt at reform will work.

In early November, angry workers refused to accept the new money and demanded to be paid in food. There were riots in Shanghai. The people wanted rice and there was almost none to be had. Merchants also refused to accept the new money, and, as a result, the value of the yuan fell to about four cents in the black market.

Before the middle of the 1930's, China was the world's greatest user of silver coinage. When the armies of Japan began to overrun the country, however, the silver went into hiding. It was hoarded by the people. This,

to help China. For instance, the China Aid Act of 1948 provided for the establishment of the Chinese-American Rural Reconstruction Commission. This group is composed of two Americans and three Chinese. It is trying to work in the fields of agriculture, home demonstration, health, education, marketing, credit, irrigation, home and community industries and nutrition. It has not had a chance to show any great results in the rehabilitation of the Chinese countryside, though, because of the war.

Generalissimo Chiang Kai-shek has tried to make use of the talents of China's best elder statesmen. However, their work of advising the Government was made very difficult from the very beginning. Their efforts were always interrupted, or made use-

South Koreans eagerly received news of the May elections, dropped from low-flying airplanes.

plus uncontrolled American purchases of Chinese silver, finally reduced the value of Chinese silver coinage to the vanishing point. China's hope of making her currency reform succeed has been dimmed by war. Too much money must be spent for military purposes, and not enough is coming from her industry, which the war has disorganized.

Just as the United States has gone into other lands with food, shelter and help in rebuilding, it has tried, in a limited fashion,

less, by the tragic battle news. No matter in what direction the Chinese turned, they found that all efforts to rebuild the country would have to wait until the coming of peace. The Generalissimo warned his army leaders that the war against the Communists might go on for eight more years. Whenever I think of my Chinese friends, these days, I have to remember that the outlook will continue to grow darker for them so long as they can find no peace.

Wise guidance in Japan prevented such strike scenes as this, which took place two years ago.

Fighting continued throughout the year, and the Communist armies rolled inexorably southward as the Chinese Nationalist Army crumbled before their advance. Toward the end of the year, rumors began to reach the rest of the world. The most common—and most persistent—were that Chiang's closest advisers were suggesting that he resign; and that there would be a negotiated peace with a coalition government to follow. On Christmas Day, the Communists broadcast a list of government officials whom they intended to punish as "war criminals," and Chiang's name was at the top of the list. A week later, in Chiang's New Year's Day message to his people, he offered to talk peace but only on his own terms. The offer was scorned by communist leaders, who boasted that they would soon take Nanking. As the year ended, it looked as though they might.

In contrast to China, Japan has enjoyed order and security—thanks only to the presence of the American Army of Occupation and the wisdom of its leaders. Since the defeat of Japan, a big point in the foreign policy of Soviet Russia has been to spread communist influence in Japan. During the year the principal gains of the Communists there were in the labor unions. They received much help from the Soviet representative on the Allied Occupation Council. In the closing days of the war, Russia took many thousands of Japanese prisoners. Three years later, after having received Soviet teaching in the prison camps of Siberia, they were sent back to Japan, where their activities were directed by the Japanese Communist party. This had become strong enough by the middle of the year to threaten a nation-wide strike, which would have been a grave blow to the country. As a result, General MacArthur decided that civil employees should not be allowed to strike. His idea was made into law and serious damage was prevented, at least temporarily. Thanks to stern, but wise, methods Japan has continued to make progress.

During 1948, the Philippine Islands achieved a large measure of reconstruction. The period was marked by great patience on the part of President Elpidio Quirino and false promises by the Communists. The goal of President Quirino was peace with the Communist-led Hukbalahaps, whose leader was Luis Taruc. Once, surrender terms had been arranged for thousands of these guerrilla fighters. They were to be allowed to return peacefully to their farms and other jobs. However, the orders were suddenly changed by the higher levels of the communist command.

Steps Toward a Better Life for the Islanders

While trying to restore peace to the islands, President Quirino and other government leaders also tried to put certain land reforms into effect in the hope of raising the living standards of the people. Also, the Government adopted a new policy regarding oil lands and the development of oil wells by foreigners. It will limit the amount of oil land that can be held by foreign companies and places a limit of twenty years on oil-land leases.

In August 1948, there was a rebirth of freedom in South Korea. The new Government of President Syngman Rhee was inaugurated in Seoul, and the powers of government were turned over to him by American military authorities. The new Government later was officially recognized by the United Nations, despite Soviet protests.

South Korea also has a National Assembly, which was named in free elections, and a new constitution. It had been planned to withdraw American troops soon after the new Government was installed, but they remained at the request of President Rhee. In Decem-

August 15 was the first birthday of the Dominion of India. Thousands gathered at the historic Red

ber, though, the Army announced that some were leaving. However, Korea, was at the year's end, still divided on the 38th parallel. Korea suffers from this division. The south is mostly agricultural and the north is industrial. Koreans can hardly look forward to a balanced economy and a better life so

long as the Iron Curtain drops on the 38th parallel.

For Burma, it was a most unhappy year. Politicians fought among themselves, there was rebellion and there was pressure from the Soviet Union. As the year ended, the situation of Burma was very much like that

34

Fort in old Delhi to celebrate the anniversary.

fluence in Burma simply because Burma's anti-communist leaders were not willing to settle their own political differences. Those of us who worry about the fate of our friends in Burma were deeply disturbed when the Burmese premier, Thakin Nu, demanded that his country recognize Soviet-Russian leadership.

At the same time that this was going on in Burma, the Leftist parties in the new Republic of Indonesia also consolidated under the leadership of Mohammed Hatta. Russia immediately recognized the Republic, as did her satellite governments of Bulgaria, Rumania and Poland. After this had happened, it was not surprising that the Good Offices Committee of the United Nations had to admit complete failure in trying to bring the Dutch and the Indonesians together. In Indonesia, however, there is some light in the gloom that has hovered so long over all of the Far East.

Anti-communist Indonesians and farseeing Hollanders are continuing to strive for one goal. They want to see the establishment of a United States of Indonesia that would be joined in union with the Netherlands, yet stand as an equal among the sovereign nations of the world. The people of the Netherlands did their part during the year by voting to revise their constitution to make a free Indonesia possible.

The Netherlands Government Takes "Police Action" in Indonesia

However, true peace was not to be for Indonesia in 1948. On December 19, the Netherlands launched an armed attack upon the Republic, in what was called a "police action" to prevent a threatened uprising by Republican terrorists. A number of the Republic's leaders, including President Achmed Soekarno, were taken into custody. The action of the Dutch was sharply criticized by many, and the UN Security Council acted by ordering a cease-fire on December 24. To this, the Netherlands replied that the UN had no jurisdiction in the affair.

French Indo-China became the second most important target of the Communists in East Asia. Throughout the year, the revolutionary Viet Nam regime held out in the north against as many as 120,000 French and colonial troops. It was led by a man named Ho Chi Minh, who was educated in Moscow. The French failed to reach an agreement

WIDE WORLD

of Czechoslovakia before the Communists seized power there. Following the Moscow line, the Burmese discouraged the establishment of Christian missions and created a united front of Left-wing parties. A man named Than Thun was the Red commissar of Burma. The Communists gained great in-

35

with former King Bao Dai, of Annam, who had abdicated after the Japanese surrender in Indo-China. Bao Dai is now a refugee in Hong Kong, where he spends his time playing with his favorite dogs. The chief French supporter in Indo-China is General Nguyen Van Xuan, who is leader of an anti-communist group. As I pointed out earlier in this article, the situation in Indo-China contributes to the weakness of France.

India and Pakistan Progress, but Not Toward Unity

India and Pakistan are now well along in their new status of independence. During the first year, many, many thousands of lives were lost because Moslem and Hindu leaders were not able to live together peaceably. However, instead of moving along toward unity, the two new dominions have grown farther and farther apart. Pakistan especially, with its traditional religious fervor of Islam, has encouraged what is called the separatist movement. There have been some accomplishments, though. The Government of Prime Minister Nehru of the Dominion of India has started a wide and determined program of agricultural reform to increase the production of food. Land is being reclaimed and irrigation projects have been started. There has also been a growth of industry in India which, if it is allowed to continue, will help to raise the standard of living of the impoverished Indian people. There has also been progress in the fields of education, sanitation and communications—more so in India than in Pakistan.

There is evidence, however, that India has been marked as a likely area for communist expansion. Russian agents moved their southeastern headquarters from Bangkok, in Siam, to New Delhi, capital of the Dominion of India. Moscow also opened an embassy at Karachi, the capital of Pakistan, with a branch in Peshawar. Peshawar is a city in a strategic district in the Northwest Frontier Province and the gateway to Afghanistan.

As yet, the Communist party is small and not very powerful in India, and can claim an actual membership of only 75,000. However, just as elsewhere, there are many people (sometimes called fellow-travelers) who can be counted on to do the bidding of the Kremlin. The Communists have sympathisers among the class of Indians formerly called Untouchables; among the Dravidians in the south and among members of the labor unions.

The communist leader in India is Puran Chandra Joshi. He was a very busy man during the year. In February, Russian agents in the Kashmir area used the bitter fighting between the Hindus and the Moslems to their own advantage. Many of these agents were graduates of the Lenin Institute, which is the Soviet school of revolution in Moscow. They spread the idea that rebellion could accomplish reforms. In April 1948, Prime Minister Nehru announced that he had evidence of a plot by the Communists to overthrow his Government through violence. Several communist leaders were arrested and the activities of others were banned. The Communists answered this action by organizing a "popular front" group with the Socialists who had broken away from the Congress party. In June, however, the Hindu and Moslem leaders decided that if the fighting between their people continued, it would help the Russian program. Since then, they have been trying—with some success—to bring about better relations between Hindus and Moslems. What happens in the future will depend on the success of Hindu and Moslem leaders in their efforts for peace.

Chinese Communists Cause Trouble in Malaya

In Malaya, there was the same familiar pattern. Chinese Communists worked their way into the Sungei Seiput district of the Malaya Federation and conducted a reign of terror. When trouble spread to the important tin mines at Ipoh, British High Commissioner Sir Edward Gent declared a state of emergency. The central group of the terrorists was made up of former members of the Chinese guerrilla army that had fought the Japanese in the Malayan jungles during the war. It is unpleasant now to remember that these men were equipped with American weapons and had received American combat training. Trouble in Malaya hindered the flow of rubber, tin and oil so badly needed by the rest of the world.

I like to have good things happen to my friends, but it is impossible to write about Asia this year without realizing that all Asia has been torn by political strife, and in all too many cases by military strife. The year 1949 may be a fateful one in the history of that great continent.

THE most important astronomical event of 1948, and perhaps of the whole first half of the twentieth century, was the completion of the 200-inch telescope on Palomar Mountain, California. The story of the building of this great telescope, which was dedicated on June 3, 1948, has been retold so many times that here we need to touch upon only a few of the highlights. You read in last year's ANNUAL about the planning and early work on the 200-inch glass disc. Tests made at Palomar showed that further work must still be done on the big telescope mirror before it will give a perfect image.

Think back for a moment to 1608, when a spectacle-maker in Holland invented the telescope by accident. He just happened to hold two lenses in such a manner that a weathercock on a distant church tower appeared greatly enlarged. Then the great Italian astronomer, Galileo Galilei, when he heard of this, played with lenses until he, too,

By WILLEM J. LUYTEN
Professor of Astronomy, The University of Minnesota

ASTRONOMY

during the year

had made a telescope. It is a far cry from that first crude "optic tube" that Galileo made more than 300 years ago to the great giant on Palomar Mountain. The 200-inch telescope is a triumph not only of scientific genius, but of engineering skill and precision. This colossal artificial eye gathers 1,000,000 times as much light as a single human eye.

Now that the telescope is finished, what are astronomers planning to do with it, and what do they expect to achieve with it? Those are fair questions, but not easy ones to answer, especially the second one. Edwin P. Hubble, the head of the scientific plan-

ning commission for the telescope, has given some of the answers.

First of all, the work done with the 100-inch telescope at Mount Wilson, California, and the work done with the Palomar telescope will be planned together. These two telescopes—the two largest in the world—are so valuable that astronomers are not willing to waste any precious observing time by overlapping or repetition of work. The work with these telescopes, which are only ninety

Looking through the opening in the dome of the 200-inch telescope on Palomar Mountain.

miles apart, will be closely co-ordinated. Astronomers are planning a special light-beam type of telephone, so that an observer at one telescope can easily talk with an observer at the other. The telescope is a unique scientific instrument. In no other science is there so large a proportion of all available money tied up in a single instrument. The astronomer, however, has to put all his eggs in one basket, for without the present-day big telescopes modern astronomy would be unthinkable.

Of all the important problems in astronomy that are waiting for an answer, three have been picked out for immediate attack by the big telescope. The first deals with the question of the famous "canals" on the planet Mars—are they real, or have the people who have drawn pictures of them been "seeing things"? The 200-inch telescope is so powerful that astronomers hope to photograph the canals—if they exist—with exposures of only snapshot length. The results should settle the canal argument once and for all.

What Keeps the Stars Shining? How Long Will They Last?

Another item on the program concerns the chemical composition of the sun and the stars. Are the stars really 99 per cent hydrogen, and do all other chemical elements occur in nearly equal proportions in all stars? The physicist, especially, would like to know the answers to these questions. From these answers, we may also find out just what keeps the stars shining, how long ago they began to shine, and how long they may last. We have never before been able to make the necessary observations to answer these questions. Now, with the big telescope, we hope to gather enough light from a half dozen of the brightest stars so that we may take that light apart in minute detail and find the answers.

Is Our Universe Like a Huge, Expanding Solid-Rubber Ball?

The third, and perhaps the most important, question to be tackled is that of the expanding universe. With the 100-inch telescope we have found that the deeper we peer into space, the faster everything appears to run away from us. Some of the more distant galaxies or systems of stars even seem to move with the incredible speed of tens of

thousands of miles a second. Astronomers now hope to find out whether this is actually true, and, if so, what it means. In other words, is our universe like a great expanding solid-rubber ball? Several possible explanations have been suggested, but in order to decide which one is right, we must be able to see farther than we have so far been able to. With the 100-inch telescope we reached a distance of about 500,000,000 light-years—a light-year is about 6,000,000,000,000 miles. With the 200-inch telescope we hope to reach the billion light-year mark. That, we *hope,* will be far enough!

Knowledge Is a Challenge— a Test of Human Character

Perhaps the greatest discoveries and the most important ones, however, will be made in fields we have not yet even thought of. This nearly always happens in science. We have two different sets of ideas, and then we say, "If only we could make this or that observation, then we could decide which of these two sets of ideas is right." Well—we make the observations, and suddenly we discover that neither one of our earlier theories is right. Something new has been added, and we are off to a fresh start, toward new conquests of knowledge. We also know, as Raymond Fosdick (president of the Rockefeller Foundation) said at the dedication of the Palomar Mountain telescope: "Knowledge is not a gift, but a challenge; it is not merely an augmentation of facts, it is a test of human character." In our search for truth "the telescope is the lengthened shadow of man at his best." The telescope is a unique instrument—without it there would be no astronomy, and without astronomy man would know nothing of the universe beyond the earth on which he lives.

United States Post Office Honors the Big Telescope

The great importance of the 200-inch telescope has even been recognized by the Government. The United States Post Office has issued a special stamp in its honor, showing a picture of the majestic dome on Palomar Mountain.

In 1948 a new moon was discovered in the solar system. Dr. G. P. Kuiper, at the McDonald Observatory in Texas, discovered a new satellite of the planet Uranus. Four other satellites of Uranus are known, two discovered in 1787, and two more in 1851–52. The new moon is so close to the planet—only 81,000 miles distant, or one-third the distance from our moon to the earth—that it can not be seen; it must be photographed. (The eye of the camera is much more sensitive than the human eye, and therefore we can, through the telescope, photograph numerous objects which no human being has ever seen.) This fifth moon of Uranus revolves around the planet in 34 hours and is of the 17th magnitude—more than 10,000 times too faint to be seen with the naked eye. If it is similar to our own moon in composition—but this is a big IF—it is only about 300 miles in diameter, about the same size as the state of Missouri.

Observations also made at the McDonald Observatory during the close approach of Mars last winter seem to indicate definitely that there is carbon-dioxide gas in the planet's atmosphere. It now looks probable, also, that the green markings on Mars' surface are real, and that they may be due to some sort of vegetation—something like mosses or lichens. This brings us closer to a definite YES in answer to the age-old question: Is there life on Mars?

A Rich Crop of Brilliant Comets in the Year 1948

The year 1948 also brought with it a rich crop of new comets, including three that were visible without a telescope. One, which appeared just before Christmas 1947, was visible mainly in the Southern Hemisphere. It was brighter than any comet since Halley's comet in 1910, and had a tail several degrees long before it broke in two. Another comet was visible for a week or so in May, near the constellation Cassiopeia. The most spectacular and dramatic comet, however, was first observed just before sunrise on November 6 in the constellation Virgo. It was brighter than Halley's comet, with a tail more than thirty times the diameter of the full moon.

Did the Planets Come from the Sun? Or from Clouds of Dust in Space?

A new theory on the origin of the solar system was proposed by Dr. Fred L. Whipple, of Harvard University. He suggests that the planets did not come from the sun, but that they were all formed at about the same time by the collapse of vast clouds of dust in space. Dr. Whipple believes that the sun itself, and possibly most of the stars, came into being in this same way. This idea is a very interesting one, but astronomers have not had time to study it carefully, and we do not yet know whether it is true.

A "Double Star" Is Often More than Two Stars Circling around Each Other

It has been discovered recently that a double star is often more than just two stars circling around each other. Often the stars lie at the center of a fast-whirling mass of very thin gas, a sort of outer atmosphere which has escaped from the stars and is now slowly disappearing into space. Perhaps this explains the origin of many of those great clouds of gas we see throughout the vast spaces between the stars.

Further work has been done on the "white dwarfs," and we now know more than 100 of these strange, dense stars which weigh anywhere up to 1,000 tons per cubic inch. In them we find matter existing under conditions that we can not hope to approach on the earth. In the white dwarfs the temperatures are measured in billions of degrees, the pressures in trillions of pounds per square inch. In these stars we have, in short, a laboratory in which we can study matter in the raw; from our study of them we may hope to obtain more information as to what makes the atom tick.

Astronomers all over the world are becoming interested in the building—perhaps by UNESCO—of a great, common observatory, to be used by all nations.

Astronomers from Many Countries Renew Ties of Friendship

In August the International Astronomical Union met in Zurich, Switzerland. No discoveries or startling announcements were likely to result from this meeting. To all scientists, however, such meetings are very important. In August, for the first time since 1938, astronomers from many different countries met and talked together, renewing the ties of international friendship and co-operation. There is no firmer basis for peace among nations than that which can be laid by mutual understanding between the peoples of the world. As Raymond Fosdick said at the dedication of the Palomar telescope: "We need, in this sick world, the perspective of the astronomer."

ASTRONOMY

Star Families

By Roy K. Marshall
Director, Fels Planetarium

MOST people know about the Big Dipper in the sky, a group of seven stars arranged in the form of a cup of four stars and a handle of three. This star group spends all of its time above the horizon for people who are as far north as San Francisco, Philadelphia, New York and Chicago. The Big Dipper is particularly important to those who are just beginning to know the sky, because it is easy to find and it helps us to find the North Star. By extending a line between the two stars that form the front of the dipper's cup—from the star at the bottom of the cup through the one at the rim—anyone can find the North Star, and from this star, his directions.

Go out some night and find the Big Dipper, in the northern sky. Look at the star at the bend in the dipper's handle. You will find, if the sky is clear and if there are not too many lights around, a fainter star near by. The bright star at the bend of the handle is called Mizar, the faint one, Alcor.

The distance between Mizar and Alcor appears to be a little more than a third of the width of the full moon. In reality, because the stars are much farther away than the moon, Mizar and Alcor are very much farther apart than they seem. If they were both as far away from us as Mizar, they would be many thousands of millions of miles apart— so far that light would take more than three months to travel from one of them to the other. (Light travels about 186,000 miles in one second.) But Alcor is much farther away from us than Mizar. Light has been traveling for eight years, on its way to us from Alcor, before it passes Mizar. Then the light from Mizar joins it, and the two rays of light travel side by side toward us. Together they reach our eyes about 80 years after leaving Mizar. We say the distance of Mizar is 80 light-years; the distance of Alcor is 88 light-years. (A light-year is the distance light travels in one year, about 6,000,000,000,000 miles.)

Such a combination of two stars apparently close together in the sky is called a double star. Those that can be seen with the unaided eye are called naked-eye doubles.

Reproductions of photographs of the visual binary star, Kruger 60, in upper left part of pictures. One component is seen revolving around the other. Another star is seen at lower right.

In the constellation Auriga, Capella marks the goat, and Epsilon Aurigae, the head of a kid.

Mizar and Alcor are about as far apart as two stars can be, and still be thought of as forming a double. There are other much closer pairs of naked-eye doubles in the sky. One of them is in the constellation of Lyra, east and a little north of the bright star Vega. It is called Epsilon Lyrae, and it forms a small triangle with Vega and a third star southeast of that brilliant star. The two stars of Epsilon Lyrae are less than a third as far apart as Mizar and Alcor are.

When we use even a small telescope to view Mizar and Alcor, we find a third star near by. It is too faint to be seen with the unaided eye. But the really beautiful sight is to see that Mizar itself is double, consisting of two stars so close together that the distance would need to be marked off about fifty times to bridge the gap between Mizar and Alcor. When Epsilon Lyrae is examined with a telescope, each of the two stars that can be seen with a sharp eye is seen to be double! In other words, Epsilon Lyrae is really a double-double, and so it is often called.

Sometimes such double stars as revealed by a telescope are only accidental doubles, as Mizar and Alcor are. That is, two stars which are really quite far apart—one of them much farther away from us than the other—seem to us to be close together because we see them in just about the same direction in the sky. We call such pairs optical doubles.

Sir William Herschel, one of the greatest astronomers of all time, did his astronomical work from 1774 to 1822. He found many double stars and believed that he could use them to determine the relative, or comparative, distances of the stars. He thought that all of the pairs he saw were optical pairs—like Mizar and Alcor. Herschel knew, of course, that during the year, as the earth moves around the sun, any star is seen to shift its position in the sky a little, with our change of position in the earth's orbit. A more distant star would not seem to shift as much as a closer star. You can prove this for yourself by picking out two trees, one of which is maybe twice as far away as the other. If you move back and forth across the line joining the two trees and you, you will notice that the nearer tree seems to shift much more than the distant one. As you watch, you will see the distant tree first on the left, then on the right side, of the nearer

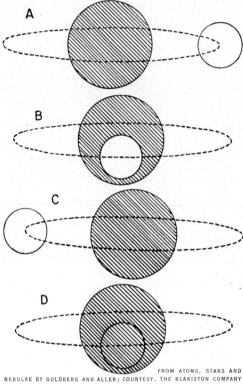

FROM ATOMS, STARS AND NEBULAE BY GOLDBERG AND ALLER; COURTESY, THE BLAKISTON COMPANY

One star in this eclipsing binary is small and bright; the other is large and dim. In A and C, each star gives its full light. In B the bright star, in front, cuts off some of the faint star's light. In D, the large faint star cuts off the bright light of the small star which is behind.

tree. Herschel thought that he might see this same sort of thing with the stars, and thus be able to judge which ones were farther away. Today we use this apparent shifting of the stars, as the earth revolves around the sun, to measure the distances of the stars.

Sir William, however, was very much disappointed. After examining hundreds of double stars, he came to the conclusion that many of them were not optical or accidental doubles at all. They were real physical pairs,

with two stars really close together, and connected with each other by the strong pull of gravity. In short, he discovered that many double stars are really binary stars, consisting of two stars revolving around their common center of gravity.

Today, many hundreds of binary stars are known, and from them we can learn much that would otherwise be hidden from us. For example, we can weigh the stars! Even in the largest telescope in the world, a star appears to be only a tiny bright point of light. We can not see its real surface, yet we can weigh it, if it is one of the members of a binary star which can be fully studied.

The way we do it is this: We compare the two stars with the earth and the sun. First, however, we study the law of gravitation and learn that the earth revolves around the sun in a period of exactly one year because it weighs practically nothing as compared with the sun. Let us see just what this means. If the earth and the sun were of equal weight, our year would be only 258 days long, instead of 365 days. Two bodies a certain distance apart, as the sun and the earth are, make one whirl around in a period which depends upon the sum of their masses—their weights, as we commonly think of it.

Astronomers Can Tell How Far Apart and How Heavy Binary Stars Are

So we study a binary pair of stars, and see how long it takes them to make one trip around. If we can measure their distance from us, then we know how far apart they are. Knowing the distance that separates them, and the period of their revolution, we know the sum of their masses, as compared with the sun.

That is a useful piece of information, but we want to go one step farther. We should like to know how heavy each one is. Here we are helped by some other information that we have gathered about a lot of stars. We know that the heavier stars always give out more light. So, if the two stars are equally bright, we know that they are equally heavy, and we can divide up the sum of their masses in two equal parts. If one of the stars is brighter than the other, then we know it has more of the total mass, and we can tell how much by measuring how much brighter one star is than the other.

It may seem puzzling that we have been able to learn that the heavier stars give out more light, when we use this fact to determine the relative masses of two stars of a physical binary. The relation between mass and true brightness, or luminosity, was discovered from a few binary stars which are easy to study because a third star is near by. Each of the stars of the binary is measured with respect to the extra star which is not a part of the system. We can then see that the two stars revolve around their common center of gravity, but that the heavier one moves in a smaller path or orbit than the other one.

In a Binary System, the Heavier Star Is Nearer the Gravitational Center

Think of a seesaw. If two people of equal weight use the seesaw, they should sit an equal distance from the center. But if one of them is heavier than the other, he should sit nearer the center. So the heavier star is nearer the gravitational center, in a binary star, and it thus moves in a smaller path. For example, we usually say that the earth revolves around the sun, as though the sun were fixed, and did none of the moving. Actually, the earth and the sun are like two people on a seesaw, but the sun is so much heavier than the earth that its center is less than 300 miles from the center of the seesaw, while the earth is about 93,000,000 miles from the center. Both the earth and the sun revolve around their common center of gravity, but the earth travels in a much larger path, because it is so much less heavy than the sun is. And, of course, this earth-sun situation is very much more complicated than this, because the other planets are pulling and tugging at the sun.

We find, from our study of binary stars, that our own sun is a star of more or less average mass. There are some stars weighing a few hundreds of times as much as the sun, and there are a few stars weighing only a hundredth as much as the sun. But our sun is a typical star, in every way. Because the stars that have the same color as the sun appear to have the same mass as the sun, we believe that our methods are sound. What is most important, however, we believe that the law of gravitation written by Sir Isaac Newton, in 1687, is truly a universal law that applies throughout the whole universe. Our results are consistent and logical; stars of the same color and the same real brightness always turn out to have the same mass, in whatever binary system we find them. Stars that have the same real brightness and color as our sun have just about the same mass as the sun. We are quite satisfied that our methods are correct.

Some binary stars observed through telescopes have very long periods—so long that we have not seen them go around once since they were discovered. There are others that

Joseph Fraunhofer, inventor of the spectroscope, discovered and measured the dark lines in the solar spectrum known today as the Fraunhofer lines. These dark lines have proved to astronomers that the stars consist of the same chemical elements that we know on earth.

go around once in only a few years. There is one with a period of only about three and a third years, and still another with a period of only a year and a half. But we know of binary stars whose periods are only a few days or a few hours. They are so close together, however, that even with the greatest telescopes they can not be separated, yet we know that they are binaries.

In the constellation of Perseus, there is a star named Algol. Its name may come from the Arabic expression for the Demon, or the Mischief-Maker. Our English word "ghoul" is related to Algol. If you watch Algol for several weeks, on every clear night, you may be rewarded by finding that it is, one night, fainter than you have ever seen it before. Its variation in brightness takes place in a period of 2 days, 21 hours, very nearly. This means that each 2 days, 21 hours it is at its faintest, which is less than half as bright as it is normally. It remains practically at its greatest brightness for more than 2 days. For 5 hours it fades to its least brightness, then for 5 hours it brightens to its greatest brightness once more.

In 1782 a young British astronomer who, it is interesting to relate, was a deaf-mute, came to the conclusion that Algol faded because it really consisted of two stars, one of them fainter than the other. When the faint star passes between us and the bright one, he said, the total light we receive from the pair is less. This reasoning of John Goodricke has been amply confirmed, over and over, in this matter of the eclipsing binaries, as stars of this kind are called.

Some Binary Systems Are Eclipsing Binaries—Others Are Not

Any binary star would be an eclipsing binary, if the motion of the two stars around each other took place in a plane which is in the line of sight. This means merely that the edge of the orbit would have to be turned toward us. The chances are that the motion will not be so exactly arranged, however, that one of the stars must, each time around, stand exactly in front of the other. If the two stars are very close together, however, the chances are better that an eclipse will occur. When the two stars stand side by side, we get light from both of them. When they are lined up, one in back of the other, either wholly or partially, we get all of the light from the one in front, but only part of the light, or none of the light, of the one in back. The pair will be seen as one star, because they are so close together, but the combination will vary in brightness.

Sometimes two stars of a binary are far enough apart so that we could see the two, with telescopes, except that one is much too faint to be seen. If the motion is arranged so that the pair is an eclipsing binary system, we know that there are two stars there, even if we can't see both of them. That is the case

with another star visible to the unaided eye, in the constellation of Auriga. Near the bright yellow star Capella there is a small slim triangle. The star at the sharpest corner of this triangle is called Epsilon Aurigae. It is an eclipsing binary with a period of twenty-seven years, the longest known for a pair of this kind. Another star of the triangle is Zeta Aurigae, an eclipsing binary with a period of about two and a half years.

We Can Determine the Diameters of Stars from Eclipsing Binaries

Epsilon Aurigae consists of a star of normal size and one which is the largest star known today. We have learned that we can discover the masses of stars from visual binaries (binaries that can be seen as two stars either with the unaided eye or through the telescope). Now we find that we can determine the diameters of stars from eclipsing binaries.

Let's consider Algol again. The two stars revolve around their common center of gravity in 2 days, 21 hours, or about 69 hours. The length of the eclipse, from the time the star begins to fade until it gets back to its original brightness, is usually given as about 10 hours. In other words, it takes the two stars 10 hours to pass each other, and it takes them 69 hours to go all the way around.

We can say, then, that the sum of the diameters of the two stars is $\frac{10}{69}$ of the length of the path that one star pursues with respect to the other. If we knew the distance between the two stars, we should know the length of the path of one with respect to the other, and could then find out the sum of the diameters of the stars.

The Biggest Star, Two Billion Miles in Diameter, Is Invisible

We can do just this, as we shall see, and out of such study we have learned the diameters of many stars. Among them there is the freak giant which is the invisible fainter star of Epsilon Aurigae, with a diameter of almost 2,000,000,000 miles, or more than 2,000 times the diameter of our own star, the sun! This star is a big, puffed-up mass of gas, so cool that it does not shine very brightly, but very thin, so that the brighter star of the Epsilon Aurigae pair is able to shine through the outer layers of it. It is the biggest star we know today, and one of the

Photograph of the seven bright stars in the Big Dipper. The star at the bend of the handle is Mizar; the fainter star, above it, is Alcor. They are often called the Horse and the Rider.

very coolest. If it had not been a member of an eclipsing binary system, we should never have discovered it.

When John Goodricke said that Algol was really a pair of stars, there was no proof at hand. It seemed reasonable to him, and other astronomers accepted his explanation, in time, but the proof did not come until more than a century had passed. The proof came from the instrument called the spectroscope, whose most important part is a prism of glass. The spectroscope permits us to know what the stars are made of, how hot they are, and how fast they travel. We are particularly interested here in learning the method by which we discover how fast the stars travel.

A spectroscope is attached to the lower end of a telescope, and starlight captured by the telescope passes through the prism of the spectroscope. Light is bent by the prism, but the blue and violet light is bent more than the orange and red light. In between are yellow and green. The prism spreads the light out into the rainbow band of color which we call the spectrum. Crossing the spectrum of a star are thin, dark lines, which tell us what is in the stars. Only certain materials give certain lines, and we can identify those materials. We find that the stars are made of the same stuff—the same chemical elements—that we find on earth; they are made of the same materials, indeed, that make up our human bodies, and so we are star dust!

We want to know how fast the stars travel, and the spectroscope tells us. To understand how this is, we must turn for a while to the field of sound, instead of light. When a source of sound comes toward you, the pitch is higher than it would be if the source of sound were not moving toward you. A diving airplane seems to whine as it approaches you, its sound falling in pitch as it turns and noses upward to go away from you. This is called the Doppler effect, after the scientist who first explained it. As the source of sound moves toward you, more waves than would normally reach your ear are arriving, so the pitch of the sound is higher. When a source of sound is going away from you, fewer waves than normal reach your ear, and the pitch seems lower than normal.

The same thing is true in light. The positions of the dark lines in the spectrum of a star may be thought of as the pitch of the light. For most stars, the lines are shifted from their proper positions, telling us that there is motion of the star with respect to us. If the lines are shifted to the redward direction from their proper positions, the star is moving away from us; if the shift of the lines is toward the violet, the distance between us and the star is growing less. The amount of the shift is a measure of the speed.

At the Harvard College Observatory, Professor E. C. Pickering found that the spectroscope gave, for one of the stars in Mizar, sometimes single lines and sometimes double lines. That is, sometimes it appeared to be a single star, sometimes a pair of stars, one going away, one coming toward us. This was the discovery of the spectroscopic binary. When the spectroscope was used on Algol, it was found that there was, indeed, motion first toward and then away from us, indicating binary motion, just as John Goodricke had suggested a century earlier.

Eclipsing Binaries Can Be Detected Only with the Spectroscope

Every eclipsing binary is a spectroscopic binary—it can be detected only with the spectroscope—but not every spectroscopic binary is an eclipsing star. If the two stars move in a plane which does not pass exactly through the earth, a shifting of the spectrum lines will be seen, but there will not be a change of light as one star lines up exactly in front of the other. Some spectroscopic binaries just miss being eclipsing binaries.

Now we can measure how fast the stars of the Algol pair move in their paths. Knowing how fast they move, and knowing that the period in which they move all of the way around their paths is two days and twenty-one hours, we can find out the sizes of their paths. Then, we can find out how large the stars are, as we have seen above.

Binary Pairs Sometimes Show One Set of Lines—Sometimes, Double Lines

Sometimes, a binary pair will consist of a bright star and a faint one, and only one set of lines will be seen. This set will shift back and forth with respect to its normal position, indicating that one star is coming toward us, then going away from us. That tells us that there is really another star there, even if we can not see the other one, or its spectrum. In other instances, the lines are all double, as the two more nearly equal stars move, one toward us, the other, away; then the lines become single, as the two stars move one to the right, the other to the left, across the line joining us and the stars. Then the lines again will double, as the star that was going away from us begins to come toward us, and the star that was coming toward us begins to go away.

From the study of the spectrum of a spectroscopic binary, we can learn much concerning the masses of stars, their distances apart, and the way their orbits are arranged

in relation to the earth. But usually these things are tangled together, unless we can observe the pair also as an eclipsing binary or as a visual binary, directly through the telescope.

There are all kinds of combinations of visual, eclipsing and spectroscopic pairs. Sometimes, as with Mizar, we find optical systems of which one or both stars will be spectroscopic binaries. Sometimes a close pair of stars will be revolving around a common center of gravity with another close pair, or a single star. Some have double, triple and even quadruple systems. We suspect even more complicated systems, in which one star of a spectroscopic binary will have another small star revolving around it.

Masses of Some Invisible Stars Are as Low as Those of Planets

A few years ago, careful measurements indicated that certain stars appeared to be swinging from side to side by a very little bit, as though stars with very low mass were revolving around them. The masses of these invisible stars were so low that they were comparable with the masses of the planets, and it was announced that planets had been discovered revolving around stars other than our sun.

With the largest telescopes we have, we should not be able to see directly any planet like those in our solar system, even if such planets were revolving around other stars. But we must be very careful about saying that these invisible objects revolving around other stars are planets, and not very faint stars. We have as yet no convincing evidence that we have discovered, either directly or indirectly, any planets moving about other stars. There probably are some, moving about many stars, but we can not say that we know definitely of any.

We can say, however, that single stars, like our sun, seem to be almost the exception. There are so many double stars that are real physical binaries of one kind or another—visual, eclipsing or spectroscopic—that we wonder why it is that our sun is a single star. We are very grateful for the binary stars, however, because from them we can learn so much that otherwise we should need to guess at.

If you would like to locate these constellations, the article Pictures in the Sky in THE BOOK OF KNOWLEDGE will tell you how—*Editorial Note.*

ATOMIC ENERGY

SERVANT OF INDUSTRY

By DAVID A. KEYS

Atomic Scientist, Chalk River, Canada

WE are living at the beginning —the very beginning—of the atomic age. While the achievements of our atomic scientists seem almost miraculous to us, they will probably be regarded by scientists of the future as merely the first paragraph of the first page of the primer of atomic science. We have learned how to get at the energy locked within the atom's heart. We can do this now by actually splitting the nucleus of the atom and using the power which that kind of explosion produces.

So far, the most spectacular use of atomic energy has been a destructive one—in the atomic bomb. We now look forward hopefully to the day when we shall have learned how to apply atomic energy to the processes of everyday peacetime life. And, indeed, we have already learned a number of things in this field.

We have read here and there about the wonderful possibilities of the atom's power. Some writers have even told us that the day may come when a great steamship, like the Queen Mary, may be powered by the energy contained within the atoms in a single glass of water. Other writers point out that you may be able, some day, to run your automobile or your airplane for years on the power hidden within a tiny piece of radioactive material about the size of a large pinhead. These dreams may come true—who knows? But they can certainly not come true in the near future. We have much work to do before they can, if ever, become reality.

As you know, all atoms are composed of

If there were any leaks in this atom-smasher, they would be found by the electronic detector. Right, worker preparing radioactive isotopes is protected from atomic radiation by lead bricks.

WESTINGHOUSE; NATIONAL FILM BOARD

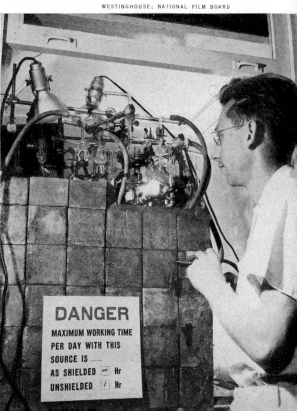

DANGER
MAXIMUM WORKING TIME
PER DAY WITH THIS
SOURCE IS
AS SHIELDED ∞ Hr
UNSHIELDED / Hr

the same kinds of almost infinitely small particles. Atoms of different elements, however, have different numbers of particles. The central core, or nucleus, is made up of protons and neutrons. The protons carry a plus or positive electrical charge; the neutrons are, as their name suggests, neutral, and carry no charge. So the nucleus is positive. Moving around the nucleus are other very tiny particles called electrons, which carry a negative, or minus, charge. The negative charge of the electrons balances the positive charge of the protons. Therefore, since there is always an equal number of protons and electrons, the atom, as a whole, is neutral and carries no electrical charge.

An Electrical Force Probably Holds the Nucleus Together

Although we do not thoroughly understand the nature of the force within the nucleus which holds it together, scientists think that it is probably an electrical force. Atomic scientists knew that this power, if we could get at it, would greatly change the lives of men. And, gradually, they discovered a way to split open the nucleus and free its power. The process by which this is done is called atomic fission. (The word fission means a splitting up and breaking apart.) Since an atom is so small we need a very, very, very tiny "bullet," or particle, to break up its nucleus. Scientists decided that the best bullet would be a particle which has no electrical charge, so that it would neither be repelled by the positive nucleus, nor absorbed by it. The neutron which, as you know, carries no charge, seemed to be the answer. And it proved to be the correct answer. Today we use neutrons as "bullets," and with them we bombard—actually *hit*—the nuclei of other atoms to break them open. When the nucleus splits, some of its tremendous energy is released. Although neutrons are used most commonly in smashing atoms, other particles are also used, such as deuterons—heavy hydrogen nuclei—and alpha particles, which are the nuclei of helium atoms.

Man-made atomic fission goes on in a special kind of atomic furnace—an atomic pile. It is called a pile because it is actually a pile of graphite blocks within which is placed the material—usually uranium—which is to be bombarded. Atomic fission in the pile is carefully controlled. As the atoms break up, the temperature inside the pile rises until a terrific heat is produced. This heat must not be allowed to become too great. So long as it is kept under control, there is no possibility that the atomic pile can explode.

To keep the temperature at the right level, liquids or gases are circulated in pipes through and around the pile to absorb its heat and carry it away. One of the main problems of scientists and engineers today is to build a special kind of atomic pile in which the heat produced by the splitting of atoms can be transformed into power for doing useful work. Much of the power which keeps the wheels of industry running today is steam power, usually produced by the burning of coal or oil in the chemical process of combustion. If, by the physical act of splitting atoms, power can be provided to supply enough steam for the needs of industry, then we need hardly worry about the scarcity of any other kind of fuel. Since steam can be harnessed to produce electric power, our electricity can also be produced as a result of the activity of the atomic pile.

There is a great deal, however, as we have seen, which we do not yet know about atomic fission. Before we can run our factories, our locomotives, our electric generators and our ships and airplanes by atomic power, much work must be done by the chemist, the physicist and the expert on metals. New types of atomic furnaces and boilers will have to be invented, among other things. In many centers scientists are now working on the technical problems of making atomic power available for peacetime uses. The Knolls Atomic Power Laboratory of the General Electric Company is especially devoted to this type of research.

Scientists Must Be Shielded from Harmful Effects of Radiation

One of the great difficulties about atomic research is that the scientists working on these problems must be carefully protected from the powerful radiations caused by atom-splitting. Both the neutrons and the gamma rays which escape from the pile are highly injurious to the health. Therefore, very strong shields of concrete and of metal which absorb the harmful radiations must be erected around the pile.

We know that there are certain forms of elements which do not have the same atomic weight as that listed for these elements in

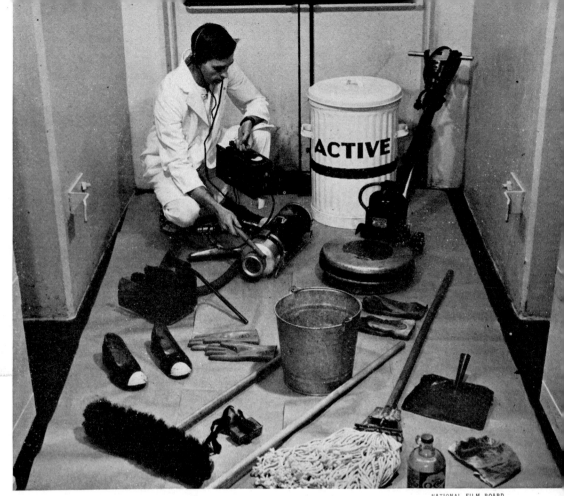

A health surveyer checks equipment used by cleaners at Chalk River for radioactive contamination.

the table of atomic weights. In every other respect, however, these elements are like the standard forms. These varying forms we call isotopes. When we place a quantity of a certain element in the pile, where neutrons are flying freely, some of them crash into the atoms of the element. Its atoms thus become heavier; the material becomes a radioactive isotope. Today we know how to produce hundreds of radioactive isotopes, and already we have discovered how to use some of them for industrial purposes, as well as in medicine and biology.

In any chemical reaction we can use radioactive isotopes just as we would use other forms of the element. But they have a more important use than that! The atoms of radioactive isotopes, because of the radiations they emit, reveal their presence, wherever they are, to the scientist. Because we can trace the progress of these "tagged" atoms,

whether through the digestive tract of an animal, in the growth process of a plant or in a chemical reaction, we call these atoms *tracers*. Scientists can follow them with sensitive instruments which register the presence of the radiations given out by them.

Tracers have already added to our knowledge of pure science. Now they give promise of being useful in controlling certain industrial processes.

They help us, for instance, to determine wear and tear on blocks of metal. It is important in certain industrial processes to know how long given metals will withstand friction and use. In one experiment, the metal block was made of beryllium and copper, with some radioactive copper isotopes mixed in. Neither the beryllium nor the plain copper atoms give off rays, but the copper isotope atoms do. During the experiment, the block was rubbed with different materials under different degrees of pressure. Tiny specks of copper, some of them radio-active, became detached from the block and adhered to the surface of the rubbing material. The amount of copper was so minute, however, that its presence could be detected only by the rays which came from it. An estimate, obtained in this way, of the amount of material worn off the original block would give a fair idea of the wearing quality of the metal.

Radioactive iron gives us another example of the use of isotopes in the control of industrial processes. In one experiment, a small amount of radio-iron was mixed with the ordinary iron used in the manufacture of aero-engines. The purpose of the experiment was to determine the wear of the engine's cylinders. In running the engine, a lubricant was used, of course, and its oils and greases picked up some of the iron isotopes mixed with the common iron in the engine. When the radioactivity of the lubricant was measured, the wear of the cylinders was easily determined.

Gold can be transformed into mercury if it is bombarded by neutrons in an atomic pile. This is the opposite reaction to that sought by the alchemists of old. They tried in vain to transform mercury and lead into gold. Mercury prepared from gold is a single stable isotope and gives a very sharply defined wave-length when its band of green light is viewed in the spectrum. For years scientists have used an unsatisfactory measuring rod for spectral wave-lengths—the band of red light in the spectrum of the element cadmium. They may now adopt the wave-length of an isotope of mercury, prepared from gold, as their standard.

Radio-Cobalt May Be Used as a Substitute for Radium

When the nucleus of an atom begins to fall apart, it sends out three kinds of rays—alpha, beta and gamma. Gamma rays behave like invisible rays of light. Radium in a pure state gives off a great number of these gamma rays. Now, by exposure in the atomic pile, ordinary cobalt metal can be transformed into cobalt isotopes having many times the gamma-ray activity of an equal mass of radium.

Radio-cobalt may be used as a substitute for radium—which is very scarce—in the treatment of certain diseases. In industry,

it may be used instead of radium for taking radiographs—pictures made by other forms of radiation than light—of thick metal castings. If there are flaws inside the castings, such as hidden cavities or cracks, the radiograph will show them up.

Radioactive gases have been used to study the flow of air in furnace ducts and in ventilating systems. They have also been used to trace the movement of gases from smokestacks under varying conditions of wind direction, atmospheric temperature and humidity.

Sewage Water in Wells Can Be Detected by Radioactive Salt

The flow of underground waters from sewage-disposal plants can be followed by adding a little radioactive salt to the water. Then, if any of the sewage water seeps into neighboring streams or wells, tests will reveal the presence of radioactivity.

Some chemical reactions take place which we would never know about if we did not have tracers to show us exactly what was going on. Certain reactions of limestone, for example, fall into this class. Limestone consists of calcium carbonate. In each of its molecules there is an atom of carbon. Now, there are also carbon atoms in carbon dioxide, which, as you know, is one of the common gases in the air. Scientists were interested in finding out whether there is any exchange between the carbon atoms of the limestone and the carbon atoms of the carbon-dioxide gas. Or does each carbon atom remain firmly attached to its original oxygen atoms?

The first step in finding the answer was to make some radioactive limestone. In making it, radioactive carbon atoms were used, as well as ordinary carbon atoms. In the air there are no radioactive carbon atoms. Therefore, if, in the controlled experiment, we found that some radioactive carbon atoms had made their way into the carbon-dioxide gas and the weight of limestone remained unchanged while its total activity was reduced, then there must have been the sort of exchange that we were wondering about. It was shown that such an exchange in carbonates does take place; the tracer atoms also enabled us to follow the rate at which this exchange occurred. In much the same way, tracers may be used to show us what happens in many other chemical reactions.

AUSTRALIA
during the
year

By Lloyd Clarke
Australian News and Information Bureau

Australia gives a heart-warming welcome to newcomers. Recently, thousands of people have gone there to live, and during the year the Government made many announcements to encourage still more immigration. Displaced persons and fugitives from tyranny are welcome, as, indeed, are all people who want to seek a full life in a new country.

This spacious continent offers opportunities for many different kinds of work and different ways of living. For those who like to work out-of-doors, there are the huge ranches of the open plains country, with their millions of sheep and cattle; rich farms and fisheries and some timberland, too, although Australia's forests are not so extensive as those of the United States and Canada.

Others may prefer to live in Australia's great, modern cities. Some of the most important work of the Commonwealth is carried on in the fields of public administration and the professions; commerce and finance; and transportation and communications. Many persons find employment in the thriving factories, where the industrial worker has a wide choice of occupations. Australia's industries include the manufacture of textiles, leather and clothing; pottery, bricks and glass; industrial metals and machines; and the treatment of many mine and quarry products, including precious metals. Recently there has been an intensive search for uranium in Australia, and the hunt for this

Docks on River Yarra, port of Melbourne.

A woolen mill on the island of Tasmania, one of the states of the Commonwealth that particularly welcomes new industries. Here, machines are combing wool fibers into parallel filaments, a process known as "gilling:" Below, Australia's great jurist, the late Sir Isaac Isaacs.

metal, more precious today than gold, has met with some success.

The beauty of the country and its many natural curiosities make Australia as interesting as it is pleasant. This is the home of the platypus, the lyre bird and those little, native "teddy bears" called koalas; the home, too, of Yellow-Dog Dingo and Old Man Kangaroo. Here are found the wonders of the Great Barrier Reef and the beauty of mountains that are clad all year round with evergreens.

The forty-hour week is the rule in Australia today. This work-week went into effect on January 1, 1948, and is one of the most important industrial reforms of recent years. The question of how long a man should be required to work came up before the Arbitration Court in 1947. It was felt that a man ought to work long enough to do his duty by the community and still have a reasonable amount of leisure. The question finally reached the High Court, which decided that no man should be required to work more than forty hours in any one week.

A reform that would touch even more people was still up in the air at the end of the year. This was the nationalization of the

Australian banks. In Australia, the biggest bank is the Commonwealth Bank. This is a government organization, somewhat akin to the United States Federal Reserve Bank, and is responsible for the issuing of Australian currency. The Government believes it would be best to have the control of all banking in its hands. Led by Prime Minister Joseph B. Chifley, the Government passed an act to bring this about.

But the private banks—called trading banks—were of a different opinion. They claimed that the Government lacked the authority to do what it had done. The High Court was called upon to decide the issue. Dr. Herbert V. Evatt presented the Government's side of the case before the High Court. Dr. Evatt, one of the country's foremost attorneys, is a former member of the High Court, and is now Federal Attorney General and Minister of External Affairs.

The proposed nationalization of the banks stirred deep interest all over the world. The High Court, after months of hearing evi-

Sting ray caught near the north-coast seaport of Darwin. Below, White Rock Light, Great Barrier Reef. This wonderful coral reef, running for 1,250 miles along the coast of Queensland, is broken into countless islands, some awash, some submerged, others beautifully habitable.

dence, finally gave its decision. It agreed in general with those who had taken the legislation to task, and it ruled the Nationalization of Banking Act illegal. The Government, not content with this decision, appealed to the Privy Council, which is the highest court of authority in the Commonwealth of Nations. The Privy Council is composed of representative members from each of the partner nations. Its judicial committee includes some of the greatest legal minds in the world today. As 1948 drew to a close, the case was still awaiting a hearing.

A Great Australian for Whom Precedent Was Broken

While all this was going on, one of Australia's greatest jurists, Sir Isaac Isaacs, died. He was the first Australian-born governor-general of Australia. The governor-general is the direct representative of the king in a country which, though completely self-governing and independent, is closely linked with Britain through allegiance to the Crown. British precedent was broken when Sir Isaac was appointed as the king's representative in Australia. Before that, it had always been the custom for the British Government to appoint an Englishman.

Sir Isaac, perhaps more than any other Australian, typified the young nation and the opportunities it offered. He died at the age of ninety-two. He was born in Melbourne, educated at a state school and at Melbourne University, and was a school teacher before he was called to the bar. By 1892 he had become a member of the Victoria State Parliament, and his brilliant legal mind made him a clear choice for the post of attorney general in the state.

Young Days, Stormy Days, and an Old Age Full of Honor

Those were turbulent days in Australia. The six colonies which were then self-governing were moving toward the Union that was founded in 1901. Young Isaac Isaacs was one of the men who helped to draw up the Constitution. Later he became chief justice of the High Court and was knighted by the King. Sir Isaac, who was governor-general until 1936, was not only a great jurist and statesman but also a great scholar. He died on February 11, 1948, and the leaders of many nations paid him tribute.

While we are talking about the political scene, we should mention one other thing of special importance. In February, Prime Minister Joseph B. Chifley announced that the Government had decided to increase the membership of the House of Representatives and the Senate. The increasing number of people in Australia, where it is compulsory to vote, made such a change seem wise. At present, the House has 75 members and the Senate has 36. The membership of the House will be increased to 122 and of the Senate to 60. Parliament House will be enlarged.

A Question That Was Settled in Favor of States' Rights

Rent control and price control! These are of great interest to Australians, just as they are to the people of certain other lands. During the year, the Government held a referendum to ask the people to amend the Constitution. The proposed amendment would permit the Government to keep control over rents, prices and certain conditions of marketing—a control that it had acquired during the war. However, there was a strong objection to the idea, so far as "the man in the street" was concerned. The reason is one with which most Americans are familiar—the question of states' rights. The popular vote went against the amendment, and the powers that the Federal Government wanted to keep were returned to the states.

Australians Love Sports and Good Sportsmanship

Australians are great lovers of sports, and this year the Olympic Games aroused their keenest interest. Though her representation was small, Australia met with most encouraging success in the Olympics. Two champions were John Winter, who won the high jump with a magnificent jump of 6 feet 6 inches; and Mervyn Wood, who rowed his way to victory in the single sculls (1,900 meters) event in 6 minutes, 51³⁄10 seconds.

In the Davis Cup matches at Forest Hills, New York, Australia did not do so well. She lost all her matches, but with the good spirit that one always expects to find in tennis. The American Lawn Tennis Association, for the first time in its history, sent a special plaque to the Australian players to honor their great sportsmanship. The Australians had only one answer: "We couldn't have lost to better people. But . . . next year we'll be back!"

HORSELESS BUGGY TO STREAMLINED BEAUTY

BOTH PHOTOS: FORD NEWS BUREAU

1896–1949—the chugging ugly duckling of fifty years ago has become a thing of grace and power.

By JOHN E. SCANLAN

Get a horse!

Get that varmint off the road!

Jeers and enraged sputterings were the unhappy lot of the brave motorist of fifty years ago, wherever he appeared. Frightened horses reared and upset their carriages at the mere sight or sound of an automobile. When a car broke down, jeering bystanders stood around, offering comic advice.

The automobile of the 1890's was a vastly different contraption from the sleek, smoothly purring monster of today. Only a few adventurous people dared own a "horseless carriage," which chugged along—when it ran—at the amazing speed of six to twelve miles an hour.

The vehicle was really a converted carriage, with a two-cylinder engine that clanked and clattered, and gave off evil smells. Sometimes the engine blew up; and it often caught fire. It broke down every few miles; and if you were no mechanic yourself, you were lucky if you could find someone in the vicinity to fix it. When driving in the country, you had to carry extra gasoline in cans, and grease and oil, for of course there were no gas stations. Gasoline was sold in hardware stores during the day and in drugstores at night.

As a matter of fact the first automobiles seldom were driven beyond the paved cities and towns. There were none of the wonderful concrete highways of today. In fact, as late as 1900 most highways were very bad. If all the hard-surface roads in the country had been laid end to end they would not have

55

Before grandfather could drive his Stanley Steamer, he had to pass an engineering test.

historians claim that the first one built in America was made by Charles E. Duryea, in Springfield, Massachusetts, in 1892–93. It was called the Duryea Motor Carriage or Motor Wagon. Others believe that the credit should go to a man named Elwood Haynes who designed one, in Kokomo, Indiana, in 1893–94. At any rate, both of their automobiles are on exhibit at the Smithsonian Institution in Washington, D. C., and the Smithsonian gives the credit to Duryea.

In those early days it was every man for himself in the making of horseless carriages. Men worked in barns and bicycle-repair shops or in their own cellars. No one knew much about gasoline engines or design, but everyone had ideas. There were cars of all shapes, sizes and designs, powered by gasoline, naphtha, steam and electricity. Over the years, more than 2,500 different makes of automobile have been manufactured in the United States alone, yet all but a few have disappeared. There were, for example, the Haynes, Duryea, Pierce Arrow, Roamer, Scripps-Booth, Cleveland, Oakland, Saxon, Apperson 8, Doris, White Steamer, Multiplex, Marathon, Russell, Winton, Pope Toledo and hundreds of others. All of those were familiar names to early drivers. Today, you could just about tick off all of the different makes on your fingers and toes.

Today, thousands of miles of concrete and macadam highways cross and crisscross the country. Horses scarcely twitch an ear as the streams of cars whizz by. The farmer could hardly get along without his car and truck; and, when we ride, it is in the luxury of soft cushions, warmth and protection from the weather, and at a speed that the driver of fifty years ago could only dream about.

reached from Boston to New York. During the summer months, the roads were deep with dust that rose in thick clouds to choke and blind the driver and his passengers. There was good reason for wearing long linen dusters, bonnets with veils, and goggles. In the late fall and early spring, roads were hub-deep with mud that trapped and held the most powerful car of the day.

The very early automobiles had no windshields or tops for protection in bad weather. Some doctors said that the wind, dust and engine fumes would cause many kinds of illness. Farmers said that the engine gases killed the grass and ruined their crops. Some people said that if the Lord had intended people to ride in automobiles, it would have been foretold in the Bible.

There is some disagreement as to who made the first workable automobile. Some

Today's car of gleaming chrome and steel, with smoothly purring engine, practically drives itself.

AVIATION

ADVANCES

By WILLY LEY

AUTHOR OF *Rockets and Space Travel*

THE chief events in aviation during the past year can be described in one word —"More!" More planes, more speed. More carrying capacity and more research. Especially, more research. The list of things that aeronautical engineers know is long, but the list of things that they still want to know is still longer.

They want to know, among other things, just how much air pressure there is at 100,-000 feet or at 150,000 feet.

They want to know whether the composition of the air up there is the same as farther down.

They want to know how a specially de-signed plane will behave at those altitudes, and how its specially designed instruments will behave.

They also want to know the easiest way of "doing something" about the instability of helicopters.

They want to know how one can prevent planes from running into mountain tops in bad weather.

And what to do about icing.

And whether aircraft engines can not be improved by new types.

For all these reasons there is emphasis on research.

Everybody is agreed that at least some of the future of aviation will lie much higher up than at present. With everybody agreed on that fact, however, there are still some curious obstacles. An airplane designer will be

AVIATION ADVANCES

quite willing to devote his skill and time to designing a plane that will fly at, say, 100,000 feet. But before he can go ahead he'll ask some questions. He might ask, for example, what the average daytime temperature is apt to be at 100,000 feet. And what the average night time temperature will be. In order to build a plane for 100,000-feet altitude he wants to know (and has to know) a number of things which could be properly answered only if somebody went to 100,000 feet first to find out. This looks like a deadlock, but researchers have found a way out.

Of course rockets go much higher even than 100,000 feet; but they move at very high speed and the instruments they carry have no time to gather much information. Therefore something else had to be found, something that would go to 100,000 feet and *stay* there for a while. It turned out to be a novel type of unmanned stratosphere balloon, consisting of a "tube" of plastic (polyethylene is the technical name of the substance). This balloon is a little more than 100 feet long. The wall thickness is very small, namely $\frac{1}{1000}$th of an inch, which is about as thick as the cellophane wrapper of a pack of cigarettes. The balloon itself weighs a little over 100 pounds and can carry 70 pounds of instruments.

Before the ascent the balloon is laid on the ground, in the direction of the wind. When everything is ready a small amount of

U. S. AIR FORCE PHOTO

Like an arrow in flight, the XF-86 turbojet flashes through the air at speeds that would tear the wings from ordinary planes.

helium gas is poured into the envelope, and forms a small "bubble" in the top of the balloon, about 15 feet in diameter. The helium fills less than $1\frac{1}{2}$ per cent of the available space. The other $98\frac{1}{2}$ per cent is there for the gas to expand in as the balloon rises.

At the instant of release by the ground crews these balloons look very strange because the plastic is just as transparent as household cellophane. The whole balloon simply does not look real; and since it also makes snake-like movements, one spectator exclaimed: "This is the ghost of a python rising to heaven."

After a few miles of altitude have been gained the snake-like shape disappears. Near its ceiling the balloon is probably pear-shaped, over a hundred feet tall and with a largest diameter of about seventy feet. Naturally, the instruments do not have to be brought down to the ground to be read. Part of the instrument load is a battery-powered radio transmitter which passes the readings on to a ground station for as long as the balloon is aloft—or at least as long as the batteries last. No results of these experiments were published in 1948, but in time these balloons will collect all the information needed for the design of the very high altitude airplane.

While this study is still in an early stage, much progress with new power plants can be reported. Two new types have advanced most during the year. Both happen to be about halfway between the conventional internal-combustion engine and the by now almost as conventional turbojet engine.

When different types of aircraft engines are being discussed it must always be remem-

The JRM-2, the world's largest flying-boat in regular service, takes off with a roar.

THE GLENN L. MARTIN COMPANY

bered that they are all alike in their final action. In the *internal-combustion engine* (piston engine) the straight-line movement of pistons in their cylinders is translated into the rotary motion of a shaft; the shaft carries a propeller (usually with gears in between) and the propeller produces a stream or jet of air which propels the plane. In the *turbojet engine* air is sucked in in front by the action of a rotating compressor, then heated by burning fuel in it. The hot mix-

combination of the 28-cylinder Pratt & Whitney Wasp Major engine and of something that goes under the long name of "two-stage General Electric variable discharge turbosupercharger." To explain the meaning of this formidable name we have to take it apart. The pistons need air for burning the gasoline. This air has to be forced in (*supercharger*); and that is usually done by having a turbine in the exhaust (*turbosupercharger*) driving a compressor. Normally one turbine

The Bell XS-1 experimental rocket ship streaks through the air faster than the speed of sound.

ture of air and combustion gases first turns a turbine wheel (which powers the compressor) and then emerges from an exhaust nozzle as a jet which propels the plane. In the end it is always a stream or jet of air, or of combustion gases, or a mixture of both, which does the actual work. The differences lie in the various methods by which such a stream is produced.

Since a large piston engine also produces great quantities of exhaust gases, one could ask why these exhaust gases were not used for propulsion. The answer to that question is not so simple as the question itself. But now it has been done. The new engine is known as the Wasp Major-VDT. It is a

can not take out all the energy of the exhaust. For this reason two units are operated, one after the other (*two-stage*). These things are not new. But even after the second stage has been passed, the exhaust gases still have energy which can be used for propulsion by means of a discharge nozzle. The difficulty was that the turbosuperchargers needed more or less power according to conditions such as altitude, speed and so forth. Full efficiency required that an adjustment between supercharger use and discharge could be made—and that explains the word *variable*. The result of all this is that the normal Wasp Major has 3,500 horse-power, the Wasp Major-VDT has over 4,000 horse-power plus a few hundred pounds of jet thrust.

The similarity in the final action of the internal-combustion engine and the turbojet also permitted another question. There is rotary motion in the turbojet. Then why not put a propeller on the shaft and get propeller thrust in addition to jet thrust? This combination was called "turboprop." Research work on it began several years ago, especially in Great Britain. The year 1948 saw the unveiling of at least three successful production types of such engines: the Napier "Naiad" with 1,500 shaft horse-power and 240 pounds jet thrust, the Bristol "Theseus" with 2,040 shaft horse-power and 600 pounds jet thrust and the Armstrong Siddeley "Python" with 3,700 shaft horse-power and 1,150 pounds jet thrust. Designers hope to develop this type to 5,000 shaft horse-power and 2,200 pounds jet thrust. This is still in the future; but the first air liner with turboprops is now undergoing trial flights: the Vickers "Viscount," a four-engined plane which resembles the DC-4 in external appearance.

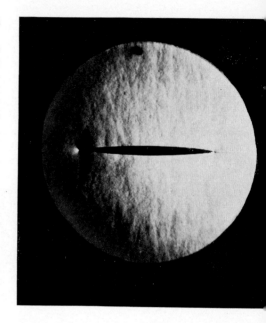

Left, subsonic speed. Center, transonic. Right, supersonic. White marks at the left or leading

Rocket and Turbojet Power Bring Speed Faster than Sound

The most important piece of aviation news of 1948 was that piloted planes had flown faster than sound. The accomplishment does not fall precisely within one year. The first faster-than-sound flight was made on October 14, 1947, but it was not announced officially until 1948. Honors for the first performance of this kind went to the Bell XS-1, rocket-powered research plane of the Air Force, piloted by Captain Charles E. Yeager. During the first half of 1948 the North American XF-86, turbojet-powered fighter plane of the Air Force, also surpassed the speed of sound but did not reach the speed of the XS-1. A little later a British research plane, the turbojet-powered deHavilland DH-108, reached the speed of sound during a one-minute dive from 40,000 to 30,000 feet.

Flight That Is Faster than Sound Is Called Supersonic Speed

Aerodynamicists, however, do not usually say that a plane flew faster than sound. They either say that it flew with supersonic speed or else they say that M was larger than 1. The letter M means the Mach number, a term that refers to an Austrian physicist by the name of Mach. He was the first to study the behavior of air at such high speeds. The reason why aerodynamicists prefer to speak about the Mach number instead of saying "supersonic" or "faster than sound" is simple. The speed of sound is not the same in various altitudes. At sea level it is quite close to 760 miles per hour, at 35,000 feet it is 663 m.p.h. and at 40,000 feet around 660 m.p.h. The Mach number is the actual speed of a plane divided by the speed of sound for that altitude. Therefore a plane which flies with a speed of 380 m.p.h. at sea level is said to travel with M-0.5 for 380 is one-half of 760. If the same plane could fly with the same speed at 40,000 feet it would travel at M-0.58.

At first glance, the use of the Mach number may look like an unnecessary complication. Actually it is not, because the behavior of air going around an airplane wing does not depend on simply the speed of the plane. It depends on that speed in relation to the speed of sound. And that is the Mach number.

Scientists now distinguish three different speed ranges. From M-0 to M-0.8 we have the subsonic (meaning "below sound") speed range. Above M-1.2 we have the super-

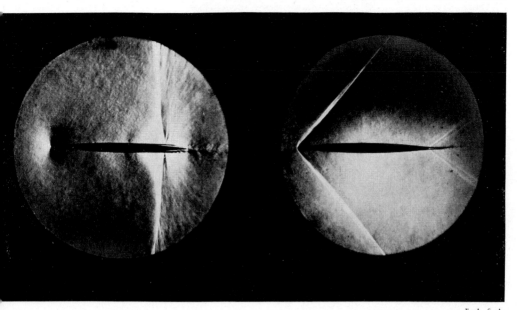

N. A. C. A.

edge, and at the trailing edge, of each wing show the amount of destructive wind shock in each range. It is worst in the transonic range and deflected at supersonic speed.

sonic (meaning "beyond sound") speed range. Between M-0.8 and M-1.2 we have the transonic ("across sound") speed range.

What would happen if planes should be fast enough to approach the speed of sound was for many years a matter for discussion among scientists. Wartime experiences with fast airplanes, approaching about M-0.6, were simply bad. There seemed to be violent forces which might shake the plane apart. Some experts were openly afraid to try for higher speeds. Others hoped that ways and means might be found to overcome what had been called "compressibility effects." A very few, pointing to the fact that the shells from large guns emerged from the muzzle with about M-2, were confident that high speeds could be reached. When the news came that the Germans had a rocket-propelled interceptor, the Messerschmitt Me-163B, which did 550 m.p.h. or M-0.7, hopes began to rise. And when V-2 appeared, doing M-6, most experts were convinced that it was just the wings on a plane that caused trouble. Obviously the fuselage could go as fast as one could push it.

It was about then that the XS-1 was designed. The designers gave it a body almost like that of the V-2 rocket, with very thin wings. They asked for a rocket motor that would burn liquid oxygen with ethyl alcohol and develop 6,000 pounds of thrust. Such a motor was supplied by the firm of Reaction Motors, Inc. This motor had another useful feature. It was really a battery of four rocket motors, each with 1,500 pounds thrust. The pilot could use one, two, three or all four motors and control his speed that way. While the XS-1 could take off from the ground, it was decided to hang it from a B-29 bomber, which would carry it up to about 30,000 feet and provide it with several hundred miles per hour of speed without using any fuel.

A large number of preliminary tests were made, during which all went well. Then the pilot who had volunteered for the job, Captain Yeager, let the motors run full blast for the first time. The date, as we mentioned, was October 14. The XS-1 passed the much feared transonic range without falling apart, as some had still predicted, and achieved a faster-than-sound flight. The official announcement was that it traveled with "M higher than one," but the trade journal Aviation Week stated that the speed was 1,100 miles per hour which corresponds to M-1.4.*

It was thus proved that an airplane de-

* According to the same source the XF-86 did 700 m.p.h. in level flight at an altitude between 30,000 and 40,000 feet.

American C-54's (above) are a part of the great Airlift bridging Berlin's blockade.

Britain spans the blockade with huge Sunderlands that land on Berlin's Wannsee.

signed for very high speed flight could attain supersonic speeds, provided only that its motor was powerful enough to push it hard enough. This does not mean that all the problems of supersonic flight have been solved. But everybody is confident now that they *can* be solved.

The "newsiest" aviation event of the year took place in Germany, and it has put everybody on this planet to thinking about what can be done by air. This was the "Airlift" as we call it, or *die grosse Luftbrücke* ("the great air bridge") as the Germans say.

Early in July 1948 the Russians decided to blockade Berlin. The city is controlled by four nations; but it is surrounded by the Russian Occupation Zone of Germany. The Russians blockaded the sections of Berlin that were controlled by the United States, England and France. These sections were thus threatened with starvation.

After a number of hurried conferences the Americans decided to deliver food and other supplies to Berlin by air, and the British and French promised to help. The Airlift actually began on July 10 with British and American planes. The first British plane which reached Berlin was loaded with dehydrated potatoes. The first American plane happened to carry raisins by the ton which led Berliners to speak of the American planes as *Rosinenbrummer*, or raisin flies.

The American planes that were available in Germany at that time were mostly C-47's (the military equivalent of the DC-3), with a carrying capacity of between only 3 and 4 tons. There were also a few C-54's (military equivalent of the DC-4 air liner) with a little more than twice that carrying capacity. While American C-54's were rushed to Germany from all over the globe, the British, who also had only medium-sized planes available during the first few days, called in their enormous Short Sunderland flying-boats. These can carry a little over 5 tons pay-load per trip. It so happens that a large lake, or rather a string of large lakes, the Havel Lakes, are in the British sector of the occupied German capital. The British could make use of these lakes, which are sheltered by wooded hills. The American planes used were all land planes, most of them landing on Tempelhof Airport.

After a few weeks, the weight of the goods carried for the relief of the blockaded city reached a record of 2,400 tons a day. That was only the beginning—in every respect! The Germans had been told that food for the city would be brought in by air. They real-

ized that this could not be an easy job. In spite of earlier evacuation and a battle fought in the city itself, Berlin still numbers close to three million inhabitants. The Germans had also been told that some coal would be supplied by air. Then the German workers who unloaded the Airlift planes saw to their surprise that the planes also brought construction materials and construction equipment to extend the runways at Tempelhof Airport and to build another airport for Berlin. The British started flying in small emergency power plants for the production of electric current. Each one weighs about 6,000 pounds and two made up the load of a British "York." They brought several hundred such power plants to Berlin.

The French do not have many airplanes at their disposal, but they flew what they had.

American planes flying the Airlift land in Berlin with food and supplies every three minutes.

COURTESY, THE NEW YORK TIMES

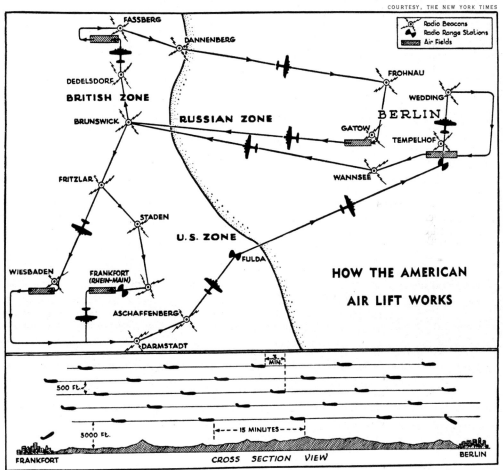

HOW THE AMERICAN AIR LIFT WORKS

CROSS SECTION VIEW

While the British ordered most of their available planes into the Airlift, the whole performance became more American every day. By October the Americans had two hundred planes on the Airlift. Of these 154 were the large C-54's; 66 more C-54's were added late in October. Even before that addition the Americans were flying 5,000 tons of supply daily in good weather and 3,000 tons daily under the worst weather conditions in which one can fly at all.

Planes Take Off and Land with Clock-like Regularity

Many of the planes make several round trips a day. They are spaced about three minutes apart and the loading of the planes at one end, unloading at the other, servicing, fueling and repair have grown into a wonderful and magnificently functioning organization. Each plane is made to carry the maximum of which it is capable. A DC-3 or DC-4 loaded to the same take-off weight as the planes on the Airlift would never be permitted to take off from an airport in America.

In October 1948 the schedule had been arranged so tightly that the ground-control system (GCA) at Tempelhof always handled several approaching planes simultaneously. If a pilot missed his approach he was ordered to return *with his load,* because there was no room in the landing pattern for a second try by any plane.

The Airlift itself was backed by commercial aircraft. These supplied spare parts and so forth by flying them across the Atlantic for the Airlift planes in the American zone. The first such supply movement took place in July, and consisted of 62 tons of military material. The second "lift," a few weeks later, consisted of 100 tons of engines. Both regular air lines and so-called "non-scheduled" air transport companies have taken part in this aerial backing of the Airlift.

Practice for Pilots; Food for People

To the military, the Airlift provided an opportunity for practice in the handling of large numbers of aircraft on a round-the-clock basis. It was a fine chance for seeing what such an organization could do. The outcome was that it proved possible to feed even a very large city by air.

"NEPA" stands for *N*uclear *E*nergy for *P*ropulsion of *A*ircraft and is one of the government projects going on at Oak Ridge. Naturally much of the work going on there is classified as "secret" for reasons which do not need to be explained. A few results of the studies have been made public, and they afford a fascinating glimpse of what the near future will bring.

What Sort of Power Next? Perhaps Atomic Energy

The Oak Ridge scientists have stated flatly that the theory of flight by means of atomic energy is "now 99 per cent complete" and that the work still to be done is one of straight engineering development. They also predicted that this engineering work should take "five years or less," so that, counting two years for construction and testing, there should be atomic-energy planes flying around seven years from now.

The main problem seems to be that of "shielding." Any kind of atomic reaction must produce dangerous radiations, which are all the more dangerous since they cause harmless construction materials that are near to turn radioactive. In an atomic pile on the ground, shielding is accomplished very simply by massive concrete structures. The same method could be used, without any change, on an ocean liner, but an airplane simply could not carry enough shielding of this kind.

Atomic Energy Brings Up New Engineering Problems

Whatever the Oak Ridge scientists want to use is their secret, but it must still be large and heavy because they say that the first atomic-energy airplane will probably be larger even than the big B-36 bomber. Other problems, new in aviation engineering, are caused by the fact that the weight of the "fuel" can not be distributed over the fuselage and wings, but is all in one spot in the fuselage. Still another problem is caused by the strange new fact that the airplane would weigh as much on landing as it did on take-off. Ordinary air liners lose tons of weight during flight because of fuel consumption. An atomic-energy airplane, however, would have unlimited range. Any distance—even around the globe at the equator—could be flown as a non-stop hop.

We'll see whether it will actually take seven years for these prophecies to come true. Maybe half the time will be enough.

HELICOPTERS
in Canada

By CHARLES CLAY
Canadian Author and Journalist

THE grizzled Fire Ranger took a long look at the helicopter sitting on the beach at the Sioux Lookout base. After a minute he turned to the Chief Ranger and said, "I'm of the opinion that the thing just can't fly."

At that moment the ungainly machine lifted off the beach and, at a thirty-foot altitude, flew sideways. Then it settled gently down on the apron in front of the Forestry building. The Chief Ranger looked at his grizzled companion with a query in his eye, but the old Ranger, scratching his head, grinned: "I'm still a bit doubtful!"

It is true that gracefulness is not one of the strong points of helicopters. They are often called "flying windmills" or "eggbeaters." All the same, they can do almost anything except fly upside down. They can take off straight up in the air, fly forward, backward or sideways and land on a postage stamp. Their hovering ability is invaluable. If there is something a helicopter pilot does not understand, he can stop in the air and look it over—or just stop and think!

"Eggbeaters" patrol forests, fight fires and perform many other important services. For instance, they fly ahead of ships to guide them through ice packs. They lead fishing vessels to runs of fish. They are used to take censuses of wild animals, to patrol highways and pipe lines and to lay telephone wires. They serve the Post Office Department, the armed services, ranching, agriculture and many other organizations and industries.

Many Canadian bush-country jobs that have always, until recently, been done from the ground can be done much better with helicopters. Take timber appraising, for instance. Over great stretches of forest and timberland where the trees are destined for logging and pulpwood, timber appraisers can fly as low and as slow as they like and so can make exact estimates of how much wood there is to be cut.

Prospecting is another job that helicopters do well. Prospecting with "flying windmills" began in Canada and is now carried on in the United States, Mexico and Venezuela. It is exciting to explore an area for gold or oil or other minerals; but when it is done on foot the job can be very slow and difficult. For instance, on foot, it would take two engineers and two helpers about seventy days to make a mineral survey of an area only five miles square. A survey of the same area with

In rescue work, the injured may be hoisted up to safety with a cable, while the helicopter hovers in the air above the spot.

RCAF PHOTO

SHELL OIL CO. PHOTO

Pontoons for marshy landings! The strange-looking tripod supports a gravity meter.

a helicopter carrying a magnetometer is a matter of hours instead of days.

A magnetometer is an instrument designed to aid man in his exploration of the earth's crust—a magnetic device used in both airplanes and helicopters. In many cases, however, the latter do a better though slower job. If you watched one in action, you would see the helicopter trailing, at the end of a steel cable, a curious cylinder which looks like a giant cigar and carries electronic gadgets that detect underground rock formations. The cabin of the helicopter is fitted with a maze of wires and charts that automatically record the findings of the trailed instrument. The magnetometer is a peacetime development of an airborne device used during the war to detect submarines.

Pack mules are no match for helicopters in the job of land surveying. In the summer of 1948 the Canadian Government sent two survey crews and two helicopters into the

Yukon. They made a topographical survey of more than 15,000 square miles of muskeg, forests and mountains. To make this survey with ground crews and pack mules would have taken from six to nine years.

In the fertile fields of the Prairie Provinces, farmers use helicopters to dust their grain crops. The Ontario Department of Mines and Resources uses them to dust jackpine and spruce against the attacks of hungry armies of budworms, while out west, in British Columbia's famous Kootenay and Fraser valleys, they are used for dusting fruit trees.

When airplanes crash in the wilderness, it is often nearly impossible to reach the scene of the disaster. If there is no near-by place for a rescue plane to land, precious time is lost trying to send in ground-rescue crews; but helicopters can usually find some small space to settle down on, even when the terrain is very rough. They can be equipped to land on either land or water.

"Flying windmills" proved their worth as rescuers at the end of World War II. Now, a search-and-rescue system has been set up by the International Civil Aviation Organization at Montreal. Canada, because of her air traffic and her great northern bush country, is playing a leading part in this work. The Royal Canadian Air Force has a small fleet of helicopters for rescue duty, with machines based at Greenwood, Nova Scotia; Rockcliffe, Ontario; and Edmonton, Alberta. They are used in co-operation with the Canadian Army and Navy, the Royal Canadian Mounted Police and other government agencies.

In the winter of 1947 the machine at Greenwood searched for four missing hunters. It moved slowly along at a very low height and was able to follow the marks the men had made in the snow, and so tracked them down to a cabin in which they had taken shelter.

Air-Sea Rescue Work Comes Face to Face with Danger

The most nerve-wracking kind of helicoptering is air-sea rescue, when the machines must hover above storm-tossed boats and angle for the victims with a hook on a strong steel cable. First, web harnesses are lowered to the sailors in distress. The harness fits under the arms, and has a ring stoutly fastened in front. The sailors put these harnesses on and then snap the dangling hook into the ring. Then a motor in the helicopter drives the hoist—which is a lifting apparatus —and up come the mariners, one by one, into the helicopter cabin. If all the victims are unconscious, then some one has to climb down the steel cable and put a harness on each of them.

Do not confuse a helicopter with an autogyro. Although both have whirling blades called rotors, the autogyro is driven forward by a regular propeller in the nose. The autogyro was being developed before the helicopter but it was not able to do the things a helicopter can, and is not generally used any more.

Helicopters are not without faults. They are still slow. They are still poor weightlifters for their size and for the amount of fuel they burn. One pilot said that trying to fly a helicopter is like trying to sit on top of a greased ball. Flying them is very difficult because they maneuver so easily that they keep the pilot constantly on the alert. The whirling rotors cause a down draft equal to a 40-mile-per-hour wind which blows up dust on taking off and landing. Moreover, helicopters are expensive. Even a small one costs about $5,000, while the larger commercial machines cost as much as $70,000 each.

The helicopter industry actually started only in 1939. The first hop was just 250 yards. Helicopters can now go 400 miles in one hop, can fly as high as 21,000 feet and can reach a speed of more than 100 miles an hour. Newest of all are jet-propelled helicopters, still in the experimental stage.

So far, the most common kinds of helicopters in Canada and the United States are the Sikorsky, the Bell, the Kellett and the Bendix. The largest have 2 rotors, one on each end. There are different designs, carrying from 2 to 10 passengers, and designers are working on models to carry 24. During World War II, the United States Army, Navy and Coast Guard and the British Royal Navy and the Royal Air Force used about 400 helicopters. They were not made in Canada until 1947, when a machine specially designed for rugged work in the northern bush country took to the air.

Vast stretches of northern Canada are covered with low, rocky, forested hills. Although there are many large lakes and rivers, there are also great areas where the lakes are too small for winged aircraft. Helicopters are ideal for such territory. That is why many experts believe that these flying machines have a more useful future in Canada than in any other country.

The M-14 Whirlajet uses jet engines of the German V-1 buzz-bomb type on the tips of its rotors.

the BALLET

The beauty and color of the ballet never loses its magic charm, and in recent years it has become increasingly popular. Here are some of today's stars. Above, left to right: Nora Kaye in *The Black Swan*; Yvette Chauvire in *Divertissements*; and Rosella Hightower. Left, center: Leon Danielian, Alexandra Danilova and Frederic Franklin. Below, left to right: Frederic Franklin; Lucia Chase in *Bluebeard*; and Alicia Markova. At the top of the next page, Alexandra Danilova in a classic pose; and below, Mary Ellen Moylan and Luis Trapaga. Right, a close-up of Miss Danilova's legs poised on the tips of the toes, or *sur la pointe*, as the position is called.

PHOTOS FROM BALLET THEATER, LIPNITZKI, FROM FRENCH EMBASSY INFORMATION DIVISION AND BALLET RUSSE DE MONTE CARLO, INC.

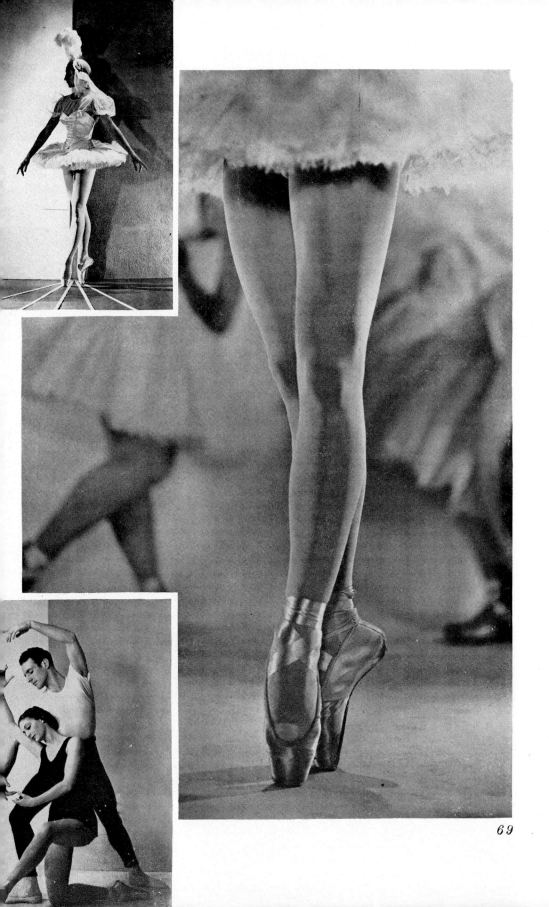

Right, the breath-taking throne-room scene in the Ballet Theater's production of *Princess Aurora*, presented by Lucia Chase and Oliver Smith.

Final scene from *La Rose Rouge* presented by the Paris Opera Ballet. The ballet is based on a story by Oscar Wilde, the music is by Paul Dukas and the choreography (dance arrangement) by Etchevéry.

In this scene based on the story of Orpheus and Eurydice, Maria Tallchief, an American Indian, and Nicholas Magallanes show us the piteous lovers on their ill-fated journey.

BALLET SOCIETY

BALLET RUSSE DE MONTE CARLO, INC.

Guests at the masked ball in *The Night Shadow*, a one-act ballet by Vittorio Rieti. The choreography of this charming fantasy was done by George Balanchine, himself a famous dancer.

71

Discoveries in BIOLOGY and MEDICINE

By MAC V. EDDS, JR.

*Assistant Professor of Biology,
Brown University*

DURING the past few years, the search for a better understanding of the crippling disease infantile paralysis has been greatly intensified. Although it may be decades before this disease is brought under control, new discoveries about it are being made rapidly. One particularly interesting finding has just been announced. Considerable evidence has been gathered over the years to show that the tiny virus which causes infantile paralysis, or polio, as it is often called, enters the brain or spinal cord by moving along nerve fibers connecting these organs with the rest of the body. Since the polio virus is too small to be seen with the ordinary microscope, however, it has

The Metasequoia, believed to be extinct for 20,-000,000 years, was found growing in China.

RALPH W. CHANEY

never been possible to follow the invading particles along this route. The electron microscope, which magnifies objects far more than an ordinary light microscope, has at last made this direct demonstration possible. Normal nerve fibers, viewed with an electron microscope, look like cables made up of numerous smaller filaments. The filaments (each one is less than a millionth of an inch in diameter) appear to have a heavy outer rind and a lighter core. Thus, they rather resemble a piece of macaroni, although they are not really hollow. Once these filaments had been seen, the question arose whether the polio virus might be conducted through them. Nerves of monkeys were therefore exposed to the virus and then examined with an electron microscope to test this possibility. The guess proved to be a good one. Many of the filaments of the infected nerves were filled with the tiny virus particles. They move along the nerve slowly, traveling about one-twelfth of an inch per hour.

One of the biggest problems of cancer lies in recognizing it early enough to treat it. This is particularly true of cancer of the organs within the body because, being hidden, they can be studied only by X rays. In the past, X rays have been used either to take pictures of internal organs or to make them visible on a special screen. The latter procedure has many advantages—it is like watching a moving picture. But even so, the pictures are very dim and their interpretation sometimes becomes almost guesswork. They can not be made any brighter without exposing the patient or the doctor to damage from the X rays.

A new device has been developed which greatly increases the brightness of these pictures without endangering anyone. It produces its effect by acting on the X rays after they pass through the patient but before they strike the viewing screen. A 500-fold increase in brightness results and internal structures can be seen with a detail never before possible. Earlier and more accurate recognition of hidden cancers should now be possible.

Penicillin is the best known and most widely used of all the germ-killing substances

This test device has proved that the brightness of X-ray pictures can be increased 500 times.

which have been discovered in recent years. This drug is now produced on a tremendous scale by growing the mold which forms it in huge tanks. Penicillin, so scarce a few years ago that few people could share its benefits, has now become available to all. But penicillin has one important disadvantage. Once injected into the body of a sick patient, it rapidly disappears. Repeated and often painful injections must therefore be given every few hours. Longer-lasting penicillin preparations have been made by mixing the drug with oils or waxes, but these left much to be desired. A recently developed mixture of penicillin, peanut oil and an aluminum soap is much better. When a single dose of this mixture is injected, it remains in the blood in germ-killing amounts for as long as four days. The usefulness of this important drug has thus been extended even further.

Altogether, penicillin may be used to treat almost a hundred different diseases. Despite this remarkable record, however, there are many other ills for which penicillin does nothing. Many scientists have therefore searched for similar drugs which would attack germs that penicillin leaves untouched. Dozens of compounds from various other lowly plants have been prepared and tested. Most of them have little value, but each year two or three new drugs are generally discovered that make more diseases curable for the first time. As more and more microbes are

thus brought under control, it is worth wondering whether Pasteur was right when he predicted that disease germs would some day be abolished. Certainly, if the war against microbes continues for another fifty years as successfully as it has for the half-century since Pasteur died, diseases caused by germs may well become nothing more than memories.

For thousands of years man has complained of the short span of human life and has envied supposedly longer-lived animals. Claims that certain animals live hundreds of years have been accepted without question. Few people have taken the trouble to check actual records to determine the truth. But now records of this kind from many different zoological parks have been gathered together and compared. The results clearly contradict popular legends about long-lived animals. Except for a few giant tortoises, man lives longer than any animal ever kept in captivity. We still know little about wild animals but it does not seem likely that they would long outlive their captive brothers.

Parrots and elephants are frequently credited with tremendously long lives. Yet no elephant is known to have exceeded 60 years. The rest rarely reach the age of 30, and 15 or 20 years seems a good average for the larger animals. Against these figures, the human life span which occasionally extends more than a century looks pretty good after all.

A fish has an acute sense of smell, although most of its nose is inside the head where it can not be seen. Indeed, the part of its brain which receives information from the nose about odors is unusually large. An interesting experiment has been performed to show just how well fish do smell. Minnows were allowed to swim in a tank through which two separate currents of water were flowing. One type of water plant had been washed in the current on one side of the tank, while another plant had been washed in the other current. The fish were soon taught to prefer one plant scent over another and to swim into the current containing it by rewarding them with food when they chose the correct odor.

Many plants and animals that once lived on the earth have long since perished; we say they are extinct. Some of them died millions of years ago, yet we know about them through skeletons preserved in stone as fossils. A few years ago, scientists were amazed to learn that a fish caught by a commercial fisherman off the coast of Africa was truly a "living fossil." Fossil records of the ancestors of this fish showed that it had once been common but had apparently died off many millions of years previously. Discoveries of this kind are very rare, of course. They are important, not only because they are interesting, but also because they show us how much we still have to learn of creatures living in out-of-the-way places.

Recently, a "living fossil" of a plant has been found. The plant is a tree, a close relative of the giant redwood trees living in the western United States. This tree, known to botanists as Metasequoia, was believed to have become extinct some twenty million years ago. It has now been discovered alive, however, near a remote village in the interior of China. Indeed, a small forest of these trees, some nearly a hundred feet tall, has survived. It is as though a segment of a distant yesterday had been preserved, escaping destruction for twenty million years. So far as we know, Metasequoia is the most ancient type of tree to be found anywhere in the world.

Radioactive Carbon Probes Secrets of Photosynthesis

Almost all living things depend on the fundamental food-making process known as photosynthesis. Photosynthesis is a chemical reaction carried out by green plants. The reaction combines carbon dioxide and water into simple sugars and occurs only in the bodies of green plants bathed by light. The sugars thus formed are changed by the plants into many other food substances, vitamins and the like which make up animal and human diets.

Photosynthesis is a very complex chemical event, even though its raw materials and its finished products are relatively simple compounds. Man has long sought to understand the details of this reaction, but progress has been slow. Now, thanks to the use of radioactive carbon, most of the process can be explained. Radioactive carbon is the same as ordinary carbon except for a slight change in weight and in its ability to give off charged particles whose travels can be measured with special instruments. When carbon dioxide is made from radioactive carbon, it is said to be "tagged" and its fate in photosynthesis can be followed closely.

Virtually all the chemical steps in photosynthesis have been discovered in this way. These same steps occur in reverse order when animals break down sugars to carbon dioxide and water. One great problem remains unexplained. Light, as we said, is necessary for photosynthesis. The problem is: How is light used in this process?

Penicillin, the wonder drug, is produced on a huge scale by the growth of mold in big tanks.

CHAS. PFIZER & CO., INC.

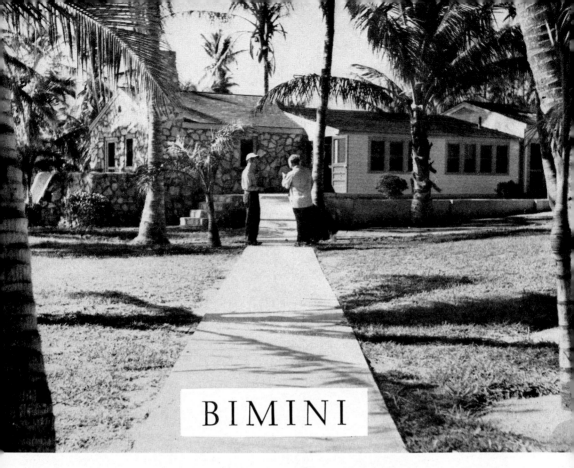

BIMINI

Scientists' Paradise

By Wayne M. Faunce

Vice-Director and Executive Secretary, American Museum of Natural History

IF you have ever gone exploring among the rocks and tide pools along the Atlantic coast, you have probably seen many strange and interesting creatures that make their home in the sea or along its margin. Sea-anemones, sand dollars, little crabs and starfish live in the sun-warmed waters of the pools left by the tide among the rocks. In the ocean itself, either near shore or in the depths farther out, live numerous kinds of animals and plants. Small creatures such as the lobster and the shrimp share the salt waters with the mammoth whale and shark. Brilliantly colored fishes, startling in their blues, yellows and reds, swim in the same sea as the silver cod and hake. Moving gently back and forth with the wash of the tide, or

deep down below the surface, the long-fingered seaweed responds to the least motion of the water.

There are several very definite and distinct branches of science that deal with marine plants and animals. Many biologists study specimens in their laboratories, far from the sea. Some work in laboratories by the sea, where they can make detailed studies of the behavior and habits of marine life in its own environment. A few scientists—William Beebe in his bathysphere, for instance—have gone down into the sea to watch the curious life that goes on below the surface of the waves.

The Caribbean Sea, which lies between the West Indies and Central and South

The Lerner Marine Laboratory on Bimini Island. The library building is built of stone.

America, is extremely rich in many forms of marine life, both plant and animal. In March 1948, on the little island of Bimini, one of the British West Indies, a new scientific laboratory was dedicated to the study of marine life in the Caribbean. Bimini lies sixty miles off the coast of Florida, due east of Miami. The island, which is only five and a half miles long and about six hundred feet wide, is now the home of the Lerner Marine Laboratory. The laboratory was presented as a gift to the American Museum of Natural

harbor there are great numbers of living corals and sea fans. Along the western side stretches a fine beach of sand composed of pulverized coral.

If, after you have gone to college, you should decide to become a marine biologist, it is quite possible that some day you might find yourself working on Bimini. The work of the laboratory is carried on by the members of the Department of Fishes and Aquatic Biology of the American Museum of Natural History. In addition, however,

On the bay side of Bimini are the piers and the stockades, or pens, in which the fish are kept.

History by Mr. Michael Lerner, president of the International Game Fish Association.

Bimini is ideally located for the study of Caribbean life, on the edge of the Great Bahama Bank. Between Bimini and Florida flows the Gulf Stream, with its many interesting and unusual forms of fish and plant life. The laboratory stands on a two-and-a-half-acre piece of land, one edge of which faces the Gulf Stream side of the island, and the other, the Great Bahama Bank side. The eastern side of the island forms an excellent but shallow harbor. At the entrance to the

other scientists who are carrying on serious research in this field can make arrangements to use the laboratory and its equipment.

If you should go to Bimini, you might very easily imagine that you had landed in a tropical fairyland, far removed from the workaday world of the scientist. The waters which surround the island are of the most intense and brilliant blue, reflecting the color of the sky above. The leaves of palms and mangroves stir with the faintest breeze. The long beach of coral sand, white and inviting under the sun, is a paradise for bathers. Little coves and inlets, partially enclosed by land, provide interesting bases for exploration, and for loafing. In spite of all these attractions, however, the laboratory on Bimini is headquarters for a hard-working and serious group of scientists.

There will be plenty of time later for you to explore the laboratory buildings. Let us go down to the docks on the bay side of the island. Here, beside the docks, are huge stockades, or enclosures, built to house the fish and other sea creatures that are being studied. As you look through the transparently clear water into one of the stockades, you notice giant sea turtles flippering their way aimlessly up and down, or traveling slowly around and around in circles. Each turtle carries with him a few free passengers —fish known as remoras—which attach themselves to turtles or sharks, or even to ships, by peculiar suction cups on the tops of their heads.

You may possibly at some time have seen schools of dolphins or porpoises playing in the water along the shore. Here, in a second stockade, are three of these fascinating animals, about eight or nine feet long. They curve through the water, leap into the air and then plunge down one after the other. They seem to be extremely playful creatures, and often, at sea, afford much entertainment to passengers on ships.

The Strange Sea-Going Adventures of a Cow-Porpoise and Her Calf

Mr. Lerner, donor of the laboratory, has tremendous collections of fish of all sizes and kinds in the Bimini stockades and undersea cages. When he decided that he would like to add some porpoises to his collection, he started on an adventure. Two porpoises—a cow-porpoise and her half-grown calf—were to be brought over from Miami in a boat chartered for that purpose. They started on the trip to their new home at dawn one morning. The cow-porpoise, nine feet long and about four hundred pounds in weight, and the calf, lay on the deck of the boat. Since porpoises, like whales, breathe air, it did not bother them to be out of the water. The crew of the boat, however, was kept busy pouring water over them, to keep their skins from getting dry. Halfway to Bimini the weather became so bad that, with a broken rudder, the boat had to turn back. In another boat the porpoises started out again, but the

Mmm, that's good! A porpoise comes to dinner.

Above, bringing in a specimen swordfish. Below, scientist at work in Bimini laboratory.

weather grew even worse, the boat lost its way, and it was 3:30 A.M. the next morning before they reached Bimini. Even then they did not actually reach the island, for the boat was grounded at low tide some distance from the dock and had to wait for high tide to float it again. At last the porpoises were dumped from specially constructed stretchers into the water of the stockade. For a day or so they showed signs of stiffness and swam about rather clumsily. In time they completely recovered and came to regard the stockade in Bimini Bay as their home.

The Landlubber Octopus Takes a Walk

A strange thing happened at Bimini which some of my friends call a whopping fish story. Coming from the laboratory building early one morning, I found a strange visitor shambling awkwardly across the dew-covered grass. This was the first time I had ever seen a landlubber octopus. This creature had been placed in one of the outdoor concrete tanks near the laboratory building. I knew that he did not care to stay in one place very long, for I never knew in which tank I should find him. When I surprised him, out on his early morning stroll, he turned and hurried back to his tank. Pulling himself up the concrete wall with the suckers on his tentacles, he plopped down into the water where he belonged. Several times I encountered this strange morning wanderer, but I was never quick enough to get a picture of him on the lawn. Finally, early one morning, we found him dead on the grass. He had wandered once too often, and too far, from his home tank.

The Beauty of the Marine Underworld as Seen from a Glass-bottomed Boat

Before you leave Bimini, you will want to go out in the glass-bottomed boat and watch the curious sea life below you. If you have luck, you may anchor over a spot where schools of many-colored fish are playing. Perhaps, near by, a twenty-foot shark may be lying on the ocean bottom, paying no attention to the frisky fish. The water is so clear that you can see down into it for sixty feet or more. You will be astonished by the beauty of the corals and the color of the sea fans.

If you aren't nervous, you can put on a diving helmet and climb down into the water

of one of the stockades. It is very comfortable to sit on the bottom of the ocean watching the fish and the long rippling tentacles of the sea weeds. You may even make friends with curious creatures peering from crevices in the rocks—lobsters, crabs or small fish.

Of course, if you happen to be a fisherman by inclination, Bimini provides a fishing paradise. Out in the Gulf Stream great marlin and other game fish are waiting for your skill in trolling. Or, if you prefer, you can fish quietly from an anchored boat in forty or fifty feet of untroubled water nearer shore. Numerous kinds of fish abound in all the waters off Bimini.

While the life of the Bimini scientists looks to the outsider almost like a vacation existence, it is really made up largely of good hard scientific work. Much remains to be learned about the creatures and plants which inhabit the sea, and almost nothing is known so far about the deep-sea or abyssal fishes. Only a few miles from Bimini the sea is 3,000 feet deep, and as time goes on exploration of these depths will yield many answers to our questions.

Bimini Scientists Hope to Make the Sea Yield More of Its Riches

As we learn more about the types of animal and plant life in the Caribbean, the picture of plant and animal behavior will become clearer. The Bimini scientists hope also to find out more about the possible economic values of the sea. Dr. Harold J. Humm, of Duke University, has already spent some time at Bimini studying seaweed. It is hoped that from certain kinds of seaweed growing there agar-agar can be manufactured. It is in cultures of this material that germs are grown for hospital study. Before World War II much of this seaweed was imported from Japan.

In the laboratory, which is one of the four buildings belonging to the institution, there is a library stocked with books on marine biology. Beyond it is a large room with tanks for smaller fishes. You may be fortunate enough to enter the tank room at the moment when the bat fish is fishing. This curious creature can, at will, extend a little fishing rod from its forehead. At the end of the rod is a moving piece of flesh that looks like a worm wriggling on the end of a fish line. When a small fish comes close, lured by the false bait, the bat fish swallows it up.

One of Lois Lenski's delightful pictures for *Boom Town Boy*, published by J. B. Lippincott.

BOOKS OF THE YEAR FOR BOYS AND GIRLS

By May Lamberton Becker

Reader's Guide, N. Y. Herald Tribune
Weekly Book Review

FASCINATING as facts can be, there still is room for fantasy in young people's reading. Among the prize-winning books of the year are some of a particularly good kind—the story that can best be described by saying that it couldn't actually happen, but if it should, this is exactly the way it would. In other words, what happens in the story may be impossible, but the details of how it happens are so true to life that they make the whole thing sound true—and delightful.

A fine example of this is THE TWENTY-ONE BALLOONS, written and illustrated by William Pène du Bois. After taking a first prize at the Children's Spring Book Festival

at the New York HERALD TRIBUNE, it also won the year's outstanding award for the best children's book, the Newbery Medal. Before airplanes were invented, when the only way to get about in the air was by free balloons floating with the wind, sportsmen took a keen interest in racing balloons. These were of enormous size, so that they would stay up as long as possible. The balloon in this story was not built for racing, however, but because its owner wanted to get off the earth for a real vacation. He built a balloon with a car like a small house hanging under it, and set off across the Pacific Ocean. Some time later, he was picked up in the Atlantic Ocean, surrounded by the wreckage of

My Father's Dragon, by Ruth Stiles Gannett. Pictures, Ruth Chrisman Gannett. Random House.

twenty-one balloons! What could have happened? What did happen makes a fascinating story that would appeal to any child and to grownups too.

The Caldecott Medal for the best picture book was won by WHITE SNOW, BRIGHT SNOW, written by Alvin Tresselt, illustrated in color by Roger Duvoisin. This is the kind of fantasy that brings out the magical quality in familiar things; its singing words tell what the first snow of the season means to children, and the pictures have the same touch of magic.

The prize book for younger children in the Children's Spring Book Festival was not only the first work of a young author, but also a fantasy of the first order. This was MY FATHER'S DRAGON, by Ruth Stiles Gannett, illustrated by Ruth Chrisman Gannett. As if a small boy were talking, it tells how "my father," when he was a little boy, met an old cat who told him about an island it had visited in its seafaring days. The island was inhabited only by wild animals, who had captured a baby dragon and were using it as a ferry boat. So "my father" sets off at once to rescue the sad little dragon, has immensely funny adventures, and sails out of the last page on the dragon's back.

If You Want to Grow Up Famous, Try Rescuing a Dragon

If an older reader knows that "my father" is the famous literary critic Lewis Gannett, he finds the book even more entertaining. A little boy, however, loves it because it is so like the tall stories little boys tell one another to prove that "my father is the most wonderful man in the world." The pictures in this book follow every turn of the tale.

DAUGHTER OF THE MOUNTAIN, by Louise Rankin, took the Spring Festival prize for "middle-aged" children's books. This told how a ten-year-old Tibetan girl, whose terrier was carried off by dog-stealers, trailed it over the wild and towering mountain passes of her country, clear to the coast. Reading it is like being in that high country, as the author was for years. The prize for older children's books went to THE CRIMSON ANCHOR, a sea thriller by Felix Riesenberg, Jr., a real sailorman, who knows what modern seamanship is. The prize of the Julia Ellsworth Ford Foundation was won by Alice Rogers Hager, for CANVAS CASTLE, a novel for girls, about a girl who longed for a permanent home.

Canadian Forest Country and Geography without Tears

There are quite a few books with scenes laid in different regions of the Western Hemisphere—especially in the north. CANADIAN SUMMER, by Hilda Van Stockum, takes the large family we met at Washington, in THE MITCHELLS, to Canadian forest country. Younger children have PETER PAINTS THE U. S. A., pictures by Arnold Bare, text by Jean Poindexter and the Junior Reviewers. This is geography without tears: when Mr. Bare was ten years old, his father took him around the United States and he carried a paint-box. The sketches he did then he has

now made into finished pictures in color.

For historical novels of the American Civil War period, young people have BITTERSWEET, by Martha Barnhard Harper, and MARY MONTGOMERY, REBEL, by Helen Fern Daringer. The colonies just before the War of Independence are a vivid background for BLUE DOWRY, by Florence Maule Updegraff; and RIVER DRAGON, by Carl D. Lane, tells about the first steamboat to go up the Mississippi River.

Flora Bailey's SUMMER AT YELLOW SANDS shows ten-year-olds the Navajo Indians as they are today; and in Lois Lenski's BOOM TOWN BOY, they find out what the discovery of oil meant to Oklahoma, and what it did for—and to—the farmers. The outstanding sports story of the year is John Tunis' HIGHPOCKETS, about baseball. Of the many excellent biographies, JEFFERSON'S DAUGHTER is among the best. It gives an especially good idea of the many-sided Thomas Jefferson through the eyes of his devoted, sensible daughter Martha.

Unexpected Treasure—More Babar, More Dr. Dolittle

Just in time for Children's Book Week came several surprises. We thought that there would be no more books about Babar, the little elephant. Now, however, ten years after the author's untimely death, his son, Laurent de Brunhoff, has produced BABAR'S COUSIN, THAT RASCAL ARTHUR. The book is dedicated "to the memory of my father," and you would really think that his father had written it and made the pictures. We thought that we should never have another Dr. Dolittle book, but when the author, Hugh Lofting, died, he left DR. DOLITTLE AND THE SECRET LAKE. The book, with the author's own illustrations, was published in time to give the children a treasure for which they had not hoped.

Clare Newberry's latest kitten picture book, SMUDGE, is about a black kitten this time; and Orlando, the Marmalade Cat, Kathleen Hale's hero who charms two continents, appears in ORLANDO BUYS A FARM. The best collection of poetry for children that has appeared for some time was published in time for Christmas. It is AN INHERITANCE OF POETRY, collected and arranged by Gladys Adshead and Annis Duff and illustrated by Nora Unwin. It holds many hours of pleasure for youngsters and grownups too.

CANADA
A RECORD OF THE YEAR

By CHARLES CLAY, *Canadian author and journalist*

IN 1848 Robert Baldwin and Louis La-
fontaine formed the first Canadian government that was responsible to the
people for all its actions. It was a government that could hold office only as long as it
had the confidence of the majority of the
people's elected representatives. Thus 1948
saw the Dominion beginning her second century of Responsible Government. To commemorate this event, the Canadian Post Office Department issued a blue-gray four-cent
stamp bearing pictures of Queen Victoria
and of King George VI.

When he retired in November, the Rt.
Hon. William Lyon Mackenzie King had at-
tained a world record as the elected leader
of a free nation. Beginning December 29,

**U. S. Defense Secretary Forrestal, visiting
Canada, inspects the RCAF Guard of Honor.**

CANADIAN ARMY PHOTO

1921, he held the office of prime minister for
a total of twenty-one years, five months,
eight days. This was nearly seven months
longer than Sir Robert Walpole, who was
prime minister of England from April 3,
1721 to February 11, 1742. Mr. King
handed over the prime ministership to the
Rt. Hon. Louis St. Laurent, who had been
elected Liberal leader on August 7.

There were other political leadership
changes during the year. The most important of them was the resignation of Progres-
sive-Conservative leader John Bracken and
the election of the Hon. George Drew to
that office. Mr. Drew, who had been premier
of the province of Ontario, at once began
touring Canada to tell the people about the
new program of the Progressive-Conserva-
tive party.

Elections were also held in five of the nine
Canadian provinces, but there were no major changes in government. The Progressive-
Conservative government won 53 of the 90
seats in the Ontario election, and the Co-
operative Commonwealth Federation government (a socialist party) won 31 of the
52 seats in the Saskatchewan election. In
both these provincial elections the governments lost a little power, but were still able
to command the confidence of more than
half of the people's elected representatives,
and therefore continued in office. The Liberal government won 47 of the 52 seats in
the New Brunswick election, the Union Na-
tionale government won 82 of the 92 seats in
the Quebec election, and the Social Credit
government won 50 of the 57 seats in the
Alberta election. In these three cases each of
the governments gained in strength.

Biggest and most far-reaching Canadian
political event of 1948, of course, was the
decision of Newfoundland, oldest British
colony in North America, to join Canada.

Twice the people of Newfoundland voted on the question before a decision was reached, and then the Government of Canada and a special delegation of Newfoundlanders met in Ottawa to work out the details of union. An agreement was signed December 11, to be approved by the Canadian and British parliaments.

Parliament gave much of its time to trade, financial and economic matters. For instance, the Government began to change Canada's trade with the United States. Up until 1948 the normal thing was for Canada to buy more things from the United States than she sold to the United States. This meant that Canada always had a trading deficit with that country. To make trade balance, the Canadian Government (1) made laws to get Canadian manufacturing companies to buy more of their raw materials and tools in Canada than from the United States and (2) started a drive to sell more Canadian goods to the United States than to British and European markets. As part of this drive, Canadians were forbidden by law to buy a great many made-in-America things, which caused much hardship because Canadian manufacturers could not produce substitutes fast enough.

Canada's export trade expanded during 1948 until it reached a peak never before achieved. As part of this expansion, Canada was very active in promoting the charter of the new International Trade Organization, which is an agency of the United Nations. Canada also co-operated in the Marshall Plan—the European Recovery Program. In 1948 the Dominion sold more than $250,-000,000 worth of foodstuffs and raw materials to Europe under this American scheme for helping Europe recover from the war.

The High Cost of Living Caused People Much Concern

During the year Canadians were very much concerned about the prices they had to pay for food, clothing, rents, home furnishings and the other necessities of life. Prices kept on going up, despite the efforts of the Government to keep them down. Indeed, some of the Government's activities caused certain prices to rise. For instance, the Canadian ban on the shipment of meat to the United States was lifted, and this made the price of meat in Canada soar; in like manner, new and higher prices for Ca-

NATIONAL FILM BOARD

Oil wells among the wheat fields of Alberta.

nadian foods shipped to Great Britain meant that Canadians also had to pay more for cheese, eggs and bacon.

To offset some of these increases, the Government kept "ceiling" prices on some of the foods, such as bread and butter. This meant that such foods could not be sold for more than given prices. In addition, the Government removed a special 25 per cent tax which it had imposed on a number of everyday articles (ranging from alarm clocks to automobiles), and this of course helped to reduce their prices. The Government also undertook to investigate the reasons for high prices of meat, working clothes, lumber, vegetables, fruits and other commodities, but by the end of the year it had not made a report of its findings to the people. While the Government was doing

© BY KARSH

The Right Honorable Louis St. Laurent, who became prime minister of Canada in November 1948.

84

these things, the women of Canada, who had organized several consumer associations, tried to get housewives to stop buying high-priced articles. But this was not too successful.

While tension mounted in Berlin between the United States and the Soviet Union, the Canadian Government began steps towards what Defence Minister Brooke Claxton called "common defence with other countries." Those steps were: to provide for (1) flexible defence of Canada's territory, (2) rapid expansion of the three armed forces if war should break out, and (3) joint action with friendly nations.

Canada Proposed a Regional Security Pact

The third step was very significant. Canada took the lead in proposing the formation of a "North Atlantic Union," which would take the form of a regional security pact uniting the United Kingdom, France, Belgium, the Netherlands and Luxemburg with the United States and Canada for defence. In addition, Canada agreed to give the United States full use of the Canadian sections of the Alaska Highway during any emergency, and to exchange military information with the United States. The latter agreement included the training of key American military forces in ways of carrying on Arctic warfare.

Canada's own defence measures were quite far-reaching. The Government spent $30,000,000 more on war preparedness in 1948 than it had spent in 1947. Recruiting standards were adjusted and educational training within the armed forces was increased, so as to attract greater numbers of young men. The Royal Military College was reorganized and began to train air-force and naval officers as well as army officers.

The Air Force itself was expanded, over $6,000,000 worth of new jet fighters were ordered, and special radar technicians were trained. The Navy was also enlarged, a new and huge aircraft carrier, called the Magnificent, was put into service, and work was begun on a large ice-breaker for use in Arctic waters. The Magnificent, accompanied by two destroyers and other vessels, took a training cruise into frigid Arctic waters.

Nor was the Army left out of Canada's preparedness activities. Some soldiers were given special parachute training, and a unique brigade of rangers (made up of trappers, fur traders, prospectors and woodsmen) was organized to help defend the north country. Many tests were made to see how army radar, transport, clothing and weapons stood up to Arctic cold, snow, and wind. The United States Army took part in such tests.

Other general defence measures included the creation of an Industrial War Board to advise the Government; the building of large military towns near the army training camps at Borden, in Ontario, and Shilo, in Manitoba; and plans for the construction, in co-operation with the United States, of a far-flung Arctic radar network, to warn against enemy planes, as a first line of defence against invasion.

In 1948 more Canadians were working than ever before. Not only were more Canadians working; they were also earning more money. The pay envelopes of industrial workers were the fattest they had ever been. Indeed, the increases in the total payments of wages, salaries and other income were general throughout the Dominion, and they

Former Premier King at the Liberal convention.

amounted to about 10 per cent more than the payments made in 1947.

Canadian farmers, like Canadian city workers, were better off in 1948 than they had been in 1947. The figures told the story. For instance, during the first six months of 1948 the nation's 750,000 farmers' cash income from farm sales amounted to $974,-212,000, which was about $242,000,000 more than for the first six months of 1947. The farmers' income for the second six months was equally high because the Western Prairies had one of their best grain crops in years, and because the Maritimes had an excellent potato crop.

A nation's chief resource, of course, is its people, and the number of Canadians increased considerably during 1948. Some of this increase was due to the number of babies born, and some was due to the great numbers of immigrants who went to the Dominion. Most of these were Europeans who had lost their homes during World War II, but some were British men and women who wanted to make new homes for themselves. Nearly 100,000 immigrants landed in Canada during 1948, and by the time the year ended there were about 13,-000,000 Canadians. That was nearly 500,-000 more than the year before.

New Sources of Petroleum, Uranium and Titanium

Exploration and development resulted in a very great expansion of the nation's supplies of raw materials. The new oil field at Leduc, Alberta, brought in more than thirty wells during the year and production soared. The oil was refined at Edmonton at a big refinery which was built during the war at Whitehorse, Yukon. After the war it was taken apart and carried piece by piece over the Alaska Highway to the Alberta capital.

Several strikes of uranium-bearing ores were made, and some of them proved to be so rich that Canada began to overtake the Belgian Congo as the world's greatest producer of uranium. Vast iron-ore beds in bleak northern Quebec were uncovered and development started. The world's largest deposits of titanium ore, also in Quebec, were discovered. Titanium is used in the manufacture of paints. Platinum was found in Manitoba.

There was great hydroelectric develop-

ment in 1948, notably in the province of Ontario, and the United States Geological Survey announced that Canada had the second largest hydroelectric-power capacity in the world. The Dominion's national-park system created a large new park in the province of New Brunswick; more than 30,-000 drought-stricken acres of western prairie land were restored; and a special board was appointed to study flood control and power development along the mighty Fraser River. This board was appointed after the Fraser River had raged in a disastrous flood during the spring of 1948.

Mapping the Arctic Regions of Canada

Development of Canada's Arctic regions went forward with vigor. The Royal Canadian Air Force mapped about 500,000 square miles of the Arctic, the Canadian Army opened its fourth Arctic radio station, the Department of Mines and Resources built the Dominion's most northerly hydroelectric station to serve the gold-rich Yellowknife area. The Department of National Health and Welfare set up the first of a series of Arctic hospitals to serve Eskimos and Indians.

The Defence Research Board conducted special investigations into the habits of mosquitoes, black flies and deer flies, in an effort to control those biting pests and make Arctic summer living more bearable. During its operational flights, the Royal Canadian Air Force discovered two new Arctic islands, one of which proved to be twice as big as Canada's smallest province, Prince Edward Island.

Canada became the first nation to carry all first-class mail by air at the regular postage rates. This made it possible for a letter to travel from Sydney, Nova Scotia, to Victoria, British Columbia, in only fourteen hours. The services of Trans-Canada Air Lines were expanded by agreements between Canada and Bermuda and the Netherlands. All major airports started installing a new system, which uses radar to guide pilots safely along the last twenty miles of each flight no matter how thick the fog may be. Manufacture of jet air liners for passenger service was begun.

The Canadian Pacific Railway introduced to North America the first automatic ticket issuing and accounting machine when it installed a specially built machine in its Montreal station. It saves time and prevents errors. The Hudson Bay Railway, long the most romantic frontier line on this continent, became part of the Canadian National Railway system.

During 1948 the Canadian sections of the Alaska Highway were thrown open to automobile traffic, and a few adventurous tourists sped along it, admiring the wonderful scenery and getting a taste of wilderness motoring.

Frequency-modulation radio broadcasting appeared in Canada during 1948, but no television was attempted. However, Canada did get an agreement with the United States which gave Canada the right to certain television channels. New Canadian Broadcasting Corporation stations were opened at Windsor, Ontario, and Sydney, Nova Scotia; and the power of other CBC stations was increased so as to give listeners better service.

The Achievements of the National Research Council

Canadians have warmer homes, safer airplanes, longer wearing clothing and many other conveniences because of the work of the busy scientists of the National Research Council. To find out what was best for Arctic weather, these scientists tested machinery and clothing in special cold rooms that registered 76 degrees below zero. The atomic-energy laboratories at Chalk River, Ontario, were expanded greatly. A huge special 5,000,000-volt generator was built to help in atomic research. The laboratories also built and operated two radioactive piles, and manufactured more than twenty kinds of radioactive isotopes for use in medical research. These atomic-energy activities put Canada in the front line of world scientific development. It was recently revealed that, during World War II, Canadian research had developed a vaccine which saved countless water buffalo from rinderpest disease. This enabled Asians to raise enough food to prevent widespread starvation throughout the Far East.

Canadians were active during 1948 in making life safer and longer. Much of this work was done by the Department of National Health and Welfare. The most important step was a federal government ten-point plan to assist the provinces in raising health standards. Parliament voted the first

$30,000,000 of a scheme which will finally run to $150,000,000. The provinces use the money for health surveys, strengthening public-health services, fighting tuberculosis and other diseases, increasing mental-health services and caring for crippled children. Formation of the Arthritis and Rheumatism Society, the Cancer Research Society and the Heart Research Institute was good news to Canadians suffering from those diseases.

In the field of sports a dazzling achievement was that of Barbara Ann Scott, who won the European Women's, the Olympic, the World and the Canadian Women's Senior Skating championships. In addition, she

WIDE WORLD

Ottawa welcomes home Barbara Ann Scott.

won the Lou Marsh Trophy for being Canada's outstanding 1948 sport competitor, and the Canadian Women's Amateur Athletic Federation's rose bowl for being Canada's most outstanding woman athlete. At the season's end the twenty-year-old champion turned professional, making her debut in New York's huge Roxy Theatre on December 22. Canada's skating honors did not end with the champion. Twenty-one-year-old Wallace Distelmeyer and eighteen-year-old Suzanne Morrow came third in the mixed-pairs event of the World skating competitions, and also third in the Olympic mixed-pairs competitions.

The Royal Canadian Air Force hockey team was victorious in the winter Olympics. The Dominion's historic Stanley Cup, emblem of hockey fame, was won by the Toronto Maple Leafs. More than 2,000 snowshoers met in Ottawa in January in the first International Snowshoe Tournament since 1937. Junior and senior ski championship contests were held in Banff in February. Lucille Wheeler, thirteen-year-old skiing wonder, came first in the women's junior events and was the best individual performer; she outpointed contestants several years her senior.

During 1948 Canadians took to the air in gliders, and set a number of Canadian records. Al Pow, of London, Ontario, reached an altitude of 11,200 feet when ice began to form on his wings and he had to come down (world record: 22,434 feet). Ovila Boudreault, of Ottawa, set a Canadian distance record by covering 46 miles (world record: 465 miles). A little later in the year Mr. Boudreault set a Canadian time record by keeping his glider in the air for 5 hours and 28 minutes (world record: 38 hours, 21 minutes). As these comparisons show, gliding is a new sport in Canada, but every year more Canadians get interested in it.

As part of its policy of greater freedom of expression for all people, the Government made a change in the election laws, so that Canadians of Japanese blood could now vote.

Steps Were Taken to Curb the Activities of Communists

However, there was one Canadian group which faced a restriction of its activities. These were the Canadian Communists. Early in 1948 the Federal Government decided it would not let any non-Canadian Communists into the country. Soon after, the Government said it would employ no member of the Communist party or any person associated with the Communist party on Canadian government work of a secret nature. Besides the steps taken by the Government, Canadian labor unions also acted against Communists. Union members who were proved Communists were expelled from the Canadian Congress of Labor; and the Canadian Trades and Labor Congress passed a resolution deploring the actions of Canadian Communists.

In spite of this clearly expressed dislike of their ideas, Canadian Communists continued to carry on their propaganda. Of the seventy-eight foreign-language newspapers printed in Canada, nineteen, or nearly one-fourth, favored communism.

Literature and the arts attracted many Canadians. Although the cost of printing and binding books was greater in 1948 than it had been in 1947, over a hundred new Canadian novels and non-fiction books appeared during the year. Plans were announced to build a national theater in Ottawa. The Canadian Broadcasting Corporation won four first awards and two honorable mentions at the twelfth exhibition of educational programs of the American Institute for Radio.

Music and the Arts Received Greater Encouragement

A move to promote and encourage music composition and appreciation was made with the formation of the National Federation of Music Associations of Canada. By 1948 films produced by the National Film Board were being shown in sixty foreign countries, and the distribution was being increased. The Saskatchewan government set up Canada's first provincial arts board, which at once began carrying culture to small prairie towns and villages.

Canadians were also active in international affairs. Besides taking the lead in the creation of a "North Atlantic Union," Canada was often the leader in the work of the United Nations. The United Nations Security Council accepted Canada's proposal to send a special committee to Indonesia to work for a lasting peace. In a dramatic vote, forty members of the United Nations General Assembly favored the international atomic-energy control plan introduced by Canada.

That would be a good note on which to finish this survey of Canada during the year. But there is, perhaps, an even more appealing note to remember. The first paragraph of this article described a special postage stamp issued by Canada to commemorate a century of Responsible Government. In 1948 there was also another anniversary for Canada: it was the centenary of friendly relations with the United States of America. Thus Canadians were proud, indeed, when the United States Post Office also issued a commemorative three-cent postage stamp. It was sky-blue and showed the old railway suspension bridge across the Niagara River gorge. It carried the words: "A Century of Friendship, United States–Canada, 1848–1948." Truly a good omen for the future.

Fort Toronto, or Fort Rouillé, from a drawing in the possession of the Dominion Archives.

Toronto, Queen City of Ontario

By Louise McDowell

ALONG Ontario's northern shore, the towers of Canada's second largest city rise above the blue waters of the lake. Its ten-mile water front is lined with docks, wharves and warehouses; and the shipping that fills its harbor comes, not only from the Great Lakes, but also from the Atlantic and even the far-away Pacific. The city's Huron Indian name, Toronto—the place of meeting—was well chosen. Railways, highways and airways meet and cross at Toronto, so that today, as in the long ago, it is a link between eastern and western Canada.

Raw materials for its hundreds of industries are brought to Toronto by land and by water—the harbor has handled more than four million tons of cargo in a single year—

and the finished products are shipped to many far countries as well as to the United States and within Canada itself.

Besides being the political and financial capital of Ontario, Toronto is a center of art, music and education. Its symphony orchestra is internationally famous, and its great university is the largest in the Dominion.

A beautiful, clean and well-lighted modern city, garlanded with lovely residential suburbs, people love to live in Toronto, and those who are not so fortunate as to live there love to visit there.

Today it is not easy, with the great modern city all about one, to roll back the years and recapture the scene as it was in 1749. Where brick and steel and concrete now stand, the

Looking eastward along King Street, as it appeared about 1834 when Toronto was incorporated.

trees stretched down to the bright lake. Only the cries of the wildfowl in the marshes and the songs of the voyageurs broke the stillness. War parties of Indians moved silently as painted shadows through the forest.

It was in October 1749 that the French Governor of Canada took steps to build a fort at the entrance to the wilderness trail that led from Lake Ontario overland to the upper Great Lakes. Although the commemorative column in the National Exhibition Grounds gives 1749 as the date of the founding of the fort, the most recent historians are agreed that it was not actually constructed until the following year. The rude building with its strong stockade, or fence of split logs, was named Fort Rouillé, but most of the fur traders and the later settlers seem to have called it by the softer Indian name, *To-ron-to*.

A few years later the fort was burned by the French to save it from the British. It was not until 1793 that the first British town was built on its site by Colonel Simcoe, the first governor of Upper Canada. The tiny capital in the wilderness was named for the Duke of York; and York it remained until 1834, when the city was incorporated and the name changed to Toronto. Thus the modern city is more than a century old.

Under either name, Toronto has had an exciting history, in peace and in war. It was burned by the Americans in the War of 1812; riot and bloodshed reached its gate in the Rebellion of 1837. In the 1850's the Queen City on the lake took turn about with Old Quebec as capital of all Canada. Today, as Toronto begins her third century of existence, her path is one of peace and industry and a well-merited prosperity.

The old cannon on Centre Island points quite peacefully toward the modern city across the bay.

THE TORONTO CONVENTION AND TOURIST ASSOCIATION

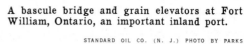

A bascule bridge and grain elevators at Fort William, Ontario, an important inland port.

Canada's inland waters find their way to the sea in four great drainage systems. They flow into the Atlantic, Pacific and Arctic oceans and into Hudson Bay. The Atlantic basin drains an area of about 420,000 square miles, mostly through the Gulf of St. Lawrence. The Pacific basin drains an area of about 400,000 square miles, partly into the Pacific Ocean through British Columbia, and partly into the Bering Sea by way of the Yukon River. The Hudson Bay basin is the largest. This enormous basin drains an area of almost 1,500,000 square miles. Some of its waters find their way from the eastern slope of the Rockies in southwestern Alberta. The Arctic basin is big enough—930,000 square miles. The greater part of this far northern

By IRENE M. SPRY
Canadian Writer

inland WATERWAYS

O N a golden autumn day, more than four hundred years ago, the French navigator Jacques Cartier climbed a mountain behind the Indian village of Hochelaga. Spread below him was the shining sweep of the St. Lawrence River and the lower valley of its tremendous tributary, the Ottawa, opening the way to the unknown northwest. Cartier, like all the other navigators of that time, hoped to find a waterway leading to the Pacific and to China, and this broad stream might well be that dreamed-of Westward Passage.

The village of Hochelaga vanished long ago beneath the brick and stone of the great city of Montreal. The rivers on which Cartier looked are now crowded with shipping from ports he never dreamed of. Cartier did not find his Westward Passage to China, nor did the other seekers who followed him. What he did find was the first of the wonderful highways of water along which a new nation was to grow and spread until it stretched clear across the continent.

area consists of the Mackenzie River system.

The Great Lakes–St. Lawrence waterway is the most important because it has been the pathway of civilization into a vast part of the interior of the continent. After the explorers came the fur traders. Then came the settlers. Farms and towns pushed the forests back from the shores of the rivers and lakes, and even when railways were built they followed, wherever possible, the gentle grades of river valley and lake shore.

The men who first followed the course of the St. Lawrence and its tributaries came in from the sea and, of course, had to follow the river back to its source to find where it came from. Today we no longer enjoy the thrill of the unknown, for every foot of this river system has long ago been surveyed and mapped.

The St. Lawrence is the only big river system in North America the main stream of which flows from west to east. It has its real beginning nearly three thousand miles from the Atlantic Ocean, where Superior, largest and deepest of the Great Lakes, receives the waters of more than two hundred streams. Out of Lake Superior into Lake Huron flows St. Mary's River, with the falls that form the first of the stair-steps in the downward course of the river system. To get around these falls, two sets of canal locks have been built at Sault Ste. Marie—one on the Canadian side and one on the United States side of the river. At the eastern end of Lake Huron, between Port Huron and Sarnia, the St. Clair River flows into little Lake St. Clair, and from there the Detroit River, with Windsor on one side and Detroit on the other, empties into Lake Erie. Between broad, shallow Erie and fish-shaped Lake Ontario is another stair-step where the Niagara River thunders over its cliffs in a drop of nearly two hundred feet. Here the Welland Canal carries the shipping between the lakes.

The main stream of the St. Lawrence leaves Lake Ontario at Kingston, where it is joined by the Cataraqui River and by the Rideau Canal from the Ottawa River. The broad waters of the St. Lawrence embrace the lovely wooded Thousand Islands for miles along its course. In its 750 miles from Ontario to the Gulf it is joined by many big rivers: from the north, the Ottawa, the St. Maurice and the Saguenay; from the south the Chaudière, the Richelieu, the St. Regis, Racquette, Grasse and Oswagatchie. Past farmland and woodland, industrial towns and cities the great stream flows, sometimes swift and deep and smooth, sometimes tumbling in rapids over the dangerous rocks.

The Indians and *voyageurs* could "portage" or carry their light craft around these rapids. Today canals at Lachine, Soulanges, Cornwall and other points by-pass these dan-

The Northland Echo glides over the broad, shining reaches of the Clearwater River in Alberta. The West has many such tranquil streams as well as the turbulent rivers that are not navigable.

STANDARD OIL CO. (N. J.) PHOTO BELOW BY COLLIER; UPPER RIGHT BY PARKS

NATIONAL FILM BOARD

Above, lake boats taking on grain; right, a freighter on St. Clair River, near Sarnia.

ger points. Ship channels have been deepened by dredging. The Department of Transport has deepened harbors and built piers, wharves, transit sheds, elevators and cold-storage warehouses. Of the eight Canadian harbors controlled by the National Harbors Board, four—Quebec, Three Rivers, Montreal and Chicoutimi—are on the St. Lawrence inland waterway.

After the turn of the century, the opening of the great wheat empire of the West gave a new importance to the Great Lakes-St. Lawrence route. From huge elevators at the Head of the Lakes, specially built boats, called upper-lakers, carry wheat to Prescott, Ontario. There it is transshipped to river vessels, canallers or lower-lakers. These take it down the St. Lawrence.

Most water-borne freight nowadays consists of bulky materials. Besides wheat and

Canada's waterways are paths for pleasure boats as well as freight carriers. This boat is passing through Soulange Canal. Below, locks 4, 5 and 6 of the Welland Canal, between Erie and Ontario.

other grains and flour, the Laurentian water highway carries coal and coke, gasoline and oil, copper and other ores, iron and steel and their products, and pulpwood and paper. The volume of traffic on the Great Lakes is shown by the fact that the tonnage passing through the Canadian and American canals at Sault Ste. Marie each year is greater than that which passes through the Panama Canal. The greater part of this traffic moves from the Head of the Lakes down the waterway to seaports, or to eastern towns and industries. Return traffic is much lighter.

Since 1854, when the Reciprocity Treaty was signed, Canadian waterways have been open to American and Canadian shipping alike. There is a heavy movement of traffic, not only between Canadian ports, but also from United States ports to Canadian ports. Traffic going from Canadian to United States ports, however, is much smaller. More than half the freight carried through Canadian canals in ordinary times comes from Canadian ports. During the war, however, it was the other way around.

One of the most vital links in the St. Lawrence waterway has been the improvement of the ship channel below Montreal. Before it was improved the river was no deeper than ten feet in some places. Work to deepen the channel was begun as long ago as 1814, but it was not until the canals on the upper river were completed that really vigorous action was taken. A new method of dredging was introduced and today the ship channel is thirty-five feet deep. In order to make navigation safer the channel was marked with buoys and lighthouses. Provision was made for a chain of radio signal and direction-finding stations and for a pilot service. Ice-breakers were used to lengthen the open season in the spring and fall. Today, ocean steamers of large size can go up the river as far as Quebec, and those not quite so large can go up to Montreal. The channel is not quite deep enough for the Queen Mary and the Queen Elizabeth.

The importance of this great waterway in developing Canadian industry becomes strikingly clear when one calls the roll of Canada's industrial cities: Montreal, Three Rivers, Toronto, Hamilton, Windsor and the rest. One metal industry in Canada was founded almost entirely on a great tributary of the St. Lawrence—the Saguenay. Ships carry bauxite and other raw materials from South America and Greenland up the river to the huge aluminum plant at Arvida, and carry the finished product away to distant export markets. The deep-water transport is cheap and the tremendous hydroelectric power provided by the river has attracted this industry. It takes a fabulous amount of electric power per pound of metal to produce aluminum.

Jackpine and Spruce Logs Float Down to the Paper Mills

Not only the minerals, but the forests of the Canadian Shield still depend upon waterways for their usefulness. Where once the great rafts of squared pine came down, spruce and jackpine logs float today, to the pulp and paper mills that have multiplied since the first World War. Every floatable tributary of the St. Lawrence and Ottawa rivers brings down a harvest of logs with its spring freshets. When the National Transcontinental Railway from Quebec to Winnipeg was completed, it opened up another series of rivers which the shantymen of the last century had not been able to reach.

The picturesque setting of the Rideau Canal, a connecting link between Ottawa and Kingston.

Draining "down north" to Hudson Bay, they float the logs north to mills along the railroad, which carries the finished newsprint to market.

The St. Lawrence-Great Lakes waterway overshadows other Canadian waterways, but there are a number of small canals, such as the Murray Canal between the Bay of Quinté and Lake Ontario; St. Peter's Canal, which connects Bras D'Or in Cape Breton Island with the Atlantic; and the Trent Canal from Lake Ontario to Georgian Bay.

Since the opening of the Hudson Bay Railway in 1931 a certain amount of wheat has been shipped abroad by way of the port of Churchill, on Hudson Bay. This is shorter than the St. Lawrence route but it can be used only for about three months in the summer.

In British Columbia the rivers had created a mining industry long before the twentieth century. Gold was found in the Fraser River in 1858, and prospectors worked their way up one river after another seeking the shining yellow dust. They used the rivers as transport routes and also for washing the gold clear of the sand and gravel in which it was found. When the Klondike gold rush came in 1898, miners swarmed northward down the Yukon River. When the placer gold and the surface veins played out, and it became necessary to use heavy machinery to get out the gold, the Yukon River remained a thoroughfare. Old-time wood-burning stern-wheelers, which once had plied the far-off Mississippi, still ran the rapids or warped painfully up them.

The Yukon River has been a part of the romantic background of countless stories of the Northwest, but few people know that it is the fifth largest river on the North American continent. It begins in the Coast Range of British Columbia, where it is called the Lewes River. Then it flows north through the Yukon Territory where, at Selkirk, it is joined by the Pelly and changes its name to Yukon. From there it twists and turns its leisurely way across the territory and into Alaska, gathering tributaries along the way, until it loses itself in the marshy coast of the Bering Sea, 2,300 miles from its source. The lower reaches are frozen during nearly nine months of the year, but steamboats can navigate it clear up to Dawson in the summer months. The Lewes and most of the big tributaries are navigable for hundreds of miles.

The River of Golden Nuggets and Silver Salmon

The Fraser is British Columbia's own river; no other province or territory shares it. Its two forks rise in the Rocky Mountains, one near Mount Robson and one near Mount Brown, and it empties into the Gulf of Georgia, joined by many rushing mountain streams as it flows. We have spoken of the finding of gold along the Fraser in the last century, but the river has brought another source of wealth in the silver horde of salmon that work their way upstream each year on the way to their spawning grounds.

So valuable are the Fraser salmon that the Dominion and United States governments together have spent more than a million dollars to help them to reach their spawning grounds. For many years the gorge at Hell's Gate was so choked by a great rock-fall that thousands of exhausted and injured fish could not pass. They floated down stream and died without hatching their eggs. To prevent the huge losses that this caused, two long fishways were designed and built around

that part of the river. These fishways are canal-like detours and are cut through the rock of the canyon walls. Since 1946, when they came into use, the salmon runs have increased wonderfully.

The Mackenzie River, Highway of the Far North

The Mackenzie is one of the longest river systems in the world. Into Lake Athabaska flow two big rivers, the Athabaska from the Rockies, and the Peace River, which rises in British Columbia and cuts through the Rockies at a height of two thousand feet above sea level. The water that these rivers bring into the lake flows out again as the Great Slave River, emptying into Great Slave Lake in the Northwest Territories. From Great Slave Lake the stream that was named for the explorer, Alexander Mackenzie, begins. It wends its way through forests of pine and spruce, birch and poplar, down to the flat, barren shores of the Arctic Ocean, joined in its course by another big river, the Liard.

Long ago the Hudson's Bay Company developed it as a fur route, building trading posts along the Mackenzie and its tributaries. Today, from June to October, the company's steamboats ply the river between Great Slave Lake and Aklavik near the Arctic Ocean. When oil was discovered at Norman Wells in the 1920's, men and machinery were carried along this waterway. It has served the radium and uranium mine on Great Bear Lake under the edge of the Arctic Circle, the booming gold town of Yellowknife on Great Slave Lake, and, during the war, the builders of the Alaska Highway and the Canol project.

Besides the great river systems of Canada there are the thousands of small lakes and streams that cover the Dominion like a spangled silver net. In the built-up parts of the country these do not play much of a role in commerce and transportation. However, in the vast northern lands, made up of forests, muskeg and rock, they are of vital importance. The air age has come to the wilderness. The waterways that yesterday knew only the dip of the paddle, are today natural landing fields for planes, fitted in summer with pontoons and in winter with skis. Much has happened since the day that Cartier gazed upon the St. Lawrence and the Ottawa, but Canada's wealth and progress are still bound up in her waterways.

By Richard Finnie
Author and Explorer

Silver birches fringe the ice-clad reaches of the Mackenzie River not far from Norman Wells.

CANADA

the northwest territories

SPRAWLED across the top of Canada, east of the Yukon and north of the four western provinces, the Northwest Territories stretch to the North Pole. This region was the first part of Canada to be explored by Europeans, yet it is still the least populated and the least known. In Queen Elizabeth's time, the navigator Martin Frobisher went there, seeking gold and also a short route to China. Later, Henry Hudson discovered the huge bay that is named for him, and perished there. Since then a succession of explorers, prospectors and fur-trappers have invaded this beautiful, remote land, but it is only within our own century that serious efforts have been made to develop it.

The present area of the Northwest Territories is 1,300,000 square miles—more than a third of the entire Dominion. It is divided into three districts. East of the Yukon and north of British Columbia, Alberta and Saskatchewan is the Mackenzie District. The District of Keewatin takes in the islands in Hudson Bay and the mainland north of Manitoba. The District of Franklin includes

An Indian pilot guides the oil-exploration boat on its course up the Mackenzie River.

Melville and Boothia peninsulas and most of the Arctic islands from Greenland to the 141st meridian.

The names of these three districts are on maps, but only the Mackenzie District is written or spoken of much by name. The other two are generally called the Western Arctic and the Eastern Arctic. A man who has visited Baffin Island or Victoria Island is not likely to tell you that he was in the District of Franklin or the District of Keewatin. Instead he will say that he was in the Eastern Arctic or the Western Arctic. If, however, he has been visiting Port Radium or Aklavik he will probably say he has been in the Mackenzie District.

In such an immense region there is bound to be some variation in geography, climate, vegetation and animal life. The Mackenzie District, through which the great Mackenzie River flows to the Arctic Ocean, is partly mountainous, partly lowland. It has countless beautiful lakes and fine forests of spruce, jack pine, birch and poplar. Summers are warm and winters are cold. In the Mackenzie Valley even ninety-degree temperatures are not uncommon in the summer. On such

warm days people often go swimming to escape the heat.

The Eastern Arctic is more like the popular idea of the Frozen North. Here are snow-capped mountains and hundreds of miles of the flat, marshy plains called tundra. There are no trees. Summers are short and chilly, and often windy, and winters are long and cold. In the Territories as a whole winter temperatures seldom drop lower than 60° below zero, but they often stand at 20° or 30° below for weeks on end. Summer temperatures may rise higher than 70° above zero, and, in places, hordes of flies and mosquitoes make life miserable for man and beast.

Winter snowfall is moderate in the Territories. In summer, the snow does not stay on the ground, nor ice on the lakes, except in very high places. However, the ice in the Arctic Ocean, though it breaks up and drifts away from the coast, never completely disappears. Throughout the land—even in the most barren sections—grow hundreds of varieties of flowering plants, shrubs and grasses.

Animal life within the Territories ranges from frogs, mice and swallows to whales, swans and buffalo. The last remnants of North American bison outside captivity roam the Wood Buffalo Park on the line between Alberta and the Mackenzie District. Near by is the most northerly breeding-ground of white pelicans. Mountain sheep graze among the Mackenzie Mountains. Small but growing herds of musk-oxen live in the Thelon Game Sanctuary (along the Thelon and Hanbury rivers), on Boothia Peninsula and on several Arctic islands. The musk-oxen were once threatened with extinction, but now they are protected.

The Territories Abound in Animal Life

There are black bears, Barren Ground grizzlies and polar bears, moose and two or three kinds of caribou. There are coyotes, timber wolves and white wolves. There are mink and marten, lynx and wolverine, white and colored foxes, muskrats and beavers, seals, walruses, whales and narwhals. There are ravens and owls, ducks, geese, gulls, swans, ptarmigan and song birds; but there are no penguins. In the lakes and rivers and in the Arctic Ocean there are many kinds of fish. The widest assortment of fur-bearing and game animals is found in the Mackenzie District, but animal life—including insects—extends to the farthest corner of the most northerly island, Ellesmere.

Furs and gold, petroleum, radium and uranium are the products that have brought fame to the Territories, and the most crowded hour of its history came during the great upheaval of World War II. The Hudson's Bay Company has had fur-trading posts in what is now the eastern part of the Northwest Territories since the last half of the seventeenth century. Then, in the early 1920's, came the rush to the oil fields at Fort Norman on the Mackenzie River. One hundred and thirty years before, the explorer, Alexander Mackenzie, had seen oil seepage on the banks of the river, but the age of fuel oil and gasoline was still far in the future, so the oil stayed in its frigid storehouse. Even in the 1920's it was difficult and expensive to transport this oil to a market and the several wells that had been drilled were closed up.

The oil boom of the twenties did two important things, however. It brought the air age to the Northwest Territories, and it made people realize that this northern region contained other valuable things beside furs.

In 1928 a group of Toronto mining men prospected the land between the Mackenzie

STANDARD OIL CO. (N. J.) PHOTO BY CORSINI

Barrels of gasoline for refueling aircraft that land at Fort Smith airport. Below, a towboat, with its tow of two barges, unloads supplies at Arctic Red River.

CANADIAN DEPT. OF MINES AND RESOURCES

In the Yellowknife River country at the north arm of Great Slave Lake, gold was discovered in 1935. Within three years a town had grown up there and the first gold ingot was poured at one of the several mines. Soon the output of Yellowknife gold was worth more than all the furs being shipped out of the entire Northwest Territories. Tungsten and other useful metals were also discovered, and hydroelectric power began to be developed in the area. Elsewhere in the Territories there were reserves of coal and iron.

The aboriginal dwellers in the Northwest Territories are the Indians and the Eskimos. The Indian tribes—Loucheux, Hares, Dogribs, Slaves, Yellowknives and Chipewyans —live in the wooded areas. The Eskimos live chiefly along the coasts of the mainland and the Arctic islands, and get most of their clothing and food from the sea and land animals and fish. There are, however, some Eskimos who live inland in the Keewatin

STANDARD OIL CO. (N. J.) PHOTO BY PARKS

Yellowknife—waiting to go down a gold mine.

Norman Wells—tracks in the snow reveal the

River and Hudson Bay by air, traveling in planes equipped with pontoons. They found deposits of copper, lead, zinc and silver. In 1930 a prospector named Gilbert LaBine found another mineral, pitchblende. The following year he started a mine on the shore of Great Bear Lake—the fourth largest lake in North America—thirty miles from the Arctic Circle. The mine was named Eldorado, and it proved to be the richest source of radium and uranium in the world. As such it played a vital part in the creation of the atomic bomb.

Eldorado required oil for its machinery, and for the boats needed to carry the mine products to the nearest railroad. This meant a steady local market for the products of Norman Wells, 300 miles to the west. The original wells were opened up and new wells were drilled. Soon Norman Wells was able to supply, not only Eldorado, but nearly all the needs of the Mackenzie District. From 1939, when the war began, aviation gasoline, as well as low-test motor gasoline and Diesel oil, could be made on the spot.

District. These live mainly on caribou and are generally called the Caribou Eskimos. There are about 4,000 Indians and 5,400 Eskimos in the Northwest Territories.

The 1941 census showed about 2,500 white inhabitants. There were only about twenty-five white settlements, perhaps half of which boasted government-aided mission hospitals and schools. At key points the Government had wireless and weather stations. Along the Mackenzie River traders and missionaries cultivated small farms and gardens, as they had done since the early 1800's. The two most progressive farms belonged to the government doctors at Fort Simpson and Aklavik. The northernmost herd of dairy cattle was at Aklavik, 120 miles north of the Arctic Circle.

At that time people and supplies traveled mainly by boat, dog-team and airplane. Only small planes were used, mounted on skis in winter and on pontoons in summer, for the lakes and rivers were the only landing fields.

heavy traffic to and from the oil refinery.

Western Arctic—Eskimos hunt the white whale.

In the Eastern Arctic the settlements still received their supplies once a year from a Hudson's Bay Company steamer. In all the Northwest Territories there was no road more than a few miles long.

Then came the Japanese war. It brought tremendous and far-reaching changes to the Northwest Territories. The Dominion Government gave permission to the United States Army to build airfields at Southampton Island in Hudson Bay, and at Frobisher Bay in Baffin Island—the island that Martin Frobisher had first visited in 1576. These fields, with others in eastern Canada, Newfoundland, Labrador, Greenland and Iceland, were used on defense patrols and for a ferry route to Europe.

An overland route, safe from attack by sea, was needed between the United States and Alaska, and so the Alaska Highway was begun. The route was to run from Alberta through northern British Columbia and the Yukon to Fairbanks, Alaska. For this huge and difficult project a great deal of oil and gasoline was needed. Tankers brought these

101

supplies to Alaska by sea, but there was always the danger of Japanese interference in the sea-lanes. The answer was to bring oil from Norman Wells in the Northwest Territories. In order to do this, more wells had to be sunk at Norman, more supplies and men and machinery had to be brought in. Ways had to be found to transport them to the oil field and also to transport large quantities of oil away from the field. Therefore the vast Canol (short for Canadian oil) project was begun.

Air Transportation Comes into Its Own

Norman Wells was a thousand miles from the nearest railway, and the Mackenzie River steamers could not handle all the heavy machinery, trucks, bulldozers and tractors that were needed. Neither could the small planes that were in use in the Territories. Big army transport planes must be used; but these planes had to have runways. They could not land and take off with skis or pontoons. In September 1942, the first transport plane delivered its load at Norman Wells, and before the end of the year a dozen landing strips had been carved out along the way.

Even the big transports could not, of course, carry the heaviest equipment. A road had to be built. During the winter the United States Army engineers and civilian contractors bulldozed a road over the thousand-mile stretch from Norman Wells to a point eighty miles north of Peace River where an older road ended. By the spring of 1943 thousands of tons of freight and equipment were being carried over this rough road.

While this was being done, exploring parties in the air and on the ground were studying the territory between Norman Wells and Whitehorse, nearly 600 miles away. They were seeking passes through the Mackenzie Mountains by which a road and a pipe line could go to the refinery being built at Whitehorse. Only a handful of white men, and not many Indians, had ever traveled over this country.

It took months to plot the route, but in the spring of 1943 camps were set up, a supply chain was forged and hundreds of men worked against time to build the road, to bridge swift mountain streams, to string and weld pipe, and to erect storage tanks and pumping stations. Surveyors and engineers,

dog-drivers, cat-skinners and crane-operators, welders and steel-workers, truck-drivers, machinists, carpenters, cooks and clerks—all worked together on the giant engineering feat. On December 31, 1943, the Canol Road was punched through; in another couple of months the last joint of pipe was welded. Thousands of barrels of oil a day could flow continuously through the pipe from Norman Wells to Whitehorse.

When the wonderful engineering project was ready to go into operation, the Japanese had already been driven from the Aleutians and the urgent danger was past. Yet there had been danger, and the Canol project had helped to provide insurance against it. Moreover, Canol had been useful in other ways. Many of the light bombers ferried to Russia for use against Germany were fueled from branch Canol pipe lines.

These northern projects, including the airfields in the Eastern Arctic, opened up little-known and remote areas. They also tapped new oil reserves, paved the way for peacetime development, and gave thousands of people first-hand knowledge of the Far North.

Nature Has Reconquered the Canol Road

Though the Alaska Highway is being maintained as a land link with Alaska, the Canol Road has been forgotten. Brush is once more growing over the northern half of the Mackenzie Valley winter road. Sooner or later, however, it will be turned into a permanent road and extended to the Arctic.

The wartime work will leave its mark on the Territories. The people will make use of the roads, airfields and town sites built during the war. The Arctic is the aerial crossroads of the Northern Hemisphere and some day it will come into its own. The airfields in the Eastern Arctic and along the Mackenzie Valley will hum with activity, as they serve giant air liners carrying passengers between the great cities of the Old World and the New. War-project workers, men and women, discovered that it is possible to live comfortably in the Far North. For some time to come, mining and fur-trading will continue to be the mainstays of commerce there. But as new mines are opened up, more and more people will settle in the north. Stock-raising, farming, fishing, transportation and all kinds of businesses will give opportunities to vigorous, self-reliant, modern pioneers.

CAREERS

Is there a story in it?

By MEYER BERGER, *The New York Times*

JOINED together, the first letters of North, East, West and South spell out NEWS. NEWSpapers are made up of reports of actual happenings in all corners of the earth—in the North, the East, the West and the South.

Before men had paper on which to write or print, even before they carved on cave walls or on tablets to tell a story or leave a message, they passed news by word of mouth. News helped them to exist.

It was important news, for example, for them to hear that game had been seen, say, to the west, or to the east. When they heard this news they knew where to hunt for food.

As the world grew and living passed the simple stage, so did the kinds of news that were part of the scheme of existence. As men's interests covered an ever wider range, so did the news.

People in one part of a city, or nation, wanted to know what people in other parts of the city, or throughout the nation, were doing. They wanted news of wars and of the making of peace. Later they came to want news of sports, books, art, plays, new inventions, of life and death among their neighbors.

The borders of knowledge and of civilization extended. Instead of being interested only in what happened near their homes, people became curious about people and

In addition to covering any assignment which he may receive from his city editor, left, a general-assignment man must be able to write the story fast, if a deadline is nearing.

events in far places. They wanted international news.

Newspapers had to use more reporters and photographers, and the newest means of swift communication—the telephone, the radio, radiophoto—to put the news before their readers in the quickest possible time.

Great syndicates were formed to get and sell news to newspapers and to radio stations that broadcast news. The three largest syndicates in the United States are the Associated Press, the United Press and the International News Service. They comb the world for items.

Today, schools teach the art of getting news and news photographs. In some schools this is merely part of the general English course. In several large colleges journalism is taught to prepare young men and young women for work on newspapers or in radio.

Men and women who cover all kinds of news are called general assignment reporters. On the larger newspapers, though, reporters specialize in one subject, the one they like best. Modern newspapers have men who specialize in science, art, real estate, radio, the theater, motion pictures, fashions, sports, finance, military affairs or politics.

The work can be exciting. Reporters who are sent after news must be quick to hear

COLUMBIA UNIVERSITY PHOTO BY WARMAN
Clacking typewriters and busy students give this class a city-room air at Columbia University.

When a big story is breaking fast, a reporter may give the facts, over the telephone, to a rewrite man who will write the copy.

The copy desk is the watchdog of the city or news room. Its members check all copy for accuracy and write the headlines.

and to see what they must pass on to their readers. They must train themselves to write rapidly, especially when events come just before edition time.

Newspaper writing, like most good writing, is best when it is simple. Then it is clear and easily understood. In all cases it must tell a complete story in the fewest possible words. It must, first of all, cover the five W's —Who, What, When, Where and Why.

In most stories these points are best told in the first, or lead, paragraph, which is more or less a summary. If a reporter went, for example, to cover a warehouse fire, he might see many interesting and exciting things, but his lead would still be simple and crisp. It might be:

> Wind-swept fire last night destroyed the warehouse at 1654 West Street. It was traced to an electrical short circuit.

The exciting details, and all the other information about the fire—how it spread, who was hurt in it, how it was fought, something of the color, the sound and the action, the amount of damage, any heroic acts—would follow. The reporter would be assigned a certain amount of space in which to tell the story, and he would put into it the most im-

Are there any errors in the written story? The copy reader (below) checks it carefully before the copy goes to the composing room.

Before you see the story in your newspaper, it receives a final check by proofreaders, who watch for typographical errors.

portant and most interesting details, and discard the others.

The lead of the greatest story in history, the story of creation in the Bible, was told with only a few simple words:

In the beginning God created the Heaven and the Earth.

A longer and more flowery lead sentence would not have been so clear or so powerful.

Feature writing does not always call for the same crisp handling as "hot" or "spot" news. Usually it deals with some subject that is apt to move a reader to pity or to laughter —sometimes to both. It may be a word-picture of a spectacle like a parade, an air review, a race, a fight, a simple burial, a pet show, a person, anything that yields what newspapermen call "color."

In feature writing, as in straight news writing, the simple words and the clear sentences are best, but the reporter has a better chance to use his writing skill. He—or she—can come closer to the fiction writer's style.

This does not mean that the feature writer's articles can be fiction. In the best newspapers even the most colorful stories do not depart from fact. They do not exaggerate for mere effect. Truth simply told can be as exciting as fiction.

Almost everything that happens is news. That simply means someone somewhere will be interested in it. News value increases, though, in proportion to the degree in which it differs from routine.

A small fire that smokes out hundreds of people in, say, a theater, hotel or school, though it does little damage, is a better item than a large fire in some lonely place that affects only a handful of people.

Keep Your Eyes and Ears Open While Out on a Story

The good reporter must develop a knack for catching the atmosphere of the event he covers. He can do a more readable story of even a routine happening if he is sensitive to what goes on about him.

He can work in the lights and the shadow. For instance, if he covered something that happened at five o'clock in the morning it might be better to say that it happened at daybreak, or if at five o'clock in the evening, say twilight, or sundown.

One simple word like that gives a warmer picture than merely telling the hour, and creates atmosphere. To make one word or phrase serve that purpose is an art which the good reporter must learn. He must catch color, sound and action, and pass it on so the reader gets a better picture of what happened. The trick is to do this without wasting words.

Practice Makes a Good Writer: Rewrite the Professionals

It is good practice, when aiming at a career in newspaper or radio work, to change what professional news writers set down, or what radio news announcers say. It is fun, sort of, to change leads in a newspaper—or even a complete story—to see how you can make them crisper, shorter and simpler. This practice gets you into the habit. You begin to watch against word waste. If a word, phrase, or sentence does not advance the action or atmosphere of a story, discard it.

At a football game, a parade or a race, watch for the color, the action and the atmosphere. Cultivate the habit of snatching interesting detail—the queer, the quaint and the unusual—from what is happening before your eyes. This is what the good news announcer does.

Television Offers a New Field for News Reporters

The freshest field for the reporter is television. This will become more and more popular as a form of news reporting. Here the reporter will have to know where to shift his cameras and his sound pick-up devices to catch what is most important. It is a new kind of reporting.

Several large newspapers throughout the country distribute, without charge, a number of booklets telling how a newspaper is run, how to get news and how to write it. They also take groups on free guided tours of their plants to show a newspaper in the making.

Write to the largest newspaper in your part of the country and ask if it has free literature on newspaper work. If no newspapers in or near where you live have such a service, write to The New York TIMES at 229 West 43rd Street, New York 18, N. Y., or have your English teacher send for the booklets. They will be extremely helpful to anyone anxious for a career in newspaper work. Your library also will probably have one or more books on journalism. They will help.

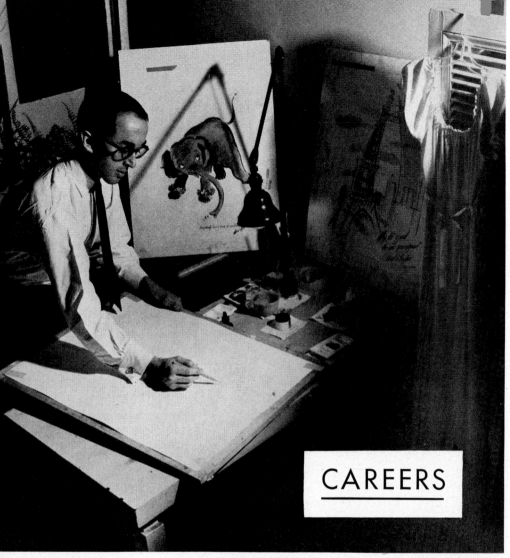

A good job and glamour too! Talented staff artists help make attractive newspaper "ads."

IN A GREAT STORE

By Dorothy Shaver

President of Lord & Taylor

CHOOSING a career is really choosing a way of life. There is a vast difference between a career and a job—you start out on a job, but a career is something you carve for yourself out of the job. On a job you are paid for your skill and experience at, say, clerical or stenographic work or selling. You make a career out of one of these jobs by using your intelligence, your imagination, your industry to arrive at a position of responsibility. In short, a career is a "plus-job"—the plus being what you yourself give to the job in addition to what is expected of you.

Now let's look at retailing as a career. Retail selling is one of the oldest forms of business. The most ancient civilizations had market days and places where tillers of the soil, artisans and craftsmen spread out their wares for people to buy. In modern life this kind of business has become very important. We have not only markets, but super-markets and chain stores. Everything we eat and wear, everything we need for comfort and use in our homes, is purchased at some retail place—a store, a shop or a market. The business section of any town or city is made up chiefly of retail stores or shops, and the merchants or shopkeepers are among the important business people of the community.

In Canada and the United States the retailing business as a whole involves billions of dollars, and gives employment and careers to millions of citizens. Every year more and more of our young people go into this kind of business, because they find it both profitable and interesting.

The modern department store is a highly specialized form of retailing. In it you can buy pots and pans, radios and phonographs, furniture and rugs (known to the trade as "hard goods"), as well as "soft goods"—clothing and accessories for every member of the family. Naturally, in such a store there is an endless variety of jobs, and opportunities for many different kinds of career. The different fields can be divided roughly as follows:

1. *Management.* People in charge of receiving, marking, packing and delivering merchandise; supervisors of maintenance—of the store's housekeeping personnel, such as painters, carpenters, porters and matrons; supervisors of mechanical and electrical equipment—elevators, air conditioning, etc.; service personnel in charge of the selling staffs; the personnel and training departments; the adjustment department—all of these are careers in management and are positions generally held by men.

In selecting people for these positions we look for a number of things: knowledge of

Backstage dressing room? Not a bit of it! This is window-display work "behind the scenes."

BEN GREENHAUS

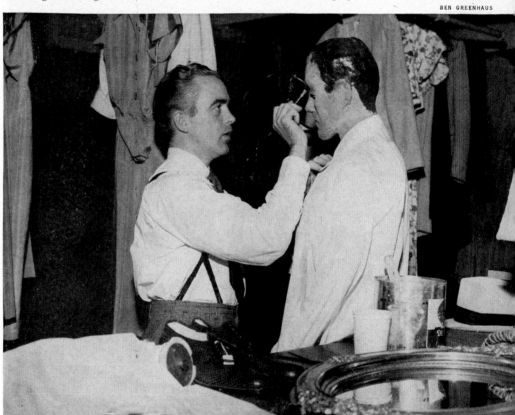

LOUISE DAHL-WOLFE

The author in her office. Miss Dorothy Shaver is one of the world's top women executives.

psychology and skill in dealing with other human beings; a knack for mastering an enormous amount of detail; the ability to judge what is important and what is not important; an open mind toward more efficient ways of doing things. Service is one of the things that makes a customer like one store better than another. It is what gives a store its personality. The service department has been one of the outstanding spots as a steppingstone to a retailing career for young men and young women too. If you think you would like a career in management, analyze your special abilities and see if your particular talents fit into this category.

2. *Merchandising and buying* (more about this later).

3. *Finance.* This includes credit, accounting, bookkeeping and control. These are pretty much the same in all businesses, so I will not dwell on them at length. In a department store, however, which is a world in miniature, the work is probably more interesting and varied than it is in many other businesses.

4. *Promotion.* This includes advertising, publicity, display and fashion co-ordination. I will have more to say later about these as fields for stimulating careers.

Now let us go back to the merchandisingbuying end of the retail business, which is really the axis around which a store turns. Everything that is sold to a customer must first be bought from a manufacturer or wholesaler—people who make or process merchandise to sell *in quantity* to retailers. People who do the buying from the wholesalers are called buyers, and each buyer must have a thorough knowledge of the special kind of merchandise he purchases. For instance, a shoe buyer must know about leather and how it is processed; how shoes are manufactured; what the wearing qualities are, and the current styles or colors in shoes. A buyer must know not only his own market, but also other markets related to it. He must have a sense of values, good taste— and must, of course, be a good salesman.

A good buyer also knows what his or her customer needs or wants, and must find new ways of satisfying those needs. A buyer is an important cog in the machinery of a department store, and the most successful buyer is one who has that extra creative spark of imagination. Although both men and women have found buying a satisfying and stimulating career, buying for a department store has an especial attraction for women. Because most of our shoppers are women, it is not surprising that women are especially fitted for department-store buying.

I know that all of you who are interested in a retail career are anxious to know what kind of training you will need for the job I have just described. I have always felt that the best training you can get is a liberal education (which gives you a broad knowledge of the world), followed by special study in your own field. For example, if you want to become a buyer, it is helpful, though not absolutely necessary, to take a liberal arts course in college and then take additional courses in merchandising and retailing. However, the most important training that a buyer can have is to sell.

The Gentle Art of Finding Out What People Like to Buy

This is so important that I am going to say it over again. There is no better way to learn what a customer wants than to learn first-hand by selling to her. If you were to apply tomorrow for a job in merchandising, the chances are that you would be assigned at once to the selling force to learn the business at its very source. Then, by finding out what people like best to buy, you will know what to look for at the wholesalers when you become a buyer. If you can get selling experience while you are in school, during vacation or whenever you have free time, then you will be one step ahead of the person who has had no experience at all in selling.

Good Taste—the Best Guidepost to Successful Merchandising

I think it is also important to mention that much of the work in a department store demands a high degree of artistic ability. I mean this in a very special sense. Fashion is, after all, a form of art, and practically every article sold in a department store is influenced in some way by fashion. A woman may not be a painter or a writer or actually practice any of the fine arts. Yet she may express her artistic sense by the way she dresses and by the furnishing and decorating of her home. The woman who is well dressed knows the value of color and line, even though she has never studied them. The people who are buying, selling, displaying or advertising clothes must know a great deal about color and line if they are to be successful. In addition to all these things, they must have that quality that we call a sense of chic —for want of a better word. It means in part a sophistication, a sense of drama, and above all a sense of the fitness of things.

Ever So Many Kinds of Jobs for Many Special Talents

This is especially true in the field of promotion, which offers jobs just as fascinating as buying, and which calls for a high degree of creative effort. There is, for example, advertising, with its art, copy and production staffs. The art department needs people who are skilled in drawing and making layouts— fitting pictures and text into an attractive and well-balanced design. The copy staff uses people with a knack for saying the usual in an unusual way. The production department needs people who have a passion for accuracy and an ability to follow through.

Department managers have to be people who know how to organize the work of others and to see that the work is carried out smoothly. Apart from paid-for publicity,

BEN GREENHAUS

Throughout the store, at Christmas time, a wonderland comes true.

there is the business of getting interesting bits of news about the store into newspapers and magazines, or on the radio or over television. There are fashion co-ordinating jobs which include getting up fashion shows and tying up the various fashion promotions in a store. People with taste, imagination and ingenuity, together with artistic ability, find window and interior display a satisfying career for their talents.

So you see, a department store presents a great variety of jobs which are worthy of making careers. One can become a promotion manager, an artist, a personnel director, a cafeteria manager, a dietitian, a buyer, an interior decorator or a merchandise manager —enough careers to satisfy a wide variety of talents and interests.

Success in the career you have chosen is a combination of knowing what you want to do and working very hard to do it. Hard work means more than sheer physical labor, more than doing your particular job to the best of your ability. It includes both of these, but it also means learning more and more about the field in which your job lies.

The More You Know about Your Work, the More Fun It Will Be

For example, a buyer of inexpensive dresses is, of course, expected to know all about the fashions in the lower price ranges. However, she must also know what the Paris designers have designed for their exclusive customers. Although she buys dresses, she should also know what is new in the sportswear market. She brings this knowledge of the whole fashion picture into her selection of the best possible dresses for her department. That is why she is a successful buyer.

From what I have said, you may think that it is not very easy to be successful in retailing. But it is not so difficult as it sounds —for if you like it, it will be exciting and enjoyable, and if it is exciting and enjoyable it is no longer hard work.

There is so much activity in the retail world! There are always new things and constantly changing fashions, as varied as the life of the community. There are always new customers and new ideas for promoting the merchandise itself. You are a part of all that activity. No other business offers such varied opportunity and excitement.

If this is what you really want, let nothing stop you. It can be yours!

111

CAREER

as an

Norman Rockwell with brush, palette and pipe.

ILLUSTRATION is a way of telling a story with pictured images instead of words. If you consider the drawings of the cave-dwellers and the picture-strips that the ancient Egyptians painted on the walls of their tombs, it is an older form of story-telling than the written word. Yet, through all the centuries during which written language has grown more flexible and more exact, the brush and pencil of the artist have kept on recording the lives of the people about him, their joys and sorrows, their moments of nobility, even their petty meannesses.

In the springtime of Western art, Giotto and many other painters told the story of the Christian religion. In the sixteenth and seventeenth centuries, Jan Steen, Pieter de Hooch, Pieter Brueghel, even Rembrandt, pictured the doings of the Flemish and Dutch people among whom they lived. Later on, Hogarth in England and Daumier in France, and many lesser lights carried on the story-telling tradition. Today the field of illustration is wider than ever before. Magazine covers and illustration, greeting cards, calendars and, of course, advertising, offer a wealth of opportunity to young artists whose talents lie in that direction.

It is true that the field is not overcrowded, simply because not every artist, however

great, has the additional gift of story-telling. In the same way, some of the greatest of singers have been ill at ease in opera, because they had not the urge or the aptitude for acting which opera demands.

When boys and girls ask me—and they frequently do—how to get started as an illustrator, I think of my own career which is, of course, the one I know most about. From my own experience, and from what I know of the experience of others, I would say that there are three qualifications which are absolutely necessary. These are: the urge to tell in pictures what you see or hear; a thorough knowledge of your craft—drawing and painting; and continuous and unrelenting practice.

The first of these qualifications is one which, apparently, you must be born with. It is made up of curiosity about everything under the sun, imagination, memory, and the desire to re-create on paper or canvas the faces and scenes that interest you.

The second qualification—knowledge of your craft—must be gained by study and by hard work. An artist, whether he paints formal portraits, landscapes, abstractions or whatever, has got to know the mechanics of his trade. So does a violinist or a carpenter or a cook. Young people sometimes think of this study and work as unbearable drudgery, and so it probably is for many people. However, if you really, deep in your heart, want to be an artist, you will welcome the chance to master the tools and methods of your art, and after a while you will wonder how anyone could possibly regard it as drudgery.

This brings us to the third qualification: practice. It is this that makes the other two really work. It may be that somewhere there has been an artist who was such a great genius that he never did any practicing at all, but if so nobody seems ever to have heard of him. Indeed, one of the most noticeable traits of the great masters of music, painting or any other art, has been their devotion to working at it.

ILLUSTRATOR

By NORMAN ROCKWELL, *Artist*

One of the questions I am often asked is, how much and what kind of education should an artist have? Of course, in any field of work the more general knowledge you have the broader your horizon will be. To the practicing artist, however, a college education can be, at the best, a pleasant sideline. At the worst, it is an interruption to his career. The reason for this is clear. Anyone who expects to make a career of art must start working at it very early in life. By the time you reach college age you should have become pretty well set in your career. If by that time you have not become a practicing artist, then by all means go to college and study for some other kind of vocation.

Art school is, however, of great importance, for there you will get technical knowledge, encouragement from people who really know the problems involved, and the stimulus of working with others who have the same general goal. In the old days, young people who wanted to become artists worked and studied with established masters—cleaning brushes, running errands, sweeping out the studio while they learned the fundamentals of their art. Today we have special schools of art and, in the regular public and private schools, art courses which can give you a great deal of the necessary training.

I won't try to give you any advice about technique or methods of painting. These are things that every artist works out for himself, according to his own experience and tastes and aims. Trying to use another person's methods is quite as uncomfortable as trying to wear someone else's shoes. It may, however, be helpful to tell some of the steps by which the earlier part of my own career progressed.

I can't remember when I was not sketching things that interested me. Long before I reached high school, drawing was the most absorbing of all occupations so far as I was

concerned. In my second year of high school I left to enter the National Academy of Design in New York. After hours at the academy, I studied at the Art Students' League; and it was one of my teachers there, Thomas Fogarty, who put me in touch with a pub-

A section of the famous Rockwell cover that tells the story of a happy homecoming.

The professor welcomes the chance to curl up with some good bacilli.

How your head feels in that first 24 hours.

THE COMMON COLD

By NORMAN ROCKWELL

COURTESY OF THE SATURDAY EVENING POST ©

The tub treatment relaxes the patient while drowning the germs.

An appreciative audience, the right acoustics, and he's off.

Officer Clancy needs no whistle. When he says "Stob!" he means "Dode go."

Many germ strategists prescribe the direct frontal attack.

lisher who wanted illustrations for some children's books. That was when I was seventeen.

Since then I have done a tremendous number of illustrations for stories, covers for magazines, pictures for calendars, advertisements, greeting cards and even a few mural paintings and portraits.

An Art Editor's Judgment Can Be Very Helpful

I can't say that I have ever had a difficult time selling my work. One reason for this is that art editors usually know exactly what they want. When they look at a picture they can tell at once whether it fills their need or not. The first time I took a couple of paintings to THE SATURDAY EVENING POST in Philadelphia, the art editor and the editor-in-chief both looked at them and accepted them at once. On the other hand, art editors usually know when they don't like a picture, and that can be a help to a young artist too. It helps him to learn where his market is, and what type of picture best suits his public.

Illustrating a Written Story Has Its Problems

In recent years I have done very little illustrating of books and stories. Covers, the Boy Scout calendars, Christmas cards and a few other pictures in which the story is told entirely by the artist, take up most of my time. Illustrating a story *written* by someone else is pleasant and often exciting, but in some ways it is more difficult than making the picture tell your own story. The cover artist, for example, tells the story himself with color and line instead of words. Illustrating another person's story is a sort of team work. You take the story written in words and try to make pictures that will give it more vividness, without taking the reader's interest from the written word.

In any branch of illustrating, faithfulness to life is of the first importance. When, for instance, I illustrated TOM SAWYER and HUCKLEBERRY FINN, I went down to Hannibal, Missouri, to get the feel of the town and the people that Mark Twain wrote about. The pictures for a story about Martha Washington were painted at Washington's Valley Forge headquarters, where the story took place. When I illustrated a WOMAN'S HOME COMPANION serial about

Louisa M. Alcott, I spent several days at the Alcott home at Concord.

I have done a great many historical pictures and enjoyed doing them, but best of all I like making pictures of the people of our own time and country—people that you

COURTESY, BROWN & BIGELOW © AND BOY SCOUTS OF AMERICA

A painting for the Boy Scout calendar, alive and authentic in every detail.

meet everywhere you go in the United States and Canada. It gives me pleasure and satisfaction to paint their activities, to show the characteristics which enable them to meet disaster and triumph, as well as the small delights and irritations of life. No two artists paint exactly alike, and no two artists paint exactly the same kind of subject. If you wish to be an illustrator—or any other kind of artist—select the subjects that it gives you the greatest satisfaction to paint. You can't go wrong.

115

CAREERS IN
Industrial Photography

By Roy Stryker
Director, Photographic Division, Standard Oil Company of New Jersey

TODAY, when it sometimes seems as if everybody in the United States and Canada owns a camera, and when newspapers, magazines and textbooks use almost as much space for photographs as they do for the written word, a career in photography has taken on a new meaning.

Years ago a career in photography meant one thing only to most people—the making of camera portraits. Every small town had at least one photographic studio, to which the townsmen came to have specially posed pictures made of themselves and their families. All of the milestones of life were recorded in light and shadow by the portrait photographer: graduations, weddings, baby pictures; the girl in her first grown-up party dress, the young soldier in his new uniform; Father and Mother on their twenty-fifth—or their fiftieth—wedding anniversary. Portrait photography is today more important than ever before, but it is no longer the chief way of earning a living with your camera.

If you study carefully the various kinds of photographs that are published day after day and week after week, you will see that, taken all together, they make a running record of the times we live in and the way we live. They cover the great events and personalities, of course. But most important of all, they show the daily life of the ordinary individual in every part of the world where a man can take a camera. Atomic explosions and automobile collisions, royal weddings, prize winners at county fairs, scenes of home life, work going on in great steel mills or oil refineries—nothing is missed by the curiosity and imagination of the questing cameraman.

This kind of photograph can be divided rather roughly into the taking of spot news and documentary pictures. As a matter of fact, the same picture can fit into both of these classes. A picture of a Dust Bowl farmer and his family running for shelter from a great cloud of wind-driven soil is a good news picture. If it is made a part of a series of pictures of farm life in the great midland plains, it becomes a documentary photograph. In recent years, many exciting books have been published that show in pictures the life and work and play of people in a particular industry or region. Many photographers have used great imagination and fine skill in selecting and taking these pictures.

Such a photographer is really a photographic reporter. In this kind of reporting the camera supplements the pencil and the typewriter in presenting a slice of life or a vivid story. The photographic reporter has an interesting and varied life. He may have assignments that take him to far countries, but in any case the very nature of his work

A simple scene with great pictorial interest.

FARM SECURITY ADMINISTRATION

A farmer and his children seeking shelter in a dust storm. This picture, taken in Cimarron County, Oklahoma, in the dark years of the great drought, is a vivid scene in a drama of desolation.

makes it unfailingly absorbing and fascinating.

The technical part of picture-making is easily learned, but it actually forms a very small part of a good photographer's equipment. Good pictures are made with the eyes and the brain, before the shutter is clicked and the exposure made. The real tools of the trade are curiosity, imagination and, especially, hard work.

I would advise any boy or girl who wants to build up a career in photography to begin right at home. Don't try to find unusual or spectacular subjects for your camera. Just say to yourself, "What's down my street?" —then take your camera and find out. If you look with real curiosity and imagination at the homely familiar scenes around you,

they will become as strange and interesting as if you had never seen them before. The curious pattern of shadows cast on a wall by an iron fence, the attitudes and expressions of a group of men talking on the Post Office steps, children playing marbles on the sidewalk—sights that you have been seeing every day without giving them a second thought—these are the materials from which you may learn to slice the essential human or pictorial interest.

When you have gotten used to looking for the unusual in the commonplace, you will begin to improve in your ability to judge as well as to take a picture. Think of the camera as a language with which to interpret the world and the people around you, and always try to tell your photographic story truthfully and sincerely.

So far as education is concerned, the more you learn about the world in which you live the deeper your understanding of your subject matter will be. Art, literature, history, social science—all of these are especially helpful in broadening your knowledge and deepening your understanding. Indeed, in photography as in most activities, you will find a use for any form of study that teaches you to use your brains and to develop your taste.

If you stick to the actual taking of pictures you will have a life-work that can not be surpassed for interest and the satisfaction of doing something worth while. But the modern field of photography has other careers in it that do not include actual camera work. Government departments and large private industries often have photographic

As a gull might view New York Harbor.
STANDARD OIL CO. (N. J.) PHOTO BY CORSINI

118

divisions. So do museums, scientific laboratories and, of course, the big picture magazines. Such enterprises need, not only skilled photographers, but research departments, photographic libraries, and editors to plan and direct the work of the photographers.

The Range and Scope of the Camera Are Almost Limitless

My own experience is proof of the range and scope that the field of photography can give, yet I do not even own a camera and I never personally take pictures as part of my work. Yet in the years that I have been directing photographic work, in governmental departments and in private industry, I have been responsible for the taking of close to half a million photographs of a documentary nature. These have included such subjects as rural slums, farm life in general in the United States and Canada, transportation on such widely separated rivers as the Mackenzie and the Mississippi, the story of a great city's milk supply, and the many and far-flung operations by which oil is brought from the earth and prepared to run the wheels of industry.

Documentary photographs must, above all, be truthful and realistic in what they portray. If they include faked or trick shots, or specially posed scenes, then they are not really documentary pictures. The very word "documentary" tells us that they are honest recordings of scenes and people and places as they really exist. For this reason documentary pictures are of tremendous value historically. When you take pictures of this type, and do it honestly and with imagination and judgment, you are making a pictorial record of the time in which you live. This record will be of benefit not only to the people of today, but will also be of value to future generations.

It is a fascinating field, as I have said before. No matter what has been your training or aims, if you are once exposed to the virus you are quite likely never to recover.

For example, I was raised on a ranch, studied at the Colorado School of Mines, worked in a settlement house on New York's East Side, and then graduated from Columbia with a degree in economics. Following graduation I taught there for several years. You might not, at first glance, think that this rather varied educational background would lead to a career in photography. Yet,

A steel guy derrick lifts its arms against the sky—one of man's powerful construction tools.

taken as a whole, it represented a broad field of related interests. Agriculture, mining engineering and first-hand knowledge of the needs and problems of the less fortunate of one's fellow-men make a firm basis for the study of economics—which deals with the production and distribution of goods and the reasons for poverty and wealth.

When I gave up teaching to take a position with the Federal Government, I was given the job of presenting some of the problems of the less fortunate in rural America, and the remedies that were being applied to their ills. It was then that I discovered the value of telling a story in pictures, and this experience is proving equally useful in presenting the story of oil to the public. Since I have been directing the photographic division of the Standard Oil Company (New Jersey), the field has broadened to take in half the world and many different kinds of life and of industrial activity.

1. King of Swat.

2. Golden Jubilee Queen.

CELEBRITIES

3. Peace-loving nobleman.

4. United States Senator.

5. Amazing Dutchwoman.

6. Former Justice.

HOW GOOD IS YOUR MEMORY FOR FACES?

Each of these people was pictured in your daily newspaper many times during the year just past.

Can you guess who they are from the clue we give with each picture?

Answers on Page 123

7. Third party man.

8. China's First Lady.

9. General of the Armies.

10. Standard-bearer.

11. Patriot and sage.

12. Canadian diplomat.

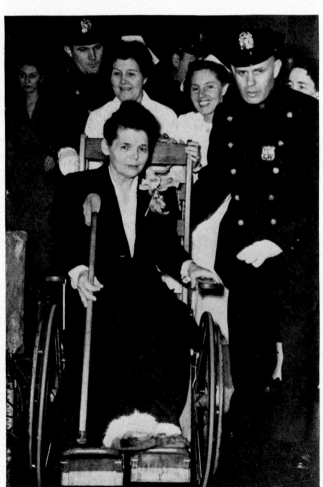

13. Israeli Premier.

14. She leaped to freedom.

1. GEORGE HERMAN (BABE) RUTH, known to millions of young and old baseball fans all over the world, died in August 1948, after a long illness. He was affectionately known by his admirers as "The Home Run King," "Sultan of Swat" and "King of Swat." He ranked with the great Ty Cobb as one of the greatest record-setters in base-ball.

2. QUEEN WILHELMINA OF THE NETHERLANDS, loved by her country-men, celebrated the Golden Jubilee (fifty years) of her reign in September. On Sep-tember 4, she abdicated in favor of her daughter, who became Queen Juliana.

3. COUNT FOLKE BERNADOTTE of Sweden died in the service of peace in May. He was head of the Swedish Red Cross and was assassinated while acting as the United Nations mediator in the fighting between Jews and Arabs in Palestine.

4. MARGARET CHASE SMITH, Maine Republican, has a new job in Washington, D. C. After serving her state as a representa-tive in the House of Representatives, she ran for the United States Senate in No-vember and was elected.

5. FANNY BLANKERS-KOEN of the Netherlands became the heroine of the 1948 Olympic Games by winning three first-place gold medals in the track events during the summer games. She is the mother of three children.

6. CHARLES EVANS HUGHES, the former Chief Justice of the United States Supreme Court, died of a heart attack in August. He had served as Chief Justice from 1930 until his retirement from the bench in 1941. In 1916 he made an unsuccessful at-tempt to win the presidency of the United States but was defeated by Woodrow Wilson.

7. HENRY AGARD WALLACE, former Vice-President and former Secretary of Agri-culture, headed the famous Third party and staged an unsuccessful campaign for the presidency.

8. MADAME CHIANG KAI-SHEK, the "first lady" of China, came to America in November to plead for more help for the Chinese Nationalist Government in its war with the Communists.

9. GENERAL JOHN J. PERSHING, hero of World War I, died in Walter Reed Hos-pital, Washington, D. C., in July. He held, in addition to many other honors, the honor of being the only American since George Washington to hold the rank of General of the Armies (which is higher than the five-star rank of General of the Army).

10. THOMAS E. DEWEY, governor of New York State, made his second bid for the na-tion's highest job in November—and lost. He ran for the presidency of the United States as the Republican candidate and, after the election was over, said that he would not try again.

11. MOHANDAS K. GANDHI, the little "spinner" of India, spent most of his life fighting for the liberation of his homeland. Shortly after the independence of the Do-minion had been proclaimed, he was cruelly assassinated by a political fanatic in New Delhi, capital of India.

12. HON. LESTER B. PEARSON, dis-tinguished Canadian, became his country's Secretary of State for Foreign Affairs after serving as a representative in the United Nations. He succeeded Louis S. St. Laurent, who became Canada's Prime Minister.

13. DAVID BEN GURION, chairman of the Jewish Agency, became the first Premier and Defense Minister of the new State of Israel following the organization of the new nation in Palestine.

14. OKSANA KASENKINA, the little Rus-sian school teacher, found a haven in the United States after creating what might be termed an international incident. When scheduled to return to Russia, she had sought to remain in America. Russian consular rep-resentatives attempted to prevent her from doing so. She tried to escape from the Rus-sian Consulate in New York by jumping from a third-story window and was severely injured. When she was released from the hos-pital, she said that she would like to teach in America after winning citizenship.

CENTRAL AMERICAN PICTURE

By Spruille Braden
*Former United States Ambassador to
Cuba, Colombia and Argentina*

THE Central American republics of Guatemala, Honduras, El Salvador, Nicaragua and Costa Rica are quite properly often thought of almost as a single unit or country. In fact, many people—including many Central Americans—have hoped for years that the five countries may some day be united in one great and powerful nation, with one central government. Certainly the United States would prefer to see a single, strong republic there rather than a number of separate and relatively weak countries.

However, the differences—and even rivalries—that exist between the republics, plus the personal ambitions of a few politicians, have prevented such a union in spite of all the advantages that it might offer. The people of each of the republics are rightly proud, too, of the ways in which their country stands out from the others. They do not like being lumped together simply as Central Americans; and it is true that any generalization about them is likely to be misleading and possibly wrong.

The Republic of Panama is also distinct in its history, in the nature and composition of its people and in many other ways. However, it is next door to Costa Rica and there are enough similarities between it and the other five countries to warrant its being considered with them in a discussion of Central America. (Panama is not generally considered as a republic of Central America because it is situated on the narrow isthmus that connects Central America with South America. When Spain controlled all of Latin America, and for some years afterwards, the area was governed as a part of the continent of South America.)

Thick jungles must be leveled and cleared, and thousands of acres of swamps must be drained.

When, in addition, the three Caribbean republics of Cuba, Haiti and Santo Domingo are included in the discussion, the differences become so multiplied that it would take a large book to tell all that there is to tell about them. In an article of this size, then, it is possible to discuss only a few of the high points relating to all these republics and the lives of their people. The author will be well rewarded if his words create in the reader an urge to visit them and to know each of them at first hand. Once visited, these enchanting countries will lure the traveler to return again and again.

Years of extensive research could not wholly unfold all of the story of the Indian tribes that once occupied these lands—or their customs, and how some of the tribes have survived from the days of the Spaniards, while others have entirely disappeared or have mixed their blood with that of the conquerors. There are thrills and romance in the story of the struggle of these republics for independence, and in the history of the way in which each republic—sometimes rapidly and firmly, sometimes haltingly—has developed and moved toward democracy as we understand the term.

No human hand could accurately portray the wealth of color with which nature has endowed Central America and the Caribbean Islands. A hundred artists, painting day in and day out for a hundred years, could not even begin to put on canvas all of the marvelous scenic beauties which invite the eye.

However entrancing all this may be for the scholar and artist, these lands demand the most careful thought by the statesman, the economist and the business man. The countries are fundamentally important to North America from the purely practical aspects of international relations and its own natural economy. This is true, whether the world is to live in a state of war or in peace —or, what now seems more likely, under conditions of the so-called "cold war" which may, without warning, turn into a full-

A never ending battle must be fought to keep the dreaded plant disease, *Sigatoka*, in check.

fledged, disastrous armed conflict.

One quick glance at the map will convince anyone of the vital importance of the Caribbean Islands and Central America to the whole Western Hemisphere in case of any major conflict. There lies the defense of the entire southern flank of North America. Should a powerful foe obtain a foothold, use of the Panama Canal might be stopped overnight and security would be imperiled.

The United States depends on Central America and the Caribbean for such essential things as sugar, bananas, coffee, fibers, some minerals and other tropical products. In turn, the United States sends them a long list of products, including wheat and rice and many kinds of machinery, equipment and tools. Of course, it would be possible to get along if the Caribbean and Central-American countries were to be eliminated both as suppliers and consumers, but life would be far less agreeable.

In peace or war, it is best for all that there be friendship and co-operation. The American republics are agreed that they should hold together as a working community of nations within the United Nations. The leadership of this group of nations has fallen upon the United States, because of its size and power. Failure to accept the responsibility might prove costly. The United States must assume that leadership, if only for self-protection against an attack on the Panama Canal and its southern flank in the event of war. Likewise, it must do so in times of peace, as a moral obligation, in order to build a community of nations co-operating for their common benefit and for the preservation of democracy as we understand it.

Is This Community of Nations Possible? Some Say Not

Some people may say that such a community of nations can not be established or operate successfully because the various republics are so unlike. Some are wealthy, some are poor. They contain many different races; and, above all, their political systems are very different. Unquestionably there are obstacles to overcome, but considerable progress has already been made. The differences in relative wealth can be improved, as living standards are raised, by raising the productive power of the workers. It can not be emphasized too strongly that the only way to raise living standards is by increasing the

UNITED FRUIT COMPANY

producing power of the people. Finally, there is an abiding urge for democracy and freedom, as we understand the words, among all these people.

When we speak of their urge for democracy, it also must be recognized that all too often these ambitions have been disappointed. Much of the cause has been due to the great lack of education, and to the fact that the change from a more or less feudal society to a working democracy is a very slow process. As a result, it is not surprising that force or revolution very often has been substituted for an election, and that one dictator after another has seized the power. It must be admitted that some of the old-type dictators were patriotic and well-meaning and really did try to advance the interests of their countries and to improve the lot of their fellow-citizens. The old-fashioned dictator, though, could be overthrown quite easily by a determined majority of citizens

armed only with machetes and a few rifles. For this reason alone, he had to respect the will of the people to some extent—which was a kind of democratic influence. The modern dictator, backed by a small, well-organized military force equipped with the most modern weapons, is better able to deal with opposition. He controls the newspapers and radio, education and the national economy, and even the courts and labor.

The United States, through its State Department, has officially declared many times that it would rather co-operate and be friendly with governments that are freely elected by the people. Such co-operation should take a practical form. The small republics should be helped to develop in agriculture, mining, industry and technology, in health and in culture.

Many of us who live in the Temperate Zone have a mistaken idea about tropical agriculture. We assume that because of the

Even when lands have been reclaimed, the struggle must still go on. Miles of piping for spraying must crisscross thousands of acres to save banana plants from the dreaded *Sigatoka* (plant disease). Invading plant and insect life must not be allowed to overrun and kill off valuable crops. Unceasing and intensive warfare must be waged, using the most modern methods yet devised by scientists, to keep the plantations from reverting to primitive jungle.

Private Enterprise Brings Millions of Dollars to These Republics

Such a vast undertaking, which has been carried forward by the United Fruit Company, is a fine achievement for American private enterprise. It has assisted in establishing a new, balanced and diversified economy, with modest profits to itself, which has greatly benefited these nations. Other cases could be cited of how American enterprise has increased the individual productive power and has made millions of dollars flow into these republics each year. For instance, with an investment of many million dollars one United States company alone, the American and Foreign Power Company, today supplies 866,000,000 horse-power hours of power per year in four of these countries. Individual output has been increased many times and living standards of the people have been raised correspondingly. Each year, the United Fruit Company sends about sixty-five young men from these countries to a company-operated school, where they receive free instruction. They are taught scientific farming, the care of farm animals and dairying.

These records of accomplishment foretell a lasting prosperity both for Central America and the Caribbean and the United States. What has already been done successfully can be repeated in the future—and on an increasing scale—for the benefit of all concerned, providing the republics will maintain a favorable atmosphere for the investment of private capital. If they will do so, standards of living, health and education will be still further improved. This, in turn, should help to keep out the virus of communism and, instead, promote the spread of genuine democracy. Good business makes good friends, especially if those friends are devoted to the same democratic principles of government and of living.

Politics and government provided the chief news from Central America and the Caribbean region during the year; and Costa Rica's election and dispute with Nicaragua made the most headlines. In Costa Rica, Otilio Ulate Blanco was elected president, but a faction opposing him tried to install his rival, Dr. Rafael Calderón Guardia, as president. The disagreement flared into an open revolt, led by Col. José Figueres, in support of Ulate. Figueres was victorious and he then installed himself as head of a provisional government. Nicaragua became involved, first by sending troops to oppose Figueres; and later when it was charged that an invasion of Costa Rica was launched from Nicaragua. Costa Rica protested and the dispute was investigated by the Organization of American States which, acting under the Rio Pact, ordered both countries to make peace. In Panama, supporters of former President Arnulfo Arias fought police during the election that named Domingo Arosmena president. Arias, charging fraud, fled to Costa Rica. Cuba elected Carlos Prio Socarrás as president, and President Castaneda Castro of El Salvador was deposed in a military coup. Left: Market day in Cartago, Costa Rica, seems placid in spite of political upheavals.

---

hot, damp climate huge crops of bananas, sugar-cane, fibers and other products abound everywhere in the nine republics, just waiting to be picked or harvested. It is true that in the Caribbean and Central-American jungles, forests and swamps, plant life sprouts forth almost overnight in surprisingly luxuriant growth. What we fail to realize is that a tremendous amount of work must be done to fight this luxuriance of growth before a crop can begin to be profitable.

Jungles must be leveled, and swamps must be drained. Malaria and other diseases must be eliminated. Highways and railroads must be pushed through forests and over mountains. Homes, schools and hospitals must be built; warehouses and docks must be constructed. Fleets of refrigerated steamers must be put into operation, and world markets must be opened. All of this requires courage and initiative. It requires organization and huge amounts of money.

AMERICAN CYANAMID COMPANY

Wool shirt on left was treated with plastic.

and carpets, but they are strong, smooth, glossy and easily cleaned.

The process for making nylon has also been improved. Formerly nylon was manufactured entirely from coal, with the addition of chemicals that are made from water and air. Recently, however, it was discovered that ordinary corncobs contain a chemical —an oily liquid—called furfural which can easily be turned into nylon. More than 100,000 tons of useless corncobs have already gone into the making of nylon stockings. By using the annual crop of millions of corncobs, which would otherwise be wasted, coal that can not be replaced can be saved for other uses.

There are new ways, too, of improving the natural fabrics, such as cotton and wool. Cotton cloth wrinkles easily when it has been wet, and wool shrinks in washing. Both wrinkling and shrinking are now prevented by soaking the cloth in plastics and then baking the cloth so that the plastic becomes a

CHEMISTRY
during the year

By GERALD WENDT
Editoral Director, Science Illustrated

ALL the materials that you can feel, see, smell or taste are chemicals, including even those materials of which your own body is made. Every year chemists learn how to make new and useful chemicals that nature has not provided. Many of these man-made chemicals are more satisfactory in certain respects than the older natural materials. Rayon and nylon, for instance, have certain advantages over cotton and wool, which are nature's handiwork.

As chemists learn more about these artificial materials, they find ways to improve them. Nylon was first familiar in the form of very fine fibers, fine enough to make excellent stockings for women. These fibers are made simply by squeezing the melted nylon through very tiny holes. Now, nylon is also pressed out through larger holes to make heavy, thick fibers. These strong and elastic fibers are used for window screens, tennis rackets, fishing lines and toothbrush bristles. We now have even rugs made of nylon yarns; they are not so fuzzy as woolen rugs

part of the fiber or yarn. When a small quantity of plastic is soaked and baked into cotton or wool, it stiffens the cloth slightly, and prevents water from entering the pores of the fabric. When made from cloth that has been treated in this way, cotton dresses can be worn in the rain and still look fresh. Woolen sweaters and stockings, and even woolen suits, with this treatment, can be washed with soap and water without danger of shrinking.

It was many years ago that chemists first began making new types of those materials that we call plastics. Glass, the oldest of all plastics, is made by first melting sand, lime and soda together. At this stage it is a thick, sticky plastic liquid. After being rolled into sheets and cooled, it becomes hard and brittle. The thick liquid, however, can be squeezed through tiny holes, as nylon is, to make very thin fibers. These thin fibers are flexible and can be woven into fabrics, or crumpled and crushed into pads. The fabrics made from these glass fibers are strong and glossy, and can not be wet by water or burned by fire. Glass pads of this type were used during the war to line the walls of submarines to keep out the cold of the ocean. Now they are used to line the walls of houses to keep them warm, or the walls of refrigerators to keep the heat out. One of the

Weed-killer 2, 4-D, used on part of this field, killed dandelions, but left grasses unhurt.

glass companies has a small office building in New York City, called the Glass House. The walls of this house are covered with glass cloth instead of with wallpaper, the ceilings are glass pads to keep in the heat in winter and to deaden sound. The desks and the chairs are covered with glass cloth, too.

Another new material in common household use now is the metal magnesium. It is extracted by a new process from sea water in Texas. During the past year or two, this material, which was formerly very expensive, became cheap enough so that furniture could be made of it. Such furniture is very light in weight, since magnesium is the lightest of the common metals. A piece of magnesium weighs only two-thirds as much as a piece of aluminum of the same size. A child's chair weighs only a pound or two, and even a small boy can lift a magnesium table with one hand. Magnesium furniture is also much lighter than wood furniture, yet stronger.

If you have read the article on fuel in this ANNUAL, you know what is being done toward producing synthetic gasoline from natural gas and from coal. An entirely new kind of fuel will be needed, however, in the new high-speed planes and in rockets. This fuel is oxygen. In ordinary engines gasoline is used as fuel. It burns in oxygen from the air that comes into the engine through the carburetor. High-speed planes and rockets fly so high that the air is too thin to support combustion. Rockets and super-jet planes must carry not only gasoline, but also the oxygen for burning the gasoline. We do not usually think of oxygen as fuel, but at the great heights where the new planes will fly, oxygen must be considered as much a fuel as is gasoline.

There is a great difference, however, between the two. Gasoline is a liquid and can be carried in tanks. Oxygen is a gas. Up to now, when we have stored or carried oxygen, we have compressed it into strong and heavy cylinders; but those are too heavy for a plane to carry many of them. Because of this difficulty a new form of oxygen has been developed. It is a liquid that is not pure oxygen, but that is very rich in oxygen—hydrogen peroxide. This is the same peroxide that is sometimes used to kill germs in a cut finger. The ordinary drug-store peroxide is a very weak solution in water, while the new rocket fuel is pure 100 per cent peroxide. A rocket, or a high-speed jet plane, can carry two fuel tanks, one containing gasoline and the other, peroxide. When the two liquids are squirted at each other in the rocket or jet engine, each "burns" in the other. An excessively hot flame is produced which roars out of the rear nozzle of the engine and pushes the rocket forward. This new fuel is still an experiment, and most of the tests made with it are being kept secret by the Army and Navy. Its uses are war uses.

We hope never to have another war between human beings, but there is a different kind of war, with enemies of the whole human race, which goes on all the time. This is the war against the many small pests which either attack us directly—such as insects and disease germs—or attack our food supply, such as rats, some insects and weeds. Until the last few years there was some danger that these pests might get the better of us because of their great numbers. New chemical inventions have now made it certain that no insect, weed or vermin has a chance of victory. Even most disease germs can be conquered.

For getting rid of rats there are now two chemicals, called ANTU and 1080, that are so poisonous to these creatures that there is no longer any reason why rats should survive. Any city, or any farmer, can get rid of them quickly and easily.

DDT Kills Many Insects Which Attack Human Beings and Crops

The fate of insects is just as sure. They die quickly when sprayed with a chemical called DDT. This insecticide is effective not only against the insects which sting or bite human beings, such as mosquitoes, wasps and flies, but also against the thousands of kinds of insects which eat vegetables, leaves and grain that are needed for human food. DDT has been in use for several years, but the new trick in the war against insects is to dissolve the DDT in a chemical which is a liquid only when it is under pressure. The DDT and this chemical are now put into small "bombs" which are strong enough to keep the pressure on the liquid. When the nozzle is pressed down to make a tiny opening, the liquid squirts out and in a flash it evaporates and becomes a gas. This gas reaches even into the tiny cracks in an insect's skin, and kills quickly. DDT alone does not kill some tiny creatures, such as the red spiders, which look like insects but which are not. All insects have six legs. Spiders and mites have eight legs and do not belong to the insect family. A new chemical, however, known as thiophos, can be added to DDT, making a combination which kills the mites also.

2, 4-D Kills Broad-Leaved Plants but Not Plants of Grass Family

One of the most successful pest controls is the plant- and weed-killer, 2, 4-D. It has been in use for some time, but each year chemists are learning more about the best methods for its use. When a grassy lawn is sprayed with this chemical, the weeds curl up and die, but the grass pays no attention to it. American farmers are now saving large quantities of such food crops as wheat, oats, rice, corn, rye and barley by using this weed-killer. Poison ivy and poison oak are easily destroyed by 2, 4-D. Great care must be taken in using this chemical, for while it does not kill plants that belong to the grass family, it does kill all plants with broad leaves.

Among man's most dangerous enemies are the tiny plants called bacteria, which cause so many diseases. In recent years chemicals have been found which keep some of these little plants from multiplying in the human body; these sulfa drugs (they contain a little sulfur) cure diseases such as pneumonia and blood poisoning. Another drug, called penicillin, is made from a tiny plant, the penicillium mold.

In 1948 the chemists went one step further, and made chemicals that seem to attack another, still smaller, group of man's enemies. The common cold and infantile paralysis are caused by an organism so tiny, called a virus, that it can not ordinarily even be seen in a microscope. It is not known whether viruses are plants or even whether they are truly alive. They do seem to come alive, however, when they get into the cells of the human body, and they destroy those cells, causing a cold in some cases, and paralysis in others. Two drugs, divarsul and aureomycin, have been discovered which end the activity of the viruses in small test animals, such as mice. It is not yet known, however, whether they will do the same for human beings.

A NEW age of pioneering is looming in the Western Hemisphere. Vast wilderness regions in North and South America are about to be opened to civilization. Since the time of Columbus, European civilization has spread steadily westward, developing the more temperate regions of the Americas. Now it is beginning a new age of expansion toward the north and the warmer equatorial zone.

A few years ago it was fashionable to say that the Americas had no more frontiers; that our age of pioneering was gone forever. People thought of pioneering as being chiefly an agricultural undertaking, clearing the forest land or breaking the plains for the kind of farming that opened our West during the nineteenth century. They looked around and saw that the only empty spaces left were near the equator or in the far north. In such places the traditional kind of individual pioneering which colonized Minnesota or Manitoba is largely impossible. Then, too, it used to be thought that, in the far north and the tropics, the soils were not suitable for modern farming and white people could not stand the climates.

Many things have happened in recent years, however, to change people's ideas about these regions. We are beginning to learn more and more about both the Arctic and the tropics, and the more we find out about them the better they seem. Thousands of people are today discovering that the climates of these two regions are not nearly so forbidding as had been supposed. For instance, most white people who live in Alaska —people who are, like most Canadians and Americans, of European stock—love that country and its scenery and climate. Indeed, many of them would not dream of living anywhere else. The same thing is true of the tropics. It used to be thought that the tropical climate robbed you of energy, and that the white man could not live there very long without deteriorating. However, experiences in Australia and at the Panama Canal have proved that idea to be wrong. Tropical climates are never so hot as most of us used to think. They are often cooler than Washington or New York or Kansas City in summer. No white person need fear living in the trop-

TOP, GRACE LINE; RIGHT, STANDARD OIL CO (N. J.) PHOTO BY PARKS
New settlements in far places: a cattle-breeding station at Tingo Maria, in Peru; and the airfield at Yellowknife, in northern Canada.

COLONIZATION

NEW WORLDS
in the
AMERICAS

By EARL PARKER HANSON
Consultant to the United States Army and Navy on World Exploration

A street in Fairbanks, Alaska. As the North is developed, Fairbanks will gain new importance.

ics if he takes proper exercise, eats a balanced diet, and follows the simple rules that prevent such diseases as malaria and hookworm.

There are several important reasons for the present interest in the possibilities of these undeveloped regions. First of all, there is the urgent need to find living space and a new life for people from the crowded and impoverished countries of Europe and elsewhere. There are many thousands of men and women who have no place to live, no means of building useful and comfortable lives. At present they must be fed by donations from the rest of the world. To most human beings, however, living on charity is not really living: it robs them of hope, ambition and the feeling of accomplishment that is so necessary to human well-being. The conviction is growing that we should do something to make room for these people, and help them to produce their own foods or otherwise make honorable and dignified livings. Certainly they would find it far pleasanter to

make new lives for themselves in the north or in the tropics than to live in Europe on charity and in semi-starvation.

Then, too, business men in both North and South America are beginning to realize that they have much to gain by developing the resources of the areas that now lie almost empty. The United States, for example, has become the richest and most powerful nation on earth because, throughout her history, her people have pushed steadily onward to develop her resources and put them to work. The feeling is growing that this work should be continued, and that the nation still has vast resources for development in Alaska. In other words, new pioneer-ventures in that territory, in farming, fishing, mining, lumbering and manufacturing would add much to the nation's wealth and standard of living. Canada, also, is looking toward her north as a source of future economic strength. The nations of South America are busily "growing up" through the development of their resources and the building of many factories of various kinds.

All of this, however, requires people who are willing to go, and live, and work where the undeveloped resources are. That, in turn,

means that we might before too long see a new pioneering movement in the Western Hemisphere.

If you stop and consider the number of people per square mile in different parts of the Western Hemisphere, you will realize how thinly populated are the vast regions of the north and along the equator, compared with South America's coastal areas and the thickly populated regions that stretch northward as far as southern Canada. The thickly settled areas have up to 300 people per square mile; in the empty lands there are often fewer than one person per square mile.

Another way of looking at it is to see how much room each of us has to turn around in. For example, New York State, with its big cities, is so crowded that there is only 0.004 square mile of land for each man, woman and child living in the state. On the other hand, Alaska has more than 8 square miles for every Alaskan—or more than two thousand times as much room as New York State has for its inhabitants. Similarly, in southern Ontario there is about 0.2 square mile per inhabitant; while in the Yukon and Northwest Territories there are 9 square miles. Mexico has about 0.03 square mile of space

An Indian boy kicking up the sparkling waters of Great Slave Lake with his outboard motor.

STANDARD OIL CO. (N. J.) PHOTO BY PARKS

NATIONAL FILM BOARD

Winter settles down on Churchill, Hudson Bay port from which grain is shipped in summer.

Near Tingo Maria the Huallaga River lies like a glassy floor against a tapestry backdrop.

for every inhabitant. In the Amazon basin, which looks blank on the population map, there are possibly more than 10 square miles per person.

That is far too much space for practical purposes. The men who want to see the Americas developed to their full capacity, in prosperity as well as security, fully realize this fact. You can not run mines, or lumber camps, or productive farms, or trading centers, or factories or outposts for defense with only one person for every eight, nine or ten square miles of space. So the needs of the Americas are beginning to combine with those of Europe's surplus population to bring about a new wave of western settlement.

From Alaska, for instance, come persistent pleas for more settlers, more workers, more people; and the United States Government has recently taken steps to open lands along the new Alaska Highway for veterans who

want to go pioneering. While this northern territory has an area one-fifth as large as all the forty-eight states combined, it has a total population of only about 75,000. If all the men, women and children in Alaska went south to watch a football game in California's Rose Bowl, there would still be room enough in the bowl for the entire population of a city like Augusta, Maine.

When the United States bought Alaska from Russia, after the Civil War, a howl of derision went up because most people thought that the territory was so cold and forbidding as to be almost useless. Today we know better. Dr. A. H. Brooks of the United States Geological Survey has written that "three quarters of Alaska has a climate entirely favorable to occupation by the white race, and better than that of Finland and much of Sweden."

It is pointed out that the countries of northern Europe—Norway, Sweden and

Finland—have a total population of nearly 14,000,000 people, whose standards of living are considered to be among the highest in the world. Not only does Alaska resemble these countries in climate, scenery and resources, but it is in many ways even better off than they are. Its area is more than 100,-000 square miles larger than theirs, it has far more arable land, more pasture, richer fisheries, more water power and far greater mineral deposits, including coal and oil. Many people who know Alaska claim that it can easily, with proper development, support a population of 10,000,000, or about 140 times as many as it supports now.

Alaska Has Many Square Miles of Rich Farming Land

While Alaska is far different from the broad prairie lands of the Middle West, it does have an area about as large as New York State where farming of the conventional kind can be done. In regions such as the Matanuska Valley the grass is rich and can support a thriving dairy industry. Spring wheat and barley can be grown, and because of the long hours of summer sunlight, such vegetables as potatoes and pumpkins grow far bigger than they do farther south. Another equally large area, while not suited to the raising of crops, is splendidly adapted to grazing. Here one comes to the consideration of reindeer, which do well in this northern territory and are an important source of food in Scandinavian countries. Alaska's reindeer herds are still rather small, but it has been estimated that the country could support several millions of these animals, and so add greatly to the world's total food supply.

As timber supplies in the states are runing low, Americans are becoming more interested in Alaska's enormous forests. There is talk of starting lumbering operations there, to ship timber south and support industries for making newsprint and other kinds of paper. Alaska's underground resources are also being investigated. In the northernmost areas, the Navy's oil reserves are proving to be extremely rich, and the explorations being carried forward by the United States Geological Survey are revealing tremendous mineral resources. Alaska's known minerals include gold, jade, asbestos, coal, chromite, copper, mercury, the platinum metals, antimony, iron ore, manganese, molybdenum, vanadium, zinc and many others. In short,

Alaska, one-fifth as large as the forty-eight states, is perhaps far richer in natural resources than any United States area of the same size.

Many of the arguments that apply to Alaska, many of the reasons for colonizing Alaska, apply equally to northern Canada. There, too, we see a growing interest in the development of the region's vast resources. For decades there has been a steady movement of agricultural pioneers westward and northward in such areas as the Peace River district in Canada, and the Canadian Government has studied pioneering problems and published many important books on the subject. The present pioneering movement differs somewhat from that which opened the old West. Modern agricultural pioneers have to compete in a highly organized world. They need roads, cars, trucks, garages, gasoline stations and railroads. They also demand such things as stores, radios, electricity and other products of civilization. Canada's present land-settlement program is therefore an orderly movement, preceded by transportation facilities and directed by the Government.

Prospecting from the Air Is a Recent and Exciting Development

Although this movement has been going on for many years, the development of aviation has given it a great stimulus. Few stories in the history of air exploration are as exciting as that of Canada's air-borne prospectors of the 1920's and '30's. These men flew all over the so-called Barren Lands, where exploration on the ground would have been a long and difficult undertaking. They penetrated the most remote parts of that vast northern region, located immense deposits of mineral wealth, and staked them out for future use. In such sub-Arctic areas as northern Manitoba, new mines and new log-cabin villages were created, often almost overnight. Farther north, development usually had to wait until means of ground transportation had been built.

One dramatic exception was the uranium deposit at Great Bear Lake. This was so rich that it paid to use airplanes to carry men, machinery and ores. These deposits were discovered almost on the Arctic Circle in the years before World War II. They played an important part in the creation of atomic power, and continue to be important for atomic development, now, and in the future.

Not far from Great Bear Lake, at Fort Norman, are important oil wells. For many years these wells have provided fuel for the planes, motor boats and tractors of northern Canada. During the war they became even more important, for it was from these wells that the Canol pipe line drew the oil that it carried to Alaska for use in the war effort. The Norman wells represent only one small tapping of an enormous oil field, which is known to be one of the richest in the world.

The Far North Is No Longer a Lost and Desolate Land

As more and more people examine Canada's north, the region loses more and more of its former terrors. It is now known, for instance, that large parts of the huge Barren Grounds were misnamed. Instead of being barren areas of mosses and lichens, they are really great prairies, with rich grass and many flowers. Near the mouth of the Mackenzie River, the Canadian Government a few years ago took steps toward changing the Eskimos from hunters into herders. Because of the inroads of civilization, with its firearms, much of the game had disappeared from that area. A large herd of reindeer was therefore driven over from Alaska for the Eskimos to tend, and for the purpose of building up the region's wealth and ability to support people.

Throughout Canada it is felt that only the lack of proper means of transportation is holding back the development of the north country. It is believed that the solving of this problem will bring a real rush of pioneering farmers, herders, miners, hotel-keepers and others to carry civilization into this land. Transportation has already begun slowly to move northward. Some years ago the Government built the Hudson Bay Railway from Winnipeg to the bay on which Henry Hudson lost his life. At its northern end, at Fort Churchill, there is now a trading post and an army camp. There Canadian and United States troops develop new items of clothing and equipment for northern military operations, and tackle some of the many problems that arise out of the climatic and weather conditions. What they learn about the far north will be useful for civilian life there, and so will help to advance Arctic pioneering.

In the west, the Alaska Highway, built as a military project, will be a tremendous aid

in the settlement of the country. The United States Government has already opened for settlement Alaskan lands along that road, and it should not be long before the road brings new settlers into the Canadian areas through which it passes.

Meanwhile, thorough studies are being made of the problem of navigation along Canada's north coast. Partly for that purpose, the United States Weather Bureau, working jointly with the Canadians, has established weather stations on the Canadian Arctic islands. The farthest north of these stations is on Ellesmere Island, within a few hundred miles of the North Pole. Just as these stations will help to solve the problem of Arctic navigation and flight, so they will also help to open Canada's north for peaceful penetration by industries and settlers.

Down in the middle of South America we see something similar going on in the tropics. Just as many a Canadian is today pointing to the north and saying "There lies the future Canada," so many a Brazilian and Peruvian points to the fabled Amazon basin and says, "There lies the future South America."

Six Nations Divide among Them the Vast Amazon Basin

Six South American nations own the Amazon basin among them. These are Brazil, Peru, Bolivia, Ecuador, Colombia and Venezuela. Like all other countries in Latin America, they are being rapidly developed and are also taking stock of all their resources, including their frontiers. They are discovering two of the same things about the Amazon basin that we have recently discovered about our northland: that it is far richer and more hospitable than had been imagined.

The basin of that one great river is almost as large as the entire United States. It reaches from the Andean crests in the west, where the climate is almost arctic, down to the foothills, and then for 2,000 miles eastward to the Atlantic coast. Along that lower stretch the climate is truly equatorial, but, as we have said before, not nearly so bad for human beings as had been thought.

On the eastern slopes of the Andes is found almost every imaginable kind of resource, including limitless water power and large valleys that are well suited for agriculture. Those regions are rich in mineral wealth, oil, timber and occasional grasslands. The nations that own them are making large

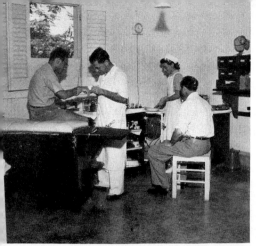

In Sosua, Dominican Republic, four hundred refugees have found a new life in a rich and fertile country. The Sosua health clinic, the dazzling white beach and a luxuriant cornfield.

plans for their development.

Active steps toward that development are already under way. Peru has completed its world-famous Tingo María Highway, which runs from the west coast over the Andes, down to navigable waters of the Ucayali River in the Amazon system. The town of Tingo María, built where once only a few thatched Indian huts existed, is a progressive modern settlement, with a bank, a motion-picture theater and a first-class tourist hotel. The people who live in the town farm the surrounding land. Soil technicians and explorers use Tingo María as a base in their studies of the possibilities of the country.

All the other Andean nations are following the example of Peru. They are building roads down to the Amazonian country, with the expectation of settling people there, opening mines and factories and raising food crops.

Farther down, along the Amazon's lower 2,000 miles, conditions are different. In that region's almost limitless rain forests there are still many wild Indians who have no contact with white men. But there are also great resources in rubber, timber, palm oils, fibers, waxes and the like. These are beginning to interest the various governments as future sources of national wealth and as raw materials for new national enterprise.

In these lowlands conventional methods of farming are not practical. Because the torrential rains very soon wash all the nourishment out of the soil, you can not cut down the forests and put the land to crops in the usual way. However, the region's many hundreds of rivers rise in flood every year, and

then fall again, leaving rich deposits of loamy soil on their banks. For thousands of years Egypt's agriculture has benefited by the same kind of action on the part of the Nile. South Americans point out that they have in the Amazon a total of thousands of square miles of flood plain that is enriched in the same way as the Nile Valley. If the Egyptians can cultivate such land successfully, so can the South Americans.

Although it is often called the Hylean Amazon (from the Greek word *hyle,* meaning woods), the lower Amazon basin is not one vast jungle, as many people think. Scattered here and there among its forests are something like 50,000 square miles of open prairie, well suited to cattle-raising.

With such things in mind, the Brazilian Government, which owns most of the lower Amazon basin, is taking active steps toward colonization and development, especially along the Tocantins River, which flows down

137

from the Mato Grosso region to the Amazon. Explorers and scientists are at work examining the resources. Development goes forward and new towns are already beginning to spring up. Investors in both North and South America are becoming interested, and concessions are being granted for lumbering, mining, transportation and colonization.

With the exception of the Antarctic continent, no region of its size is so empty of human beings as the Amazon basin's three million square miles. As man discovers its real wealth, and as he learns to adapt himself to its climate, this region is becoming more and more important in a world where population is increasing and food supplies are growing short. For this reason UNESCO (United Nations Educational, Scientific and Cultural Organization) has recently begun to interest itself in the problem of Amazonian development. In 1947 UNESCO organized the Hylean Amazon Institute, which is now at work in the Amazon basin.

Gathering Knowledge about a Little-Known World

The institute is not directly concerned with colonization; its main purpose is scientific research. It will gather together and make available all of the information that already exists about the Amazon country. To this will be added the results of a vast program of study which is now under way. It includes the study of the physiography of the region, the nature of the soil and its agricultural possibilities, the plant and animal life —especially the insects—and the minerals. The scientists of the institute will also study the Indians who live there, their languages, customs, ways of living, diseases and so on.

Never before has so vast and far-reaching a program of exploration and study been undertaken, and it will be thrilling to watch the results. All of the information that the institute gathers will be of great help to the nations who are planning to colonize the region. It will also be useful to the peoples of other tropical regions.

Other parts of tropical Latin America are having their own pioneering movements, but on a smaller scale. In the Dominican Republic, for example, there is the Sosua Project, where some 500 displaced persons from Europe have been settled in a planned venture that is based on agriculture. This is, of course, a small project, and the Dominican

Republic is too small a country to absorb many settlers. Nevertheless the experiment has proved valuable, for it shows that Europeans can get along well in the tropics if they work hard, eat well and observe a few important rules of health.

Similar small ventures have gotten under way recently in Mexico and other Latin American countries. However, most of these are in countries which are already well filled with people. It is, therefore, to the more or less empty lands that we must look for the real pioneering movements of the future.

Pioneering in the Far Southland That Stretches to the Horn

One more such area is the land which stretches south through Patagonia to Cape Horn, at the tip of South America. While this land tapers down to a point and is therefore much smaller than our own broad Arctic and sub-Arctic, its pioneering development is going on much more rapidly than are those in our north. Both Chile and Argentina, who share this region, are discovering riches there, building roads, establishing air lines and settling it with people. Within the last twenty years or so Tierra del Fuego has seen a great increase in its sheep-ranching. Moreover, little more than a year ago, oil was discovered there, and thousands of men flocked into the region to take part in a major oil boom. Tourist resorts, hotels, summer hunting lodges and winter ski fields are springing up near the Straits of Magellan, in a country that has been considered for centuries one of the world's most inhospitable lands. The Chilean city of Puntas Arenas, on the strait, is the most southerly city in the world, and a modern and comfortable one.

Just north of the Straits of Magellan, in the beautiful fiord region near the town of Puerto Aisen, the Chilean Government is carrying out a systematic colonization program. Chilean farmers by the thousands are taking up land, organizing co-operatives and making new homes for themselves, while taming what was only yesterday an uninhabited wilderness.

Whether we look to the gleaming lands of the north, to the windswept fiords of the far south, or the forests and savannas of the equatorial regions, we may see a vision of the future. The twentieth century may well go down in history as one of the great pioneering ages in the Western Hemisphere.

DEEP SOUTH

By Arthur F. and Martha J. Raper, *writers on agricultural economics*

THE modern commercial city of Memphis, Tennessee, stands on the Chickasaw Bluffs, high above the Mississippi River. Its skyscraper office buildings look down on the spot where, four centuries ago, Hernando de Soto first came upon the giant inland river. Across from Memphis and linked to it by long railroad and highway bridges, are the low, rich farm lands of Arkansas. Below Memphis, in Mississippi, the Yazoo Delta begins, a leaf-shaped plain of great fertility that reaches down through the state to Vicksburg.

Where the great river flows, from Memphis to New Orleans, is the heart of the region known as the Deep South. Besides Louisiana, Mississippi and Alabama, this region includes the southeastern part of Arkansas

Cotton grows luxuriantly in the rich soil of the Yazoo Delta in Mississippi. Pickers leaving the

and the southwestern corner of Tennessee. In the northern part, the uplands rise gently to the Appalachian Mountains in Alabama and to the Ozark-Ouachita Mountains in Arkansas. The basin of the Mississippi and its southern tributaries, and the land along the Gulf of Mexico, are low-lying—in many places less than 200 feet above sea level.

The Deep South is chiefly an agricultural country. The rich soil, the long, hot summers and the abundant rainfall have made it ideal for growing cotton. Many other crops are raised there—corn, fruit and vegetables, pecans and peanuts, tung trees for the oil that is used in paints and varnishes, sugar-cane and rice—but cotton is the major crop. The cycle of planting, cultivating, harvesting and marketing cotton has done much to shape the pattern of life in the Deep South. Business and industry, education and politics have all been influenced by it.

The Deep South is a land of rivers, and the trade and industry of the region are centered in a number of old water-front cities. Along the Mississippi, between Memphis and New Orleans, the most important commercial cities are Baton Rouge in Louisiana and Vicksburg in Mississippi. On the Arkansas River, a western tributary of the Mississippi, are Little Rock and Pine Bluff, Arkansas. Farther south, in western Louisiana, there is Shreveport on the Red River, which also flows into the Father of Waters. Up the Alabama River, which flows into the Gulf, are Montgomery and Selma. The chief seaports are New Orleans, Baton Rouge and Lake Charles in Louisiana, and Mobile in Alabama.

For generations these river cities have served the planters and farmers in the territories surrounding them. Each is also a manufacturing or distributing center for one or more industries. Hardwood flooring and furniture are specialties of Memphis and of Little Rock, the capital of Arkansas. Montgomery, the capital of Alabama and once the capital of the Confederate States of America, has many manufactures, among them brick and tile, chemicals and food products. Cottonseed oil and meal, glass-making and petroleum refining are big industries in Shreveport. Baton Rouge, the capital of Louisiana, has one of the largest petroleum refineries in the world.

Mobile and New Orleans are famous for shipbuilding and as ports for shipping pine and cypress lumber. These two cities and Memphis export the largest amount of cot-

Vicksburg, where the United States Government has its Waterways Experiment Station, still remembers its days as the Gibraltar of the Confederacy, and the long siege that finally opened the Mississippi River to the fleets of the Union forces. At Natchez the present-day visitor can still see magnificent gardens and columned porticoes of a hundred years ago, when cotton flourished and the steamboat traffic brought great wealth to the city, Natchez has been under five flags: French, Spanish, British, United States and Confederate, and each nation has left traces of its occupation in customs, architecture and names.

Biloxi, the first permanent white settlement in the Mississippi Valley, is today devoted to play and to fishing. It is both a summer and a winter resort, and its shrimp and oyster fleets add to its picturesqueness as

Giant generators furnish power for the industries of northern Alabama and Mississippi.

TENNESSEE CONSERVATION DEPARTMENT

FSA PHOTO BY POST

field with their sacks filled with snowy bolls.

ton. Since New Orleans and Memphis are the northern and southern gateways to the Deep South, both are great railroad centers. Indeed, all southern transcontinental freight and passenger traffic must flow through them.

Up in the red hill country of northern Alabama, where coal and iron are found, are the foundries and steel mills of Birmingham, the Pittsburgh of the South. In recent years the hydroelectric development of the Tennessee Valley has brought many textile mills and other industries to the smaller cities of northern Mississippi and Alabama. Far down in the lowlands of southern Louisiana the salt and sulfur mines are growing in importance.

In a region so large and so varied in soil and climate there are bound to be differences in the character of the towns and cities. It is in the ancient river towns, dreaming in the sun of the glories of their youth, that we find the air of romance the writers of fiction and songs have led us to expect. No matter how much business activity goes on, or how progressive the local trade organizations are, the business and progress are managed with a grace and leisure that makes you forget how much hard work is really being done. Always, too, there is a sense of the past.

well as to the prosperity of its citizens.

Demopolis, on the Tombigbee River in Alabama, was founded by a group of Napoleonic exiles in 1817. These people, whose lives had been passed in salons and military quarters, set out to cultivate grapes and olives in the Tombigbee wilderness. They worked hard and cheerfully, but the climate and soil were not suited to vines and olives. Most of the colonists moved to New Orleans and other French settlements. Today their enterprise is remembered only in the names of a few families and places, and in the name that they gave the town, Demopolis, city of the people.

Mobile, garlanded with azaleas, flowers that were first brought there in 1745 from the gardens of King Louis XV of France; Tuscaloosa, a university town, whose century-old water oaks line the streets above the Black Warrior River; New Orleans, the most colorful and enchanting city in the United States and third ranking seaport; all are cities where the past still lingers to give grace and charm to the present.

Many books and articles have been written about New Orleans. It is the largest city in the South. It lies a hundred miles from the mouth of the Mississippi, on what is practically an island between a great bend of the river and Lake Pontchartrain. Most of the city is several feet below the level of the river, and giant pumps throw millions of gallons of water back up into the river every hour. Graves are built above the surface of the ground. The tall buildings stand on piles driven deep into the soft river soil.

In the old part of the city, houses and buildings remain from the days when it was ruled by France and later by Spain. Many of them are built around inner courtyards, and balconies with lace-like ironwork reach out over the streets. The Creoles (white people of French or Spanish descent) still carry on their traditional social and cultural life, though nowadays they mingle more freely with the newer American stock. Cookery, architecture, the theater and the winter carnival season have made New Orleans famous all over the world.

Carpenter Dam on the Ouachita River in Arkansas. Its pine-fringed lake is stocked with fish.

The people of the Deep South have many problems, but they are neither gloomy nor bitter, and more worrying is done about them than by them. The people, rich and poor, enjoy life and enjoy one another. They are sociable and friendly and have a keen interest in what is going on around them. Strangers chat on streetcars; storekeepers and clerks visit with their customers. Conversation revolves around the news of friends, relatives and acquaintances.

Party-giving, Party-going, and Visiting Back and Forth

They are also a hospitable people. They love giving parties and going to them. Almost everyone has friends and relatives scattered throughout several states and there is a great deal of visiting back and forth—each visitor furnishing an excuse for a round of morning, afternoon and evening parties.

Among the country people the "all-day sing," or "singing convention" is a popular pastime during the slack work seasons. Whole families attend these gatherings, coming from miles around the countryside and bringing picnic baskets with them. A leader announces a song, and all who have learned the "tone lengths" and "tone shapes" join in. Then another person becomes the leader, for each must have his turn. He may select some old song that dates back hundreds of years, or a new one for which he himself has just written the words and music.

At noon the women spread basket dinners on a large table under the trees, and the singers come outside to enjoy ham, fried chicken, potato salad, pies and cake. Smiling mothers in big white aprons preside over tubs full of lemonade, and, in season, there are watermelons and more watermelons. After lunch the singers, refreshed and restored, go back to their singing again.

Barbecues are a favorite institution in most parts of the South, but especially in Mississippi. Often they are purely social occasions, but sometimes they are held as part of a political meeting. Someone has said that cotton and politics are the subjects of greatest interest to Southern whites of all classes. Even cotton, however, can not compete with the fascination of politics.

A political meeting and barbecue may be announced for a community of perhaps only a hundred people, but a thousand people may have gathered before the first speech

TUSCALOOSA CHAMBER OF COMMERCE, PHOTO BY PAUL DAMOND

A leafy, sun-dappled street in old Tuscaloosa.

begins. A man will travel miles to hear a candidate he has no intention of voting for. Speeches are cheered for the strength of their invective. The speaker who can reel off the longest, strongest string of words unfavorable to his opponent has the delighted appreciation, if not the support, of his audience.

After the morning speeches are over, everyone lines up to be helped to barbecue, Brunswick stew and other good things to eat. The whole night before, men have sat beside trenches dug in the earth, burning wood to make a deep bed of coals. Over these glowing embers they slowly roast the halves of dressed hogs, turning and basting them often. On the morning of the great day, wives may watch the final roasting and even offer advice, but the cooking of barbecue is a man's job. Indeed, almost every district has one or more men who make a business of arranging barbecues, and the really good ones are in great demand.

Finally the meat is cut up and laid on platters. Then the barbecuers test the Brunswick stew simmering in huge cast-iron pots. This

143

is a wonderful thick soup, usually made from chicken, okra, fresh corn and tomatoes and, in fact, practically every vegetable that is in season. Barbecues are usually held in a shady grove, with wooden trestle tables to which people take their plates.

The group activities of the Negroes center in their churches, fraternal lodges and benevolent societies. In the back-country districts, church services, usually held monthly, are combinations of singing conventions and revivals. The ministers are often local farmers who illustrate their sermons from daily happenings. Out of these meetings still come folk songs akin to those of slave days.

Saturday afternoon is a holiday for all. No matter how badly the cotton may need chopping or picking, the farmers leave their fields at noon on Saturday for their weekly gathering at the county seat.

It is a gay time, with much talk and friendly visiting on the streets and in the

stores where the country people buy next week's supplies. The farm people also crowd into the county seat during court week, and in the fall when the county fair is held.

The bayou region in southern Louisiana is quite different from other parts of the Deep South. Here the land is low. There are many rivers and swamps. The bayous are winding, sluggish creeks that carry the overflow of swamp and river and form a back-country drainage system to the Gulf for the rains.

The people who live in the bayou country, south and west of New Orleans, are of French ancestry—Creoles and Cajuns. The name Cajun is a local word that was originally applied to the Acadians who went to Louisiana from Canada in the eighteenth century. Nowadays the word takes in many people who have no Acadian ancestry at all, but most of them are at least partly French.

The Cajuns enjoy life together. They usually marry and remain within their own com-

Pirogues slip silently through the dim cypress swamps and bayous of southern Louisiana. The great trees, with their swollen roots, are often shrouded with ghostly fronds of Spanish moss.

PHOTOS BELOW, AND UPPER RIGHT PAGE 145, BY WEBB, FLAHERTY PRODUCTION SHOTS

munity. Much of the bayou country is too wet for farming, and wherever the land drains well it is thickly settled. Many Cajun homes are built on the slightly raised strips along the bayous and the oxbow lakes formed where a river has changed its course. The houses are close together in a long line and have to be reached in small boats.

Near the Gulf many bayou people make their living from fishing and fur-trapping. It is a charming sight to see a fishing village turn out to watch the priest bless their shrimp boats before the men start out into the Gulf. Hundreds of small boats come for the ceremony, each one gaily decorated with flags. The priest wears his most gorgeous vestments, and lovely water hyacinths float by as he sprinkles the holy water.

The French part of Louisiana extends southeastward from New Orleans and westward almost to the borders of Texas. It is a mysterious and fascinating land, with wind-ing roads beside winding bayous; white plan-tation houses glimmering through the aisles of live oaks draped with Spanish moss; aza-leas splashing vivid color against the dark cypress trees, and the creamy cups of mag-nolias filling the air with perfume. Down be-low New Orleans the Barataria country—a maze of marshes and islands—is the home of shrimpers, fishermen and trappers of musk-rat for the northern fur markets. Many of these people are descendants of the pirates and smugglers of whom Jean Lafitte is the most famous. They are a simple, kindly peo-ple today, and their colorful ancestors have bequeathed them little of their fierce, adven-turous dispositions.

This is the Deep South: from the scarred hills of Georgia to the green Passes of the Mississippi delta, it is a land of contrast and variety, of the very new and the ancient; the land and its people forever marked by the great river flowing through its heart.

Scenes of Louisiana life: upper left, blessing the shrimp fleet; upper right, hanging muskrat skins to dry; lower left, working with the oyster fleet; lower right, getting the barbecue pit ready.

ALL PHOTOS EXCEPT UPPER RIGHT, LOUISIANA DEPARTMENT OF COMMERCE AND INDUSTRY

DOLLS

The happy of a doll

By FRANCES PARKINSON KEYES

Author of DINNER AT ANTOINE'S *and many other books*

Violet and her cocker spaniel.

ALL my life I have been interested in dolls. The causes for this interest, and the ways in which it has revealed itself, have varied greatly. But, in a sense, I was as truly a collector at six as I am at sixty.

I had a family of dolls, and like all normal families, it grew. Whether small or large, it received my absorbed attention. I lavished upon it the same sort of care which I myself received. My dolls—and their clothing—were regularly washed, and their hair was faithfully brushed and combed. They were dressed in the morning, put down for naps in the middle of the day and undressed at night. They had their own beds and bureaus and desks and toilet articles.

Since I traveled a great deal with my mother—which meant that the dolls traveled too!—they had a miniature Saratoga trunk, a miniature shawl strap and all the other accessories considered as essentials for voyaging in those days. And as ladies carried their

146

jewels and travel funds secreted in little bags on their persons at this period, one of the dolls even had such a money bag, with a red C for her name, Carol, embroidered on it!

Their wardrobes were replenished in New York and Paris; tiny gloves, gauzy fans, smart bonnets and lace-trimmed parasols were bought for them in the course of these magic expeditions. A few dresses were also purchased at such times—best dresses for my mother, best dresses for me, best dresses for the dolls. But most of the everyday dresses, mine and the dolls' both, were made at home; and by the time I was twelve years old, I took great pride in copying my own clothes for my dolls, using pieces of left-over material—pink satin, creamy striped gauze, gay taffetas, serviceable ginghams, warm plaids and broadcloths.

I still have most of these doll dresses, packed away in their Saratoga trunk, together with the gloves and the fans, the bonnets and the parasols. And I have the dolls

experiences
collector

This is Carol.

themselves. Somehow they have survived both time and tide, in spite of my many wanderings. When I married, I took my dolls and their belongings to my new home, with the hopeful expectation that soon I might be making dresses for my daughters' dolls. (It was not very long since I had stopped making them for my own, since, as I have just confessed, I was still doing so at the age of twelve and I was married at eighteen.) But instead of daughters I had sons, and for a long time, Carol and Violet and Phyllis and all the other dolls remained in seclusion under the eaves of a capacious New England attic. Then, without deliberate intention or effort on my part, dolls again began to play an important role in my design for living.

It was this way: Early in the course of a writing assignment which was to take me around the world, I stopped in Panama. Like most visitors there, I was enchanted with the quaint native costume called the *pollera*, which is still worn at carnival time and on

other festive occasions. When I left, Doña Beatriz, one of the hospitable ladies at whose home I had been entertained, and who had heard my exclamations of admiration, presented me with a doll she had dressed for me herself—in the *pollera*. Everything was perfect—the full, drop-shouldered dress of white muslin, figured in scarlet; the heelless green slippers which matched the ribbons securing the bodice and the skirt; the long, flexible gold chain—the *cadena carta*—with the cross at the end; the multitudinous twin ornaments placed on either side of the parted hair.

"I hope this little gift will keep your memories of us and our festivals fresh and pleasant," Doña Beatriz told me with a gracious smile as she handed me the doll, which, of course, was forthwith named after her.

Her hope was more than fulfilled. The doll served as a constant reminder of the hospitality which had been shown me in Panama and of the lovely things I had seen there. It

A family doll. Below, the Dixie Doll's bridal procession, courtyard, Beauregard House.

also supplied the incentive to collect dolls from other countries, to serve the same purpose. Some of these dolls I bought, watching carefully for the types which were really representative of the places from which they came. Others were given me by persons who learned of my interest in costume dolls and the special reasons for it.

The trip around the world, which lasted a year and a half, was followed by numerous others, all undertaken primarily as writing assignments. I spent a year in South America, an autumn in the Near East; I went repeatedly to Europe. All the time my family of dolls kept growing, as it had when I was a little girl.

The most beautiful doll, in my opinion, which belongs to this phase of my collecting, is one dressed in the costume of a *tapada* of Lima. This is the name given the highborn ladies of the Viceregal Period in Peru, who covered half their faces with their black *rebozos* (shawls) in a most provocative manner when they went about the streets, and thus earned for themselves the name of *las tapadas*—the covered ones. It is said that the partial concealment served as an excuse

for a great deal of unauthorized and clandestine flirting. At all events, this particular form of attire was finally forbidden, on just such grounds, by viceregal decree. The era had been one of great elegance; and my doll, Doña Margarita, dressed on purpose for me in old-rose brocade, has real lace on her underwear and real jewels on her arms. As is her due, she occupies a place of great honor in my collection.

Two Beautiful Old Cabinets for My Cherished Dolls

Naturally, the time came when the question arose of a suitable setting for my dolls. After several experiments, I placed the collection in an old cabinet of beautiful plain pine, which came from Marmion, in King George County, Virginia. (Marmion has long been one of my favorite haunts and supplied the background for my novel, HONOR BRIGHT.) Later, as the collection grew, I secured a second cabinet, similar to the first, and also from Marmion. These now stand, face to face, in the big study of my house at Crowley, Louisiana. Of course the dolls which had been so long secluded under the eaves were taken from their retreat as soon as I began collecting again in earnest. To my delight, I found not only those I remembered so well, like Carol and Violet and Phyllis, but others which I had forgotten: costume dolls from Switzerland and Holland and Italy which I had added to my early family during the course of my first trip to Europe.

To my further delight, several fine old American dolls were given me by relatives and friends who said that they had no special use for these themselves, and that they would rather see them in a collection, where they would be cherished and preserved, than left to the casual care of descendants who had no special interest in dolls. So Carol and Violet and Phyllis acquired some watchful maiden aunts. Doña Beatriz and Doña Margarita and the others from distant lands found that several predecessors from lands no less distant were already at hand to help in making them fit into the general picture. And then, once more without deliberate effort on my part, my collecting took a different turn.

I heard a story—a true story—about a doll that a Southern girl had given to a Northern soldier during the War between the States; and this story seemed to me so

Above: the Little St. Theresa dressed very much like this at her First Holy Communion. Background, Church of St. Jacques at Lisieux. Below: a lady from Lima, Peru.

Lovely lady of olden days—an exquisite French wax doll dressed in a riding habit of the Empire period. The ladies who once lived in the Château de Malou (background) must have looked very much like her when they went for a canter through the near-by woods and countryside.

charming and so touching that I asked permission to present it to the public in fiction form. This permission was graciously granted, and my own little story, beautifully illustrated, was published in THE HOME MAGAZINE as THE DIXIE DOLL.

Its appearance resulted in an enormous amount of fan mail. Among the letters which came from total strangers was one written by Miss Helen Walter, the presiding genius of the Just-Folks Doll House in Staunton, Virginia. Miss Walter, one of the foremost authorities on dolls in the United States, is not only a collector but a creator; and she made two requests, both of which I was delighted to grant. She asked if she might come to see my collection, and she asked if she might dress a doll for me in the bridal costume of the sixties, which would be *her* interpretation of *my* creation!

The Dixie Doll arrived in due course, and a place of honor was found for her, too; but her surroundings seemed to lack something needed to make them complete. I gave the matter thought, and first decided that, like most brides, mine should have attendants and at least one member of her family with her. I consulted Miss Walter, and soon the Dixie Doll was companioned by three other dolls. One was elegantly but soberly dressed to represent her mother, and a doll of the same size as these was gaily dressed to represent her maid of honor. A much smaller doll —a beautiful little blonde bisque which, incidentally, represents a much rarer type than the black-headed china dolls of the same period—was daintily dressed to represent a flower girl. An entire shelf in one of the old cabinets was set aside for the procession formed by these additions, and the Dixie Doll immediately lost her lonely look!

In the course of my trip around the world, I had bought a doll dressed like a Japanese bride. Her black kimono, faced in scarlet and embroidered in cherry blossoms, and the bands of scarlet silk encircling her elaborate coiffure provided a striking contrast to the bodice and hoop skirt of cream-colored brocade, the lace veil and orange blossoms of the Dixie Doll. But Suki, the Japanese, did not fit into our traditional procession. She too looked lonely and slightly incongruous on a shelf all by herself. So, one by one, other foreign bridal dolls were found to place beside her: a Syrian, gorgeously gowned but veiled in black, her dowry in a diadem formed of small gold coins; a bride from the Spreewald, near Berlin, wearing an enormous white ruff around her neck to supplement her enormous headdress; a Breton bride, with long streamers on her cap and a peach-colored silk apron; a Hopi "Butterfly Bride," made entirely of wood, but adorned with feathers and painted in bright colors; a demure Danish bride, a candle-slim Chinese bride, a second Indian bride—this one clad from top to toe in doeskin—all these now form their own procession and there is nothing incongruous about it. They harmonize wonderfully well with each other.

As I have said, the Dixie Doll was the happy result of a story I had written—the generous contribution made by one kind of a creator to another.* But as time went on, I found that sometimes the dolls came first

Above: Mexican dolls, the left in peasant dress, the right wearing the "China Poblana." Left: costume of the plateau near Cuzco, Peru.

and the stories afterwards! This was especially true when my writing assignments abroad changed to the field of hagiography —that is, the writing and critical study of the lives of saints.

The first of these assignments took me to Lisieux. This picturesque little Norman city is chiefly famous as the home of Thérèse Martin, now called the Little St. Theresa, to distinguish her from the Great St. Theresa of Avila, and more familiarly designated as the Little Flower. I had never done any writing of this kind before, and I felt very hesitant about attempting it. Only a strong conviction that a real need existed for a simple, straightforward story of Thérèse Martin, told with the help of her former teachers and classmates and of her surviving relatives, impelled me to do so. I needed all the assistance of every kind that I could get. I went to

*The story of my Dixie bride has often been erroneously told. I am extremely grateful to Eleanor St. George for giving a correct version of it in her excellent work entitled THE DOLLS OF YESTERDAY, published by Charles Scribner's Sons.

151

Creole elegance in the eighteenth century! This doll, in handsome, striped-silk skirt and muslin bodice, is opening a Norman chest, or ditty box, at the foot of a Creole half-canopy bed.

live in the ancient abbey of the Benedictines, where Thérèse had received her early education, and I talked with everyone I could find who had known her. I even acquired dolls which would make the very clothes she had worn and those which she was accustomed to see about her appear more familiar to me.

A Little French Girl Dressed for Her First Communion

One of the most significant occasions in Thérèse Martin's life was her First Holy Communion. She wrote about it herself, most movingly, in her autobiography, and all her best biographers have been quick to sense the profound effect which it had upon her. The communion rail in the chapel of the Benedictines was marked with a plaque commemorating the fact that this was the place where the important event had taken place. Pilgrims and tourists alike were ushered in to see it. Last but not least, the dress and the veil she had worn were carefully preserved in the museum at Carmel. In all Latin countries—at least in all those of which I am qualified to speak—a little girl, in spite of her tender age, wears a full-length dress for her First Holy Communion, and a veil that is almost as long. Often these dresses and veils are comparable to those of a bride in delicacy and costliness. The general celebration differs from ours too; the religious services are closely allied with gala breakfasts and luncheons, and the gifts bestowed on the young communicant are by no means confined to religious objects. These observances do not lack reverence in the Latin mind, nor should they do so to us. Actually, they reveal a close affiliation between earthly joys and spiritual joys which is wholesome and beautiful. But, as an Anglo-Saxon, I was slightly startled shortly after my arrival in Lisieux, when I saw the windows of the leading confectioner. They were filled with dolls dressed like First Communicants and, upon investigation, I discovered that the long, full skirts of these dolls concealed tubular candy boxes which served at the same time as standards! The mild shock I had sustained did not prevent me from buying one of the dolls and placing her on the desk in my workroom, which had been the pupils' refectory when Thérèse Martin was a student at the abbey. It was not long before I persuaded the nuns that a fitting companion for her would be a doll dressed like those little girls who had

once eaten their meals in that very place. She should have a plain, dark serge uniform, saved from severity by the fetching white bonnet that went with it, and the brightly colored bretelles and belt worn over it— green for one class, orange for another, violet for another and so on. (My doll belongs to the violet class.) The next step was to get dolls dressed like the Benedictines themselves: a Benedictine novice, with a serviceable blue gingham apron to protect her habit, and a warm capuchin of white wool to shield her from the heavy rains and strong winds of Normandy while she went about her appointed tasks; also a Benedictine Mother, wearing the ceremonial choir-cowl and carrying in her hand the little lantern used to light the way about the premises after dark. And finally I achieved a doll dressed like a Carmelite—a doll so sweet of face and dignified of bearing as to suggest Thérèse Martin herself.

After my return from Lisieux my collec-

Sweethearts in their Sunday best—a fine pair of bisque Canadian peasant dolls. The background is Caen Cathedral, in Normandy.

tion began to grow along two different lines. The first dolls dressed as nuns suggested the acquisition of others, representing different Orders, and I am indebted to many kind Sisters who themselves have outfitted dolls correctly garbed to the last details of their habits. (Among the Orders thus represented in my collection are the Visitation, Dominican, St. Vincent de Paul, St. Joseph and the Good Shepherd.) And the success of WRITTEN IN HEAVEN, The Life on Earth of the Little Flower, resulted in writing assignments which took me back, over and over again, to Normandy and other parts of France, to Mexico and to South America. So I have an exquisite French wax doll in an Empire riding habit, which I associate with the Château de Malou, the scene of CAME A CAVALIER. At one time the lovely ladies who lived there must have looked and dressed very much like her. I have peasant dolls which seem to fit naturally against the background of the Auberge du Vieux Puits, at Pont Audemer, where Flaubert wrote much of MADAME BOVARY and where I have pursued my own calling in a far less distinguished way. I have a *Peruviana* from the highlands near Cuzco and the gay *China Poblana* as well as the humbler *India* of Mexico.

The story of the *China Poblana* costume has been told very often, but it still bears retelling. Many, many years ago, an immensely rich merchant, a citizen of Puebla, brought home with him a Chinese bride when he returned from a voyage to the Orient. It was natural that she should become locally known as *La China*, because of her origin. Soon her loveliness, her graciousness, and above all her charitableness made her known in other ways. Instead of vying with the ladies of her acquaintance in wearing the latest fashions, she chose one colorful but serviceable costume and, regardless of passing modes, wore it year in and year out. The adaptation of it, which is sometimes made of costly material, elaborately embroidered, still follows the style chosen by the original *China Poblana* for her own use and is a tribute to her memory.

Louisiana, Treasure-Trove for the Collector

Apart from the assignments which take me abroad, much of my present writing keeps me in Louisiana, another region which is a treasure trove for the collector, as it is for the chronicler of either religion or romance or both. I now have a doll dressed like Evangeline, from her own Acadian country; a doll dressed in the regal costume of a carnival queen; a doll in the somber perennial mourning of a conservative Creole widow; a doll carrying her tiny trunk on her back, like the "casquette" girls who came overseas as wives for the first settlers, and hooded and cloaked as these girls were. But my favorite in this group is a doll wearing the full striped-silk skirt and sheer muslin bodice characterizing the early days of Creole elegance. And I have found her a bed which I think is worthy of her—a bed with the half-canopy which is also so typical of Louisiana. At the foot of the bed is placed one of those chests, ornamented with birds and apples, which the Norman sailors formerly used as their ditty boxes—and in which the little girls at the Abbaye des Benedictines kept their chalk and their pencils and their small personal treasures. So again there is harmony between the things that came from far away and the things that are part of our own tradition.

A Doll Collection Need Not Be Expensive

From the very beginning it has been a happy experience for me, this casual collecting of dolls. All my life, it has been associated with my home, my travels, my amusements and my work. I have not brought great knowledge to it, for I am not an authority on dolls, and I have not spent large sums on it. Only a few of my dolls have much intrinsic value, and most of those have been given to me—among them the superb pair of bisque Canadian peasant dolls which are my latest acquisition and one of my finest. But from my dolls I have *achieved* learning which might not have come to me in any other way, and the money I have spent on them has proved a wise investment in many respects: in keeping fond memories fresh, as Doña Beatriz hoped they might; in familiarizing me with costumes and customs of many lands; in helping me to correlate objects and ideals which seemed, at first glance, alien to each other.

I do not see why a similar form of collecting should not be an equally happy and rewarding experience for almost any girl. If I have succeeded in proving this, I have found another reason why my own collecting has been so worth while!

The Year in EUROPE

By LAWRENCE M. LEVIN

Premier de Gasperi speaks in Milan five days before the Italian elections of April 18–19.

THE year 1948 saw most of the countries of Europe divided into two hostile camps. One of these sought to spread communism by all the means at its disposal; the other opposed communism just as vigorously. The result was a "cold war," in which political propaganda, economic pressure, strikes and sabotage replaced the bullets and shells and aerial bombs of a shooting war.

At the beginning of the year the supporters of communism included Soviet Russia and the countries which had adopted communist or pro-communist governments—Poland, Yugoslavia, Rumania, Hungary, Bulgaria and Albania. In these lands the governments in power tried to prevent the people from coming in contact with any ideas except those favored by their rulers. It was as if an iron curtain had dropped between this pro-communist bloc (group) of nations and the rest of the world. Hence, it was often said of these countries that they were behind the iron curtain.

The anti-communist group was made up of most of the countries of Western Europe; it was often called the West, or the Western bloc. This group included Belgium, Denmark, Eire (Ireland), France, Great Britain, Greece, Iceland, Italy, Luxemburg, the Netherlands, Norway, Portugal, Sweden, Switzerland and Turkey.

Several countries were outside of the two camps. Two small neighbors of Soviet Russia—Czechoslovakia and Finland—tried desperately to remain neutral. Little Czechoslovakia had been swallowed up by nazi Germany a short time before the outbreak of World War II and had been freed by the Allies. Finland had been an Axis partner in the war and had paid the penalty. It had given up considerable territory to Russia and had agreed to pay that country a war indemnity

155

of $300,000,000. Both Czechoslovakia and Finland had suffered terribly in the war; both asked only to remain at peace with all nations.

The Nations of the West Refuse to Accept Spain as a Partner

Spain was certainly not in the Soviet camp, since it was a fascist state and as anti-communist as could be. But the nations of the West did not accept Spain as a partner. It was not easy to forget that General Francisco Franco, the *caudillo,* or chief, of Spain, had been openly friendly toward the Axis countries in World War II until it had become clear that they were losing the war.

Two former Axis countries—Germany and Austria—were jointly occupied by Russia, the United States, Great Britain and France; they were really divided up into Russian and Western areas. The two countries were not treated in the same way. Germany, as the most guilty member of the Axis, was under complete Allied military control and had no organized government of its own. Austria had been gobbled up by Germany in March 1938, and had been forced to fight at the side of the Nazis. After the war it had been separated from Germany; it had been permitted to set up its own government, with a president, premier and national legislature.

This, then, was the situation in Europe at the beginning of 1948. Both camps sought to strengthen the ties that bound their member nations. The communist bloc was united, for one thing, by its unquestioning acceptance of Russian leadership. Another bond was the Cominform (Communist Information Bureau), which had been set up in September 1947, with the aim of warring on "American imperialism." As time went on, it became clear that the Cominform was really an international agency, under Russian leadership, for the promotion of communism.

The nations of the West also felt the need of a bond that would knit them more closely together. In part, this was supplied by the European Recovery Program (ERP), first suggested by United States Secretary of State George C. Marshall in June 1947. The ERP proposed to help the nations of western Europe to get on their feet again by means of funds and materials supplied by the United States and other countries of the Western Hemisphere. The United States was to play the principal part in this program, which was

to be carried on for a period of four years.

Sixteen European nations were to receive help from the ERP. They included the fifteen countries that we have already mentioned as belonging to the Western bloc. Austria (that is, the part occupied by the Western powers) was also to be eligible for aid under the European Recovery Program. Each of the ERP countries was to receive help from available funds and materials according to its needs; it was to contribute to the plan according to its means.

In December 1947, the United States Congress appropriated $522,000,000 for emergency relief for France, Italy and Austria. It was not until April 1948, however, that Congress officially approved the European Recovery Program. Two months later, it authorized the spending of $5,055,000,000 for the ERP for a period of fifteen months, but with the understanding that, if the President approved, the sum could be spent in twelve months.

How European Recovery Program Funds Were Allotted

On April 16, the sixteen Western powers taking part in the European Recovery Program had set up an Organization for European Economic Cooperation (OEEC). A council of the OEEC, meeting in Paris in September, reached an agreement on the division of ERP funds for the year ending June 30, 1949. The money was to be allotted as follows:

Austria	$217,000,000
Belgium and Luxemburg	250,000,000
Denmark	110,000,000
Eire	79,000,000
France	989,000,000
Great Britain	1,263,000,000
Greece	146,000,000
Iceland	11,000,000
Italy	601,000,000
Netherlands	495,000,000
Norway	84,000,000
Sweden	47,000,000
Trieste (a free territory at the head of the Adriatic Sea)	18,000,000
Turkey	50,000,000
American and British zones of Germany	414,000,000
French zone of Germany	100,000,000

The ERP, then, served to link the countries of western Europe. There were other ties.

In 1947, Belgium, the Netherlands and Luxemburg had agreed to form a customs union. Because of their close co-operation, the three small nations had come to be known as the Benelux countries, or simply Benelux. (The name is formed by combining the first two letters of BElgium and NEtherlands and the first three lettters of LUXemburg.)

On March 17, 1948, this three-country alliance was broadened when the Benelux countries joined with Great Britain and France in signing a fifty-year treaty. The pact, drawn up in Brussels, Belgium, provided for mutual defense and other forms of co-operation. Some months later (September 28) the five nations set up a common Permanent Defense Organization.

The Brussels Pact brought to men's minds the idea of European union. In May, an important meeting was held at The Hague, in the Netherlands, to discuss this important matter. The 700 delegates to the conference formed what became known as an unofficial Congress of Europe; they included representatives of the Western bloc nations as well as exiles from eastern Europe. The Congress issued a report on May 10, calling upon the nations of the Continent to adopt political union, free trade and a common currency. Another Congress of Europe, meeting at Interlaken, Switzerland, on September 1–4, urged Great Britain, France and the Benelux countries to consider proposals for a European Assembly and a federal constitution for the nations of Europe.

The Pro-Communist Forces Take the Offensive

Thus the members of the two opposing camps of European countries sought to draw their lines closer for the cold war. In this struggle the advantage of the attack lay with the pro-communist forces. Because most of the Western powers believed in free speech and freedom of the press, they permitted Communists and their sympathizers to carry on their activities openly within their boundaries. These Communists of the Western bloc made no secret of their opposition to the European Recovery Program and their support of the policy followed by Soviet Russia. On the other hand, in the countries behind the iron curtain any opposition to the govern-

ment in power was called treason and it was severely punished.

Toward the end of February, the pro-communist nations scored a great victory in the cold war by adding another country—Czechoslovakia—to their alliance. On February 23, the Czech minister of the interior, Vaclev Nosek, a Communist, claimed that he had discovered a "reactionary plot" to seize the Government. With this plot as a pretext, communist "action committees" throughout the country began to remove anti-Communists from federal and local offices. There was great indignation among the country's moderate elements.

In order to avoid bloodshed, President Eduard Benes, a world-renowned liberal, agreed to accept a Cabinet made up of Communists and of those willing to work with them. From now on Czechoslovakia was definitely in the pro-communist bloc. All anti-Communists were kept out of the Government; they were often persecuted.

The national elections of May 30 resulted in a victory for the new Government, but it was a meaningless victory. In the first place, the Government had kept the vote from all those who had "sinned against the republic, the nation and the people's democratic state" —meaning all those who had actively op-

Czech President Eduard Benes and his Cabinet.

WIDE WORLD

posed communism. Again, following common practice in both fascist and communist countries, there had been only one slate of candidates, made up of government supporters. Citizens could either vote for these candidates or leave their ballots blank. Naturally the government candidates won.

Several days after the election (June 7), President Benes resigned, because he was unwilling to sign a new constitution drawn up by the Communists and their allies. He retired to his country home, where he died on September 3, 1948. He was succeeded as president by Premier Klement Gottwald, a Communist; another Communist, Antonin Zapotocky, became premier.

The Communists were not quite so successful in Finland. To be sure, at Russia's urgent invitation, Finland signed a ten-year pact of mutual defense and friendship with Soviet Russia on April 6, 1948, and promised to

French soldiers on strike duty at a coal mine.

have closer trade relations with that country. As a reward, Russia agreed to lop off about $75,000,000 from the war reparations that Finland had promised to pay.

But if Russia expected the Finns to show their gratitude by turning to communism, she was disappointed. In the parliamentary elections, held on July 1–2, 1948, the People's Democratic Union, a radical group made up of Communists and Socialists, was badly defeated. It had formerly been the leading group in the 200-seat Parliament; it now dropped to third place among the parties represented in that body.

In June 1948, the Cominform suffered a setback when a violent quarrel broke out between Yugoslavia and the other Cominform nations. The Yugoslav premier, Marshal Tito, whose real name is Josip Broz, had apparently been one of the most faithful allies of Soviet Russia. The world was amazed, therefore, when, on June 28, 1948, the Cominform denounced Tito's leadership of the Yugoslav Communist party. It accused Tito of carrying on a "hateful and slanderous policy" toward Russia and of showing sympathy with Western methods. The Cominform warned the Yugoslav Premier and other party leaders that they must follow the policies set by Soviet Russia or else get out of office.

Yugoslavia Is Isolated Because of Her Quarrel with the Cominform

But the Yugoslav leader defied the Cominform and in so doing he defied Moscow. It soon became clear that he had the firm support of most of his countrymen. Yugoslavia now faced the wrath of the other members of the Cominform. They showered the Yugoslavs with abuse; but that was not all. On July 3, Albania cut off trade relations with Yugoslavia; it was soon followed by Rumania and by other members of the Cominform. And so Yugoslavia, from the point of view of the pro-communist bloc, was an outcast. Yet this Cominform family quarrel did not bring the Yugoslavs into the ranks of the Western bloc.

The chief battlefield of the cold war was Germany. It was shortly after the surrender of Germany in World War II (May 1945) that the country had been divided into Russian, American, British and French zones. The capital city of Berlin, which was well within the Russian zone, also had its Rus-

A tried and true British industry—textiles. This is a modern spinning machine.

sian, American, British and French sectors. The occupying powers had agreed to work together in order to make their rule of the country as effective as possible. But the three Western powers differed with Russia and, to a lesser extent, among themselves, over occupation policies. Therefore each of the four German zones tended to become more or less isolated from its neighbors.

Toward the end of 1947 the United States and Great Britain decided to bring about closer relations between their two zones, which thereafter were often lumped together under the name of Bizonia (two-zone land). At first the French held back. They were afraid that if the three Western zones of Germany were united, the Germans might again be in a position to build up war industries. This threat would be particularly great if Germany were to control the industrially rich Ruhr district. The French wanted this area to be internationalized.

Later, the French became more favorable to the idea of combining the three Western zones. In May, French delegates met in London with representatives of the United States, Great Britain and the Benelux countries and they agreed on the policy to be adopted toward Western Germany. (1) Delegates from the three Western zones would meet on September 1 to draw up a constitution for a limited Western Germany government, to be established early in 1949. (2) A seven-nation authority, made up of representatives of the United States, Great Britain, France, Benelux and Western Germany, would control the coal, coke and steel of the Ruhr district. (3) American, British and French troops would remain in Germany "until the peace of Europe would be secured." (4) The three Western allies would consult with one another if, at any time, Germany again became a menace to world peace.

Western German Representatives Draw up a New Constitution

On September 1, a sixty-five-member Parliamentary Assembly, made up of Western Germans, met in Bonn and began to draw up a provisional constitution. On October 1, the assembly decided that the new government would be known officially as the Federal Republic of Germany.

The Russians angrily denounced the efforts to unite the three zones of Western Germany; they claimed that area would become a Western puppet state. For their part, the Russians caused plans to be drawn up for a People's Republic of East Germany. A constitution for the proposed government was approved on August 3 by the communist People's Council in the Russian sector of Berlin.

Soon there was another source of friction between Russia and her former allies—the problem of setting up a new currency for Germany. The need for this move was great. The imperial mark (*Reichsmark*), the German unit of money, was worth little. Cigarettes had come to serve as a substitute for money; black markets flourished. The four occupying powers had started negotiations to set up a new currency, but had failed to come to any agreement.

The three Western countries decided, finally, that the situation was too critical to permit any more delay. On July 19, therefore, they announced that a new "German mark" (*Deutsche Mark*) would replace the almost worthless imperial mark in their zones. The three Western sectors of Berlin continued to use the old currency for a time. Russia was furious because the Western powers had acted without her. She introduced a new currency for her own zone and insisted that the Western sectors of Berlin should adopt it. The Western powers replied by bringing in their new German marks into their Berlin areas.

The Russians Set up a Blockade of Berlin's Western Sectors

Russia determined to drive her former allies out of Berlin by bringing about anarchy in their sectors of the capital city. We have already pointed out that Berlin was well within the Russian zone; therefore all land traffic from the West to Berlin had to pass through a narrow corridor. The Russians now bottled up this corridor by forbidding shipments of any kind from Western Germany to Berlin by rail or highway. They also cut off electric-power service from the Russian sector to the other sectors of Berlin. They claimed that they had acted because railroads, highways and power lines were in bad condition. This pretext fooled nobody.

Later the Russians also shut off deliveries of food and fuel from the Soviet zone to the Western sectors of Berlin. As for the Western allies, they put an embargo on all shipments to the Soviet zone from the West.

The blockade of the Western zones of Berlin was now on in good earnest; the inhabitants were threatened with industrial chaos and starvation. The Allies determined to meet this challenge by flying in supplies. They at once increased the number of daily cargo flights from 50 to 100 in order to bring in 200 tons of flour and other foods, as well as medical supplies. This was the beginning of what came to be known as Operation Vittles—that is, the bringing in of "vittles" (the popular spelling of victuals, or food).

Operation Vittles proved to be a great success. In time the number of planes used to bring in cargo was greatly increased. From the comparatively modest beginning of 200 tons daily, air cargo reached a total of 5,000 tons daily and more, in good weather. Allied planes (chiefly American and British) brought in not only food and medical sup-

Barbed-wire prison. These Greek rebels were

plies but also coal and equipment.

The supplying of Berlin by air was effective but costly; besides, the Allies did not relish the idea of carrying on Operation Vittles in the stormy winter months. Therefore, they sought to put an end to the blockade by means of negotiations. With this in mind, envoys of the United States, Great Britain and France began a series of talks with Russian officials in Moscow on July 30.

For a time it seemed that the negotiations had succeeded, for on August 30 the Russians consented to lift the blockade. In return, the Allies agreed to use the new Soviet currency in their Berlin sectors, provided that this currency would be under four-power control. But Marshal Vasily Sokolovsky, the Russian military governor of Berlin, refused to lift the blockade unless the Allies permitted the Russians to inspect all planes entering the city, as well as all trains, trucks and other vehicles used for land transportation. The Allies refused to accept these conditions,

WIDE WORLD

caught by Government troops, northern Greece.

Bulgaria, Czechoslovakia, Hungary, Rumania, the Ukraine and Yugoslavia—sent delegates to this conference. The only Western powers represented were the United States, Great Britain and France. It soon became clear that the pro-communist countries intended to make up their own rules. The pact that was finally adopted set up a Danube Control Commission on which there was not a single representative of the Western powers. Naturally the Western delegates to the conference refused to sign the pact.

The Cold War Hampers the Recovery of All the Nations of Europe

The cold war had an unfortunate effect on all the nations of Europe. It hampered European recovery by preventing the free exchange of goods between East and West. Both sections of the Continent suffered as a consequence.

Reliable news about the nations behind the iron curtain was rather scanty throughout the year. Foreign correspondents were forbidden to send out items of which the governments in power did not approve. Favorable news was apt to be strongly flavored with propaganda. The officially approved news dispatches painted a fine picture of unity and increasing prosperity; but some of the refugees from the iron-curtain countries had a rather different story to tell.

It seemed clear, at least, that Russian industry was gradually recovering from the blows that the German invasions of World War II had dealt it. As a further sign of progress, the Soviet Union announced, in October 1948, that it would begin a far-reaching fifteen-year "Stalinist strategic offensive" against drought. A vast reclamation project would protect the great wheat belt of southern and central Russia from periodic drought winds from Asia. The Russians planned to provide 3,000 miles of forest shelter belts to slow down these winds. They also planned to create 45,000 reservoirs in the wheat-belt area.

They claimed that such agricultural planning was not possible in a capitalistic country. Officials of the United States Department of Agriculture took a somewhat different view. They produced figures to show that the United States had actually done more in introducing conservation practices in the last fifteen years than Russia had made even preliminary plans for in the next fifteen.

which had not been included in the Moscow agreement.

The negotiations continued to drag on for a time; but they definitely broke down on September 21. On the 29th the Allies referred the Berlin blockade to the United Nations Security Council as a threat to world peace. The council voted on October 25 in favor of a resolution calling upon Russia to give up the blockade; in return, the three Western powers would agree to negotiate the Berlin currency problem and other questions affecting Germany as a whole. This resolution was vetoed by two council members, Russia and the Ukraine, and nothing came of it. (Although the Ukraine has a seat in the United Nations, it is really a part of the Soviet Union.)

Another battle in the cold war took place when representatives of ten countries met in Belgrade on July 30, 1948, to draw up rules for the navigation of the Danube River. Seven pro-communist countries—Russia,

As for the allies of Russia, their industries were hampered by the fact that they now had to get from the Soviet Union the machines, tools and equipment which the West had formerly furnished. But Russia was not in a position to supply these goods in adequate quantities and would not be in such a position for some time to come.

Premier Alcide de Gasperi Maintains His Hold in Italy

In Western Europe, the absence of censorship in most areas made it possible to have a clear picture of what was going on. In many cases the picture was not a pleasant one. Italy had a particularly difficult year in 1948. At the beginning of the year the Government was headed by Premier Alcide de Gasperi, who represented the moderate, pro-ERP elements. He was bitterly opposed by the Popular Front, made up of Communists and Left-wing Socialists and numbering millions of supporters. He was no less bitterly opposed by the Italian Social Movement, a group which was openly fascist. It upheld not only the memory but also the policies of the late fascist dictator, Benito Mussolini.

It was generally agreed that the Communists had a good chance to win the April 18–19 elections to the Italian national legislature —a result which would have been a deadly blow to the Western bloc. But the elections resulted in a clear-cut victory for De Gasperi. His Christian Democratic party won a 53.5 per cent majority in the new Chamber of Deputies. However, the Popular Front, with 30 per cent of the seats, was still a force to be reckoned with. It succeeded in stirring up unrest throughout the year and in holding back the recovery of the country.

France also passed through a disturbing year. For the first half of 1948 she was under the leadership of Premier Robert Schuman, a member of the MRP (*Mouvement Républicain Populaire*: Popular Republican Movement). He was supported by a coalition (union) of parties, made up of the MRP, the Socialists and the Radical Socialists. This coalition represented a "third force," which was opposed to both the Communists and the conservative Rally of the French People, a party led by General Charles de Gaulle. Premier Schuman proposed to restore French prosperity by combating inflation. To do this, he tried to keep both wages and prices from rising, but without much success.

His shaky Government lasted longer than most people had thought possible. But it fell at last when Schuman's Socialist allies refused to support his plan to spend 313,500,-000,000 francs (about $1,465,000,000) for the armed services for one year. Premier Schuman resigned on July 19 and was succeeded by André Marie. But Marie could not unite the country behind him, and on August 28 he too was forced to give up his post. Schuman again returned to the premiership, but he remained in office this time only about two days.

His successor, Dr. Henri Queuille, was a friend of General de Gaulle, but he kept to the middle-of-the-road policies of former Premier Schuman. Like Schuman, he urged Frenchmen to keep both wages and prices stable; he also pleaded with his countrymen to produce more as the best means of solving France's problems. But production was held back in the last months of the year by a series of damaging strikes, particularly a disastrous coal strike.

The British Empire Undergoes Important Changes

There were several important changes in the British Empire in 1948. On January 4, Burma, formerly a British possession, became an independent republic. Exactly a month later (February 4) Ceylon became the seventh dominion of the British Commonwealth of Nations. In 1948, too, the British gave up their mandate over Palestine, which had been intrusted to them by the League of Nations on September 29, 1923. The last British troops left the area on June 30.

On July 5 Britain's cradle-to-the-grave security program went into effect. This program consists of five parts. An Insurance Act provides benefits for unemployment, sickness, old age and death, and gives help to expectant mothers, widows and orphans. An Industrial Insurance Act insures workers against industrial accidents and diseases. Family Allowances aid children of school age. National Assistance helps those who would not be eligible for benefits under the Insurance Act. Finally a National Health Service provides free medical care for every person who requests it.

There was a major political upheaval in Eire in 1948. In the February elections to the Dail (Parliament), Prime Minister Eamon de Valera's Fianna Fail party lost its majority in the Dail. After sixteen years in office, de Valera had to give up his post. On February 18, the members of the new Dail elected John A. Costello prime minister.

In December, the Dail passed a bill setting up the Republic of Ireland, an independent state free of the British Crown. Though signed by President. S. T. O'Kelly, the bill did not go into effect in 1948.

Civil war in Greece continued throughout the year between the government troops and the rebel forces, made up chiefly of Communists and headed by General Markos Vafiades. Vafiades and his followers had set up a new "Free Greek Government" in August 1947. They received help from several of Russia's allies, particularly Albania, Yugoslavia and Bulgaria. The government forces had the open backing of the United States, which supplied them with money and military advisers.

The fighting remained indecisive. The government troops, prodded by their American advisers, launched several drives against the rebels: in Epirus, in February; in central Greece, in April; in the Mount Grammos area, near Albania and Yugoslavia, in June; in the Vitsi Mountain area, in northwestern Greece, in August. Yet, although government troops claimed important gains, the rebels continued to defy them.

There was discontent among the Greek people because of the Government's failure to take active steps to improve conditions. Though the Cabinet was headed by a liberal premier, the aged Themistocles Sophoulis, the very conservative Populist party had great influence and succeeded in warding off reforms. Many Greeks also were shocked at the mass executions of political prisoners in 1948. Some of those who were put to death had been in prison since 1944.

A New Queen Mounts the Throne in the Netherlands

The year 1948 marked the end of an era for the Dutch. On August 31 their beloved queen, Wilhelmina, gave up the throne after a reign of fifty years. She had been in ill health for some time and her only child, Princess Juliana, had served as regent since May 14, 1948. On September 6, Juliana became the queen of the Netherlands.

Spain edged closer to the nations of Western Europe in 1948. On February 7, the Franco-Spanish frontier was reopened, after having been closed for two years. Several months later (May 14) British and French delegates signed a one-year trade agreement in Madrid. Certain Western statesmen openly suggested that it would be well to admit Spain into the anti-communist camp as an ally against Russian aggression. But the move met with much opposition.

On October 7, the British Foreign Office announced that the exiled Socialists and Monarchists of Spain had reached an agreement on a coalition government-in-exile. This agreement was worked out by the socialist leader, Indalecio Prieto, and the monarchist representative, José María Gil Robles. Communists were to be barred from the new group, which hoped to win the support of the Western powers.

A new queen—Juliana of the Netherlands.

THE NETHERLANDS INFORMATION BUREAU

Jan. 1. British railroads are nationalized.

Jan. 3. Winter-aid program gets under way for France, Italy and Austria as U. S.–Italian agreement is signed in Rome.

Jan. 6. American and British military governments in Germany are to form single bizonal administration (Bizonia).—80th U. S. Congress opens.

Jan. 7. In his State of the Union message to Congress, President Truman recommends: a $40 cost-of-living credit to every income-tax payer and dependent, but no reduction in income taxes; quick action to halt inflation; speedy approval of the European Recovery Program.

Jan. 10. Iraq and Britain agree to a new treaty of alliance, recognizing Iraq's com-

Burma's flag is hoisted as the country becomes an independent republic on January 4.

WIDE WORLD

164

plete independence in foreign affairs.

Jan. 11. The Jewish Agency names Moshe Shertok as its officer to deal with the UN Palestine Commission.

Jan. 15. A severe cold wave sweeps over the U. S. east of the Rockies.—Canada restores price ceilings on meat and butter and controls on other items.

Jan. 17. Indonesia and the Netherlands Government sign a truce agreement.—Henry A. Wallace is endorsed for president at first annual convention of Progressive Citizens of America.

Jan. 19. India and Pakistan agree to submit their differences to a UN mediation board.

Jan. 20. W. L. Mackenzie King announces his intention to retire as prime minister and head of the Liberal party of Canada.

Jan. 21. German papers are made public by the U. S. State Dept. which reveal that in their 1939 agreement Russia and Germany proposed to divide Europe between them.

Jan. 22. Britain's new foreign policy is presented to Parliament by Foreign Secretary Bevin, centered around "a consolidation of western Europe . . . a spiritual union."

Jan. 26. A Polish-Russian trade agreement is signed in Moscow, covering the exchange of more than a billion dollars' worth of goods in the next 5 years.

Jan. 29. President Petrillo of the musicians' union agrees to end ban, on February 1, against duplicating musical programs on FM radio stations.

Jan. 30. Gandhi is assassinated in New Delhi, by a Hindu.—The 5th Winter Olympics opens in St. Moritz, Switzerland.

Jan. 31. The UN Appeal for Children opens its first global fund-raising drive.

Feb. 2. The U. S. and Italy sign a 10-year treaty of friendship, trade and navigation, the first post-war pact of this kind to be made by the U. S. with any European nation.—President Truman urges a 10-point civil rights program.

Feb. 3. College and training benefits for veterans are increased by at least $350,-000,000 in 2 bills passed by the U. S. House of Representatives.—1,500,000 workers go on a food strike in Bizonia.

Feb. 4. The island of Ceylon becomes a self-governing dominion within the wide-rang-

By Helen Merrick

ing British Commonwealth of Nations.

Feb. 6. Barbara Ann Scott, Canadian figure skater, wins women's title in Winter Olympics.

Feb. 7. Gen. Omar N. Bradley becomes U. S. Army chief of staff, succeeding Gen. Dwight D. Eisenhower.

Feb. 8. Sweden wins Winter Olympics.

Feb. 11. Aconcagua, the highest peak in the Western Hemisphere, in Argentina, is scaled by a 5-man team.—Russia's leading music composers are accused by the Communist party central committee of being "ideologically incorrect."

Feb. 12. Sir Oliver Franks is named to succeed Lord Inverchapel as British ambassador to U. S.

Feb. 14. Part of Russian reply to U. S. publication of secret German documents declares that Stalin was forced to sign the non-aggression treaty with Hitler in 1939 in order to gain time.

Feb. 16. The UN Palestine Commission reports to the Security Council that partition can be carried out only with "military forces in adequate strength."

Feb. 17. In election in the Bronx, N. Y., to fill a vacancy in Congress, Leo Isacson, American Labor party candidate endorsed by Henry Wallace, wins surprising victory. —President Gonzales Videla of Chile lands at Discovery Bay, South Shetlands, to claim Antarctic and other areas, including the Falkland Islands, off tip of South America, in dispute with Britain.

Feb. 18. John A. Costello is elected premier of Eire, ending 16-year government of Eamon de Valera.

Feb. 24. Prague and other communities in Czechoslovakia are taken over by communist "action committees."

Feb. 25. Communists take over the government of Czechoslovakia in a "bloodless revolution."

Mar. 2. The partition of Palestine is accepted by Russia in the UN Security Council as a solution to the Holy Land problem.

Mar. 7. Henry A. Wallace accepts nomination for president at organizing convention of "Progressive party of Pennsylvania."

Mar. 8. The U. S. Supreme Court rules that

SWISS FEDERAL RAILROADS

The American team marches into the stadium as the Winter Olympics open at St. Moritz.

C-47's, of the Berlin Airlift, on the unloading line at Tempelhof Airport.

U. S. AIR FORCE PHOTO

165

The ruins of Vanport, Oregon, which was buried in the disastrous Memorial Day flood.

tion Charter is signed by 53 of the 56 nations attending the UN Conference on Trade and Employment in Havana.

Mar. 27. In Paris, delegates of 16 nations agree on a draft charter for an "Organization for European Economic Cooperation."

Mar. 30. Pan-American conference of 21 nations opens in Bogotá, Colombia.—President Truman signs bill extending rent controls.

Mar. 31. A Russian order to Soviet troops to inspect all American, British and French trains entering or leaving Berlin is opposed by U. S., British and French authorities in the city's Western sectors.

An air show marked New York City's Golden Anniversary, celebrated during the summer.

religious instruction in public schools involves the use of tax-supported property and is unconstitutional.

Mar. 10. Jan Masaryk, non-party foreign minister of Czechoslovakia, dies in Prague under mysterious circumstances, reported as suicide.

Mar. 11. U. S. film-makers and British Government reach a 4-year agreement by which Britain will end its 75% tax on imported motion pictures and Americans will take out only $17,000,000 a year.

Mar. 15. Conference on European aid program opens in Paris; 16 nations are represented.—In a wildcat strike, more than 200,000 U. S. soft-coal miners leave pits and threaten a general shutdown of industry if their demands for an old-age-pension program are not met.

Mar. 16. The walkout of soft-coal miners spreads; and U. S. meat production is cut in half as strike of 100,000 CIO workers in 140 packing houses enters second day.

Mar. 17. In a message on foreign affairs to a joint session of Congress, President Truman renews plea for universal military training and a temporary draft, and recommends quick adoption of European Recovery Program.—Britain, France and Benelux sign a 50-year treaty pledging military, political and economic partnership.

Mar. 23. Dr. J. M. Uhrich is named lieutenant-governor of Saskatchewan, after death of Lieutenant-Governor R. J. M. Parker.

Mar. 24. The International Trade Organiza-

Apr. 1. Air transport of food into Berlin by U. S. Army begins.—Secretary Marshall tells Pan-American conference that while U. S. is ready to increase its economic aid to Latin America, it must continue to give top priority to Europe.

Apr. 2. Congress overrides President Truman's veto of tax-cut bill.

Apr. 3. The European Recovery Program bill is signed by President Truman.

Apr. 6. Finland and the Soviet Union sign a 10-year mutual defense and friendship treaty.

Apr. 7. The U. S. Senate confirms the nomination of Paul G. Hoffman as Economic Cooperation Administrator, head of ERP.

Apr. 9. Jorge Eliécer Gaitán, Liberal party leader in Colombia, is assassinated in Bogotá.

Apr. 12. Soft-coal miners begin returning to work in U. S.—On 3rd anniversary of death of Franklin D. Roosevelt, Britain unveils memorial statue of him in London.

Apr. 15. President Roxas of the Philippine Republic dies suddenly.

Apr. 16. A special session of the UN General Assembly opens to consider the Palestine problem—17 countries, including western Germany, sign convention creating the Organization for European Economic Cooperation, Europe's half of the ERP machinery.

Apr. 17. The 5-power Western bloc of Europe forms a permanent Council of Foreign Ministers.—Elpidio Quirino becomes president of the Philippine Republic.

Apr. 19. The U. S. Atomic Energy Commission announces that a secret test of "an atomic weapon" has been held in Eniwetok Atoll.—Burma is admitted as the 58th UN member.

Apr. 20. In Italian elections, the Christian Democrats receive about 49% of the vote and win a 53.5% majority in the Chamber of Deputies.

Apr. 21. Chairman Lilienthal of the U. S. Atomic Energy Commission reports that radioactive cobalt, a by-product of atomic-energy research, promises to rival radium in cancer treatment.

Apr. 26. King George VI and Queen Elizabeth celebrate their 25th wedding anniversary.—The inter-American conference in Bogotá approves charter creating an organization of American nations.

Apr. 28. A UN truce to safeguard Walled City of Jerusalem is accepted by Zionists and Arabs.

Apr. 30. Gen. Hoyt S. Vandenberg succeeds Gen. Carl Spaatz as U. S. Air Force chief of staff.

May 1. Citation wins 74th Kentucky Derby.

May 2. Gen. Dwight D. Eisenhower retires from the Army.

May 5. Britain receives $33,500,000 of Marshall Plan funds to buy food from Canada.

May 7. Winston Churchill calls for a U. S. of Europe and a world government at unofficial Congress of Europe, meeting in The Hague.

May 10. Threatened nation-wide railroad strike in the U. S. is halted, after President Truman orders the Army to run the lines. —In South Korea election for a National Assembly, supervised by the UN, Dr. Syngman Rhee's anti-communist independence party wins majority.

May 11. Vice-Premier Luigi Einaudi is elected first president of Italy.

May 14. The Jewish National Council, meeting in Tel Aviv, proclaims an independent State of Israel.—The British mandate over Palestine ends at midnight Palestine time; and a few minutes later President Truman issues American recognition, in fact, of Israel.

May 15. Arab troops from Lebanon and Egypt invade Palestine.

Miss Elizabeth Bentley, chief witness before the House Committee on Un-American Activities.

ACME

May 16. Dr. Chaim Weizmann is named first provisional president of Israel.

May 17. Russia grants recognition to Israel. —The White House reveals that 3 "atomic weapons" were exploded successfully in recent Eniwetok tests.

May 20. The UN Security Council names Count Folke Bernadotte, of Sweden, to act as mediator in an effort to bring peace to Palestine.

May 21. President Truman signs $3,198,-100,000 Air Force and Navy aircraft bill, authorizing a 70-group Air Force.

May 26. Gen. Smuts and his United party are defeated in parliamentary elections in South Africa.

May 28. Charles Franklin Brannan is confirmed as U. S. Secretary of Agriculture. —Dr. Daniel F. Malan, leader of the isolationist Nationalist party, becomes premier of South Africa.

May 30. Flood waters sweep through Oregon and Washington toward the sea, leaving 60,000 homeless and a trail of damage estimated at $75,000,000; Vanport, Oregon, is buried.

June 3. The world's largest telescope is dedicated at Palomar Mountain, California.

June 7. Dr. Eduard Benes, elected president of Czechoslovakia for life in 1946, resigns. —Gen. Eisenhower assumes office as the 13th president of Columbia University.

June 10. Former King Michael of Rumania and Princess Anne of Bourbon-Parma are married.—Secretary of Labor Schwellenbach dies.

June 11. A 4-week truce begins in Palestine, on terms laid down by Count Bernadotte.

June 12. U. S.–British women's Wightman Cup tennis matches are won by the U. S. —President Truman signs bill providing for the enrollment of women in the regular armed services.

June 14. Klement Gottwald is elected president of Czechoslovakia by Parliament.

June 18. The UN Commission on Human Rights adopts draft of a declaration on human rights; among other provisions, it would end dscrimination because of race, religion, sex or nationality.

June 19. The economy of the western zones of Germany is cut off from the Russian zone (except in Berlin) by replacing practically worthless Reichsmark with a new currency, the Deutsches Mark.

INTERNATIONAL

A new light in the sky—the brilliant comet which made its celestial bow in November.

June 20. The 80th U. S. Congress closes session.

June 21. The Republican National Convention opens in Philadelphia.—Chakravarthi Rajagopalachari becomes governor-general of the Dominion of India, succeeding Earl Mountbatten.

June 24. President Truman signs the peacetime Selective Service bill.

June 25. Gov. Thomas E. Dewey of N. Y. is nominated Republican candidate for president, with Gov. Earl Warren of California as his running mate for vice-president.— President Truman signs bill which will admit 205,000 refugees into the U. S.—Joe Louis retains the world heavyweight championship in a bout with Joe Walcott.

June 26. Air shuttle service to supply food and medicines to the 2,250,000 inhabitants of the Western powers' sectors of Berlin begins.

June 27. Zavah Haganah, new army free of independent groups, is sworn in by the State of Israel.

June 30. More than 200 American and British planes carry food and essential supplies into western sectors of Berlin over Russian blockade.

July 1. The N. Y. International Airport opens at Idlewild, N. Y.

July 3. In elections in Finland, the Agrarian party replaces the Communist bloc as the country's strongest single political group.

July 5. The government medical and dental care plan goes into effect in Great Britain.

July 7. The U. S. Navy swears in its first peacetime enlisted women.

July 9. The U. S. Government returns the railroads to their owners.—The 4-week

Palestine truce ends.

July 12. The Democratic National Convention opens in Philadelphia.

July 14. The entire Mississippi delegation and half the Alabama delegates walk out of Democratic convention.—Palmiro Togliatti, Italian communist leader, is shot and seriously wounded.

July 15. President Truman is nominated as Democratic presidential candidate; Senator Alben Barkley of Kentucky is nominated for the vice-presidency.—Gen. John J. Pershing dies.—The UN Security Council orders Israel and the Arab states to end fighting in Palestine within 3 days.

July 17. Revolting Southern Democrats, meeting in Birmingham, Alabama, nominate Gov. J. Strom Thurmond of South Carolina, for president, and Gov. Fielding L. Wright, of Mississippi, for vice-president.

July 19. The Schuman Cabinet falls in France.

July 20. Twelve top U. S. Communists are arrested, charged with conspiracy to overthrow the Government.

July 22. Newfoundland votes for confederation with Canada.

July 24. Henry A. Wallace is nominated for president, and Senator Glen H. Taylor, of Idaho, for vice-president by the Progressive party.—André Marie becomes premier of France.

July 26. The U. S. Congress begins special session.

July 28. Explosion and fire wrecks the I. G. Farben chemical works in Ludwigshafen, Germany; hundreds of persons are killed and thousands injured.

July 29. King George opens the Olympic Games in London.

July 30. A 10-nation Danube-River conference opens in Belgrade.

July 31. Elizabeth T. Bentley, former communist spy, begins testimony before House Committee on Un-American Activities.

Aug. 5. An agreement is announced by which the French zone of Germany will practically become united economically with the British and U. S. zones (Trizonia).—The U. S. House of Representatives completes action on granting a $65,000,000 loan to the UN for construction of permanent headquarters.

Aug. 7. Louis St. Laurent, Canadian Minister of External Affairs, is elected to succeed Prime Minister Mackenzie King as leader of the Liberal party.

Aug. 12. Mrs. Oksana Stepanova Kasenkina, Russian teacher, leaps from a third-floor room of the Soviet Consulate in New York City, suffering serious injury.

Aug. 13. Maurice J. Tobin is sworn in as U. S. Secretary of Labor.

Aug. 16. Babe Ruth, famed American baseball player, dies in New York City.

Aug. 18. The invention of a new method and machine for casting steel in one step, instead of many expensive steps, is announced.—The Danubian conference closes with the passage of a Russian-proposed draft for exclusive East European control of the waterway.

Aug. 19. A new Chinese currency based on gold is announced.—The U. S. Federal Reserve Board issues regulations, effective September 20, putting controls on install-

Christening day—December 15—for Great Britain's new "Bonnie Prince Charlie."

WIDE WORLD

169

Indonesian Republic leaders: Premier Sjahrir, President Soekarno, Vice-President Hatta.

ment buying.—The U. S. demands the recall of N. Y. Russian Consul General Lomakin.

Aug. 22. A world council of main Christian faiths, except Roman Catholic and Russian Orthodox churches, begins meeting in the Netherlands.

Aug. 26. Numerous deaths and prostrations occur as eastern U. S. swelters in an extreme heat wave.—Thousands of German Communists in Berlin, many of them storming the City Hall, force a postponement of a meeting of the City Assembly.

Aug. 27. Charles Evans Hughes, former U. S. Chief Justice, dies.

Aug. 28. The French Cabinet of André Marie resigns.

Aug. 30. The International Refugee Organization becomes a full-fledged UN specialized agency.

Aug. 31. The 4 military governors of Berlin begin discussions on ending the blockade of the city and solving its currency problem.—Col. Gen. Andrei A. Zhdanov, member of the Soviet Politburo and frequently mentioned as the possible successor to Stalin, dies.—Robert Schuman becomes French premier.

Sept. 1. The Chinese Communists announce the creation of a "North China People's Government."

Sept. 2. Shipping on the West Coast of the U. S. is tied up as longshoremen, joined by seagoing unions, go on strike.

Sept. 3. Eduard Benes, former president of Czechoslovakia, dies.

Sept. 4. Queen Wilhelmina of the Netherlands ends reign of 50 years, giving up the throne in favor of her daughter, Juliana.

Sept. 7. Prime Minister Nehru of India demands that the Indian Army reoccupy parts of Hyderabad.—French Schuman Cabinet resigns.

Sept. 10. Lester B. Pearson is appointed Canadian Minister for External Affairs.

Sept. 11. Mohammed Ali Jinnah, governor-general of Pakistan, dies.—Premier Henri Queuille forms new French Government.

Sept. 13. Hyderabad is invaded by Indian troops.

Sept. 14. Kwaja Nazimuddin becomes acting governor-general of Pakistan.

Sept. 17. Count Folke Bernadotte, UN mediator in Palestine, is assassinated in Jerusalem.

Sept. 18. Hyderabad forces surrender to Indian troops.

Sept. 19. Social Democrats keep their parliamentary leadership in Swedish elections.

Sept. 20. The Palestine report of Count Bernadotte is made public; it suggests a revision of boundaries, ceding the Negeb to the Arabs.—On second reading, the British Commons passes, 319 to 192, the bill to curb the power of the House of Lords.

Sept. 21. The UN General Assembly opens meetings in Paris; Australian External Affairs Minister Evatt is elected president.

Sept. 26. Efforts to solve the Berlin problem end in failure after more than 6 weeks of discussion.

Sept. 27. It is announced that a cache containing papers left by Peary polar expedition has been found.

Sept. 28. A permanent military organization for the defense of western Europe is announced by the defense ministers of Britain, France and Benelux.

Sept. 29. The Berlin blockade is referred to the UN Security Council.

Oct. 3. The Israeli Government announces that it will oppose removal of even part of the Negeb from Israeli territory.

Oct. 4. Cleveland wins the American League baseball championship.

Oct. 5. Dr. Karl T. Compton is appointed as successor to Dr. Vannevar Bush as chairman of the Research and Development Board of the National Military Establishment of the United States Government.

Oct. 6. The Japanese Cabinet of Premier Yoshida resigns.

Oct. 8. Norway, Cuba and Egypt are elected to the UN Security Council, for terms beginning January 1, 1949.

Oct. 11. Cleveland wins the World Series.

Oct. 12. Gen. Eisenhower is formally installed as president of Columbia University.

Oct. 14. Chinhsien, Manchurian port, falls to Chinese Communist troops.—The Japanese Diet elects Shigeru Yoshida premier.

Oct. 17. A French decree fixes the exchange rate of the dollar at 262 francs in export-import transactions.

Oct. 18. Israel rejects UN cease-fire proposal for Negeb, but agrees to hold peace talks with Egypt.—Foreign-trade activities in the French zone of Germany are joined with the merged American-British zones.

Oct. 19. Joe Louis announces that he will defend his heavyweight title in a bout scheduled for June 1949.—At Loire pits, French troops battle Communist-led strikers.

Oct. 21. Beersheba falls to Israeli forces, cutting Egypt's last links with the Negeb and the Jerusalem area.

Oct. 23. A practical state of siege is declared by the French Government as infantry is rushed into central France to drive barricaded miners from the coal pits.

Oct. 24. A 15-year reclamation project is announced by the Soviet, to develop about 300,000,000 acres including the barren steppes.

Oct. 25. Defense Minister Claxton discloses that Canada is co-ordinating her defense plans with those of other Western powers so as to fit them into an eventual North Atlantic pact.—French troops take over numerous coal mines.

Oct. 30. Mukden, biggest city in Manchuria, falls to Chinese Communist troops.— French coal mines resume production.

Oct. 31. Girl Scout Week opens.—With ⅔ of Palestine said to be under its control, the Israeli Government orders cease fire. —Five Chinese Nationalist armies are routed.

Nov. 3. President Truman wins the election over Governor Dewey; both houses of 81st Congress will have a Democratic majority.

Nov. 4. Nobel Prizes are awarded to: T. S. Eliot, American-born poet and dramatist, literature; Patrick M. S. Blackett, British atomic scientist, physics; Arne Tiselius, Swedish biochemist, chemistry; Dr. Paul Mueller, of Switzerland, medicine.

The winning side in China—Communist soldiers cheer their victories in Manchuria.

Nov. 6. A new comet appears, one of the brightest and most spectacular in the 20th century.

Nov. 7. It is announced that James Boswell manuscripts lost for more than 150 years, including 1,300 pages of the working draft of his life of Johnson, are recovered.—De Gaullists pick up 98 seats in election for French upper house, but fall short of a majority.

Nov. 8. Members of the Commonwealth of Nations sign a $220,000,000 trade agreement with Japan.—Three Johns Hopkins doctors reveal development of a mass X-ray test for gastric cancer.

Nov. 10. Dock workers begin strike tying up Atlantic coast of U. S.—Martial law is proclaimed in Nanking and Shanghai.

Nov. 12. Hideki Tojo is sentenced to hang by Allied tribunal.—A million Chinese are in battle as Nationalist defenders of Suchow attempt to hold lines against onrushing Communist forces.—Kwaja Nazimuddin is appointed governor-general of Pakistan.

Nov. 13. President Evatt of UN General Assembly and Secretary-General Lie appeal directly to the heads of the U. S., British, French and Russian governments to begin "immediate conversations" to resolve Berlin issue.

Nov. 14. A son is born to Princess Elizabeth and the Duke of Edinburgh.

Nov. 15. Louis Stephen St. Laurent takes office as prime minister of Canada, as William Lyon Mackenzie King resigns, after heading the Canadian Government for more than 21 years.

Nov. 16. Chinese Nationalists claim a major victory over Communists east of Suchow.

Nov. 17. British Commons passes steel nationalization bill

Nov. 19. First combined trade agreement for U. S., British and French zones of Germany is signed with France.

Nov. 22. King George VI indefinitely postpones all engagements because of illness.

Nov. 24. Venezuelan Army takes over government and ousts Pres. Rómulo Gallegos.

Nov. 25. It is announced that George McCullagh, publisher of the Toronto GLOBE & MAIL, Canada's largest morning newspaper, has bought the Toronto EVENING TELEGRAM, the nation's leading Conservative newspaper.

Nov. 27. French General Confederation of Labor calls off 8-weeks' coal strike.

Nov. 29. Dominion of India officially abolishes Untouchability.

Dec. 2. French National Assembly rejects American-British plan for German trusteeship over Ruhr industries.—Chinese Communists announce capture of Suchow.

Dec. 3. House Committee on Un-American Activities announces find of "pumpkin papers" in spy inquiry.

Dec. 5. Western Berlin voters defy communist threats in election for City Assembly members; Social Democrats poll nearly ⅔ of votes.

Dec. 8. It is announced that the Palomar Mt. telescope has some flaws; and it may be a year before the instrument is in working order.

Dec. 9. UN General Assembly approves a convention outlawing genocide.

Dec. 10. UN General Assembly adopts a universal Declaration of Human Rights, which defines political, social, economic and other rights considered essential for every human being.—U. S., Canada and Brussels Treaty countries begin Atlantic security talks.

Dec. 11. Agreement arranging for admission of Newfoundland as 10th Canadian province is signed in Ottawa.

Dec. 15. Son of Princess Elizabeth and the Duke of Edinburgh is christened Prince Charles (Philip Arthur George) of Edinburgh.

Dec. 16. France announces the development of an atomic-energy pile.

Dec. 18. Netherlands Government announces that it is undertaking "police action" against "terrorists and undesirable elements" in Indonesia.

Dec. 19. Acting UN Mediator Bunche declares that the State of Israel is "firmly established" and war in Palestine is over.—Dutch airborne troops capture Jogjakarta, capital of Indonesian Republic, and arrest Republic's leaders.

Dec. 22. Former Premier Tojo, Gen. Muto and 5 other Japanese war criminals are hanged.

Dec. 24. Canada announces recognition, in fact, of State of Israel.

Dec. 28. U. S., Britain, France and Benelux announce agreement for an international authority in the Ruhr.

Dec. 31. Chiang Kai-shek offers limited peace terms to Chinese Communists.

EXPEDITION *from* NAIROBI

By JAMES L. CLARK
Leader, Central African Expedition,
The American Museum of Natural History

ALL PHOTOGRAPHS IN THIS AR-
TICLE, JAMES L. CLARK, CEN-
TRAL AFRICAN EXPEDITION

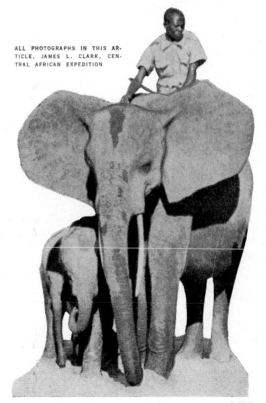

IT'S lots of fun to go on an expedition, but it's also lots of work! Most expeditions go to strange and far-away places, where there are no stores. This means that the expedition must take with it practically everything that will be needed—tents, food, guns, cameras and a thousand-and-one other things. Sometimes just the planning takes a full year. Long lists must be made, with nothing left out. Then the equipment must be bought, and this often takes a great deal of shopping. Passage on the steamer, and baggage space, must be arranged well ahead of time.

If just one man were going on the expedition, getting ready would be complicated enough. But when many men are going, all the equipment must be multiplied just so many times. Before you realize it, you may have many truckloads of equipment and sup-

Above, the expedition trucks in the game country of southwestern Kenya. Below, a mother elephant and her baby at the Government Training Station Camp in the Belgian Congo.

Stepping out tonight? African tent boy, who does odd jobs around camp, using charcoal flat-iron to press clothes of expedition members.

plies. What you take, of course, depends on where you are going—to Africa, Asia, Australia or Alaska. Getting everything together is like buying all the things for a new house —a new house all alone in the midst of a vast wilderness. If you forget anything, you will probably have to do without it.

Although I had been to Africa four times

Bandi natives in front of their hut in south-eastern French Equatorial Africa. Mangoes, reddish yellow fruit, are hanging on trees.

before, I wanted to go back to visit some parts of the country that had almost never been explored. I wanted to learn something about the native people and how they live, and to study the animal and plant life. So, on November 1, 1947, I left New York City and sailed over the Atlantic Ocean across the equator to Capetown, at the very southernmost tip of Africa. I took with me 6 trucks and 133 pieces of baggage. Capetown is about 6,500 miles from New York, and the trip took 19 days. Although it was almost winter when we left New York, it was summer when we arrived in the modern city of Capetown. The Northern and Southern Hemispheres, as you know, have opposite seasons.

Last-Minute Arrangements in Nairobi— 29 Native Boys as Cooks and Helpers

While the steamer carrying all my baggage continued up the east coast of Africa to the port of Mombasa, I flew by plane from Capetown up through Africa to Nairobi. I had planned to start my expedition from this little town. Here, while waiting for my baggage, I hired my white guide and twenty-nine native black boys to act as cooks and helpers. I bought my hunting licenses and some equipment which I had known could be purchased in Nairobi.

Nairobi, which is the capital of Kenya Colony, is nearly 6,000 feet above sea level, in beautiful highland plains country almost on the equator.

On Our Way—from the Wooded Highlands across the Grassy Plains

When the boat carrying my baggage arrived, I went down to the coast on the train, and brought all the luggage back to Nairobi in the six trucks. By the time everything was ready to start, the four other members of the expedition party had arrived in Nairobi by plane from America. On January 20, our whole party rolled out of the little town to begin our work in the field. From the native villages on the wooded highlands, we dropped down over open grassy plains. Towering above us were the impressive and majestic cones of extinct volcanoes. As we crossed the plains of this beautiful country we saw herds of antelope. During the daytime it was very hot, but the nights were cool and comfortable.

After traveling two hundred miles, we

came to our hunting country—open, pleasant grasslands. Here there were many kinds of antelope, and herds of zebra, rhinoceroses, elephants and lions. We photographed these creatures in color. We had no trouble with any of them: they pay little attention to automobiles. If we were careful, we could ride up very close to any of them, even the lions, and take pictures.

One scientific member of the expedition collected and studied the insect life of that

wild animals got water. One day, when some of the boys went down to get water for the camp, they came running back to tell me that there were two lions down there, drinking. The boys could not get near the water hole and they wanted me to come down and shoot the lions so they could get some water. Lions are very independent creatures, and while they will not ordinarily attack you if you keep your distance, it is still not safe to provoke them at close range. Fortunately,

One of the expedition safari trucks, carrying expedition equipment and members, about to cross an African stream. The "gangplank" of rough boards leads on to a ferry made of native dugout canoes covered with boards. The ferry is manned by interested African natives.

part of the country. Others collected some specimens of animal life. The photographer and I were very busy taking motion pictures of the animals and the country.

We had selected a pretty camp-site and our many boys went cheerfully to work, pitching our tents and making the camp comfortable for a long stay. They were thoroughly happy now because there was plenty of fresh meat to eat. Near by was a water hole from which not only we but the

when we reached the water hole with our guns, the lions had moved on, having drunk their fill.

After we had finished the work we had to do in this camping-place, we turned westward. We passed over the rich highlands of western Kenya, which are 8,000 feet above sea level, and dropped down to Lake Victoria, the head of the Nile River. This beautiful lake is the largest one in Africa and the second largest fresh-water lake in the world.

We skirted its northern shores through tropical Uganda and traveled on to the base of snow-tipped Ruwenzori, breath-taking in its beauty and its great height. This lofty mountain once was supposed to be in the mythical mountain range known as the "Mountains of the Moon." Modern explorers have found no such range of mountains, although there are many high peaks in this region. We spent several days exploring and photographing on Ruwenzori, which is much like the Alps in its beauty and majesty. Then we circled its southern base and went north, through the rich Belgian Congo.

In this part of Africa, near Niangara, is located the Elephant Training Station where the capturing and training of the African elephants is carried on by the Belgian Congo

This native African village, with its round, thatched huts, is built in the cone of an extinct volcano on the shore of Lake Kivu in the Belgian Congo. The government authorities have taught the natives much about health and sanitation, and the huts of this village are arranged according to gov-

Government. The station was located here because there are many wild elephants roaming the near-by forests. When more elephants are needed for training, the men go into the open forests on horseback after the animals. Along with them go many natives, carrying strong ropes, and several trained elephants with their drivers—mahouts—riding astride their necks. When a small herd of elephants is located, the horsemen cut off the young elephants from the others, and drive the rest of the herd away. Then they circle around —all this with the help of the trained elephants—and tie up the protesting youngsters. This is very dangerous work for both the men and the horses, since the angry mother-elephants often charge into the group trying to free their young.

We Make Friends with the Pigmies, Gay and Cheerful Little People

In this beautiful, fertile country of the Congo, with its big-tree forests and its little pigmies, we found many happy and friendly natives. The pigmies, a gay and cheerful little people, are about four and a half feet tall. Like tiny black gnomes, they roam stealthily through the deep forests, hunting for antelope or elephants to supply the meat which is their main diet. When they have more meat than they need, they trade their surplus to other natives for vegetables, tobacco and salt. When these are used up, they disappear again into the deep forest on another long hunting trip. One day they took me hunting with them, and showed me how they string their long net snares through the undergrowth to catch the smaller game. They crawl up very close to the large animals, even the elephants, and kill them with poisoned spears or shoot them with poisoned arrows. The pigmies trail the wounded animals which die within a short time. Then they cut away the flesh around the wound, and eat the rest of the meat, either raw or after it has been toasted over a fire.

The Whole Pigmy Family Travels through the Deep Forest

These little people travel through the forests in small groups made up of a few families. The children go along with the grownups; the babies are carried by their mothers. Each family owns one earthen cooking-pot, a basket, a long net for catching game and a few spears and knives. You can see that they are not overburdened with possessions. When the end of the day comes, they make simple small huts from sticks and big leaves. They have no beds, but always sleep on the bare ground.

After we had said good-bye to the pigmies, we continued westward through the big rain forests, where enormous trees towered high above us on either side of the narrow road.

ernment regulations. Most of the volcanoes on the shores of Kivu are extinct, but some of them send wide streams of molten lava into the lake.

177

EXPEDITION FROM NAIROBI

We were delighted with the thousands of exquisitely beautiful butterflies, and especially with the little white ones that looked like so many big snowflakes.

Along the Wide Congo River, We Found Friendly and Contented Natives

When we came to the wide Congo River, we found the black people living in the river basin friendly and contented. Their round huts of sticks and mud, with grass-covered roofs, are seen all along the winding roads. Each family hut, or group of huts, has its own little kitchen garden of native bananas and vegetables, as well as its own chickens, goats and dogs. The big moist forests, with their many bamboos and palms, cast a pleasant shade over the native men working in their gardens, on the white man's plantations, or on the roads. The women care for the huts and do the cooking, while the children help their mothers or attend the mission schools.

Turning north, the expedition headed for French Equatorial Africa, where very little exploring has been done. For some distance the country is much the same as the Congo, but as we moved northward into a warmer, drier climate, we found a more open land, with smaller trees. The native people, although of a different tribe, looked much the same and lived in much the same way as the others we had seen. Although they were poorer, because the country was less fertile, they seemed contented and were willing to help us all they could in our work.

The Native Children Were Given Trinkets for the Specimens They Collected

This was the country from which I wanted especially to collect animals for our museum. I hunted the large ones. The small animals, such as mice, frogs and fishes, which would also be valuable scientific specimens, were more difficult to obtain than the larger ones. So I hired the native children, who knew where to find the small animals, to catch them and bring them to me at the camp. When they brought the animals in, I would pay for them in bright-colored beads, candy or small trinkets. It was very hot during the day, with the thermometer at 105 degrees, but the nights were comfortably cool. We secured our water from deep native wells, or from little streams which had not dried up.

In this country, as in most of Africa, there are just two seasons, the rainy season and

the dry season. The rainy season is the African winter, cooler but not cold. When the rains come, little traveling can be done because all the ground is very wet and muddy, like our farm lands in spring. For this reason, expeditions must do their work during the dry season when the ground is hard and one can move about without difficulty.

The dry season was now nearing its end and the big rains were about due in this northern country. We wanted to be back in Nairobi before they came. So back we went again through the Congo, by another road which took us into the beautiful mountainous country called the Kivu.

Volcanoes Light the Skies Above the Kivu

Here, along the north shores of Lake Kivu, were many volcanoes—mostly old ones not now active. Two big ones, each about 13,000 feet high, still had great pits of fire burning in their cones. There was also a very active little "baby" volcano which had just broken out of the ground five weeks before I arrived. This sputtering little fellow was spilling over and sending two rivers of molten lava four miles down a wide valley into Lake Kivu. When I went over to photograph these flows, I saw great columns of steam shoot up into the air as enormous clumps of this red-hot lava broke off and tumbled into the water. At night there were five big red spots on the high clouds. These red spots were caused by the glow from the molten rock in the three volcanoes and from two forest fires set by the burning lava flows on their way down the valley. As we watched the strange red glows in the sky, and saw around us the high mountains covered with the forest haunts of the ferocious mountain gorilla, we did indeed know that we were in a far country.

Home Again, After Three Months and 8,500 Miles of Travel

After another week of travel through this mountainous country, and down to Lake Victoria, we followed the familiar road through western Kenya back to our starting-point. We had been out over three months, and had traveled 8,500 miles. We brought back with us many scientific specimens for the American Museum of Natural History, many valuable notes and records, and three miles of colored motion pictures.

178

FOLKLORE

Wandering Myths

By Marius Barbeau
Folklorist for the Canadian Government

IN the treasure trove of myth and fairy
lore there are many tales that have been
told in all lands and in all ages. There
are the stories of the knight that slays the
dragon and rescues the maiden; of the phoe-
nix, which, Ovid tells us, lives on frankin-
cense and other fragrant gums; the roc—
the giant bird that carried Sindbad the
Sailor to the Valley of Diamonds; the well-
frog that swallowed all the water in the
world; and a host of other stories. In one
form or another, such tales as these are
familiar in many countries throughout the
world.

One of the most widely told of these stories
is familiar to us from the ancient Greek
version—the story of Orpheus and Eurydice.
Orpheus was the ideal poet and musician of
the Golden Age. So sweet was the music of
his lyre that it charmed men and beasts
and even the trees and rivers. His bride,
Eurydice, was the loveliest of the nymphs.
They lived in a world of beauty and happiness, but, alas! one day Eurydice trod on
a snake and died of its poisonous bite.

Then Orpheus sought her in the world of
the dead, Hades. Passing through crowds of
ghosts, he played his lyre and sang of his
deep sorrow to the rulers of the realm of
shades, Pluto and Proserpine. They were
moved by his grief and devotion, and told
him that he could take Eurydice back again
to the world on one condition. He must not
turn to look at her until they had reached
the upper world.

As the two reached the great portals of
Hades, Orpheus disobeyed and glanced behind him. And so he lost his beloved bride,

A carved pole of the Haida Indians tells the
story of Gunarh and his wife, one of the North
American versions of Orpheus and Eurydice.

179

Orpheus imploring Pluto and Proserpine, rulers of the underworld, to let him take his beloved Eurydice back to the world of the living.

for Eurydice vanished, to dwell among the shades for ever. Unhappy Orpheus lived very little longer. Some beautiful nymphs called maenads tried to win his affections, but they found that he had no thought for anyone but Eurydice. This made the maenads so jealous that they slew him.

This ancient tale of enduring love has a simple theme that you can recognize even when you meet it with different characters and many variations in detail. In every country where it is told, you will see that the pattern is the same. Someone journeys to the realms where the spirits dwell and tries to bring back a beloved spirit to the land of the living. Like a chameleon, however, the story takes on the color of its surroundings.

For instance, let us see how they tell this story in Japan. There, it is the goddess Izanami who dies. Then her husband, Isanagi, journeys to the Land of Gloom (Yomotsukuni) to find her spirit and bring it back to the world of the living. The god-

dess begs her husband not to look at her while they are still in the nether world. Yet, like Orpheus, he disobeys, and loses his beloved again and for always.

The Hawaiians had much the same story, but they gave it a happy ending—which is quite unusual in the folklore of any people. In a Hawaiian tale of Polynesia, Hiku, the grieving husband, disguises himself as a butterfly. He captures the ghost of his wife and succeeds in bringing her safely back to life in spite of the difficulties in his path.

Some of the important variations that are found in this tale of two lovers arise out of the beliefs and legends of different peoples about the world of ghosts and shadows. In some places in North America, among the Indians, the native hero makes a perilous and difficult journey into the sky, instead of journeying into the nether world. Among the seacoast Indian tribes of the far north, as among the Eskimos, it is believed that souls after death dwell under the ocean. The Tahltans of the northern Rocky Mountains believe that souls travel to the sky on snowshoes, and then follow the Milky Way west-

ward. Among the Tsimsyans of the north-western coast, the home of the dead is in the killer-whale center at Kwawk, far out to sea.

Sometimes the Indians would tell their myths to the missionaries and other white men who visited them; and sometimes the

the North American Indians was made by Father Brébeuf, who established the first mission to the Hurons of Georgian Bay in the early 1600's.

In the story as told to Father Brébeuf, the hero makes a journey to the Village of Souls to look for his lost sister. He finds her, but is unable to touch her. Her soul is so small that he can put it inside a pumpkin. This he does, and is allowed to embark in the "white stone canoe" and carry it home—on one condition—that "no one raises an eye to observe." On the homeward journey, when the soul is on the point of coming to life, a curious witness looks and the soul shrivels up and is lost forever.

As we have mentioned, to the seacoast tribes of the northwest, the home of the dead is the undersea abode of the killer whales. In their version of the story the hero has the harsh-sounding name of Gunarhnesemgyet. This name has a lovely and lyrical meaning: "Listen, and you fall under a spell!" The episodes in this tale of Gunarhnesemgyet show vividly the seacoast background of the story-tellers.

Every day a white sea otter passed in front of the village on the seashore. The hunters tried in vain to capture it. At last Gunarh (as we may call him for short), the most skillful of all the hunters, found this beautiful animal asleep on the water. He managed to catch and kill it and gave its wonderful pelt to his wife. While she was working on the otter skin, she broke some rule, or taboo, which aroused the wrath of

A carving of the killer whale carrying the Tsimsyan woman to the undersea home of Kwawk, abode of the dead.

white men would write them down. In this way, many Indian tales and beliefs have become a part of our historical records. The earliest written account of this legend among

the sea-dwelling spirits. Breaking a taboo is a dreadful offense, and the offender is always punished. And so it happened in this case. Unnoticed by anyone the magic sea otter

181

started to drift away from the shore, carrying Gunarh's wife with it.

When the people on shore realized what was happening, they saw that the white otter had two dorsal fins, so they knew that it was Gilsadzant, a great spirit of Kwawk, and that he was taking Gunarh's wife to the world under the sea. Gunarh, with some friends, set out at once in a dugout canoe and tried to overtake the swift otter. They were too late. The otter disappeared at the spouting hole that was the entrance to the undersea abode of Kwawk.

Gunharh's Adventures in the Spirit Land beneath the Northern Seas

Gunarh anchored his canoe at the hole, and climbed down a rope. The Giant Mussel guarding the portal tried to hold him back, but Gunarh killed it by chanting a magic spell and choking it with a handful of snuff. Next the Giant Clam tried in vain to stop him. Then a crowd of blind women appeared, calling out, "We smell Gunarh!" The clever Gunarh, however, knew what to do. He rubbed saliva in their eyes, which restored their sight. So grateful were the women that they promised to help Gunarh rescue his wife.

Farther down the undersea trail stood the Giant Crane, which was also blind. "I smell Gunarh!" cried the Crane. But Gunarh also restored its sight, thus gaining another friend. "Your wife is just ahead," warned the Crane. "A Giant Man called Gilsadzant guards her; but he is too fat. If you trip him, he will never be able to get up again."

Soon Gunarh reached the House of the Killer Whales, where a fire was burning and they were making a blackfish cloak for his wife. Stealing softly in, Gunarh quickly put out the fire, seized the soul that he loved so dearly, and fled, swift as lightning, from the ghost house. The giant Gilsadzant would have stopped him, but Gunarh tripped the enormous man who, falling, blocked the narrow trail to those who were pursuing the fugitives. The Giant Crane also helped to block the trail, crying, "Rush on, Brother, you will escape!" The women who had been blind, who were Geese Women in disguise, helped to hold back the vengeful pursuers. At last, triumphant, Gunarh reached the anchor rope of his canoe, and his friends pulled the hero and his wife aloft to the light of day.

Gunarh's story, you will notice, is next of kin to the tale of Hawaii. Just as Hiku, disguised as a butterfly, brings Kawalu back to life, so Gunarh successfully returns from the depths of the sea with his wife. It is curious to note how often the folk tales of pagan and savage peoples have sorrowful endings. These two stories are among the rare exceptions.

The North American Orphic hero, just like the hero of ancient Greece, has inspired sculptors and painters. Here in the north country, however, the adventures have been carved and painted on totem poles and tribal symbols. A far greater number of versions of this tale have been traced in North America than have come down to us from the Greeks and Romans. Folklorists have collected many of them. Miss A. H. Gayton, in her ORPHEUS IN NORTH AMERICA, tells us that stories "of the recovery of the beloved person from the dead are common in North American mythology." Like Miss Gayton, Stith Thompson has built up a long list of different versions in his TALES OF NORTH AMERICAN INDIANS.

The Same Tale Is Told in Many Lands under the Palm and under the Pine

Another story-pattern, called by the name of its Greek version, is that of Cupid and Psyche. Part of the story is repeated in such tales as that of the Scandinavian maiden who married the prince who was enchanted as a polar bear. Both the Norse maiden and Psyche were forbidden to look upon their husbands in their natural form; both yielded to overwhelming curiosity and were punished by having to undergo great hardships. The Psyche story has another device that is shared by countless folk and fairy tales. The heroine (in some stories the hero) is set three impossible tasks as a condition to winning her heart's desire. Wherever this occurs in a folk tale, whether it be those collected by Perrault or the brothers Grimm, the Arabian Nights, or the lore of Celt or Norseman, the solution is the same. The tasks are successfully accomplished, but with the help of some friendly supernatural power.

These are but a few examples of the amazing way in which the pattern of fancy is repeated in the fabric of folklore and legend. The weaving of the tales may be elaborate or crude, depending upon the art and skill of the weavers, but the themes are the same, in all times and in all places.

The Forty-niners

THE GOLD RUSH A HUNDRED YEARS AGO

By Marguerite Aspinwall
author of LOST TREASURE
TRAILS *and other books*

I'll scrape the mountains clean, old girl,
I'll drain the rivers dry.
I'm off for Californy—
Oh, Susannah, don't you cry.

Oh, Susannah!
Don't you cry for me.
I'm off to Californy with
My wash bowl on my knee.

SO runs a song of the gold-rush days, a hundred years ago, when one of the great treasure hunts of all time took place in far-away California. This territory was then a new addition to the United States. It had only recently been acquired from Mexico, and had not yet been taken into the Union as a state. California was so far from the settled portions of the country, and both travel and communications were so poor in those days, that Americans as a whole had not shown much interest in the new land to the west.

Then something happened to bring California startlingly into the limelight. In January of 1848, gold was discovered by a man named James Marshall, who was building a sawmill at Sutter's Fort at the junction of the American and Sacramento rivers.

Men in the immediate neighborhood began a sort of crude placer mining, and were amazed by the richness of the deposits they uncovered. It is said that gold nuggets were found in the roots of bushes, and that with only a hunting knife, men could dig wealth out of easily reached pockets in the rocks.

There is a story that a Mormon named Sam Brannan, who had set up a store near Sutter's Fort, rode into town one day holding aloft a bottle filled with gold dust, and shouting, "Gold! Gold! Gold from the American River!"

A crowd gathered, and presently a stampede began to the scene of the discovery. By spring, tales of the fabulous gold strike had spread over all of California. Men from every walk of life—doctors, lawyers, merchants, laborers—dropped everything and started in hordes on this spectacular treasure hunt. Soldiers deserted their duty; sailors left their ships. Everyone in California was headed for the gold fields, to stake out his own claim and dig himself a fortune.

Fortunes *were* dug, too. Some men made as much as $15,000, $20,000 or $30,000 in a week's work; others, of course, were less lucky, and gained barely living wages from their exertions. It was largely a matter of chance as to whether or not the site chosen contained pay dirt.

The news finally reached the Atlantic seaboard. There was plenty of exciting talk, but at first most people did not believe it. Then a letter from Governor Mason to the War Department was made public. "There is more gold," said the letter, "in the country drained by the Sacramento and San Joaquin rivers than would pay the cost of the late war with Mexico a hundred times over."

That made men prick up their ears! Times were hard, and people needed money and jobs. The California trek caught at every man's imagination that winter. From January 1849 on, the great rush was in full swing. Men dropped their everyday responsibilities and set off for the gold fields, sure they would become millionaires. Some actually did return as rich as their hopes; some never came back at all.

There were three ways of getting west to California, all of them long, all of them dangerous. One way chosen by the Forty-niners —who are sometimes called the Argonauts— was by ship around Cape Horn, and up the west coast to San Francisco. This way was

The little wooden town of San Francisco, the gateway to the gold fields, as it looked in 1849.

the easiest but was also much the longest.

The second was supposed to be the shortest of the three and was therefore the most popular. This was by sea to Chagres on the Isthmus of Panama; then by canoe on the Chagres River to a little inland place called Cruces; and from there by muleback along a deeply mired jungle trail to Panama City on the Pacific. From Panama the travelers proceeded north to San Francisco by whatever boats were running. Unfortunately, there were far fewer craft on the Pacific than on the Atlantic. The Pacific Mail Steamship Company had three side-wheelers plying the route: the California, the Oregon and the Panama. The other boats available were a motley lot—some unseaworthy, usually ill provisioned, and always overcrowded. Bad as they were, there were not enough vessels. Wild with impatience, men fought for passage aboard them. There were necessarily long waits in Panama, where because of the crowding, dirt, poor food and generally unsanitary conditions, cholera, yellow jack and jungle fevers added to the human misery in the place. Many Forty-niners perished on the isthmus, never even coming anywhere near their golden goal.

The third way—the hardest and most desperate of all—was by wagon train across the

Plains. Some died by the hand of Indians, some died of starvation and disease. Thirst killed many another in the terrible alkali desert of the Humboldt Sink. For greater safety small groups of Forty-niners usually met at Independence or St. Joseph, Missouri, which then were civilization's last frontiers. Here they joined forces and set out in long wagon trains for the hazardous final stages of their journey.

Some of the Forty-niners took their families with them across the Plains. There is an account of a family party that crossed the Plains successfully, taking with them two small children and a ninety-year-old grandmother. Many other groups never arrived at their destination; and many more left members of their families in shallow graves along the trail. The sufferings of these heroic adventurers were very great. However, a vast number of them struggled through to their journey's end, only to find other hardships awaiting them.

At the gold diggings prices were high, and goods of any kind sold for fantastic amounts. Onions were a dollar apiece. So were potatoes. A live fowl brought $16. A cooking stove with its fixtures, which had cost $60 back east, brought $400 in the mining camps. Beads, purchased for $.10 a bunch,

The modern city of brick and steel, stretching down from Nob Hill to the Golden Gate.

could be sold to the Indians for $10. The camps were infested with rats which had escaped from ships' holds and multiplied ashore. Cats were in great demand to hunt them down, and any cat could be sold for as much as $16.

Naturally, the first thought of those who had come so far, and with so much hardship, was to begin digging the moment they reached the gold fields. Excitement was all around them. Lucky miners were striking rich pockets of ore on one side, while, on the other, discouraged men were giving up a losing fight and going away with less than they had brought with them. No one knew who would be the fortunate winner in the next hour.

During the first months, before the great flood of fortune-hunters began to arrive from all parts of the country, the camps were free from violence and theft. Men left cans full of gold dust on the shelves in their tents, without fear of robbery. Such trust was not possible a year later, when the rough characters of the land, the thieves, gamblers, and even murderers, began to invade the fields.

In the camps Sunday was a day of rest from digging, though not one of quiet. This was the day the hard-working miners played. There were fortune-tellers, wandering fiddlers, artists who would sketch a man's likeness for a high price in gold dust; and of course the saloons and gambling halls were wide open to take away as much of the men's earnings as they could get by fair means or foul. This was the day, too, for the so-called "miners' meetings," when a duly elected judge dealt out justice in matters of property quarrels and offenses against camp law.

The end of the day was usually marked by a dance, in which—because women were scarce in the gold fields—certain men were told off to act as "ladies" and dance with the partnerless miners.

Not all of the gold-seekers returned home when they left the camps. Many drifted into San Francisco and other towns, and, going into various businesses there, helped to build up the new country.

Only a hundred years have gone by since the days of the Forty-niners. Yet what changes there have been! The journey to "Californy" is no longer fraught with peril. The miles that were once so hardly won are now traveled in safety and comfort. As the spirit of adventure beckons us westward, we may choose whatever magic carpet we like the best—great, rolling highways, luxurious trains or flashing air liners—to visit the land of the Argonauts' dreams.

185

FUEL

more *POWER* to you!

By JOHN E. SCANLAN

OLD King Coal, the strong man of the fuel world, is stretching his muscles.

For many years he has been doing a good job of furnishing heat and steam power for the world, but up to now we have never given him a chance to use all of his vast amount of energy to the best advantage.

Now science is experimenting with coal to find other and better ways of making it produce energy or power. Some of these experiments have been made with coal in a fluidized form. That is to say, the coal is turned into a powder as fine as talcum, so that when it is mixed with air it flows like water through pipes into the furnaces where it is burned. These experiments have been quite successful. As a result, within the next few years we shall probably be getting power from coal in a number of new ways.

For one thing, we shall probably be making gasoline and Diesel oil from fluidized coal. It may seem odd that a liquid fuel can be produced from such a solid thing as coal, but that is exactly what scientists are doing in experimental plants right now.

Also, it has been discovered that coal in fluidized form will burst into very hot flame when it is ignited. This makes for less expensive power, per pound of fuel, than can be obtained from burning lump coal. Scientific engineers are now working on a new type of railroad locomotive that will burn coal in powdered form.

Let us look first at the method of producing synthetic or artificial gasoline and oil. The original process was developed in Germany, just before World War II, by two chemists named Franz Fischer and Hans Tropsch. Their principal raw materials were ordinary lump coal and a catalyst of cobalt in hard pellet form. From these they were able to get Diesel fuel, and a low grade of gasoline which had to be improved by further processing.

It remained for American chemical engineers to improve upon the Fischer-Tropsch method by fluidizing both coal and catalyst. By this method, a high grade of gasoline, in addition to Diesel oil and industrial chemi-

Water (steam)! Coal! Air! These are broken down and their atoms of hydrogen, carbon and oxygen are made to combine in molecules of gasoline and other necessary substances. Two important steps of this chemical process are pictured here.

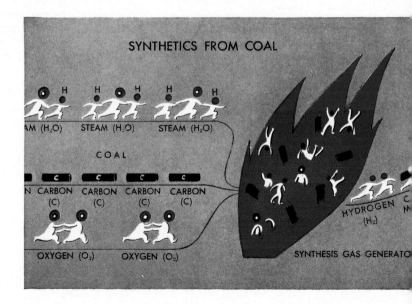

SYNTHETICS FROM COAL

STEAM (H₂O)   STEAM (H₂O)   STEAM (H₂O)

COAL

CARBON (C)   CARBON (C)   CARBON (C)   CARBON (C)

OXYGEN (O₂)   OXYGEN (O₂)

HYDROGEN (H₂)

SYNTHESIS GAS GENERATOR

186

cals, can be produced in fewer operations.

In the United States and Canada there are enough untapped petroleum reserves to keep us supplied for a long time, but the demand for oil is increasing and the expense of taking it from the ground is mounting. More people are installing oil burners for home heating; railroads are using more and more oil-consuming Diesel locomotives; and there are more automobiles on the highways than ever before in history. Both commercial and military aviation use tremendous amounts of gasoline; and shipping is turning to oil as a more efficient fuel. Synthetic liquid fuels are thought to be at least part of the answer to this rapidly growing fuel problem.

At first, American scientists used only natural gas as the raw material for making synthetic fuels—not only because it contained the necessary chemical elements, but because it was cheaper. However, they know that coal is still our largest source of potential energy.

Untouched coal reserves in the world are very great. It is estimated that there is enough undug coal of all grades in the United States alone to keep us supplied with fuel for thousands of years.

Experiments have now progressed to the point where one ton of bituminous or soft coal can be made to produce a hundred gallons of gasoline and Diesel oil, plus other chemical products.

In the making of synthetic gasoline and oil, almost any kind of fuel can be used— even corn husks could be used. The Germans used a very low grade of lignite called brown coal which, ordinarily, is not much good for anything. American chemical engineers are using bituminous coal because there is so much of it, although they could use lignite because there are vast reserves of it in the far west.

We call the Fischer-Tropsch method the hydrocarbon synthesis process. If you have studied chemistry, you know that a hydrocarbon is a chemical compound of hydrogen and carbon, and that synthesis is the process of uniting elements or simple compounds to make a more complex compound. Petroleum, from which we get oil and gasoline, is a very complex mixture of hydrocarbons.

In the first step of the fluidized solids process, powdered coal is burned in a generator. Blasts of steam and oxygen are shot in at the same time. The oxygen and steam react with the carbon in the burning coal and form a mixture of carbon monoxide and hydrogen. This mixture is called the synthesis gas.

The synthesis gas then flows through pipes into huge chambers called reactors. The bottom of each reactor is filled with many water tubes. (These tubes help to control the temperature, which is very important.) A special catalyst—a substance which speeds up and assists the chemical reaction without changing its own form—is densely packed around

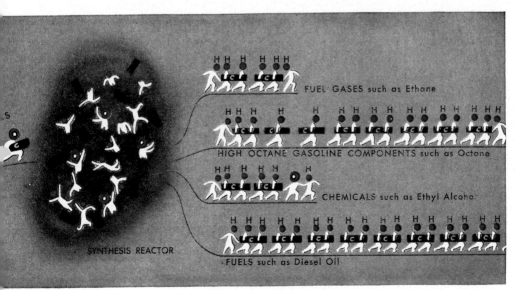

SYNTHESIS REACTOR

FUEL GASES such as Ethane

HIGH OCTANE GASOLINE COMPONENTS such as Octane

CHEMICALS such as Ethyl Alcohol

FUELS such as Diesel Oil

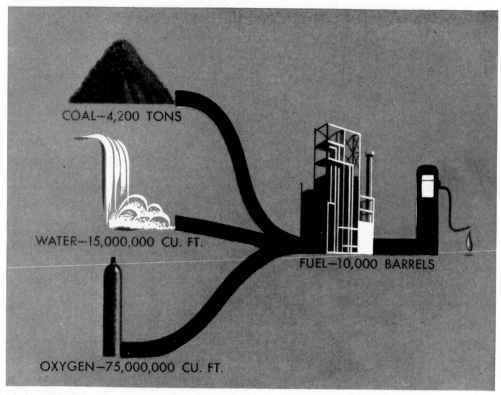

COAL—4,200 TONS

WATER—15,000,000 CU. FT.

FUEL—10,000 BARRELS

OXYGEN—75,000,000 CU. FT.

Look at this drawing—then turn back to the chart on pages 186–187, where the same story is told in greater detail. The catalyst used to speed up the reaction is not shown in these diagrams.

the tubes. This catalyst is a bed of iron particles ground to the fineness of powder. The gas is forced up through this mass from the bottom of the reactor. As it passes through the catalyst, the synthesis reaction causes an intense heat. The heat and gas, acting together, greatly disturb the catalyst so that it billows and seethes like boiling water in a pot, although it is not actually in liquid form. The boiling action helps to spread the heat more evenly in the reactor, and throws the gas and the catalyst into closer contact with each other.

As a result of all this, the synthesis gas is broken up into the complex hydrocarbon molecules of oil and gasoline. These substances rise to the top of the reactor as a mixture of gases and vapors. Then they are piped off to condensers, where they are separated and the vapors are condensed to form the primary products—oil and gasoline.

Scientists do not know exactly what causes this strange transformation to take place. It may be the kind of catalyst, or it may be the

tremendous amount of heat. They do know that if the catalyst were not there, nothing of the sort would happen.

Diesel engines using oil for fuel are, in the main, the most efficient for mobile equipment today. This is because a Diesel engine makes better use of its fuel than engines powered by coal or gasoline. For this reason, more and more railroads, for instance, are replacing wornout steam locomotives with Diesel locomotives to haul their freight and passenger trains. However, the fact still remains that coal—even though its price has been going up—is still a cheaper fuel than oil made from natural petroleum.

So, engineers asked themselves, why not build something that will use coal more efficiently? They found their answer in a gas turbine engine, which works very much like that of a turbojet fighter plane. By the time you read this, a new type of locomotive powered by fluidized coal burned in a gas turbine will probably have had its first trial runs.

As we said earlier, it has been discovered

that coal powdered as fine as talcum, or finer, bursts into very hot flame very quickly. In the gas turbine, though, the flame is not used to make steam as in the old-type steam locomotive or factory engine. Instead, the burning coal heats the air in which it is burned. The air expands and is forced through a wheel having blades or vanes arranged something like the blades of an electric fan. The terrific speed of the expanded air pushing against the vanes makes the wheel spin around furiously.

The vaned wheel is called a turbine and is connected with a generator that generates electricity for eight electric motors. These drive the big wheels that roll the locomotive along the tracks.

Let's see just how the whole operation is performed. First, the coal is in lump form in the engine's coal bunkers. From the bunker, the lumps are fed to a crushing machine which grinds them up into very small pieces —about the size of percolator coffee. Even this, though, is not small enough. A mechanical conveyor then carries the coal to a pump, which drops the tiny bits of crushed coal into a compressed air pipe through which the air and coal flow into an atomizer. In the atomizer, each bit of coal is thrown against a target of the hardest metal available, and

the particles are broken into still finer bits. Now finer than face powder, the coal goes on its way to the combustor or burner, where it burns fiercely and heats the air which drives the turbine.

However, before the heated air is ever allowed to touch the turbine wheel, it must go through a cleaning machine. This is called a dust separator and it serves a very important part in the operation. In this device the ash of the burned coal, which has been carried along with the air, is taken out. Were this ash not taken out, its sharp particles would soon wear away and ruin the blades of the turbine wheel.

The new type of locomotive will have several advantages. For instance, it will be cheaper to run than an oil-fired or Diesel engine because of lower fuel cost. It will be less expensive to maintain than the old coal burner because there will be no boilers to inspect and fewer moving parts to keep in repair; it will operate better in extremely cold weather; and it won't need to carry water. Fluidized coal will also be of help to the home owner. Experiments with powdered coal for use in a house furnace are going on. Here, the coal burns very much as oil does in a furnace. The results will be more heat and less smoke and ashes.

The fierce heat in a synthesis gas generator must be watched and controlled. It is kept between 1600 and 2000 degrees Fahrenheit.

The end of the process—drawing off synthetic oil. A synthetic product is one that has been made by combining atoms "to order."

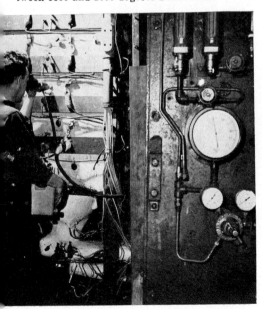

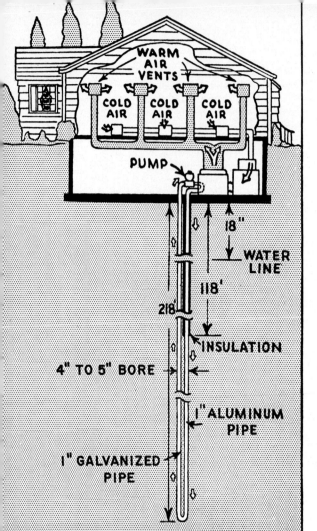

Labels on diagram:
WARM AIR VENTS
COLD AIR COLD AIR COLD AIR
PUMP
18"
WATER LINE
118'
218'
INSULATION
4" TO 5" BORE
1" ALUMINUM PIPE
1" GALVANIZED PIPE

The liquid refrigerant passes through the coil of pipe, taking heat from the earth. On its return to the surface, its temperature is raised by compression. The hot liquid then flows through other coils, heating the air.

COURTESY, SCIENCE AND MECHANICS

will be no soot from the burning of oil to spread its ugly black mantle over the white snow of the countryside. The houses, indeed, may have no chimneys at all, for we may by then be heating our homes from the great furnace in the earth.

In the ground, whether it is covered with the green cloak of summer or with cold white layers of snow, there is a great deal of heat—an actual furnace in the earth. Below a certain level, the earth never freezes. How far down that level is found depends on your position on the globe. Below this freezing line, whatever its depth, the ground remains at the same temperature throughout the year. In New York, for example, the temperature of the earth thirty feet below the surface is always about 52°. (All degrees mentioned in this article are Fahrenheit.) To the north the temperature at that depth is generally colder —to the south, it is warmer. For each additional sixty feet of depth, the temperature increases by one degree.

Engineers have now learned how to draw heat from this great furnace in the earth. This warmth can be used to keep our homes comfortable in cold weather—without coal, wood or fuel of any kind. The new kind of

FURNACE

W HEN you go for a walk in the country on a cold winter afternoon, you notice little wisps and rising plumes of smoke curling up from the houses that dot the countryside. Each house has its furnace and possibly its fireplaces. Coal or oil or wood is burning away merrily to keep these homes warm, and inside all is cozy and as comfortable as on a summer's day. The wood to feed fireplaces, however, has to be cut; the coal to keep furnaces going has to be shoveled, and oil has to be delivered by truck to the house and piped into the cellar. This involves a great deal of work.

Twenty years from now all of this may be very much changed. On your walk through the country in that far-away time you may see no smoke from burning coal or wood pouring from chimneys. Perhaps, too, there

miracle furnace which taps the heat reserves in the earth is known as the heat pump.

We usually think of a pump as something down on grandfather's farm, which is used to draw water from a well. The heat pump, however, is quite another kind of pump. It reaches down into the earth in your own backyard, even in the dead of winter, and comes up, not with air or water, but with heat to warm your house. It will give you all the hot water you need. It will heat steam tables for cooking, and, actually, it will also run your icebox and your deep freezer. All this without using any fuel or causing any smoke, dust or ashes!

The heat pump itself is not a very large machine. It could be encased in a steel box about six feet high, six and a half feet long and three feet wide. It could be kept up in the attic, or down in the cellar, or even under the kitchen steps.

To draw on the vast, ever present supply of heat within the earth, the heat pump burrows deep underground. One kind of heat pump has a loop of one-inch pipe that runs from the pump down to a depth of two hundred feet below the surface of the earth. This loop of pipe then arches back up through the earth and into the pump again. Circulating through the pipe and the pump is the vital bloodstream of the heat pump, a liquid known as a refrigerant, a word which comes from the Latin word meaning coolness. This liquid carries the heat from the earth into your house.

The heat pump, strangely enough, works in very much the same way as does the refrigerator in your mother's kitchen. In your refrigerator, cold air is not pumped into the compartment where the food is kept, as so many people imagine; instead, heat is taken away from the food. In a chamber in your refrigerator a gas which will easily turn into liquid—perhaps ammonia or sulfur dioxide —is put under great pressure. The gas is then forced into another chamber and into metal coils where it is cooled to such an ex-

in the earth

By MELVIN ROSENBAUM
Science Writer

tent that it becomes a liquid. After this the liquid passes into the coils inside the food chamber of the refrigerator, where it changes back into a gas. As it evaporates, it takes up heat from the food stored in the refrigerator. Then the gas, containing the heat absorbed from the food, passes out of the food compartment. It is again put under pressure, cooled to liquid form, and pumped back through the coils.

The heat pump, instead of extracting heat from food as does the gas in your refrigerator, draws heat from the earth. Let us see

what happens to the liquid refrigerant in its journey through the pump and its coils of pipe. When it starts down through the pipe into the earth, the liquid is cold, but as it travels downward the fluid begins to pick up heat. The farther down it travels, the more heat it collects. On its return trip to the pump, the liquid runs no risk of losing the heat it has gathered, since the upper half of the pipe through which it passes back to the pump is well insulated, or protected, against the loss of heat. Before the refrigerant enters the pump itself, the heat it picked up from the earth is widely scattered throughout the liquid. Then, in the pump, the liquid is compressed or squeezed together into a smaller space and the heat is concentrated. As a result of this, the temperature of the liquid shoots up.

When the "hot" refrigerant passes out of the pump, it flows into still other coils, which warm the air passing over them. This warm air is then distributed throughout the house. The refrigerant has now given up much of its heat. It is further cooled by being allowed to expand. By this time it is ready to return once more to its duties of picking up heat from the earth.

The heat pump can draw heat, not only from the earth, but also from the air, or even from the water in deep wells, from any source with a year-round temperature between 40° and 80°. With a heat source of only 50° the pump can warm a house to 70°.

You may wonder how heat can be extracted from well water, which is famous for being cold. Well water is usually at a temperature somewhere between 50° and 55°, which makes it a good source of heat for the pump. Everything contains some heat, even if it is cold by our standards. Only at absolute zero (−459.6°) is there no heat whatever. Even in a cold stone there is heat that could be used if there were some way of getting at it.

When summer comes, the heat pump proves its usefulness in another way. A turn of a switch or of a valve will reverse the direction in which the liquid flows in the coils. Then the refrigerant will pick up heat from your uncomfortably warm house, transfer it to the earth which will be cooler than the air, and return to the house bringing coolness. The air in the house, as it passes over the coils of the pump, gives up its heat, and the house is cool.

191

GOVERNMENTS

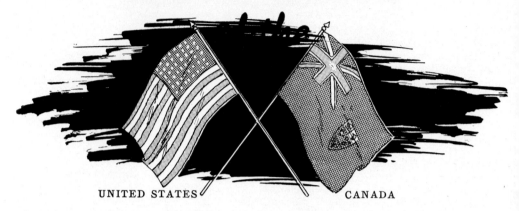

UNITED STATES   CANADA

WESTERN HEMISPHERE

By LAWRENCE M. LEVIN

THE governments of the Western Hemisphere, like governments the world over, show a wide variety of patterns; no two are the same. Yet they fall into four pretty definite groups. (1) There are twenty-two independent republics. (2) There is a self-governing dominion of the British Empire. (3) There are three departments, or states, of the French Republic. (4) Finally, there are a number of colonies and other dependencies belonging to Great Britain, Denmark, the Netherlands, France and the United States. (A dependency is a territory which is under the rule of another state.)

THE INDEPENDENT REPUBLICS

The United States is the oldest republic in the New World and has served as a model for practically all the rest. Its form of government is not altogether the same now as it was when George Washington, the first president, took office in 1789. Among other things, Americans have changed the method of electing the president, vice-president and senators. They have given women the right to vote. They have abolished slavery, which was once established by law. They have permitted the Federal government to tax the income of the citizens.

Yet, throughout the years, the United States has remained a government of the people, by the people and for the people. It has been a very stable kind of government. Whatever changes have been made in it have been brought about by legal means. There has never been a dictator in the United States; there has never been a successful revolution.

The United States is made up of forty-eight states, two organized territories and a number of possessions in the New World and in the Pacific. There is also a Federal district —the District of Columbia—which contains the national capital.

Each state has a certain amount of self-government. It elects its own governor; it has its own legislature; it has its own courts, too. The states have authority over private property. They punish crimes against individuals. They control education. They pass laws concerning marriage and divorce. They construct and maintain highways. However, they can not enter into treaties with foreign governments, nor coin money nor declare war. All these matters and others, too, are left to the Federal government.

The Federal government has three branches—executive, legislative and judicial. The executive (carrying out) branch sees to it that the laws are enforced. It leads the nation in time of war. It also makes treaties with other countries; but the Senate must approve these treaties before they can go into effect. The legislative (law-making) branch of the government passes all kinds of laws. The judicial (judging) branch interprets laws, assigns penalties for breaking them and settles disputes. The three branches of the government are kept separate from one another. In this way each keeps the others from becoming too powerful.

The chief executive of the United States is the president. He is elected for a four-year term by a special group of electors, chosen by popular vote; and he is eligible for reelection. Until recently there was an unwritten law—really a custom—that no president was to have more than two terms. But in the present century President Franklin D. Roosevelt served three full terms and part of a fourth (1933–1945). The two-term custom seems to be a thing of the past.

The president may be impeached (charged with misbehavior in office) by the House of Representatives. He is then tried by the Senate, with the chief justice of the Supreme Court presiding. If at least two-thirds of the members of the Senate declare the president guilty, he is removed from office. Only once in the history of the country has a president been impeached (Andrew Johnson, in 1868); and he was acquitted by the Senate.

The president is assisted by a nine-man Cabinet, consisting of the Secretary of State, the Secretary of the Treasury, the Attorney General, the Postmaster General, the Secretary of the Interior, the Secretary of Commerce, the Secretary of Labor, the Secretary of Agriculture and the Secretary of Defense. The members of this body are chosen by the president, are responsible to him alone and may be removed by him. Each incoming president ordinarily selects his own Cabinet. However, a vice-president who succeeds a president in office before the end of the latter's term generally keeps the old Cabinet.

The second most important executive is the vice-president, who is selected in the same way as the president. The chief official duty of the vice-president is to act as presiding officer of the Senate. He becomes the nation's chief executive if the president with whom he was elected fails to complete his term of office. Seven vice-presidents have

The Althing House in Reykjavik, Iceland, home of the oldest parliament in the world.

U. S. ARMY PHOTOGRAPH

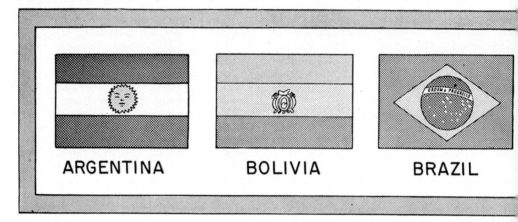

ARGENTINA   BOLIVIA   BRAZIL

succeeded to the highest office in the land in this way.

Formerly the next in order of succession to the presidency, after the vice-president, was the Secretary of State, followed by the other Cabinet members, in the order in which their posts were created. In July 1947, Congress passed a law changing the rules of succession to the presidency. If the vice-president can not complete the term of office as president, he is now succeeded by the Speaker of the House of Representatives. Next in the line of succession is the senator who has taken the former vice-president's place as presiding officer of the Senate. Then come the Secretary of State and the other members of the Cabinet.

The legislative branch of the Federal government is the United States Congress, made up of a Senate and a House of Representatives. The Senate has 96 members—two for each state; the House of Representatives has 435 members. Both senators and representatives are elected by popular vote; senators serve for six years and representatives for four. The Senate and the House work to a considerable extent through committees.

Both houses of Congress vote on all bills; but measures having to do with taxation are introduced only in the House of Representa-

tives. The Senate alone approves or rejects treaties made by the executive power. It also approves or rejects men named to high office by the president.

The Supreme Court, sitting in Washington, is the chief judicial body. It consists of a chief justice and eight associate justices. The other Federal courts are the Circuit Courts of Appeal and the District Courts. Federal judicial bodies are entirely separate from those of the states. They try men who have broken the laws of the United States; they also judge disputes between American citizens and those of other lands. The Supreme Court can pass upon the constitutionality of any act. If the court declares it unconstitutional, the law is wiped out.

In recent years the Federal government has taken a more active interest than ever before in the activities of industry, farmers, labor and citizens in general. A Federal body, called the Securities and Exchange Commission, regulates stock speculation. The Federal Housing Administration busies itself with housing problems. The Federal Crop Insurance Corporation protects farmers from losses caused by bad weather, insect pests and the like. The Tennessee Valley Authority (TVA) built a great electric power and flood control development in the valley of the Tennessee River; it now operates the development. These are only a few of America's Federal agencies.

To the south of the United States we find the twenty Latin-American republics, which once formed part of the Spanish, Portuguese and French possessions in the New World. They are: Mexico, on the North American mainland; Costa Rica, Guatemala, Hon-

| YELLOW | GREEN |
| RED | BLUE |

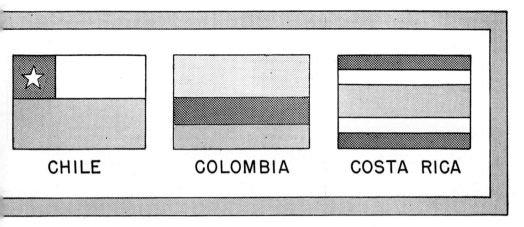

CHILE   COLOMBIA   COSTA RICA

duras, Nicaragua, Panama and El Salvador in Central America; Cuba, the Dominican Republic and Haiti in the West Indies; and Argentina, Bolivia, Brazil, Chile, Colombia, Ecuador, Paraguay, Peru, Uruguay and Venezuela in South America.

When these countries won their independence they adopted constitutions on the American model. They have amended these constitutions again and again and in many cases have replaced them with new constitutions. Still, on the whole, the governments of the Latin-American republics are like that of their northern neighbor.

Like the United States, the typical Latin-American republic consists of a number of states, which have a certain amount of self-government. These states are generally called provinces (also states and departments). The capital of the country is usually located in a federal district, corresponding to America's District of Columbia. In addition to the states, certain countries have territories or other dependencies.

The federal government in each of the Latin-American republics has three branches —executive, legislative and judicial. We find the same separation of powers as in the United States. Sometimes, however, a strong executive may seriously weaken the legislative and judicial branches for a time.

The chief executive is the president. In most of the Latin-American countries he is chosen by the direct vote of the people. In Argentina and El Salvador, as in the United States, he is selected by a special group of electors; in Haiti and Uruguay, by the national legislature. The term of office ranges from four to seven years. In most Latin-American countries the president can not succeed himself in office.

In every Latin-American republic we find a presidential advisory body, called a Cabinet, or Council or Ministry. This body has much the same duties as the United States Cabinet. The number of Cabinet members varies considerably in the different countries of Latin America; Cuba, for example, has seventeen, while Haiti has only six.

The federal legislature of most of the Latin-American republics consists of two houses: The upper house is generally called the Senate; the lower house, the Chamber of Deputies. The members of the lower house, without exception, are selected by popular vote. In some cases the senators are also chosen in this way; in other cases, they are chosen by a special body of electors or by the legislatures of the provinces. In six countries—Costa Rica, Guatemala, Honduras, Panama, Paraguay and El Salvador—there is a single legislative body.

The judicial system varies from republic to republic in Latin America. However, all twenty have a federal judicial body corresponding to the United States Supreme Court. In most cases this tribunal is called the Supreme Court or the Supreme Court of Justice, and it sits in the nation's capital. (The principal court of Haiti is the Court of Cassation; that of Venezuela, the Federal and Cassation Court.)

The federal government plays a prominent part in supervising the activities of the citizens in some of the Latin-American countries. This is particularly true in Argentina. In that nation a far-reaching five-year plan, started in 1947, is now in effect. The federal

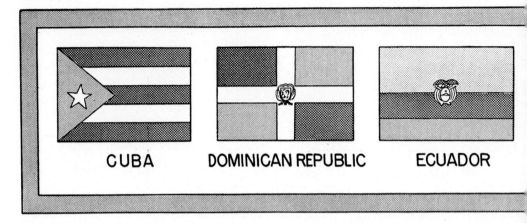

CUBA DOMINICAN REPUBLIC ECUADOR

government has undertaken to develop the nation's industries, transportation, public works and natural resources. It also aims to reorganize education, labor legislation and social insurance. In carrying out the plan, the orders of the president have the force of laws. The federal government is also very powerful in Mexico and Brazil.

The Latin-American republics, as you see, have much in common with the United States. The people themselves are the rulers. The three powers of the state—executive, legislative and judicial—take much the same form as in the United States and in almost every case they are kept separate. In some of the Latin-American countries, too, we see federal governments supervising the activities of the citizens.

Yet there are certain differences between the government of the United States and those of the other independent countries of the two Americas. For one thing, political violence plays a more important part in Latin America than in the United States. Revolutions have been fairly common, and a considerable number of them have overthrown the existing government. Within the last ten years there have been successful revolutions in most of the twenty Latin-American republics.

One reason for this state of affairs is that a political machine sometimes remains in power for one administration after another. This machine, generally headed by a "strong man," controls elections; it silences, or imprisons or exiles critics. As a result the enemies of the administration in power have little chance of bringing about a change in government by legal means, and so they re-

volt. There are other reasons for starting revolutions. Sometimes a reform administration makes enemies of those whose interests it attacks. Sometimes the administration in power is blamed for hard times.

We must not forget, however, that revolutions have been common throughout the ages; some of the most firmly established governments in the world have had their share of them. The important thing to note is that representative government is on the march in Latin America. More and more the citizens are insisting on choosing their rulers freely; they are insisting, too, that these leaders should be the servants and not the masters of the state. Only a few "strong men" are now in power. Democracy is a living and growing force in Latin America.

In 1944 Iceland became the twenty-second republic of the Western Hemisphere. Until the year 1944 this island in the North Atlantic belonged to Denmark. To be sure, from 1918 Iceland had been called a sovereign state; but its ruler was always the king of Denmark. On May 24, 1944, the voters decided, by an overwhelming majority in a special election, to cut all ties with the Danish Crown. In the following month the Icelandic Althing (Parliament) proclaimed Iceland a republic.

For administrative purposes Iceland is divided into sixteen provinces, each with a governor at its head. There are also ten urban municipalities (city communities); they form administrative districts which are entirely independent of the provinces.

The chief executive of Iceland is the president, who is elected by popular vote for a four-year term. He does not have as much

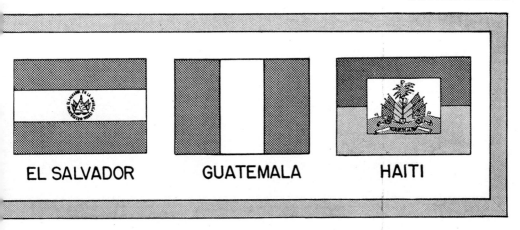

EL SALVADOR GUATEMALA HAITI

power as the president does in the other Western Hemisphere republics. The real executive authority is in the hands of a Cabinet of six ministers, headed by a prime minister. All Cabinet members must belong to the Althing and are responsible to that body. They can be impeached by the Althing. In that case the case is decided by a special tribunal, the Landsdómur, which is called on to serve only in case of impeachments.

The Althing is the world's oldest parliament, going back to the year 930. Its members are chosen by popular vote. After the election the Althing sets about dividing itself into an upper and lower body. The members elect one-third of their number to serve as an upper house; the other members form the lower house.

Canada

So far we have been dealing with the independent nations of the Western Hemisphere. We come now to the Dominion of Canada—a big country which is a member of the Commonwealth of Nations, yet which is truly self-governing. Canada has certain ties with the mother-country. It acknowledges allegiance to the British Crown; it has a governor-general named by the king. A part of its constitution is based on the British North America Act of 1867. The Dominion must apply to the British Parliament for permission to amend any part of this act. The Canadians, however, are masters over their own trade, commerce, navigation, shipping, banking, coinage, foreign policy, national defense and education. The Dominion has its diplomatic representatives in Great Britain, the United States, the Netherlands

and other countries. It is a member of the United Nations.

The Dominion of Canada is made up of nine autonomous (self-governing) provinces and two territories. In July 1948, as we shall see, Newfoundland voted to join Canada as its tenth province. However, Newfoundland did not officially become a member of the Canadian family of provinces in 1948.

The chief administrative officer in each province is the lieutenant-governor. He is appointed by the governor-general of the Dominion, acting on the advice of his Cabinet. Each province has a popularly elected Legislative Assembly; Quebec also has a Legislative Council. The Northwestern Territories and the Yukon Territory are each administered by commissioners. In the Northwest Territories there is a six-man council, appointed by the governor-general of Canada; in the Yukon Territory, an elective three-man council.

The provinces have authority over education, property, civil rights and, in general, over "all matters of a merely local or private nature." Such matters as trade, commerce, banking, coinage, national defense, navigation and shipping are left to the Dominion government.

The chief executive of the Dominion, in name at least, is the governor-general, appointed by the British Crown. He always acts, however, upon the advice of his twenty-member Cabinet, headed by a prime minister. The prime minister and the other Cabinet members represent the real executive authority; the governor-general serves rather as a link with the mother-country. Only members of Parliament, the Dominion legis-

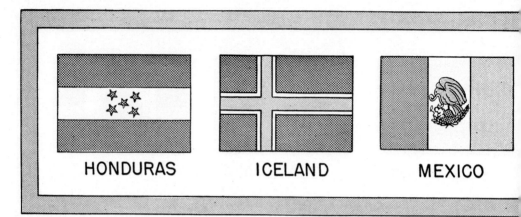

HONDURAS   ICELAND   MEXICO

lature, can be in the Cabinet. The Cabinet is responsible to Parliament and holds office as long as it retains the confidence of that body.

The Parliament consists of a Senate of 96 members and a House of Commons of 245. (A bill adopted in 1946 provides that, beginning with the next general election, the House of Commons shall consist of 255 members, elected on the basis of one member per 45,000 inhabitants.) The members of the Senate are appointed for life by the governor-general, acting on the advice of the Cabinet. The members of the House of Commons are elected by popular vote for a term not longer than five years.

The provincial courts handle most judicial matters; they enforce federal laws as well as provincial laws. The Supreme Court, founded in 1875, acts almost entirely as a court of appeals from the decisions of the provincial courts. Formerly Canadians could appeal even from decisions of the Supreme Court to the judicial committee of the British Privy Council. (The Privy Council is a body of men appointed by the British Crown to advise it in matters of state.) In January 1947, however, the judicial committee declared that it did not have the right to act on such appeals.

Three French Departments

Just as Canada is a member of the Commonwealth of Nations, so French Guiana, Guadeloupe and Martinique are part of the French Republic. Yet there is an important difference. Canada, as we have seen, is really an independent country, though it is bound to Great Britain by certain ties. French

198

Guiana, Guadeloupe and Martinique are departments, or states, of France, just as Massachusetts and Illinois are states of the United States.

They became departments on January 1, 1947; before that date they had been French colonies, ruled by a governor appointed in Paris. They are now governed in just about the same way as any other French department. Each has at its head an administrative officer called a prefect, who is assisted by a prefectorial council. Each is represented in the national legislative bodies of France—the Council of the Republic and the French National Assembly.

Dependencies

There was a time when most of the New World was divided up among a few European powers, particularly Spain, Portugal, France and England. In the course of the past century or two, European holdings in the Western Hemisphere have been greatly reduced.

Great Britain has far more colonies in this area than any other European state. It has a number of islands in the West Indies—the Bahamas, Barbados, Jamaica, the Leeward Islands, Trinidad and the Windward Islands. There are the Bermuda Islands, in the Western Atlantic, and the Falkland Islands, in the South Atlantic. There is British Honduras in Central America, and British Guiana on the northeast coast of South America. Finally there is Newfoundland, an island off the east coast of Canada; it has a dependency, Labrador, on the mainland.

The pattern of government is much the same in most of the British colonies in the New World. The chief administrative officer

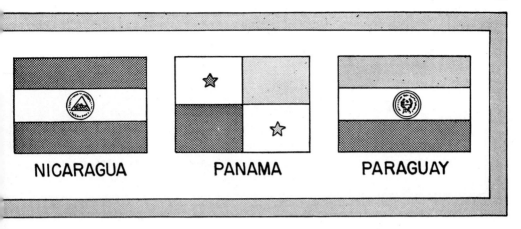

NICARAGUA · PANAMA · PARAGUAY

is the governor, named by the British Crown; he is assisted by an Executive Council and a Legislative Council. In four of the colonies there is also a colonial legislature—the House of Assembly, in the Bahama Islands, Barbados and Bermuda; the House of Representatives, in Jamaica.

Newfoundland is in a different position. It was formerly a dominion of the British Empire; but in 1934 it lost this standing because of financial difficulties. For some time afterward, a governor, named by the Crown, exercised both executive and legislative power. He was assisted by a six-man Commission of Government, made up of three Britons and three Newfoundlanders.

On November 6, 1947, Canada invited Newfoundland to become a regular province of the Dominion. In a special election, held on July 22, 1948, the Newfoundlanders voted, by a narrow margin, to join the Dominion as its tenth province. Before the change in government could become official, the United Kingdom would have to make the necessary arrangements and the Canadian Parliament would have to give its approval. This double-barreled program was not completed in 1948.

Denmark rules over far more territory in the New World than any other European country does. It has but one colony, Greenland, but this is the largest island in the world, covering more than 800,000 square miles. There are only about 20,000 inhabitants, however, for most of Greenland is covered by a huge ice cap.

The island as a whole is administered by a Board of Governors, sitting in Copenhagen, the capital of Denmark; they are responsible to the Danish premier. For administrative purposes Greenland is divided into three districts—North, South and East Greenland. To represent the Danish government on the spot there are two *landsfogeder* (governors), one in North Greenland and the other in South Greenland. In 1946 an extensive five-year plan for Greenland was drafted in Copenhagen. This plan aimed to increase native self-government in Greenland, to develop the resources of the island and to raise the living standards of the inhabitants.

The Dutch have two "overseas territories" in the New World. One of these, Curaçao, consists of five islands in the West Indies—Curaçao, Aruba, Bonaire, St. Eustatius and Saba—and part of a sixth, St. Martin. (The other part of St. Martin belongs to France and is a dependency of Guadeloupe.) A governor, named by the Dutch Crown, administers the islands; he is assisted by an Executive Council. There is also a territorial legislature, called the Staten. Islands other than Curaçao are governed directly by officials called gezaghebber, appointed by the governor.

The other Dutch possession in the Western Hemisphere is Surinam, or Netherlands Guiana, on the northeast coast of South America. Surinam is governed in much the same way as Curaçao; here, too, we find a governor, Executive Council and Staten.

Now that French Guiana, Guadeloupe and Martinique have become departments, there is only one French colony in the New World. It consists of the islands of St. Pierre and Miquelon and certain other islands off the Grand Bank, south of Newfoundland. A governor, named by the French president, ad-

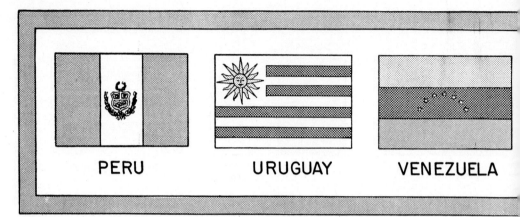

PERU   URUGUAY   VENEZUELA

ministers the colony. He is assisted by a Council of Administration, consisting of appointed officials and elected members. The colony sends one representative to the Council of the Republic and one to the French National Assembly.

The United States has several possessions in the New World outside the limits of the country proper. One of these possessions, Alaska, forms the northwestern tip of North America. Alaska is one of America's two organized territories (the other is Hawaii); but the chances seem to be good that it will be a state before long. It is a land of great promise, with its fisheries, its fur industry, its mines and its military importance as an outpost of the United States.

The chief administrative officer of Alaska is the governor, appointed by the president of the United States. He is assisted by a secretary, also named by the president. The secretary acts as governor of the territory when the governor himself is absent. There is a territorial legislature, made up of a Senate and a House of Representatives; regular sessions of this legislature are held every two years and they last sixty days. The United States Congress makes certain kinds of laws for the territory. Alaska is represented in Congress by a delegate who is elected by the people for a two-year term. He sits in the House of Representatives but has no vote.

Puerto Rico, in the West Indies, is also passing through a period of change. It is not certain, however, whether it will one day be a state of the United States or whether it will become an entirely independent country. The chief administrative officer, the governor, was formerly appointed by the presi-

dent of the United States. However, the Butler-Crawford bill, passed by the United States Congress in August 1947, gave Puerto Rico the right to select its own governor by popular vote. The first election for governor was held in November 1948.

Puerto Rico has its own legislature, consisting of a Senate and a House of Representatives. A resident commissioner, elected by popular vote, represents the island in the United States Congress. He has the right to speak in Congress, to serve on congressional committees and to introduce bills, but he can not vote. The president of the United States appoints the justices of the insular Supreme Court; he names the auditor, an important financial officer; he appoints an official, called a co-ordinator, to supervise Federal civilian activities.

The Virgin Islands of the United States, in the West Indies, once belonged to Denmark and were known as the Danish West Indies. They were sold to the United States in 1917 in the course of World War I. The president of the United States appoints the chief administrative officer, the governor. This official has the help of two Municipal Councils and a Legislative Assembly.

The Panama Canal Zone was acquired from the Republic of Panama by treaty in 1904. It is a strip of land ten miles wide, across the Isthmus of Panama; through this strip runs the Panama Canal. The Zone is really a government reservation for the operation, upkeep and defense of the canal and all of its equipment; no land in the Zone is privately owned. It is administered by a governor appointed by the president of the United States.

GREENLAND

The MOST NORTHERLY COUNTRY

By VILHJALMUR STEFANSSON
Arctic Explorer and Author

MORE so even than Tibet, Greenland has been a "closed country." For instance, up to World War II, if someone from Canada or from the United States wanted to see Greenland, he had to be more than just a tourist. He had to state that he was an artist or a scientist and that he wanted to study the land or people—wanted to paint landscapes or portraits, or to study Eskimo music, botany, glaciers or what not.

Once he had permission to enter the country, however, everything was even simpler than if he had wanted to visit Denmark, to which Greenland belongs. He would sail to Greenland on an official ship; his passage would cost nothing, and he would pay only

"The sun was shining on the sea,
Shining with all his might. . . .
And this was odd, because it was
The middle of the night."
THROUGH THE LOOKING GLASS

The midnight sun lights these icy waters.
U.S. ARMY SIGNAL CORPS PHOTO

a small amount for his meals.

The chief purpose of the Danes in keeping visitors away from Greenland was to try to keep out contagious diseases. They also wanted to preserve the native way of life, so that the people would eat the seals they could catch instead of wanting to import beef; would eat their own fish instead of demanding canned sardines and anchovies; and would dress in their own fashion from their own materials instead of demanding clothes from the outside world.

Everyone seems to agree, however, that the Greenlanders have increased in numbers, while their Eskimo cousins in Alaska and Canada have been decreasing; that the Greenlanders are healthier, better educated, more self-supporting and, as a result, more self-respecting.

Today there is a strong group in Denmark that wants Greenland opened to the world, but the island is still difficult to enter.

Greenland is so long that if its northern edge were in Canada near Winnipeg, its southern tip would be down in the Gulf of

Greenlanders read fishing, weather and political news in the weekly paper founded in 1860.

Cutting blocks of gleaming white marble in the quarries at Marmorilik, in north Greenland.

Mexico. It is so wide that if it were set on top of the eastern United States it would spread all the way from the Atlantic seaboard to the Mississippi.

Except around the edges, most of Greenland is covered by a tremendous ice cap, which is called the inland ice. This is the only ice cap of great size in the Northern Hemisphere and it covers more than four-fifths of the island. Curiously enough, the northern end of Greenland has no ice cap at all. In summer, northern Greenland, called Peary Land, is one of the largest snow-free areas on the island.

In many sections, the inland ice is like a great, solid river ponderously making its way to the sea, where it breaks off to float away as icebergs. There are other parts of the coast where the distance from sea to inland ice is nearly two hundred miles.

Between high, rocky banks, narrow inlets of the sea, called fiords, penetrate far inland from the coasts. Great icebergs, breaking off in the fiords, reach the open ocean after a journey of many miles. The only part of Greenland where few or no icebergs are produced is the north coast.

One of the coldest spots in the world may be in the interior of Greenland. The coasts are lower and warmer. The famous New England explorer, Donald B. MacMillan, spent one of his many Arctic winters on the coast of Greenland, eight hundred miles north of the Arctic Circle. The coldest temperature he recorded that year was 37° below zero. During World War II, airplanes took off again and again from Maine airports where it was colder than at the Greenland bases where they landed.

Greenland's coastal weather is changeable —sunny one minute and cloudy the next. One of its surprises is a mighty wind called the foehn. Although this wind comes down from the inland ice, the temperature, instead of growing colder as you might suppose, becomes much warmer. Greenland is famous as a weather-maker, and her weather is of great importance in predicting weather on the North Atlantic and in western Europe.

There are no proper forests in Greenland, but there are clumps of willow and alder. Some of these trees reach a height of thirty feet. The island is not a farming country in the ordinary sense, though sheep do very well. In parts of the island some vegetables may be grown during the short summer.

Wild flowers bloom with great brilliance during their brief season. As for bird life, some sixty species are native. The animals include the reindeer, polar bear, ermine, Arctic fox, white hare, wolf and musk-ox.

Today, most of the twenty thousand people who live in Greenland are either pure Eskimos or are descendants of whites and Eskimos. Some people think of all these people as Eskimos; others call those who are half white or more, "Greenlanders." However, as time goes on, the name "Greenlanders" seems to be given to more and more of the inhabitants. Perhaps after a while all will be given that name except recent immigrants. At present there are about five hundred of these immigrants, most of them Danes in civil service. There are also a few outsiders. For instance, during World War II the United States set up a number of air bases in Greenland, and some of these were maintained after the close of the war.

The Greenland Administration, a bureau of the Danish Government, governs the island. The official language of the country is

Wrinkled by wind and weather, lighted by laughter, strengthened by sorrow, the faces of these Greenlandic women of Upernavik might have been painted by some old Flemish or Dutch master.

Eskimo, for Denmark, as we have seen, encourages the islanders' native speech and ways. The Soviet Union has, in this respect, a like policy toward the Eskimos of northeastern Siberia. By way of contrast, in Alaska, English is the language of the schools where Eskimo children go. In Canada it is English or French. Many Greenland Eskimos speak Danish as a second language; many Siberian Eskimos speak Russian.

Sheep Whose Ancestors Crossed the Northern Seas

Most Greenlanders still live by hunting and fishing, as they have done for centuries. However, in 1915, the Danes brought 170 sheep from Iceland to Greenland. The sheep prospered—perhaps even better than in Iceland—so that in twenty years there were 7,000 that fed out most of the winter. Dairy cattle have been brought in, too, but they need longer stabling and more hay.

It is not certain whether Greenland was discovered first by American Indians or by European whites. The Eskimos, who are one sort of North American Indian, may have arrived there between 3,000 and 1,500 years ago. Greenland may have been seen by the British several hundred years before Christ; or, in the fourth century B.C., by Pytheas, a Greek who was one of the greatest explorers that ever lived. It is possible, too, that Greenland was known to the Irish in the fifth and sixth centuries of our era. Ancient books, however, do not mention this great island until around 900, when Gunnbjörn, an immigrant from Norway, sighted land to the west or northwest of Iceland.

The first exploration of Greenland known to history was made by Eric the Red, who was born in Norway but became a citizen of Iceland. Eric left Norway as a child with the family of his outlawed father. Then, in his turn, Eric was outlawed from Iceland. He decided to spend the three years of his exile in exploring the "land seen by Gunnbjörn." So he spent the seasons 982–985 exploring, probably as far north as Disko, on the west coast some two hundred miles north of the Circle.

Between coasting voyages the Eric party spent the winters, it seems, about as if they had been at home in Iceland. They built barns for their sheep and cattle, made hay and sheared the sheep for woolen clothes. They hunted and fished little, for the Icelanders of that day were pastoral in their ways.

It was apparently during the third winter that Eric made the decision, recorded in ERIC'S SAGA, to try to secure colonists to settle the country. For this reason he decided to give the great island a fair name, Green Land, so that "people might all the more desire to settle there."

Eric returned to Iceland in the autumn of 985. He turned out to be such a good promoter that, in the fall of 986, he was able to land again on the southwest coast of Greenland with fourteen ships carrying about thirty persons each. That adds up to more than four hundred colonists—a band larger than those which more than six hundred years later founded Jamestown, Virginia, and Plymouth, Massachusetts.

The Icelanders in Greenland found themselves in a country much like the one they had left. They had brought with them their farm animals and methods of animal husbandry. Their cattle, sheep, horses, pigs and chickens did well. From the start, the colonists carried on a brisk trade with Europe, especially Norway.

There Were Churches in Greenland Nine Hundred Years Ago

The settlers in Greenland adopted Christianity in the year 1000; by the twelfth century there were sixteen churches as well as a convent and a monastery. For several centuries the Greenlanders were in touch with Europe. At last, however, this contact was lost and the Greenlanders were left to themselves. Just what became of them is not wholly clear. The colonists began to do less and less farming and more and more hunting. For a hunting people in the Arctic the Eskimo way of life is better than the European, so the whites gradually abandoned their European ways. They moved north, where the hunting is better than in the south; and they left their churches, some of which may still be seen though in ruins.

When the Danes took possession of Greenland in 1722, they met only what looked like the savagery of the North American Indians of those days. It would seem, however, that most of the people of Greenland have in their veins some of the blood of the 10,000 Scandinavians who were living there between 1100 and 1200, at the height of the colony's European-style prosperity.

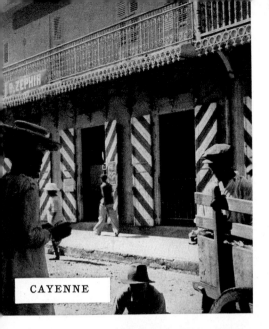

CAYENNE

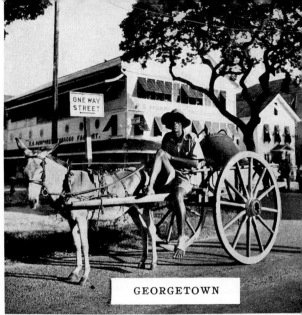

GEORGETOWN

THE GUIANAS
SHINING TOWNS AND STORIED JUNGLES

By ALFRED MÉTRAUX
Author and Anthropologist

WHEN the Americas were first discovered, Spain claimed exclusive rights to the whole New World. The other European nations were not at all convinced by these claims, and set about ignoring them to the best of their ability. Within a few years the French, English and Dutch were busily trying to grasp a share of the Spanish Main by force of arms. Today all that is left of the empire each tried to found on the mainland of South America are three sleepy countries: French, Dutch and British Guiana. Not long ago even these were looked upon as unprofitable nuisances.

The adventurers of the sixteenth century, however, thought the dark jungles of Guiana concealed fabulous wealth. Somewhere inland they believed they would find El Dorado, the Golden, and the treasure city of Manoa, about which Sir Walter Raleigh wrote, ". . . . . for the greatness of its riches, and for the excellent seate, it far exceedeth any of the world." Manoa was sup-

PARAMARIBO

posed to stand on the shore of Lake Parime, a body "of salt water 200 leagues long." Raleigh risked and lost both his fortune and his life in the quest for Manoa and its gold. Indeed, it was not until the nineteenth century that the great scientist Friedrich von Humboldt finally proved that Manoa existed only in dream, and that the lake was merely a dry plain, occasionally flooded in the rainy season.

The Dutch Gave Up Manhattan for Tropical Guiana

The low, fever-ridden Guiana coast promised wealth of a different kind to the Dutch, French and English planters who settled there in the seventeenth century. They raised tobacco and sugar-cane. The Dutch originally occupied what is today British Guiana, while the English landed in the present Dutch Guiana (also called Surinam). The Netherlands must have found Guiana a profitable colony, for they thought they had made a good bargain when, in 1667, they traded away the little island of Manhattan and their settlements along the Hudson River for their present colony of Surinam. Much of the prosperity of Dutch Guiana was due to the efforts of Portuguese Jews who had found a haven there.

During the eighteenth-century wars between England, France and the Netherlands, the colonies passed from hand to hand. At last, in 1816, they were divided among the three powers. England received the lion's share, about 90,000 square miles. Holland got about 54,000 square miles, and France about 35,000 square miles.

The Capitals of the Three Guianas Are All on the Coast

The colonies share the same climate and resources. The narrow coastal belt of each is covered with marshes and lagoons, crisscrossed by rivers and creeks, choked with sand bars and mangrove trees. In such surroundings the Dutch made ready use of their long experience with dikes and canals. The three capitals—Georgetown (British), Paramaribo (Dutch) and Cayenne (French) —are all on the coast.

None of these three cities is very large, and the white population of all of them is quite small. Curiously enough, each of the capitals reminds the visitor very much of the far-off European lands to which they be-

long, in spite of their tropical setting. Georgetown, on the Demerara River, is a gleaming white city garlanded with green foliage, but the Gothic towers of church and market, the many playing fields for cricket, football and hockey, the tennis courts and the golf course might have been transplanted from Surrey or Kent. It has a population of about 73,000.

Paramaribo is a Dutch city, with its solid, spotless buildings, spacious squares and straight canals. Its broad streets, paved with finely crushed shells, are lined with tall trees that form green arches overhead. Paramaribo is also on a tidal river, the Surinam, and its population is about 71,000.

The Many-colored City of Cayenne Nestles among Its Gardens

The capital of French Guiana, Cayenne, is situated on an island in a river—both named Cayenne. It is much smaller than the other two capitals; about 12,000 population. It is a town of many gardens, and the houses are painted in colors as bright as the tropical flowers. Indeed, many of the houses have each story painted a different shade—light blue, dark blue, yellow, red or rose. Like the other two capitals, Cayenne is a seaport, but the harbor is so shallow that vessels that draw more than fourteen feet of water must anchor six miles out and unload passengers and cargo by means of small boats and lighters.

About fifteen to fifty miles inland, the ground begins to rise and gradually lifts up into a chain of mountains and plateaus. The rounded summits and hills of the Tumuc-Humac, which separate French and Dutch Guiana from Brazil, are a largely unexplored country. The rivers of this region are shown on maps as dotted lines, so little is known about them. The Carib and Tupi-Guarani Indians there live and die much as their ancestors did before the discovery of America. At the western edge of British Guiana, Mount Roraima, with its perpendicular reddish cliffs, towers like a natural fortress, 8,600 feet above the rolling savannas and jungles. Conan Doyle used this as the setting for his LOST WORLD, with its prehistoric monsters.

Deep tropical forest covers most of the Guiana uplands. The rivers are the only gateways to the interior. Everywhere there is an unbroken range of gigantic trees, whose leaves are so thick that the sun can not pierce them. Creepers passing from trunk to trunk and over the tree tops mat the whole forest together. The air is heavy with a strong, sweet scent. In the swamps grow thick palm groves, and the brooks are lined with tall ferns. Everywhere orchids bloom on the ground and in the trees.

The jungle hides countless birds. Now and then a cock-of-the-rock or a parrot flashes by like a fireball. Peccaries, tapirs, jaguars and other animals, large and small, lurk everywhere, hidden from the eyes of all but the most expert hunters. Fish swarm in the rivers, but fishing is dangerous. Man-eating pirai, paralyzing electric eels and sting rays are a constant menace to the unwary.

The rivers are almost the only routes for travel, and these are not open ways. Except in their lower courses, they are continually blocked by rapids and falls. Canoes must be hauled through the rapids with ropes, or dragged over paths hacked out of the jungle. Short railways now connect the navigable stretches of some rivers in British Guiana.

One of the greatest waterfalls in the world is in British Guiana. It is the Kaieteur, formed by the Potaro River as it drops 822 feet from a cliff. The foaming curtain of water, 370 feet wide, the tremendous sand-

A native woman fishes for her lunch from a two-hundred-year-old sea wall in British Guiana.

EVELYN DE LONG FROM THREE LIONS

stone walls, and the tropical forest create a scene of unequaled magnificence. In several regions of the interior uplands there are beautiful rolling savannas, covered with tall grasses and clumps of trees.

Because of the weakening effect of the climate, the Guianas have attracted few European colonists. The temperature remains almost constant throughout the year at about 80°, and the humidity at about 60 per cent. In the British colony only about 3 per cent of the people are white. Man-power has always been a problem.

The colonists first tried to enslave the Indians, but here as elswhere they failed in their purpose. The Indians preferred to die, and soon the planters gave up the attempt.

On the whole, the destiny of the Indians in the Guianas has been better than in the Spanish and Portuguese colonies. There are about 14,500 of them today, and they are allowed to live more or less as they please. Though they use the white man's guns and

some tools and goods, they are still as good Caribs and Arawaks as in the days of Sir Walter Raleigh. To the Guiana Indians science owes the knowledge of curare, a mysterious poison which has become most important in medical research.

In the early colonial days, the planters brought in Negro slaves to solve the manpower problem; and for a long time Paramaribo was one of the great slave markets of the Caribbean. Here were brought many cargoes of Africans, mostly from Nigeria, Dahomey and the Gold Coast. Many of these Negroes preferred the jungle to the cruel plantation life, and thousands escaped into the interior, where they founded villages on hidden creeks. In time these bush Negroes became a serious threat to the planters. Troops were sent against them, and from 1726 until 1777 constant war was waged. Finally, however, the Dutch were forced to grant them their liberty. Their descendants, called Djuka, or bush Negroes, number

Contrasting scenes in Dutch Guiana: a bauxite factory at Moengo that furnishes the raw material for our aluminum, and a group of Djuka with the drums their ancestors brought from Africa.

about 19,000 today. They still keep their dearly bought independence, though their *granmans* (chiefs) must be approved by the Dutch authorities.

The Djuka speak the Takeetakee tonga, a language which has an English vocabulary with some Dutch and Portuguese words added, and which is spoken according to the rules of African grammar. Because most of the Djuka Negroes ran away to the jungle soon after they were brought over, their descendants have kept many of their original customs and beliefs. In some ways the Djuka Negroes are closer to seventeenth-century Africa than are their modern cousins there. They still worship many of the old African gods, such as the Sky God and the Earth Mother. The tales they tell are the same as those still heard in the great forests of the African coast. Up to the present they have kept their great skill as wood-carvers, but they have developed a tradition of their own. They still make wooden idols. They also make handsome trays, seats, combs and other wooden objects which they cover with symbolic designs in raised carving. One of their favorite subjects is the serpent.

After slavery was done away with in 1863, Hindu and Javanese and some Chinese laborers were brought to the Guianas. Today the Hindus form the largest single racial group in the area. A person who wanders through the streets of Georgetown or Paramaribo meets members of most of the races of mankind.

When the Eyes of the World Were Focused on French Guiana

French Guiana acquired a bad reputation because of a special type of colonist. In 1854 it was made a convict settlement. Every criminal in France who was sentenced to more than ten years' imprisonment was deported to Devil's Island, or to Saint Laurent du Maroni on the mainland. So harsh was the life of these prisoners that French Guiana came to be called the "dry guillotine." Nevertheless, many convicts escaped into the jungle, and after incredible adventures a few were able to reach Venezuela or Panama.

In 1894 the eyes of the whole world turned toward Devil's Island. A French army officer, Captain Alfred Dreyfus, through an error of justice, was sentenced to end his days there. Many people in France took up his cause, and a struggle took place that al-

EVELYN DE LONG FROM THREE LIONS

A town crier, once a convict, beats his drum and tells the news in the streets of Cayenne.

most caused a revolution in France before he was set free five years later. In 1946 the French Government abolished the penal settlement, and the following year French Guiana was made a regular department of the French Republic.

The resources of modern science can do much to create better living conditions in the Guianas. If this is done, and if settlers can be drawn to the old colonies, some of the dreams of the first adventurers may yet come true. The Guiana upland is a continuation of the Brazilian plateau, which is rich in gold and diamonds. The export of gold is already quite important, and in the year 1936 a million dollars' worth of diamonds came from British Guiana.

More important than gems or precious metals is Guiana bauxite, the ore from which much of the aluminum used in the United States and Canada is made. There are also many other products which may some day become sources of wealth: rosins, gums, timber, cabinet woods and, above all, balata, from which beltings for machines are made. The treasures of the Guianas are greater than Sir Walter Raleigh himself imagined, but El Dorado can be created only by using science, courage and hard work.

209

GUIDED MISSILES

•

PRESENT AND FUTURE

By WILLY LEY

AUTHOR OF *Rockets and Space Travel*

I T used to be the usual thing, after the end of a war, for the officers and men who fought in it to fill the military magazines with personal recollections, telling first-hand stories of battles lost or won.

This time it is different. True enough, the magazines for professional soldiers and for the reserves still have many things to say about past battles. Yet a surprising amount of space is now given, not to the past, but to the future. In talking about the future, in trying to see what may be coming, one of the main topics is a new military instrument that came into use toward the end of the second World War—the missile.

According to the dictionary, a missile is a weapon thrown, or designed to be thrown. As far as this definition goes, a coconut heaved by one monkey at another monkey is as much a missile as a V-2 rocket fired against a target two hundred miles away.

Military men have a different definition. In their language, there are a good many things that a missile is *not*. For instance, to a military man, a projectile fired from an artillery piece is not a missile. Neither is a 4.5-inch bombardment rocket, which is used in the same manner as a 4.5-inch howitzer. Neither is a bomb dropped from an airplane.

On the whole, military men think of offensive weapons as falling into four classes:

1. Guns
2. Rockets
3. Airplane bombs
4. Missiles

Class 4 is not very definite. It just contains things that do not fall into one of the first three.

A missile has to be an offensive weapon. Nobody would think of calling a naval mine a missile. On the other hand, a naval torpedo *is* a missile, and the fact that it is not usually regarded as one is only because naval torpedoes have been around for half a century.

Some airplane bombs are missiles in the military sense, which puts them in Class 4 instead of in 3. Many missiles are rocket-propelled, or will be, and yet do not belong in Class 2. The thing that really distinguishes the missile from all other weapons is the possibility of guiding it.

Once an artillery shell has left the muzzle of its gun barrel, the artillery man who pulled the lanyard has no control over it any more.

Once a firing button for a battery of bombardment rockets has been pressed, there is nothing the gunnery officer can do about it any more.

Once the bombardier in an airplane has pulled the release and the bombs are tumbling out of the bomb bay, he can not influence them any more.

Missiles, however, can be more or less guided while they are traveling on their way. There are some airplane bombs where this is possible and consequently such bombs are missiles, not just bombs.

There is, for example, a bomb called Azon. After releasing this bomb, the bombardier can influence its trajectory—that is, the curve that it makes in space. He can guide it to some extent to the right or to the left of the path that it would have taken without guidance. In a later model of this bomb, the Razon, the bombardier can also influence the range.

One missile that was in use in the Pacific

How fast will a guided missile fly? Will its flight be straight and true? To find out, new models are tested in the high-speed wind tunnels at Aberdeen Proving Ground, Maryland.

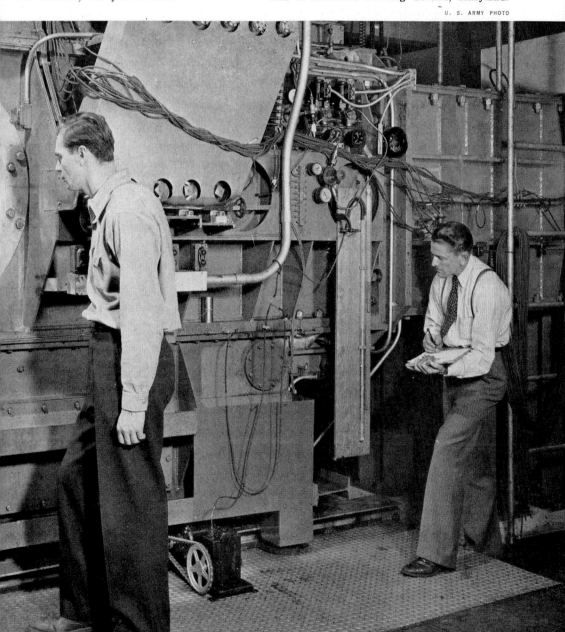

against Japanese shipping was the Bat, so-called from its shape. The Bat was a kind of small, unmanned airplane. It consisted mostly of a bomb, which was the body, with wings and guiding surfaces attached to it. When it swooped down on a Japanese ship like a fast glider, the bombardier could flatten or steepen its path, or make it move sideways, or both.

These three missiles did not have anything to propel them except gravity. They traveled with speed and force because they had been carried aloft by an airplane and were released from a height considerably above that of the target. This is an important point because it shows that a missile does not need to have any special kind of propulsion in order to be classified as a missile. What counts is the guidance, not the propulsion. Almost as if to prove this point, the Germans produced a missile, the Hs-293, that operated very much like the Bat, but had a rocket unit for propulsion.

Missiles can have all kinds of shapes. They may look like bombs or like small airplanes. They may look like torpedoes or even like slender blimps. They may have any kind of propulsion: gravity, gasoline engines, turbojets, ramjets or rockets.

Military men classify missiles according to their use. If a missile like the German V-1 (or the U. S. Navy's Loon, which is an improved V-1) were on the drafting boards today, the officer in charge of the project would refer to it as a GTG missile, meaning ground-to-ground. If it were intended for use from aircraft carriers, the classification would read STS, meaning ship-to-shore.

A missile such as the Bat and the German Hs-293 would be classified as ATG (air-to-ground), although the Navy would be likely to write ATS (air-to-ship). A missile that is to be sent up to intercept enemy bombers or enemy V-1's would be called GTA (ground-to-air). The German V-2 was a GTG or possibly an STS missile.

Warhead with Wings—the German V-1 Flying Bomb

Let's look first at the German V-1 flying bomb. It had the general shape of an airplane, with a fuselage 25.4 feet long and a wingspread of 17.7 feet. The purpose of this missile was to carry a 2,200-pound bomb over a distance of about 150 miles. The bomb is called a warhead, a term used first

for the explosive charge of the naval torpedo.

The guidance of the V-1 was built in. It was simply a robot pilot that was set to keep the missile on a straight course and at a certain altitude—high enough to clear all natural or artificial obstacles in its path.

For the propulsion of the V-1, the Germans developed a kind of intermittent jet engine called an impulse duct or pulsejet. In order to do its job, however, the missile might have been powered by an ordinary airplane engine or by practically any kind of jet engine. In fact, American engineers had been working in 1918 on a 400-mile missile of just this type, powered by a Liberty engine, one of the early American airplane engines. The chief reason why the Germans chose the impulse duct was that it was much cheaper to make in quantity than either aircraft engines or turbojets.

Taking Their Oxygen with Them, True Rockets Can Fly High

After the flying bomb came the V-2, which was a true rocket. The thing that makes a rocket different from all other kinds of missiles is the fact that it carries its own oxygen, and so can go up to high altitudes where the atmosphere is very thin. Engines that depend on the oxygen in the atmosphere can not operate at anything like such heights.

The take-off weight of the V-2 rocket is 15 short tons or about 13 long tons. It was designed to carry a warhead weighing one long ton over a distance of about 200 miles. To do this job, the rocket had to take off vertically and stay on a vertical path for the first ten miles or so. Then it was slowly tilted in the direction of the target to an angle of 45°. The guidance consisted in supplying instruments and servo mechanisms (small motors operating the fins) that would cause the proper tilt at the proper time.

The guidance was sketchy and somewhat crude in both the V-1 flying bomb and the V-2 long-range rocket. The robot pilot could not deal with emergencies. For example, in several cases, V-1 bombs were damaged by English fighter-plane fire and began circling round aimlessly until their fuel supply was exhausted. One or two even turned around and flew back to the German-held French coast where the Germans then had to shoot down their own missiles.

Things must have gone wrong with the V-2 rockets, too, because the German firing reports and the British reports about impacts do not agree at all. It is certain that about 20 per cent of the V-2's fired against London did not get there—but nobody knows what happened to them. The robot mechanism may have failed to produce the proper tilt. If so, the rocket, instead of rising to an altitude of some 70 miles and traveling a horizontal distance of 200 miles, may have risen as high as 100 miles and crashed some thirty miles from the firing point into the sea, unobserved by either Germans or English.

It is clear that one would want to guide a guided missile for the whole length of its flight, or at least for the greater part of it. The Germans had an example of this type too—the Rheintochter, which means Rhine-maiden. This was an anti-aircraft rocket or, as it would now be called, a GTA (ground-to-air) missile.

Rheintochter was to be used against American Flying Fortresses. The principle was to use two radar beams, one to follow the airplane to be shot down and one to follow the missile. By co-ordination of these two radar beams the missile was to be guided to the airplane, ending in the destruction of both. This particular weapon, however, was never used. The Germans probably ran into too many practical difficulties.

Missiles with Humans to Guide Them— That Was the Kamikaze Way

The Japanese overcame the difficulties of guidance from a distance in their own peculiar manner—they simply piloted their missiles. Their so-called Kamikaze squadrons were nothing but suicide squadrons. While the Japanese used many types of planes for Kamikaze attacks, they also developed for this purpose a special missile that became known as the Baka bomb. It was much like a German V-1 except for two points: The Baka was rocket-propelled and was launched from the air, where it was carried underneath a larger bombing plane. It was interesting to find that the Germans, too, had developed a type of V-1 to be guided by a pilot, but could not use it because they could not find volunteers.

At this moment it is not at all certain just what use missiles may find in a future war. In fact, that is the question that takes up much space in the military journals. One can be sure of only a few principles.

OFFICIAL U. S. NAVY PHOTO

Bat bomb, carried under the wing of a U. S. Navy Privateer. Radar guides such bombs.

There is little doubt that there will be anti-aircraft or GTA missiles. These might be either medium-sized rockets, say twenty-five feet long with a take-off weight of three or four tons, or small, unmanned jet planes taking off with the aid of rocket boosters.

It is quite likely that these missiles will be equipped with "seeking" devices, which means robot pilots that are "excited" by something. For instance, one may imagine a robot pilot that will make the missile that carries it follow the *sound* of an aircraft engine. Or one that will make its missile follow the *heat* of an aircraft engine, especially a jet engine with a nice, hot exhaust. Or one may imagine a robot pilot that works with a radarscope, and just makes a bee line for anything that appears in that scope. When it gets close enough to the center of attraction, the missile would be exploded by a proximity fuse.

It is less likely that ground-to-air missiles will be guided from the ground in the manner tried by the Germans with their Rheintochter. Such an experiment might work well when you have just one target plane and one missile in the air at the same time. It is a different story when there are hundreds of planes overhead and dozens of missiles in the air, for the radar beams would cross-splash all over the place, confusing both the equipment and its operators.

213

GUIDED MISSILES

For their weight, missiles have great range and power. At sea, the missile has one chief advantage over guns. A ship can carry missiles that are the equal of guns much too large for that ship. For example, the warhead of a V-1 flying bomb weighs about as much as a projectile for a 16-inch naval rifle. The bomb has a range of 150 miles. The 16-inch rifle has a range of only about 30 miles. It needs a full-fledged battleship to carry 16-inch rifles, but a V-1 flying bomb could be fired from a destroyer or even from a submarine if these vessels were properly equipped.

On land, things happen to be much more complicated than at sea, simply because it is land. Suppose two battle fleets 150 miles apart open fire at each other with missiles. The chances are that there will be nothing but water in the space between the fleets. Over 150 miles of ground, however, many interceptor units of the enemy may be hidden.

For this reason, it seems there is not too much use for guided missiles in and near the battle lines themselves. Anything within a range of ten miles is a good target for artillery fire (which is highly accurate); for area-beating by bombardment rockets (which are not accurate but thorough); and for assault by hedge-hopping planes. Within the combat zone, the only guided missiles that could possibly be useful might be some very accurate air-to-ground missiles such as the Azon and Razon bombs, provided that the enemy can not interfere with their guiding.

The realm of the missile is likely to begin beyond the immediate combat zone, from 50 to about 250 miles. What missiles can be used for these ranges? The airplane-like flying bomb. The long-range rocket of the general design of V-2. And, of course, either bombs or air-to-ground missiles carried by ordinary bombardment aircraft.

Which is most practical? This can be decided only from case to case. Each one has a number of drawbacks and limitations.

In the case of the ordinary bomber, the bombs are cheap but the airplane is not. The bomber might have to have fighter cover, and the safety of the crew manning the bomber must be considered.

The flying bomb and the long-range rocket have the great advantage that they are not piloted and have no crews whose lives might be lost. Furthermore, they are never

Testing a Loon, an improved V-1, at the **Naval Air Missile Test Center, Point Mugu, California.**

grounded by bad weather. They are an all-weather air force.

A missile of the V-1 type is comparatively cheap. Yet it has the disadvantage of being limited to altitudes where the air is dense enough to give lifting power to its wings. It can be reached by defending fighter airplanes, which can climb to the same altitude and fire away at it, and the missile can not even shoot back. These missiles are also within the range of anti-aircraft fire.

The German V-1's suffered heavy losses because of having to fly so low. Only one out of four reached London, the target city. That figure, however, is misleading and makes the performance of the V-1 sound better than it really was. One out of four is the figure for the whole V-1 assault. It includes the first days of the attack when there were few counter-measures. In the last days of the V-1 assault, after the proper counter-batteries had been set up, only one flying bomb out of twenty slipped through the defenses.

Can Missiles of the V-1 Type Be Made a Great Deal Better?

It is possible to improve this type of missile in a number of ways. One would be to increase its speed. The first V-1's had a speed of about 350 miles per hour. It is more difficult to hit a faster missile, although the advantage is not so great as one might think.

Another improvement would be a dodging device in the robot pilot, so that the missile would suddenly change its direction (left, right, up or down) when a defending fighter plane came near. However, if the missile is kept dodging for a long time it would fail to reach its target because it would use up its supply of fuel. Moreover, the dodging device would have to be so good that the robot pilot would return to its original course after each dodge.

Another possibility would be to forget about robot pilots and to install a television sender instead, so that the missile could be guided by an operator who remains on the ground. This sounds wonderful, I know. Yet it would give the enemy a chance to interfere not only with the missile itself but also with the television transmission.

The long-range rocket is superior to the flying bomb in every respect except one. It is almost as expensive as a manned airplane. A German V-1 cost about 850 man-hours of work to build; a V-2 rocket, 13,000.

A V-2 can not be intercepted with any great amount of success. It shoots up to heights where the atmosphere is too thin to support the very best airplane wing. Because of carrying its own oxygen, the V-2 rocket goes far beyond the reach of missiles or planes that depend on the oxygen in the air. On its way down it falls more or less vertically at speeds of about a half mile per second. Probably there will be interception missiles in the future, but some rockets will come through. And if they carry atomic warheads, only one needs to get through.

The Bigger the Long-Range Rocket, the Costlier It Grows

There are limitations to the long-range rocket. The only type that can be mass-produced in a hurry, if necessary, is the V-2, which has a range of 200 miles. The rocket A4-b, also a German development, was a V-2 with short, stubby wings. It traveled a slanted, instead of a nearly vertical, downward path. This rocket had a range of 300 miles, but it was not used during the war. For longer ranges, the rocket would have to be very large and would be just that much more expensive and difficult to handle. All this means that rockets will be the rarer the bigger they are.

Greater range also means less accuracy, for naturally a rocket becomes less accurate the longer the distance it has to travel. Guiding from the ground by radar is possible. Yet radar beams, like light-waves, travel in straight lines, and the horizon gets in the way rather soon. As a result, guiding over very long ranges would have to be done to a large extent from bases between take-off point and target. These bases would, of course, be closer to the enemy; and if the bases can be that much closer, the rockets could, in many cases, be fired from them in the first place.

We can draw four conclusions about the use of guided missiles in the near future.

1. The most promising use of missiles is over long ranges.

2. The most promising long-range missile is the long-range rocket.

3. It will probably be a good while before the range of the long-range rocket increases beyond eight hundred miles.

4. The long-range rocket, because of its small warhead, can be decisive only if it can be made to carry an atomic bomb.

HURRICANES are always big news. Each year hurricane experts are at their wit's end to forecast the unusual behavior of some of the storms that reach our coasts. Recently, however, scientists have managed to pry much deeper into the secret places of the hurricane to find out what makes it behave as it does. A group of scientists flew in B-29 airplanes into the heart of the worst hurricane of 1947, passing back and forth, underneath and above the top of the great cloud system that made up the storm. They were "taking its pulse" and finding out what made its heart beat. They carefully measured delicate changes in temperature, pressure and wind force, all through the hurricane. It was dangerous work. They stuck the nose of their plane into dark ugly clouds which were sometimes more than six miles above the earth's surface. No one knew whether the plane could stand the strain. The scientists felt that it was worth taking the risk, however, for they wanted to find out what the upper part of a hurricane is like. They were fairly certain that it is this upper part which determines the size of the storm and its path.

We know from early records that hurricanes caused death and destruction in the Western Hemisphere long before white men came. When Columbus first set foot in the New World, he found Indians who worshiped a fearful deity named Hunrakan, god of the big wind. According to the Indian legend, when Hunrakan was angry, he sent his mon-

hurricane is going and such a storm sometimes strikes quite suddenly. The hurricane's power to destroy is probably greater than any other force known to man, except possibly the tornado. It has been estimated that the energy of destructive winds in a large hurricane is greater than the energy stored in twenty atomic bombs. (In a hurricane, of course, the energy is spread out over many miles and could never do the damage of even one atomic bomb.) It has happened twice in India that with one sweep along a coastline a hurricane has drowned more than 150,000 people. In 1900 more than 5,000 people lost their lives in this way in Galveston, Texas.

For many years now the Government has assigned to special agents from the United States Weather Bureau the duty of tracking down this Public Enemy No. 1. They study his behavior in order to learn more about his next moves, and then send out warnings of his whereabouts. Hurricanes have been difficult to study because until lately they could be examined scientifically only from the surface of the earth. Now that we can fly right into their very hearts, we can learn much more about them.

Have you ever been in a hurricane? If you have, you will probably agree with one man who described such a storm as "a lot of wind going somewhere in an awful hurry." Actually, a hurricane is a huge whirlpool of cloud and air moving swiftly in a spiral around a small central area known as the "eye" of the storm. The eye is a curious con-

looking down on a
HURRICANE!

sters of wind and raging seas to kill or destroy those with whom he was displeased. Columbus himself was caught in one of these severe storms near the West Indies. Since then many of these violent West Indian storms have been reported. In time they came to be known as hurricanes, after the old Indian god, Hunrakan.

The hurricane is one of Mother Nature's "bad boys." It is hard to predict where a

trast to the rest of the hurricane. It is usually cloudless and within it the air is serenely calm, undisturbed and almost indifferent, it would seem, to the fury surrounding it. The hurricane as a whole is often very wide, 500 miles or more of whirling streams of air. An ordinary hurricane would cover an area the size of Alabama and Mississippi combined. The stronger and more dangerous winds are near the center, next to the eye, and gen-

By R. H. SIMPSON

*United States Weather Bureau,
Washington, D. C.*

erally extend outward less than 150 miles. The eye is small in comparison, usually covering an area less than 30 miles wide.

These great storms form in the Caribbean Sea or in the tropical part of the Atlantic Ocean between the West Indies and Africa. As the hurricane grows in size, the wind whirling around the center reaches speeds of 75 to 100 miles an hour, or even more. The entire whirlpool of air usually drifts slowly westward at first, but later turns northward, sweeping into the Gulf of Mexico or up the Atlantic Coast. Most of its life is spent over open water. When it moves inland, the eye is destroyed and the whirl gradually disappears, leaving behind only cloud and rain. The forward movement of the storm, as a whole, is usually slow compared to the speed of the whirling winds within it. It ordinarily arrives at a coastline moving only 10 to 20 miles an hour, like a spinning top edging slowly across a sloping floor.

Let us imagine that you are watching a

Hurricane ahoy! Observers 30,000 feet above sea level in a B-29 look into a big blow.

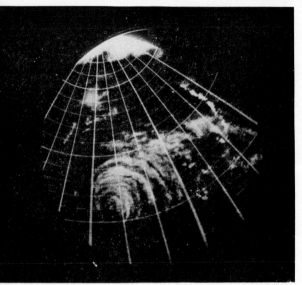

Picture of hurricane on plane's radar screen shows storm in relation to islands and coast.

hurricane as it passes directly over your town. First, the sky is covered with clouds and little showers quickly come and go. The wind begins to blow gustily from the northeast or the north. Then the rain comes down harder and the showers last longer as the wind blows faster and faster from the same direction. First the wind bends the trees over at a sharp angle. Then it strips branches off. Other trees are completely uprooted. Timbers are carried through the air, shingles are ripped off roofs, and some roofs are even lifted right off the houses. The rain finally comes down in torrents and streaks out into horizontal sheets, blown by the wind. Suddenly the wind dies down, the rain stops and the sun pops through the clouds. You breathe a sigh of relief and rush outdoors to look at the damage.

If you are really hurricane-wise, you realize that the storm is only half over, and that you are now in the center—the eye of the storm. In thirty or forty minutes the sun will again disappear and the wind will return with all its fury. This time, however, it will be blowing from the opposite direction, from the south or southwest. For the next few hours things will happen exactly as they did before the center of the storm struck you— but with one difference. Everything will be in reverse order, with the storm gradually

slowing down and the clouds slowly breaking up.

If a storm can be so violent at the earth's surface, how bad will it be two, four, or six miles above? Because they did not know the answer to this question, airplane pilots were careful to keep away from hurricanes before 1943. In that year the United States Air Force, in a daring flight over the Gulf of Mexico, proved that a fairly small plane could be flown through a hurricane and come out still in one piece. In 1944 and 1945 many flights into hurricanes were made, but mostly for the purpose of locating the storm centers for weather forecasters. The planes which made these trips generally flew only at low levels and were not equipped to make scientific studies of the storms.

In 1946 a high-flying B-29 plane was sent out to explore a hurricane. It made history by climbing up on top of the storm clouds, although its crew could make only limited measurements of the inside of the storm. The complete picture of the hurricane, from top to bottom, was beginning to take shape in the minds of scientists, although many details were still lacking. The flight of this B-29 proved that at last a plane had been built which could fly into every nook and cranny of a hurricane to explore its many secrets. Plans were made at that time to explore thoroughly the first big hurricane of 1947, whenever it might come.

I was privileged to help plan some of these operations and to take part in several of the flights. The flights were to be from Bermuda, an island far out in the Atlantic Ocean, where a number of new B-29's were based. These planes were specially rebuilt for the purpose of making weather observations and they contained every kind of existing weather instrument that could be used in flight. The plastic nose, originally designed for the bombardier, had been converted into a magnificent weather observatory.

Radar's Magic Eye Sees Through Clouds and Haze

The most important piece of weather equipment aboard the plane was the radar. With this instrument one could "see" through cloud and haze for scores of miles ahead. We could "see" islands and coastlines, and tell how far the sea was below the plane. Most important of all, the hurricane, with all its tentacles of cloud and rain, together with its cloudless eye, could be viewed clearly. The position of each part, in relation to the plane, showed clearly on the radar screen.

Radar Sees by Radio Signals Reflected from Solid Objects and Rain

On this screen every object beneath the plane, or in the air around the plane, appeared as it would on a map, with the plane in the center of the map. Radar might be thought of as a sort of television camera which sweeps all the way around the horizon showing on its screen everything within sight for 100 miles or more in all directions. Radar "eyesight" is different from television, however. It "sees" by means of radio signals or impulses which are sent out in rapid succession like bullets from a machine gun. When these radio impulses strike an object they quickly bounce back and are collected again by the radar set. The radar shows on its screen only those objects which reflect the impulses. These radio impulses are reflected from rain as well as from solid objects.

It is this ability of radar to "see" rain that makes it helpful in locating and flying through a hurricane. It was learned during World War II that a hurricane not only contains a great deal of rain, but that the heaviest rain always seems to lie in lines or bands which spiral inward toward the calm center of the storm. Since the storm center itself has few clouds and no rain, the radar sees the hurricane as a pinwheel-like object. The picture on page 218 is an actual radar photograph of a hurricane. An observer with a good radar can look ahead of his plane a hundred miles or more, see the storm center, and know exactly how far it is from the plane.

Preparing for a High-Altitude Flight into the Heart of a Hurricane

On September 12, 1947, all was ready for a series of high-altitude flights into the first big hurricane that might come along. On this very day one was reported by a ship far out in the Atlantic Ocean, although the storm was still too far away for us to fly into it. Crews were alerted, last-minute preparations were made; and everyone stood by for the storm to come close enough so that we should not waste too much gasoline going and coming.

At dawn on the morning of September 14, ten of us lined up in front of the plane for final instructions. We knew more or less what to expect of the hurricane and what to do if the plane should be forced down into the water. We were so loaded with clothing and equipment that we might have been mistaken for strange creatures from Mars. In addition to our regular clothes, cameras and other equipment, we were either wearing or carrying flying coveralls, flying jackets, "Mae West" life preservers, parachutes and oxygen masks. Soon after we climbed aboard, the big plane rose gracefully from the long runway and soared off south over the Atlantic into an almost cloudless sky. We planned to fly into the edge of the storm, which was still some distance away. We were to climb on top of the highest clouds, and then fly back and forth, measuring the temperature and pressure of the air. We hoped to descend over the center of the storm into the calm air of the eye, taking pictures and making special measurements.

Hurricane-hunters at work in a B-29, observing winds, barometric pressure and temperature.

Before long the sheet of high cloud which always extends far out, ahead of the storm, appeared on the horizon. A little later the radar began to show a few long curved fingers of rain far ahead in the actual storm area. The sea was becoming rougher now, and occasionally a ship could be seen tossing around below us.

We Catch Up with What the Radar Screen Saw Miles Back

We moved in under the high cloud sheet, and the sun gradually faded from view. Ahead, it began to look dark and uninviting. We were seeing now with our eyes what the radar had seen many miles back. Below us, the wind was blowing at the rate of more than fifty miles an hour. As we crossed first one, and then another, of the bands of heavier cloud and rain, the plane bumped slightly on each. In between these bands the air was very smooth, and we rode in complete comfort. It was fascinating to consider how peaceful it was in the cabin of our plane when down below the winds were racing over a frothy and angry sea.

At this point the pilot began the climb according to our original plan. Higher and higher we went, wondering how far we should have to go to reach the top of the storm. In a hurricane the year before, a B-29 had climbed to a height of 33,000 feet and had reached the top. When we reached 30,000 feet, however, nearly six miles above sea level, we saw the cloud base still high above us. Not until the plane reached 33,000 feet did it enter the clouds; and not until it had climbed to its ceiling of 36,000 feet did we break out into the sunshine above. NOW WE WERE ON TOP!

We Fly Through an Ice-Crystal Cloud into the Eye of the Storm

We were on top of one of the biggest hurricanes that had crossed the Atlantic in many years. Looking down we saw an ocean of white cloud—peaceful-looking cloud—but we knew that seven miles below things were not so peaceful! We were completely dependent on our radar now, because all view of the sea surface was completely shut off. With the radar we set a course for the storm center. Before we reached the center, however, the tops of the cloud below us began to rise, and we were forced to fly into it since the plane was unable to climb any higher. From here

on we depended entirely on radar.

Occasionally a brilliant halo could be seen overhead, reflected in the ice-crystal cloud through which we were flying. We reached the storm eye and circled it. Even though the radar indicated that there was no rain below the plane, the high clouds in which we were flying did not break away as we had expected, and we could not take the pictures we had hoped for. Because we had had to climb higher than we had expected to, we had used much more gasoline than we had counted on using. In addition, moisture from the cloud had begun to freeze on the plane, making it so heavy that further flying in the storm was too dangerous. There was nothing for us to do but return to Bermuda, even though we had not yet gathered all the information we wanted.

Learning to Predict the Path of a Hurricane

As soon as another plane could be made ready, we were back in the hurricane again. On this second trip we tried flying no higher than six or seven thousand feet, and avoided or stayed in between the bands of rain which surrounded and spiraled into the hurricane center. In this way the plane could fly almost into the eye without losing sight of the surface, and without bumping.

After we had explored the lower part of the hurricane, we made further attempts to climb on top. We succeeded in reaching a height of 37,000 feet, and on the next flight, 38,000 feet, but on neither of these flights did we succeed in breaking out on top of the clouds. This was because the hurricane had grown so much larger since we made our first flight, in spite of the fact that we had lost as little time as possible.

With each flight, however, the true picture of what makes up a hurricane has become a little clearer. Gradually we are learning how to tell where a hurricane is going to move. We have discovered that the storm tends to point out its future path by a layer, or tongue, of warm air which extends from its middle and upper portions. As more flights are made into hurricanes, we may in time be able to predict from almost the first day exactly what such a storm is going to do. Some scientists dream of the day when we shall know how to control, or at least partially control, the direction in which a hurricane is going to move!

ICELAND

ISLAND OF FROST AND FIRE

By HALLDÓR HERMANNSSON

*Curator, Fiske Icelandic Collection,
Cornell University*

F AR in the North Atlantic lies an island
of frost and fire. It was given the name
of Iceland, and yet it is one of the most
volcanic regions in the world. Some of its
many volcanoes have long since become ex-

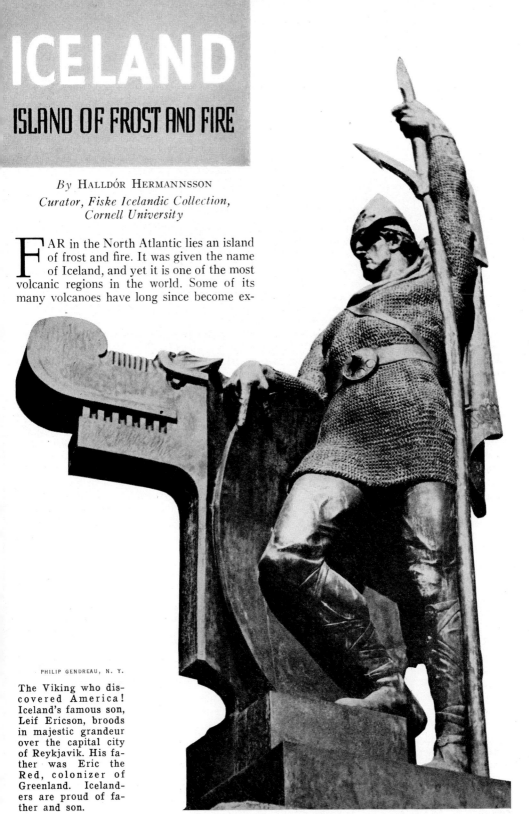

The Viking who dis-
covered America!
Iceland's famous son,
Leif Ericson, broods
in majestic grandeur
over the capital city
of Reykjavik. His fa-
ther was Eric the
Red, colonizer of
Greenland. Iceland-
ers are proud of fa-
ther and son.

221

tinct, but others lie slumbering, biding their time. The most famous, Mount Hekla, erupted as recently as 1947.

When you approach Iceland from the southeast, as voyagers from Europe always do, a wonderful sight meets the eye—a cup-shaped glacier of immense size. This is Vatna Jökull, the largest glacier in Iceland. As you keep on along the coast, you see other, smaller glaciers, so that at first sight Iceland seems to live up to its shivery name. Yet, as if to remind you of the island's hidden fires, you can see in the distance, well back from the coast, the snow-capped summit of Mount Hekla, 5,108 feet high.

Wild Winds Blow on the High Plateau but Farms Lie Snug in the Valleys

Long ago, active volcanoes built the island into a high plateau. Today, the plateau is about as desolate a place as you could imagine, with barren deserts of lava and vast fields of ice and snow. No one can live on the high tablelands of the interior, for the winds are too fierce and the climate is too cold.

The snug farms and brightly painted cities of Iceland are not found on these bleak heights, but in sheltering fiords and valleys and on parts of the low-lying fringe of coast. Here summer brings green pastures, gracious meadows and grassy slopes, where sheep and cattle are a familiar sight. Here, too, are large tracts of soft-colored heather, which is excellent natural pasturage for the sheep. Many fields of grass and hay, however, are cultivated with the greatest care to make good fodder, for livestock-raising is Iceland's most important industry. Fishing is next in importance to farming. From late winter on, the fishing boats set forth, often on lengthy journeys, to return laden with cod, herring and other delicious fish.

The Dazzling Northern Lights That Flame across the Sky

The Arctic Circle crosses Iceland's northernmost tip. As a result of their northerly latitude, Icelanders are treated to one of the most magnificent sights in the world—the wonderful aurora borealis, or northern lights, that flame across the night sky in the most glorious displays. Days and nights on this beautiful island are different from those we know in our temperate zones. Winter days are very short, but in summer it seems as though the sun would never set.

Iceland is so far north that her climate would be bitterly cold if it were not for the warm Gulf Stream which almost encircles the island. In the capital, Reykjavik, it is not unusual for women to wear cotton dresses in the summertime. The mean annual temperature in this charming, modern city is 39.4°. Reykjavik is in the southwest, which is the section where the Norsemen first settled long ago, and which is still the most thickly populated part of the island.

About 130,000 people live in Iceland. It is a very little country, not quite so big as the state of Kentucky, and at the most not more than one quarter of it is inhabited.

Iceland has no railroads and none of its rivers are navigable. In the old days, horses used to be the only means of transportation. Now there are airports and roads, and automobiles have been brought in. Nevertheless, the small Icelandic pony—one of the loveliest, strongest and most intelligent of animals—is still very useful.

The Treeless Hills of Iceland Have a Beauty All Their Own

One of the first things that a stranger notices about Iceland is the lack of trees. Curiously enough, the fact that trees are scarce gives the island an attractiveness all its own. The bare, craggy hills and mountains stand out sharply and look much higher than they really are. Dwarf birches and clumps of willow are found in some of the valleys and in other sheltered places, and sometimes a rowan tree may reach a height of thirty feet. Yet the forests are mostly brushwood. There is so little timber that Icelanders nowadays build most of their houses and many other buildings of concrete.

Because of the many glaciers and the moist climate there are countless streams and waterfalls and small, lovely lakes. Fishing is a favorite summer sport, for most of the lakes are well stocked. There is good trout-fishing in the lakes and streams and salmon-fishing in the rivers. Of all the lakes, Mývatn, in the north, is perhaps the most famous for its beauty. Its setting is pure enchantment, with volcanoes and craters all about. Wild ducks and other waterfowl abound on its waters and make their homes on its islands. Mývatn fills a shallow depression between two streams of lava; its greatest depth is less than nine feet.

The deep-hidden fires of Iceland keep hot

springs boiling or steaming throughout the island. This hot water, in turn, is used to heat the buildings of Reykjavik as well as many greenhouses. Vaporous springs near Reykjavik gave the city its name, which means Bay of Smokes. Some miles away there is a group of geysers. Earthquakes are frequent and every once in a while they do a great deal of damage.

How Iceland Received Its Undeserved Name

As you can see, the name Iceland fits this little country very poorly. A visitor once spent a winter on the island and nearly perished from lack of provisions. By early spring, when the pack ice began to drift down from the Arctic Ocean bringing with it cold, mean weather, the visitor was at his wit's end. He was so discouraged that he called the country Iceland. Later, however, he returned to live there the rest of his life.

When foreigners hear its name, they are likely to imagine that the island is filled with Eskimos and polar bears. Nothing could be farther from the truth. Once in a while a polar bear may pay a visit to the island, if he has happened to get caught on drift ice from the north. Very few animals are native— probably only the foxes, white and silver and blue. Even the reindeer were brought there a good many years ago. Iceland has neither frogs nor snakes. Apart from land animals, there are seals and whales and water birds, including the eider duck and the whistling swan.

All of the people are Icelandic. This means that they are of Scandinavian stock, with a bit of Irish and Scotch. Their language, Icelandic, is closely akin to Norwegian.

In its history, the island is a part of Europe. Unlike other European countries, however, Iceland was uninhabited in prehistoric days. The Irish were probably the first people to live in Iceland, but they left when the Norwegians came.

The King Whose Angry Nobles Set Sail for a Distant Isle

Norsemen discovered the island about the middle of the ninth century. A little later, in 874, King Harold Fairhair was uniting Norway under his sway and he made many of the aristocratic families so angry that they sailed away to their newly discovered country. Some went first to the Orkney and Fae-roe islands and some married into Scottish and Irish families before going on their way. This accounts for the Celtic traits that are found to this day among the men, women and children of Iceland.

The Icelanders took pride in preserving their traditions and their native tongue, and they created a wonderful literature. The Eddas are famous and so are many of the stories called sagas. Icelanders have never lost their ancient love of literature. They write many books, their schools are very good and there is no illiteracy on the island.

Because so many Norsemen fled from Harold Fairhair long ago, Icelanders today are able to say that they have the oldest parliament in the world. The Norse settlers made Iceland an independent republic with a parliament called the Althing. Somewhat later, the Icelanders lost their independence, for Norway became master of the island. Then, in the fourteenth century, both Norway and Iceland passed under Danish rule. Iceland remained Danish for nearly six centuries but at last, in 1944, she broke her ties with Denmark. Iceland became an independent republic for the second time in her history, and her parliament is still called the Althing, as it was in days of old.

Siglufjordin, in the shelter of the hills.

INDIANS
of
SOUTH
AMERICA

By ALFRED MÉTRAUX
Anthropologist

Indian Panpipes make weirdly beautiful music.

Long before the Spanish came, a Peruvian Indian made this silver statuette of a man wearing a feather headdress.

THERE are nine million or more Indians scattered over South America from the Guianas to Tierra del Fuego. Most of them are today peaceful farmers, herders and workers, but in many out-of-the-way regions their old life continues. Arrows may whiz past the ears of travelers in the jungles of the upper Amazon, and now and then scalps are taken in the Paraguayan Chaco.

Nevertheless, the 400-year-old drama is playing itself out. In the tropical forests and plains many of the old tribes have vanished in futile combat, or have fallen prey to disease. As new roads are cut through the jungle and airplanes land on unnamed lakes and rivers in search of rubber and other products; as oil wells are drilled and modern farming settlements spring up, native customs die out and the Indians are engulfed in the new population.

Peru, Ecuador and Bolivia, however, continue to be essentially Indian countries, where some seven million backward and neglected natives are slowly becoming aware of modern times and struggling for a happier life. The Indian is neither a romantic character nor an inferior being; he appears to be the man on whose shoulders rests the des-

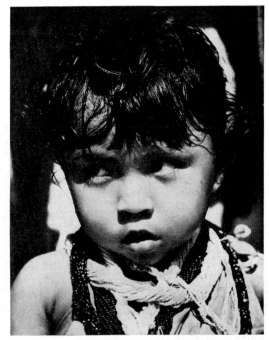

He lives near Cuzco, first home of the Incas. Right: her ancestors were Carib warriors.

tiny of several young republics.

Where did all these Indians come from? Although there are important physical differences among them, they all show strong resemblances to our North American Indians. Most anthropologists (the scientists who study the beginnings and growth of the human race, and the ways of primitive peoples all over the world) believe that the very earliest ancestors of both the North and South American Indians were wandering Mongolian tribesmen of northeastern Asia. They think that these people crossed Bering Strait into Alaska. From there they spread over North America, and traveled down into the southern continent.

The earliest tribesmen from Asia did not bring with them much in the way of worldly goods, but the dog seems to have been their companion. What appears to have happened is this: The waves of travelers scattered over the two western continents and settled by themselves for long periods of time. In this way the many widely separated groups developed their own peculiar ways of living. Some groups remained in one locality or became, from time to time, wanderers. Others, growing numerous and powerful, set out to conquer their neighbors. From these cross-ings and recrossings of paths arose the modern Indians as they have been known since Columbus first saw them.

No one can say what would have happened if the peoples of the New World had been left alone for a few hundred years longer. However, one must realize that some Indians, lucky perhaps in where they lived, made tremendous advances, and were quite as original and inventive as mankind in other parts of the world. The builders of these great civilizations had taken some of the decisive steps toward modern life and we may well honor their ingenuity.

For all its fame, the Inca empire was not the first high civilization of the Andes region. Instead it was the last heir of many advanced cultures. Some had flourished and died centuries before the Incas arose.

The most famous of these ancient cultures is called Chimu. Its center was in the region of Trujillo, in northern Peru. The Chimu people lived in large cities made of adobe— sun-baked clay. They built their temples on huge terraced pyramids. Archeologists, digging in the ruins of these cities, and in Chimu burial grounds, have discovered that they were an agricultural people, getting most of their food from the soil. They are perhaps best known for their amazing skill in making wonderfully beautiful pottery. Thousands of their vases have been unearthed. Many of them represent people, houses, fruits and scenes from everyday life, and all are beautifully painted.

Another early valley civilization grew up at Nazca, in southern Peru. Nazca pottery ranks next to Chimu pottery in beauty and originality. While Chimu art is very realistic, that of Nazca is famous for its symbolic designs, in which cats, demons and ferocious warriors are pictured. Pieces of Nazca cloth have been found, some of it beautifully embroidered. These people discovered by themselves every single important type of weaving known to man. They wove tapestries in a way very much like that used in making the famous Gobelin tapestries of France.

While these two civilizations were in existence, in the early centuries of the Christian Era, another one developed in the dreary highlands of Bolivia, on the shores of Lake Titicaca. The lake lies some 12,000 feet above sea level. The vanished grandeur of this ancient culture may still be sensed from the ruins of its capital near the Indian village of Tiahuanaco.

The early Tiahuanaco people took pride in shaping enormous stone slabs and fitting them carefully to form the walls of their great buildings. You can still trace the advance of their civilization across the highlands by means of these structures. In their capital, among colossal blocks transported in an unknown way from far-distant quarries, stands the Sun Gate, one of the marvels of the Americas. It was cut from a single tremendous block of stone. In its center is the carved image of a god, surrounded by other beings with condor or fish heads. Gigantic human statues are scattered among the ruins.

Tiahuanaco was already a dead city when the Incas conquered the region. They believed that the giant stone statues were the first men, created by the supreme being, Viracocha, and later turned into stone by him. The present day Aymará Indians of La Paz and the Bolivian highlands are probably descendants of the Tiahuanaco people.

The Inca tribes were the last of the great native civilizations to flourish before the conquest of South America by the Spaniards.

When speaking of the Incas, it must be remembered that they were not a single tribe. The name Inca—the English spelling of Ynca—is a Quechua Indian word meaning ruler or king. No one tribe was known as Inca, although there are Indians in northern Bolivia today who claim to be descended from this ancient line of rulers and who call themselves Incas.

The first Incas were a few Quechua-speaking Indians who lived on a lofty, cold plain

The ancient Peruvians made wonderful painted pottery. Left, Chimu jar; right, Tiahuanaco urn.

BOTH PHOTOS, AMERICAN MUSEUM OF NATURAL HISTORY

in the Andes not far from the pleasant valley of Cuzco. Their land was not very good for agriculture, and their life—herding llamas—was not an easy one. About 1100 A.D. they apparently decided that there must be an easier way to make a living. The near-by valley of Cuzco looked to them like the answer to their problem—it was warmer, the land was better, and it was well watered by the roaring Hautanay River. Life would be much pleasanter there.

The Inca Legend of the Golden Son of the Sun

According to legend, the highland Indians convinced the valley people that one of their number, a young boy, was the son of the sun and had been sent by his father to rule the valley. One story is that the valley people were convinced of the truth of this by a trick. One morning the boy was dressed in a golden robe and made to stand at the entrance to a cave high up on one side of the valley. This cave faced the east. As the sun came up its first rays were reflected from the robe with dazzling brilliance. The valley people were simple and superstitious. When they saw the strange and beautiful sight they believed that the boy really was the son of the sun and accepted him as their ruler. The boy, who thus became the first Inca, was given the name Sincha Roca (War Chief Roca).

For nearly 400 years the Incas ruled with remarkable success. The little valley of Cuzco became the center of an enormous empire, including parts of Ecuador, Peru, northwestern Argentina, Bolivia and northern Chile. Its capital was the city of Cuzco in the valley.

While these early civilizations of a high type arose and declined, there were hundreds of other Indian tribes and sub-tribes scattered over the rest of South America, among them the Caribs, Arawaks, Tupi-Guaranis, Mapuches, Puelches, Tehuelches, Yahgans and countless others. Some tribes were fierce and warlike; others were peaceful. Some lived by cultivating the soil; others lived by hunting and fishing. Some lived in villages; others were wanderers.

Jungle Indians made long voyages through the complicated water system of the Amazon River, for they were excellent canoemen. They also used the streams of the Cassiquiare region of Venezuela. These, in flood season, connect the basin of the Ori-

This Indian girl, with her gorgeously feathered pet, is one of the Chunchos of upper Brazil.

noco with that of the Amazon. The Indians were thus able to travel deep into the interior of the continent.

Indian peddlers carried on an active trade between distant tribes in such goods as hammocks, graters, dogs, bows and arrows and hunting poisons. Seventeenth-century Spanish explorers found the Indians of the Amazon using knives and axes that the Dutch had traded a few years earlier to the tribes on the Guiana coast.

The jungle Indians today live in very many small tribes. They have long been looked upon as being extremely wild and primitive. This is principally because they usually wear no clothes, avoid white people and sometimes—but rarely—practice cannibalism. Unfriendliness between tribes is common, and attacks on neighboring tribes are of frequent occurrence. Under such circumstances you would expect wide differences in language and culture. Yet, oddly enough, a single language—such as Tupi-Guarani—may be spoken throughout immense areas, sometimes by natives living thousands of miles apart.

On the whole, most of the tribes have a fairly high type of civilization. Most of them live in clearings in the forest and grow corn, sweet potatoes, yams and manioc for food. They depend mainly on manioc, a very nourishing tuber. Sweet manioc can be boiled and eaten like potatoes, and a kind of bread can be made of it. Bitter manioc contains a deadly poison—prussic acid—which these Indians long ago learned to remove. This they do by grating the tuber into shreds, and then squeezing the shreds in one way or another until all the juice—which contains the poison—is squeezed out. Left standing in the sun, or boiled, the poison quickly evaporates from the juice. From what is left we get our tapioca. The dried manioc flour is usually made into flat cakes and baked on the hearth.

Among the wildest of these jungle tribes are the Chavantes. They live in a rich part of the Mato Grosso, deep in the interior of Brazil, and are seldom visited by travelers. It is only recently that they have begun to show any friendliness toward white men. They live in round huts made of palm thatch, about thirty feet in diameter and about ten feet high at the peak of the roof. These are grouped around a bachelors' hall, or men's club. Plenty of space is left between the hall and the huts for feasts and dancing.

The Indians' Knowledge of Plants Helps Them in Hunting Game

The jungle does not abound in game, but the Indians are good hunters and have invented many ingenious ways to catch animals and fish. They have a remarkable knowledge of plants, which is of great value to them. For instance, some tribes make a poison known as curare from a certain type of vine. This they put on the points of their arrows and blow-gun darts. It is such a strong poison that it immediately paralyzes the animal or bird that is hit, yet it does not make the meat unfit to eat. Other kinds of plants are used to catch fish. When the leaves are crushed and thrown into the water, they give off a juice that drugs the fish and makes them float to the surface, where they are easily lifted out. The Indians also shoot fish with arrows.

Most tropical Indians know how to weave fabrics or to make bark cloth, yet they prefer to go without clothes. They do wear many kinds of beautiful ornaments, however, especially feather ornaments. With the brightest plumage of parrots and other tropical birds, they make gorgeous headdresses, collars,

anklets, bracelets and long, rich cloaks.

The Indians also show great skill in building, although they have only a few kinds of tools. Such tribes as the Witoto and Macusi build great huts, large enough to shelter a whole community of 200 or 300 persons. These houses are not divided into rooms; each family simply swings its hammocks between posts, leaving the central part of the building free for cooking, meetings and dances.

The Indians also show great skill in basketry. Every hut contains a wide variety of plaited articles, from kitchen utensils to knapsacks and artistically woven storage boxes for feather ornaments and knick-knacks. Pottery is known to all these Indians. Today most of it is plain, but archeologists digging at the mouth of the Amazon have revealed that people once lived there who made beautiful ceramics. These vanished artists probably were Arawaks, related to the Indian inhabitants of the West Indies, where pottery of the same type is also being

The jungle sharpshooter brings down his quarry with a blowgun and deadly, poisoned darts.

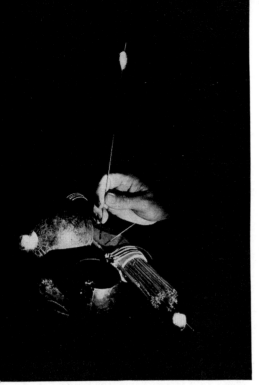

Before each hunting trip, the Indians dip their darts in a syrup of curare and snake venom.

The Indians feel that man could not cope with the spirits without the help of shamans —medicine men. Every tribe has at least one. It is not easy to become a shaman. The young candidate must study for many years and must undergo terrible ordeals, such as being stung by ferocious ants, going without food for weeks, and drinking pure tobacco juice. After a certain amount of this he begins to have visions in which he sees spirits and talks with them. This is a sign that he has become a shaman, for the power of the shaman depends on his familiarity with one or more spirits.

The main business of the shaman is to cure sick people. The Indians believe that all ailments, even the most common ones, are caused by the spirits. If a spirit grows angry at someone, or if a witch orders him to, he can shoot a thorn, a stone, or some other object into that person's body. It is then the shaman's task to heal the ailing person by enlisting the aid of other spirits. Sometimes the shamans complete their cure by prescribing herbs or special diets. When this is done, not only the sick person, but his whole family are often required to take the treatment.

Masked Dancers Blow Trumpets to Please the Spirits

The Indians believe that they can control the will of the spirits by wearing masks which they think resemble the spirits, and by dancing and acting out pantomimes. Sometimes they make huge trumpets to represent the spirits. The men keep these trumpets in special huts, hidden from the women, who would be killed if they were to see them.

The dances which the Indians perform are often of a religious character and are meant to have a favorable effect upon crops, game and fish. The music of flutes and Panpipes accompanies the dance. Dancers shake rattles, which are believed to be the voices of the spirits.

Since the Indians are convinced that every death is caused by the sorcery of outsiders, they live in fear of neighboring tribes. When a death takes place in their own tribe, they feel that they must have revenge. After consulting with their shaman to find out which tribe was responsible for the death, they make a surprise attack at dawn, killing and capturing a few people. Then they hurry home and celebrate a victory.

South of the forests lies a region of wide

dug up by modern archeologists.

Long before Columbus came, these Indians made rubber balls. They played a game something like soccer, in which they butted the ball with their heads or shoulders. They also made rubber syringes and waterproof pouches. It took Europeans an amazingly long time to appreciate the properties of rubber.

The forest Indian's life is governed by spirits. He sees all nature as animated by spirits. Some are the souls of animals and plants, and others are the ghosts of the dead. Any unusual happening is believed to have been caused by these supernatural beings. The attitude of the Indians toward spirits is chiefly one of fear, because the spirits are considered to be malicious, or, at the least, unpleasant. The very look of the spirits is frightening. They are supposed to be hairy and crooked, they walk with their toes turned up, and they have glowing eyes—altogether, not comforting-looking characters to meet in a lonely place on a dark night. Sometimes, to deceive people, a spirit will take human shape. A few spirits may show gratitude for human help, but even these are unreliable and touchy companions.

plains, covered partly by short, thorny bush, and partly by prairie grass. The part that is dry bush is called El Gran Chaco—the great hunting ground. The grassy areas are the fertile pampas of Argentina. In both areas the Indians long ago lived mainly by hunting, fishing and gathering wild fruits and vegetables.

The Fierce Warriors of the Chaco Learned Some of the Inca Arts

The Chaco Indians were more civilized than their southern neighbors, for they were in contact with the Incas of Peru. They wove beautiful fabrics and made pottery. Their houses, however, were rather crude, hastily thrown-together shacks, since they moved frequently from place to place. Most of them were warlike tribes who scalped their enemies.

The Indians of the pampas and Patagonia, on the other hand, lived a miserable existence. They dressed in skins, lived in skin tents, and lived by hunting the swift, ostrich-like rheas and the guanacos. They were often attacked and enslaved by the Chaco tribesmen.

The coming of the Spanish in the sixteenth century brought about a great change in the way of life of these peoples. The Spaniards brought horses to Buenos Aires in 1536. Some of these horses escaped, and a hundred years later big herds of wild horses covered the pampas. Many Indian tribes of the Chaco and the pampas, like the Plains Indians in North America, took to the horse. Once mounted, they could fight with the Europeans on equal terms. They soon became the scourge of the frontier. The Chaco Indians even conquered large territories in Paraguay.

In these raids the Indians acquired clothes, weapons, tools and silver. They also captured hundreds of Indian and white prisoners, whom they made slaves.

In the eighteenth century, new horsemen appeared on the plains. These were the Araucanian Indians, who had victoriously resisted the advance of the Spaniards in Chile. For a century the Araucanians ruled the plains, even forcing the Argentinian government to pay tribute to them. It took a large Argentinian army to force the Araucanian chief to surrender in the 1870's. Today the Araucanians are crowded on reservations.

The Tehuelches lived south of the pampas.

These were the giants whom Magellan discovered and named Patagones—Big Feet. Today they have almost vanished. Only a few families are left, around the southernmost lakes of Patagonia. The weapon that the Patagonians used in hunting, and even in warfare, was the bola—two or three stone balls connected by sinews—which they hurled at their prey or their enemies.

Perhaps the most primitive Indians of South America are those who live in Tierra del Fuego and the islands off the tip of the continent. Some, like the Ona, are hunters of the guanaco and a kind of rabbit. Others, like the Yahgan and the Akalakuf, are water nomads who spend most of their lives fishing in small bark canoes. No people surpass them in hardiness. In that exceedingly cold, raw climate, the Yahgan wear only short skin capes, and can plunge into freezing water without seeming to feel at all uncomfortable. In their canoes they keep a fire going continuously, and as soon as they step on land they build a fire there. These people live in small family groups and are always on the move.

Broken Bottles Made Glittering and Deadly Arrowheads

These Fuegian fishermen, when they were first visited by white people, used bone harpoons very much like those of the ancient cave-dwellers of Europe. After the Scottish ranchers came to the Tierra del Fuego, the Ona, who had been making their arrow-heads of flint, quickly began to make them of broken bottle-glass, of which there was a great deal around the white settlements. In their struggle for life the Ona were greatly helped by their furry dogs, which they trained to drive herds of guanaco towards the hunters.

Today these simple people are almost extinct. After they began wearing the white man's clothing, many died of lung diseases. Others, forced to hunt the sheep of the ranchers because the guanaco had begun to disappear, were themselves hunted and killed by the ranchers.

These millions of Indians, with their great variety of characteristics and customs, form a real problem for the countries in which they live. In the past little has been done to help them to advance in civilization and well-being, but there is reason to believe that the future will hold much greater opportunity for them.

INDUSTRY'S SEVEN-LEAGUE BOOTS

By E. C. McDowell, *Consulting Engineer*

BETWEEN Shipshaw and Arvida, in Quebec, over the deep, rushing currents of the Saguenay, a bridge is being built. It will not be the longest or the highest bridge in the world, but for all that it is unique. It is the first bridge to be built entirely of aluminum.

In a curious way the Arvida bridge is a symbol of the romance of modern industrial development, for it has been made possible by power and transportation, the seven-league boots which have carried industrial development so far and so swiftly, in so short a period of time.

The aluminum industry at Arvida was built up just in time for World War II. Power from the hydroelectric development of the Saguenay called for the creation of industries to make use of it. Transportation made it possible to bring bauxite and other raw materials to Arvida from as far away as tropical Guiana and arctic Greenland. Engineers, mechanics and administrative workers came from all over Canada and from the

United States to build and carry on the industry. Its products, both during and after the war, were shipped to many parts of the world.

Industrial production is of great importance to the growth, in prosperity and civilization, of any country. To be prosperous a country must have a good agricultural production too, but there is a limit to the number of people who can be supported by agriculture, and a limit to the area of land that can be put under cultivation. There are only two things that can put a limit to industry's growth. These are giving out of supplies of

armorers' quarters. The master workmen or merchants of these trades were organized into guilds. In the various shops the owner usually worked with his men. The families generally lived close around the shop they worked in.

This gives you an idea of how industry was carried on in all countries down to recent modern times. Different countries, even different cities, specialized in certain products which they made better than anyone else did. These were transported by caravans, trains of pack horses, or ships, long distances to foreign markets. Most of the products

Descending the river in a "broadhorn" flatboat, so named from its two long steering oars.

raw materials from which products are manufactured, and the lack of a market for increased production. The growth of power and transportation prevents these things from happening.

From the most ancient times until less than two hundred years ago nearly everything people used or wore was made by hand labor. There were no machines to help turn out the work and much of the manufacturing was done by people in their homes. Yarns were spun by hand, and cloth was woven on simple hand looms. In the cities each trade or vocation was carried on in a separate street or neighborhood. There would be the street of the glove-makers, or the furriers' or

that were sold in lands far from the place of their manufacture were luxuries; they had to be light enough to handle easily on the long journeys.

At various times in the past, China excelled in the making of porcelain and silks, India and Persia in rugs. Ancient Damascus and the Spanish city of Toledo were famous for their fine swords and armor, their silverware and silks. In some of these places manufacturing was done by groups of people on a large scale, but any machines used were very simple, and the output depended upon the handwork of skilled craftsmen. Since even the most skillful hand worker can do only so much between dawn and dusk, the output could not be very great, and prices were so high that only the well-to-do could buy the products. The great mass of the people had to depend upon their household industries and upon local craftsmen. Thousands of things that we today can buy in abundance and cheaply were unknown then, or were entirely too expensive for the average person.

About the time the British colonies in America declared their independence, near the end of the eighteenth century, another revolution started up in western Europe. It was called the Industrial Revolution. It was at this time that industry began to try on its seven-league boots and begin to step out, and ever since it has been moving faster and with longer strides. There have been many revolutions of one sort or another throughout the world, but the Industrial Revolution, which is still going on, has done more to advance material progress than any other event, with the possible exception of the invention of printing.

The British Isles took the lead in this revolution during the eighteenth and nineteenth centuries.

The Use of Coal Leads Up to the Age of Steam

Coal had been used in small ways for several hundred years, but in the eighteenth century it began to be used more and more, first for fuel and later for smelting iron and other metals. Then the steam engine was invented, and by the end of the century had been perfected enough to be used for driving machinery. This brought about the invention of many machines to do the work of hand labor.

In the textile industries, the power loom took the place of the old hand loom and could weave many more yards of cloth in a day. The spinning-jenny, which spun yarns on many spindles, took the place of the old spinning-wheel with its one spindle. In 1793 the cotton-gin was invented to separate the cotton fiber from the seeds, and this provided an abundance of raw cotton to be used for fabrics. Up to this time most of the textiles were of linen and wool, which were not too abundant. Knitting machines and sewing machines were invented later on.

Thus it came about that the textile industry was one of the first to start the factory system, with power-driven machinery turning out as much cloth as fifty or more hand weavers could have done. Improvement in machinery and methods has been going on ever since. Within the last year a Frenchman has invented and put into operation looms of an entirely new and different type, which can weave nearly three times as many yards of cloth as the standard loom of today can do.

The beginning of the nineteenth century brought a revolution in iron production. With the steam engine to give the power, rolling mills were built which could squeeze a huge mass of white-hot iron into long bars or plates or sheets. Also steam hammers were

STANDARD OIL CO. (N. J.) PHOTO BY ROSSKAM

Mississippi stern-wheel towboat and barges.

made that could forge large pieces of iron into different shapes. Before that time iron had had to be forged by hand, just as the blacksmith forges horseshoes with hammer and anvil; and that meant that it was not possible to forge very large pieces of metal.

Iron and, later, steel manufacturing began to grow and expand like the jinni in the Arabian Nights story. People thought up endless new uses for the metal. The use of electric power in steel-making caused the industry to grow still more, until now it is almost impossible for us to imagine our world without it.

These two classes of industry are examples of the swift progress that has been going on since industry came into its chief source of power, which was, and to a large extent still is, steam. Today, electricity, generated by steam or water turbines, has given rise to still other big industries, and has greatly lightened labor and speeded up production throughout the industrial world.

In the past seventy years, two other sources of fuel and power—petroleum and natural gas—have come into use. Huge refineries have been built to produce the various types of gasoline and oil which are the basis of the vast automobile and airplane industries. Now the world is looking forward with the expectation that, in the near future, airplanes, and probably other means of transportation, will be driven by atomic energy. Expert engineers, designers and scientists are now making studies to find a practical way of carrying this out.

We have seen the part that power has played in the building up of modern industry. Power has made it possible to manufacture all sorts of articles in abundance. Power has also enabled industry to gather its raw materials from far and near, and to send its completed products all over the world.

When power-driven machines first began to increase production, better and cheaper ways of transportation had to be developed to carry these products to a wider market and to bring raw materials to the mills and factories. The invention, in England, of the steam locomotive, to haul coal from the mines, took place at this time. This was the real beginning of the railway systems that now haul freight on land all over the world.

Steam power was also applied to navigation, and ships were no longer at the mercy of winds and calms. Ocean transportation took a long step forward in speed and safety. Ships could take the most direct route to their destinations, and could follow the coasts more closely, without the danger of being driven ashore by on-shore winds. The steamboat solved the problem of river navigation, and the rivers of the world became highways of traffic.

Before 1811, when the first steamboat appeared on the Mississippi River, this great stream could be navigated conveniently only downstream. Fleets of large flatboats floated

Power and transportation have made possible scenes such as this—an automobile assembly line.

FORD NEWS BUREAU

down the river, laden with the products of the Midwest, to New Orleans. Going upstream against the current was a different matter. Only small cargoes of merchandise in light boats could do it, and the boats had to be rowed. In swift stretches of the river the boat would be brought near the shore and some of the men would walk along pulling a tow-line, while those in the boat pushed with long poles. Sometimes, when the wind happened to be right, a sail could be used. Often it took a whole day to go eight or ten miles. Today, both the flatboats and the big white steamboats have gone from the Father of Waters, but in their place a much heavier barge traffic has been built up. Powerful steel towboats with Diesel engines take tows of steel barges up and down the Mississippi River and all its larger tributaries, carrying all kinds of raw materials and finished products. These barges are of 2,000-ton capacity, and six or eight of them are lashed together and handled by one towboat. Often one towboat will handle 16,000 tons of freight—as much as three or four hundred railway freight-car loads.

Most of Our Big Cities Are Built on Navigable Waterways

You may have noticed that nearly all the great inland cities of Canada and the United States are situated on navigable rivers, or on the Great Lakes where there is deep water navigation. Chicago, which is on Lake Michigan, is also connected by a canal with the Illinois River, and by way of this, with the inland barge routes of the Mississippi River system.

Another barge route will, when completed, speed up the service of industry in the coastal waters of the East. The United States Government is building a series of waterways along the Atlantic and Gulf coasts to connect all the chief harbors, bays, inlets and lagoons into one continuous barge route from Boston, Massachusetts, to Brownsville, Texas, at the mouth of the Rio Grande. This route will also connect most of the navigable rivers that flow into the Atlantic and the Gulf of Mexico.

In the industrial countries of Europe, nearly all the manufacturing centers are situated on navigable waters. Water transportation is the cheapest, and commodities can be shipped in much larger bulk by water than in any other way. Industry, therefore,

has naturally located where water transportation is most convenient.

The world-wide means of transportation over the oceans and seas and the inland waterways have given industry a way to draw raw materials from almost every region of the world and the means of shipping products to those regions in return. The railroads now connect water transportation with most of the land areas of civilized countries, and with parts of uncivilized regions. Until the beginning of the twentieth century, however, local traffic to and from the railroads and waterways depended upon horse-drawn vehicles of all kinds, traveling over roads that were often far from good. In the Orient and in some parts of Africa and South America, traffic is still carried on by caravans of various kinds of pack animals where there are no wagon roads.

The automobile brought about the building of vast networks of concrete and other hard-surfaced highways in Canada, the United States and most European countries west of Russia, and in parts of more advanced countries in other regions of the world. Then there grew up lines of trucking companies that, in North America, at least, cover practically the whole continent. They carry freight and merchandise between cities and towns, and bring farm products long distances to markets. Some of the larger trucks can carry loads of fifteen tons or more. They have a capacity equal to that of many of the old freight box cars that the railroads used about seventy-five years ago. They save time and expense by what is known as making "door-to-door" shipments—carrying merchandise directly from factories to warehouses and retail stores, often hundreds of miles away.

Industry Adds Wings to Its Seven-League Boots

Now the latest means of transportation, the airplane, is rapidly coming into use for still faster movement of almost everything that the motor truck and express companies carry. The load limit of freight-carrying planes is being increased as new planes designed for that purpose are being developed. In this latest means of transportation, industry may be said to have added wings to its seven-league boots—making them like the winged sandals of Mercury.

Besides its great speed, the airplane has

made it possible to carry freight to and from regions once considered inaccessible. The glittering vastness of the Canadian and Alaskan northland, as full of mineral treasures as the cave of Ali Baba, has been opened to development by the airplane. Large-scale development of these regions will probably have to await the building of railways, for bulk transportation by plane is still very costly. Nevertheless, we have recently seen an example of what air transport really can do—the remarkable feat of hundreds of American and British planes carrying fuel and food to beleaguered Berlin to supply more than two million people.

Many Kinds of Transportation Are Needed by Industry

These four systems of transportation are what may be called the life-blood of industrial production. They are, as we have seen, water-borne transportation, railway, highway and air transportation. No one of them, by itself, could meet all the needs of gathering raw materials and distributing finished products.

There are other means of transporting materials, especially overland. The most useful and economical of these are the systems of pipe lines through which petroleum is pumped. First the crude oil is carried from the oil fields to the refineries; then the refined products, such as gasoline and fuel oil, are pumped long distances across the country to be stored for further distribution. During World War II, when German submarines largely prevented Texas and Louisiana tank ships from carrying oil to the Atlantic seaports, pipe lines saved the day. These were two great pipe lines, one twenty-four and the other twenty inches in diameter, known as Big Inch and Little Inch. Starting down in the southwest, they carried petroleum products to the industrial northeast.

Big Inch and Little Inch are still on duty, but now they carry natural gas from the Texas and Oklahoma gas fields to the East. Natural gas is also piped from these fields to southern California. The greatest pipe line, thirty inches in diameter, is now being built across Arabia from the oil fields about the Persian Gulf to the eastern end of the Mediterranean Sea. There the oil will be transferred to tank ships to cross the seas. This is an outstanding example of how every possible means is used to cut costs of transportation and save time, for transport by pipe line is the cheapest, fastest and most direct means of carrying the oil.

Pipes are also used to carry materials in powdered form. This is done by means of compressed air. Such materials as cement, sugar, starch, carbon black, flour and so on, which must be protected from weather while being transferred from freight cars to storage bins, are blown through pipes from car to bin. This method is also being used in the building of big engineering projects, such as dams. In one case, the railway cars carrying the bulk cement could not get within three-quarters of a mile of the site of the dam, which was also at a much higher elevation than the railway tracks. Trucking the cement through all sorts of weather would have been slow and costly, so it was blown from the cars for three-quarters of a mile on the level, and then six hundred feet up to where the concrete-mixers were. French engineers, planning a hydroelectric dam in the southern Atlas Mountains of Algiers, met a similar problem. The spot where the dam was to be was twenty miles away from the nearest railway, across very rugged country. They considered building a road so that the cement could be trucked to the site. However, it was finally decided that it would be much cheaper and quicker to have a series of compressed-air stations, and blow the cement the twenty miles through a four-inch pipe.

Moving the Factories to the Fields and Mines

One way of cutting down the cost of transportation of raw material from the source to the factory is to move the factory to the source. For the past fifty years cotton mills in the northeastern United States have been steadily moving south to the heart of the cotton belt, in the south Atlantic and Gulf states. In Brazil there are large deposits of high-grade iron ore and coal—the two basic ingredients of steel. It would not pay to ship this high-grade ore up to the steel plants in the United States, so American financiers and steel experts, with the help of the Brazilian Government, have built a big steel plant in Brazil. It will be seen from this that transportation and power play the most important parts in increasing and cheapening production. By means of them modern industry moves through the world with the strong, sure strides of a young giant.

INSECTS

in flight

By C. H. CURRAN

American Museum of Natural History

THE fastest flyer in the animal world, faster even than any of the birds, is the tiny deer botfly. When it is traveling at top speed, this little insect probably covers about 400 miles in an hour's time.

Insects were old hands at flying when the dinosaurs first lumbered their heavy way across the face of the earth. During these long ages insects have tried out many different ways of flying, and, strangely enough, all those types of flight are still used by the varied kinds of insects that live today. Because one insect flies one way, and another flies another way, we can compare their methods of flight and find out which are fastest and best.

Among the very earliest flying insects there were great numbers of cockroaches. Theirs, however, may not have been the first method of flight used by insects. Cockroaches lived dangerous lives and depended for their safety upon their ability to hide from their enemies. Because their front wings were narrow and heavy, they could easily hide in narrow cracks and under stones. The heavy front wings protected then, as they do today, the delicate flying wings that fold under them.

Some warm summer day, when you are sitting in a sunny meadow abuzz with insect sounds, watch how the different insects fly. You will notice that the wings of some seem to go every which way and that they do not move in the same direction at the same time. This gives an effect like that of a helicopter. You will notice, too, that these insects move

ahead slowly and uncertainly. Certain kinds of moths and the grown ant-lions fly this way. They are readily tossed about by the wind. They seem much more anxious just to stay in the air than to get to any place in particular.

This kind of flying, so much like that of a helicopter, is the simplest kind of flight. It is very well suited to the needs of some insects that do not have to fly far to find good feeding places for their young. Often young insects grow up within a stone's throw of the spot where their parents lived out their whole lives. For this type of insect "helicopter" flying serves very well.

We do not understand perfectly even the simplest kind of insect flight, in spite of long years of study. There are many secrets of flight which can not be uncovered by a study of an insect's external organs. We do know, of course, that the flight of our fastest flies depends largely upon the wings, upon the shape of the body, and upon those little knob-like rods called halteres. The halteres are organs which help the fly to keep its balance. They are found below the wings on the thorax, the middle part of the body. But inside the fly's body there are many muscles which play an important part in flying. There are also nerve cells which perform special duties as the fly speeds along. Scientists hope the time will come when they can ac-

SPERRY GYROSCOPE CO., INC.

The haltere of this model drone fly is the white spot, like a pinhead, below the wing.

High-speed photography of drone fly held by wax on pin reveals some secrets of insect flight.

tually watch what goes on inside the bodies of flying insects.

The fly's wings, as they push down and backward against the air, drive the little creature forward. Some wings are better than others for flying. An insect with large wings often will not fly as rapidly as one with small wings. The crane fly, for instance, which looks like a big mosquito, has large wings but its flight is slow and heavy.

Have you ever carefully watched insects flying? If you have, you may have noticed that the wings of bees and flies, as they move up and down, seem to form a figure eight. Almost every student of insects has been taught that this is true. Recent motion pictures of the drone fly, taken at high speed, show that the movement of the wings does *not* form a figure eight. The high-speed camera proves that what seems true to the eye in this case is an illusion. The great speed with which the fly's wings move creates this illusion.

The pictures of the drone fly show that in both the downward and the upward stroke the fly's wings are generally at an angle of

forty-five degrees. The heavier costa, or front edge of the wing, is carried up or down ahead of the fine, thin hind border of the wing. Because of this rotating or circular motion, we think we see a figure eight as the wings move.

The driving power of the wing is greater because it is flexible and not rigid. As the wing begins its downward stroke the membrane of which the wing is composed presses strongly against the air. The pressure of the air on its under side causes the thin membrane to balloon upward as the air fills it. The hind edge of the wing is still curved upward from the previous downward stroke. Just the opposite is true, of course, when the wing begins its upward stroke. This peculiar movement of the wings in both bees and flies gives the impression of a figure eight. It is this movement, also, which makes it possible for flies to fly in a straight line.

The slow flyers among the insects beat their wings fewer times per second than do the fast flyers. In the crane flies the wings probably beat less than 100 times each second. When the house fly flies at top speed, its wings beat about 180 times a second. Mosquitoes in flight probably move their wings up and down at a slower rate than the house fly.

Butterflies and moths generally fly slowly. Most of them have large wings. Because of their large wings and the light weight of their bodies, the butterflies and moths fly with a wavy motion and not in a straight line. This wavy motion is a protection to the insect. Birds, bats and other insect enemies find it difficult to catch an insect which flies this way and that. During the war, ships which were being chased by submarines often escaped by just this kind of zigzagging.

The Great Speed of Hawk Moths Has Never Been Clocked

Among the moths, however, there are some that fly with great speed. No one has any idea how fast the hawk moths can fly. It seems probable that some of them can fly almost as fast as the fastest flies. Hawk moths are sometimes known as humming bird moths, and like humming birds, they hover over flowers and suck the flower nectar with their long tube-like mouthparts. Hawk moths are among the few creatures that can fly backward. Other backward-flyers are the humming birds, the sun birds, some large tropical damsel flies and some bee flies.

The fastest of the hawk moths are almost perfectly streamlined. The head and thorax have the weight and strength that is necessary for rapid insect flight. The body, however, tapers gracefully to a narrow point. The wings, too, are wonderfully designed for rapid flight. They are long and narrow, more or less pointed, and very strong.

For untold ages man has been interested in the honey bee. He has watched it carefully because it produces one of the richest foods we know. In flight the front and hind wings of the honey bee are locked together by a series of hooks. The front and hind wings, because of this, act like a single pair of wings. Butterflies and moths also "hook up" their front and hind wings.

Most insects whose front and hind wings do not act as a single pair are poor flyers. The dragon fly is an exception to this rule, however. Like the heavy-bodied flies and hawk moths, the dragon flies are ideally built for rapid flight. They have large heads and thoraxes, and slender or flattened abdomens. As yet we have no proof of the way the wings

of the dragon fly behave during flight. All of the evidence, however, seems to prove that the front and hind wings, instead of being hooked together, work against each other. When the front wing moves upward, the hind wing seems to make a downward stroke. This gives a shimmying of the up-and-down motion that produces flight in a straight line. In spite of this queer method of flying, the dragon fly's wings probably move as rapidly as those of a fly, but the upward and downward stroke is less.

Man himself, during the last fifty years, has become a "flying" creature. As he has become more and more interested in airplanes, he has become more interested in the flight of insects. If flight engineers and scientists can learn how insects fly so well and so fast, they may be able to design and build better and faster airplanes. Yet it seems likely that one reason for the high speed of insects lies in the fact that they can move their wings, while an airplane can not.

PHOTOS, SPERRY GYROSCOPE CO., INC.

Whole new techniques have been worked out for handling and photographing insects in flight.

Tillamook Rock

LIGHTHOUSES

By KATHARINE LANDON FUGUET

WAVE-SWEPT lighthouses are built on dangerous rocks and reefs, always lonely and often far from shore. To build those difficult towers is an adventure unlike any other, and the builder, besides being skillful, must know the sea and its ways.

At Tillamook Rock, where thousands of sea lions used to play, heavy seas wash over the rock and may batter the lighthouse tower. Landings used to be very dangerous on that steep, rocky islet, which rises sharply out of the Pacific about a mile from the Oregon coast. When the time came to build a lighthouse there, the construction foreman who set out to examine the site was drowned in attempting a landing.

The hazards of landing are almost always the first peril that must be met in working on rocks or reefs that are washed by the sea. At Tillamook, the problem was solved by carrying the men and materials from the

supply ship to the rock by means of a cable and traveler run from rock to ship. Later, a derrick was set up on the rock, and vessels were brought within reach of its boom. Today the hoisting derrick on Tillamook Rock is a familiar sight and is taken for granted as the proper way to land men and materials from boats.

If most of the workmen are landsmen, as they were at Bell Rock, the builder has his hands full in caring for their safety. Bell Rock, Scotland, is a famous sunken reef. A good-sized area is exposed at low water, but the tides are tremendous. At high water spring tides—the highest of all—the rock is covered to a depth of as much as sixteen feet. To make a landing, the workmen had to fight their rowboats against strong currents, and at least two seamen had to be stationed in each boat to help them do it. Walking on the wet, rugged rock was, to say the least of it, risky. Seaweed flourished all over the rock, and much of the slippery stuff had to be cleared away so that the men could go about their business without breaking their legs or falling into the water.

Skill in engineering is another necessity. Faulty towers are no match for the sea. There was once an iron tower where Minot's Ledge Light now stands, on the sunken reefs of Cohasset not far from Boston harbor. It was the first lighthouse in the United States to be placed where the full sweep of the Atlantic could pound it.

Those sinister reefs had been the scene of many grievous wrecks. One of the ledges, the Outer Minot, was just barely exposed at low tide and was chosen for the site of the tower. It was a difficult place to work. Landings on the ledge could be made only at low spring tides, and, even so, could not be made except when the sea was smooth. Under such circumstances, only a few hours of work could be done on the foundations in the course of a year. At length, holes were drilled in the solid rock, wrought iron piles were wedged into them and an iron-frame tower was completed. Its light was shown on January 1, 1850. The balance of the structure seems to have been all wrong, or perhaps there was some other weakness. Its light was last seen from Cohasset at 10 o'clock on a stormy night in April, 1851. When morning came, the tower and the keepers who were in it had vanished.

The tower that now stands on Minot's Ledge is one of the finest pieces of lighthouse engineering in the world—a granite cone, nearly ninety feet high, built with great mass and strength. The poet Longfellow, who visited it, wrote that it "rises out of the sea like a beautiful stone cannon." Its door, forty feet from the base, is reached by climbing up a ladder. Minot's Ledge Light was completed in 1860, after five years of bulldog persistence.

Towers That Are Triumphs of Engineering Skill

There are many famous wave-swept towers: Skerryvore, which was the work of Alan Stevenson, Robert Louis Stevenson's uncle; Bishop Rock, Wolf Rock, Dhu Heartach, off the Cornish and Scottish coasts; and Fastnet, off the southwest coast of Ireland. There are Wolf Trap Spit in Chesapeake Bay, Spectacle Reef on Lake Huron, and The Graves in the approaches to Boston.

Light station, East Gloucester, Massachusetts, with housing for fog signal and radio beacon.

If we think of lighthouses that are well known in literature, we are back, at once, at Bell Rock. This is the rock of Sir Ralph the Rover. Southey tells in his ballad, THE INCHCAPE ROCK, how Sir Ralph cut down the warning bell and how, because of this piece of villainy, his ship struck the rock and sank.

Inchcape or Bell Rock lies off the east coast of Scotland, some miles from Dundee. There had been several attempts to set up a beacon on the rock, but none of them succeeded until Robert Louis Stevenson's grandfather, Robert Stevenson, was appointed to build a lighthouse there. He wrote the story

Hatteras Light, North Carolina—one of the most dangerous spots on the Atlantic coast.

of the building of the tower, telling about every little happening in the course of the work, much as Robinson Crusoe tells about his daily life on the desert island. Many people spoke of Stevenson's ACCOUNT as The Robinson Crusoe of Civil Engineering. Robert Louis came very near to being a lighthouse engineer, as his father and uncle and grandfather were. When he was young, he visited the Northern Lights, as the Scottish lighthouses were called. He found his grandfather's ACCOUNT so interesting that he put it into the book that he wrote about his family, called A FAMILY OF ENGINEERS. You will find it there, shortened a little, in the chapter called The Building of the Bell Rock.

Eddystone is probably the most famous lighthouse in existence. The storied rocks of Eddystone lie fourteen miles off Plymouth, a port in the south of England. They were a menace well known to Sir Francis Drake a century and more before the first lighthouse was built there. Altogether, there have been four towers on the Eddystone Rocks. The designer of the first one was Winstanley. France was at war with England while the building of the tower was going on, and French privateers captured Winstanley and his men and took them from the rock. That was in 1697, during the reign of Louis XIV. The story goes that the King ordered their release because, said he, he was at war with England but not with humanity.

Candles Once Shed Their Beams from This Curious Pagoda

Poor Winstanley! We would laugh at his timber tower today. Stevenson calls it a "strange pagoda, with its open gallery, its florid scrolls and candlesticks: like a rich man's folly for an ornamental water in a park." Yet Winstanley had such faith in this creation that he wanted to be in it during a mighty storm. In 1703 his wish was granted, but he and the tower and the others who were in it—all were swept away.

The next Eddystone lighthouse was simpler, but still made of wood, and before fifty years had passed it was destroyed by fire. Then came Smeaton's tower, made of stone. The famous engineer, John Smeaton, was the first to use dovetail joints for the stones of a lighthouse, and the stones he chose averaged a ton apiece. As time went on, however, water began to undermine it. A higher

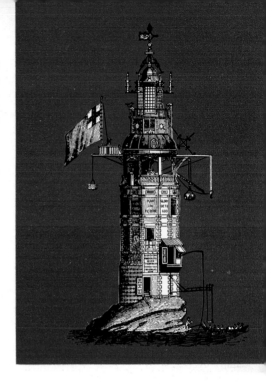

Earliest Eddystone Tower, completed in 1699.

tower was wanted, and so the fourth Eddystone Light was begun. This time the builder, Sir James N. Douglass, took particular pains with the base. He made it solid and vertical, a massive cylinder that breaks up or turns back heavy seas, so that even in storms nothing but spray rises up to the lofty lantern. His tower, completed in 1882, is still in use today.

One of the tallest of the reef lighthouses is the iron skeleton tower at Sombrero Key, Florida, 160 feet in height. Tall towers are required on the generally low-lying Atlantic coast. Very short towers are more common on the rugged Pacific coast, for there they are often built on high bluffs. Lights more than 500 feet above the sea include those at Lehua, Hawaii (707 feet); Point Ritidian, Guam (573 feet); Kaula Rock, Hawaii (562 feet) and San Nicolas Island, California (556 feet).

The earliest lighthouses used to be made of masonry, but steel is more generally used in new construction today. There are a few made of wood, such as the one on Seal Island, off the coast of Nova Scotia. In many places where warnings are needed it would be sheer folly to try to build a lighthouse, so lightships are used instead, permanently stationed and riding at anchor in every weather.

A lightship guides the big ships to the deep, wide Ambrose Channel, entrance to New York Harbor.

Ambrose Lightship, for instance, marks the entrance of Ambrose Channel, through which the largest ocean liners enter New York harbor.

Lighthouses built on land often have comfortable houses for the keepers and their families, but rock towers seldom have room for so much luxury. Living quarters, storerooms and everything else must be fitted in-side the tower. The rooms follow the shape of the walls, one above another, with steps winding higher and higher until they reach the light itself. Most of these lonely towers have a staff of four keepers. Three tend the light while the fourth is on shore, turn and turn about.

Wrecks have often occurred because of mistaking one lighthouse for another. To

Winding the weights that turn this great, revolving lens. Montauk Point, Long Island.

At Father Point, on the St. Lawrence River, there is room for the keeper's house near by.

prevent such disasters each tower is identified in a number of ways: by its light, its fog signal, its color and shape or—more recently —by its radio beacon. Radio stations installed at lighthouses, on lightships, or at other points well-known to mariners, work automatically, sending out signals in all directions. Passing ships that receive the signals can identify the station and get their bearings by means of direction finders.

The color of a lighthouse is chosen to make it stand out clearly against its background. The old Portland Head Light is sparkling white against dark, Maine rocks. The red brick tower of Jupiter Light, Florida, gleams like a jewel against a background of sand and water. Bold patterns also help. There is no mistaking the barberpole bands of Hatteras and St. Augustine. At Sankaty Head, Nantucket and Montauk Point, Long Island, the towers are girdled with a broad band of color. Diamond shapes mark the tower at Cape Lookout, North Carolina. On many minor light structures, color marks the channel. As you enter it from the sea, red marks the right and black marks the left, just as these colors do on buoys.

A Welcome Sound to Mariners— the Ear-Splitting Diaphone

When fog shuts down, the foghorns begin. Each fog signal station is known by the number of its blasts and by the silences in between. The various kinds of fog signals differ in sound, which helps to tell them apart. Most familiar is the great, hoarse bellow of the diaphone—often two-tone blasts, first high, then low. A diaphone has a piston with a slot in it and is worked with compressed air. Diaphragm horns sound altogether different; two or three may be used to produce a chime signal. Reed horns, sirens, whistles and bells are also used. Bell buoys are still used where the bell responds to the motion of the waves, like the bell of Sir Ralph the Rover:

On a buoy in the storm it floated and swung,
And over the waves its warning rung.

The oldest form of warning is still the light itself. Ancient records tell of Egyptian towers, topped with fire and tended by priests. The most famous, the Pharos, was one of the Seven Wonders of the World. It gave its name to many a lighthouse built by the Romans and the French made it a part of their language. The French word for lighthouse is *phare*. The Pharos was built in the third century B.C., on the island of Pharos in Alexandria Bay.

Wonderful Modern Lenses, Beautiful as Jewels

There was no really brilliant light for lighthouse use until the nineteenth century, when Augustin Fresnel, the French physicist, developed his very wonderful system of lenses. The rays of the lamp shine on all the many pieces of beautifully cut and highly polished glass. As a result, the rays are focussed so that they stream forth in the desired direction in a brilliant, horizontal beam. The first Fresnel lens in the United States was installed at Navesink Light, New Jersey, in 1841.

Nowadays, lenses are assembled in a wide variety of types, depending on the kind of light that is wanted. Fixed lights are continuous and steady. Others, called flashing lights, show a single flash at regular intervals, and the duration of light is always shorter than the duration of darkness. Occulting lights are the other way round— steady lights, eclipsed at regular intervals, with the period of light as long as, or longer than, the period of darkness. These characteristics are also varied in certain ways, for every possible means is used to give each light a special character of its own. In some situations, lights of different colors alternate regularly. Standard light colors for lighted aids to navigation are white, red and green.

In most of the larger lighthouses, electricity is now used for the light itself. Electric incandescent lamps shining on the larger lenses can produce lights of enormous candlepower. A recent list of the principal lighthouses maintained by the United States Coast Guard shows the great variety of candlepower in use today. Boston Light, Massachusetts, the first lighthouse built by any of the colonies in North America, has the brilliance of 100,000 candles; Fire Island, New York, 300,000; Cape Elizabeth, Maine, 500,000; Cape Charles, Virginia, 700,000; Cape St. Elias, Alaska, 1,000,000; Pully Point, Washington, 2,000,000. The three most brilliant lights on the list are White Shoal, Michigan, 3,000,000; Liston Range, Delaware, 5,000,000 and Hillsboro Inlet, Florida, 5,500,000.

Maps
AND
NEW INVENTIONS

By ERWIN RAISZ

Institute of Geographical Exploration,
Harvard University

THERE was great excitement in the harbor of medieval Genoa. The seamen gathered around a man in Oriental garb, who displayed a dark, heavy stone with some magic in it. If you rubbed a needle with this stone and floated the needle in a glass of water, it always turned until it was pointing directly north and south.

Land and sea, fifth century B.C. The world as it was known to Herodotus, the historian.

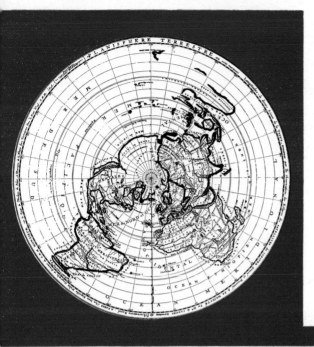

This was great news. These seamen had been able to reckon their hourly run to a mile, but direction—that was another matter, particularly at times when clouds hid the sun or stars. Now they had not only distance but direction as well. Add the two together and you have the basis for a map.

With the wonderful magnetic needle new surveys were made, and the result was the famous portolan chart of the Mediterranean region. It was far more exact than any chart that had been made before. Thus a new invention—the compass—introduced a new era in the art of cartography, which is the making of maps and charts.

Early in the seventeenth century came the invention of the telescope, which led to a solution of the problem of how to measure longitude. As a result, in the latter part of the century, Jean Dominique Cassini made the first really accurate map of the whole known world. This was a large-scale map,

Cassini world map of 1696. The meridians of longitude are shown spreading farther and farther apart instead of merging at the South Pole. Below, the Multiplex, a modern aid to map-making.

PUBLIC ROADS ADMINISTRATION AND U. S. GEOLOGICAL SURVEY

STANDARD OIL CO. (N. J.) PHOTO BY COLLIER

With the help of these stereoscopic binoculars, mountains, hills and valleys show up in high relief. The photographs from which the map-maker is drafting his map were taken from the air.

drawn on the floor of the Paris Observatory.

About half a century later an Englishman, John Harrison, invented the chronometer, an extremely accurate kind of clock. His invention made it possible to find the exact longitude of a ship at sea, and it gave England the leadership in marine chart-making that she still holds.

Today we are again on the threshold of a new era in cartography. For the first time in history we are able to fly in airplanes high above the earth and to see its patterns—patterns we were not aware of when we merely moved about on the earth's surface. Furthermore, we can photograph these patterns with cameras of great perfection.

Imagine that you are in a B-29. In the bottom of the plane is installed a trimetrogon—three cameras mounted in fixed positions relative to each other. Push a button and the cameras take pictures automatically every few seconds until the rolls of films are used up. Each roll can take as many as 500 pictures, although generally there are less.

Every shot makes three pictures: one straight down, the other two sideways, with a combined sweep from horizon to horizon. Each of the three pictures overlaps the one next to it by 60 per cent, or more than half, so that every point that is to be used appears on at least two pictures. One loading can photograph a strip of the earth's surface 1,000 miles long and 5 to 20 miles wide, supposing the plane flies at 20,000 feet.

This is a far cry from the toil of the surveyor of yesteryear, who slowly and laboriously dragged his heavy instruments over swamp, mountain and forest to provide us with maps. Nowadays, from the glaciers of Alaska to the mangrove marshes of Venezuela or the icy ramparts of the Himalayas, nothing is hidden from the eyes of the camera. What once took months to survey can now be photographed in hours.

Taking aerial photographs is but half the story. Maps can be drawn from detailed photographs with the help of the most marvelous plotting machines. The operator of the ma-

247

Drafting a detail map. Here, a small section of an aerial map is enlarged with accuracy.

chine can plot every house, every field, meadow and stream. One of these machines, the Multiplex, projects the overlapping pictures, one with a green light, the other with a red, and the operator wears green-red eyeglasses. The parts that the two pictures have in common appear in high relief, as in an old-fashioned stereoscope. The operator has a special pointer whose motion is carried over to the map he is working on. Suppose he wishes to plot the outlines of a mountain. He can lead his pointer around the sides of the mountain at whatever height he selects and can be sure that the pointer follows this height faithfully, for if the pointer goes above or below that altitude it appears double. This is the modern, time-saving way to draw contour lines.

Contour lines connect points at, let us say, 100, 200 and 300 feet above sea level. If you should take a relief model and place it in the sink and pour in more and more water, you would get higher and higher shore lines. These shore lines would be contour lines. Sea level is the zero contour line.

New inventions also help the maker of charts for ships at sea. No more soundings with wire and weight! The fathometer strikes a "ping" and it echoes back from the bottom of the sea. From the time between "ping" and its echo, the depth of the water can be told, for we know that sound travels through water at about 5,000 feet per second, depending on the density of the water.

By repeatedly sounding these echoes, instruments can draw a continuous profile of the bottom of the sea as the ship sails along. This makes it possible for us to learn more in a year about the land under the sea than we could have done in many times ten years in the past.

The best sounding is useless, however, unless we can plot it on a chart. To do so, we have to know exactly where the ship is when each sounding is taken. Today's surveying ships use an adaptation of radar known as shoran (short-range navigation) to find their position if they are within 200 miles of shore.

If they are farther out they use still another form of radar known as loran (long-range navigation).

Loran was developed in World War II before shoran came into existence. A ship using loran has a loran receiver which receives the radio signals sent out from loran transmitting stations on land. The position of these stations must be known to the ship. Usually

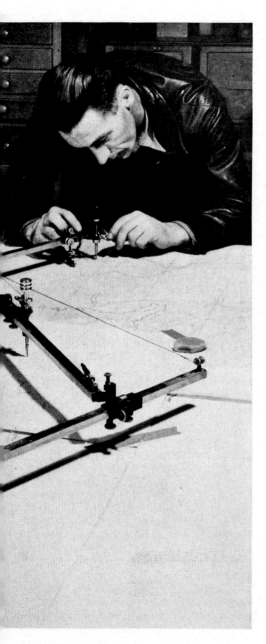

he makes his loran reading and computes his position in only a few minutes.

Shoran is used to locate the soundings of a surveying ship within two hundred miles of shore. Instead of three shore stations, shoran has only two. The ship sends out radio impulses to the two stations on shore, and these impulses are immediately rebroadcast back to the ship. A sensitive instrument on the ship records the time that it takes these radio waves to make the round trip from ship to shore and back again. Then the distances from the ship to each station can be figured, because it is known that radio waves travel at the speed of light (about 186,000 miles a second). Once he has found out what these two distances are, the navigator can use them, together with the known distance between the stations themselves, to find the position of his ship.

Radar Maps That "See" in Storm and Darkness

A plane, shrouded in rain clouds, can fly in complete darkness over an unseen city, and yet the pilot can "see" the city almost as clearly as on a sunny day. His radar is giving out very short waves in all directions, and these waves are echoed from hills, buildings, ships and railways, but are absorbed by water, ground and vegetation. In hilly land, slopes facing the plane reflect more than slopes away from it. These reflected waves show up on a screen as an ever changing relief map of the land below.

We can not yet use ever changing movie maps. However, the United States Aeronautical Chart Service has prepared sixteen-mile-to-the-inch radar charts imitating the effect of the radar screen. Thus another invention—radar—again changed our style of maps.

Hills and Dales, as Plain as the Nose on Your Face

When France, Okinawa, Iwo Jima and so forth were to be invaded, it was very important that every man should know exactly where he was to go and what he was expected to find. Many of our soldiers had difficulty reading maps. To help them, detailed relief models were made of the landing beaches, on which every house, field and hill was clear. The models were reproduced in rubber and could be rolled, squeezed or immersed in salt water without damage.

there are three loran transmitter stations which operate as a group—a master station and two slave stations. They are usually separated by distances of from 200 to 400 miles and they give out signals at definite intervals. The navigator receives signals from the master station and one of the slave stations; then from the master station and the other slave station. From these two sets of signals

For making the relief model on the left, contours were cut from cardboard and assembled in a series of steps. The thickness of each piece of cardboard represents the height of the contour interval. In the next picture, modeling clay has been applied over a stepped contour base.

Light and inexpensive relief models are also made of a synthetic resin called vinylite, which you may have seen used for raincoats and window shades. A map is photographed on a thin vinylite sheet that has been sensitized. Then the sheet is made hot and pliable and is sucked into a plaster negative mold. When cooled, it makes a fine, semi-transparent model with the map on it.

A strong copper or zinc model can be made by pasting a contour map on the sheet of metal. Then, with an electric hammer, you push the mountains up to the height that the contour lines show.

One does not need complex equipment to make models. During the war some clever topographers made models from any material they could lay their hands on. They called them "egg-crate" models. Contours or profiles were cut from old boxes. Canvas was stretched over them and painted and sanded. Sponge-rubber trees, wooden houses, plastiline cliffs and so forth were used for natural-looking models to brief the attacking soldiers. (It might be interesting to study the geography of your own neighborhood

and make a detailed model).

Pity the old-time cartographer! His back is bent and his eyes are red from all the fine lettering and minute ruling of patterns upon the map. His art was perfected by lifelong training. Nowadays the names and patterns are printed on sticky cellophane, and a young girl can paste them on the map. There are also sheets printed with dots, lines and other symbols—for instance, of forests or swamps —that help to make our maps expressive and attractive.

The old letter press printed small maps from zinc or copper plates with raised lines, which wore out after a few thousand copies. The modern offset presses print from large metal sheets on which the lines are not raised but are held in place chemically, as on a lithograph stone. These metal sheets are bent around a cylinder from which the design is "offset" (transferred) to a rubber cylinder, and the rubber cylinder prints on a continuous roll of paper. In this way, fine lines can be printed on coarse paper at great savings in cost. Some huge offset presses may print several thousand four-by-five-foot

The finished clay model is called the "master" model. Exact likenesses of it can be made by means of a plaster-of-Paris mold. Wet plaster of Paris is poured over the model and removed after it has hardened but before it has become dry. It is then checked for accuracy (above, right).

Plaster molds are used to make rubber reproductions of relief maps, such as the two here. Rubber relief maps have many advantages, for they can be rolled or immersed in water without harm.

251

maps in an hour, printing two colors in one operation.

It would take pages and pages to describe all the new devices that aid the modern cartographer. But did airplane photography, Multiplex, echo sounding, radar and so forth change our usual style of maps immediately? No. During the war there was such an urgent demand for maps and more maps that there was no time, at first, to change from old styles to new. The demand was for quantity. Tons of maps were shipped out daily from the enormous plants of the United States Army Map Service. More than 30,000 different maps were prepared and a half billion individual sheets, weighing 20,000 tons, were shipped out from this office alone.

A Torrent of Maps and a New Trick or Two

Add to these equally huge numbers of charts of the Coast and Geodetic Survey, the Hydrographic Office, the Aeronautical Chart Service and the maps of the Office of Strategic Service and the different topographic battalions. These sky-rocketing figures were matched by the British, and later we learned that Germany was in no way behind.

The first result of the new cartography was enormous coverage, using mostly the results of airplane photography. Even so, these maps did not differ essentially from pre-war kinds. Slowly, however, new styles crept in. Maps had to be read by night flyers under a red, amber or ultraviolet light. Soon strange-looking maps appeared, with purple tints printed on fluorescent paper, which lighted up weirdly in the darkness. Even more ghostly were the maps on which the lines were printed with phosphorescent paints.

Forest, Swamp or Grassland? Information Wanted!

In New Guinea the bushwhacking and machete-swinging foot-soldiers demanded maps showing forest, swamp, grassland and vegetation. The topographic battalions prepared some for them and the idea caught on in Washington. Soon this kind of information was overprinted on many maps.

Before the war, charts and maps were two different things. Charts, of course, are for navigation, and land is shown only so far as it is interesting to seamen. Maps are designed for use on land. However, with amphibious

operations, both charts and maps had to be used so that, at the end of the war, it was often hard to tell the difference between them.

The Photo-Map—a Mosaic of Aerial Shots

Many soldiers had difficulty reading the usual contour maps, which do not show the kind of country and its vegetation, cultivation, fields, clearings, fences and so on. They would have preferred airplane photographs if these had been clear enough and properly labeled. To help them, the Army Map Service issued the photo-map. Small airplane photographs of an area were joined together to form a mosaic. These mosaics were reproduced by an extremely fine halftone screen with white and black lettering and with color overprints added. Sometimes the regular map was on one side of the paper and the photo-map on the other.

A Great Change Coming— the Land-Type Map

All of these improvements point to the greatest change still to be made in the usual kind of map. Every day thousands of people, traveling by air, can look down on the marvelous patterns of the earth. Flying over long distances, one can not fail to be impressed by the constant changes in the country underneath. Yet even the best of our present-style maps do not do justice to the richness of these patterns. They hardly suggest the difference between the meadow-patched forest of New England, the lake-dotted rock and muskeg country of the northland, the striped wheat fields of Canada and the strange formations of the frozen ground of the Arctic coastal plain. In the usual type of map, for instance, any lowland is painted green, whether it happens to be a steaming jungle or the sandy desert of the Sahara.

The new "land-type" map tries to show the land more or less by its natural colors and patterns, even if in a symbolized way. On these maps the mountains are shown by plastic shading or by "landform" symbols, and the map is reproduced by three-color process. Roads, railways, lettering and so forth are overprinted in red or black. The land-type map is still in an experimental state but it holds promise of closing the altogether too large gap that is still ordinarily found between land and map.

mardi gras

Rex, monarch of Mardi Gras, rules in glittering gaiety.
ACME

HERE comes the king!
King who?
Why, Rex, of course. King of Carnival! Once a year, on Mardi Gras, this delightful king rules the city of New Orleans. In the afternoon, merrymakers from far and near pack Canal Street to see his magnificent parade. Bands and maskers and prancing horses herald his coming, while confetti and colored streamers flutter in the air. Before the day is over, you will see almost every sort of masquerade costume imaginable. In fact, on this day of many wonders, you may turn into a pirate yourself, or a knight in armor, a bright red devil or perhaps a ballet dancer.

As Rex's parade comes into sight, the crowds burst into cheers. Above the uproar rises the music of one of the many marching bands. It is playing a traditional carnival song—IF EVER I CEASE TO LOVE. The words for this song, it is believed, were first written for Grand Duke Alexis of Russia when he was a guest in New Orleans for the Mardi Gras of 1872. Of its many verses, the one the Grand Duke liked best went this way:

> If ever I cease to love,
> If ever I cease to love,
> May the Grand Duke Alexis
> Ride a buffalo in Texas,
> If ever I cease to love.

The distinguished visitor clapped so hard that he split the seams of his white gloves wide open—or so the story goes.

The torchlit Mardi Gras parades held in New Orleans bring mystery and enchantment to the

Rex sits aloft on a glittering throne on a float as gay as a wedding cake. His crown and scepter and regal robes are resplendent with wondrous jewels and his mantle is a marvelous sight. It stretches the entire length of the float. The two little page boys who stand at the foot of his throne are having the time of their lives, tossing trinkets to the crowd. Every time they throw a string of beads or a toy or what not, there is a wild scramble. The trinkets are not valuable so far as money goes, but each one is priceless as a remembrance of Mardi Gras.

The rest of Rex's parade is as beautiful as skilled designers can make it, and when the last of the floats has passed, the streets are given over to revelers.

Evening brings the torchlit splendor of the last great parade of the carnival season—

the magnificent procession of Comus, Merry Monarch of Mirth. Old-fashioned flares and bright flambeaux light the way for the Merry Monarch. The flickering flames break up the night into dancing, goblin shadows and cast a weird, red glow over the dream-like scene. The light plays on burnished floats and gorgeous costumes, turning the parade of Comus into a fantastic, unforgettable sight.

Mardi Gras night winds up with splendid balls for Rex and Comus. As another famous party once did for Cinderella, the balls end instantly the minute the clock strikes twelve. It is Ash Wednesday now. Lent has begun and the carnival is over for another year. There have been parades and parties and gaiety throughout the carnival season, but Mardi Gras, the day before Lent, was most wonderful of all.

streets of the old French city by the Mississippi.

around its neck. Behind the ox rode a little boy who was crowned King of the Butchers. After the parade was over, the ox was butchered, the meat was sold, and many good dinners were enjoyed.

Carnivals Are Held in Many of the World's Cities

In the United States, carnivals are held on Mardi Gras chiefly in Louisiana and Alabama, where the influence of old France is still felt. In parts of Canada, which also has close ties with France, children go from house to house gathering gifts, as many boys and girls do on Hallowe'en. Many of the Shrove Tuesday carnivals held in Europe and in South America before World War II were famous. Among the best-known were those held in Rome, Venice, Turin, Naples and Florence, in Italy; Paris and Nice in France; and in Mainz, Bonn, Cologne and the Rhine Valley in Germany; in Havana, Cuba; and in the beautiful seaport city of Rio de Janeiro in Brazil.

In some parts of England, Canada and France, Shrove Tuesday is called Pancake Tuesday. Many good things that could not be eaten during Lent were thriftily eaten the day before, and the custom arose of using up some of these delicacies by making them into pancakes.

Many and Quaint Are the Shrove Tuesday Customs

In the village of Olney, England, an old-time ceremony was recently revived. At a certain time during the day, when the bell in the village church rings out, the housewives of Olney rush to their kitchens and begin frying pancakes. When the bell rings out a second time, they pick up their frying pans and hurry to the village pump. There they wait for a third peal of the bell. When it comes, the ladies—pans, cakes and all—race each other to the church. The first one to arrive without spilling any of her pancakes wins the prize—a "kiss of peace" from the church bellringer.

A curious Pancake Tuesday ceremony is known in France. People not only eat their pancakes, but they feed some to the chickens. It is believed these pancakes will make the hens lay more and bigger eggs. However that may be, the chickens seem to be none the worse for having this special Mardi Gras of their own.

To feast before fasting is far from new. Early Roman Christians feasted before the Lenten-tide, and the custom spread to many parts of Europe and later to the Western Hemisphere. In time, pageants and beautiful processions became a part of the merrymaking. Today, the most colorful and best-known carnival in North America is held in New Orleans. The word "carnival" comes from two Latin words, *carnis* (flesh) and *vale* (farewell).

The name Mardi Gras came from France, where Shrove Tuesday, the day before Ash Wednesday was a day to dine on "the fat of the land." *Mardi* means Tuesday and *gras* means fat. In Paris and other French cities it was the custom to parade a fat ox through the streets. Its horns and its hooves were gilded, and garlands of flowers were hung

NEARLY everything that has been written about Mexico in the past has told about the colorful natives and their picturesque towns. Most of the pictures have been beautiful, artistic photographs of ancient buildings, Mexicans in their native costumes, or primitive ways of getting about, such as the ox-cart or the little burro. Perhaps these used to be the most interesting things one could tell about Mexico.

But things are changing in Mexico, just as they are in all countries. If you were to visit that land today, you would still see some of the poorer natives wearing simple clothes and big sombreros (hats). Thousands of workers still wear sandals instead of shoes, and serapes (blankets) instead of coats. One still passes the slow burros along the highway, and may see ox-carts along country roads. Hundreds of old churches and villages look about the same as they have for centuries. Nevertheless, Mexico has changed in many ways.

Recently an American boy and his little sister were touring in Mexico with their parents. They had driven to Mexico City in their own car. While they were driving through the city's new industrial district, the little boy said: "These buildings look just like some of the factories in Chicago." His sister, who was just a little younger, said: "Yes, but they are a lot cleaner."

Industria electrica—this Westinghouse plant is

MEXICO

By RALPH HANCOCK

These two children saw a great many things in Mexico that they would not have seen in their own country. They also saw a great many things that reminded them of their own home town, and these things are all a part of the many changes that are taking place in Mexico. Therefore, instead of looking at the sort of pictures that we are used to, let us see what some of the changes are that are making Mexico more and more important as a nation.

One of the things that made Mexico a picturesque country was its large number of poor and ignorant natives. There are still many poor people in Mexico, but not so many of them are ignorant. A few years ago the Government realized that Mexico would never become a strong nation if large numbers of its people could not even read or write. There are now many schools for children, and most Mexican boys and girls

Oil refining—an important Mexican industry.

one sign of Mexico's rapid modernization.

TODAY

AUTHOR OF *The Magic Land*: *Mexico*

seem to enjoy going to them regularly.

By the time these boys and girls have grown up, most of the people of Mexico will have had some education, but that will be a few years yet. Meanwhile, there are many grownups who were not able to go to school when they were children, and the Government is especially interested in teaching these persons. Many of these people have children who can read and write, so the Government asked the children to help teach their parents. The children helped, the Government helped, neighbors who were able to read and write pitched in and helped too. Altogether, in the past four years, they have taught more than a million persons, and there are now 18,579 schools or government centers where adults can learn to read and write.

A man who knows how to read is better able to improve his condition in life than one who can not. Therefore, one of the results of

Olden ways still hold their charm. Querétaro.

this new educational campaign in Mexico has been to improve the living conditions of its people. Thousands of new homes have been built for workers. Hundreds of miles of plumbing and electric wires have been used to make these houses modern. New factories have grown up to make things that people want. There are no big, black chimneys to make smoke, however, because Mexican factories are all run by electricity or oil. There are no chimneys in Mexican homes, either, because the climate is warm all the year around, and furnaces are not needed.

More than four thousand new factories were built in Mexico last year. These produced a great variety of things—radios, refrigerators, automobiles, automobile tires, shoes, clothing, electric motors and light bulbs, soap, books, paper and paper products, such as bags and paper cups, phonograph records and sugar.

Many of these factories were built with the help of Americans. The new sugar refinery, for example—the largest in the world— was built by an American contractor with money supplied by both Mexican and American investors. This mill is situated in the tropical state of Veracruz. American investments in Mexico now amount to more than $500,000,000.

Factories pay lower taxes in Mexico than they do in Canada or the United States.

White-hot—handle with care! Mexico's iron and steel industry is growing by leaps and bounds.

Sometimes, if a new industry is especially needed, the Mexican Government will charge no taxes at all for the first five years or more. This enables the new factory to get started and well established. Wages are comparatively low. Workers in Mexico make only about half the money that Canadian or American workers get for the same kind of work. For these two reasons alone, Mexican factories are able to make greater profits than factories north of the border can make —frequently two or three times as great.

Because of the low taxation and labor costs, many Northern firms are opening branch plants in Mexico, partly to supply the Mexican market, and partly to make goods to sell to other Latin-American countries. However, for the past year business has been so good in Mexico that very few firms have been able to produce a surplus to sell outside the country.

Another industry that has been important in Mexico for many years is petroleum. Most of the oil wells in Mexico were developed by foreign companies, especially British and American firms. Some years ago the Mexican Government decided to take over all the oil

business in the country. Foreign oil companies were made to give up their property and were obliged to leave Mexico. Their oil properties were put under the control of a government-owned firm which is now known as Pemex. Unfortunately, the wells and refineries were not so well operated by Pemex as they had been by the foreign companies, for the Mexicans had less experience in the manufacture of petroleum products. Any visitor to Mexico in the past few years knows that Mexican gasoline was of very poor quality.

This year, for the first time, Pemex has invited foreign companies to come back and help with its oil problems. Hundreds of thousands of dollars are now being invested in Mexico by American and British companies. They hope to develop many new fields, and are going to help Pemex produce more oil. Perhaps they will assist Pemex in producing better gasoline.

Factories and petroleum and mining (Mexico is the world's biggest producer of silver) are all very important, yet the one industry that is doing most to change the country is agriculture. Farming is the oldest industry in Mexico. The ancient Aztecs tilled thousands of acres of the land before the white man came. They had no beasts of burden to help them; all their farming was done by hand. Then the white man brought horses, mules and oxen, and the Indians soon learned to use them. Today one can still see the slow-moving oxen pulling plows in Mexican fields. In small fields one can also see Indians planting and cultivating and harvesting their crops entirely by hand, just as their forefathers did a thousand years ago.

The Mexican Government wishes to develop the use of modern farming methods. For this purpose it has established many large farms on which new agricultural methods are used, with tractors and many kinds of farm machinery. The Government hopes that thousands of farmers will learn from this example. What they are really aiming for is more food production. Imagine a climate where it is never winter, and yet where the people do not produce enough food for themselves.

The TVA of Mexico, Where the Papaloapan Flows

One of the largest and newest projects is in the tropical southern part of the country, where the Government is building many big dams to control the rivers and provide electric power. This is often spoken of as the TVA of Mexico because it is more or less modeled on the great Tennessee Valley development. In time, more than 17,000 square miles of wilderness and jungle will be turned into rich farming land. The whole project lies in an area drained by the Papaloapan River, and it is called the Papaloapan River Basin Irrigation and Electric Power Project.

The dread aftosa, or hoof-and-mouth disease, spreads rapidly, and is one of the worst diseases of cattle. When it broke out in Mexico, cattlemen north of the border became badly frightened, for it might jump the border and infect their cattle. That would mean the loss of millions of dollars. The sooner the disease could be wiped out, the better, so the United States and Mexican governments formed a joint commission to deal with it. Hundreds of thousands of cattle were vaccinated. In some cases sick cattle had to be killed, and the owners were paid for the loss. Some of the more ignorant farmers did not understand what was happening and did not want to have their cattle killed. The educated people, however, fully understood why

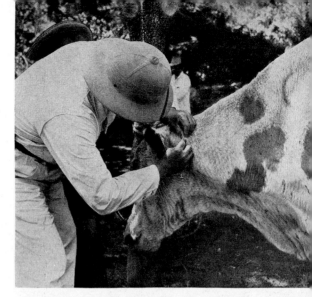

UNITED STATES DEPARTMENT OF AGRICULTURE

Aftosa, a disease of cattle, has brought Mexico and the United States together in trying to stamp it out. Vaccine helps; so do fences such as this one for quarantining cattle.

these measures were necessary. Thus, education played an important part in this campaign to stamp out a terrible disease.

Yes, the picture of Mexico is changing swiftly. Its scenery is magnificent. Its little shrines and great cathedrals and other works of days gone by still glow with ancient beauty. But in its civilization, Mexico is rapidly leaving old ways for new.

The Middle

By E. S. FERGUSON

*Formerly Deputy Administrator General
of the Finances for Iran*

KEYSTONE PICTURES INC.

Glubb Pasha, the Englishman who trained the
army of Trans-Jordan, and King Abdullah.

ONE of the most important events of
the past year was the creation of
the new Jewish state of Israel. How
it was born and the problems surrounding its
survival are of vital interest to the world and
especially to us. The other major developments in the Middle East during the past
year are all closely related to the happenings
in Palestine. They are the aims of rival Arab
countries, the control of the huge oil reserves
existing in the Middle East and the role of
Soviet Russia in this part of the world. We
in Canada and the United States have great
concern in all of these affairs.

You will remember from your studies of
ancient history that the ancient Jewish state
came to an end in 70 A.D. with the capture
and ruin of Jerusalem by the Romans. The
next important change came with the capture
of Palestine by the Ottoman Turks in 1516.
The Turkish Empire was broken up after
World War I. The League of Nations gave
Great Britain a mandate over a wide area in
the Middle East which included Palestine.
This was separate from the mandate over
Mesopotamia which later became the kingdom of Iraq. From a part of the Palestine
mandate Great Britain created the Arab

state of Trans-Jordan in 1946. Emir Abdullah became King Abdullah Ibn Ul-Hussein.
He is a member of the same family which
rules Iraq. We shall return later to King Abdullah and his ambitions for an Arab empire.

Great Britain continued to govern the rest
of the Palestine mandate under exceedingly
difficult conditions. Both the Arabs and the
Jews wanted the mandate lifted, but each
wanted to rule over the other. The Jews
based their claim on the Balfour Declaration
of November 2, 1917, which pledged the
British Government to "establishment in
Palestine of a national home for the Jewish
people." The Arabs contended that pledges
had also been given to them which would
protect Arab sovereignty in Palestine.

Following the end of World War II the
difficulties of governing Palestine increased
greatly for the British. Great Britain had
been seriously weakened by the war and
could not afford the expense of maintaining a
large armed force in Palestine. Also, as a result of the growth of air power, Great Britain
began shifting the basis of its over-all defensive strategy. Air bases in Africa were to replace naval fortresses and military forces in
the Middle East. Moreover, the United
States had assumed a major role in Middle
Eastern affairs during the last war. Great
Britain was willing, therefore, to end her
mandate rule of Palestine.

The problem was placed before the United
Nations and on November 29, 1947, the
United Nations General Assembly voted to
partition (divide) Palestine, and give part to
the Jews, part to the Arabs. This was a very
dramatic event. The outcome was not suspected until just a few hours before the final
vote was taken. It is generally agreed that
the United States was the deciding factor in-
fluencing the vote in favor of partition. The
Jewish people were greatly pleased with the
decision, but the six Arab member states
withdrew from the assembly in angry protest.

Throughout 1948 Palestine remained in

East

DURING THE YEAR

the headlines. Great Britain announced that the Palestine mandate would be given up on May 14 and that British troops would leave Palestine. The United Nations set up a commission to carry out the plan of partition and to find means for governing and maintaining order in the area. The immediate problem confronting the United Nations commission was to seek and maintain a truce between Jews and Arabs.

With the expiration of the British Palestine mandate on May 14, 1948, the Jewish leaders proclaimed the state of Israel. Within a few minutes of this proclamation President Truman recognized the Jewish provisional government as the *de facto* authority. (This was not a full legal recognition, but a partial recognition.) One of the major issues con-

Dr. Chaim Weizmann, first president of Israel. Below, Arab recruits in ancient Nablus.

fronting President Truman at the year's end was the question of giving full recognition to Israel. Israel also desired membership in the UN and a large loan from the United States.

Dr. Chaim Weizmann, a famous chemist and long a champion of Zionism, was made president. It was Dr. Weizmann who was mainly responsible for securing the Balfour Declaration from the British. Another important leader is David Ben-Gurion, premier and defense minister. He organized the first defense force which later grew into the Haganah, the Israeli army.

Fighting Begins Again on the Age-Old Battleground of Palestine

Fighting broke out between the Jews and Arabs immediately following the withdrawal of British troops. From all sides Arabs moved to attack the new state of Israel. The Egyptians sent a column from the south, Trans-Jordan and Iraq attacked from the east, and Syria and Lebanon from the north. The Jews attacked the Arab city of Jaffa adjoining Tel Aviv and occupied it. Practically all the Arab population had left, however, while the British still were there. What information has been made public shows the Jewish army, Haganah, to be well organized, adequately equipped and of high caliber. The Arab armies, with the exception of King Abdullah's army from Trans-Jordan, appear poorly organized, ill equipped and lacking in leadership. The Arab armies were being decisively beaten when both sides accepted a truce arranged by the United Nations commission. This truce was later broken and a second one established. Each side claims that the second truce was not observed by the other side. Foreign Minister Moshe Shertok of Israel reported that the Arabs were violating the truce. The Arabs on the other hand complained that the Jews were not obeying the truce.

A major problem of the war in Palestine has been the large number of Arabs, over 325,000, who have fled from their homes. They are scattered throughout the different Arab countries, where they are hungry, helpless and living under unsanitary conditions which cause an increase in disease.

On September 17 the world was shocked by the assassination of Count Folke Bernadotte, United Nations mediator for Palestine and a nephew of King Gustav of Sweden. Count Bernadotte was shot by unidentified gunmen

in uniform in the Jewish-controlled area of Jerusalem. The gunmen also killed André Serat, chief United Nations truce observer for Jerusalem, who was a colonel in the French Air Force. It was generally believed that the Stern Gang, a radical group in the Jewish state, was responsible. Public officials of Israel expressed great indignation and took the most energetic steps to catch the assassins.

In Bernadotte's report, completed just before his death, he recommended that Israel be recognized and admitted to the United Nations; that northwest Palestine be given to the Jewish state, the southern Negeb area to the Arabs; that Jerusalem be made international territory under United Nations' control. Neither the Israelis nor the Arabs were agreeable to all of these proposals.

What solution can be found for the problems of Palestine? There are only two to choose from. Either the Jews and Arabs fight it out among themselves or some other power strong enough to control the area takes over.

The second choice is unlikely for a number of reasons. No international body such as the United Nations has the military power to do the job. The nations which are in a position to contribute a strong force for use by the UN could not agree on who would control such a force. The issue would immediately become a point of debate between Soviet Russia and the United States as they are the only two powers in a position to assume such a responsibility. Neither wants the other to extend its influence in the Middle East. We shall return to this question later. It seems, therefore, quite probable that the state of Israel will have to fight its own way. This is, of course, what it desires to do.

Israel Can Bring Great Benefits to the Middle East

The new state of Israel has much to offer neighboring Arab countries. Apart from Turkey, it is the only Middle-East country where the knowledge of modern civilization is being widely used. Jewish people from all over the world have returned to Palestine with the belief that they can create a strong Jewish nation. They have brought with them the knowledge acquired in great centers of learning throughout the world. They are prepared to use the scientific learning of modern times to transform the deserts into food producing areas; to establish centers of learning; to promote health and to enforce just government. Such an example on the borders of Arab countries could not fail to stimulate Arab people to improve their present animal-like existence. The Jewish and Arab peoples must learn to co-operate with each other instead of one ruling the other. Without undue interference from other powers this is a likely prospect. None of the Arab states adjoining Palestine is strong enough to conquer the people of Israel.

Egyptian Affairs Are in a Troubled State

Egypt's population is very poor. The Government has many problems facing it, the most important one being to stay in power. The army can not be sent far from home as it may be needed to maintain order. Strikes of the police during 1948 in Alexandria and Cairo showed this. The army prevented looting in Cairo, but Alexandria suffered badly as there were not enough troops to replace the police. The British have withdrawn their troops from Egypt. On December 28, Premier Mahmoud Fahmy Nokrasky Pasha was shot and killed by a member of the recently outlawed nationalist Moslem Brotherhood. A new Cabinet was formed at once, headed by Ibrahim Abdul Hadi Pasha. The new Premier was expected to continue the same policy toward Israel. The fighting still went on.

The strength of Trans-Jordan rests almost wholly upon assistance from Great Britain. The well-trained but small army is not likely to be used up by King Abdullah in a "holy war" against the Jews. It is reported that he is short of ammunition for his armed forces; and Glubb Pasha, a British general who with other Britishers trained the Trans-Jordan army, went to England to seek a loan for the Government, presumably to secure supplies and equipment. King Abdullah is known to be ambitious to set up an Arab empire which will take in Syria, Lebanon and parts of Palestine.

Neither Syria nor Lebanon forms a serious threat to Israel. Lebanon is a country of peoples with divided religions. This does not allow for a vigorous foreign policy as both religions must be represented in the government. Syria has not recovered from the French mandate of that country following World War I, and from the events of World War II.

Iraq has not put forward a very strong ef-fort in support of the Arabs. Only a brigade of troops was sent to the fighting front, and a larger number is not likely to be sent. The unruly tribes of that country will make it necessary to keep most of the army at home.

Saudi Arabia has given no military support to the Arab cause. King Ibn Saud does not want to strengthen other Arab states at the expense of his country. The oil developments by American interests in Saudi Arabia are of more concern to him. The impossibility of growing food in Saudi Arabia without costly irrigation works has made it necessary for that country to import more than 75 per cent of all basic foods. Farms are very small. Most of them range from less than an acre to around five acres. A few farms of forty to fifty acres are considered large operations. The Arabian American Oil Company, holder of an extremely large and valuable oil concession, has been helping the country to build irrigation systems so that more foodstuffs can be grown.

It will be seen, therefore, that Pan-Arabism, as sponsored by Abdul Rohman Ozzam Pasha, secretary-general of the Arab League, has not the unity of purpose that some people think it has. The unity, if there is any, between the Arab nations, is a common objection to the creation of a Jewish state in Palestine. But no Arab country has much interest in securing benefits for any other Arab state. This is further borne out by the announcement of the Arab League on Septem-

Rioters in Alexandria, Egypt, burn streetcars.
INTERNATIONAL

ber 20 of the formation of an Arab government for Palestine, over the protests of Trans-Jordan and Iraq. Ahmed Hilmy Pasha, who had been the Arab military commander in Jerusalem, was named premier of the new state. King Abdullah of Trans-Jordan opposed creating the Arab state because it meant that the Arab League recognized the partition of Palestine. The members of the Arab League are: Egypt, Yemen, Saudi Arabia, Trans-Jordan, Iraq, Lebanon and Syria.

Israel and the Arabs, If Left to Themselves, Might Agree

It would be possible for Israel and the various Arab states to get together and try to establish some co-operative arrangement. If only the Jews and Arabs were involved, this might be done. But this is not the case. Two others elements further complicate conditions in the Middle East. They are Soviet Russia and oil.

The oil deposits of the Middle East are probably the largest in the world. They are concentrated mostly around the Persian Gulf area. British and American companies have gained extensive oil concessions and are rapidly expanding their operations. Huge pipe lines are being constructed to carry the oil from the Persian Gulf area across the desert to ports on the Mediterranean Sea. (See the article called Pipeline in Arabia, on page 307). Practically all American concessions have been granted by the Arab states, Saudi Arabia being the most important to date. It can readily be seen that the Arab states would use their position to attempt to influence American policy toward Palestine. The Arab rulers have threatened to cancel United States oil concessions and to appeal to Soviet Russia for aid. Neither threat has been seriously regarded by the Americans. The Arabs need the money from oil royalties and their threat of appeal to Soviet Russia is a hollow one as the Arabs have no real desire for Russian help. On the contrary they are fearful lest the Russians gain a foothold in the Middle East.

If one moves out of the Arab countries into Iran and Turkey, whose borders adjoin those of Soviet Russia, Palestine is no longer the main problem. These two nations are really afraid that Soviet Russia will attempt to dominate them. The United States has taken extensive measures to bolster their in-

dependence. Several American military missions are working hard in Greece, Turkey and Iran. Huge loans or gifts have been granted. During the past year a credit of $26,000,000 was granted to Iran by the United States to cover the cost of surplus military equipment. Even greater aid has been given to Greece and Turkey. It is very doubtful, however, whether Iran is capable of putting up very much of a defense of its borders. The leadership of the Iranian army is not rated very highly, and an army with poor leaders is a weak army. Moreover, the Iranian nation is not equipped to withstand any prolonged struggle. Turkey possesses a good army which would very likely give an excellent account of itself even against the Soviet Russian armies. Still, the strain of keeping the country on a military basis is a great drain upon the nation's economic life.

It is now clear that the major urgent problems of the Middle East will not be solved by the countries of that area. The issues raised in the Middle East are but a part of a bigger problem, namely that between the Western powers and Soviet Russia. It now appears likely that a long period of uncertainty lies ahead.

The United States as the leading world power carries a great responsibility to bring order and justice back into world affairs. This responsibility is being met with courage and determination. Success comes very slowly, and the utmost patience is required. The world has been broken up into new parts and it will take a long time to fit these parts together so that the leading nations of the world will respect each other without fear. The countries of the Middle East are but one part of the whole world puzzle. The solution of this puzzle depends largely upon the outcome of the struggle between the great powers of the world.

The Outlook for Peace in Palestine Brightens

By the end of the year peace had not yet come to the Holy Land, but a great deal of progress had been made. Efforts were being made by the Security Council to bring about an armistice between the Israelis and the Egyptians in the disputed area of the Negeb. King Abdullah had been recognized as their ruler by the Palestine Arabs, and it was expected that he would soon formally annex this area to the kingdom of Trans-Jordan.

MONKEY business

By FRANK A. BEACH,
Professor of Psychology, Yale University

BULA, the little chimpanzee, stood stock-still and listened. Far off she could hear her lonely friend, Bimba, crying forlornly in her cage. Bula did not rush to the door of the room and pull the door handle, trying to get out. She had learned better. Instead, she scrabbled around among the many-colored plastic chips on the floor, picked out a yellow one and shoved it into a little slot by the door. Then she ran to the scientist who was with her in her cage, held out her arms to him, begging for a ride on his shoulders to the cage where Bimba was. She expected to get that ride, too, for she had paid for it, had she not, with the yellow chip? And sure enough, almost before she knew it, she was back at home in her cage with Bimba.

Bula was one of the six chimpanzees —small apes—who were learning to use "money" under the watchful eye of a scientist at the Yale University Laboratories of Primate Biology. Their money was not the kind you carry around in your pocket or in your pocketbook. It was a queer kind of money—round, flat plastic chips, white, blue, red and yellow.

The scientist used a machine which he called the Chimp-O-Mat in teaching his chimpanzees to use money. It was rather like an ordinary slot machine—when you put in one of the plastic chips, something good to eat would come out into a little cup or into your hand. No one had any idea how long it would take the chimpanzees to learn to work the Chimp-O-Mat. The experimenter was delighted when the six-year-old male, Moos, after watching him just once, walked up to the Chimp-O-Mat, picked up a chip and slipped it into the slot in the proper manner. Then he put his hand into the cup and waited for the ripe grape to fall into it. Moos had learned to use "money."

At first, in these experiments with the

"I think you're holding out on me! Where are the yellow chips that I earned? And my piggy-back ride?" Chimpanzees can now be trained to do work for "money"—that is, chips of different colors.

265

chimpanzees, only white chips were used. These were mixed with brass slugs which could be put into the Chimp-O-Mat slot, but which were of no value since nothing came out of the machine when they were put in. The chimpanzees at first picked up the slugs as often as they did the white chips, but they soon learned that the slugs were not "good money." After that they never made a mistake. They paid no attention to the brass slugs and picked up only the white chips, each one of which brought a ripe grape from the Chimp-O-Mat.

"Keep Busy at the Work Machine. There Are Grapes inside It."

Then the experimenter set out to discover whether the chimpanzees would actually work in order to get the grapes which they prized so highly. He introduced them to a "work machine" which was so arranged that each time a chimpanzee raised its handle, which was attached to a heavy weight, the animal could reach into an opening and take one grape. Then the handle would return to its first position and would have to be lifted up again before another grape appeared. The little apes worked hard at the machine, and continued to work, until they were tired out, or until they had all the grapes they wanted for the time being.

After Hard Work, the Chimpanzees Insist on Prompt Service

The scientist's next idea was to make the chimpanzees operate the work machine in order to get the white chips, which they could later exchange for grapes. They were perfectly willing to work for the chips, each one of which stood in their minds as a symbol for a luscious grape. They would not, however, work at all when the work machine was loaded with the useless brass slugs. They had learned that these were no good and would not buy anything.

Some of the chimpanzees were even willing to work hard for the white chips and then wait until the next day to spend them for grapes. Moos, in one ten-minute period, lifted the eighteen-pound handle 185 times, accumulating a huge pile of chips. When they had to wait until the next day to spend their earnings, the chimpanzees insisted on prompt service and were most unwilling to wait even a minute or two after they had placed their chips in the Chimp-O-Mat.

They became very impatient and would repeatedly shake the machine in their rage.

Later, the investigator tried the chimpanzees with chips of different colors—white, blue, red and yellow. One white chip still bought one grape, but a blue chip bought two grapes. A red chip was worth a drink of water for a thirsty chimpanzee, and a yellow chip, most wonderful of all, meant a piggy-back ride. Very soon the chimpanzees learned that a blue chip was worth two white ones, and then the white chips were left until all the blue ones had been used. If a chimpanzee was thirsty, he would spurn the white and blue and yellow chips and pick up a red one, for which he would receive a drink of water. As in the case of Bula, who wanted to be taken to join her lonely friend, the yellow chips were in demand for piggy-back rides.

Bula Buys a Piggy-Back Ride to Escape from a White Rat

There were other times when piggy-back rides seemed more important to Bula than even the most delicious food. One day the experimenter went into Bula's room and opened a box containing a white rat. The rat sat quietly on the floor, but Bula was scared nearly out of her wits. She had never seen a rat before. She stopped buying grapes at the Chimp-O-Mat, and with great care and watchfulness skirted her way around the rat, keeping as far from it as possible. Then she hurriedly grabbed a yellow chip from a pile on the floor, placed it in the slot by the door, and jumped on the scientist's back. In no uncertain tones she made it clear that she wished to be carried away—the quicker the better—from the terrifying creature on the floor.

Bula Is Bimba's Friend but Not Her Banker

Perhaps the most amusing thing happened to the chimpanzees and their money one day when, instead of grapes, the Chimp-O-Mat was giving out slices of orange, unpeeled. Bula and Bimba, the two little females, were in the same cage. They were given a big pile of white chips, with which to buy the slices of orange. Bula, the more aggressive of the two, quickly took possession of almost all the chips. Bimba naturally did not like this and protested, whining. She held out her empty hand, hoping that Bula would give her some of the chips. This seemed particu-

This little fellow enjoys picture-taking, but now he is in a hurry to work the Chimp-O-Mat.

larly reasonable to expect, since the two were good friends. Bula, however, knew quite well what she wanted to do with the chips—and that was *not* to give them to Bimba. She did give her one chip, though, which she carefully and reluctantly selected from her enormous pile. As Bula put chip after chip into the Chimp-O-Mat and consumed one luscious bit of orange after another, Bimba became more and more unhappy. Finally Bula turned impatiently toward Bimba and threw an orange peel in her direction.

These experiments have shown us that chimpanzees, like people, can learn to use symbols. Money, after all, is merely a symbol for those things which it can buy; it has no value in itself. The chimpanzees' colored chips stood for the pleasure of eating ripe grapes and oranges, for the joy of a drink of water when a little animal is thirsty, or for a much wanted piggy-back ride.

MOTION PICTURES

NOW SHOWING —

THE J. ARTHUR RANK ORGANIZATION

On the opposite page, Sir Laurence Olivier, as Hamlet, speaks one of the famous soliloquies in his film of Shakespeare's play.

METRO-GOLDWYN-MAYER

Right, *The Search* is a moving story of a Czechoslovak boy and his mother, reunited after wandering over war-torn Europe.

RKO

Below, left, Loretta Young and William Holden in *Rachel and the Stranger,* a story of pioneer life in the old Northwest.

METRO-GOLDWYN-MAYER

Below, right, Athos, Porthos, Aramis and D'Artagnan thrill a new generation with their adventures in *The Three Musketeers.*

Red River, a really fine Western, glows with the color and romance of the Chisholm Trail.

Left, Ingrid Bergman as Joan of Arc defends herself before the tribunal which finds her guilty of witchcraft.

Below, Cary Grant and Myrna Loy in *Mr. Blandings Builds His Dream House.*

Humphrey Bogart, Walter Huston and Tim Holt in *Treasure of the Sierra Madre.*

270

In it is Montgomery Clift, who played the American soldier in *The Search*.

Right, *The Red Shoes*, a British film, blends reality and fantasy in a story of life behind the scenes in the world of ballet.

Melody Time brings us Johnny Appleseed, tree-planter and friend of animals.

Below, Katharine Hepburn and Spencer Tracy in *State of the Union*.

271

MUSICAL EVENTS

By JOHN TASKER HOWARD
Author and Composer

A scene from the modern opera, *Peter Grimes,*

TWO exciting and important musical events in 1948 were the Rachmaninoff Fund award for young pianists, and the Henry H. Reichhold symphonic award for composers. The Rachmaninoff Fund contest has been going on for several years. Regional contests were held in different centers throughout the United States, then the winners of these took part in district contests from which five young pianists were chosen to appear in the final concert at Carnegie Hall in New York.

April 29 was selected as the date for the five young people to meet their final test in the famous hall where so many of the world's greatest artists had played. The contestants were Seymour Lipkin, of Detroit, Ruth Geiger, Grace Harrington and Gary Graffman, who at different times had been regional winners in Philadelphia, and Jeanne Therrien, regional winner of Boston. At the deciding concert each of these young pianists played a solo number, and a movement of a concerto with the National Broadcasting Company orchestra, conducted by Fritz Reiner.

The winner was twenty-year-old Seymour Lipkin, and the prize was of a kind to thrill the heart of even an experienced concert artist. The two largest concert bureaus in the country—Columbia Concerts, Inc., and National Concert and Artists' Corporation—undertook together the management of this boy's career, and he was given a contract to make recordings for RCA-Victor. Under this contract he was immediately given a check for $1,000 as an advance against future royalty payments. After winning the award, Lipkin's first engagement was to play as soloist on the Telephone Hour radio program.

Gary Graffman was given a special national award and a Carnegie Hall recital in the following season, and Grace Harrington received honorable mention. Both will be allowed to enter the next final contest of

the Rachmaninoff Fund, without having to win any more preliminary or regional contests.

The Reichhold award gave money prizes totaling $32,500 to three winners. More than four hundred composers from North and South America submitted symphonic works. Two of the prize winners were from the United States—Leroy Robertson, professor

by the English composer, Benjamin Britten.

of music at Brigham Young University, Provo, Utah, and Albert Sendrey, of Los Angeles. The third was from Brazil— Camargo Guarnieri, of Sao Paulo. Robertson won the first prize, $25,000, with a composition called TRILOGY. This was played for the first time by the Detroit Symphony Orchestra under Karl Krueger on December 11, 1947. Three days later the orchestra played

it again on its Sunday evening broadcast. Guarnieri won the second prize of $5,000, while the third prize, $2,500 went to Sendrey.

The giver of these prizes, Henry H. Reichhold, is the Detroit business man who reorganized the Detroit Symphony Orchestra and for several years paid for its Sunday evening broadcasts.

Until March 1948 television was not allowed to present "live" music—music that is televised while it is actually being played. The reason for this was that James Caesar Petrillo, the head of the American Federation of Musicians, would not let its members take part in televised shows or concerts. Suddenly this ban was lifted. The result was to advance television to a wonderful extent. Television, like radio, depends very much on music of one sort or another, from popular ballad singers to symphony orchestras—in fact, without music it is almost impossible to build a well-rounded series of programs day after day and week after week.

When the ban was lifted, some of the televisors were ready with studios and equipment and could begin right away to broadcast music. Others had to hurry their preparations to catch up with the procession. Because the announcement of the ban's removal was made on a Friday, many people supposed that Toscanini and the NBC orchestra would be the first important musical organization to be televised. It did not turn out this way, however, for it happened that the Philadelphia Orchestra's regular broadcast on CBS came at five o'clock, just one hour and a half before the NBC hour. Therefore the Philadelphians, led by their director, Eugene Ormandy, had the fun and the distinction of being the first symphony orchestra to be seen by the television audiences.

An even more exciting event was the first telecast of an opera from the stage of the Metropolitan in New York. This took place on the opening night of the 1948–49 season, and the opera was Verdi's OTELLO.

In the summertime music goes outdoors, and some of the musical year's most exciting events take place under the stars, to the accompaniment of passing airplanes and cooling breezes. The 1948 summer season of the Philharmonic-Symphony Society of New York at the Lewisohn Stadium was a great success artistically, but suffered from bad weather during its last weeks.

The most popular events on the program

Students at Toronto's opera school in a scene from *La Serva Padrona*, by Pergolesi.

thorne, who lived in a little red house on the estate. During this festival an exact copy of Hawthorne's house was dedicated in the presence of two of the great author's descendants and also a grandson of the poet Longfellow. This was the result of the efforts of Mrs. Guy Patterson Gannett, past president of the National Federation of Music Clubs.

Central City, Colorado, picturesque relic of Western mining days, celebrated the seventieth anniversary of its famous opera house with three weeks of opera. The works performed were Offenbach's TALES OF HOFFMANN and Mozart's COSÍ FAN TUTTE. The opera season was followed by a number of performances of the Broadway production of Ferenc Molnar's THE PLAY'S THE THING.

Other summer centers of music enjoyed their usual seasons. Among them was the Hollywood Bowl, which opened with a performance of Mahler's Eighth Symphony, conducted by Eugene Ormandy. The annual opera season in Cincinnati, held at the Zoological Gardens, presented, among other works, SALOME, DER ROSENKAVALIER, BORIS

Eugene Ormandy, conducting the Philadelphia Orchestra, the first orchestra televised.

were the debut, on July 7, of the young pianist Vera Franceschi; the Sigmund Romberg program of operetta selections, to which 18,000 people came; a dance program conducted by Richard Korn; and a program conducted by Alexander Smallens and devoted entirely to the works of Richard Rodgers and Oscar Hammerstein II. On the program were pieces from ALLEGRO, CAROUSEL, STATE FAIR and OKLAHOMA!, and the soloists were Annamary Dickey, Thomas Hayward, Gladys Swarthout and Robert Weede. At the end of the concert Rodgers spoke to the audience and said that he was glad the affair was given while he was alive.

The annual Berkshire Music Festival opened with the Boston Symphony under Sergei Koussevitzky, playing to an audience of 7,500, including 1,500 people who sat outside the music shed on the lawns. Another interesting event was the playing of Mahler's second symphony, THE RESURRECTION, conducted by Leonard Bernstein, the brilliant young American conductor. Tanglewood, where the Berkshire Festival is held, is associated with the memory of Nathaniel Haw-

GODOUNOV, AÏDA, MARTHA and RIGOLETTO. In Washington, D. C., the Watergate series was held with Howard Mitchell conducting. In Philadelphia, the Robin Hood Dell season was cut short by money troubles. The concerts had been announced to run for seven weeks, but were suddenly canceled at the end of the fourth week. The president and manager resigned, and a new president was appointed to reorganize affairs for the 1949 season.

Strange doings have been reported from Russian musical circles. Seven of the leading composers of the Soviet Union, all of whom had been winners of the Stalin Prize, found themselves out of favor with the Government early in the year. The Central Committee of the Communist Party itself censured the composers. First on the black list was composer Vano Muradeli. The Committee said that his opera GREAT FRIENDSHIP was "musically inexpressive and poor," with "no organic connection between the musical accompaniment and the development of the action on the stage." It was also said that Muradeli had not made the proper use of the "wealth of folk melodies, songs, tunes, and dance motifs in which the creative art of the USSR is so rich," and that he had "scorned the best traditions and experience of classical opera in general and Russian opera in particular."

The committee went on to say that Muradeli's opera was not the only example of the wrong attitude that Soviet composers were taking toward music. Serge Prokofieff, Dimitri Shostakovitch, Aram Khatchaturian, Vissarion Shebalin, Nikolai Miaskovsky and Gabriel Popov were all blamed for showing "anti-democratic tendencies in music, alien to the Soviet people and its artistic taste. . . . . ."

All of these composers, the greatest in Russia today, admitted that they had been wrong and promised to do better in the future. Prokofieff even thanked the committee for its scolding, and Muradeli said that he considered his opera a "creative defeat," and promised "with all his heart" to mend his ways.

Franz Lehar, Viennese composer whose operettas have charmed two generations of

The young singers of the Opera School of the Royal Conservatory of Music of Toronto present Gluck's poignant opera *Orpheus*. Here we see the dark-robed Greek chorus with their masks.

music lovers, died at his home at Bad Ischl in the Tyrol, October 24, 1948. Among his most popular works were THE MERRY WIDOW and THE COUNT OF LUXEMBURG.

A Composer of Operas, and One of Favorite Songs

Two other famous composers died: one, the composer of favorite operas; and the other, of simple songs. The opera composer was the Italian Ermanno Wolf-Ferrari, composer of twelve operas. The best-known of these are THE SECRET OF SUZANNE and THE JEWELS OF THE MADONNA. Wolf-Ferrari died in Venice, January 21, at the age of seventy-two. The other song-writer was Oley Speaks, composer of SYLVIA, ON THE ROAD TO MANDALAY, MORNING and more than 250 other songs. Speaks died in New York, August 27, at the age of seventy-four. He was born and brought up in Ohio, and before becoming a musician he worked for a year in a railroad office in Columbus. Then he went to New York to study singing. Besides appearing in concerts he was baritone soloist at the Church of the Divine Paternity and at ·St. Thomas' in New York. A number of years ago he retired from his singing career to devote all his time to song-writing.

Opera Workshops to Train the Artists of the Future

Opera workshops are being established in widely separated parts of North America, in universities and conservatories and by enthusiastic groups in the larger cities. If we are to become an opera-conscious people, there must be laboratories and workshops. They are needed for the training of young artists, conductors and technicians, as well as for experimentation.

One of the most important of these workshops was started two years ago in Toronto —the Opera School of the Royal Conservatory of Music. Edward Johnson, general manager of the Metropolitan Opera Association in New York, himself a native of Ontario, was made chairman of the conservatory's board of directors. A high degree of talent has been found among the nine thousand students of the conservatory, and it is planned to produce full-length operas. At the opening performance of the workshop, scenes were given from several operas, including FIDELIO, DER ROSENKAVALIER, FAUST, LA TRAVIATA and LA BOHÊME.

Opera-goers in New York and radio listeners everywhere had good reason last August to fear that they would not hear any performances by the Metropolitan Opera Company during the following season. On August 5, 1948, the directors of the Metropolitan announced that they had not been able to reach new contract agreements with five of the twelve unions that represent the opera company's employees. The directors said that the company's payroll had increased by $353,000 during the past season. On the other hand, the total expenses of the season had been $220,000 greater than the amount of money taken in. For this reason, it would be impossible to grant any further wage increases.

An Agreement Is Reached and the Opera Goes On

The unions replied that they asked no further wage increases, but requested the establishment of unemployment insurance and old-age benefits. The Metropolitan is not a profit-making institution, so its employees are not covered by Social Security. For more than two weeks it seemed that both sides seriously meant what they said, but on August 23 an agreement was finally reached. The opera company offered to bring itself under the Federal Social Security Act as soon as the law made it possible for non-profit institutions to do so. In the meantime, the company promised that it would try to get old-age benefits from broadcasting and recording companies for time devoted by Metropolitan employees to the company's broadcasting and recording.

A Symphony Orchestra Considers the Problems of Parents

Because so many of its subscribers have young children, and find it difficult to get someone to stay with them on concert nights, the Buffalo Symphony Orchestra has thought up and carried out a brilliant plan. It finds baby-sitters for parents who buy season tickets. Arrangements were made with a baby-sitting agency when it was found that hundreds of young married persons could not buy tickets for the ten concerts unless they were sure that their children would be looked after on those evenings. The price of the tickets does not, however, cover the payment to the sitter. The season-ticket holders pay the baby-sitters fifty-five cents an hour.

NEWFOUNDLAND
villages by the sea

By Alexander Lacey
Victoria College, Toronto

THE old coastal towns of Newfoundland have harmonious and lovely names. Twillingate, Trinity, Heart's Content! Harbour Grace, Bonavista, Port-aux-Basques! Long ago, they were settled by fishermen who gave them the names of the homes they had left behind them—in southwestern England and in the Channel Islands, in Ireland and in France.

There are more than a thousand of these picturesque fishing villages scattered along the rugged coast of the island. They all look much alike from the sea. Each is a cluster of box-like, wooden houses backed up against the hills. Around each of these "outport" settlements are endless stretches of wooden platforms, covered with boughs, where fish are spread to dry in the sun.

Some of the fishing villages are almost entirely Irish. At Fortune Harbor and Tilting, for instance, an Irish brogue comes naturally to the tongues of Newfoundlanders who have never been to Ireland. In other villages where the people are of English descent, you can hear the accents of Devonshire, Somerset and Dorset. On the north coast, the villagers speak a West Country English that has an Elizabethan flavor.

"She's a wonderful fast sailer, that boat," says the Newfoundlander.

Bonavista, on the eastern cape where John Cabot may have made his first landfall in America.

"Those potatoes are wonderful small."

The touches that the islanders have added to standard English are full of color and charm. A Newfoundlander's word for bread is "loaf." He calls a loaf a "bun." So when he wants a loaf of bread, he asks for a "bun o' loaf."

He says "good evening" for "good afternoon," and when he is going visiting in some distant village he says he is "going for a cruise."

They are neighborly people and enjoy visiting back and forth when they can, but there is not much time for leisure in a fishing village. In summer and autumn the men fish offshore or trawl for cod off the coast of Labrador. In winter they overhaul and mend their nets and build new boats.

Living a more or less pioneer life they must be jacks-of-all-trades, and indeed they are masters of most of them. They build their own houses. They make their own fishing equipment, including boats, sails, nets and lobster pots. They hunt rabbit, grouse and other small game, and if they ever run out of other chores there is sure to be firewood that needs cutting.

Fishermen's wives also have plenty to do. Besides their usual housework they make the clothes for all the family and make rag rugs out of some of the pieces that are left over. Hooking rugs, which they call "mats," is a favorite winter occupation for women and girls.

During the fishing season the women, wearing their home-made sunbonnets, help the men in the work of curing the fish. It is a picturesque sight to see them spreading the fish in the sun on the drying platforms, called "flakes." In the evening, they heap the fish in neat, circular piles. Handling fish takes skill, which every fisherman's wife acquires through many years of practice.

Tending the family garden patch is also woman's work. Most families on the island have small garden patches where common vegetables do very well. The growing season is too short for most domestic fruits although there are varieties of plums and apples, for example, that ripen in certain parts of the country. Delicious wild berries, such as blueberries, strawberries and raspberries, are plentiful. There are also a sort of wild cranberry called "partridge-berry," and yellow-

Sun cure! The horse waits patiently while the cartload of salted fish is spread on the flake to dry.

PHILIP D. GENDREAU, N. Y.

ish berries known as "bake-apples." These are about the size of a raspberry and grow only on marshy ground.

The women also look after the family livestock, which may be sheep, goats, or a pig or two, or perhaps a cow. Cows, however, eat a great deal of hay and this is difficult to raise along the coast. Goats are much easier to please. In summer they are left to fend for themselves, and they wander around cropping grass or whatever else they can reach. A billy goat leads his little band to the hills in the morning and back home to the milking pails in the evening. Some of the goats wear bells that tinkle pleasantly as they move.

In spite of the family gardens, fresh fruits and fresh vegetables are always scarce and in winter they vanish completely. Fish is the mainstay of the Newfoundlander's diet. In winter it is almost his only food. Codfish is the most abundant and important, herring comes next, then salmon, then lobsters. There is a wide variety of fish to choose from, for the yearly catches include halibut, haddock, ling, pollock, swordfish, smelts, squid, caplin, eels, flounders, turbot and trout.

Yet in Newfoundland the word fish means only cod. All other fish are called by their own names. This is more than a habit of speech on the island—it is a legal fact. Some years ago, the local courts decided that when the word fish is used all by itself it means cod and nothing else.

Easy to Make and Delicious to Eat— Newfoundland's National Dish

If you eat breakfast in Newfoundland, especially on a Sunday morning, you will have a chance to enjoy the national dish, fish and brewis. The fish, which may be either salted or fresh, is always cod. Brewis, as any Newfoundlander knows, is made of hardtack, which is baked in large quantities at St. John's, the capital. These small, oval biscuits are hard as rocks, so they must first soak all night long in water. In the morning the brewis is put in a knitted bag, called a "brewis net," and boiled for twenty minutes. Then it is served with portions of the boiled fish. At the time of serving, melted pork fat is poured on the brewis, together with crisp little "scruncheons"—the tiny bits of pork fat that have survived the melting. Brewis is a very tasty dish, and is easy to make even without a brewis net. The important thing is

LEE WULFF PHOTO FROM NEWFOUNDLAND TOURIST DEVELOPMENT OFFICE

A "wonderful fast sailer" in the making!

to make sure that the hardtack has been soaked long enough.

Until nearly the end of the nineteenth century, the people of Newfoundland depended for their livelihood almost entirely upon the products of the sea. Then a railway was built connecting St. John's, at the eastern end, with Port-aux-Basques in the west. Soon new industries were begun in the interior and new inland towns grew up around them. Today these industries are even more valuable than the island's famous fisheries. The most important are pulp and paper-making and mining.

In winter, many of the outer settlements receive mail and supplies by dog-sled or not at all. Winter puts an end to traveling by water. When the ice has frozen, motor boats and steamers can no longer make their way from one fishing village to another. On the east coast some of the older towns, such as Fogo, Twillingate and Exploits, are on small islands. Drift ice often cuts them off from the main island for weeks at a time.

Then the dog teams come into their own. With a good team of dogs one can go almost anywhere as long as the ice and snow last. It is always an exciting time in a Newfoundland village when the mail arrives by sled after a hard and often dangerous trip over miles of rough ice.

PALESTINE: FROM DAN TO

By ILSE LICHTENSTADTER

The Asia Institute

A LAND flowing with milk and honey, where the locust's sweet bloom perfumed the night air, and the tall, sharply pointed cedar towered against the sky—this was Palestine many years ago. The watchful shepherds guarded their flocks by running brooks, and slept in peace under the stars of night. And yet from the earliest times Palestine has been a peaceful country only at intervals. Besieged, conquered and bowed beneath the yoke of tyrants, the people of Palestine have risen again and again in the attempt to make of their country a free land.

Here, in a region about the size of Wales or New Hampshire, men began to believe in the One God, the Creator of the Universe. On this belief are founded three great religions, for Palestine is holy ground to Christian, Jew and Moslem alike. This small land has played a big part in the history of the world because of its religious importance. It was here that Isaiah and Jeremiah thundered their warnings to the Hebrew people. Here lived the great poets of Biblical times. Jesus was born in a stable in the little town of Bethlehem, in Galilee. With His disciples

BEERSHEBA

He walked by the Lake of Galilee and tramped the hills near by. Just outside the city of Jerusalem He died upon the Cross. Mohammedans believe that their Prophet once ascended into Heaven from Jerusalem, in a vision.

The Holy Land was not always called Palestine. In Biblical times all the country from Dan, in the far north, to Beersheba, in the south, was known as Canaan. The Canaanites, who lived in Palestine as early as 3000 B.C., spoke a language similar to Hebrew. When the Israelites entered Canaan—the Promised Land—under the leadership of Joshua, they conquered many of the peoples

Left (below), Bethlehem, with vineyards and olive trees. Above, the Garden of Gethsemane.

Landmarks in the city of Jerusalem. Above, the famous Wailing Wall of the Jews. Below, the Damascus Gate through the ancient wall.

who lived there. Among these conquered peoples were the Philistines, who lived in the southwest along the Mediterranean Sea. Today the whole country is called Palestine, or the land of the Philistines. Modern Palestine extends from Egypt in the south, to Syria and Lebanon in the north, and from Trans-Jordan in the east to the Mediterranean Sea in the west.

Canaan Was a Land of Promise to the Hebrews

To the Hebrews, who had long lived an unsettled and nomadic life in the desert, Canaan seemed indeed a land of promise, rich in soil and growing things. In the spring, after the rainy season, wild flowers—anemones, pinks, cyclamen—carpeted the land, as they still do today. It is easy to understand why the love poems of the Song of Solomon sing of the fragile beauty of spring and the color and profusion of flowers. Palestine was a land of largess, where the olive, grape and fig and great waving fields of wheat supplied man's needs. Even before the Israelites conquered Canaan, their spies brought back to them samples of luscious huge grapes and figs, to show the richness of the land which they were destined to call home. The people of Palestine lived mainly by agriculture. Forests covered the hills and protected the soil from erosion, and trees were sacred to the early inhabitants. In ancient times, a proud and upright man was compared with a cedar of Lebanon. Many a place connected with some Biblical happening was marked, in antiquity, by a tree.

Early People of Palestine Used Asses, Camels, Oxen and Sheep

In early days, the people of Palestine used the sturdy little ass and the grotesque and dignified camel to carry themselves and their burdens. The ox plowed the fields, and sheep covered the hillsides, their white wool to be spun into fine cloth. In later times the people kept horses for domestic purposes, and today many peasants in Palestine drink the milk of goats. Thousands of years ago the prehistoric peoples of Palestine were familiar with the elephant, the hippopotamus and the rhinoceros. In Biblical times, foxes, hyenas and jackals roamed the hills of Judea, a part of Palestine, as they still do today.

Like other Mediterranean countries, Palestine has a moderate climate, at least in

Shepherds tending their flocks, as did the shep-

part. The summers are hot and dry, and in winter heavy rains fall. Snow sometimes falls in the hills of Judea and in the mountains of the north. The most fertile region, along the Mediterranean coast, is watered by little rivers that take their rise in the hills of Judea. At Haifa, the modern port at the foot of Mount Carmel, which is washed by the waters of the Mediterranean, the plain bears inland to join the valley of the Jordan to the east.

The hills of Judea form the backbone of the country, running from north to south through its center. The Hebrews and still earlier peoples built their strongholds in these heights, which rise to 3,000 feet or more above sea level. North of the Plain of Esdraelon, in Galilee, the hills rise higher still. In Syria, on the border of modern Palestine, Mount Hermon's snow-capped summit dominates the landscape from a height of more than 9,000 feet.

Many rivers flow through Palestine, but none of them are large, and many run dry for part of the year, only to overflow at the

herds of old, near the town of Bethlehem.

Chapel in Bethlehem's Church of the Nativity.

rainy season. Holy to both Jews and Christians alike is the River Jordan. The children of Israel had to cross the Jordan before they could enter the Promised Land, and John the Baptist and Jesus bathed in its waters. Although the Jordan is small indeed in comparison to the Amazon, the Ganges or the Mississippi, no other river in the world has so many historical and religious associations. It coils like a great serpent through the Jordan Valley, turning and twisting upon itself endlessly. Although the valley is only 65 miles long, the river, with all its curves, is about 200 miles in length. The Jordan Valley is extremely dry and almost unbearably hot during a good part of the year. The temperature in the shade is often 120° Fahrenheit. During the winters, however, the climate is delightful.

The Jordan River comes to its end in the Dead Sea, which is nearly 1,300 feet below the level of the Mediterranean, in the deepest land depression on earth. Because of the rapid evaporation of its waters, the Dead Sea is five times as salty as the oceans. Fish can not live there, and only the lowest forms of animal life survive.

For centuries, many different peoples of widely differing cultures have met in Palestine. Its position on the shores of the Mediterranean, between Africa, Asia and Europe, has made the country not only a trade link between east and west, but also a bridge between various cultures. In ancient times, the caravan routes connecting Egypt with Assyria and Babylon, in Asia, ran through Canaan. Palestine was also the connecting link between India and Rome, for purposes of trade. Through this crossroads of the world passed countless merchants and adventurers. Along the well-marked trade routes endless lines of camel caravans plodded along, laden with fine silks dyed with the richest colors, fragrant spices from the East, carpets and rugs fit for the palaces of princes, and perfumes and scents for ladies of fashion.

Many peoples, however, have approached Palestine not for the friendly purpose of trade or the interchange of ideas, but for conquest. Again and again the country has been invaded. These struggles began long before the days of written history. Thousands of years ago successive waves of invaders left their imprint on the life of Palestine. Jericho, the ancient fortified city on the Jordan, had been a fortress for at least 2,000 years before it was conquered by the Israelites under Joshua, in the middle of the fourteenth century B.C. Megiddo, the Armageddon of the Bible, is another famous fortress of about the same age as Jericho. This city was built in the northwest, where it barred the way to invaders from north or south, and protected the plain of Esdraelon.

Palestine Has Been Conquered Many Times in History

The list of the kings and empires which at various times in its history conquered Palestine is a long one. At different times, the people of Palestine paid tribute to the Egyptians, the Assyrians, the Persians, the Greeks, the Romans, the Turks, the Arabs and many others. The history of the country is the story of one conquest after another, with numerous uprisings by the people against the power of foreign conquerors. From the seventh century A.D. to the sixteenth century, Palestine was ruled by the Arabs. For four centuries after that it was subject to the Ottoman Turks who captured Egypt in 1517 and also gained control of Jerusalem. During the period from the end of the nineteenth century to the beginning of the first World War, two outside movements began to take shape which indirectly involved the destiny of Palestine. One of these was an Arab nationalist movement; and the other, a Zionist movement which had as its purpose the return of the Jews to Palestine.

During the Middle Ages, Merchants and Pilgrims Streamed into Palestine

During the Middle Ages an ever growing stream of merchants and pilgrims poured into Palestine and its holy cities. Regarded as infidels by the Moslems who ruled the country, these visitors to the Holy Land, like the Christians who lived there, were subjected to annoyances, restrictions and, sometimes, to serious persecution. Violence broke out again and again.

Roused by these persecutions of their fellow Christians, the people of western Europe, under the guidance of the Roman Catholic Church, set out on the Crusades to deliver the Holy Land from the Saracens, as the Moslems were called. Although for a time the Crusaders were able to hold the Kingdom of Jerusalem, their continued attempts to conquer the country (from 1096 to 1272) failed. The Crusaders' Castle, a stronghold of the Templars—a religious and military order which grew up in Jerusalem during the time of the Crusades—still stands at Athlit, south of Haifa.

Sandwiched in between all its wars and invasions, there have been comparatively few periods of peace and quiet in Palestine. Under David and his son Solomon, the country lived through a period of security known as the golden age of Israelite history.

King Solomon built the first great Temple in Jerusalem. After the Babylonians destroyed it, a second one was built under Ezra and Nehemiah. This Temple was enlarged and decorated by Herod in the time of Jesus, and it was here that He worshiped. One wall of the Temple still survives, the Wailing Wall before which Jews for centuries have mourned the lost glory of Israel and prayed for the coming of the Messiah. In the seventh century A.D., the pious Caliph Omar restored and consecrated the remains of the Temple to the service of Allah, the Moslem Supreme Being.

Many Attempts Have Been Made to Identify Places of Biblical History

Considerable effort has been made to find the actual places in and about Jerusalem which the figures of the Old and New Testaments once frequented. The so-called Tower of David in Jerusalem is actually one of the three great towers of the palace of the Herods described by Flavius Josephus, the Jewish historian of the first century A.D. Jesus' birthplace in Bethlehem is marked by the Church of the Nativity. An underground structure in the Temple area is popularly called Solomon's Stables, but, though dating from his time, was actually used as a stable only by the Crusaders in the Middle Ages.

The tombs of King David and his successors have not as yet been found, nor has the tomb of Jesus. The Garden of Gethsemane, in which Jesus was betrayed, is tended by Franciscan monks.

(Current events in Palestine are discussed in the article The Middle East during the Year, in this issue of the ANNUAL.)

PARAGUAY

"PLACE OF THE GREAT RIVER"

By MORRILL CODY

Chief, American Republics Branch, Public Affairs Program Staff, Department of State

PARAGUAY is a delightful country to visit, a land of flowers and courtesy, picturesque and *simpático*. Tucked away in the interior of South America, it is tiny as South American countries go. It is about twice as big as the British Isles, or much the same size as New England, New York State and Pennsylvania combined, with New Jersey thrown in twice for good meas-ure. Of course, it has a much smaller population. In some parts of the country you can travel a hundred miles without meeting a single inhabitant.

Paraguay is in reality two countries. From the map, you will see that it consists of roughly two half-spheres, which are divided from one another by the broad Paraguay River, where alligators drowse and grin in

The Gran Chaco is a flat region of grassy plains, rank jungles, dark swamps and palm groves.

the sunlight. The right-hand half, somewhat lower on the map than the other, is the home of practically everybody in the country. On the left of the river is the vast expanse of swamp and thorny jungle known as the Gran Chaco.

Go ten miles inside the border of the Gran Chaco and you are in a great wilderness. Except for a couple of religious colonies and one or two military camps, its only inhabitants are a few small tribes of Indians—perhaps 25,000 or 30,000 altogether. Some of these Indians have never seen a white man. They are wanderers, traveling from place to place and living in groups in one-room *toldas,* mere roofs of grass or leaves with open sides.

Some day the Gran Chaco swamps will be drained, and this wild country will become prosperous farm and cattle land. A band of hardy Mennonites has proved that good farms can be developed in the Chaco. These

Paraguayan vaqueros—cowboys—in the corral.

Mennonites came from Canada, the United States and Europe. They now live in two colonies in the very center of this area. They found an ideal retreat in the Gran Chaco, but they had to wage a mighty battle with nature before they established their now relatively prosperous cattle ranches and cotton plantations.

East of the Gran Chaco lies the real Paraguay, between the Paraguay and the Paraná rivers. Here is fertile land for growing sugarcane, cotton and tobacco, excellent grapefruit, oranges and alligator pears; and the cattle-grazing is generally good. The forests contain hardwoods of great beauty and durability—some so dense that they sink in water. The chief export products are cotton, meat and *yerba maté,* which is sometimes called Paraguay tea.

Paraguay is often very hot in summer, but the heat is usually dry and easily borne, and there are great compensations for it. A profusion of flowers grows and blooms all the year round; huge flowering trees amaze the visitor with their red and yellow brilliance; and there are quantities of wonderful birds, gaily feathered and surprisingly tame.

As for the people—but that is a longer story, taking us back into the romantic history of the country. The original Paraguay, as it is shown on early maps made by the Spanish conquerors, was very large. It included what is now Uruguay, much of Argentina and part of Brazil, and was inhabited by the Guarani Indians as well as by many smaller tribes.

The Language of the Once Powerful Guarani Is Still Spoken

Little is known of the history of the Guaranis in the days before Columbus. Yet there seems little doubt that they, along with their blood brothers, the Tupis of Brazil, were once very powerful. The English "jaguar" is one of a number of words that we have derived from the Guarani language. Today, the official and commercial language of Paraguay is Spanish, but Guarani is still widely used.

In 1537, the first permanent colony in this part of South America was founded at what is now Asunción, Paraguay's capital. The Guaranis of Paraguay welcomed the Spaniards in a friendly way, and the colony's leaders were intelligent enough to keep them friendly. The moderation and tolerance that prevailed in Paraguay was due in great part to the influence of the Jesuit missionaries.

The Jesuits first came to Paraguay from Spain in 1609, and they largely ruled the country for the next 150 years. In the course of time, the Jesuits established some fifty colonies, or *reducciones,* as they called them, in different parts of the country. The handful of Jesuits—seldom more than one to a *reduccion*—invited the Guaranis to come and live under the benevolent wing of the Church, to build houses of brick and stone, to cultivate the fields and orchards with systematic care and to share equally in the benefits thus brought to the community.

The priests taught their parishioners the virtues of discipline, honesty and thrift, and taught them to live without fear, though in poverty. The Jesuits encouraged marriage between Guaranis and Spaniards, and in many ways laid the basis for the character of the Paraguayans of today.

The Indians Learned to Love the Churchmen, Who Protected Them

There were some other and less happy developments, however. Slowly a feeling of jealousy and antagonism grew between the swaggering Spaniards of Asunción and the Jesuit colonies. Some of the Spaniards, believing the Indians should be slaves, tried to carry off the Guaranis in spite of all the priests could do to stop them. Raiding parties came from São Paulo in Brazil, fighting the churchmen and their followers and sometimes capturing hundreds of natives. As a result, the Guaranis learned to fear and shun the Spaniards.

At last the Indians lost their protectors. In 1767, the Jesuits, for political reasons, were ordered to leave Paraguay, but for many years the Indians remembered them and revered their teachings. Their influence left a permanent mark on the character of the people. Although the *reducciones* finally became a thing of the past, the Spaniards and the Guaranis continued to marry and the Paraguayans became more and more closely united into one people.

Meanwhile, Spain was losing her hold on her South American colonies. On May 14, 1811, Paraguay obtained her independence from Spain in a bloodless revolution and established herself as a republic. In a very short while, the new government was controlled by José Gaspar Rodríguez de Fran-

cia, the dictator known as *El Supremo* (the supreme ruler).

De Francia ruled Paraguay with an iron hand until his death. His administration may seem very severe to us today, but nevertheless he probably saved his country from being absorbed by Argentina on the south.

The first thing Francia did was to close the frontiers to all outside communication. No foreigners could come in to Paraguay, and those who were already there were not allowed to leave. Even Paraguayans were not permitted to cross their own frontiers except to return home from abroad. Francia neither sent out nor received any diplomats but built a self-sufficient state, completely cut off from the rest of the world.

Obedience to this dictator was unquestioned. So great was his personal power over the people that many dared not pronounce his name, and he became known simply as *El Supremo.* After his death in 1840, the poorer people spoke of him in hushed tones as *El Difunto*—The Deceased.

To turn his people from thoughts of pleasanter living in other lands, Francia drew a terrifying picture of foreigners—evil creatures ready to devour and destroy if ever they could gain an entry to the country. He succeeded in making his people highly suspicious of foreigners.

At the same time, Francia united the Paraguayans in a feeling of common descent and tradition which today sets them apart from all other nations of South America. Among themselves they speak of the Paraguayan "race," by which they mean their mixture of Spanish and Guarani blood and also the special characteristics which were developed under the Jesuits and Francia.

A Dictator Whose Rule Was Mild and Benevolent

The next dictator, Carlos Antonio López, was a man of quite different ideas. His rule, which lasted for twenty-two years, was milder and more benevolent. He immediately opened the frontiers to foreigners; he invited other countries to send representatives to Paraguay and he encouraged new industries and international commerce. At his death he left the country prosperous and the people happy.

At this point in Paraguayan history appears its most romantic figure, Francisco Solano López, son of Carlos Antonio. Before the death of *El Supremo,* young López, who was born in 1827, was old enough to know and understand the power that Francia had over the Paraguayans. The boy was the apple of his father's eye. Great emphasis was placed upon his military education and at eighteen, with the rank of general, he was placed in command of the growing Paraguayan army. Then, to round out his background, he was sent to Europe with his pockets full of money. From this venture he returned with new ideas about the importance of nations and the value of an international reputation.

Meanwhile, year by year, the Paraguayan army was becoming more powerful. When his father died in 1862, Francisco Solano came to the presidency, determined to make the army stronger than ever. An arsenal was built in Asunción, and a small but excellent inland navy of river steamers was constructed and manned. Paraguay hummed with industry and preparation for a war for which there appeared to be no cause.

Trouble, however, had been brewing for many years. There was civil strife in Argentina and in Uruguay, while, to the north, in the vast empire of Brazil, there was a growing ambition to absorb the little republic of Uruguay.

López Is Beset by Enemies Without and Fifth Columnists Within

López, backed by what was considered to be the best army in South America, watched these three neighbors like a hawk. Then, in 1864, Brazil attacked Uruguay and López attacked Brazil. The following year he invaded Argentina. Meanwhile a pro-Brazilian government had been set up in Uruguay, giving him a new enemy. To overthrow him, all three countries joined together in a Triple Alliance.

During a five-year struggle, the Allies gained ground only in hard-fought battles, for the Paraguayan army showed a stubborn courage scarcely paralleled in history. The population of Paraguay was reduced from about 900,000 to less than 250,000, while many of those left alive were permanently injured or too old or too young to lift a musket. Most of the survivors were women, who outnumbered the adult males by ten or twelve to one.

The war ended in 1870, when López was killed in battle. His once great army of more than 80,000 had been swept away, Asunción was occupied and the country laid waste. Fortunately the Allies contented themselves with a few boundary gains. Brazil took some territory in the north and Argentina took some in the south and west, but they returned the main part of the country to self-rule and independence. The question of boundaries between Paraguay and Argentina was finally settled by President Rutherford B. Hayes of the United States, who acted as arbiter.

Paraguay Took Half a Century to Recover from the War

Paraguay now began life again under a new constitution designed to prevent any more dictators from gaining control of the country. The great loss of man-power in the War of the Triple Alliance made it very difficult for Paraguay to get back on her feet. Today, however, there are almost as many men as women in the country; the total population is estimated at about one million. There are many newcomers, for immigration was encouraged, but Paraguay could easily absorb tens of thousands more. Most of the newcomers are Italians, Germans and Ukrainians, but there are also some Australians, British, Swiss, French, Spaniards and Argentinians. There is even a colony of about four hundred Japanese families.

At no time since the disastrous days of López have the citizens of Paraguay known good fortune. There are so few local industries that almost all manufactured goods have to be imported. Distances and lack of transportation within the country itself make it impossible for Paraguay to export as much as she should. Whatever progress Paraguay has made, in the face of extreme poverty, has been due to the fact that she is a land of health-giving sunshine and fertile soil.

In 1932, the Paraguayans had another test of their indomitable spirit in war. This time they fought Bolivia for control of the Gran Chaco. The Bolivian army was German-trained and twice the size of that of Paraguay. Nevertheless, the Bolivians made one error which cost them the victory. They had not taken into consideration the great might of the Chaco itself and the Paraguayans' knowledge of its ways. European military training was not much help against the drought, heat, insects and disease of that great swampland. Most of the Bolivians

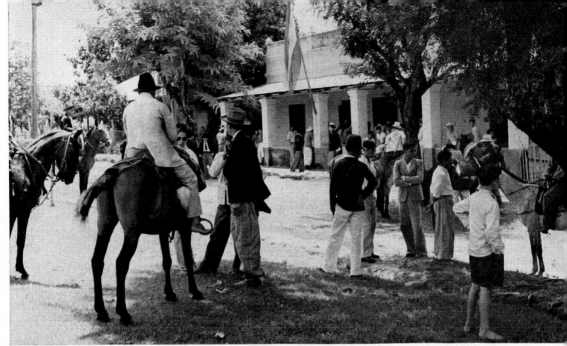

Passing the time of day in the plaza of San Bernardino, a pleasure resort on Lake Ypacaray.

came from the highlands and were unused to the tropical climate, and soon the Chaco made them easy prey for the Paraguayans.

Paraguay began the war without much equipment and had no money to buy it, but it was not long before she found herself well supplied with captured stores, some of which can still be seen in the arsenal at Asunción. The commander-in-chief of the Paraguayan forces in the Chaco war was José Félix Estigarribia, who led his men to victory. The war ended in 1935 and the peace was signed three years later. Paraguay was given about three-fourths of the disputed part of the Chaco; Bolivia, an inland country, was granted a free port on the Paraguay river. In 1939, Estigarribia was rewarded with the presidency of his country.

In August 1940 Paraguay adopted a constitution which provides for a popularly elected president to serve a five-year term. So far, this new constitution has not worked out exactly as was intended. In September 1940 Estigarribia was killed in an airplane accident, and General Higinio Morínigo was appointed to succeed him as provisional president. Then, in the 1943 election, Morínigo was elected president and ruled as a virtual dictator.

In February 1948 an election was held in which there was only one presidential candidate, Juan Natalicio González. Although Morínigo's term of office was due to end in August, in June he was forced to resign by the supporters of the president-elect. On August 15, González was inaugurated for a five-year term.

During World War II, Paraguay found herself faced with the necessity of taking sides in the conflict. She chose quickly and decisively, despite certain opposing influences; she broke relations with the Axis and offered her resources for Western Hemisphere defense.

With the help of the United States Government, Paraguay began a period of public-works construction and educational development, especially in agriculture and public health. New hospitals were built and a modern vocational school was started. The study of English is making great progress, with British and American help.

Unfortunately for Paraguay, a solution has not been found for all of her economic problems, and the mass of her rural population still live in poverty. Nevertheless, the Paraguayans are generally cheerful and hopeful in their outlook. Their deep-rooted loyalty and honesty have not wavered since the days of the Jesuits. They are good friends, people you can trust. With their native intelligence and energy, these hardy people will surely some day bring prosperity to their country.

Robert E. Peary, Arctic explorer and discoverer of the North Pole, on his ship, the Roosevelt.

Robert E. Peary, Explorer

By Marian Lockwood

THE helicopter circled slowly over the small pile of dark rocks which stood out like black light against the whiteness of the snow. The endless white blankness stretched from horizon to horizon, but here, right below, was the treasure for which the men in the helicopter were searching. The rocks formed a cairn in which Robert E. Peary had left the records of his expedition in 1906, on one of his attempts to find the North Pole.

United States Task Force 80, an expedition of the Navy and the Coast Guard, with some Canadian naval officers and civilians along, had successfully made the long trek north to latitude 85°. This was farther north than any point ever reached by any other vessel under its own power. The expedition

had gone north to bring supplies to weather stations in that region, and to make surveys for new stations to be established there under joint authority of the governments of the United States and Canada. The men of the expedition had hoped, also, to find the cache of which Peary had spoken. After several attempts had failed, however, the men of the three ships involved—the Navy ice-breaker Edisto, the Coast Guard ice-breaker Eastwind and the Navy cargo vessel Wyandotte—had almost given up. They were due to turn back in a couple of days, for the sun would soon be sinking below the horizon for the long months of Arctic night. Huge ice-packs, also, were threatening to crush and block the ships.

But luck was with the men of Task Force

80. In the pile of rocks they found not only the records left by Peary to prove that he had actually visited that particular spot, but also copies of records left there by members of a British expedition searching for the pole in 1875–76. Peary himself had brought back the original records of the British expedition and had left copies of them in the cairn. The records were discovered on Cape Sheridan, which is about 450 miles south of the North Pole.

The name of Robert E. Peary is written high on the list of the great explorers of the world, along with such names as Columbus, Magellan and Cortes. Just as truly as did those earlier explorers, Peary, with courage and perseverance, conquered the unknown in his attempts to find the North Pole. Faced again and again with almost certain defeat, blocked by obstacles which seemed insuperable and almost overcome by fatigue

and difficulties, Peary still never knew the meaning of the word failure. He had for many years only one goal—to find the North Pole. Toward this end the energy of much of his life had been directed.

Later, after his great discovery, he wrote these lines: "I have always been proud that I was born an American, but never so proud as when on that biting, sunlit Arctic day I saw the stars and stripes waving at the apex of the earth, and told myself that an American had set Old Glory there. As I watched it fluttering in the crisp air of the Pole, I thought of the 23 years of my own life which had been spent in laboring toward that goal, and realized that at last I had made good; that I could now lay at the feet of my country a trophy which the greatest nations of the world had been struggling to attain for nearly four hundred years."

Have you ever wondered how explorers

The cairn on Cape Sheridan in which were found the records of Peary's expedition as well as records of previous Arctic exploration. The "R" on the cross stands for the ship, the Roosevelt.

are made—why they become explorers? Just what it is that makes a man willing—even anxious above all else—to give up the comforts and certainties of civilized life and start forth again and again on long, uncomfortable and dangerous journeys whose end may very possibly be death?

Perhaps we shall better understand the answers to these questions by learning more about Peary, both as a boy and a man, for he was certainly born to be an explorer. No fairy godmother could have chosen for him gifts more precious than were his. Courage, both of the body and of the mind, perseverance, faith in himself and the importance of his work, a vision of far horizons always opening up before him—these treasures were bestowed upon him who was to discover the top of the world.

Peary's Ancestors Were Sturdy Outdoor People

Peary's ancestors had, for generations, been men who lived and worked out-of-doors —lumbermen in the thick forests of Maine. His father and his uncles migrated from southwestern Maine to Pennsylvania, where they were in the "shook" business—making staves from which barrels and hogsheads are manufactured. Robert was born in the little town of Cresson, Pennsylvania, on May 6, 1856, in a tiny four-room house built of rough boards. When he was three years old, his father died, and his mother moved back, with her son, to her old home in Maine, where she settled on Cape Elizabeth, south of Portland.

The Young Peary Was Interested in Natural History and Sports

Robert found the outdoor world of Maine a true wonderland. He swam and fished in the waters of Casco Bay, he took long hiking trips through the woods and on the mountains, but above all, he spent his time studying the life of nature around him. From his earliest days he was fascinated by birds and when he grew older he collected bird skins and bird eggs. He became an expert taxidermist; and in an upper room of the house which his mother later bought in Portland, he kept his collection of birds which he stuffed and posed in lifelike positions. Robert advertised his birds in one of the Portland papers, and from their sale he was able to help out with the family finances.

His friends found in young Peary a remarkable combination of virtues. He was an athlete of unusual ability and a superior student. He seemed to have no fear and would gladly climb to the top of a dangerously tall tree just to secure one bird's egg that he wanted for his collection. He loved books, almost as much as the outdoor world, and would allow nothing to interfere with his studies.

Peary's Days at Bowdoin Were Happy Ones

When it came time for him to go to college, his mother went along to Bowdoin with him. In the little town of Brunswick, Maine, she made a home for the tall, blonde, blue-eyed young man whose feet were already restless for the feel of far countries. Peary had no money to spend for his college years, but was fortunate in winning a scholarship which he held for the entire college course. One of his greatest interests in college was in his collection of birds—mainly eagles, hawks and owls.

An Old Book on Greenland Aroused Peary's Interest in the Arctic

After his graduation from Bowdoin in 1877—second in his class of fifty-one—he became interested in surveying, and in 1879 took a position in Washington on the Coast and Geodetic Survey, for which he received $10 a week. Soon he passed the examination for the admission of civil engineers into the Navy and was given the rank of lieutenant. Much of his early work in the Navy was done in Nicaragua, where he learned much about exploring under difficult conditions and among primitive people.

Peary's interest in Arctic exploring was first seriously aroused in 1885 by an old book he discovered about the inland ice of Greenland. Almost immediately he made up his mind that he wanted to go and see that northern land for himself, and in 1886 he secured a leave of absence for that purpose. From then on, most of his energy and his interest was tied up with trips which took him deeper and deeper into the wilderness of snow and cold and ice.

Of exploring, Peary himself said, "The true explorer does his work not for any hope of reward or honor, but because the thing he has set himself to do is a part of his being."

PERU

By CARLETON BEALS
Author and Lecturer

GRACE LINE

Llama.

PERU is a land of countless surprises. The equator cuts across the northern part and yet you can find temperatures as cold or as springlike as you please by simply going up or down the lofty ranges of the Andes Mountains. Although the whole country lies in the Torrid Zone, glaciers and snow are found on the majestic summits all the year round.

The Andes run up and down the length of Peru, splitting it almost as neatly as you could split a string bean. They are so high that the land on one side is altogether different from the land on the other. Rain is almost unheard of on the west of the mountains. Day after day the sun blazes down on sandy deserts and green, irrigated valleys facing the blue Pacific. Here are busy harbors and one of the loveliest cities in the Americas—Lima, the capital of Peru. You might think that the sun-drenched coastal strip would be as hot as pepper. Instead, especially around Lima, the climate is cooled by one of the great wonders of the Pacific ocean—the cold Humboldt Current, which sweeps north from the frozen south.

Hot, mysterious jungles and dense tropical rain forests are found on the other side of the mountains. This eastern region is a lush, rich, rainy country, where torrents roar down through the gorges of the Andes and join to make Peru's greatest rivers. Two of the headwaters of the Amazon, the Marañon and the Ucayali rivers, join a little above the jungle city of Iquitos, from which rubber, quinine and other products of the tropics are shipped all the way down the Amazon to the distant Atlantic. The rain forests run up the eastern foothills of the Andes to cooler heights, in some places as far up as eight thousand feet. Vast stretches of jungle and forest are almost impenetrable. Here are little towns and tribes of Indians that have long been cut off from the rest of Peru.

This astonishing land even seems to offer you a choice of centuries to live in. You will find the twentieth century in Lima, the most completely Spanish and European city in Peru. More than 657,000 people live here, and much of the city is very modern indeed. Yet, in the older parts, you can fancy yourself living in the sixteenth century, in the romantic days of Pizarro and the bold Spanish conquistadors.

In the highlands of the Andes, you can go back still farther into the days of long ago.

293

GRACE LINE

Loading copper at one of Peru's many mines.

STANDARD OIL CO. (N. J.) PHOTO BY COLLIER

Coastal fishermen bring their catch to harbor.

GRACE LINE

Rich farmlands nestle below the high Andes.

STANDARD OIL CO. (N. J.) PHOTO BY COLLIER

Buy a basket, some oca or olluco or a spoon!

Ruins of wonderful fortresses and palaces and temples tell of the ancient glories of a great empire built long before the coming of the Spaniards.

Time seems to have stood still in the little villages in the mountains, where Quechua and Aymará Indians live in thatched, stone huts very much as their ancestors did for centuries. These highland Indians still speak their native languages, but many of them also speak Spanish. They have kept their colorful costumes as well as their ancient songs and dances.

Quechua women wear bright, embroidered blouses, fringed shawls of many colors and quantities of wide skirts. They deck themselves with rich silver jewelry and, as a final touch, top off the splendid effect with sedate derby hats. Aymará women wear wide, flat, black hats or else tall stovepipe hats painted white. The men wear blouses and woolen trousers and bright sashes, and their ponchos are every color of the rainbow. They wear wide, flat-crowned hats or wool caps with earlaps.

Highland Indians eat many of the same dishes that were relished by their ancestors. Frozen potatoes, called chuño, are an ancient favorite. Other old-time foods include oca and olluco, which are native roots; charqui, which is dried meat; and cuyes, a sort of guinea pig. Anticuchos, sizzling on bamboo sticks, are chunks of ox-heart spiced with chile.

There are two everyday sights in the Andes that must have been familiar to Pizarro. One is the amusing and haughty llama. The other is the method of terrace-farming that is still in use today. Miles of terraces run up the sides of many mountain and coastal valleys, making lovely patterns, row upon row. Some of these terraces have stone sides that were built long ago. They make it possible to grow crops on steep slopes right up to the edge of the lofty pasture lands where the llamas and alpacas graze. Higher yet, above the pastures, live vicuñas and chinchillas.

The great use of the llama is as a beast of burden, although his coarse wool is also useful. For centuries he was almost the only means of transportation in the Andes. He walks with sure-footed dignity over difficult mountain paths, but he is somewhat touchy. If he is given too heavy a load he lies down and refuses to move an inch, and if he is annoyed he has a horrid habit of kicking. This relative of the camel was domesticated in Peru long before the Spanish conquest.

In ancient times, the Quechua Indians of Peru were ruled by the Incas, a wonderful people who once held sway far beyond the present boundaries of the country. The empire of the Incas included Quechuas and many other Indian tribes. Today, we use the word Inca for all the peoples of this great empire.

The Golden Empire of the Incas Ends in Tragedy

The story of the Incas is a tragic one, written in gold and silver and blood. Their wealth was fabulous, and tales of their boundless treasure at last reached the ears of certain bold, brave Spaniards whose leader was Francisco Pizarro. Although he had only a handful of men to help him, Pizarro was resolved to conquer the Inca empire.

Happily for the Spaniards, the Incas were engaged in a civil war for the succession to the throne, and so their empire was in a weakened condition. Another piece of good fortune for Pizarro was the fact that the Incas were only too used to doing what they were told to do. The government of the Incas was so highly organized and planned so many details in the lives of its subjects that the people had become very dependent and were lost without their leaders. In 1532 Pizarro captured Atahualpa, one of the rulers, and from then on the rest of the conquest was easy.

The story of Atahualpa is famous. Pizarro was impatient for all the treasure he could

Pipes gather oil from wells near Talara.

get, and he offered to set Atahualpa free in return for a tremendous amount of silver and gold. Atahualpa kept his part of the bargain and filled a room with exquisitely wrought golden vessels and other priceless treasure. Then Pizarro turned upon Atahualpa and put him to death.

With the capture of the magnificent capital city of Cuzco, 11,000 feet high in the Andes, Spain became master of the Inca empire. Peru remained under the Spanish yoke until the nineteenth century. She declared her independence of Spain in 1821. The period following the conquest is the time when many Spaniards, fired by marvelous reports of this strange new land, came to seek their fortunes or to settle in Peru. Today, many Peruvians are of Spanish descent, while others are a mixture of Spanish and Indian blood and are called mestizos. About half the people of Peru are Indians.

Small wonder that many Spaniards set sail for Peru when they heard the tales the conquerors had to tell! When Pizarro and his men entered the capital of the Incas, they stepped from the field of battle into a city of fairy-tale magnificence. Old chronicles dazzle us with its marvels. They speak of sheets of gold hung in the Temple of the Sun, of golden flowers and golden doors, and of palaces and princely dwellings where gold was lavished in adornment, both inside and out.

The Spanish conquerors, the conquistadors, were followed by missionaries, and many of Cuzco's buildings were soon turned into convents, monasteries and churches. Cuzco is a fascinating mixture of Spanish and Incan days.

Through the tip-tilted streets of this picturesque mountain city, gaily costumed Quechaus lead their llamas as of old. According to legend, Cuzco was founded by Manco Capac, son of the sun-god worshiped in the temple.

A stone-built, thatched cabin near Arequipa.

Some of the gigantic stones with which the Incas fortified the city are still standing, carefully fitted together without any mortar.

The newly conquered empire was to be ruled from Spain, and so Pizarro looked about for a good site that could be easily reached from the sea. He chose the valley of the Rio Rimac, on the Pacific coast, and laid out a new capital, Lima, a few miles up the valley. Today, the principal plaza of Lima and the wide avenues leading away from it are still very much as they were when built by Pizarro. The great cathedral and many churches and other buildings are splendid examples of the days of Spanish colonization. Eight miles from Lima is Callao, the most important port in Peru.

Although the coast of Peru stretches for 1,400 miles from Ecuador on the north to Chile on the south, there are few good harbors. Much of the coast meets the sea in steep bluffs, especially toward the south. This sunny coastal strip is almost rainless. Great stretches of desert follow the coast all the way to Chile, but in between the deserts are many brief rivers and streams that are fed by the melting snows of the Andes. These rivers are not navigable. Nevertheless, many of them have carved out fertile valleys that are broad and beautiful. By means of irrigation, important crops are grown in many of

Modern capital; ancient citadel. Above, Lima. Below is the Inca fortress of Machu Picchu.

the valleys. North of Lima, they are used for crops of sugar-cane and cotton. In others delicious fruits are grown—oranges, lemons, peaches, pineapples, bananas, chirimoyas, olives and grapes.

Soil is so precious in these pleasant valleys that Peruvians do not waste it by building their houses on it. The valleys are tilled right to the edge of the sand. Tiny Indian villages cling to the bluffs on either side. Some of the huts are made of cane and roofed with palm leaves. Others are made of sun-dried bricks, with homely roofs of corrugated iron. Sometimes, near by, a great landowner may build a splendid mansion with flower gardens all about.

It is very pleasant to come upon one of these lovely green valleys after riding through miles of barren desert, and yet the coastal sands have a beauty and fascination of their own. Stretching for 200 miles south of the Ecuador border, there is almost no sign of vegetation. Winds drive the sand thousands of feet high against the Andean cliffs, so that whole deserts are sometimes found on plateaus 10,000 feet above sea level. Their color effects are magnificent. Barren hills may be tinted orange, yellow, brown, blue, lilac, purple or gray or any combination of these colors. The curving drifts of the dunes are often as pleasing to the eye as a masterpiece of sculpture, with wind tracings on the sand as delicate as a piece of old lace.

To these beautiful, barren lands, there could be no greater contrast than the teeming life of the Humboldt Current. This tremendous mass of cold water, 150 miles wide, is alive with hordes of strange and wonderful fish. Over the waters, the air is filled with myriads of birds that follow the current to prey on the fish. These millions of ocean birds hunting their dinners are one of the marvelous sights of Peru. There are so many of them that they cover the near-by islands with one of Peru's most curious sources of wealth—the valuable fertilizer called guano. The Humboldt Current comes in part from the icy Antarctic. It brings moist, cool breezes and life-giving mists far up the coast before it finally veers away to the west. This is the current that set the Kon-Tiki raft on its adventurous way toward the Polynesian islands.

The highlands of the Andes are a very different sort of world. Their towering ranges are rugged and jagged and sharp. They look like monstrous saws with teeth turned upward toward the sky. Peruvians call the Andean highlands the *sierra*—a Spanish word meaning saw.

The Lofty Mountain Wall Divides the East and West

You have to go higher than Mount Marcy, in the Adirondacks, in order to cross the Andes at all. The very lowest pass in the ranges is more than 7,000 feet high. This is just about the same height as Harney Peak in South Dakota. Other passes are far higher. One of the highest in use today is 17,400 feet above sea level. This breath-taking height is only about 3,000 feet lower than the highest mountain in North America, Mount McKinley. The highest railroad in the world crosses the Andes at about 15,800 feet. Even Mont Blanc, highest peak in the Alps, is not so lofty. Partly in Peru and partly in Bolivia is the highest navigable lake in the world—Titicaca, some two miles above sea level.

The snow-crowned peaks of the Andes reach still nearer to the sky. In the Cordillera Occidental, loftiest of the Peruvian ranges, at least ten peaks rise above 20,000 feet. Huascarán is the highest, 22,180 feet. To find any mountains higher than these you will have to go to Chile or Argentina or to

the highest on earth, the Himalayas.

Although nowadays a skillful pilot can whisk you over the barrier of the Andes in a glorious journey, it has always been very difficult to get from one side of Peru to the other. The products of the western part must be shipped out of western ports. These products include the oil that is found on the coast and the copper and other minerals of the western mountain mines. Cerro de Pasco, the greatest copper-mining center in Peru, lies at an altitude of 14,300 feet. The mountains around it are enormously rich in deposits of copper, gold, silver, vanadium and other minerals.

The Jungles and Rain Forests Hide Untold Treasures

The wealth of the tropical areas, on the other hand, must be shipped down the Amazon River. The jungles and rain forests hold untold treasures of rare woods and spices and rubber, as well as most brilliant birds, butterflies, orchids and other tropical life. There is oil in the eastern foothills as well as on the coast. When this eastern oil is developed, the river port of Iquitos, once a boom rubber town, may flourish anew as an oil metropolis. Peruvians look forward with great enthusiasm to the development of the eastern region, which they call the *montaña*. Although this Spanish word means mountain, Peruvians use it in a sweeping way to include the jungles of the upper Amazon basin and the forested plains and foothills of the eastern Andes.

Most Peruvians are engaged in farming, mining and commerce. There are a number of important textile mills and factories, but modern industry is still very young. Cotton has recently become the chief crop and it is cultivated in a great many coastal valleys. One of the native varieties is very valuable because of its long fiber. The second largest crop is sugar-cane, and the third is rice.

Peru's new aim is to produce more manufactured goods, so that the country will be less dependent on exporting raw materials. A big new power project on the Santa River, north of Lima, will provide electricity for half of Peru and for many new factories. The hope is to improve living conditions throughout the country, not only in the cities but in the lost and lonely villages of the *montaña* and in the difficult highlands where so many Indians dwell.

PETS

our friends from the wild

By Lee S. Crandall

General Curator, Bronx Zoo

PERHAPS you have a pet dog or cat which is almost as important as any other member of your family. It may be a golden canary you love, singing his gay song in the morning sunlight, and flinging wide the spray from his morning bath. So familiar and so dear to us are these companions of our everyday life that we often forget they are descended from wild creatures of the forest, the plain and the sea.

On a winter's night your dog lies close to your feet in front of the fire, sometimes pushing against your hand with his friendly wet muzzle. It is only by a stretch of the imagination that you can connect him with the half-wild wolf-dog, skulking about the camp-fires of early man. That wolf-dog, however, has developed into the wonderful breeds we know today.

It is even possible that there may have been a real wild dog which no longer exists. The sandy-colored dingo of Australia is closer to the dog we know than any other wild type. It must have been carried to Australia by primitive men long ago. Yet in all the rest of the world there is no living wild dog from which the dingo could have sprung. Perhaps the dingo is a half-way point in the development of the domestic dog. We do not know the whole story of the dog's history. We can only say that he has developed from some wild ancestor.

It is strange, indeed, to realize that the tiny, hairless Chihuahua and the delicate and dainty Pomeranian come from the same ancestral stock as the ponderous St. Bernard and the out-size great Dane. One has only to visit one of the large dog shows of today to realize the tremendous hold that dogs of every type have upon our hearts. The poor boy who picks up a mangy stray dog in the alley shares with the proud owner of a champion the happiness and satisfaction that come from a dog's trustful affection.

The story of the cat, like that of the dog, is not entirely clear. It is, however, probably much more simple than the dog's history. Scientists have found cat mummies, dried-up remains, in the ancient tombs of Egypt. This proves that cats have been kept as pets from those early times.

There is a wild cat found in North Africa today, and another very much like it in Europe. Both are very much like the cats we keep as pets, at least like those of the same color, gray, with narrow black stripes on the body and cross markings on the legs. Our "striped tabbies" are so much like these wild cats of Africa and Europe that there can be no doubt of their origin.

Many beautiful kinds of cats have been produced through the centuries. You may

Chickens are friendly pets. They cluck and talk about all sorts of things.

wonder that I use the word "produced." This is just the right word to use, since man himself has played a great part in selecting and breeding the cats, and other animals, that he wanted to keep as pets.

The fuzzy Persian cat is simply a long-haired breed, sometimes known as the Angora. One of the most ancient breeds of cat is the Siamese, which has blue eyes and a cream-colored coat, and brown ears, feet, tail and face. The Siamese is so different from other cats that somewhere along the way it may have had at least one unusual ancestor.

The cat that arouses the greatest curiosity is the Manx, with its very short tail and very long hind legs. The Manx is a great jumper and is often called the "rabbit cat." Some people mistakenly think it is a cross between a rabbit and a cat; but it is all cat.

Because there are so many kinds of domestic rabbits, one might think they came from different kinds of ancestors. Actually, they are all descended from the common wild rabbit of Europe. The rabbit must have been tamed at a very early date, though we do not know just when. Now it is one of the most loved of all pet animals. There are woolly haired Angora rabbits, and lovely

What's the matter? Are you afraid of me?

Couldn't we possibly be friends?

PHOTOS BY BUBLEY, STANDARD OIL COMPANY (N. J.)

velvet-coated animals of the Rex varieties. The lop-ears have great, leathery ears as much as twenty-seven inches long. There are large breeds, such as the Flemish giant, and tiny ones, like the Polish rabbit.

The domestic rabbit has been developed in a great variety of colors and markings. Dutch-marked rabbits are solid in color with white collars, an even stripe up the forehead and white feet. English markings consist of dark ears, tail, nose, back streak and tiny round spots on the sides of the body, which is otherwise pure white. The Himalayan rabbit, too, is mostly white, with colored nose, ears, feet and tail.

When the Spanish explorers first visited Peru, in the sixteenth century, they found small animals running freely about the houses of the native Incas. These animals were guinea pigs or cavies, tamed descendants of a small wild type of animal still found in western South America. These little creatures had been tamed and kept as pets by the natives, who also probably used them for food. Nowadays no one thinks of the guinea pig as other than an endearing pet. It is small, harmless and friendly, always ready to squeak a greeting to its owner. There are

This little deer could run away, but he is having a fine time right where he is.

Wake up and play with me.

Not much more than a handful.

three principal breeds of guinea pig: the short-haired English, the long, silky haired Peruvian and the wiry haired Abyssinian. They come in a great variety of attractive solid and broken colors.

Because feathers do not lend themselves to stroking as readily as fur, birds usually can not be fondled as freely as small animals. They are also very timid. Yet many birds are kept purely as pets. The canary is one of the few pet birds whose history is fully known. Wild canaries are still to be found in the Canary Islands, Madeira and the Azores. During the sixteenth century the little greenish-yellow birds were taken to Europe, where they soon became loved for their sweet songs. In time these strangers were induced to breed in cages. From these beginnings came our popular golden songster.

Some Canaries Learn Their Songs from a School Master

Strange though it may seem, not all of the many kinds of canaries are bred for song alone. The heavy, blocky Norwich, the slender, elegant Yorkshire and the top-knotted crest are bred entirely for type and color. The songs of all three are loud and coarse.

The roller is the best singer among the canaries. It learns its beautiful song by hearing a well-trained canary known as the "school master." For those who want a pet canary with a louder song, one that can compete with radios and street noises, there is the chopper. This is a bold, powerful songster whose notes can be heard above the din of cities.

Pigeons are among the most popular of the feathered tribes. No other tame creature is found in such a wide range of color, marking, form and plumage. The pigeon has been a tame bird for nearly 5,000 years. In spite of this, modern pigeons still retain in many cases the colors of their common ancestor.

The Slate-Blue Pigeon Has Not Changed His Color in 5,000 Years

All pigeons are descended from the wild rock dove which is still found from the cliffs of England across Europe and most of Asia. This bird is slaty blue, with dark head, breast, tail and wing-tips. The wing itself is crossed by two narrow black bars. Pigeons of this color may be seen begging peanuts in any city park, or in the lofts of pigeon fanciers anywhere. This color of our modern pigeons is still the same, after 5,000 years, as the color of the rock dove from which they are descended.

Pigeon breeds are so numerous that it is difficult to select those which are most popular as pets. Among the great favorites, however, are the pigmy pouter, the fantail and the gay, acrobatic little house tumbler.

Bantam Chickens Are Friendly and Affectionate Pets

Domestic fowl, such as chickens, are likely to be valued as producers of eggs and as plump roasters, rather than as pets. This is true in general of the larger breeds, but the bantams are kept almost entirely as pets. If you think of a hen as a hopelessly stupid bird, you will receive a pleasant surprise when you come to know a really tame bantam. The little feather-legged Cochin bantams make wonderful pets because of their gentle friendliness. Even the flighty rose comb will make ample return for kindness bestowed upon it.

Like all their relatives, both large and small, the bantams are believed to have descended from the red jungle fowl still found in eastern India, Malaya and some of the islands to the south. The cock of this wild fowl wears pointed, bright chestnut feathers on the neck and lower back. The breast and tail are black. This beautiful color pattern is still found in many of our tame bantams known as the black-breasted reds. Except that the jungle cock has a very small comb and carries his tail at a gracefully low angle, he looks very much like a game bantam cock of the same color.

The Goldfish Is a Tame Pet from China and Japan

One does not think, somehow, of a fish as being tame. Yet the goldfish is tame. It has been developed by the Chinese and the Japanese from a brownish green carp-like fish found in eastern Asia. In the Far East families have devoted themselves, generation after generation, to the breeding of curious beautiful and perfect varieties of fish. If left to themselves for generations goldfish quickly take on a plain olive color, instead of the shining gold so much admired. Also there are beauties of form as well as of color that must be preserved by careful selection. The fan-tail, the veil-tail and the telescope are only a few of the many fine varieties.

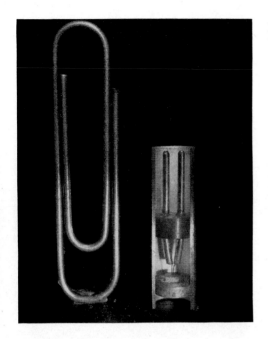

planets revolve around the sun. The nucleus contains neutrons which carry no electric charge, and protons which are positive. The positive charge of the nucleus balances the negative charge of the revolving electrons, so that the whole atom is neutral.

What, then, is the meson? Why are scientists so excited over it? What are mesons like, and what can be done with them? How were they discovered?

The existence of mesons was first suggested by Dr. Hudeki Yukawa, a Japanese scientist, in the 1930's. Reasoning from theory, he reached the conclusion that there must be still other atomic particles—tiny particles that bind the nucleus of an atom together. Only in this way could he account for the fact that the positive protons do not repel each other. Dr. Yukawa's calculations and conclusions aroused great interest

The transistor, a new type of radio tube, shorter than an ordinary paper clip (left).

Physics ADVANCES

By SAMUEL RALPH POWERS
Professor of Natural Sciences, Teachers College, Columbia University

THE most exciting thing that happened in atomic research during the year was the separation, in the laboratory, of a nuclear particle called the meson or the mesotron. The existence of this particle was not even suspected twenty years ago. Mesons, like protons, neutrons and electrons, come from within the atom. These tiny particles, once their secrets are mastered, hold forth to man the promise of vast new stores of energy.

In last year's BOOK OF KNOWLEDGE ANNUAL we explained something about the structure of the atom. Electrons, which carry a negative charge of electricity, whirl in fixed orbits about the positively charged nucleus, or heart of the atom, somewhat as

Communication with the speed of light! Ultrafax, combining radio-television and photography, can transmit 1,000,000 words a minute.

among scientists. Physicists scurried to their instruments to check the Japanese scientist's mathematics. Their findings supported Dr. Yukawa's theory. A few years later, as a result of his studies of cosmic rays, Dr. Carl D. Anderson, at the California Institute of Technology, announced the discovery of the meson, a particle that fitted Dr. Yukawa's predictions.

The meson, scientists tell us, is a very strange kind of atomic particle, if, indeed, it is a particle at all, in the usual sense of that word. There are five different types of mesons. The most common kind weighs about two hundred times as much as an electron, or a little less than one-ninth as much as a neutron. Electrons are always negatively charged, but mesons may be either positive, negative or neutral.

And now for the strangest part of the story—and in this story mesons are unlike ordinary atomic particles—the life-span of the meson is only about two-millionths of a second! Tremendous quantities of energy, such as that derived from cosmic rays or from powerful atom-smashers, are required to release them from the atomic nucleus. The mesons must therefore carry enormous quantities of energy during the brief periods of their existence.

Mesons, which are very numerous, swarm in great abundance in the earth's atmosphere. In the upper reaches of the envelope of air that surrounds the earth, powerful cosmic rays from outer space collide with nuclei of atoms of gas molecules. Each collision creates mesons. Because of their short life-span, however, mesons remained undetected in early studies of the atmosphere.

Higher and Higher, in Search of the Short-lived Meson

Mesons have been studied in research centers atop high mountain peaks, in the cockpits of specially-equipped B-29 "flying laboratories," and, more recently, with delicate instruments stowed away in the nose of a stratosphere-bound V-2 rocket. Wilson cloud chambers, Geiger counters and sensitive cameras have aided scientists in tracking down the elusive meson. Studies made on the top of Mount McKinley show that the energy of the mesons derived from cosmic-ray collisions varies between 150,000,000 and 400,000,000 electron volts. This is a greater amount of energy than scientists ever controlled before

the building of the giant atom-smashers. Scientists next sought for methods of separating mesons at will from atomic nuclei. Early in 1948 two scientists, working with the giant cyclotron at the University of California, first succeeded in obtaining mesons in the laboratory. They fired alpha particles

For generating power measured in millions of

(the hearts or nuclei of helium atoms) at targets of carbon or beryllium, under very high voltage. As a result, mesons were obtained and their paths photographed.

What can scientists do with mesons? In the future the meson may be used, as is the almighty neutron, as the "trigger" in setting off atomic bombs. A meson can produce fission in uranium and create enormous quantities of nuclear energy. Furthermore, the meson "triggers" will, it is believed, release 50 per cent more energy from uranium than does the neutron.

Meson research is still far from completed.

electron volts! The cyclotron shown here is used by physicists at Columbia University.

COLUMBIA UNIVERSITY PHOTO BY WARMAN

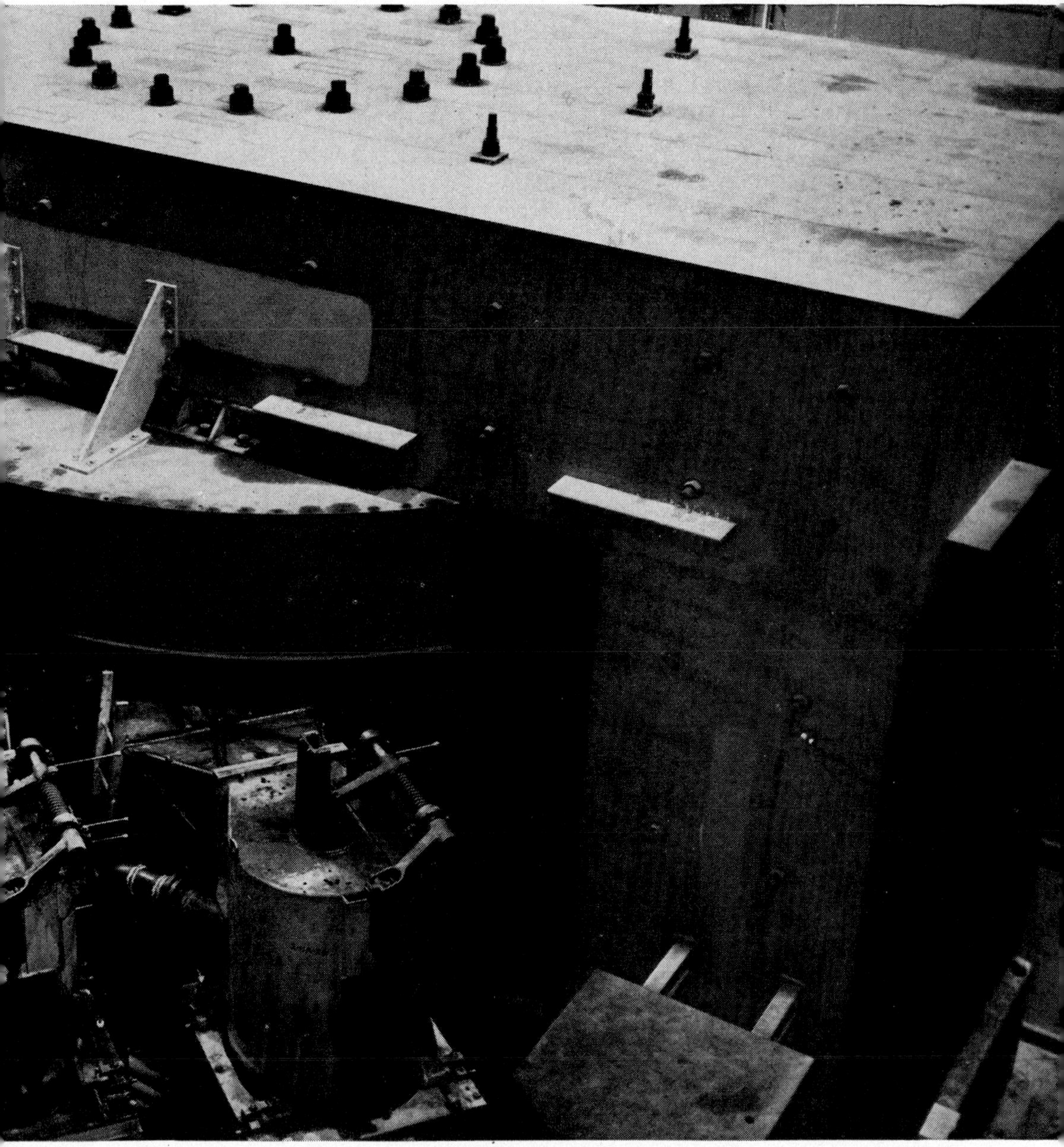

In fact, it may have only begun. Is the meson a particle or a compact bundle of energy? Is it the unit within which matter and energy are the same? How does the meson bind an atomic nucleus together? Now that scientists have learned how to obtain mesons at will, physicists can study these problems at their leisure. Once we understand how atoms are converted into energy, we may discover how to convert energy into matter.

Chemists have already succeeded in creating artificially elements which do not exist in nature. They now believe that they can create elements even heavier than curium (96), which is the heaviest element known to man. At least two more elements, numbers 97 and 98, can be created, chemists say. The new heavy elements will have masses as high as 247 or 248. The mass of hydrogen, the lightest element, is 1, and the mass of the heaviest variety of curium is 242. The tiny, short-lived meson, and the discoveries which scientists will no doubt make while studying it, will play an important part in the creation of these heavy elements.

New and invaluable tools are being devised for the use of scientists, tools to bring more and more energy under control. Two enormous new atom-smashers are under construction in the United States. Each will generate billions of electron volts, far exceeding the power of any atom-smasher now in existence. One of the machines, a 110-foot cyclotron, will be installed at the Radiation Laboratories of the University of California. The other, a 30-foot synchrotron, will belong to the Brookhaven National Laboratories on Long Island.

Ten Thousand Tons of Magnet in the "Race Track" Cyclotron

The California cyclotron will generate about 10,000,000,000 electron volts, pouring forth 20 times more power than the largest atom-smasher now in operation. Ten thousand tons of magnet will form its gigantic core. Atomic particles, in this instance protons, will be fed into the machine, speeded up and whirled in giant circles around a covered "race track" 110 feet in diameter. Because of the great energies involved and the tremendous heat generated, the cyclotron will operate for 2 seconds at a time, and then be shut off for a few minutes.

The Brookhaven synchrotron will reach energies of 3,000,000,000 electron volts. In this machine the atomic bullets will travel at almost the speed of light, 186,000 miles a second. A proton reaching an energy of 3,000,000,000 electron volts will make 3,500,000 trips around the track within the instrument, a distance of about 150,000 miles, in less than one second!

A new discovery, the magnetic oil clutch, may well change the operation of every automobile in the world. The clutch is a very simple device—a cylinder of oil filled with millions of iron particles or other magnetic material. When the clutch is engaged, an electric current passes through the iron-filled oil cylinder. The iron particles become magnetized, and act as though they formed a rigid iron bar. Perhaps even more important will be the use of magnetic clutches on heavy power equipment such as printing-presses.

Diamond Chips as Electric-Current Amplifiers

In last year's BOOK OF KNOWLEDGE ANNUAL we told you about the use of diamonds as Geiger counters. Each time a diamond crystal is struck by a fast-moving atomic particle, a current is set up within the diamond. This current can be detected, and the atomic particles counted by means of the current generated within the diamond. Thus the diamond acts as a Geiger counter. Now, as a direct result of this earlier discovery, there comes an announcement from the Bell Laboratories that a diamond can also amplify an electric current. Tiny gold-coated diamond chips about the size of a snowflake have amplified electric currents as much as five hundred times.

The common radio tube which has been in use for some forty years may soon be a thing of the past. A new type of radio tube, called a transistor, has many advantages over the familiar type. The transistor is only about an inch long; it is slimmer than a pencil and contains no grids, glass or plates. It heats up instantly. Like the conventional radio tube, the transistor can either amplify or oscillate an electric current. The essential material of the new tube is germanium metal, specially treated to make it semi-conducting. The ability of a semi-conducting metal to carry an electric current can be controlled. Although germanium may be used as the heart of the new tubes, other available semi-conducting metals include silicon and the oxides of selenium and copper.

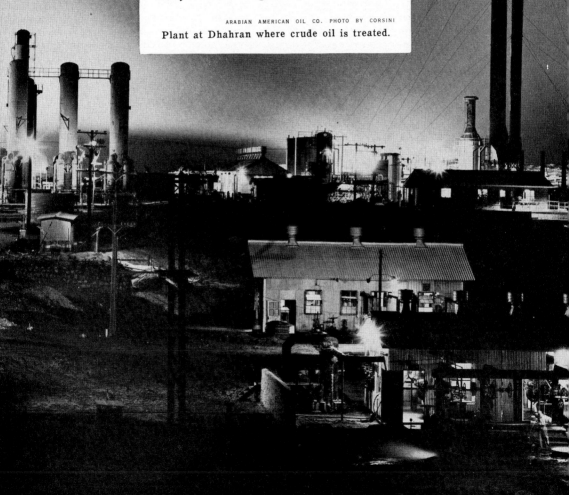

pipeline in *Arabia*

By RICHARD FINNIE
Author and Explorer

S AUDI ARABIA is at once one of the poorest and one of the richest of countries. Inland from the Red Sea and paralleling it there is a mountain chain some of whose peaks rise to 9,000 feet, but much of Saudi Arabia is low, rolling or flat land of sandy desert and gravel plains. There are

Plant at Dhahran where crude oil is treated.

many wadis, or river beds, but water flows in them only during the occasional rains of winter. A few days after a rainfall grasses and shrubs sprout magically but soon wither. The general aspect of utter barrenness presented by most of the Arabian hinterland is relieved only by an occasional oasis. In winter the climate is moderately warm, although in the higher regions the temperature may drop to freezing at night. In summer the heat becomes terrific. From May to October temperatures as high as 120 degrees in the shade are common.

This land of Saudi Arabia has a population of some four and a half million people, the inheritors of an ancient civilization. Among them are merchants and soldiers, fishermen and date-growers, craftsmen and professional men. But most are nomads, moving back and forth with their camels, sheep, goats and donkeys in constant quest of water and pasturage. For many generations the largest national source of income was from the pilgrims who, each year, come from all over the Mohammedan world to Mecca, the shrine of the prophet Mohammed.

In 1925 the country was unified by a shrewd and powerful ruler, King Abdul Aziz ibn-Saud. Nine years later a find was made in the province of Hasa, near the shore of the Persian Gulf, which marked the turning of Saudi Arabia into a land of fabulous wealth. Oil was discovered by the Arabian American Oil Company, to whom the King had granted a drilling concession. This was treasure far greater than the gold of King Solomon's mines, one of which had recently been brought to light in another province of Saudi Arabia.

A New Town Springs Up on the Shores of the Persian Gulf

Near the site of the original well a town sprang up, inhabited by American oil-workers with, later, their wives and children. The town was called Dhahran, after two near-by hills. Soon many wells were drilled in the surrounding area, and a refinery was built on the shore of the Persian Gulf. Pipe lines were laid to this refinery as well as to another on near-by Bahrein Island, the location of an earlier oil discovery. Petroleum products were henceforth sent to European and Middle Eastern markets aboard tankers.

There was one commercial disadvantage in this arrangement. The distances which

had to be sailed by the tank ships to dispose of their cargoes were very great. To reach the Mediterranean Sea, along the shores of which lay the oil-receiving ports, the tankers had to sail a roundabout course. They had to pass from the Persian Gulf to the Arabian Sea, southwesterly through the Gulf of Aden, then northward through the Red Sea and the Suez Canal, where tolls had to be paid. That was a voyage of 3,600 miles, which was slow and expensive.

By 1944, when the world was at war and more and more oil was needed, officials of the Arabian American Oil Company pointed out that a pipe line might be built from the oil center of Saudi Arabia to a port on the Mediterranean. The distance would be only a thousand miles. If the pipe line were big enough, it could take the place of the tankers and be more economical. The United States Government considered sponsoring such a project but finally decided to leave it to private industry.

Planning and Exploring the Route through Five Countries

In 1946 the Arabian American Oil Company (Aramco for short), began to make right-of-way agreements, or conventions, as they were called, with the countries through which a pipe line might pass. Besides Saudi Arabia there were Trans-Jordan, Syria, Lebanon and Palestine. The following year an affiliated company was formed to build and operate the new pipe line. It was called Trans-Arabian Pipe Line Company (Tapline for short). Parties of engineers and construction men explored possible routes by air and overland. They saw no obstacles too great to be overcome. A big pipe line could be laid, one that would carry more than 300,000 barrels of oil a day. Oil would be needed to support the economic recovery of Europe. Oil would be needed, too, by the countries through which the pipe line was to pass, adjoining Saudi Arabia.

The plan was to build from both ends. The Mediterranean base was to be at Beirut, the capital city of Lebanon, just a few miles south of which the line was to have its outlet. A contract for the construction of the westerly third of the line was awarded to Williams Brothers, of Tulsa, Oklahoma, while the easterly two-thirds was to be laid by International Bechtel, Inc., a San Francisco company already engaged in public-works projects in Saudi Arabia. The pipe line was to start at Abqaiq, a large oil field forty miles south of Dhahran.

The main receiving port for supplies was to be at Ras el Misha'ab, an uninhabited point on the desert at the edge of the Persian Gulf near the Neutral Zone between Saudi Arabia and Kuwait. This was about 190 miles northwest of Abqaiq. There were several reasons for the selection of Ras el Misha'ab. It had the best potential harbor north of the already developed ports along the Persian Gulf coast of Saudi Arabia. Those other ports were small and already too crowded. And from Ras el Misha'ab access roads could be built to bring materials to widely separated points along the route of the pipe line to the Mediterranean.

Active planning and purchasing for the job started in the spring of 1947 in San Francisco, 11,000 miles away from the Persian Gulf. The arrangements were as complete as for an army invasion. All materials had to be shipped from the United States because of an almost total absence of local supply sources . . . not only the materials

for the pipe line and pumping stations, but also construction and transportation equipment, repair facilities and spare parts, housing, all foodstuffs and supplies essential for the livelihood and well-being of the hundreds of American workers who had to be recruited and sent to Arabia.

The project was to be fully equipped for an initial period of at least nine to twelve months. If any one item were forgotten, six months might elapse before it could be delivered. After being properly approved, thousands of different articles and pieces of machinery were to be bought, received, packed and shipped. Every shipload, whether from the Pacific Coast or the Atlantic Coast of America, would take forty days or more to reach its destination halfway around the world.

The planners knew that the Arabian section of the pipe line was to pass through a wilderness without roads, its only inhabitants the wandering Bedouins; a wilderness lacking water or food resources; a wilderness of sand dunes, eroded valleys, briny sinkholes and vast gravel plains; a wilderness subject

Along the shaded line oil will flow, through Saudi Arabia, Trans-Jordan, Syria and Lebanon.

ADAPTED FROM A MAP SUPPLIED BY RICHARD FINNIE

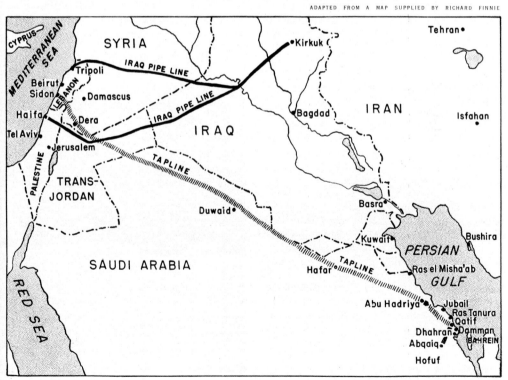

The Skyhook's spidery legs march into the sea.

to high winds and blinding sandstorms; a parched wilderness whose dusty trails are sometimes turned into rivers of mud by heavy rains. They had to consider these things and make provision for them. Special trucks had to be built with oversize water tanks and fitted with low-pressure tires that would roll over soft sand. Refrigerators and cold-storage chambers had to be provided to preserve food in the desert heat. DDT and sprayers had to be provided to protect workers against the flies forever swarming across the sands. Distillation units would be needed to convert brackish well water or even sea water into water pure enough for drinking and cooking.

On June 19, 1947, the first contingent of Americans left for Arabia to meet the first shipment of supplies for Tapline. By December the planning had been finished and 90 per cent of the requirements for the job had been shipped or were at dockside awaiting shipment. There were more than 5,000 separate purchase items. These did not include spare parts, which numbered over 30,000.

On July 12, 1947, a small party of engineers, construction men and a few Arab helpers set out with a truck convoy from Ras Tanura, Aramco's refinery center on the Persian Gulf, and drove to Ras el Misha'ab. Trails were rudimentary and the 140-mile journey took three days. The sight which met the eyes of the newcomers was uninspiring . . . an expanse of sand at the edge of the turquoise sea. The temperature was at least 120 degrees in the shade, but there was no shade. The men attempted to erect three tents in a freshening breeze. They succeeded in getting up only one. The breeze turned

into a dreaded *shemal*, a blinding sandstorm, that lasted for three days. Meanwhile a truck had been sent to fetch drinking water from a well forty miles inland. Before it got back the last bottle of precious water in the party was accidentally dropped and broken.

From this adventurous beginning Ras el Misha'ab grew in nine months into an imposing modern town with a population of 500 Americans and 1,500 Arabs. It was complete in all respects, with power plant, sewage disposal and water system, a score of 24-man barracks, a 500-man mess hall, a laundry, machine shop and garage, warehouses and office buildings, radio station, nurses residence and family dwellings. There were also Saudi Arab customs and immigration buildings and a residence for the local emir, or ruler. There were two causeways for berthing barges, and a three-mile ship-to-shore "Skyhook" aerial cableway for unloading pipe.

All main camp and harbor construction was soon finished. The Skyhook, the only one of its kind in the world, has been in operation since early May. During the first twelve months of the Tapline project, sixty-five ships from America discharged cargoes at Ras el Misha'ab totaling 200,000 tons. The surveying was completed, from the Persian Gulf to the Mediterranean. A substantial amount of pipe was not only laid but actually placed in service. All of this adds up

At Ras Tanura, on the Persian Gulf, a canal

to one of the greatest feats of logistics ever performed by private industry.

While work went on apace at the Persian Gulf end of the pipe line, Tapline's activities at the Mediterranean end were slowed down and temporarily halted because of unsettled political conditions there.

In January 1948, the Trans-Arabian Pipe Line Company modified its plans. Its directors decided to change the course of the pipe line slightly to pass through several local oil fields with an alternative outlet at Ras Tanura, the refinery center and ocean port sixty miles from Abqaiq. In this way the first portions of the pipe line to be built could be placed into service as soon as they were completed. The oil they gathered could be refined and loaded aboard tankers for immediate delivery.

On February 16, the first pipe from Ras el Misha'ab reached the right-of-way. It had been received at the main camp in 31-foot lengths and welded by automatic machines into 93-foot sections. Hauled by giant trucks, it was loaded aboard trailers each of which carried 9 sections weighing nearly 40 tons. The pipe, 30 inches in diameter, was lifted from the trailers by big tractors with cranes.

Meanwhile the right-of-way had been prepared for the pipe. Earth-moving machines and pile drivers had been busy. There were bulldozers, draglines, backhoes, ditching ma-

carries cooling sea water to the oil refinery.

chines and giant plows. Some of the pipe was to be placed in trenches and buried. Some of it was to lie above ground on piles. The pipe had to go through sand dunes fifty or sixty feet high. It also had to cross swampy mud flats called *sabkhas*.

The big pipe was placed end to end and welded together, mile after mile. Americans and Arabs worked side by side. The critical jobs were done by the Americans, who were more experienced. But the Arabs were learning. They did some of the welding, truck-driving and other tasks.

Arabs and Americans Learned Much from Working Together

The Americans had to adjust themselves to differences in language and religious customs. Arabic is a difficult tongue which few foreigners ever master, but many American construction men pick up in a few months a hundred or more words and phrases which serve them well. Their Arab companions often acquire a little English. All Saudi Arabs, who are devout Moslems, pray five times a day. Americans have to get used to seeing their Arab friends quietly walk away, one at a time or together, turn in the direction of Mecca, and prostrate themselves for as long as a quarter of an hour. The Moslem holy day is our Friday, and accordingly Americans in Arabia have come to observe their Sunday on that day too.

By early May the pipe-liners had built 44 miles of line. The pipe was tested, and since then there has been a steady flow of about 120,000 barrels a day of oil to the Ras Tanura refinery. The pipe-liners went ahead with their task. They had on hand enough pipe to lay 238 miles of the line, to connect with other oil fields near the Persian Gulf. When that was done, 823 miles remained to be laid to the Mediterranean. Just when the job could be completed would depend on two factors: how soon more steel would arrive from America, and the political situation in the Middle East.

The first stage of the trans-Arabian pipe line introduced new methods of construction previously untried in Arabia. It was carried out in varied terrain presenting most of the problems to be expected along more than half the 1,067-mile route to the Mediterranean. So it will have served as a pilot line and a model, thus making easier the balance of the job.

By LOUISE McDOWELL

THERE is no magic spell so ancient and so powerful as the naming of places, people and things. Even in our day the spell is still honored in the seriousness with which we treat the naming of a new baby, a new residential community or a new brand of soap. Of course, a name is chiefly needed for identification—to enable us to tell one object from others of its kind. But there are many other things that influence the selection of a name. The fond and hopeful people who name babies and soaps and real-estate developments always try to choose attractive names or names that have pleasant associations. Just consider the names that have come down to us from the Bible. There are still many people named Joseph and Samuel and Peter, Mary and Rebecca and Anne, but few little children are named Cain or Judas or Jezebel.

When it comes to the names of places—towns and states or provinces, mountains and rivers and swamps—the desire to give a pleasant impression is not nearly so evident. This is especially true of names that were given long ago, to places where civic pride was not concerned, and the main idea was

to show in the name what the place was like. The man—whoever he was—who first named the Dismal Swamp in Virginia really felt that it *was* dismal. So with the Badlands of the West and the Barren Lands of the Far North. Yet these baldly stated, unalluring names have come to have a romantic appeal that no Sylvan Shades or Paradise Valley can equal.

In the "older" continents, such as Europe and Asia, most of the place names are so old that their original meanings have been lost or buried under the weight of the centuries. In the Western Hemisphere, and especially in North America, it is quite different. There are many places in the United States and Canada which were founded and named within the memory of people now living; and even where the reason for a name has been forgotten, it is not difficult to guess what influenced the minds of the people who named it.

The maps and postal guides of Canada and the United States are fascinating to read as records of the origins, ideals, fads and fancies of the different peoples who have shared in the building of the two nations.

If you spend a few hours studying the maps and guides you will begin to see a pattern in what, at first glance, seems to be a mere hotchpotch of unrelated names. There are many cases in which you can tell about when a place was settled by the kind of name it has, and, of course, the nationality of the pioneer settlers quite frequently shows up in the name.

Many Names Can Be Grouped and Classified and Labeled

One of the refreshing things about our North American place names is the rugged individualism exercised in their selection. In spite of this there are at least six different types of names that appear over and over again on the maps:

(1.) Indian names.
(2.) Religious names—saints, holy days and Biblical names.
(3.) Names of places in the European homelands of the settlers.
(4.) Classical names—Greek and Roman places and historical characters.
(5.) Famous people—statesmen, national heroes, etc., both native and foreign.
(6.) Fanciful or descriptive names.

Perhaps the loveliest names of all, and often the most difficult to spell, are those which have come down to us from the first dwellers in our forests and mountains and plains. Four Canadian provinces, more than twenty states, many towns and cities and an endless number of rivers and mountains and lakes preserve for ages to come the half-forgotten tongues of the Indian tribes. Even the Indian names, however, give us a hint of the nationality of the white settlers who first adopted them. Our North American Indians had no written language, and their names for places and people were, of course, spelled out in Spanish or French or Dutch or English, according to which European explorers and pioneers first came in contact with them. Not all of these European missionaries and soldiers and adventurers had keen and precise ears for words, so it is quite possible that some of our Indian names would sound very strange to the braves and sagamores who first gave them to the white people.

You will notice that the Indian names that have come to us from the Spanish and French are softer and more musical than most of those that were written down by the English, Scotch, Irish and Dutch. Still, they all have an air of far away and long ago—Schenectady, Saskatchewan, Tuscaloosa, Wyoming, Shenandoah, Canarsie, Snoqualmie, Athabaska, Rapidan and hundreds of others. The Indians are being swallowed up in our civilization, but the names that they gave us brood over our lands and cities like the Great Spirit that they worshiped.

All the way across the continent, from the Gulf of St. Lawrence to the Gulf of California, there are names of a religious origin. There are hundreds of names of saints, such as St. Anne de Beaupré, St. Charles, St. Louis, St. Paul, Santa Barbara and San Francisco, most of them given by the French and Spanish missionary fathers. The state of Florida takes its name from Pascua Florida —flowery Easter—for it was first seen by the Spanish explorers on Easter Sunday. Cape Gracias á Dios reminds us that navigators often had reason to give thanks to God for bringing them safely in sight of land.

Some of the names given to settlements by the Spanish priests and explorers were beautiful and majestic in the extreme. Today people in all parts of the world know of the City of Our Lady Queen of the Angels, but few people know it by that name—either in Spanish or in English. Most of us call it Los Angeles, and all too many simply use the doleful initials—L. A. Of all the people who, in the last few years, have sung about traveling on "The Atchison, Topeka and Santa Fe," how many know that this railroad goes to the Royal City of the Holy Faith of Saint Francis? In our more hurried day it is simply Santa Fe, New Mexico.

Names That Were First Heard Thousands of Years Ago

Quakers, Mennonites, Baptists and other religious sects, including the Puritans of Massachusetts, have left us names out of the Old Testament: Bethel, Hebron and Salem among others; and we find, scattered across the land, such places as Jericho, Antioch, and Babylon, towns far different from the ancient cities that their founders read about in the Holy Scriptures.

It is a curious fact that the French people who settled Canada and Louisiana did not seem to care about naming their new settlements after the towns and cities of Old France. In the province of Quebec today, and in the states that were once the French province of Louisiana, you will look in vain

313

for places named Paris or Amiens or Auvergne or St. Malo. Orleans, the city where Joan of Arc won a victory that changed the history of two nations, is commemorated in New Orleans, Louisiana, and the island of Orleans in the St. Lawrence River, across from Quebec. Then there are Vincennes, Indiana, and Chambord and Verdun in Quebec.

On the other hand, the English who settled New England would seem to have known no other names than those of the towns they left behind them. The Pilgrim Fathers, who set sail from Plymouth, England, had hardly stepped on the famous Rock before they named it and their new home Plymouth. The settlers around Massachusetts Bay named their towns after Boston, Bedford, Cambridge, Waltham and other towns on the east side of England. All up and down the Atlantic Coast, from Nova Scotia to the Virginia Capes, you will find the names of cities in England.

Not only the English but the Dutch and the French Huguenots named their towns for the Old-World cities from which they had come. Flushing and New Utrecht, New Rochelle and Amsterdam—all in what we now call New York State, are reminders of the people who first owned that region.

Farther north and west in New York State, you will find classical names thickly clustered—Troy, Ilion, Athens, Attica, Carthage, Corinth, Ithaca, Utica, Palmyra, Rome, Syracuse. What is more, some or all of these names appear in Pennsylvania, Ohio, Illinois,

Indiana, Tennessee, Mississippi, Georgia and Alabama. Few if any names of Greek and Roman cities are found in Canada, New England, the Atlantic Coast or the land west of the Mississippi River. The reason for this is one of those fads and fancies that history is full of.

After the American Revolution, the people of the young Republic liked to compare their country to the Greek and Roman republics, by way of contrast with the European monarchies of the time. Western New York and Pennsylvania and the greater part of the other states we have mentioned began to be settled about the time that this interest in classical times was at its height, and that is why there are so many Romes and Athenses south of the lakes, between the Alleghenies and the Mississippi.

About the same time, or a little earlier, Upper Canada was settled by the United Empire Loyalists. The Loyalists were not the least bit interested in Roman and Greek republics—indeed, they had had quite too much of the American Republic. The names that they gave their cities reflected their loyalty to the Crown and its defenders. The Loyalist strain has given Ontario its characteristic distinction even to this day. Besides the royal names of Guelph, Hanover, Queenston, York and Georgetown, you will find the names of British statesmen such as Chatham and Dundas, and of military heroes such as General Brock, who was killed fighting for King and Country at Queenston

Heights in the War of 1812.

Among the names that are picturesque and descriptive without having any especial historical association, there are too many hundreds to tell about here. The West, both in Canada and the United States, is full of them. Kicking Horse Pass in the Canadian Rockies; Medicine Hat in Alberta; Tombstone, Arizona, are a few that most of us have heard of. Medicine Hat is said to have got its name from the ceremonial headdress of an Indian medicine man. It is easy to imagine the incident from which Kicking Horse was derived; and Tombstone speaks for itself. Manyberries, Alberta, sounds like a wonderful place for pies and shortcakes. Misery Gore, in the state of Maine, is more mysterious and tantalizing. You might think that such a name came from some terrible tragedy enacted in a remote village. However, Misery Gore is not even a village. It is a strip of land, twenty-five miles long and half a mile wide, left over when township boundaries were straightened out.

Some people think the name is a corruption of "misericorde" (mercy), a name often found where the Catholic missionaries have carried the Cross. It is also true that the word "gore" is an ancient Anglo-Saxon unit of land measurement—but this would not account for the "misery" part of the name.

The game of thinking up names for new towns still goes on, and some of the names are arrived at in curious ways. Arvida, Quebec, where the great new aluminum industry has been set up, is named for the founder of the industry, Arthur Vining Davis, using the first two letters of each of his names. This is like Kenora, a district in northern Ontario, made from the first two letters of three other place names—Keewatin, Noranda and Rat Portage. Delmarva (Delaware-Maryland-Virginia) and Texarkana (Texas-Arkansas) are other examples of these word-puzzle names.

There are towns named for their principal industries, such as Gloversville, New York, Oil City, Pennsylvania, and Ironton, Ohio. Mechanicsville and Mechanicsburg sound like busy manufacturing centers—and so they are. Frostproof, in Florida, must be an ideal place for a person who feels the cold, or who wants to grow oranges.

Whatever their origin, the names that give color and interest to timetables and maps are a true index to the imagination and to the activities of the people of Canada and the United States.

The Story of
HARRY S. TRUMAN

By KATHARINE L. FUGUET

Harry S. Truman was born in the small town of Lamar, Missouri, on May 8, 1884. His father, John Anderson Truman, and his mother, Martha Ellen Young Truman, were descended from pioneer American stock, mostly Anglo-Saxon. In Harry Truman's own words, "We're a little of everything—Scotch, Irish, Dutch. If you shook the family tree, anything might fall out."   •

In 1842, some years before the great Gold Rush sent hordes of people to the hills of California, Truman's grandparents migrated from Kentucky to Missouri, which in those days could still be called a frontier. His mother's father, Solomon Young, was a large landowner and a business man in the best tradition of America's pioneers. From 1846 to 1860, the wagon trains of Solomon Young wound their way on long, difficult journeys into the western wilderness, for Solomon was a prosperous freighter.

Young Harry was not likely to forget the stories he was told about those exciting days. The letter "S" which is his middle initial is a constant reminder of his grandfathers, Solomon Young and Anderson Shippe Truman.

When he was six years old, Harry's parents left Lamar and settled on a farm at Grandview, near Independence, Missouri. From then on, Independence was his home town. There was a little girl, Bess Wallace, who went to the same school Harry did. He was seven when he met little Bess, and they attended many classes together. At that time they went to the same Sunday School, too. These childhood sweethearts grew up together and became engaged just before Harry went away to serve his country in World War I.

Soldiering had long appealed to the boy. He had set his heart on going to the United States Military Academy at West Point. Although he was slated for appointment, he was never able to realize his cherished dream. He was rejected because of poor eyesight.

Besides, any money that he could earn was needed. After he was graduated from the Independence High School in 1901, he went to work as a timekeeper on a railroad construction job. Next, he was an employee in the mailing room of the Kansas City STAR. Then he worked as a bank clerk in Kansas City.

Meanwhile, Harry's father was growing older, and the care of the 600-acre farm near Independence was becoming a little too much for him. Harry was called back to the farm to help. During his boyhood he had learned the meaning of the word "chores," for he had grown up, as they say, "between plow handles." Now he proved to be both a good farmer and a good manager. One of his neighbors remembers him as "the weed-fightinest guy I ever knew."

He had good need to be a fighter. The year 1914 made great changes in his life, for that was the year his father died and the year when the first World War began. After the death of John Anderson Truman, Harry set out to modernize the farm and went in for such "newfangled" ideas as crop rotation, soil conservation and the keeping of records. These innovations paid, however, and won for Harry the widespread admiration of neighbors whose methods had remained old-fashioned.

Harry kept on farming until 1917. He had joined the National Guard at an early age, and the training he received helped him to make an excellent record in the wartime service of his country. He enlisted in the Field Artillery, and his regiment was sent for training to Camp Doniphan, on the Fort Sill Reservation in Oklahoma. He won promotion to the rank of captain; and in April 1918, was sent to France. As commander of

Once a farm boy in the state of Missouri, Harry S. Truman rose to be president of his country.

Battery D, 129th Regiment, 35th Division, he was in the thick of action, most notably in the great Argonne offensive.

His home town, Independence, heard tales of his exploits and when peace came and he went home he found himself a hero. He came back a thirty-five-year old veteran with major's leaves on his shoulders. There were his mother, his sister, the farm—and Bess! Six weeks after his discharge from the army, he and Bess Wallace were married, June 28, 1919. They had many interests in common, among them a love of music. This interest was inherited by their daughter Margaret, who grew up with an ambition to make music her career.

Harry Truman, the newlywed, soon branched from farming into business, investing his savings in a haberdashery in Kansas City. He and his partner, Sergeant Jacobson, made money for a year or so; but in 1922, the business failed. Truman was left with a personal debt of about $21,000. Thirteen years later, when he came to the Senate, he was still paying it off. He might have escaped this burden by going into bankruptcy, but his sense of honor made him pay off every single cent of the debt.

After his disastrous venture into business, Truman went back to his home town and did some hard thinking. What should the next step be? During the war, Captain Harry had shown a knack for organization and leadership which was very much admired by one of his fellow-officers in the regiment. This was young Jim Pendergast, nephew of the Democratic leader of Jackson County, of which Independence is the county seat. In 1922, veterans in Independence began urging Truman for local political office. In November, he was elected to a county judgeship for a two-year term. About this time he began reading law and was a student at the Kansas City Law School, 1923–25.

There was a split in the Democratic party in 1924, and Truman was defeated that year for re-election; but in 1926 he won a four-year term as presiding judge of the county court. In this position, Judge Truman was the chief administrative officer of the county government, a post which he held until his election to the Senate in 1934. His personal reputation and his host of friends stood him in good stead, for it was during this first term in the Senate that the organization that had been of such help to him, the Pender-

gast machine, fell to pieces. At the next election, in 1940, the people of Missouri showed their confidence in Truman by sending him back to the Senate for a second term.

Those first six senatorial years, however, were largely a training period. With his talent for studious application, Senator Truman set out to learn all he could about the work of the Federal Government.

He helped draft railroad legislation; wrote a bill for the Federal licensing of motor-vehicle operators in interstate traffic; and helped draft the Civil Aeronautics Act. He was, furthermore, a hard worker on many committees—Appropriations, Military Affairs, Interstate Commerce, and the Committee on Public Buildings and Grounds. He gave his hearty support to President Roosevelt's domestic program, and after the outbreak of World War II, in September 1939, he also supported Roosevelt's policy of preparedness.

A committee that was his own idea was the one that first brought the future President nation-wide fame. This was called the Truman Committee. As a veteran of the earlier world conflict, he had watched with indignation the extravagance and profiteering that had followed in its wake. As a senator, he wanted to prevent such waste if he could. The job of the Truman Committee was to investigate waste or alleged waste in the war effort. As a result, the Government was saved more than $200,000,000 in the early days of the war.

In 1944, Truman was President Roosevelt's running mate on the Democratic ticket and was elected vice-president in November of that year. On Roosevelt's death, April 12, 1945, Harry Truman became president of the United States.

His new responsibilities were staggering. The war had not yet been won. The atom bomb was still in the future. President Truman was faced with decisions that would involve the welfare of the whole world.

Through the final dark days of the war and through the many stupendous problems that followed, the humble man from Missouri could only do his best. Was it enough? Would the people trust him as "Captain Harry" had once been trusted? The answer to these questions came on the 2nd of November 1948. The presidential election held that day was a victory for Harry S. Truman as well as for his party.

PROTEIN

the builder

By JOHN J. O'NEILL

Science Editor, New York Herald Tribune

HARVARD UNIVERSITY NEWS OFFICE

Dr. Robert B. Woodward pouring synthetic protein on a sheet of glass.

WHEN you eat meat, cheese, eggs, fish, milk and many other foods, you are feeding your body the proteins it must have. No living things, plant or animal, can exist without proteins. Sixty per cent of the solid matter in our bodies is protein. Your body changes the proteins you eat into other proteins which build your muscles, your stomach, your heart, your skin and fingernails, your hair and many other parts of your body.

There are, of course, other chemical substances which are necessary to life, but none are more strange than those we know as proteins, for in these the processes of life take place in all living things. These proteins within the body are much more wonderful than any machine that man can make. They have the power to grow and to repair and to reproduce themselves.

Proteins are very complex chemical substances. They are made up of huge molecules which are groups of smaller molecules called amino-acids. The amino-acids are made of still simpler particles called atoms. There are four principal kinds of atoms in amino-acids and proteins—carbon, hydrogen, oxygen and nitrogen. Proteins are different from other substances mainly because they contain nitrogen.

Let us watch the building up of some protein molecules, beginning with the atoms. Atoms, although they are very tiny, have something which we may compare to hands, although they are, of course, not actually hands in our sense of the word. These "hands" make it possible for atoms to take hold of other atoms and thus form groups of atoms called molecules. Hydrogen has one hand, oxygen has two hands, carbon has four hands, and nitrogen, five. Chemists call these "hands" by another name—valence bonds. Although nitrogen has five hands, it usually keeps them all in its pockets, or pulled up, hidden in its sleeves. In other words, nitrogen shows no great tendency to take hold of other atoms. When a way is found, however, to make nitrogen hold hands with other atoms, strange things happen in the games it plays.

A tiny bacterium, a very simple, one-celled form of plant life which lives in the ground, knows how to get the nitrogen atom to take its hands out of its pockets and join hands with some atoms of hydrogen. This group then joins other atoms. Plants take these groups, or molecules, containing nitrogen atoms through their roots as food, and build them into other groups called amino-acids. These amino-acids, in their turn, join together in more complicated molecules of substances known as proteins, which the plant stores in its fruit and its tissues.

We eat the plants as food, just as animals do. Our bodies break down the proteins from the plants into their amino-acids, and then change these into new combinations. Some of them are changed into other kinds of amino-acids. There are twenty-three amino-acids altogether that exist in nature. When

319

we eat meat, we get from it special kinds of amino-acids which the animals have made from the amino-acids in the plants they have eaten. There are eight amino-acids that our human bodies can not make. These we must secure in our food, either plant or animal, if we wish to remain alive and in good health.

The twenty-three different kinds of amino-acids join themselves together in many ways, forming many thousands of combinations. Among these combinations are the substances we know as hair, skin, nails and so on.

An amino-acid may be likened to a football team, lined up for the kickoff, and taking the form of a capital T. Down the stem of the letter T are located the "center" and the various "backs," quarter, half and full. Across the top bar of the letter are the right and left end members of the team.

In most amino-acids the backs, down the stem of the letter, are represented by a string of carbon atoms, each with a hydrogen atom on either side of it. The make-up of the top cross bar of the T is more interesting. The two sides are different. The left side is made up of a nitrogen atom with two hydrogen atoms attached. This is called the amino group. The right-hand end is made up of a carbon atom with two oxygen atoms attached to it. To one of the oxygen atoms a hydrogen atom is hooked. This is called the carboxyl group.

In a football team, each member of the team has a certain position and certain duties. In the amino-acid molecule the groups of atoms in different positions have different properties or characteristics. The stem of the

REPRINTED FROM SCIENCE ILLUSTRATED

CHECK THE AMINO ACIDS IN YOUR DIET
YOU MUST HAVE THESE FOODS

Listed below are the six foods richest in protein. Nutritionists suggest that the best meal contains a blending of at least two or more of the six.

Lean meat — especially steak, chops, liver—is the finest source of protein and amino acids.

Milk, an excellent protein food, is a prime source for the manufacture of many acids.

Cheese contains a full complement of the 20 amino acids and is rich in high quality proteins.

Eggs—at least one a day —offer a goodly share of proteins necessary to keep your body healthy.

Nearly all fish contain a wide assortment of both essential and non-essential amino acids.

The lowly soybean, in almost any of its varied forms, provides most of the necessary acids.

OTHER FOODS: Many of the so-called healthy foods, high in other food values, are low in amino-acid content. Tomatoes, mushrooms, carrots, apples, asparagus, oranges, are especially deficient. But, many low-protein foods are necessary because they provide needed vitamins, fats, and carbohydrates.

amino-acid T likes to mix with oils and fats, because it has the same structure as oils. It will not, however, mix with water. Both ends of the top bar of the amino-acid T love water. The amino group at one end is strongly alkaline and likes to mix with and neutralize acids. The carboxyl group at the other end is strongly acid, and likes to mix with and neutralize alkalis or salts. With all these properties gathered together in one small molecule, it is not strange that amino-acids can join together in thousands of ways. In this way they form a great variety of protein substances with different properties.

The Skin That Covers Your Body Is Waterproof Protein

Our skin, for example, is a special kind of protein which is waterproof. If it were not waterproof, the water from our baths would leak through the skin to the inside of our bodies. The protein which forms our fingernails is another special kind, also that of our hair.

The amino-acids join hands in various ways. Very often the amino group of one amino-acid joins the carboxyl group of another. They form a long line like

TTTTTTTTTTTTT

with the top bars joined. The lower end of the stem can act like a chemical hand. It can take hold of other groups, cre-

TTTTTTTTT

ating structures like TTTTTTTTT. Some amino-

TTTTTTTTT

acids have two amino groups. This gives them a total of four hands for making connections. We may imagine that these four hands make a figure something like an X, so

XXXXXXXX

we can get combinations like XXXXXXXX.

XXXXXXXX

At other times they form long lines linked together here and there as in

——X——X——X——X——
X——X——X——X——X
——X——X——X——X——

Long threads like this can form hair or fur, or such threads can be formed in layers and built up crisscross one on top of the other to form a thick broad surface like skin. They can be formed, also, into hard, thick materials such as nails, hoofs and horns.

Protein molecules, made up of chains, sheets or masses of amino-acids, are the largest molecules known. The smallest protein molecule contains more than 2,000 atoms and the largest contains many millions.

We know many proteins very well. The white of an egg is protein. It is called albumen. When the egg grows into a chicken the albumen breaks up into amino-acids. These amino-acids are then put together in a different way to form new kinds of proteins. These new proteins form muscles, skin, feathers, beak, stomach, eyes and other organs. This is what our bodies do in a different way with the proteins they get from food. They break them into amino-acids and then put them together in different ways in various parts of the body.

Scientists would like to find the way to make proteins as nature does. A long step was recently taken in this direction at Harvard University. Dr. Robert B. Woodward, Dr. William E. Doering and C. H. Schramm succeeded in making substances which greatly resemble the protein that nature makes. They started with materials that were very much like amino-acids. They consisted of a chain of carbon atoms, with an amino group at one end, and a carboxyl group at the other end. They put these substances in water and let them set quietly. In time they found that the molecules had joined, end to end, and had formed materials with properties much like those of proteins.

If Scientists Could Make Protein Foods, Famine Would Vanish from the Earth

Think what it would mean if in time scientists could make proteins that we could use for food. Then there would be plenty of food for all people everywhere. Scientists are, however, very doubtful that this will ever happen. Living bodies are very particular about the kind of amino-acids and proteins they will use for food.

There are two kinds of each amino-acid. Both kinds of each acid have the same number and kind of atoms put together in the same way, but they differ in structure like left- and right-hand gloves. Nature makes and requires the left-hand kind. The kind man makes usually turns out to be the right-hand kind.

It is certain, nevertheless, that scientists will be able to make artificially many useful materials of protein. Artificial fur, rubber, "real" artificial silk and many other substances will be produced in great quantities for people all over the world.

Doris Brown, a bright star of television.

RADIO AND

By Hubbell Robinson, Jr.
*CBS Vice-President
in charge of programming*

THERE are thousands of men and women—young men and women, many of them—who are taking part in the work of putting radio and television (TV) programs on the air.

Just how many different kinds of skills are required to put programs on the air can be seen better from a network's Master Control Room than from almost any other one place. Let's look in on one of these "nerve centers." They are called this because all of the "nerves" of a network—all of the lines that carry programs—are controlled from this one place.

In mid-afternoon—about 3:15—this might be seen from a look at the lines hooked up by Master Control:

1. Studios 26 and 28 are both "on the air" and each is being "fed" to a different part of the network; that is, two programs are being sent out at the same time to two different groups of stations on the network.

2. Studios 7 and 25 are just completing their rehearsals and will make final tests with Master Control prior to "taking air" at 3:30.

3. Two field technicians are making tests from a suburban hospital, where one of the 3:30 programs will originate.

4. One of the big nighttime shows is feeding its dress rehearsal from its studio to a recording company so that the program may be heard and criticized by its producers before it is aired; and the same kind of

thing is going on from another studio.

5. Several announcers are being auditioned (tried out) from a studio. Their tests are being "piped" on telephone lines to program executives listening in their offices.

These are some of the program activities that might be going through the Master Control Room of a network at one and the same time. Behind all of these operations we can see the hundreds of actors, musicians, producers, directors, writers, researchers, announcers, engineers, technicians, program assistants and many others. This kind of a bird's-eye view—a view of programs "on the air," programs "in rehearsal," and programs or talent "in audition"—shows radio as most of the people who work in it know it. As television networks stretch across the country, the pattern in TV is becoming more and more similar.

One article can not cover the many things that have to be done to put programs on the air by radio or by TV. It can scarcely even suggest the swift-paced excitement, the disappointments and hard, persistent work that are all part of program operations. There are some facts, however, with which we can start. We should have in mind who the principal people are, and what they do. Let's take just a few of them, people like the:

Producer. The person responsible for preparing and presenting a program.

Director. The person who casts and rehearses a program, and who directs the actual air performance. He may also write or rewrite the script.

Writer. Like producers and directors, a writer may be a free-lance operator, that is, an individual who contracts to do particular programs for an advertising agency, a station or other organization; or a writer may be "on staff" of a network or station to handle the varied writing assignments that come up. These range all the way from short continuities to tying musical selections to a dramatic broadcast.

Studio Technician. The person who "mixes" the various elements of a program to produce a proper sound-volume balance. By

TELEVISION PROGRAMMING

Television's Howdy Doody and Bob Smith.

means of controls in the Studio Control Room, he can make sure that pickups from the studio are of good, uniform quality. He also makes the split-second switch of a lever so that the particular studio can take the air and, similarly, go off the air.

Sound Man. The studio technician who produces, either manually or by recordings, the desired sound-effects.

Television has the same kinds of people. It also has a good many more. Some day there will probably be more jobs in television than there now are in radio; because the fact is, it takes more people to do *the same thing* in television.

For example, to produce the Ford Theatre on the CBS radio network takes a crew of ten people, over and above the cast and the orchestra. This includes a producer, director, associate director, talent buyer, editor, writer, two sound men and two engineers. But to produce the Ford Theatre as a separate production for the CBS television audience takes a crew of forty people, in addition to cast and musicians.

Some of these additional people are: four cameramen; two men on audio (the sound portions of the program); a "dolly-pusher" for one camera (a man who rolls the movable camera to different positions on the set); two camera-control men; five men in a control room to co-ordinate the different channels of material flowing in from the program itself and from a separate room where the

advertising announcements are prepared for inclusion in the program at the right time. In addition, there are thirteen stagehands and helpers, as well as people to build the sets and produce other visual materials for the program, such as the titles and credits (to author, talent, producer and others).

On an entirely different kind of program, Winner Take All, the comparison is much the same, ten people for radio and thirty-four people for television. So this is why television, when it becomes fully established throughout the country, should become an even bigger market than radio is for people who want to "help put shows on."

Television shows, by the way, are of three main types: *original productions*, that is, programs built entirely with the television audience in mind; *simultaneous programs*, that is, programs which are televised as they

Larry LeSueur uses a walkie-talkie to interview people at a national political convention.

Broadcasting from "the bubble." This glass-enclosed studio on wheels can go anywhere.

are being broadcast for the radio audience; and *adapted programs*, that is, programs that have been popular in radio but which require alterations and additions to make them popular on television too. Much television programming is being done by means of film. The film may be full-length movies, selected shorts, or productions specially prepared for television. Many companies are already in the business of providing program material for television on film. If TV develops as now appears likely, film will be important for the many hours the television program departments must fill. Many people will actu-

Actors awaiting a cue from the control box.

ally be "in television," but will be working for a film company that makes films for television.

Dramatic shows in television require the same kind of patient, painstaking production that good movies and good plays require. For example, this is the procedure used to get one first-class dramatic production ready for television. Rehearsals begin three weeks before the program is scheduled, and continue six to eight hours a day for the next week and a half. Meantime, music is planned; and schedules worked out for cameramen, sound men and technicians. Then comes the almost magic fusion with the many other elements, such as costumes, makeup and scenery construction. Finally, the director is ready to offer his play.

If it were a radio production he would have enough to worry about—engineers, a

sound man, the performances of his actors. In television he has a larger number of people to direct and a larger technical apparatus in use. So he can worry (if he wants to) about cameramen; about men handling the "boom mikes" (microphones on the ends of long poles which can be handled to pick up the actors' voices at close range without getting in the angle of the camera); lighting men; property men; floor supervisors; and many others. Then, too, there is the worry as to whether actors will remember their lines in TV, a worry which does not happen in radio because they read scripts.

There are many such points of comparison with radio; and these comparisons can help us understand some of the special features of both radio and TV. Imagine, for example, that you are the director of a discussion program, and that you do one version for radio, and another for television. Your own imagination will suggest the differences in the way you will have to go about preparing each show.

Radio and Television Methods Often Differ Widely

In TV, you can make use of film sequences from newsreels, charts, pictures, maps and cartoons; you have a chance to *show* how things work, or how things happened. In radio the moderator can direct the discussion a good deal more than he can in television. In radio, he can signal one person to hold back and let another person air his views; but in television, such an attempt, unless very skillfully done, might look like bias to the audience at home and produce letters of complaint. These examples are merely intended to indicate the kind of special thinking required to put on programs in either medium.

All broadcasts, of course, do not come from the controlled conditions of streamlined studios. Many of radio's best-remembered broadcasts have been from scenes of disaster or other great excitement, from the World Series or national political conventions, from high in the sky and from deep in the sea. Television, too, is taking its place as a "reporter" of such events. Already adequate mobile equipment and staff for field operations has a big place in TV, as it has in radio.

Each non-studio or "remote" pickup requires special planning so that it comes off with the split-second timing we take for granted. In a remote pickup from a regular land point such as an auditorium, plane hangar or sport arena, the field men set up complete studio technical facilities and feed a special telephone line to Master Control. Sometimes, if adequate land facilities are lacking, the signal must be short-waved to a point where it can be connected with the telephone line carrying it to Master Control.

Many exciting stories have been written about the "special events" men who, like the good reporters they are, have rushed to scenes of important news and brought the story through, regardless of hazards and difficulties, to the millions of people listening comfortably in their homes. TV, too, has performed some great exploits in direct on-the-spot pickups and in getting film versions for later showing. The long election night coverage of 1948 gave TV one of its biggest "special events" jobs up to that time.

Already, more than fifty TV stations are on the air several hours each day, and already there are networks which are sending out programs regularly to their affiliates. In the case of radio, programs are carried by special telephone wires to the transmitter of the local station, where they are actually broadcast. In the case of TV, more elaborate equipment is required to connect stations. This may be either a coaxial cable or a microwave relay system. The latter involves sending the TV signals straight out through the air and then relaying them from point to point by means of booster stations. These booster stations are necessary because TV signals only carry, as a usual thing, some fifty miles. The theoretical distance is "to the horizon," which depends, of course, on how high the transmitter is. There are many exceptions to this limited distance for TV signals. Direct reception has been reported several hundred miles from a TV transmitter. However, booster stations every thirty to thirty-five miles are necessary at present.

Radio and Television Have Drawn New Talent

This fascinating business of radio and television has attracted many people who have had no previous training. For the most part, they are people with ambition and intelligence who have learned "on the job." But there are many highly trained experts, too, people like George J. Stoetzel, lighting consultant and designer of a studio lighting sys-

tem which enables actors to work in a temperature of not more than seventy-four degrees; formerly the huge banks of powerful studio lights, believed necessary to illuminate the scene properly, made the artists swelter during a long rehearsal or show.

There are lots of people in radio-TV, too, who have had their sights set on putting on shows, or being in shows, since they were very young. One of these is Fletcher Markle, the brilliant twenty-seven-year-old director of Ford Theatre. Markle formed his own acting unit, in British Columbia, when he was only eighteen. There, too, he wrote, directed and

WGN

Radio plays need careful and expert direction.

starred in a sixty-five-week series of full-hour plays. Finally, after other theatrical, movie and radio ventures, his road led to CBS and to almost immediate success.

Doris Brown, who is seen on two CBS-TV shows, began her interest in "shows" while at summer camp, continued it at college, and then in summer at college, and then in summer stock companies. Her road led to an audition for a TV show and finally to her popular role on children's TV programs.

Since 1947, BROADCASTING YEARBOOK has published annual lists of books on all phases of radio and TV, together with some description of what the books contain. Here, the boy or girl who wants to get into the program side of radio or television will find many good books on the various kinds of jobs, on the terms used in radio and TV, and on the techniques one has to know.

. . . what happened in

By FRANK LEUER KELLER

*Assistant Professor, Latin American
Geography, Rutgers University*

BEFORE talking about the year's events in South America, we should first think about a few of the things that continually influence current affairs in this region of the Western Hemisphere. It may help us to understand some of the problems that face the republics to the south of us.

For instance, there is the problem of language. If you were to take a trip to South America, the people with whom you might speak would reply in one of three different but related Latin languages. It might be Spanish, Portuguese or French—except, of course, in those countries that straddle the long Andean mountain chain. There, the majority of the inhabitants speak only their strange Indian tongues, centuries old.

Most of the people live by agriculture. They either have farms of their own or, more likely, work on country estates of great land-owners. They differ greatly from us in the kind of clothes they wear, the architecture of their homes, and their ideas about life. The Latin also likes to live in towns, whether it be a large city or a small *pueblo* (village). As a result, the population of the larger cities has increased rapidly in recent years.

It is this city population whose ways of living are most like ours. The people wear clothes styled as ours are instead of native dress. They have a money economy—that is, they use coin or currency to buy what they need—rather than the barter system. They are factory workers and business men. However, at this point the similarity to our way of living ends.

There are two ways of life going on at the same time in Latin America. One, at the top, is made up of a thin layer of people who live very much as do North Americans. They

KOPPERS COMPANY, INC.

The fiery blast and open-hearth furnaces of this steel mill (above) will soon cast their eerie glow into the night sky of Concepcion, bringing a new industry and new prosperity to Chile.

Bright flowers and magazines are very popular with the city-dwellers of Argentina.

have a wide viewpoint and many have a broad education. The second layer lies far below this level, leaving a wide gap in between the two. Its people live in poverty and neglect—often without land of their own to cultivate—and in ignorance. In recent years farsighted officials have been trying to bring these two layers closer together—to narrow the gap and provide a better way of life for the people of the second layer. Much of the news that has come out of Latin America during the past year was based on the ceaseless struggle of these two widely separated groups to find a common meeting ground.

Perhaps the event of greatest importance for the future of the Western Hemisphere was the meeting of the Ninth International Conference of American States. It was held in Bogotá, Colombia, from March 30 to May 2, 1948. Here, in the former home of South America's liberator, Simón Bolívar, the twenty-one nations of the Pan American

SOUTH AMERICA

Union agreed to the charter of the Organization of American States.

By signing the charter of this new organization, the countries bound themselves into a working association of nations—a miniature United Nations for the republics of the Western Hemisphere alone. They pledged themselves to economic co-operation and to achieve better ways of living. They pledged themselves to try to settle all disputes peaceably, to protect their weaker neighbors from aggressor nations and, in many other ways, to help assure peace in the Western Hemisphere.

The Organization of American States will not replace the Pan American Union. In fact, the union will become even more important than it has been in the past, because it will serve as the secretariat of the new organization, with much the same duties as the secretariat of the United Nations. The former governing board of the union will be the executive council of the organization.

Peru's ancient valleys are producing food with the aid of modern farm machinery.

to Bolivia

Pacific Ocean

Antofagasta
to Salta - 559 mi.
(sea level)

CHILE

ARGENTINA

Socompa

Pocitos

San Antonio de los Cob

Abra Chorrillos Pass
(15,760 ft.)

to Santiago

to Bolivia

Salta
3,960 ft.

TRANS-ANDEAN SHORT CUT

TIME MAP BY V. PUGLISI; COURTESY OF TIME, COPYRIGHT TIME, INC.

On this relief map, the mountains have been sliced off to show you the line of the new railway.

South America can be divided into three broad geographical regions, based on the kind of raw material that each produces. The areas growing such food as bananas, cacao, sugar and coffee (Caribbean region and central Brazil) regard the United States as the natural customer for their products. The countries of the Temperate Zone (Argentina, Uruguay, Paraguay and southern Brazil) chiefly produce agricultural products similar to those of North America. Therefore, they do not find any important markets in the Western Hemisphere. These products have always been sold to the United Kingdom and to continental Europe. The countries that produce minerals depend on the manufacturing areas of western Europe and the United States to buy the output of their mines.

Thus, the tropical areas depend more on United States markets. The agricultural countries of the Temperate Zone, and the mineral-producing countries of the Andean region need European markets for continued prosperity. However, during and after World War II, the European markets dried up to a great extent. The European countries have not been able to manufacture the goods with which to buy their share of Latin America's raw materials. Because of this the year has been largely a repetition of other post-war years for South America. That is, efforts have been mainly directed toward re-establishing the flow of foreign trade with western Europe.

The Marshall Plan (European Recovery Program), however, flashed a ray of hope on

the scene. As you know, the program is one by which the United States will try to provide Europe with enough agricultural products and industrial machinery for it to regain its old position in world trade. Many of these agricultural and mineral shipments will come from South America. In fact, by mid-year $32,000,000 in food and raw materials had been authorized for shipment to Europe from Latin America. For example, Chile received $12,000,000 to export copper to Italy, France, Britain and the Netherlands. Venezuela prepared to send $12,000,000 in petroleum products to Italy. It must not be thought, though, that Marshall-Plan spending alone will be enough to rebuild the foreign trade of Latin-American nations. Nor will it build up their home industries or raise their very low living standards.

Many Latin-American nations operate on what is called a one-crop economy. This means that they produce only one principal crop or other product for trade with other nations. There have been recent attempts to change this system. Trade agreements have been made between some of the countries. Loans of money from the Export-Import Bank in the United States, and the World Bank of the United Nations are helping, too. For example, a steel plant is being built in Concepcion, Chile, by the Chilean Development Corporation and the Koppers Company of Pittsburgh, Pennsylvania. The development corporation is a government organization formed to help build up Chile's home industries. The plant is being built with

Chilean money and credit from the Export-Import Bank. It is employing Chilean workmen and specialists from the United States. Chile was the first Latin-American country to receive a loan from the World Bank. The loan totals $16,000,000, of which $13,500,000 will be used for building new hydroelectric plants. The rest of the money will be used by the Chilean Development Corporation to buy farm equipment and farm machinery.

Sugar for Chileans and Rice for Peruvians

An important example of the kind of trade agreement that is being made is this one, between Chile and Peru. The agreement was worked out in 1947, but its good effects did not begin to show until 1948. Chile and Peru agreed to exchange agricultural and mineral products. Forty thousand tons of Chilean rice were traded for 84,000 tons of Peruvian sugar. These countries have also removed the import taxes on their important fertilizer products—Peruvian guano and Chilean nitrate—for each other. This is a step that is helping to improve agriculture in both countries.

Another example of this beneficial kind of trade agreement is one between Argentina and Bolivia. Bolivia depends on Argentina for many kinds of food. Argentina needs such things as tin, antimony, lead, petroleum and rubber. Bolivia is rich in these resources, but they are not well developed. So Argentina is investing almost $27,000,000 in Bolivian industry to help increase the production and export of these things from Bolivia. Argentina also has loaned Bolivia another $27,000,000 for the construction of public works.

The Peruvian Government is giving direct help to the country's farmers by buying farm machinery and renting it to the farmers for a very low price. This is increasing the amount of land under cultivation and is speeding up the production of food.

Probably the most important economic agreement between any Latin-American republic and a foreign nation was made between Britain and Argentina in February of last year. Fifteen thousand miles of British-owned railways in Argentina, plus British fuel and manufactured goods, were exchanged for large shipments of Argentine meat and corn. The purchase of the railways

shows that at least one of the more advanced Latin-American nations is prepared to rely more on its own efforts than on foreign exploitation to develop itself. During the war Argentina also supplied the Allied armies with huge quantities of food. In this way, the Government built up a large amount of surplus credit in foreign countries. This kind of credit is very much like the kind that a farmer's wife might build up at the village store by sending in her eggs every day. The storekeeper does not actually pay her for the eggs each day. Instead, he keeps track of the amount of money that he owes her for them. At the end of a week, or a month, he will owe her a certain amount of money, which is her credit at the store. If she buys something, the price is subtracted from the total amount. However, if she does not use up all of her credit at once, the remaining amount would be her surplus credit. Argentina is now using up her surplus credit by ordering materials needed for her home industries.

The Airplane Makes Neighbors of Tropic Villages and Modern Cities

The airplane has played an even more important part in modernizing South America than it did in the United States or Canada. Hot, steaming jungles and towering mountain ranges have to be crossed in South American travel. Ordinarily, tropical villages set in the midst of dense jungle or vast swampland are weeks away from civilization when you travel by burro or canoe. The magic of airplane wings, though, has brought them within hours of the large cities. So it is not surprising that the nations of Latin America should be very much interested in expanding their air services.

During the year, Colombia, Ecuador and Bolivia worked out agreements with the United States which will be beneficial to everyone. The United States will furnish airplanes and technical experts to help them enlarge their air services. Chile, Venezuela, Uruguay and Brazil also are co-operating, although less formally.

Three South American nations were involved in revolutions during the year. In April, Jorge Eliécer Gaitán, a leftist Liberal Party leader of Colombia, was shot and killed in the streets of Bogotá. His murder touched off the spark of revolution, and for four days there was a reign of terror in the city.

The meeting of the Ninth International Conference of American States, which was going on at the time, was nearly broken up. Mobs of rioters looted shops and burned many buildings before government troops were able to control them. Hundreds of people were killed during the rioting.

Peru saw three revolutionary uprisings. In July, soldiers rebelled in Juliaca—in southern Peru—but the disturbance was quieted in just a few days. On October 3, Peruvian sailors and civilians tried to start a revolution in the seaport city of Callao and in near-by Lima. They attacked the Peruvian Naval Academy, a naval armory and Fort Royal Philip. They seized a cruiser and a destroyer of the Peruvian Navy. The revolt lasted only one day, though, and was quickly put down by the government. It was reported to have been started by the Left-wing Apra Party, which was opposed to President José Luis Bustamante y Rivero. Later, the Apra Party was outlawed. President Bustamante had been elected in 1945 by a coalition of Liberals, Leftists and Rightists.

Rightists Depose President José Bustamante

Peru's third revolt against the government began on October 27. It was launched by General Manuel Odria, leader of the so-called Rightists, in the southern city of Arequipa. Two days later it had spread to Lima, the capital, and on October 29 President Bustamante was deposed. He took refuge in Buenos Aires, Argentina. The next day General Odria set up a provisional government and named a cabinet composed of Army, Navy and Air Force officers. The cabinet was to govern Peru until free elections could be held and a truly democratic government could be elected, General Odria said.

Venezuela held the first popular election of its history, and President Romulo Gallegos took office in February 1948. His election was a triumph for the Democratic Action party, for it won a sweeping victory over its more conservative opponents. Out of a total population of 4,000,000, about 1,500,-000 people cast their secret ballots. All adults over the age of eighteen were permitted to vote. However, on November 24, he was deposed in a short, swift military coup headed by Lieutenant Colonel Delgado Chalbaud, and was exiled to Havana, Cuba. Former President Gallegos is an educator and

author. He wrote the famous novel *Dona Barbara*, which has been translated into several languages. He is known as a progressive and liberal politician and wants to abolish illiteracy and improve agriculture and sanitary conditions in his country.

Antarctica and the Falkland Islands (Islas Malvinas) were the cause of a dispute between England and two South American nations—Chile and Argentina—in February. All three countries claim parts of Antarctica including Palmer Peninsula (Graham Land) and the Falklands. President Gabriel Gonzalez Videla of Chile led a flag-planting expedition to Palmer Peninsula to underline Chile's claims. The Argentine Navy held maneuvers near the Falkland Islands, and England sent the cruiser Nigeria from South Africa to uphold its claims. President Videla

Furious over the death of Liberal leader Jorge

threatened to invoke the new Inter-American Defense Treaty, which had been signed by the member nations of the Pan American Union the year before. Although all the claims have not been settled as yet, there was no serious trouble. In fact the controversy ended on a sort of Gilbert and Sullivan note. Members of the crew of the British cruiser played a game of soccer with a team from one of the Argentine ships at Deception Island. The British team won.

Education also came in for its share of attention during the year. Some leading statesmen feel that a future closer understanding among people of the world must come from the young people within each nation. In 1936 the American republics agreed to the Convention for the Promotion of Inter-American Cultural Relations. Through it, each country agreed to exchange students with other American republics and grant fellowships for their support while studying. During the war years the program could not be carried out to any great extent. However, last year showed that the program will eventually be a success. In the years to come more Latin-American and United States university professors will be exchanged, to teach in each other's schools.

The architectural beauty, intriguing history, hospitality and splendor of many South American capitals are attracting many international, especially inter-American, conferences. For instance, the Ninth Pan American Child Congress was held in Caracas, Venezuela, in January 1948. The meetings lasted for five days. The representatives discussed ways of improving welfare and health.

Eliécer Gaitán, revolutionists rioted through the streets of Bogotá, Colombia, for four days.

WIDE WORLD

THE odd-sounding word "spelunk" comes from a Latin word meaning cave. Within the last few years this old word, which was out of use and obsolete for a long time, has come back again into common usage. Cave-exploring is now known as spelunking.

Those of us who think spelunking is fun come by our taste honestly. Your forefathers and mine not only explored caves—they lived in them. We are descendants of these cave-dwellers, men who hunted the great hairy mammoth and the saber-toothed tiger with flint-tipped spears. With the coming of night these prehistoric men retreated from the unknown terrors and dangers of darkness into the security of the caves that were their homes. Here, also, they were relatively safe from the attacks of wild animals, and pro-

By Vincent J. Schaefer
Research Chemist

SPELUNKING

tected from the icy winter winds and the severe heat of summer. Every now and then one of these ancient men, tiring of the cave home he and his family had occupied for some time, set out to explore other caves, hoping to find one he liked better than his own. Often, out of curiosity, he explored deeper into the passageways to find out what lay in the mysterious darkness beyond the flickering light of his campfire and his smoky torch. That same curiosity about the unknown still shows itself in our present-day interest in exploring the strange underground world of caves and caverns.

Most caves are formed by the action of water flowing underground, through such soft material as limestone which is gradually worn away by the force of the water. Caves which serve as underground stream beds are best visited either in periods of very dry weather or in the wintertime. A cave with a stream of water flowing through it is harder

to explore than one which is comparatively dry. In some parts of the country where the caves are "dead," where they no longer serve as water courses, any time of the year is suitable. Many caves, however, are wet and even muddy, for their very existence and the formation of the stony shapes which make them so beautiful depend upon the effects of flowing or dripping water.

It is probable that the caves you might want to explore in your part of the world may be of little importance when compared to such wonders as Mammoth Cave in Kentucky or the Carlsbad Caverns of New Mexico. You can have a great deal of fun, however, exploring even a small cave, and, quite possibly, exciting adventures. While you may never have the thrill of discovering a cavern which has not been explored before, you may always discover something new or unusual in the cave itself.

Several years ago I was exploring the cliff

UNITED STATES DEPARTMENT OF THE INTERIOR

edge along a swampy stream in the limestone region of the Helderberg Mountains in eastern New York. Under some huge virgin pines I saw a small hole at the base of a rocky ledge. The cool breeze flowing from the hole told me that here was the entrance to a cave. I dropped flat on the ground, lighted my flashlight and wiggled into the hole. After slow progress for a dozen feet or so, I saw that the hole was becoming larger, and soon I was able to stand nearly erect. A packed clay passageway wound in crooked fashion through a rocky channel cut by an ancient stream through the Onondaga limestone. Here and there on the walls were flint outcroppings where the harder stone had resisted the eroding effects of the flowing water. I found fossil coral in the walls, too, and now and then a fossil animal or shell. Occasionally I came across a fossil brachiopod, a creature much like our present-day clam or mollusk, with hinged shells that close tightly.

Newly discovered section of Mammoth Cave, found when these explorers examined a small avenue leading off from the main cave.

This is the kind of discovery that anyone may make while spelunking, and that adds so much to the fun of poking around underground. I realized that more than a hundred million years ago these cave fossils had been living creatures moving about in the shallow sea that, the geologists tell us, covered New York at that time.

While I was excitedly examining the fossils, I became aware that all around me the walls and ceiling of the cave were glittering with what appeared to be luminous pearls. The light of my flashlight was being reflected from myriads of tiny water droplets or dewdrops which had formed when moist air condensed on the cold rocky walls and ceiling. They seemed to be perfect spheres, supported on tiny spider webs.

Finally, after much trouble, I managed to

333

get my camera into position for a picture of these cave gems. As I was struggling with my tripod, I heard a series of squeaks. Some living thing obviously resented my presence in the cave. I soon discovered that the noise came from a small furry lump hanging from a tiny ledge near by. A little brown bat had been disturbed by my light as it was resting from a night spent in catching mosquitoes and other flying bugs. I took its picture and then retraced my steps, leaving the cool underground to enter once again the normal world of brightness, wind and weather.

In Daddy Longlegs Cave I Found a Scene of Crystal Wonder

While on a cross-country ski trip many months later, I slid down into a little valley and after some search found the cave again. The entrance was nearly hidden by snow, but the gentle flow of air from the cave kept the opening from being completely covered. I had trouble entering the cave, but finally succeeded in spite of the snow and ice. When I reached the higher part of the cave, I turned and looked back at the entrance. Here was a rare and beautiful sight. The huge many-shaped frost crystals that encrusted the roof and sides of the entry hole formed countless prisms that reflected the light from my torch. The cave-explorer who sees a sight like this has had an experience known to only a few.

On the same trip I discovered something else of great interest in this cave, which I named Daddy Longlegs Cave. On the ceiling were large groups of daddy longlegs or harvestmen, grouped so closely together that their long jointed legs overlapped. This produced an effect almost like that of a hairy mat. Near them sat a pale brown cave cricket—almost like a guardian or sentry.

Cave Moths, Frost-covered, Sleep Away the Winter

You may come across other kinds of living creatures in your exploration of caves. A certain variety of reddish moth is often found near cave entrances, sleeping away the winter season. I have found these moths covered with a coating of dew or frost crystals. When warmed, however, they soon start to crawl around as though spring had come. Even the daddys begin to move about at normal speed a few minutes after they have been disturbed by the flashlight.

Caves are sometimes occupied by porcupines and skunks, although such animals are usually found in places too small for human exploration. I have never run into any of these modern cave-dwellers, although I have often wondered what would happen if I should meet one face to face in a narrow passageway.

Gigantic Icicles, Formed by the Dripping Water

The beauty and grandeur of some caves can hardly be grasped by one who has never visited them. Imagine a vast and lofty cavern from whose ceiling hang hundreds or thousands of gigantic icicles, formed not of ice but of deposits left by the dripping waters. These formations, called stalactites, sometimes take the form of huge, elongated cones, with their points downward. Sometimes they look like elephant ears, waves, or fantastic forms of no recognizable shape. Often, almost meeting the stalactites, and sometimes even fusing with them to form gigantic pillars or columns, similar formations called stalagmites, also caused by dripping water, rise from the floor of the cave. Many stalactites and stalagmites are hundreds of years old and have been formed very gradually by the addition of paper-thin layers of calcium-carbonate deposit from the waters flowing or seeping through the cave. Sometimes these formations take on other colors from minerals which were originally in the water of the underground streams.

Perfect Fossil Leaves from Lime in Cave Streams

Another interesting kind of deposit is often associated with caves. If there happens to be a stream running through a cave, a white deposit is often found at the place where the stream emerges from its underground journey. This is called tuffa, a precipitate of lime which forms a natural cement. Leaves and other types of vegetation in the stream become coated with this lime deposit. Then, as the organic matter decays, a perfect replica remains which looks like a fossil leaf. While it generally takes many centuries for a real fossil to form, these cave-stream fossils form in a few months.

I have mentioned only a few of the features which make caves interesting to visit and to study. I hope you will have fun someday exploring a cave!

SPORTS

Plain of Olympia-1948

By FRANK BUTLER
Sports Columnist, London Daily Express

THE story of the fourteenth modern Olympiad, held in war-scarred London in the summer of 1948, is one of color, pageantry, thrills and excitement.

Five thousand men and women from fifty-nine countries competed for honors with good will and good sportsmanship.

The ancient Olympic Games, originated by the Greeks hundreds of years before the coming of Christ, were held until 394 A.D. Then they were stopped by the Roman Emperor Theodosius, who said that they no longer served their original purpose—that of fostering good will among nations.

The Olympic torch-bearer races into the stadium to light the Olympic flame. Legend says that the first Olympic flame was set ablaze in ancient Greece by the sun's rays.

A French nobleman, Baron Pierre de Coubertin, revived the games in 1896. Since then they have been held once every four years, except for interruptions caused by World Wars I and II.

The 1948 games were almost without controversy, disproving the opinion of many who argue that the games usually misfire—causing ill will rather than good will among nations. The words of Baron de Coubertin were prominently displayed in London's huge Wembley Stadium throughout the two weeks of the games: "The important thing in the Olympic Games is not winning, but taking part. The essential thing in life is not conquering, but fighting well." They best explain the Olympic spirit. No one nation can win the Olympics, even though the United States gained the most successes—its athletes winning thirty-eight first-place gold medals.

This was England's first opportunity in forty years to play host to the Olympics. Happily, the day of the opening ceremony, July 29, was a blaze of sunshine. Eighty-four thousand people packed the stadium to welcome the thousands of contestants. King George VI and Queen Elizabeth were to open the games. In 1908, King Edward VII and Queen Alexandra had opened the games for just a few more than fifteen hundred athletes from only eighteen countries.

The Parade—a Pageant of Color and Countries

The march past began just before the arrival of the King. Picture this great pageant of color. Greece, as originator of the games, led the way. Great Britain, as the host country, came last. The rest of the countries marched in alphabetical order. Following Greece came the Afghans, in their sheepskin hats, led by a Boy Scout proudly carrying their identifying banner.

Little Denmark provided the brightest blaze of color as its men and women swung by in scarlet and white. The Pakistan athletes, in their green tunics and white turbans, might have stepped directly from a Hollywood screen. The United States representatives were smart in blue blazer jackets, white hats and white trousers (skirts for the girls). The Yugoslavians wore slate gray, and contestants from the new Dominion of India light blue with blue turbans. Never in the history of the games had there been a parade

so endless, and so grand.

There was courage to be seen, as well as might. Malta, little island of the Mediterranean whose people won the George Cross for courage under wartime bombing, strutted past with a single sprinter. Tiny Singapore had only two athletes. But they had nearly a hundred thousand cheering admirers!

Kings and Queens, Princes and Princesses Were There

The King and Queen arrived with their younger daughter, Princess Margaret, and Queen Mary, the King's mother. The Duke and Duchess of Gloucester were in the royal party, too, and the Duchess of Kent, as well as Prince Bernhard of the Netherlands and the Shah of Iran.

Following a short welcoming address by Lord David Burghley, chairman of the British organizing committee, King George spoke the traditional, simple words: "I proclaim open the Olympic Games of London celebrating the fourteenth Olympiad of the modern era." Booted and spurred trumpeters of the Household Cavalry, in uniforms of cloth of gold, sounded a brazen fanfare. The Olympic flag—white with its five interlocking rings of blue, yellow, black, green and red—fluttered slowly to the peak of its mast. For the next fourteen days the rings on their rippling field of white would symbolize the unity of the five great continents of the world.

Seven thousand homing pigeons soared into the bright sky and, after circling the arena, disappeared in the distance. Their flight symbolized the sending of the Olympic message of good will to all parts of the earth. There was a thunderous salute of twenty-one guns. Then came the most impressive and dramatic scene of all—the arrival of the torch-bearer who would kindle the Olympic flame with fire which, in myth, had come from the rays of the sun.

The honor had been given to John Mark, a former British runner. He was the last one of more than a thousand athletes who, in relays, had raced the blazing torch from ancient Olympia to this modern Plain of Olympia in London. In its great white bowl at one end of the stadium the flame would burn day and night until the end of the games on August 14. The crowd rose to its feet and cheered. The marchers, who had formed into ranks after the parade, broke their long orderly lines for the moment to get a clearer view of this part of the historic ceremony.

Now the ceremony took a more solemn tone. The Olympic hymn was sung, and was followed by a dedication address by the Archbishop of York and singing of the HALLELUJAH CHORUS. Finally, the athletes took the Olympic oath by which they swore that they were true amateurs. The oath was actually taken by one man, veteran British athlete D. O. Finlay, for all of the contestants. They raised their hands in agreement as it was given. There was not a movement in the crowd as the oath was taken. Only the flag fluttered gently in the breeze.

The games began the next day. The first week's attraction, of course, was the athletics in the stadium itself. What a wonderful week it was, too! Records were broken on the first day. Emile Zatopek, an army lieutenant from Czechoslovakia, had the crowd roaring wildly as he set up a most wonderful test of endurance. He won the 10,000-meter championship in the fast time of 29:59.6, an Olympic record six seconds better than the record set during the 1932 games in Los Angeles. Another record went the same day. A Swedish runner clocked 0:51.9 in the semifinal of the 400-meter hurdles. Runner Roy Cochran of the United States then went on to lower the record even further with a running time of 0:51.1 in the final.

That Incredible Dutch Woman— Three Times a Winner!

None of the spectators are likely to forget the speed of the American sprinters Mel Patton, Harrison Dillard and Barney Ewell. Then we saw the incredible Dutch woman, Fanny Blankers-Koen, win three titles by winning the 100-meter and 200-meter dashes and the 80-meter hurdles in the women's track events. She also played a big part in helping Holland to win the 400-meter relay for women. Her name will go down in Olympic history with that of the great Finn, Paavo Nurmi, and the American sprinter, Jesse Owens.

Many of the huge crowd will best remember the Marathon, the most grueling race in the games. The contestants run 26 miles and 385 yards (or 42,195 meters). The race began at half past two in the afternoon, the runners circling the track once before leaving the stadium. Shortly after five o'clock the first runner reappeared. It was Gailly,

a Belgian. His face was white and drawn; he was exhausted, and could hardly walk. Behind Gailly came the Argentine runner Cabrora, strong and fresh-looking, who went on to win the race easily.

Beauty, Grace and Shenanigans at Wembley Pool

At near-by Wembley Pool, people watched the grace and power of the men and women swimmers and divers. The boxing events also were held near the pool and there were many exciting scenes. Once there was a procession of protest by some Uruguayans who disagreed with a decision. They carried their beaten boxer from the ring while the crowd cheered because the decision was a bad one. On the night that Lajos Papp, the Hungarian boxer, won the middleweight title both he and his trainer jumped into the pool and swam around in their clothes in sheer jubilation. Boxing fans from Argentina did the same thing when their countryman, Rafael Iglesias, won the heavyweight championship.

Throughout the fourteen days there was always something doing. Some people, who were not interested in the athletics, were thrilled by other events. There was the magic horsemanship of the Mexicans, the great strength of Turkey's wrestlers. The French, Italians and Hungarians excelled in swordsmanship, and the Swedes were skilled at soccer.

So it continued until the last day of the summer games, until August 14, and the closing ceremony. On that day, the president of the International Olympic Committee— Sigfrid Edstrom of Sweden—gave the flag to London's Lord Mayor to hold until the next games in Helsinki, Finland, in 1952.

However, long before London was ready for the summer Olympics, the winter games had been held in the snowy and picturesque setting of St. Moritz, Switzerland. Many Europeans and Americans took winter holidays to see the skiing, ice hockey, cresta run, bobsledding, slalom and ice skating.

There was some controversy over the ice hockey (which Canada won), but all was forgotten at the sight of the grace and skill of Canada's Barbara Ann Scott who won the world skating title for women.

As in the summer Olympics, no one country wins the winter games, although Sweden and Switzerland unofficially tied for first place on the honors list.

CHAMPIONS OF THE

Men's Track

100-Meter Dash—Harrison Dillard, U. S. A., 0:10.3. (Equals Olympic record.)

200-Meter Dash—Mel Patton, U. S. A., 0:21.1.

400-Meter Run—Arthur Wint, Jamaica, 0:46.2. (Equals Olympic record.)

800-Meter Run—Malvin Whitfield, U. S. A., 1:49.2. (Olympic record.)

1,500-Meter Run—Henri Eriksson, Sweden, 3:49.8.

5,000-Meter Run—Gaston Reiff, Belgium, 14:17.6. (Olympic record.)

10,000-Meter Run—Emil Zatopek, Czechoslovakia, 29:59.6. (Olympic record.)

Marathon Run—Delfo Cabrora, Argentina, 2:34:51.6.

400-Meter Relay—United States, 0:41.3. (Time is that of second-place British team, originally declared winner.)

1,600-Meter Relay—United States, 3:10.4.

10,000-Meter Walk—J. F. Mikaelsson, Sweden, 45:13.2. (Olympic record.)

50,000-Meter Walk—J. A. Ljunggren, Sweden, 4:41:52.

110-Meter Hurdles—William Porter, U. S. A., 0:13.9. (Olympic record.)

400-Meter Hurdles—Roy Cochran, U. S. A., 0:51.1. (Olympic record.)

3,000-Meter Steeplechase—Thure Sjoestrand, Sweden, 9:04.6.

Pole Vault—Guinn Smith, U. S. A., 14 feet 1¼ inches.

High Jump—John Winter, Australia, 6 feet 6 inches.

Broad Jump—Willie Steele, U. S. A., 25 feet 8 inches.

Hop, Step and Jump—A. Ahman, Sweden, 50 feet 6¼ inches.

Discus Throw—Adolfo Consolini, Italy, 173 feet 2 inches. (Olympic record.)

Shot-Put—Wilbur Thompson, U. S. A., 56 feet 2 inches.

Javelin Throw—Kaj Rautavaara, Finland, 228 feet 10½ inches.

Hammer Throw—Imre Nemeth, Hungary, 183 feet 11½ inches.

Decathlon—Robert Mathias, U. S. A., 7,139 points.

Women's Track

100-Meter Dash—Mrs. Fanny Blankers-Koen, Holland, 0:11.9.

200-Meter Dash—Mrs. Blankers-Koen, 0:24.4. (Olympic record, first time run in Olympics.)

80-Meter Hurdles—Mrs. Blankers-Koen, 0:11.2. (World and Olympic record.)

400-Meter Relay—Holland, 0:47.5.

High Jump—Alice Coachman, U. S. A., 5 feet 6⅛ inches. (Olympic record.)

Broad Jump—V. O. Gyarmati, Hungary, 18 feet 8¼ inches. (Olympic record, first time held in Olympics.)

Javelin Throw—H. Baume, Austria, 149 feet 6 inches. (Olympic record.)

Discus Throw—Micheline Ostermeyer, France, 137 feet 6½ inches.

Shot-Put—Miss Ostermeyer, 45 feet 1½ inches. (Olympic record, first time held in Olympics.)

Men's Swimming

100-Meter Free-Style—Walter Ris, U. S. A., 0:57.3. (Olympic record.)

400-Meter Free-Style—Bill Smith, U. S. A., 4:41.0.

(Olympic record.)

1,500-Meter Free-Style—James McLane, U. S. A., 19:18.5.

100-Meter Back-Stroke—Allen Stack, U. S. A., 1:06.4.

200-Meter Breast-Stroke—Joe Verdeur, U. S. A., 2:39.3. (Olympic record.)

800-Meter Relay—U. S. A., 8:46. (World and Olympic record.)

Springboard Diving—Bruce Harlan, U. S. A.

High Platform Diving—Dr. Sammy Lee, U. S. A.

Women's Swimming

100-Meter Free-Style—Greta Andersen, Denmark, 1:6.3. (Tied Olympic record of 0:65.8 in trial heat.)

400-Meter Free-Style—Ann Curtis, U. S. A., 5:17.8. (Olympic record.)

100-Meter Back-Stroke—Karen Harup, Denmark, 1:14.4. (Olympic record.)

200-Meter Breast-Stroke—Nel Van Vliet, Holland, 2:57.2. (Olympic record.)

400-Meter Relay—U. S. A., 4:29.2. (Olympic record.)

Springboard Diving—Mrs. Victoria Manalo Draves, U. S. A.

High Platform Diving—Mrs. Draves, U. S. A.

Wrestling (Free Style)

Flyweight—V. L. Viitala, Finland.

Featherweight—Gazanfer Bilge, Turkey.

Bantamweight—Nassuh Akar, Turkey.

Lightweight—Celal Atik, Turkey.

Welterweight—Yasar Dogu, Turkey.

Middleweight—Glenn Brand, U. S. A.

Light-Heavyweight—Henry Wittenberg, U. S. A.

Heavyweight—George Bobis, Hungary.

Wrestling (Greco-Roman)

Flyweight—Pietro Lombardi, Italy.

Featherweight—M. Octav, Turkey.

Bantamweight—K. A. Petersen, Sweden.

Lightweight—G. Freij, Sweden.

Welterweight—Gosta Anderssen, Sweden.

Light-Heavyweight—Karl Nilsson, Sweden.

Heavyweight—Armet Kirecci, Turkey.

Canoeing

10,000-Meter Canadian Singles—Frantisek Capek, Czechoslovakia, 62:05.2.

10,000-Meter Kayak Pairs—Sweden, 46:09.4.

10,000-Meter Canadian Pairs—U. S. A., 55:55.4.

10,000-Meter Kayak Singles—Gert Frederiksson, Sweden, 50:47.7.

1,000-Meter Kayak Singles—Frederiksson, 4:33.2.

500-Meter Kayak Singles for Women—Karan Hoff, Denmark, 2:31.9.

1,000-Meter Canadian Singles—Josef Holececk, Czechoslovakia, 5:42.0.

1,000-Meter Kayak Pairs—Sweden, 4:07.3.

1,000-Meter Canadian Pairs—Czechoslovakia, 5:07.1.

Yachting

Firefly Class—Denmark, 5,543 points.

Dragon Class—Norway, 4,746 points.

Star Class—U. S. A., 5,828 points.

Six-Meter Class—U. S. A., 5,472 points.

Swallow Class—Great Britain, 5,625 points.

Weight-Lifting

Featherweight—I. Fayad, Egypt, 732½ pounds (world and Olympic record).

Bantamweight—Joe Di Pietro, U. S. A., 677½

1948 OLYMPIC GAMES

pounds. (Olympic record, first time held in Olympics.)

Lightweight—I. Shams, Egypt, 793¼ pounds (Olympic record).

Middleweight—Frank Spellman, U. S. A., 859½ pounds (Olympic record).

Light-Heavyweight—Stan Stanczyk, U. S. A., 920 pounds (Olympic record).

Heavyweight—John Davis, U. S. A., 997 pounds (world and Olympic record).

Pentathlon

Individual—Capt. W. O. G. Grut, Sweden, 16 points (Olympic record).

Team—Sweden.

Shooting

50-Meter Free Pistol—E. Vascuez Cam, Peru, 545.

25-Meter Rapid-Fire Pistol—K. Takacs, Hungary, 600 points.

50-Meter Small-Bore Rifle—Arthur E. Cook, U. S. A., 599.

300-Meter Full-Bore Rifle—Emil Grunig, Switzerland, 1,120.

Team—U. S. A.

Water Polo

Team—Italy.

Fencing

Men's Individual Foil—Jean Buhan, France.

Men's Team Foil—France.

Women's Individual Foil—I. Elek, Hungary.

Men's Team Epee—France.

Men's Individual Epee—G. Cantone, Italy.

Men's Individual Saber—Aladar Gerevich, Hungary.

Men's Team Saber—Hungary.

Rowing (1900 Meters)

Eights—U. S. A., 6:10.3.

Fours With Coxswain—U. S. A., 6:56.8.

Fours Without Coxswain—Italy, 6:39.0.

Pairs Without Coxswain—Great Britain, 7:21.1.

Pairs With Coxswain—Denmark, 8:00.5.

Double Sculls—Great Britain, 6:51.3.

Single Sculls—Mervyn Wood, Australia, 6:51.3.

Equestrian

Individual Dressage—Capt. H. Moeser, Switzerland, 492½ of possible 500 points.

Team Dressage—Sweden, 1,336 of possible 1,500 points.

Three-Day Individual Test—Capt. B. M. Chevallier, France, 4.

Three-Day Team Test—U. S. A., 161½ minus points.

Prix des Nations, Team—Mexico, 34¼ faults.

Prix des Nations, Individual—Lieut. Col. H. Mariles Cortes, Mexico, 6¼ faults.

Cycling

2,000-Meter Tandem—Italy, 3:55.1.

1,000-Meter Time Trials—B. J. Dupont, France, 1:13.5.

4,000-Meter Team Pursuit Race—France.

1,000-Meter Sprint—Mario Ghella, Italy.

121-Mile Race—J. Beyaert, France, 5:18:12.6.

121-Mile Team Race—Belgium, 15:58:17.6.

Field Hockey

Team—India.

Soccer

Team—Sweden.

Boxing

Flyweight—Pascuel Perez, Argentina.

Bantamweight—Tibor Csik, Hungary.

Featherweight—Ernesto Formenti, Italy.

Lightweight—Gerry Dreyer, South Africa.

Welterweight—Julius Torma, Czechoslovakia.

Middleweight—Laszlo Papp, Hungary.

Light-Heavyweight—George Hunter, South Africa.

Heavyweight—Rafael Iglesias, Argentina.

Team—South Africa, 29 points.

Basketball

Team—United States.

Gymnastics—Men

Horizontal Bars—Josef Stalder, Switzerland, 39.7 points.

Pommeled Horse—P. J. Aaltonen, V. A. Huhtanen and H. Savolainen, all of Finland, 38.7 points.

Parallel Bars—M. Reusch, Switzerland, 39.5 points.

Twelve Exercises—V. A. Huhtanen, Finland, 229.7 points.

Long-Horse Vault—P. J. Aaltonen, Finland, 39.1 points.

Rings—K. Frei, Switzerland, 39.6.

Free Standing Exercises—F. Pataki, Finland, 38.7 points.

Team—Finland, 1,358.3 points.

Gymnastics—Women

Team—Czechoslovakia, 445.45 (no individual competition).

Speed Skating

500 meters (547 yards)—Finn Helgesen, Norway, 43.1 seconds (Olympic record).

1,500 meters (metric mile)—Sverre Farstad, Norway.

5,000 meters (3⅛ miles)—Reidar Liaklev, Norway, 8:29.4.

10,000 meters (6¼ miles)—Ake Seyffarth, Sweden, 17:26.3.

Figure Skating

Men's—Richard Button, Englewood, N. J.

Women's—Barbara Ann Scott, Canada.

Pairs—M. Lannoy, P. Baugniet, Belgium.

Skiing

Men's slalom—Edi Reinalter, Switzerland.

Women's slalom—Gretchen Fraser, Vancouver, Wash.

Men's downhill—Henri Oreiller, France.

Women's downhill—Hedy Schlunegger, Switzerland.

Men's Nordic combined (11-mile cross-country and jump)—Heikki Hasu, Finland.

Men's Alpine combined (downhill and slalom)—Henri Oreiller, France.

Women's Alpine combined—Trude Beiser, Austria.

Special ski jump—Peter Hugsted, Norway.

18-kilometer (11 miles) cross-country—Martin Lundstroem, Sweden, 1:13:50.

40-kilometer (25 miles) relay—Sweden (Nils Oestensson, Nils Taepp, Gunnar Eriksson, Martin Lundstroem, 2:32:8.

50 kilometer (31 miles)—Nils Karlsson Sweden, 3:47:47.

Bobsledding

One-man cresta—Nino Bibbia, Italy.

Two-man—Switzerland (Felix Endrich-Fiederich Waller).

Four-man—United States (Francis Tyler, Lake Placid, N. Y., pilot; Pat Martin, Lake Placid; Ed Rimqus, Schenectady, N. Y.; Bill D'Amico, Lake Placid).

Ice Hockey

Canada—Won seven, tied one.

PITCHING THRILLS

By BOB FELLER
Pitcher, Cleveland Indians

ONE spring day in 1928 my father came into the living room of our farm house in Van Meter, Iowa. His arms were filled with packages. Mother looked at him and smiled. She knew how much he liked baseball, and how much he wanted me to be a player.

I was only nine years old, but I remember the scene as though it had happened yesterday. It was my first big thrill in baseball, for in the packages was a complete outfit—a baseball suit, spiked shoes, a glove and a bat that was stained green. Then Dad built a baseball diamond for me.

Eight years later, after many practice sessions on our home diamond, and after playing with amateur teams in Des Moines, I reported to the office of the Cleveland Indians at old League Park in Cleveland. I had no idea, then, that within a few short weeks I would be pitching against a famous major league club, the St. Louis Cardinals.

The date was July 6, 1936, and it was an exhibition game. There were 10,000 people there to see the famous Cardinals of that day—Dizzy Dean, Frankie Frisch, Leo Durocher, Pepper Martin and all the others. Cyril Slapnicka, the vice-president of the Indians, decided that this was as good a time as any for a beginning.

I was the starting pitcher for Cleveland. Behind the plate was patient Steve O'Neill, noted Cleveland catcher and the team manager, who had caught the Cleveland team when it won the 1920 World Series. In that first game with the Cardinals, I was very fast —and wild—which was too much for the cautious Cardinals. They did not want to get hurt in an exhibition game. Leo Durocher was my first strikeout victim. Altogether, I struck out eight men in three innings, and

allowed one unearned run. We won the game, 7 to 6.

The next month was an exciting blur. I was only seventeen and had to learn the ways of a big-league ball club. I had to learn all of the little arts of traveling and was glad to discover that my five feet, eleven inches of height fitted comfortably into a Pullman berth. I had to learn how much to tip waiters and bellboys, and I began signing my first autographs.

About a month after the exhibition game with the Cardinals, I was given the chance to start my first league game. We were playing the St. Louis Browns at League Park. Another rookie, Charley (Greek) George, was my catcher. Naturally, both of us were nervous. Yet, when the game ended fifteen Browns had been fanned—just one under the American League record, and only two shy of the major league record held by Dizzy Dean. The Indians won the game, 4 to 1, and I considered myself a veteran, although I would not be eighteen until November.

That was a big day, but there was a bigger one coming up in September. We played the Philadelphia Athletics on September 13, at League Park. In the Athletics' lineup were such stars as Wally Moses, Frank Hayes, Pinky Higgins and Bob Johnson. That day I struck out seventeen batters. In the ninth inning Outfielder George Pucinelli swung at a curve ball for the seventeenth strikeout, and Dean's major league record was tied.

There were many thrills and many headaches throughout the 1937 season, including a game in which I struck out sixteen Boston Red Sox. But the next record day did not come until the last game of the 1938 season. That was the year in which big Hank Greenberg made a bid to break Babe Ruth's record

BOB FELLER: PHOTO BY ARTHUR A. SOMERS; COURTESY CLEVELAND BASEBALL CLUB

of sixty home runs in one season.

We were playing the Detroit Tigers at the Cleveland Municipal Stadium, the biggest ball park in the country. Greenberg, who played first base and the outfield for Detroit, had fifty-eight home runs entering the final series. He didn't get any home runs in the series, but on the last day I set a record for one game that is still unbroken—eighteen strikeouts. Again it was in the final inning of the game. A third strike past Outfielder Pete Fox accounted for the seventeenth. Then Chet Laabs came to bat again. I had already struck him out four times in the game. The first pitch was a strike; then came a ball. He took a curve for strike two, and then stepped out of the box. When he stepped back into the box, a fast ball over

the inside corner of the plate finished him off. Strike three! He never made a motion to hit it, and Umpire Cal Hubbard waved him out for the record. However, there was a bitter pill to swallow. I lost the game!—even though I had managed to fan eighteen Tigers. Harry Eisenstat, a clever southpaw, won from me because I was wild and had allowed several hits in bad spots.

The seasons whirled by and it was April 16, 1940—opening day in Chicago—and we were starting the season with a game with the White Sox. It was a dark and chilly day. I felt tired, while warming up, and the ball felt heavy. Yet, despite all the bad omens, it turned out to be a banner day and game for me.

Edgar Smith, an old mound rival, pitched for the White Sox. He was a roly-poly southpaw who could be very good, and he was good that day. We went along, inning after inning, chalking up goose eggs on the scoreboard. After the sixth inning I began to think about a no-hit game. Nobody in the dugout said anything about the chance, though. That is a firm rule in baseball. The possibility of a no-hitter is not to be discussed.

Then came the ninth inning. We led, 1 to 0, entering the ninth as the result of a triple by Jeff Heath and a single by Rollie Hemsley, our catcher. Still I had not allowed a hit. The ninth inning of a no-hit game is always the worst, of course. There is great tension. Your team mates want to help you pitch a hitless game, and the other team naturally wants to prevent it.

I walked Lew Appling, and struck out the next two batters. Then Taft Wright came up to bat. He was always one of the most difficult players for me to get out. Wright rapped a sharp grounder to the left of Ray Mack, our second baseman. Mack broke fast, made a one-handed stop out on grass and threw out Wright to keep the game a no-hitter. You have got to be lucky to pitch a no-hitter, and I was lucky. That year, until 1948, was the closest we came to winning a pennant in twenty years. I lost the game that clinched the pennant for the Detroit Tigers in Cleveland Stadium. Rudy York hit a home run with one on, and an unknown pitcher named Floyd Giebel beat me, 2 to 0, to give the Tigers the 1940 flag.

I had another fine season in 1941, winning twenty-five games, but it did not seem im-

341

portant then. War was coming to the United States. I joined the Navy in December 1941. The most exciting part of my Navy career was spent aboard the U.S.S. Alabama. She was a new battlewagon and ranged the principal theaters of war on the sea. I was a chief petty officer, in charge of an anti-aircraft gun crew. She figured in action at Kwajalein, Truk, Saipan, Tinian, Formosa, Leyte and the battle of the Philippine Sea.

The most dangerous of our assignments was off Saipan, a short time after the war had ended in Europe. For thirteen hours we took part in what was called a "turkey shoot." Hundreds of Japanese fighter planes, many of them Kamikaze, were shot out of the air.

We came home from the Pacific in January 1945, and in the spring I became manager of the Great Lakes Naval Training Station team. This was a break for me, for I did considerable pitching for Great Lakes that summer so that I was ready to go back to the big leagues after my discharge in August. That was a happy night—back in Cleveland Stadium pitching against Hal Newhouser and the Detroit Tigers! I won that homecoming game and was able to win five victories before the end of the season.

My Best—A No-Hit Game Against the New York Yankees

In many ways, I think, the season of 1946 will always remain as my greatest in baseball, although there is always the chance of a deeper thrill around the corner in the game. The season was not very old before we came to the game that I consider to be the finest I ever pitched. It was my second no-hit game, and was pitched against a team that had always been my most bitter rival—the Yankees. It was in Yankee Stadium in April 1946. What made it especially sweet was that the Eastern newspapers had hinted broadly, before the game, that I was slipping. More than 30,000 fans were there to find out for themselves. The Yankees had all of their stars back from the war—Joe DiMaggio, Charley Keller, Tommy Henrich, Bill Johnson, George Stirnweiss and Bill Dickey.

Boudreau really saved the second no-hitter in the first inning with a miraculous stop and throw that prevented an almost certain hit by Stirnweiss. The ball hopped and bounded to the left, or first-base side, of second. Boudreau crossed over on the dead

run. He scooped up the ball between hops, made an underhand throw to Les Fleming at first, and turned a somersault, all in what appeared to be one motion.

I was wild throughout the game and walked five men. However, I bore down with all that I had in the pinches, using a fast ball. Frankie Hayes hit a home run off Floyd Bevans in the ninth, and we led, 1 to 0, entering the Yankee half of the final inning. Stirnweiss, who was first up, bunted to Fleming at first, who fumbled in his eagerness for an error. Henrich sacrificed and the Yankees had the tying run on second with DiMaggio and Keller coming up.

Mack Throws Keller Out, and the Game Is in the Bag

DiMaggio fouled off pitch after pitch until the count was 3–2. Then he drove a hot grounder to Boudreau for the second out. Stirnweiss moved to third. Only Keller stood between me and my second no-hit game. I believe he hit the first pitch, and it was a high, bounding ball to second-baseman Ray Mack—the man who had saved my first no-hitter. Mack started forward with a sudden burst, stumbled, and fell to his knees. I still don't know how he did it, but he got up and threw out Keller and my most prized game was in the bag.

We didn't go any place that season, but I set another record that I value highly. As the weeks rolled by I decided to set my sights on Rube Waddell's record of 343 strikeouts for one season. By September, my season total was 337 strikeouts. I needed only seven more as we moved into the final series of the year against the Tigers in Detroit. Lou Boudreau decided to give me my chance for the record by announcing that I would pitch five innings of relief ball in the opening game. I struck out six men to tie the record. In the last game of the season I pitched against Newhouser. For five innings it appeared that he would break a strikeout record, not I. He struck out six in three innings. I struck out nobody in four. In the fifth, it was Newhouser who enabled me to break the record that had stood for forty-two years. He was my 344th strikeout of the year. I went on to get four more and hang up a record of 348.

As we entered the 1948 season, I had won 158 games in what amounted to seven full seasons and had fanned 1,836 batters.

pecially built for you. Today, if you want a small and inexpensive boat for racing or day sailing, you can buy one ready-made, as you would a suit or a dress. There is a boat dealer in almost every town near sailing water. In fact, you can even get a boat in a department store in the larger cities. You will find a wide choice of types, sizes and prices.

When buying your boat it is always wise fastenings and so on. A youngster who can handle simple hand tools can put this good little boat together and have a lot of fun doing it. For somewhat larger sailing boats, in completed form, prices begin at just under $500, but will vary depending on the size, quality of construction and finish, equipment and other things. Many of the most famous racing skippers do much of their racing in

HAGERTY COMPANY

These four young sailors are having a happy time of it in their Sea Shell dinghy.

SKANEATELES BOATS, INC.

Most racers prefer a sloop rig, with a main sail and jib, as in this Comet.

to select one of a class that is already popular in your sailing neighborhood. Then you will be sure to have a boat that is suitable for local conditions. You will also be assuring yourself of plenty of good competition after you have learned to race.

The minimum cost for a boat that will really sail is just under $100. This is an eight-foot pram-type centerboard sailing dinghy and can be purchased in knockdown form. This includes all parts of the hull, rig,

ten-, twelve- and fourteen-foot sailing dinghies.

The boat will be rigged either with a single sail, called a cat rig, or as a sloop with a mainsail and a jib. Cat rigs are easier for the beginner to manage, but the sloop rig is more popular with experienced sailors.

Two qualities are especially desirable in a boat for the beginner. One is that she should be capsizable, that is, a centerboard boat, with or without ballast; and the other, that

345

she should float even when capsized and full of water. The first of these two requirements may sound odd, but there is a reason for it. The person who learns to sail in a light boat that can be capsized by poor handling in a strong breeze learns faster and better. Probably a few duckings will result. However, since no one should sail until he can swim well, and since the boat itself will float, a capsize is not necessarily dangerous, for the crew can hang onto the boat until rescued. It goes without saying that your early sailing should be done in protected waters, where help is always at hand and where there is no danger of being blown out to sea.

There Will Be a Few Duckings before You Get the "Feel" of Your Boat

The lessons that you learn in a boat of this kind will soon develop a sense of balance— what the sailor calls the "feel" of a boat— that will be good for you to have if you ever sail a larger, keel-racing yacht, or a seagoing cruising yacht. Sailing is rather like riding a bicycle. You get a few spills but soon acquire an instinctive balance which makes it almost impossible to go over.

Take Good Care of Your Boat! The Work Can Be Fun

One of the important things in boating, and one which may mean success or failure in a race, is the care of your boat. It is work that can be part of the fun of the game. The hull must not only be kept painted with good marine paint; it must always be smooth. Use scrapers and sandpaper to get a slippery bottom surface. The bottom should be covered with an anti-fouling paint which helps to prevent the growth of grass, barnacles and other marine life. The bottom, sides and decks must be kept tight. Use calking and seam compound between the planks. Your boat must be kept bailed out, and her mooring must be secure so that she won't drift away in a storm. Rigging must be trim and in good condition, and the sailor soon learns the simpler knots, splices and other kinds of rope work which go toward keeping a shipshape and smoothly working craft. Sails must be dried out after each wetting with rain or spray, and decks and trim should be touched up with paint and varnish occasionally to keep her looking right. It's enjoyable work and it results in your having a boat you can be proud of, and one which, if you sail her

properly, will win races for you.

There is no one best boat, but there are hundreds of good boats. People who own boats in your locality are always ready to advise you as to the type of boat most suitable for your local water, and to give you pointers on how to sail it. Learning to sail is easy, yet it is a game in which there is always something more to learn. You may become a fairly safe and proficient boat-handler in a few days of practice, within limitations, but the oldest hands at the game will tell you that they are still learning. They will tell you that no season goes by without teaching them some new skill or knowledge. That is one of the fascinations of the sport, and one of the things that make it popular with people of all ages.

No Matter What Anyone Says, a Good Book Is Helpful

It has often been said that you can not learn to sail by reading a book. However, that does not mean that the books should be ignored. Dozens of books on how to sail have been written, and most of them are good. They are written for sailors in all stages of development. The beginner should get one or two of them—the kind that uses many pictures and diagrams is excellent—and read them over before trying to sail. Then get into your boat and go to it! Take an experienced hand along the first few times to provide advice and moral support.

You'll Make the Wind Take You Where It Doesn't Want To

The actual practice will seem, at first, quite different from the simple descriptions of the book; but further practice will translate into practical maneuvers the principles that you have learned from the book. Before long you will find yourself full of confidence. You will be able to keep your boat on her feet even in squally weather, and make the wind take you not only where it wants, but where it doesn't want to take you. You will do this with a series of tacks to windward that will take you in the very direction from which the wind is blowing. Once you reach this stage of sailing, you can keep on learning about boats, winds, seas, weather, sails, rigging and a hundred other things as long as you like. You will have a lot of fun, and if you acquire the real racing-skipper touch and technique, you will win a lot of prizes.

(LEFT) T FORMATION

UNIVERSITY OF NOTRE DAME

SPORTS

T or SINGLE WING?

By GEORGE H. SAUER, *Football Coach, United States Naval Academy*

W HEN Michigan trampled all over the Roses and Southern California (Michigan 49—USC 0) on New Year's Day 1948, the game added new fuel to the fire of an old argument. Which is more effective, the T formation or the Single Wing?

As a result, every college football coach became a quiz contestant, and the $64 question was "Why do you like the T, or the Single Wing, as the case may be?" Fans who watched Penn State and Michigan roll through an undefeated season in the fall of

HARVARD ATHLETIC ASSOCIATION

(RIGHT) SINGLE WING

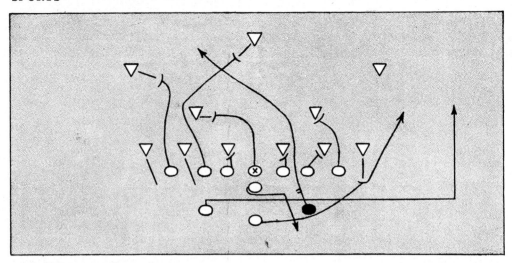

HAND-OFF: The Right End blocks the linebacker. The Right Tackle uses a right-shoulder block and moves the defensive Left Tackle out. The Right Guard uses a left-shoulder block on the defensive Left Guard and moves him out of the play. Right Tackle goes down the field on the snap of the ball and blocks the safety man. Left End starts down the field and blocks the defensive Right Halfback. The Left Halfback goes into motion in an attempt to "loosen" the defensive team. The Quarterback makes a reverse pivot on his right foot and quickly hands the ball to the Right Halfback, who breaks through the line and cuts to his left to pick up the Left Tackle and Left End. The Fullback, on the snap of the ball, runs to the left defensive end then goes down the field for a possible touchdown.

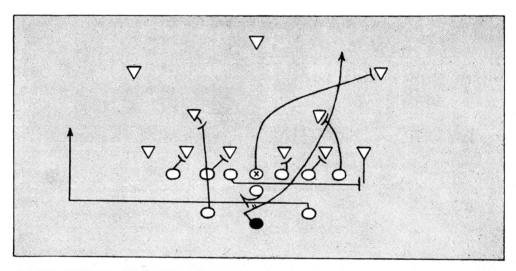

INSIDE COUNTER PLAY TO THE RIGHT: The Right End blocks the linebacker. The Right Tackle uses a right-shoulder block and moves the defensive Left Tackle out. The Right Guard uses a left-shoulder block and moves the defensive Left Guard in. The Center goes through the line and blocks the defensive Left Halfback. The Right Guard pulls, runs parallel to the line and blocks the defensive Left End. The Left Tackle lunges to his right, on the snap of the ball, and uses a left-side body block to stop the defensive Right Guard. The Left End charges head-on into the defensive Right Tackle and keeps him out of the play. The Right Halfback goes into motion. The Quarterback makes a reverse pivot to the left and fakes first to the Left Halfback, who goes through the line. The Quarterback steps back quickly and hands the ball to the Fullback, who has taken a dip step to the left. The Fullback then steps back quickly and goes on through the line for what should result in considerable gain in yardage.

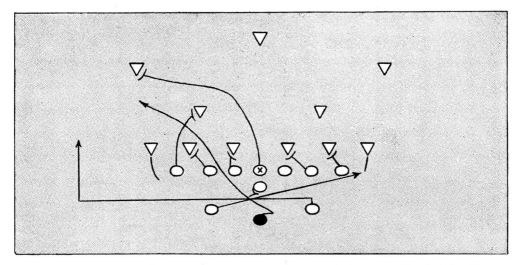

INSIDE CROSS-BUCK TO LEFT: The Left End blocks the linebacker in. The Left Tackle uses a left-shoulder block and moves the defense Right Tackle out, while the Left Guard uses a right-shoulder block and moves the defense Right Guard in. Center goes through the line and blocks the defense Right Halfback. Right Guard pulls, runs parallel to the line and blocks out the defense Right End. Right Tackle lunges left and uses a right-side body block to stop the defense Left Guard. Right End charges head-on into the defense Left Tackle and stops him. The Right Halfback goes into motion left. The Quarterback makes a reverse pivot right, faking to the Left Halfback who crosses first, and steps back quickly. The Fullback, who has dip-stepped right, takes the ball, steps back quickly, and goes on through the line.

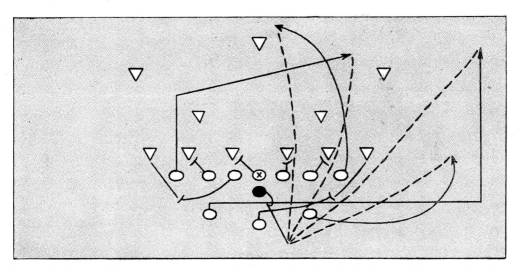

PASS PLAY, FOUR RECEIVERS: The Right End goes up the field about twelve yards, then angles left about forty-five degrees. Right Tackle blocks the defense Left Tackle out. Right Guard blocks head-on and keeps the defense Left Guard out. Center takes a quick step left and blocks the defense Right Guard out. Left Guard pulls quickly out of the line and puts himself between the passer and the defense Right End. Left Tackle blocks the defense Right Tackle. Left End goes up the field about eight yards, cuts sharply right, and should be free at the point shown in the diagram. The Left Halfback goes into motion to his right, and on the snap of the ball, goes as far up the field as possible. The Fullback steps forward with his left foot, fakes to take the ball, then blocks the defense Left End. The Right Halfback runs right and acts as trailer to the Left Halfback. The Quarterback makes a half turn right, fakes the ball to the Fullback, continues back and spots his best receiver.

1947 pooh-poohed the T formation, while supporters of Notre Dame or Texas viewed the Single Wing with about as much enthusiasm as they would an old ladies' bike race.

I would like to point out right now that the old system—namely, eleven good football players—has not been topped by either of them. I do not know which of the two systems is better, but I think that the material at hand should be the deciding factor for the coach. I have coached both systems, and plan to use the T at Annapolis.

The Single Wing Is Successful If the Coach Has Enough Men

Michigan was successful with the Single Wing because there were enough fine players to build up both offensive and defensive teams. Of course this was an ideal setup and is one that very few college coaches are ever given. Because of the two teams, Michigan could concentrate on each particular phase, and insert, polish and perfect the Single Wing offense so that it had trickery as well as power.

On the other hand, Notre Dame had an equal abundance of power and used individual perfection to win over their opponents with the T formation. I believe that either team could have switched systems with no loss in performance.

Our reason for using the T at the Naval Academy is because we do not have the abundance of man-power needed for two or three teams which can be substituted without losing something. With the T a good passer, a good receiver and a good breakaway runner can very often score, even if all blocking is not perfect. I do not mean to say that blocking is not important, but merely want to point out that knocking a man completely out of a play is not always necessary. Timing, a swift but effective block and speed are the things that make a T go. Deadly blocking, hard running power and speed are the fuel for a well-geared Single Wing attack. We do not have the size in any position, or the depth, to match our opponents, so we plan to use the T for offense at the Academy. We feel that we can do more with the T than with the Single Wing.

Today, the specialist has become a big factor in the game of football. Naturally, we all have to use the specialists because of the keen competition. However, while great emphasis has been placed on the specialist, the boy who can do all jobs well is the one who is best for the team—and who will most likely make the grade.

Twenty years ago, a boy was taught to do everything on the team, and had to do it well if he wanted a place on the first eleven. I would like to see a return to the past and see the youngsters well taught in every phase.

Don't just try to be a great kicker, a great passer or a great runner. Rather, set your sights on being a great player—on being a valuable player for your team, whether you are carrying the ball or covering the punt. A great performance by one man may be very satisfying for a few people, but victory for the team is the goal of the game.

Work on your blocking and tackling first of all. Then, if you intend to be a back, improve your running ability. From there on, passing and kicking should receive attention. Be well rounded in every department so that you can react in the most useful way to every situation, no matter how unexpected it may be. A good passer can be a handicap to his team if his throw is intercepted and he is the only man between the interceptor and the goal line and he is unable to tackle. Likewise, should one of his team mates intercept a pass, he should be able to block as well as tackle to help his team.

Really Great Players Can Do All the Jobs Well

I have always believed that a good athlete is well co-ordinated enough to learn how to do all the necessary jobs well. Too many boys are being groomed as specialists in the lower schools. If you examine your really great players in college today, you will find that they are men who can do everything—and do it better than the next fellow.

Along that same line, remember the importance of your assignment as a link in the chain of any play. Learn your plays well and carry out your assignment on every play as though you were personally conducting the ball player into the end zone. Bear in mind that there are eleven units which must mesh as one if the play is to succeed. Remember that the first rule of any great football player is: "Be demanding of yourself, and never be satisfied."

There are four plays on the two center pages. Picture yourself in your own position and determine whether you are able to carry out your job.

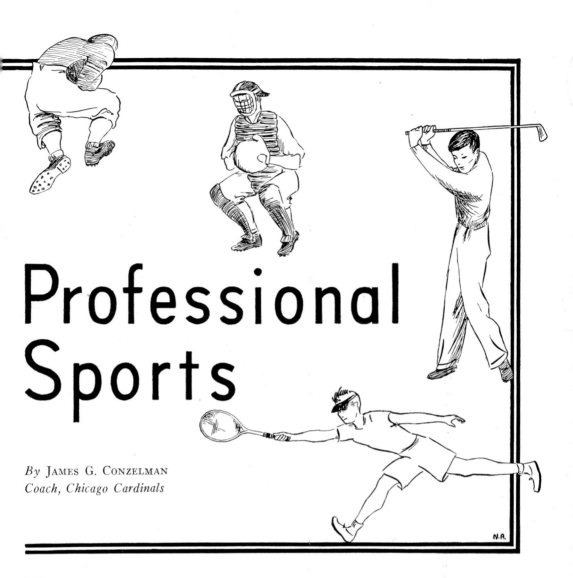

Professional Sports

By JAMES G. CONZELMAN
Coach, Chicago Cardinals

PROFESSIONAL sports has grown to be one of the biggest businesses in the country. The play-for-money boys are cashing in on their athletic skills as never before in the history of organized sports, a history which goes way back to the days of the Greeks and the Romans.

It was not so many years ago that the term "professional," particularly in regard to sports, carried a dubious meaning for some people. In very early times, professional athletes were often professional soldiers as well, who would fight on the side offering the most money. People looked on their double trade as shoddy, though they were tolerated and even sought out in times of danger to the country.

Times have changed! Although there is still a sharply drawn line between professional and amateur athletics, you are no longer stepping beyond the pale of polite society if you turn pro. Football, baseball, tennis, golf, swimming—pick almost any sport you like, and you will find plenty of boys and young men just out of high school and college reaping a golden harvest. However, it must never be forgotten that today's professional is one of yesterday's best amateurs.

The first appearance of the professional athlete in recorded history is generally credited to that period following Rome's conquest of Greece in 146 B.C. For centuries, participation in the Olympic Games had been limited to free-born Greeks whose personal life showed no violation, however small, of the rules of state or of manhood. Indeed, permission to compete in the games was in itself the highest honor that Greece could bestow upon an individual.

The Greeks Played While the Romans Watched

For many years after the conquest by Rome, the games continued to be the personal athletic property of the Greeks. The Romans did not take part, although they watched with interest. Later, however, they began to encourage their own youths to acquire skill in the Greek sports. The result was that the Romans finally began to take part in the games.

With athletes from both Greece and Rome competing, the contests continued on a friendly basis for several generations. Trouble began, though, when the Greeks accused some of the Roman champions of making use of their popularity by appearing in other cities and accepting money, or its equivalent in material gifts. This, the Greeks said, violated the amateur code and made the guilty ones ineligible for the Olympics.

The Romans denied the accusations and continued to send these contestants to the games. At a later Olympiad the Romans, angry because of the charges of professionalism made against some of their athletes, set fire to the buildings around the stadium. They wrecked everything in sight. After this happened, the Roman Emperor Theodosius abolished the Olympic Games.

Today's professional has his own events, leagues and organizations which present the paid athlete and his own particular skills to the public either as an individual or as a member of a team. He has many types of sport in which to star.

Great Sports Spectacles from B.C. to Today

Boxing, which was popular for hundreds of years before the Christian Era, is still one of the great sports spectacles. Horse racing and bullfighting, depending on state and national laws, flourish in many countries. Billiards, automobile racing and motorcycle racing, and aviation often are sponsored by manufacturers whose products are used in the events.

Six-day bicycle racing, like wrestling, is directed by syndicates which move the contestants from city to city for racing meets. Soccer football is very popular in England, continental Europe and South America, and draws large crowds in those countries. Tennis, with its paid performers picked from the Davis Cup winners, very often shows profitable years. Professional golfers swing their way across the nation in annual tournaments that offer substantial cash prizes to the top players.

Professional Basketball Is Settling Down

Following the pattern of major league baseball, hockey and professional football have settled down into solid organizations. Basketball has effectively put over its professionalized version, but needs a few more years to develop stability and permanent roots.

It seems to me that the first group of athletes to win respect for professional sport was the baseball players.

After 1900, the major leagues of baseball settled down into a somewhat permanent pattern, properly supervised by executives who demanded that the rules be obeyed. Baseball became the national game. Its victories and defeats, its player as well as team records began to be published in detail in the newspapers. The general public got to know the stars of the diamond, how much they received in salaries and something of their private lives off the field.

A Word to the Wise—Learn a Business, Too!

For boys who are thinking of entering any of the professional sports, however, there is one warning. Prepare yourself for a business career in later years. Experience in industry, or business, can be gained through ordinary effort during the months that you are not playing. By getting this experience, the professional athlete is able to cushion his retirement from sport and make the change from sport to business an easier one.

Only a few stars earn the fabulous sums of a Babe Ruth, a Jack Dempsey or a Charley Trippi, which might enable them to retire after their athletic careers have ended. Unfortunately, most of the professional sports require youth. Even the age of thirty can be old in games such as football and basketball. Baseball players have a few additional years before spent muscles call for retirement.

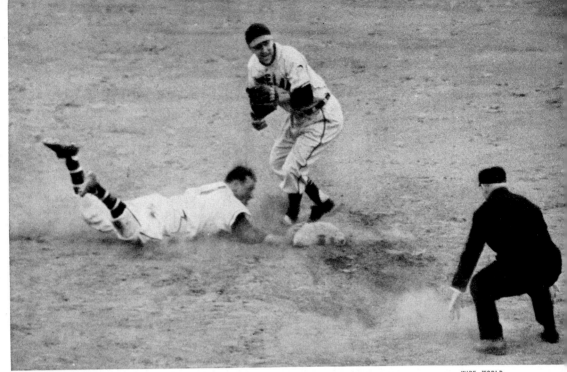

Was Phil Masi really safe at second in that famous eighth inning Feller-to-Boudreau pick-off play that came during the Series opener in Boston? The fans and Lou Boudreau thought not.

Sports Review

By LEO WALDMAN
Courtesy of A. G. SPALDING & BROS., INC.

THE first post-war revival of the greatest of all athletic carnivals—the XIV Olympiad of the modern era—and the sensational comeback of the Cleveland Indians led the parade of many thrilling sports events in 1948.

The Olympic Games, as you know, were held in London's Wembley Stadium from July 29 through August 14. More than 1,000,000 spectators, from all parts of the globe, were there.

The United States sent 341 contestants, the largest number of all, who won 38 first places to lead all other countries. Sweden was a distant second, with 17 gold medals, and Hungary was third with 10. Great Britain, the host nation, was able to win only one first place—in rowing. (There is more about the games in the article, Plain of Olympia.)

The irrepressible Cleveland Indians not only won the American League pennant from the Boston Red Sox, but went on to take the World Series from the Boston Braves of the National League, four games to two. Cleveland's victory was the twenty-eighth for the American League, compared to seventeen for the National League. Also, it was the first pennant and World Series for a Cleveland team since 1920.

The Braves got off to a good start in the Series, winning the first game 1 to 0 on the strength of Johnny Sain's four-hit pitching. Bobby Feller pitched for Cleveland, and allowed only two hits to Sain's four. However, a single by Tommy Holmes in the eighth inning scored Phil Masi and the only run of the game. Feller, one of the greatest pitchers in American League history, had waited ten years to pitch in a World Series. It was his hard luck to become the second pitcher ever to lose a two-hitter Series game.

Lou Boudreau and his Indians came charging back, though, just as they had been

WORLD SERIES RESULTS

First Game — R. H. E.

Cleveland (A.)..0 0 0 0 0 0 0 0 0–0 4 0
Boston (N.)....0 0 0 0 0 0 0 1 ..–1 2 2
Batteries—Feller and Hegan; Sain and Salkeld, Masi (9).

Second Game

Cleveland (A.)..0 0 0 2 1 0 0 0 1–4 8 1
Boston (N.)....1 0 0 0 0 0 0 0 0–1 8 3
Batteries—Lemon and Hegan; Spahn, Barrett (5), Potter (8) and Salkeld.

Third Game

Boston (N.)....0 0 0 0 0 0 0 0 0–0 5 1
Cleveland (A.)..0 0 1 1 0 0 0 0 ..–2 5 0
Batteries—Bickford, Voiselle (4), Barrett (8) and Masi; Bearden and Hegan.

Fourth Game — R. H. E.

Boston (N.)....0 0 0 0 0 0 1 0 0–1 7 0
Cleveland (A.)..1 0 1 0 0 0 0 0 ..–2 5 0
Batteries—Sain and Masi; Gromek and Hegan.

Fifth Game

Boston (N.)...3 0 1 0 0 1 6 0 0–11 12 0
Cleveland (A.).1 0 0 4 0 0 0 0 0– 5 6 2
Batteries—Potter, Spahn (4) and Salkeld; Feller, Klieman (7), Christopher (7), Paige (7), Muncrief (8) and Hegan.

Sixth Game

Cleveland (A.)..0 0 1 0 0 2 0 1 0–4 10 0
Boston (N.)....0 0 0 1 0 0 0 2 0–3 9 0
Batteries—Lemon, Bearden (8) and Hegan; Voiselle, Spahn (8) and Salkeld, Masi (9).

doing all season. They won the next three games—4 to 1, 2 to 0 and 2 to 1—in a beautiful display of pitching and air-tight defensive play by both teams. Bob Lemon, Cleveland's twenty-game winner during the regular season, accounted for the Indians' first victory. Gene Bearden, twenty-seven-year-old freshman southpaw and Purple Heart winner, gave up only five hits in scoring his shutout triumph. Steve Gromek, who had been used sparingly during the last two months of the season, surprised everyone by coming through with a 2-to-1 success.

Trailing three games to one, Boston came back in the fifth to win an 11-to-5 victory. Warren Spahn, veteran lefthander, relieved Nelson Potter in the fourth inning and held Cleveland to one hit over the last five and two-thirds innings. Cleveland, however, finished it all by taking its fourth and clinching contest with a thrilling 4-to-3 decision. Lemon started in the box for Cleveland and, although he had to be relieved by Bearden in the eighth, he was given credit for the game. He was the only pitcher in the series to win two games.

It was a record Series, both in receipts and attendance. A total of 358,362 fans turned out for the six games, and paid $1,633,685.56 to see them. The largest crowd ever to see a World Series game—or even a regular season game, for that matter—saw the fifth game in Cleveland. The stadium was packed with 86,288 people. Winning players' shares of the series were $6,772.05 apiece, also a record. Each of the players on the

Boston team received as his share $4,651.51.

Both teams were evenly matched at the plate and on the mound, but Cleveland came out on top because of its decided edge in the field. Both teams hit four home runs, and both scored seventeen runs. The Braves had forty-three hits and the Indians had thirty-eight. However, the comparison ends here. The Braves committed six glaring defense errors, compared to Cleveland's three. Cleveland's infield rattled off nine double plays—four in the important final game—while Boston was able to make only three in all six games.

Cleveland came close to losing its chance to play in the World Series. On the final day of the season, the Indians lost to Detroit, 7 to 1, and the Boston Red Sox beat the Yankees 10 to 5. The two teams wound up in a deadlock for the American League pennant. It was the first American League deadlock in the forty-seven-year history of the league, and the second one in major-league history. However, Cleveland, a fighting ball club if ever there was one, whacked the Red Sox 8 to 3 in the all-important play-off at Boston.

In taking the National League flag, the Braves—oldest club in organized, professional baseball—won their first pennant in thirty-four years. Sain, a veteran right-hander, was the mainstay of the Boston pitching staff, with twenty-four victories to his credit. The big guns of the Braves' attack were the outstanding players Tommy Holmes, Alvin Dark, Jeff Heath and Bob Elliott.

The final standings of the teams in both leagues, as published in Spalding's Baseball Guide, follow:

AMERICAN LEAGUE

	W.	L.	Pct.	G. B.
Cleveland	97	58	.626	—
Boston	96	59	.619	1
New York	94	60	.610	2½
Philadelphia	84	70	.545	12½
Detroit	78	76	.506	18½
St. Louis	59	94	.386	37
Washington	56	97	.366	40
Chicago	51	101	.336	44½

NATIONAL LEAGUE

	W.	L.	Pct.	G. B.
Boston	91	62	.595	—
St. Louis	85	69	.552	6½
Brooklyn	84	70	.545	7½
Pittsburgh	83	71	.539	8½
New York	78	76	.506	13½
Philadelphia	66	88	.429	25½
Cincinnati	64	89	.418	27
Chicago	64	90	.416	27½

Stan Musial, fleet-footed outfielder of the St. Louis Cardinals, was the outstanding hitter of the season in both major leagues, batting .376. In addition, he paced the National League in doubles, 45; triples, 18; runs-batted-in, 131; runs scored, 135, and hits, 230. Ted Williams of the Boston Red Sox was not far behind Musial, with a high of .369 in the American League. Johnny Mize of the Giants and Ralph Kiner of Pittsburgh wound up in a tie for home-run honors, each with 40, for the second successive year. They both finished the season with 51 in 1947. Joe DiMaggio, the Yankees' great fly chaser, led both leagues in runs-batted-in with 156.

American League players also chalked up a victory in the fifteenth major-league all-star game. The game score was 5 to 2, and it was the eleventh time that the American League had won this annual contest with the National League.

There were two no-hit no-run games during the season, one in each league. Cleveland's Bob Lemon moved into baseball's ranks of fame by blanking the Detroit Tigers, 2 to 0; and Brooklyn's Rex Barney sank the Giants by the same score. Pat Seerey, Chicago White Sox outfielder, got his name into the record books by slashing out four home runs in a single game with the Philadelphia Athletics. Only four other major-league players have ever accomplished this feat—Lou Gehrig, Ed Delahanty, Bobby Lowe and Chuck Klein.

In the more important minor-league pennant races, Montreal captured its third International League championship in four years, and also the play-offs. Indianapolis came out on top in the American Association, but lost the play-offs to St. Paul. Montreal took the Little World Series from St. Paul, four games to one. Nashville won the pennant in the Southern Association, Fort Worth in the Texas League, and Oakland won in the Pacific Coast League.

A sad note was injected into the baseball season by the death of the sport's greatest player—George Herman (Babe) Ruth. He died on August 16 at the age of fifty-three. He had become one of the outstanding figures of American life, and was probably the most famous baseball player of all time. It was not only his tremendous diamond feats that made him one of America's idols, but also his love of children and his untiring efforts to help them. Even though he played

BABE RUTH'S BASEBALL RECORDS

Most home runs (lifetime) 714	Highest World Series batting average .... .625
(World Series included) 729	Most World Series played 10
Most home runs (one season) 60	Most runs batted in (total series) 33
Most years leading league in homers 12	Most home runs in a series game (twice) . 3
Most years with forty or more homers ... 11	Most total bases (total series) 96
Most times hitting two homers in one game 72	Most bases on balls (total series) 33
	Most strike-outs (total series) 30
Three homers in one game 4	Pitched most consecutive scoreless innings
Most homers in consecutive games 7	(total series) 29
Most runs in a season 177	Most runs scored (total series) 37
Most runs batted in 2,209	Batted .300 or over for most single
Most bases on balls 2,056	series 6
Most strike-outs 1,330	Most extra bases (total series) 54
Most years on world's championship club . 7	Most total bases (one series game) 12

his last game of baseball in 1935, people still cheered him and begged for his autograph. During his twenty-two years of baseball he played in 2,502 games.

Boxing had a very active year. There were twelve championship fights, with at least one in each of the eight recognized divisions. Joe Louis headed the action with the successful defense of his heavyweight title against contender Jersey Joe Walcott. Walcott was knocked out in the eleventh round of their second fifteen-round bout at Yankee Stadium. Louis won a close decision in their first bout, the previous December. However, there was no question of his superiority the second time. After ten dreary rounds, Louis suddenly came to life and ended the fight with one punch. It was a right to the jaw and shook Walcott to his toes. The challenger pitched forward on his face, then rolled over on his back. He tried to get up, but was still on one knee as the referee reached the final count of ten. The knockout came two minutes and fifty-six seconds after the eleventh round had begun.

The Champ Will Fight Again: Either Charles or Baksi

After the fight, Louis announced that he would retire from the ring. However, he changed his mind in September and announced that he would fight a title bout in June 1949. He said that his opponent would be either Ezzard Charles or Joe Baksi, if either of them put up a good fight in a bout that was scheduled for November 12.

Two American fighters lost their championship crowns to Europeans during the year. Gus Lesnevich, world light-heavyweight titleholder, fought in March and knocked out Billy Fox of Philadelphia in one round in Madison Square Garden. Then he went to England and lost a fifteen-round decision to Freddie Mills in London's White City Stadium. Mills thus became the first Briton to hold the world's light-heavyweight title since 1903.

Gary, Indiana, Loses to Paris, France: Zale vs. Cerdan

Tony Zale, the "steel" man from Gary, Indiana, like Lesnevich, was up and down the ladder during the year. He regained the world middleweight championship by demolishing rough, tough Rocky Graziano of New York in three rounds. They fought in

356

Ruppert Stadium, Newark, New Jersey. In September, though, Zale was the victim. He lost the crown to challenger Marcel Cerdan of France in Roosevelt Stadium, Jersey City.

Ike Williams, lightweight ruler from Trenton, New Jersey, was the most active champion—successfully defending his crown three times during the year. First, he won a close 15-round decision from Enrique Bolanos of Mexico, in Los Angeles. Then he knocked out the former champion, Beau Jack, in 6 rounds at Philadelphia, in July. He put Jesse Flores to sleep in 10 rounds at Yankee Stadium in September.

The Going Gets Tough in the Welterweight Division

In the welterweight division, Sugar Ray Robinson had a tough time defending his title against a 22-year-old Filipino boxer. He had to call on all of his tremendous resources of speed and sharpshooting power punches to balk Bernard Docusen, the courageous challenger. They fought at Comiskey Park in Chicago. It was Robinson's third defense of the title that he won from Tommy Bell in 1946. Robinson had won 88 victories in 90 professional fights.

Among the smaller champions, Willie Pep, the fancy featherweight from Hartford, Connecticut, provided the shock of the year. He went down before the punishing gloves of New York's Sandy Saddler in the fourth round of a title bout at Madison Square Garden in October. No one had ever stopped Pep before, and no one except lightweight Sammy Angott had ever taken a decision from him in 137 fights. Saddler, the new champion, is aggressive, fast and a wickedly sharp hitter with both hands.

Bantamweight Manuel Ortiz Keeps His Title

Manuel Ortiz of El Centro, California, champion of the bantamweights, retained his honors for the eighteenth time by knocking out Memo Valero in eight rounds. Valero is the Mexican titleholder, and they fought in the bullrun in Mexicali, Mexico. Across the sea in Belfast, Ireland, Rinty Monaghan gained undisputed possession of the world flyweight title by stopping Jackie Paterson in seven rounds.

Little Ben Hogan of Hershey, Pennsylvania, was the big noise in the golfing world of 1948, winning four tournaments and collecting $30,000 in prize money. The diminutive powerhouse won the National Open at the Riviera Country Club in Los Angeles with a record score of 276. He defeated Mike Turnesa, 7 and 6, to win the National PGA title for the second time. Western Open honors came with his defeat of Ed (Porky) Oliver, and he claimed the Denver Open with a smashing 270 for 72 holes.

Willie Turnesa Becomes a Two-Time Winner

Likeable Willie Turnesa of Elmsford, New York, was top man in the amateur ranks. He won the National Amateur championship for the second time in his golfing career by defeating Ray Billows of Poughkeepsie, New York, 2 and 1, in the final round at the Memphis Country Club in Memphis, Tennessee. It was exactly ten years ago that Turnesa beat Pat Abbot at Oakmont, Pennsylvania, for his first National Amateur crown. Grace Lenczyk, a student at Stetson College, took the Women's National Amateur Tournament. She beat Helen Sigel of Philadelphia, Pennsylvania, 4 and 3, in the final round at Pebble Beach, California. The twenty-one-year-old winner had previously won both the women's Intercollegiate and Canadian titles.

Americans won two of England's most important golfing honors. Frank Stranahan of Toledo, Ohio, stroked his way to the British Amateur championship, and tiny Louise Suggs of Atlanta, Georgia, captured the Women's Amateur title. Stranahan defeated Charles Stowe of England, 5 and 4, and became the ninth American to win the British men's title. Miss Suggs, who defeated Jean Donald, champion of Scotland, 1 up in the final, became the second American woman to win that title. Mrs. Mildred Didrikson Zaharias came home with the honor last year.

Women's Curtis Cup Team Victor Over British

In other championship-golf competition, John F. Riddell, Jr., of Garden City, New York, won the United States Senior crown; Mrs. Zaharias, now a professional, won the Women's National Open; Mike Ferentz of Long Beach, California, won the National Public Links title; and Claude Harmon of Mamaroneck, New York, took the famed Masters Tournament at the Augusta (Georgia) National Course. The United States Women's Curtis Cup team turned back its opponents from England, 6½ to 2½ points, and Henry Cotton coasted to his third British Open championship by a five-stroke margin.

In tennis, the Davis Cup stayed in the United States for another year. Australia lost its chance at the cup in a surprisingly easy 5 to 0 sweep by the United States. The first day of play, Frank Parker of Los Angeles downed Billy Sidwell of Australia 6–4, 6–4, 6–4; and Ted Schroeder of Las Crescenta, California, turned back Adrian K. Quist, the challengers' captain, 6–3, 4–6, 6–0, 6–0.

Talbert and Mulloy Win Doubles to Assure Davis Cup Victory

Victory was assured on the second day when the United States doubles team stopped the Australian doubles combination. William Talbert of New York, and Gardnar Mulloy of Miami, Florida, defeated Colin Long and Sidwell 8–6, 9–7, 2–6 and 8–6 for the necessary third victory. On the final day, United States players made a clean sweep of it. Schroeder crushed Sidwell 6–2, 6–1, 6–1, and Parker smothered Quist 6–2, 6–2, 6–3.

Coming from Nowhere, Pancho Gonzales Sweeps the Singles Field

However, before the end of the 1948 season, an even greater surprise was due for the tennis world. Richard (Pancho) Gonzales, an unknown, flashed through a field of veteran, experienced players to capture the men's National Singles championship at Forest Hills, New York. With a thundering service and a touch of the master in his volleying, the twenty-year-old Californian defeated Eric Sturgess of South Africa 6–2, 6–3 and 14–12 in the final round. Although seeded seventeenth in national listing, Gonzales furnished the most exciting climax in the history of this annual tournament.

Mulloy and Parker won their fourth National Doubles crown by overcoming Parker and Schroeder 1–6, 9–7, 6–3, 3–6 and 9–7. In the Women's National Singles, Mrs. William duPont, the former Margaret Osborne, wrested the championship from Louise Brough, the titleholder, 4–6, 6–4 and 15–13. Tom Brown, Jr., and Miss Brough came out on top in the mixed doubles by defeating Mrs. duPont and Talbert 6–4, 6–4.

357

The approaching summer Olympics brought keen competition in track and field, both in indoor and outdoor events. Gilbert Dodds, the espistle-packing parson from Boston, Massachusetts, was doomed to disappointment, though. Dodds, who was undisputed king of the milers after winning the National A.A.U. outdoor mile race, injured a leg in training and was forced to the sidelines for the remainder of the season.

During the indoor season the soft-spoken Dodds left something for future milers to shoot at. He shattered his own world record in winning the Wanamaker Mile in the remarkable time of 4:05.3 during the annual Millrose Games at Madison Square Garden. The previous record, also held by Dodds, was 4:06.4. Unbeaten in both indoor and outdoor competition, Dodds chalked up thirty-five consecutive mile victories before being forced out of training with his injured leg.

New Yorkers' Winged Feet Win Two Track Titles

The runners and jumpers from the New York Athletic Club again won the two major team championships—the National A.A.U. outdoor and indoor crowns. The winged footers captured the outdoor title for the eighth consecutive year, with a total of 84 points. The Los Angeles Athletic Club was second with 69⅓ points and the San Francisco Olympic Club was third with 28 points. In taking the indoor laurels, the N.Y.A.C. stars had a close call, just beating the New York Pioneer Club, 16 to 15.

In college competition, the University of Minnesota surprised by winning the National Collegiate Athletic Association team title for the first time in the 27-year history of the meet. The upsetting Gophers racked up a total of 46 points to win. Southern California's favored Trojans placed second with 41½ points, and the University of Texas was third with 40 points. Fortune Gordien, who won the discus throw and placed second in the shot put, and Lloyd Lamois, who won the hop, step and jump and placed sixth in the broad jump, were the individual stars in Minnesota's march to victory.

Yale and New York University dominated the I.C.A.A.A.A. competition. The Elihu stars won the outdoor championship—their first since 1924—with 37 points. N.Y.U. was runner-up with 33. However, the Violets

had their chance to cheer at the indoor title meet, winning it with 31½ points. Yale wound up second with 23¼ points.

The Ohio Buckeyes Top the Big Nine Indoors and Outdoors

Ohio State University was complete boss of the Big Nine track and field world. The Buckeyes won the outdoor honors with 53⅓ points, and the indoor laurels with 43 points. Michigan was second in the outdoor meet, while Illinois was runner-up in the indoor competition. The Southern California standard-bearers won the Pacific Coast Conference championship for the eighth consecutive time. A complete list of team and individual champions in both A.A.U. and collegiate competition will be found in Spalding's track and field guide.

Not to forget the stamina stars, Johnny Kelley of West Acton, Massachusetts, won the National A.A.U. marathon championship; Gerard Cote, 34-year-old policeman of St. Hyacinthe, Quebec, came out on top in the fifty-second annual Boston A.A. marathon; and Bob Mathias, the 17-year-old high-school student from Tulare, California, started toward his smashing Olympic triumph by taking the National A.A.U. decathlon championship.

Bartlesville, Oklahoma, Oilers Win Olympics Basketball

In basketball, the Phillips Oilers of Bartlesville, Oklahoma, an amateur quintet, swept aside all competition in sight to qualify for the Olympics. Then they went on to win the Olympic championship. In the final tryout at Madison Square Garden, the Oilers won from the best team in the United States —the University of Kentucky—53 to 49 in a thrill-packed contest. Bob Kurland, a seven-foot center, paced the victors' attack with 20 points. Kentucky had established itself as the outstanding college team of the year by winning the annual N.C.A.A. tournament, downing Baylor University 58 to 42 in the final round. St. Louis University, playing in its first post-season court championship, won the eleventh annual National Intercollegiate Invitation Tournament by turning back New York University 65 to 52.

In other intercollegiate basketball competition, Columbia won the Eastern League championship for the second successive year, with a record of 10 victories against one defeat. Michigan came out on top in the Big Nine tourney with a record of 10 triumphs in 12 starts, and Navy won its annual skirmish with Army, 49 to 36.

Canada, as usual, swept all major hockey honors. Paced by their brilliant captain and playmaker, Syl Apps, the Maple Leafs won the National League pennant and then went on to down the Detroit Red Wings in four straight games for the coveted Stanley Cup. It was the third Cup victory in the last four years for Toronto. The final standings in the National Hockey League follow:

	W.	L.	T.	Pts.	Goals F.	A.
Toronto	32	15	13	77	180	142
Detroit	30	18	12	72	186	146
Boston	23	24	13	59	167	168
Rangers	21	26	13	55	176	201
Montreal	20	29	11	51	147	170
Chicago	20	34	6	46	195	225

The horse world had its heroes, too. Citation, called the greatest thoroughbred since Man O' War, was named "Horse of the Year." The three-year-old colt owned by Calumet Farms easily won the major honors, including the Triple Crown, in racing. He won the seventy-fourth running of the Kentucky Derby by three and a half lengths from his stablemate, Coaltown. Two weeks later he captured the famed Preakness Stakes by six lengths from C. V. Whitney's Vulcan's Forge. Then, a month later, he pranced to victory in the Belmont Stakes—eight lengths ahead of Better Self, owned by the King Ranch.

The famous trotting classic, the Hambletonian Stakes, was won by Harrison Hoyt's Demon Hanover in two straight heats at Goshen, New York. The two most important racing events in England were the Epsom Derby and the Grand National. A French-bred colt, My Love, won the Derby, and an Irish mare, Sheila's Cottage, won the National. Stymie, who had won more money in purses than any other horse in American racing history—$911,335—broke a small bone in his foot during the middle of the season and had to be retired.

For the second successive year, the University of Michigan football team was the unanimous choice as national champion of the collegiate world. The Wolverines were undefeated and untied in ten games. California, Army, Notre Dame, Clemson and North Carolina also established outstanding records during the season. Major Bowl games saw Northwestern turn back California, 20 to 14, in Los Angeles' Rose Bowl; Texas upset the University of Georgia Bulldogs, 41 to 28, in Miami's Orange Bowl; and Oklahoma's powerful squad down North Carolina, 14 to 6, in Sugar Bowl play at New Orleans. Doak Walker, outstanding star of the season, paced Southern Methodist to a thrilling 21–13 triumph over Oregon in the Cotton Bowl at Dallas, Texas. In professional football, the Philadelphia Eagles captured their first National League crown, and Cleveland took the All American Conference title.

Champion Rock Ridge Night Rocket, a Bedlington terrier owned by Mr. and Mrs. William A. Rockefeller, monopolized the two major prizes in the dog world. For one, the blue-coated terrier became the first Bedlington ever to win best-in-show at the annual Westminster Kennel Club show at Madison Square Garden. He followed this triumph by winning best-in-show for the second successive year at the annual Morris and Essex Kennel Club outdoor show.

Washington Scullers Stroke to Victory at Poughkeepsie

The University of Washington had a field day in the annual Poughkeepsie Regatta. Its rowers swept all three races, duplicating a feat that they had accomplished first in 1936 and again in 1937. California came in second in both the varsity and junior varsity races, while Navy was runner-up in the freshman event. The University of California, however, gained more than its share of the laurels by defeating Harvard in the final Olympic tryouts at Princeton, New Jersey.

Harvard called it a successful rowing season by virtue of its victory over Yale in their eighty-third meeting. The Cantabs gained their victory by establishing a new downstream course record for the Thames River. They covered the four-mile course in nineteen minutes, twenty-one and two-fifths seconds. This broke the record—by more than half a minute—set by the Yale crew of 1934.

Dick Button of Englewood, New Jersey, and Barbara Ann Scott of Canada won nearly every figure-skating championship. Button, who plans to enter Yale, won the Olympic championship, the men's world championship and the senior men's national honors. Miss Scott won the Olympic, world and European championships.

"And they worshiped the beast . . ." Revelation 13:4. From Scenes from the Apocalypse, 14th century. Museum of Tapestries, Angers.

Part of the first of the set of five hangings, Scenes from the Life of the Virgin. Late 15th century. Church of Notre-Dame, Beaune.

A HISTORIC DISPLAY—TWO HUNDRED TAPESTRIES, BROUGHT TO THE METROPOLITAN MUSEUM OF ART WITH THE HELP OF THE FRENCH GOVERNMENT.

TALES

The long file of tapestries . . . . spreads before your eyes a poem, now rustic and pastoral, now sumptuous and regal; it may be religious or warlike. Our own era adds a paean of liberty. Through its whole length, across five centuries, rings the lyric spirit of our land . . . You will read here, also, a story in which the humble labors of the field take on an air of legend, while the celestial figures of martyrs and angels hover on the blue horizon of our familiar countryside. . . . And since we can not send you our cathedrals, our palaces, or our white villages, our parks or our furrowed fields, we offer you in this long poem the happiest picture a people has ever given of its own life.

GEORGES SALLES   *Director of the Museums of France*

IN  Tapestries

No matter how many castles a king or a prince might build in those long-ago days called the Middle Ages, the royal halls were chilly and their great stone walls were grim.

Tapestries brought them warmth and color. The rich reds, yellows, greens and blues that we admire today for their soft, gentle tones were once brighter by far—as you would see if you could examine the backs of some of these priceless hangings, especially those with protective linings.

The "ancient and lovely art of woven pictures" lost much of its beauty of design in the nineteenth century. Very recently, leading French artists have been creating fresh, vigorous designs for such time-honored looms as those of Gobelin and Aubusson.

"And there was given me a reed like unto a rod . . ." Revelation, 11:1. Another scene from the Apocalypse, Museum of Tapestries, Angers.

Part of one of twelve tapestries telling the legend of St. Stephen. Woven some time between 1488 and 1500. Now in the Cluny Museum, Paris.

From The Visit of Louis XIV to the Gobelin Manufactory. Wool, silk, silver and gold. Mobilier National, Paris.

Nobleman and lady. Detail from one of six pieces called "La Vie Seigneuriale" (Courtly Life). About 1500.

The group of figures from the tapestry Wool-working, about 1500. The young woman is weaving cloth; the man is winding wool; the old woman shears a sheep. The animals and birds seem cheerfully unconcerned. They prefer to enjoy the countless exquisite flowers ("millefleurs").

The series is one of the treasures of
the Cluny Museum, in Paris. The
threads can be seen in this close-up.

Royal stag hunt in the eighteenth century.
From the Gobelin tapestries, The Hunts
of Louis XV. Château, Compiègne.

Though there was not room here to show you quite all of this spirited tapestry, you will find many
reminders of one of the world's best-loved cities. Woven in 1940, it was designed by the artist
Gromaire, who calls it Spring, or Paris. Now in the Mobilier National, Paris.

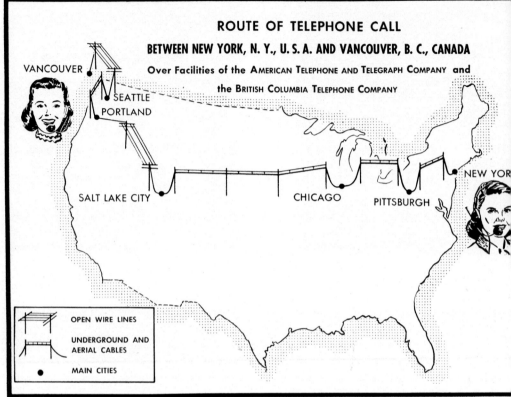

ROUTE OF TELEPHONE CALL
BETWEEN NEW YORK, N. Y., U. S. A. AND VANCOUVER, B. C., CANADA
Over Facilities of the AMERICAN TELEPHONE AND TELEGRAPH COMPANY and
the BRITISH COLUMBIA TELEPHONE COMPANY

VANCOUVER
SEATTLE
PORTLAND
SALT LAKE CITY
CHICAGO
PITTSBURGH
NEW YOR

OPEN WIRE LINES

UNDERGROUND AND
AERIAL CABLES

MAIN CITIES

TELEPHONES
Long Distance, Please!

By CARL E. WIDEBERG
American Telephone and Telegraph Company

SUPPOSE you live in New York and want to talk to your friend John Smith who lives in Vancouver, British Columbia, 2,600 miles away. You merely pick up the receiver of your telephone and call or dial the long-distance operator. If John is at home when his telephone rings, probably you will be talking to him in a little over a minute's time.

It is as easy as that—as easy as that because hundreds of people and thousands of pieces of complicated equipment are helping to make your call.

When you pick up the telephone receiver and dial, or ask for, long distance, a series of lights flash on a special switchboard in the telephone building. Below the lights are rows of sockets, or jacks. In less than four seconds an operator inserts a cord into one of these jacks and answers your signal.

364

Your answer comes rapidly because there is usually more than one switchboard—in what is called a multiple arrangement—and at least one operator is almost always free to answer your call.

A long-distance operator takes down the details of your call on a ticket. She notes that the call is person-to-person. This simply means that the one making the call wishes to speak to a particular person. In this case it would be John Smith. If, on the other hand, you are willing to talk with anyone who answers the telephone number you are calling, the call would be listed as a station-to-station call.

Thousands of Voice Highways Crisscross the Country

Now, since your call is to Vancouver, the long-distance operator must find out which route your voice is going to travel. There are thousands of routes, or voice highways. In a bulletin beside her, the operator finds that calls to Vancouver are routed through Seattle, Washington, 130 miles south of Vancouver. She plugs in on a line to one of the toll-tandem switchboards, which aid the long-distance switchboards in large cities. These toll-tandem boards contain direct circuits to many, many cities that serve as junctions, or transfer stations. It would be impossible for one operator to manage a switchboard large enough to handle incoming calls from local customers who want to make long-distance calls, and, at the same time, to connect them with circuits to locations all over the continent.

When the operator plugs in on a line to one of the toll-tandem boards, she hears an order tone, or "Zip-zip." This sound tells her that a tandem operator is on the other end of the line and is ready to receive the name of the desired city.

"Through Seattle," you hear the long-distance operator say, and the tandem operator plugs in on a circuit connecting you directly with Seattle. This circuit travels over a cable that sometimes runs underground, and sometimes overhead on poles. Mile after mile the cable stretches westward, through Pittsburgh to Chicago, across the prairies and desert to Salt Lake City—then northward over the Rocky Mountains to Portland, Oregon, and up the Pacific Coast to Seattle. When the tandem operator plugged in, she sent an electric impulse over this highway

that lighted a lamp on the Inward switchboard at Seattle.

"Seattle," says the operator as she comes on the line.

"Vancouver," replies the New York long-distance operator.

If the Seattle operator has an open circuit to Vancouver, she completes the connection, rings it and answers, "Right!"

Hardly a minute has passed. The telephone operator in Vancouver is on the line saying, "Vancouver." The New York operator gives John Smith's telephone number to the Vancouver operator, who rings it.

"Mr. John Smith, please. New York is calling," the New York operator says to the voice that answers the telephone. It is John himself; and as you and he exchange greetings, the long-distance operator in New York takes the ticket—on which she has recorded the details of the call—and slides it into a calculagraph. This is an electric clock mounted on the switchboard. It records the time to the nearest second on the ticket. After you and John have finished your conversation and have hung up, a lamp lights on the New York switchboard. This shows the long-distance operator that the call is completed, and she again stamps the ticket in the clock. The total time of the call is thus recorded. The charge for this call, which you will find on your next telephone bill, will be figured from the details listed on the ticket.

Behind every telephone call you make stands the work and progress of one of the most highly developed industries in the world today. Operating and maintaining this industry are thousands of men and women who are continually working to provide better and faster telephone service.

A Whole City of Men and Women Keep Our Telephones Working

The United States leads the world in telephone development. The Bell Telephone System, for instance, owns and operates 30,000,000 phones—three-fifths of the total number of telephones in the world. More than 660,000 men and women—equal to the population of Washington, D. C.—are employed by the Bell System. If you were to take all of the Bell System telephone wire in the United States and stretch it along the equator, it would encircle the earth almost 4,600 times.

When you made your long-distance call

to John Smith, you talked with the long-distance operator in New York. You could hear one or more operators putting your call through to Vancouver. You did not hear all the laboratory scientists, engineers, technicians, linemen and many others whose work had a part in the operation.

Amazing developments constantly improving telephone equipment come from the laboratory. Furthermore, experts learn just how many telephone wires are needed between different places by studying our increasing population figures and the number of telephone calls that are made. Routes that telephone lines shall follow, the construction and maintenance of equipment necessary to operate a telephone business also are problems that must be met.

Abraham Lincoln said of Niagara Falls: "I wonder where all that water came from." If we were to go down into the cable vaults of a big telephone building we would find another kind of Niagara—a torrent of electrical impulses pouring through wires packed into the cables that enter the vaults. Where did this torrent of impulses come from? Your voice, and the thousands of other voices being carried along at the same time, makes them.

The Telephone's Electric Ear Hears Your Voice

Electrical impulses are caused by the action of your voice as you speak into the transmitter of your telephone. The transmitter is an electrical ear. It hears what you say and sends the words by electrical impulses over wires. The air molecules that have been set in motion by your speech strike against a thin, flat disc called a diaphragm. This vibrates, as does the human eardrum when sound-waves strike against it. There is a little chamber behind the diaphragm of the telephone. It contains tiny grains of roasted coal, each smaller than a pinhead.

An electric current is flowing through the grains of coal. When the diaphragm vibrates inward, they are pushed tighter together and more current flows. When it bends outward, the pressure on the grains is released and less current flows. So the flow of the current is changed as the diaphragm vibrates, and electrical impulses are created. Carrying these impulses, which your voice has caused, requires thousands of pieces of apparatus.

Among the most important devices used to carry your voice across the miles are the repeaters or vacuum-tube amplifiers. They are the seven-league boots that have made long-distance telephoning possible. The impulses created by your voice become weak and would finally fade into silence—just as the sound of your voice does when you shout into the distance—were it not for these repeaters or amplifiers. So they are inserted into telephone lines at intervals of 50 to 300 miles to pump new energy into the impulses. The distance between them depends on the type of cable that is carrying your voice.

Mechanical Watchmen Give the Alarm When Trouble Comes

There are many other important types of equipment devices that help to give you fast and prompt service. For instance, there are devices that sort out wires, that permit circuits to be changed and that protect the system by giving alarm in case of trouble along the line. A large staff of trained technicians keeps a constant check on this equipment.

Testboard men watch over the performance of telephone circuits. They use special equipment to determine whether the circuits are working properly; and if trouble comes, they locate the exact spot quickly.

Probably you have seen telephone linemen climbing down under city streets to repair an underground cable, or perched high up on a telephone pole beside some country road. These trouble-shooters in the field make sure that nothing stops your call from getting through. Floods, storms, the blazing desert sun, the icy blasts of wintry mountains—these are all a part of the job of the telephone lineman. In time of disaster, when the rest of us are seeking safety, the lineman is on the job—repairing fallen wires and broken connections and keeping the telephones operating when they are needed most.

There have been many changes, indeed, since the day that Alexander Graham Bell predicted that the country would be tied together by telephones. As many as 750,000 messages a day pass through the long-distance circuits alone. Beside the long-distance wires that carry your calls are other wires, in the same cable, that may be carrying a transcontinental radio broadcast, or perhaps a television program. The Bell System Laboratories are constantly finding new uses for long-distance communication.

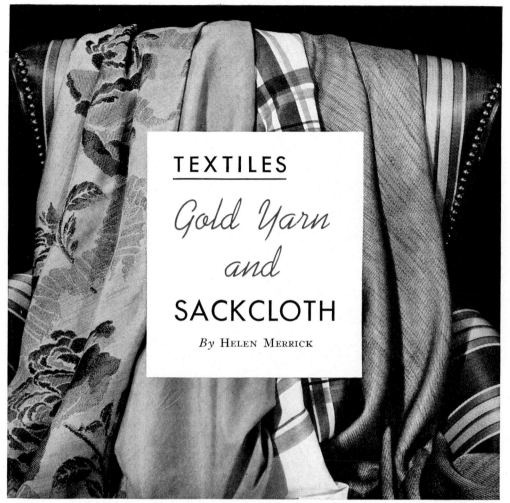

TEXTILES

Gold Yarn and SACKCLOTH

By HELEN MERRICK

ALMOST any kind of fiber is apt to turn up in textiles, these days. The gleaming threads in some of the loveliest fabrics may be the same kind of metal as your mother's frying pan, or they may be plastics like your bathroom tumbler. We have become familiar with nylon and rayon—even Fiberglass—as well as cotton, linen, silk and wool; and now metals and plastics are taking to the loom.

Lurex is a plastic-coated metallic fiber, or yarn, that won't tarnish. It gives upholstery materials great elegance, as in a black twill (a twill weave has a diagonal line) with a gold stripe of Lurex. Such a fabric would make an Empire sofa, with its rolled arms, doubly handsome, and the stripe would stay bright. In one printed drapery material sil-ver metallic threads are used with gray, yellow, orange and green. Metallic yarns may be used to point up a single color—gold threads match gold wool, or cotton or rayon, and silver may be used with gray-blue—so that you catch just a glint of the metal and must examine the fabric closely to see what it really is.

A few textiles have been made entirely of woven plastic, such as Lumarith. They are rather stiff and are more suitable for upholstery—or place mats. The first fabrics that were made of glass yarn crushed like linen, but some Fiberglass materials have been given a new finish which makes them softer and less likely to wrinkle.

Polyplastex is a new combination of glass fibers and plastic which has a number of

367

"Mother made these play clothes for us from dyed cotton bags. Aren't they pretty?"

uses, from lampshades to wall panels. Variations of it, depending on how the glass fibers are swirled and the thickness of the plastic, go by the names of Synspun, Syncurl, Synskyn and so on.

There are only a few yarns of really new materials, however, and these few may not get into large-scale production for a year or two. In August 1948 the Du Pont company announced that it had made a synthetic yarn which would fill the gap between nylon and rayon. The new yarn, described as "nylon's brother," is named Orlon. Nylon is made from coal tar, petroleum or even corncobs or oat hulls; and rayon, from wood pulp or cotton or other cellulose. Orlon is manufactured from natural gas or petroleum, or both. It will be less expensive than nylon, and stronger than rayon is when damp. Since Orlon is especially resistant to sunlight, it will have many outdoor uses, such as auto tops, awnings and sails. It doesn't take color as well as other textiles, but is easily washed.

Another new yarn, called Vicara, has been developed from peanuts, though little information about its qualities is yet available.

Ramie, a woody fiber from a tropical Asi-

atic plant, has been known in the textile industry for some years, usually under the name of "China grass." It makes a silky, very strong yarn, though it is unfamiliar to the general public because more often it has been combined with other yarns—to weight silk, for instance. Before the war ramie fiber was imported from the Far East. The process of preparing it for market was extremely tedious, and this made production in America far too costly. Ramie is now being grown successfully in the Florida Everglades, and improved methods have been developed for preparing the fiber. So you may be hearing more of ramie textiles in the next few years.

Nylon Is Given a Permanent Wave

We have all become familiar with the filmy stockings made of nylon, and perhaps your toothbrush has nylon bristles or your mother may have a slip or blouse made of nylon fabric. Up until the past year nylon yarn was produced in very long threads. Now nylon thread can be given a permanent wave and cut into lengths of a few inches, called staple, so that it can be handled like wool or cotton. Wool-like nylon is being woven into thick, extremely long-wearing rugs and knitted into fluffy sweaters and quick-drying socks. The sweaters do not need to be blocked after washing: Garments knitted of this nylon yarn are also surprisingly warm, because in making the fiber tiny locked-in air cells are created—and air is a poor conductor of heat. Also on the market are felt, velvet and upholstery fabrics made entirely of nylon, with all its wonderful resistance to wear and soiling.

Staple nylon can be used in combination with other short fibers. Even a little nylon with wool makes a material much stronger than if it were wool alone. Combined with cotton, nylon gives the fabric greater strength and resistance to rubbing without losing the softness of cotton.

Textile experts have also produced an extremely sheer curtain fabric made of nylon. It is as fine and filmy as silk gauze and, though yet quite expensive, is far more practical than it looks.

Upholstery fabrics with a homespun, somewhat rough appearance (decorators call it a "textured" look) are quite popular today. In line with this trend is a new rayon yarn called "Thick and Thin"—which describes it exactly. A fabric of this yarn has a very irregular surface, which breaks up the light. This quality gives a material of a single shade of color the appearance of having two shades. Too, the texture brings out woven stripes more distinctly. "Thick and Thin" yarn combines well with other yarns. In one taffeta, for instance, "Thick and Thin" is used as the filling (the cross threads) on a cotton warp (the lengthwise threads).

The interest in texture is seen in other upholstery fabrics, in all price ranges. It may be found in a basket weave, rather open with fairly thick yarn; a nubby bouclé, in which the yarn is knotty; and other fancy weaves. Some of these materials have especially clear colors because the yarn is bleached before it is dyed.

Your mother probably has some damask napkins and tablecloths, or you may have seen them in stores. The flat pattern of damask is made by using two weaves—perhaps a twill pattern on a satin ground. In some new damasks for upholstery, textured yarns are used for the pattern against the plain satin-weave ground. Pattern and ground may also be in contrasting colors, and the fabric can be reversed. A lovely example of this kind of damask has a medium-sized Chinese design in a textured yarn of yellow on a green satin-weave ground. This side of the fabric is subdued in color. Turn it over, however, and you have a gay fabric which is mostly bright yellow, with a delicate design in green.

Another new weave for upholstery uses a mixture of spun rayon and cotton yarn in two contrasting colors. The two kinds of yarn are woven together so that the over-all color effect changes according to the other colors with which the fabric is used.

Wool floor covering is often textured today. One kind of wool carpet has the shaggy look of a fine hand-loomed tweed fabric. Another kind of carpet has different pile levels; the design is made by clipping only part of the pile, leaving the rest looped. (The pile of a rug or carpet is produced by an extra set of filling yarns that form raised loops.) This carpet looks as if it had been 'built" rather than woven.

A Wardrobe or Draperies "in the Bag"

For a number of years farm women have been making dish towels and underclothes from cotton feed bags. Such bags were usually white or cream-colored, but they are now being manufactured in an astonishing array of well-designed prints. A new wardrobe for a girl or a woman, or new draperies for the farmhouse living room, may be "in the bag." The brand name on the sacks is in wash-out inks or they may have paper labels, easily removed. It is also easy to rip out the thread with which the bags are sewed together. A hundred-pound bag contains about one and a quarter yards of material, and four bags will make a dress. Too, the plain white or cream-colored sacks take dyes very well. The print bags are the most popular, however, and the designs range from florals and cherubic figures to stripes and checks, and even Currier and Ives prints. Would you ever guess that the play clothes in the photograph had been made from cotton sacks?

The most beautiful, and most expensive, printed fabrics today are usually screen prints; and screen printing is a slow process requiring highly skilled labor. Mass-production printed materials are usually roller prints, in which the design is printed on the goods by copper rollers with the design engraved. There is a separate roller for each color. Now textile experts and photographers are working on a method of printing textiles somewhat as a photograph is printed on film. This would give print designers an even wider field; though at the present stage of development, it is only a hint for the future.

A textured wool floor covering. The long tufts are woven fast and will not shed.

FRED ELDEAN ORGANIZATION, INC.

THEATERS FOR

No grownups admitted without a little boy or girl! Adult actors bring story-book people to life in such plays as these, where the bad Witch captures Hansel and Grethel; the Wolf almost gets Little Red Riding-Hood; and the Giant and his wife read fairy tales in *The Golden Apple*.

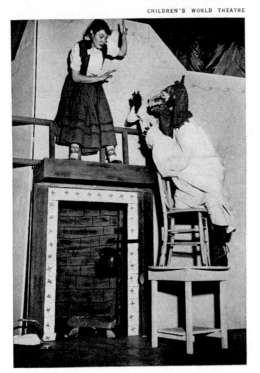

CHILDREN'S THEATRE, FORT WAYNE

CHILDREN

Peter, Peter, pumpkin-eater, and his wife welcome their friends to the new pumpkin-shell home, in the play based on the beloved and famous old Mother Goose nursery rime.

Aladdin is lucky, as anyone can see, for a genie as wonderful as this one would naturally be able to grant all his requests. For Aladdin, he brings riches and a palace.

GOODMAN MEMORIAL THEATRE, CHICAGO

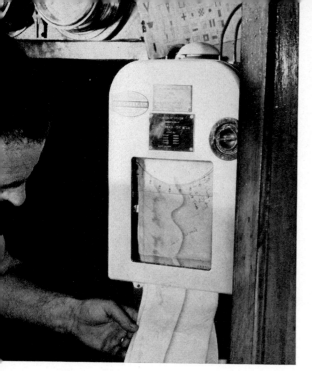

they make are beyond the range of your human hearing. These sounds can, however, be detected with special instruments.

These strange sounds which are too high for you to hear are called ultrasonics. "Ultra" means beyond, and "sonic" refers to sound. Ultrasonic waves vibrate so rapidly that they produce sounds too high for the human ear. Ultrasonics is also the name of the science which studies this type of sound.

How will this science of ultrasonics affect our lives? Let us take a peek into a laboratory where scientists are busy finding out what they can do with ultrasonic waves. The tubes of a strange-looking apparatus glow brightly. A peculiar humming noise grows louder and louder as more electrical current is fed into the large coils of the machine. On a table at one side is a small dish of oil connected underneath by wires to the complicated maze of apparatus that is spread around the room. Suddenly the surface of the oil in the dish trembles. It rises slowly and

Ultrasonics

By Sir Edward Victor Appleton
English Physicist and Nobel Prize Winner

O N a summer's day the sunny meadows are filled with sounds of life. Grasshoppers and crickets shrill their cheerful calls from their own special grass blades, and the hot air is awhir with the noise of tiny voices, high and thin. Many thousands of these little creatures are singing songs which you do not hear; the sounds

forms a mound. The force causing the oil to rise is so powerful and violent that in a short time the oil bubbles and froths like a tiny volcano. Drops of oil shoot from the mound and rise to a height of twelve inches.

Although we find it hard to believe, we learn that this disturbance is being caused by waves of sound. We hear nothing, however, for these waves are ultrasonic, beyond the reach of our ears. At the bottom of the dish lies a small metal plate. It appears perfectly still, but actually it is moving a tiny distance up and down through the oil hundreds of thousands of times a second. This moving metal plate is sending out inaudible sound-waves.

A small glass rod, pointed at one end, is passed through the oil from above and touches the metal plate. If we hold a piece of wood against the rod, we soon see a spiral of smoke curling upward. In a few moments the vibrations transmitted to the glass rod by the metal plate have burned a hole completely through the wood. All of this is done by noiseless sound.

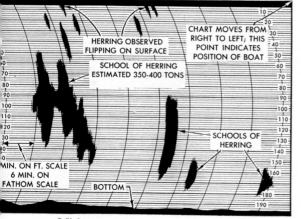

CHART MOVES FROM RIGHT TO LEFT; THIS POINT INDICATES POSITION OF BOAT

HERRING OBSERVED FLIPPING ON SURFACE

SCHOOL OF HERRING ESTIMATED 350-400 TONS

SCHOOLS OF HERRING

MIN. ON FT. SCALE
6 MIN. ON FATHOM SCALE

BOTTOM

To understand how these powerful, silent waves of sound work we must first understand the nature of the ordinary sounds which we hear constantly.

Every day we hear the sound of electric bells ringing—doorbells and telephone bells, for instance. When an electric bell rings, many things happen. First, the tiny clapper beats vigorously against the side of the bell, making it vibrate back and forth. The vibrations of the bell set up a disturbance among the molecules in the surrounding air, causing them to move back and forth in step with these vibrations. As the side of the bell vibrates outward, it pushes the air molecules away from the bell. As it vibrates back to its original position, the molecules of air dart back to fill up the space. The molecules strike their neighbors and set them in motion, back and forth. Each molecule passes on its motion to the next molecule, forming a moving wave of air. You know what happens when you throw a pebble into a pool of water. Waves, or ripples, move outward in ever larger circles, starting from the spot where the pebble hit the water. The water itself is not moving outward, but each particle of water pushes against the next particle. This motion forms a wave. In much the same way, a moving wave of air travels from the bell, and finally, when the wave of air reaches your ear, you hear the ringing of the bell.

The molecules of air that strike against your ear drums are not the same ones that were first set in motion by the bell. Each one of the billions of air molecules set in motion by the vibrations of the ringing bell has passed this motion on to its neighbors.

Seining boats, like those below, often carry depth recorders (upper left) which show the presence of solid objects between the ships and the ocean floor. A sonic beam is reflected from any solid object in its path. Chart shows schools of herring.

BOTH PHOTOS, IMPERIAL OIL LIMITED. DIAGRAM, BENDIX-MARINE SKETCH: COURTESY POPULAR MECHANICS MAGAZINE

Three things are necessary for the creation of sound. There must be vibrations from the source of the sound—a bell, a violin string, a riveting machine—to set the air molecules in motion. There must be a medium—air, for instance—to carry the sound-waves as they are formed. These waves can also move through liquids and through solids. If you were to ring a bell in a vacuum, however, you would hear nothing, for in a vacuum there are no molecules to carry the sound to your ears. Last, but no less important, there must be a receiver—perhaps your own ear—to hear the sound. Scientists use very special and delicate receivers to detect those sounds which are beyond the range of human hearing.

Sound-waves carry energy, although the amount of energy or force is usually very small. Imagine a million people in an enormous hall, all talking steadily. If all of their

Ultrasonic waves homogenize milk, breaking it up into fine particles, in this oscillator.

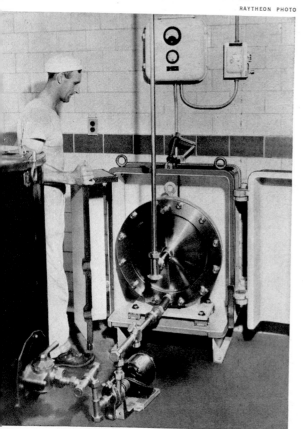

voice energy could be converted into heat, they would have to talk constantly for an hour and a half to create enough energy to heat a single cup of tea!

Sound Does Not Always Travel at the Same Rate of Speed

Waves of sound travel very rapidly. In air at normal temperatures the speed of sound is 1,120 feet a second, but with changes in temperature the speed varies. In cold air sound travels more slowly than in warm air. The speed of sound is also affected by the density and elasticity ("spring") of the substance through which it is passing. Sound travels about four times as fast through water as it does through air, and almost fifteen times as fast through steel.

Why are some sounds high, and others low? In other words, why do they differ in pitch? This quality of a sound depends on how rapidly the object (the source of the sound) vibrates. The speed of the vibrations is called the sound's frequency. An object which vibrates more rapidly than another will give out a higher sound. The human ear can hear sounds with frequencies anywhere from 20 to 20,000 times a second. Sounds which come within this range of frequencies are said to be within the audible range of sound. Middle C on your piano has a frequency of 256 vibrations a second, while the A string of the violin, to which all the instruments of an orchestra are tuned, vibrates 440 times a second.

Some Sounds Are Too High to Hear, Some Are Too Low

Sounds that vibrate less than 20 times a second are too low in pitch for the average human ear to hear. They are said to be in the sub-audible range. Sounds that vibrate more than 20,000 times a second—ultrasonics—are too high in pitch for us to hear. Ultrasonic sounds are sometimes called supersonic sounds. In these days of jet-propelled planes and rockets, however, the word "supersonic" is more commonly used to describe speeds greater than that of sound. An airplane that travels faster than the speed of sound is said to travel at supersonic speeds.

Certain meadow grasshoppers make sounds that vibrate 40,000 times a second. Bats give high-pitched squeaks, some of which we can hear, although others are in the ultrasonic range. Scientists believe that

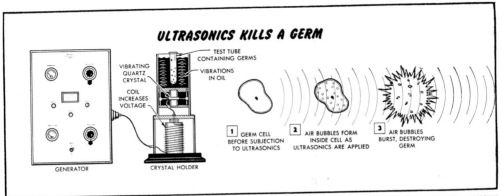

ULTRASONICS KILLS A GERM

TEST TUBE CONTAINING GERMS

VIBRATING QUARTZ CRYSTAL

VIBRATIONS IN OIL

COIL INCREASES VOLTAGE

1 GERM CELL BEFORE SUBJECTION TO ULTRASONICS

2 AIR BUBBLES FORM INSIDE CELL AS ULTRASONICS ARE APPLIED

3 AIR BUBBLES BURST, DESTROYING GERM

GENERATOR

CRYSTAL HOLDER

COURTESY, POPULAR MECHANICS MAGAZINE

Ultrasonic vibrations create bubbles inside germs, which are killed when bubbles burst.

these inaudible squeaks, which they have detected in the laboratory, guide the bats past obstacles in their paths when they are flying through pitch-black caves. The bats can tell how near the obstacles are by the rapidity with which the echo of the squeak comes back to them.

If you have a pet dog, you may perhaps own one of the "silent" whistles which will call your dog to your side, but which you yourself can not hear. Its notes are so high that they are in the ultrasonic range. These notes are easily heard by dogs, for their ears have a wider range than ours.

The first man to make practical use of ultrasonic waves was Professor Paul Langevin, a French scientist. During the first World War, Professor Langevin and his staff of assistants worked in a closely guarded building on the water front of Toulon, the great French naval base. Here they perfected an instrument that created ultrasonic waves which sent powerful bursts of inaudible sound into the sea. These bursts of sound traveled in straight narrow paths like beams of light. When the sound-waves struck an obstacle, like the hull of a submarine, an echo traveled back. Professor Langevin used a large tank of sea water for some of his experiments. When the ultrasonic waves passed through the tank, schools of small fish swimming through the beam of the sound-waves were killed. Millions of tiny air bubbles formed instantly in the tank and rose to the surface of the water. When one of the scientists held his hand in the path of the powerful ultrasonic waves, he felt intense pain, as though his bones were being heated. After the war two Canadian scientists used Pro-

fessor Langevin's discoveries in a device for detecting treacherous icebergs and submerged reefs. Here, as in the case of the bats in the dark caves, the obstacles could be detected by the reflected echoes.

You are probably wondering how men produce ultrasonic waves. In 1880 the Curie brothers, Pierre and Jacques, discovered that a quartz crystal cut in a special way would generate an electric voltage if pressure were applied to it. It was also found that if an alternating voltage were applied to it, the crystal would expand and contract in rhythm with the alternations of the voltage. This regular rhythm is used today in most of the machines that produce ultrasonic waves, both in industry and in scientific laboratories. Scientists also use other types of instruments to create these waves. One is a kind of super-siren, built on the same general principle as the silent dog whistle.

Each time the alternating voltage in the quartz-crystal type of ultrasonic generator changes direction, the crystal expands or contracts. This, in turn, causes small metal plates fastened to the crystal to move up and down. Usually the crystal and the metal plates are immersed in a dish of light oil, the medium which transmits the sound-waves.

We have seen that ordinary sound-waves carry little energy. Why, then, are ultrasonic waves so powerful? The answer can be found in the up and down motion of the metal plates on either side of the quartz crystal. These plates move through very tiny distances that can be measured in ten-thousandths of an inch. They change their direction hundreds of thousands of times a second, however, and move at enormous speeds. A

375

body shooting into space at such speeds would be about a million miles away in ten seconds.

Scientists and engineers are using these powerful ultrasonic waves in strange and fascinating ways. A machine called the reflectoscope shoots short bursts of inaudible sound into a steel bar. The sound echoes are reflected back from irregularities in the bar and are flashed on a cathode-ray screen, a special kind of fluorescent screen. Any irregularity or defect in the metal is instantly shown up by the position of the sound echo on the screen.

Ultrasonic Devices Help to Keep Air Free of Smoke and Fog

Plants manufacturing lampblack, which is used in making varnishes, paints and certain kinds of ink, are installing ultrasonic generators in their chimney flues. The energetic vibrations of the ultrasonic waves push the lampblack particles together and cause them to roll back down the chimney instead of escaping to the outside air. Fog and mist around airports and harbors can also be cleared by ultrasonics. In time, perhaps, these strange waves will be used in clearing large industrial areas of smoke and soot.

Sonar Reveals the Presence of Fish or Submarines—Gives Depth of Sea

During World War II an under-water sound device called sonar played an important part in halting the attacks of German submarines. Sonar was based on the same principles as those used by Professor Langevin in World War I. Ultrasonic waves were sent out into the sea. When they struck a submarine, an echo bounced back to the receiving apparatus. The length of time between the original sending of the ultrasonic waves and the return of the echo gave the submarine's distance and its position. In much the same way navigators can determine the depth of the ocean, or obtain a "sounding." A beam of sound is directed down to the ocean floor. The depth of the water can be determined by the length of time taken by the sound impulse on its trip down and its return trip as an echo. The new sonar instruments are so sensitive that they can detect the presence of schools of fish. Some up-to-date fishermen cruise about in boats equipped with ultrasonic apparatus, which guides them to the best fishing grounds.

Sonar is so sensitive that during the war submarine hunters were somewhat confused by the unexpected ultrasonic noises made by shrimps in the depths of the sea.

Ultrasonic Waves Have Many Astonishing Uses

Biologists found that the powerful ultrasonic waves actually shake living cells to pieces. Small fish, frogs and even mice have been killed by the beams of silent sound. Milk exposed to ultrasonic waves is almost completely pasteurized in a few seconds.

In England, ultrasonics is leading the way to quicker and better laundering. The ultrasonic waves break the electrical attraction that binds dirt to fabrics and shake the grime loose from the clothes.

American and Russian plant scientists have treated seeds with silent sound. The Russians reported that potato plants flowered a week earlier and showed crop increases up to 50 per cent more than did the untreated plants.

Ultrasonic waves may also take the place of the surgeon's knives and scalpels in certain types of operations. Doctors at Columbia University ground the quartz crystals for ultrasonic generators so that the sound-waves could be focused on a particular spot inside the brain of a dog or a cat. The energy of such a concentrated sound-beam can be 150 times as great as that of an unfocused beam. The highly concentrated beam is able to destroy a selected area of the brain in a few seconds. A brain operation is usually a long and delicate one, but with ultrasonics it would be over almost before it started.

These Strange Waves of Noiseless Sound Affect Human Beings

Ultrasonic waves sometimes have strange and startling effects on human beings. If you were to grasp a glass which was in contact with the rapidly vibrating metal plates, your fingers would be severely burned. If you stood in the path of the waves, you would feel confused and depressed, and you would lose control of your movements. A mathematician reported that for several days after she was exposed to silent sound, she was unable to work out even the simplest arithmetic problems.

As yet we know only a few of the uses that will surely be made of ultrasonics as time goes on.

The UNION of SOUTH AFRICA

UNION OF SOUTH AFRICA GOVERNMENT INFORMATION OFFICE

The veld farms seem lost in the vast golden grassland, broken by strange, flat-topped hills.

By CLAIRE NEIKIND

Journalist and Foreign Correspondent

THE Union of South Africa is like a buckle at the waist of the Southern Hemisphere, where the Indian Ocean meets the Atlantic. Land of the legendary Cape of Good Hope and its Flying Dutchman, it is a buccaneer country of gold and diamonds, jungle beasts and wind-swept veld.

For four centuries white men have struggled for a foothold in its uncharted wilderness and, after unimaginable hardship, have built it into the most modern nation on the African continent.

Although it is a vast country with almost 1,000,000 square miles of territory, its population is less than 11,000,000. This is partly because large tracts of land are uninhabitable, like the Kalihari Desert, and the rocky mountain country of the northeast, with its great peaks, such as Giant's Castle, over 10,000 feet high.

Throughout its four provinces—the Cape, Transvaal, Natal and the Orange Free State —South Africa is a study in contrasts between ancient African ritual and Western civilization. There are huge stretches of land where the only sign of man's habitation is the thatch-roofed native kraal. Yet in the same country, there are cities like Johannesburg, capital of the Transvaal and heart of the gold-mining industry, filled with twentieth-century skyscrapers, trolley cars and all the busy industrial and commercial life of a city like Pittsburgh or Toronto.

In spite of the inroads of Western civilization, however, much of the wild spirit of

377

Delicate morsels of fish, fresh from Cape Town trawlers, are expertly fried to a golden brown.

Africa remains in the countryside. South Africa still has its exotic trees, such as the wild banana and red milkwood, the kaffir-boom and the baobab, the mahogany and the white pear. It still has its High Veld in Basutoland, blanketed with pink, white and mauve cosmos and aloes. It still abounds in wild creatures—antelope and lion, crocodile and springbuck, black wildebeest and long-tailed sugar bird.

Even though the white man has almost wiped them out, there are also still a few quagga and white rhinoceroses, leopards in the mountain *kloofs,* cobras and deadly imambas, zebras and elephants. Indeed, a few hours' drive from Johannesburg will bring you to the Kruger National Game Reserve, where many of these animals roam free and can be watched safely through your automobile window.

Europeans were drawn there as long ago as 1600, a century after Vasco da Gama discovered the Cape of Good Hope. They came with the Dutch East India Company and made Cape Town a key way-station along the east-west trade routes. The first settlers were Dutch, and these were soon joined by French Huguenot refugees who quickly mixed with the Dutch.

Two hundred years later the British invaded the country and annexed it, and the Dutch "free burghers," or Boers, fled northward in the Great Trek through territory that was later to form part of the Union. They were stopped at the Great Fish River, where they met African tribes roaming downward, and fought great wars with the

Bantus, and with such tribes as the Tembus, Swazis and Zulus. These were finally put down in 1838, in the famous battle with the Zulu chief Dingan. This victory is even now celebrated throughout South Africa as Dingan's Day. From then on, the white man's rule was firmly established.

Some time later, in 1870, South Africa's greatest riches were discovered. The world's largest diamond mines were found at Kimberley. Ten years later the gold rush began on the Witwatersrand at Johannesburg. From these mines South Africa was destined to supply the world with three-quarters of all its gold.

It was during these years that the renowned diamond king and statesman, Cecil Rhodes, began his efforts to unite the four colonies into one nation. His dream was not realized until the bloody Boer War had been fought between the Dutch and British colonists, stirring up passions all over the Western world. In 1910, some years after the British won, South Africa was officially united and became a dominion of the British Empire.

South Africa today is important for other things besides gold and diamonds. Maize, wheat, kaffir corn or sorghum, and subtropical fruits such as pineapples, papaws and mangoes are the principal crops. Wool and mohair and dairy products come from her great sheep and cattle farms. Recently she has developed automobile-assembly plants, chemical and textile factories and an iron-and-steel industry. In addition, she has been developing her resources of silver, asbestos, corundum, platinum, tin and copper.

Under the influence of the Europeans, the descendants of the native tribes have learned many Western ways. Nevertheless, they have preserved many of their ancient customs to this day. Even in the cities, native workers, on their days off, still perform their exciting rhythmic tribal dances, with home-made wind instruments and brilliant colored feathers and beads. However, their contact with Europeans has not been a very happy one for either group. One of South Africa's great problems is the friction between the two million Europeans and nine million natives, colored peoples and Asiatics. At the heart of this is the dissatisfaction of the natives with their lot when it is contrasted with the way Europeans live. Native wages are extremely low, housing conditions are bad, and facilities for education of native children are seriously limited. There are also grave health problems, with a high rate of tuberculosis.

In recent days, this conflict has revolved around the right to vote, since none but a handful of the colored people in the Cape Province are represented in South Africa's Parliament.

The battle has been particularly sharp between the Europeans and the Indians, of whom there are about 225,000, mostly in and around Durban, in the province of Natal. The majority of these were brought over from India at the turn of the century, to work the sugar plantations as indentured servants. It was in fighting for their rights to full equality that Mohandas Gandhi, then a young lawyer in South Africa, first developed his famous "passive resistance" campaigns.

In the last two years, the matter of Indian rights has become important enough to be taken up in the councils of the United Nations.

Smuts, the Long-loved Leader, Is Finally Defeated

There is some friction, too, between the Dutch Boers and the British, as there has been since before the Boer War. Although the Boers outnumber the British slightly, they have been governed for many years by a mainly British party, the United party, led by Field Marshal Jan Christiaan Smuts. General Smuts is a Boer by birth, but his leadership as prime minister was based on his deep loyalty to the British Crown.

In the summer of 1948, however, the venerable Prime Minister, who is world-famous as a statesman and diplomat, was defeated for re-election by the predominantly Boer Nationalist party. This party is led by Daniel François Malan, who has now become the prime minister.

The main program of the Nationalist party was greater independence of Britain and more attention to the Afrikaans language and culture in the nation. This language is used chiefly by the Boers and is, of course, a form of Dutch. It is one of the country's two official languages, the other being English.

The election caused some concern in the Western world, not only because of the defeat of General Smuts, who is highly thought of throughout the world, but also because of South Africa's increased military importance. In the last war, because of her geographic location, she became of vital importance to the Allies' defense and supply plans. Since then, the discovery of uranium there has made her even more valuable.

Since many of the Dutch population were against South Africa's entry into World War II, on the side of the Allies, the fact that the Nationalist party is now in control has been considered unfortunate by Western nations.

Contented monarch! Lions and many other wild beasts roam at will in Kruger National Park.

UN scientists test water for malaria larvae.

"PEACE on earth, good will to men"—nearly two thousand years have passed since those words first echoed in men's hearts, yet the world is still troubled with the misunderstanding, fear and hatred that lead to war. Through all the long centuries wise and earnest men have worked to make peace and good will living realities among the peoples of the earth. Often their efforts have failed. Sometimes they have made mistakes. Nevertheless the struggle has been worth while. People and nations everywhere have become more and more aware of the need for settling disputes in a peaceful way. The terrible destructiveness of modern warfare has made people even more anxious for peace and security and the well-being of all humanity. That is why, at the end of the second World War, the United Nations was formed.

People are sometimes impatient because the United Nations has not yet been able to solve the world's problems and bring about a lasting peace. We must realize, however, that a state of affairs that has existed for thousands of years can not be completely changed in three years. It is going to be a slow, difficult job, needing great patience and the co-operation of the governments and people of all the countries.

THE UNITED NATIONS AND

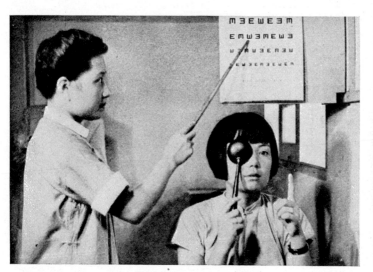

The United Nations' services to mankind include setting up eye clinics in China, rebuilding

In addition to the basic aim—peace among the nations—the United Nations has planned and is carrying out a tremendous program to improve the lives of people everywhere. Divisions and agencies of the United Nations are concerned with health, education, child welfare and many other matters that are vital to the welfare of human beings. Let us see what has been accomplished so far in some of these fields.

Among the most urgent needs created by the war was that of relief for the devastated countries. While immediate aid had to be rushed to these countries, plans had to be made for more permanent assistance. It was not enough to feed the starving and shelter the homeless. Help was needed to rebuild the lives, industries and general welfare of the people. The United Nations has had studies made of conditions in these countries, both in Europe and in Asia, and of their need for outside assistance. The General Assembly of the United Nations has called upon member countries to help meet these needs, and the machinery has been set up to enable the members to work together smoothly and without overlapping.

An Economic Commission for Europe and one for Asia and the Far East are both at work helping to solve the economic problems of the various regions in those parts of the world. One thing these commissions do is to study the resources that each country has and to advise the different governments on the best ways to use them. For example, the Economic Commission for Europe has brought about an agreement which is expected to help the transportation of goods in western Europe. For a period of six months, goods carried over roads and highways are to move between Czechoslovakia, Denmark, France, Italy, the Netherlands, Switzerland, Sweden and the western zones of Germany without being held up by frontiers.

The International Bank for Reconstruction and Development has arranged for loans to be made to several countries, including France, the Netherlands, Denmark and Luxemburg. This is for reconstruction purposes.

The United Nations Educational, Scientific and Cultural Organization—usually called UNESCO—has found out what the war-ruined countries need in the way of school textbooks and scientific equipment. A number of volunteer organizations are working through UNESCO to supply these much needed tools of education.

Still another problem that has been taken up is the development of the vast uncultivated areas in different parts of the world.

WORLD WELFARE

By Trygve Lie
*Secretary-General of the
United Nations*

bridges destroyed during the Japanese invasion and flying thousands of refugees to new homes.

A Child Writes to the United Nations . . .

A little Bulgarian girl was so happy over the sweet, fresh milk she and her sisters were receiving from the United Nations, that she wrote a thank-you poem. The poem is printed below, in Bulgarian as the little girl wrote it, and also in English.

Hurry up
Or there won't be any milk
If you delay . . .
There is fresh milk,
Drink it quickly, smoothly . . .
And thank the United Nations.
Through the open windows
The sun smiles upon us,
But in our bright room
A cloud of dust arises.
But we do not mind
For we know
That today we have drunk milk,
And we are thankful to
The United Nations.
All my little sisters and I
Are smiling today.
Again we thank
The United Nations!
Long live the United Nations!

For example, there are huge areas in Central and South America—jungle and forest and plain—which have been scarcely explored. Much of this land would be splendid for growing food and other necessary products. Other parts are rich in minerals. An Economic Commission for Latin America has been set up to advise and assist the governments of the various countries in this work. At the same time the Food and Agriculture Organization of the UN is already working out ways of using the wonderful forest resources of Latin America.

However, in spite of all that may be done in these fields, it is generally agreed that healthy international trade is needed to give real prosperity to the peoples of the world. The UN is therefore trying to get its member nations to make it easier to exchange goods among themselves and with outside countries. In 1947, 23 countries made agreements to lower tariffs on various important articles. Altogether, 123 different agreements were signed, dealing with more than 45,000 items. These agreements will affect more than 70 per cent of the world's export-import trade.

The UN Fulfills the World's Greatest Need by Feeding the Hungry

The greatest material need in the world today, however, is food. The General Assembly and the Economic and Social Council of the UN have advised governments to do everything possible to save and increase food supplies. The Food and Agriculture Organization, which has most to do with the problems of food and nutrition, has suggested that governments distribute scarce foodstuffs and fertilizers to those who need them most. Over 90 per cent of these suggestions have been carried out by the various governments.

One of the most important works of the United Nations is caring for the undernourished children of the countries that suffered in the war. For this purpose it has established the International Children's Emergency Fund. People in all walks of life, school children, churches, business concerns and many others besides the member governments have contributed to this fund. At the end of April 1948, the gifts and pledges amounted to about $57,300,000. The money was being used to help the governments give needed food to children in Albania, Austria, Bulgaria, Czechoslovakia, Finland, France, Greece, Hungary, Italy, Poland, Rumania and Yugoslavia. The first shipments of needed supplies had already been sent to China, and money had been set aside to help children in other parts of the Far East. Clothing as well as food is provided for the children. Besides all this, $4,000,000 has been set aside to fight the spread of tuberculosis among the undernourished children.

One of the saddest problems left by the war is that of the refugees and displaced persons. The United Nations has realized that as many as possible of these people should be returned to their homes. However, there are many who, for various reasons, do not want to go back, and for these new homes must be found. Therefore, in July 1947, the Preparatory Commission of the International Refugee Organization began to look after these homeless people. In the nine months following, about 71,900 were restored to their own countries, and new homes were found for 147,000.

Through the World Health Organization much is being done to fight the spread of epidemics. One of the most interesting and unusual of its efforts has to do with China. The water buffalo that the Chinese need to help cultivate their rice fields have been dying at the rate of a million a year from a disease called rinderpest. Of course, if the Chinese farmers should lose all their farm animals, they would not be able to produce the rice on which the people of China depend for food. The United Nations has set up a laboratory in Nanking, China, to make a serum that will control this disease. By 1948 plans had been made for using this serum on 15,000,-000 of these buffalo.

The International Labor Organization, which is now attached to the United Nations, has been concerned with working conditions ever since it was founded in 1919. In the last two years it has taken up such questions as social insurance, the organization of employment services, labor inspection and vocational guidance.

Working Toward a Freer and Fuller Life for All People

The United Nations has an even greater purpose than the physical well-being of humanity. Its ideal is that every human being may have the opportunity to live his or her life freely and fully. To help fulfill this ideal, an "International Bill of Human Rights" is being drawn up. After it is approved by the General Assembly, the member governments may enact laws adopting its provisions for their own countries. The human rights that it lists include the right to life, liberty and security of person; the right to fair trial; the right to a nationality; freedom of thought, conscience and worship; freedom of peaceful assembly; the right to work; and the right to social security.

All of these are only a few of the activities of the United Nations. UNESCO, for example, is working to promote friendship and understanding among the nations by having them exchange teachers and students, and by encouraging the people of each country to read the literature of other lands. The General Assembly has asked UNESCO to help governments with programs to teach the school children about the United Nations.

The United States

A RECORD OF THE YEAR

By Lawrence M. Levin

Twelve thousand people filled Convention Hall

WHEN America's victorious armies returned from World War II, they looked forward to a "brave new world" of peace and prosperity. In 1948—three years after the end of the war—the world still seemed to be a giant battlefield. Fierce fighting raged between Jews and Arabs in Palestine, between Moslems and Hindus in the Indian states of Kashmir and Hyderabad. There were civil wars in China, Greece, the Indonesian Republic, Korea, Peru and other areas.

Besides these shooting wars, there was a "cold war," in which the weapons were political propaganda and economic pressure. In this struggle, communist Russia and her allies faced the United States and the nations of western Europe. In our article on Europe in 1948 we tell you about this cold war. The chief issue was communism, which had already spread to almost all the countries of eastern Europe and which threatened to swamp the rest of the Continent. The United States played a very important part in the fight in 1948, particularly with its European Recovery Program.

This project began as a rather informal proposal. In June 1947, United States Secretary of State George C. Marshall had said that the United States would be willing to give aid on a large scale to the free peoples of Europe if they would do all in their power to help themselves. In its final form, the Marshall Plan, now called the European Recovery Program (ERP), aimed to supply aid only to the nations of western Europe. In carrying out this far-reaching program,

ACME

in Philadelphia, on the night of October 6, 1948, to hear a campaign speech by President Truman.

the United States, with the help of other Western-Hemisphere nations, proposed to supply both materials and money over a four-year period. The European countries benefiting from the program would contribute as much as they could to the common cause.

Congress Authorizes Relief Funds for Three European Nations

As an emergency relief measure, Congress appropriated $522,000,000 for France, Italy and Austria in December 1947. It was expected to approve the European Recovery Program in the regular session beginning January 6, 1948. But the ERP ran into difficulty in Congress. January and February passed, and still no action had been taken. The friends of the European Recovery Program were very much alarmed.

Toward the end of February, the democratic world was stunned when the Communists of Czechoslovakia seized power. They set up a new government, in which only Communists and those willing to work with them were represented. As time went on, it became clear that Czechoslovakia was becoming a communist state after the pattern of Soviet Russia. Communism had overwhelmed another country; when would its westward march stop?

Congress was now thoroughly aroused. On April 12, 1948, it passed a $6,098,000,000 Foreign Assistance Act. Of the amount in question, $5,300,000,000 was set aside for the first year of the European Recovery Program. Congress actually appropriated $5,-055,000,000 for the program. The sum was to be spent over a fifteen-month period; but, if the President so recommended, it could be spent in twelve months.

Before any country would be eligible for help under the European Recovery Program, it would have to sign a pact with the United States, with certain important provisions. (1) The country would agree to make itself self-supporting within the four-year period covered by the ERP. (2) It would balance its budget as soon as possible, stabilize its currency and lower its trade barriers. (3) It would make strategic materials (those necessary for war industry) available to the United States.

We tell you more about the European Recovery Program in the article on Europe in 1948. It proved to be a powerful weapon in

the cold war. By giving aid to the nations of western Europe, it served to prevent the spread of communism, for this movement flourishes particularly where there is great poverty and widespread discontent.

The cold war was carried on in many areas. The front even extended to the United States, where American Communists and other friends of Soviet Russia worked openly to bring about the failure of the European Recovery Program. One of the most striking skirmishes on the American front involved two Russian teachers, Mikhail Ivanovich Samarin and Mme. Oksana Stepanova Kasenkina. They taught in a school maintained by Russia for the children of her citizens living in New York City. When the time came for the two teachers to return to Russia, they disappeared.

On August 8, the New York TIMES published a letter written by Samarin, in which he denounced the Soviet Union. Several days later he turned up at a meeting of the House Un-American Activities Committee (August 12). After that he remained under the protection of the committee.

Members of the Russian Consulate in New York traced Mme. Kasenkina to a farm near Valley Cottage, New York—a place which housed a number of refugees from Russia. According to the official Russian version, Mme. Kasenkina had been dragged to this "den of bandits" after being drugged. According to those who lived at the farm, she had come there to seek refuge.

Mme. Kasenkina's Daring Escape from Her "Protectors"

The Russian officials brought Mme. Kasenkina to the Consulate in New York. Here she was protected from American kidnapers (Russian version) or kept prisoner (American version). Unfortunately for the Russian version, Mme. Kasenkina jumped from the third floor of the Consulate in an effort to escape. Badly hurt, she was brought to a New York hospital. Later, in an interview with representatives of the press, radio and newsreels, she said that she had determined never to return to Russia because she was very much opposed to the Soviet Government.

On August 19, the United States State Department ordered the recall of Consul General Jacob M. Lomakin, who had played an important part in the Kasenkina affair. The State Department claimed that Mr. Lomakin had made unjust charges against American officials; that he had hindered police investigation of the Kasenkina case; that he had defied the laws of the United States.

Russia retaliated by closing her two consulates in the United States—at New York and San Francisco. She demanded that America should give up her one Russian consulate at Vladivostok, and she put an end to plans for another at Leningrad. The Kasenkina affair marked a serious worsening of relations between the United States and the Soviet Union.

In view of the cold war, most Americans agreed that the country's defenses should be kept strong. But America's military leaders were not satisfied with existing conditions. It is true that the United States had over a million men under arms at all times in 1948—a huge peacetime force by American standards. But this big force had certain weaknesses. In a report issued on March 24, 1948, Secretary of Defense James V. Forrestal pointed out that, of the 544,000 men in the Army at that time, almost half were serving as occupation troops in the Far East, Germany, Austria and Trieste. Most of these men had insufficient military training. Thus, of the 98,000 men in Germany and Austria, only about 30,000 were available for combat.

As for the troops stationed in the United States, there was only one Army division that could take the field at a moment's notice—the 82nd Airborne. There were only two antiaircraft battalions in the United States, whereas forty were considered to be the minimum needed in case of enemy air attack.

Congress Acts to Strengthen the Nation's Defenses

Congress took several steps to strengthen the nation's defenses in 1948. It voted a budget of $10,516,727,413 for the period from July 1, 1948 to July 1, 1949. It also raised the man-power strength of the armed forces to 2,005,882. The Army was to have 837,000 of this total; the Navy and Marines, 666,882; the Air Force, 502,000. (By way of comparison, the actual strength of the armed services on June 1, 1948, was: Army, 548,000: Navy and Marines, 469,000; Air Force, 382,000.)

To provide enough recruits for America's war machine, Congress passed a draft bill on June 19, 1948. This measure provided for the induction of young men from 19 through 25

ACME

Soviet Consul General Lomakin reluctantly pauses to answer a reporter's questions.

years of age to serve for 21 months. It permitted 161,000 youths of 18 to enlist for one year, after which they would serve for 6 years in a reserve unit or in the National Guard. Most veterans of World War II were exempt from the draft; so were married men, men with dependents and certain others. College students were permitted to finish a school year before answering a draft call; high-school students were deferred until they graduated or reached the age of 21. Registration under the draft began on August 30.

America's military machine, then, was assured of enough funds and man-power, for the future at least. It was still hampered, however, by rivalry between the three armed services—the Army, the Navy and the Air Force. Though they were combined in a single Department of National Defense, they did not work together very harmoniously.

They all agreed that if war with Russia began, it might well be won in a comparatively short time by a knockout blow from the air. The men of the Air Force held that their arm of the service should be entrusted with this knockout blow. The Air Force, therefore, should be greatly strengthened and provided with adequate bases. The Army people agreed partly with this viewpoint. But they insisted that a big army would be necessary to capture and to hold air bases within

387

effective bombing distance. Navy men scoffed at the idea that Russia's big air force and her giant armies would let Americans establish and maintain bases at effective bombing range. They believed that the main striking force should consist of long-range bomb-

A cartoonist comments on the new draft law, under which many a young man in the 19–25 age group was measured for a new uniform.

ers based on giant aircraft carriers.

There were other matters of dispute. Would the Air Force play an important part in anti-submarine warfare, or would the Navy have complete charge of such a campaign? Would the Army be entrusted with landings on enemy territory; or would that duty be left to the Marine Corps?

The quarrel between the armed services became so bitter at last that Secretary of Defense Forrestal decided that something must be done. Therefore he called for a meeting of the Joint Chiefs of Staff at Key West, Florida, to discuss the situation. The meeting resulted in a series of compromises.

It was agreed that the Army would concern itself chiefly with fighting on land. The Navy would take over naval operations and would be in charge of anti-submarine warfare. Landing operations would be entrusted

to the Marine Corps. The Air Force would play the chief part in launching long-range bombing attacks on enemy territory.

The three services would support one another at all times. If it were advisable to do so, the Navy might operate long-range bombers taking off from the decks of large aircraft carriers. The Army would contribute men to combined operations by land and sea. All three services would help to defend the nation against air attack.

Air Force authorities had claimed originally that the nation's safety required a 70-group air force. The number of planes in each group would vary according to its nature. A long-range bomber group would consist of 30 or more planes, while a fighter group would have 75 planes.

After the Key West agreement, Secretary Forrestal proposed a 55-group air force in order to provide the proper balance between the various services. But Congress disregarded the Secretary's request. It voted in April to set up 70 groups, totalling 3,500 fighting aircraft. (This would be a peacetime figure; in war the number of planes would be greatly increased.)

Angered by this new triumph for the Air Force, the Navy went ahead with its plans for big navy bombers operating from giant aircraft carriers. In October 1948, it announced that it would soon begin construction of a 65,000-ton carrier capable of launching planes well over 50 tons in weight. This craft would be the largest vessel in naval history.

Two of the nation's three armed services changed leaders in 1948. On February 17, General of the Army Dwight D. Eisenhower turned over the post of chief of staff of the Army to General Omar N. Bradley. General Hoyt S. Vandenberg succeeded General Carl Spaatz as chief of staff of the Air Force on April 30. All four men had distinguished themselves greatly in World War II.

Western-Hemisphere Countries Remained Good Neighbors

During this war, the friendship between America and most of her Western-Hemisphere neighbors had proved to be a great asset. In 1948, with the cold war at its height, America continued to enjoy friendly relations with her sister-republics of the New World.

On April 30, 1948, these ties were strengthened when the representatives of twenty-one

American republics signed an agreement at Bogotá, Colombia. The delegates set up the charter of a new Western-Hemisphere body —the Organization of the American States. They agreed that they would settle any future disputes among themselves peacefully. They decided on full economic co-operation. They adopted an anti-communist resolution, stating that international communism would not be permitted in the Western Hemisphere.

The year 1948 was, on the whole, a period of prosperity in the United States. The wheels of industry kept turning rapidly, although the output of automobiles and certain other products was still not great enough to meet the public demand. Employment figures were higher than ever before; they remained well over the 60,000,000 mark. Yet all this prosperity was threatened by rising inflation. Except for several months in the course of

the year, most prices rose continuously.

Various factors contributed to this steady advance. An important one was an increase of wages in many industries—the third round of increases since the end of the war. Workers of the automobile industry led the way. They were followed by train workers, employees of the steel and meat-packing industries and many others. Labor leaders maintained that increasing prices made these wage rises necessary.

Government support of farm prices was another factor in inflation. When the prices of various important crops began to fall below 90 per cent of a certain level, called parity, the Government would sometimes buy up the surplus. In other cases it would take over the surplus in exchange for a loan amounting to 90 per cent of parity. The farmer could get his crop back by repaying the loan; or

Bidding farewell to the Army, General Eisenhower salutes the colors at Fort Myer, Virginia.

else he could keep the money and the Government would keep the crop. Later the Government would dispose of its holdings, generally at a loss.

The cost of this policy was great. In August 1948, Secretary of Agriculture Charles F. Brannan informed the Senate Banking Committee that the Government had lost $170,169,000 because of its support of potato prices during the 1943–47 crop years. Of course the nation's taxpayers had to make good these losses. In other words, the consuming public was taxed for the privilege of continuing to pay high prices for food!

The High Cost of Living Is a Growing Problem

The rearmament program and the European Recovery Program were not as important factors in the high cost of living as those which we have just mentioned. Yet they contributed to it. Furthermore, most people agreed that as these programs got well under way, their effect upon the cost of living would become increasingly greater.

Could anything be done to check the rising tide of inflation? President Truman believed that the answer was "Yes." In January, he urged Congress to carry out a far-reaching anti-inflation program; it would involve price control, rationing, fair distribution of raw materials and government control of credit. He also urged Congress to substitute a "flexible" program of farm-price support instead of setting up the fixed rate of 90 per cent of parity. Congress did not act upon any of these suggestions in the regular session.

Again President Truman pressed for anti-inflation measures in the special session of Congress that began July 26. This time Congress passed a very mild anti-inflation bill. The measure gave the President authority to set up restrictions on consumer credit and to tighten credits by increasing the reserves which Federal Reserve banks were required to hold. President Truman signed the bill (August 16, 1948). He claimed, however, that it provided only a tiny fraction of the controls needed "to protect us from the inflationary dangers which threaten our prosperity."

Prices and wages went steadily upward in 1948; but, surprisingly enough, taxes came down. On March 24, Congress passed a law reducing individual income taxes considerably. President Truman protested. He claimed that the tax cut would "undermine the soundness of our Government's finances at a time when world peace depends upon the strength of the United States." He vetoed the bill; but Congress passed it over his veto on April 2 by wide margins in both houses.

Among the provisions of the new tax-reduction bill were the following: (1) Reductions ranged from 12.6 per cent in the lowest income brackets to 5 per cent in the highest. (2) Persons making $600 or less were not required to pay any tax (the old rate was $500). (3) There was to be a $600 exemption for each dependent, instead of $500. (4) Taxpayers of 65 years of age or older and blind people could claim an additional exemption of $600. (5) Husbands and wives were permitted to split their joint income for taxation purposes. (Suppose the husband made $6,000 a year and the wife $2,000. The joint income would be $8,000; the husband and the wife could each pay the tax on $4,000. Thus the husband would not have to pay the increased rates for incomes over $5,000.) All of the above provisions were to be effective as of January 1, 1948.

The housing shortage continued to be a serious problem in 1948. In the special session that began on July 26, Congress passed a housing bill. It proposed to encourage private construction of low-cost housing by giving increased loans to builders. President Truman signed the bill on August 10, because he said that it would "be of some help." But he accused Congress of neglecting "those large groups of our people most in need of adequate housing—the people who are forced to live in disgraceful urban and rural [city and country] slums."

Congress Extends Federal Control of Rents

Because of the housing shortage many people felt that it was important to extend rent control, which was due to expire March 31, 1948; otherwise rents might rise steeply. Congress agreed. In March, it passed a bill extending Federal rent control for another year (through March 31, 1949).

The Taft-Hartley Act, passed over the President's veto on June 23, 1947, was very important in the labor picture throughout 1948. This measure had put a number of restraints upon organized labor (and, in certain cases, upon employers). Labor leaders had angrily denounced the act as a "slave labor bill" at the time that it was passed. They continued to attack the measure throughout 1948.

Certain provisions of the bill were upheld in the course of the year by the National Labor Relations Board (NLRB), or the courts, or both the NLRB and the courts. One of the most widely disputed sections of the measure was that which called upon labor leaders to present affidavits (sworn statements) that they did not belong to the Communist party. On June 21, the United States Supreme Court backed the "non-communist clause"; it refused to upset a lower-court decision which had declared that this clause was constitutional.

The NLRB and the courts upheld the provision of the Taft-Hartley Act which barred foremen and other supervisors from joining unions. They approved the ban on mass picketing. They backed the union-shop section of the act. This forbids the closed shop in new contracts; it provides, however, that a union shop is to be adopted if it is favored by a majority of the workers in a given factory or office. (Only union members can get work in a closed shop. Non-union workers may be hired in a union shop, but they must join the union within a certain fixed period.)

The Taft-Hartley Law Is Tested by the Courts

On the other hand the courts set aside the section of the Taft-Hartley Act which barred political spending by labor unions. In July 1947, the CIO (Congress of Industrial Organizations) had deliberately defied this ban. It had published an indorsement of a Maryland candidate for Congress in its official newspaper, the CIO NEWS. On February 11, 1948, a Federal Grand Jury indicted both the CIO and its president, Philip Murray, for violating the Taft-Hartley Act.

In the following month Federal Judge Ben Moore threw out the indictment. He declared that the Taft-Hartley Act's ban on union political spending was unconstitutional, since it deprived unions of the rights of free speech and a free press. In June, the Supreme Court upheld Justice Moore's decision.

At the end of 1948 opinions about the Taft-Hartley Act were sharply divided. However, it seemed pretty clear that the measure had not prevented unions from continuing their steady growth. In September 1948, a

Seventeen hundred tons of flour made up the first shipment to Greece under the ERP.

directory of unions issued by the Bureau of Labor Statistics proved that this was so. It showed that total union membership in the United States had risen to nearly 16,000,000 —an increase of 1,000,000 since the passage of the Taft-Hartley Act. The AFL (American Federation of Labor) had 7,200,000 members; the CIO, 6,000,000. There were 2,500,000 workers in independent unions.

The year 1948 saw bumper crops of wheat, corn, potatoes, cotton and other farm products. The American farmer had never been better off. For several years in succession there had been big crops and a world-wide demand for them. The Government had kept up farm prices with its crop-support program. Furthermore, the farmer faced the future without fear, for the government agency known as the Federal Crop Insurance Corporation protected him from losses caused by bad weather, insect pests and other factors.

There were several Cabinet changes in 1948. On April 22, Secretary of Commerce W. Averell Harriman resigned in order to become special United States representative abroad for the Economic Cooperation Administration. (This is the organization which administers the European Recovery Program.) President Truman named Charles Sawyer, a Cincinnati lawyer, as Mr. Harriman's successor. Secretary of Agriculture Clinton P. Anderson resigned on May 8 so that he might seek the Democratic nomination for senator in New Mexico. He was replaced by Charles F. Brannan, who had served as Assistant Secretary of Agriculture since 1944.

On June 10, Lewis B. Schwellenbach, who had been Secretary of Labor since 1945, passed away in Washington after a long illness. The post of Labor Secretary remained unfilled for two months. Finally on August 11, Maurice J. Tobin, former governor of Massachusetts, accepted President Truman's offer of the secretaryship.

The Eightieth Congress, in which the Republicans had a majority, did not get along well with Democratic President Truman. It failed to pass a number of measures which the President had proposed, and he denounced its record vigorously. In a speech in Spokane, Washington, on June 9, he referred to this Congress as "the worst we have ever had."

Republican leaders defended the record of the Eightieth Congress. They pointed out that it had backed the Administration's foreign policy and had thus enabled the country to present a solid front in the cold war. As for the Administration's domestic policy, Republican congressmen said that they did not feel called upon to support measures of which they did not approve.

The chief reason, perhaps, why the President and Congress did not work together harmoniously is that both were thinking and acting with the 1948 presidential elections in mind.

There Were Many Candidates for the Republican Nomination

In spite of a lively fight for the presidential nomination, the Republican party succeeded in preserving unity within the party. At the Republican convention, held in Philadelphia on June 21-25, the chief candidates were Governor Thomas E. Dewey of New York, Senator Robert A. Taft of Ohio, Governor Earl Warren of California and former Governor Harold E. Stassen of Minnesota. Governor Dewey showed unexpected strength and won on the third ballot by a unanimous vote. Governor Warren was selected as the Republican candidate for vice-president.

Long before the Democratic convention there was a serious revolt in the party. On December 29, 1947, Henry A. Wallace, who had been Democratic vice-president under Franklin D. Roosevelt from 1941 to 1945, announced that he would run for president in 1948 on a third-party platform of peace and abundance for all. He violently attacked both the older parties as war-minded and corrupt. Wallace's new political group came to be known as the Progressive party. It won the aid of such men as Senator Glen Taylor, who became its vice-presidential candidate, Representative Vito Marcantonio and Dr. Rex Tugwell, a former "brain truster" under Roosevelt. It also gained the enthusiastic support of the Communist party.

As time went on it seemed likely that there would be another split in the ranks of the Democrats. President Truman had asked Congress to adopt a civil rights program. This called for the abolition of poll taxes and the passing of legislation forbidding employers to discriminate against employees because of color or creed. Many Southerners denounced the program; they felt that it was an effort to change existing conditions in the South.

The Democrats Seemed at First to Be Divided

The Democratic party convention was to be held on July 12 at Philadelphia. As the time for the convention drew near, many Democrats from both North and South urged President Truman to withdraw from the race for the presidential nomination in the interest of party harmony. They urged that General of the Army Eisenhower should be drafted as a compromise candidate.

General Eisenhower had previously declined to enter the race for the Republican nomination. He now refused to run on the Democratic ticket. The anti-Truman movement within the Democratic party soon collapsed; from now on, the President's supporters had things all their own way. The convention put a strong civil rights plank in its platform, and President Truman was nominated on the first ballot, receiving 947½ votes out of a total of 1,234. Senator Alben W. Barkley of Kentucky was nominated for the vice-presidency.

Thirty-five delegates from Mississippi and Alabama had walked out of the convention after the passing of the civil rights plank. They formed the nucleus of a new party, made up of discontented Southern Democrats. These rebels met in Birmingham, Alabama, and on July 17 they nominated Governor J. Strom Thurmond of South Carolina for the presidency and Governor Fielding L. Wright of Mississippi for the vice-presidency on a states' rights platform. On July 24, the group adopted the name of States' Rights Democrats. The members of the new party were popularly known as Dixiecrats.

In the pre-election campaigning, President Truman continued to speak for the measures that he had tried to push through Congress: price controls, large-scale public housing, civil rights for all, Federal aid for education; he attacked the Eightieth Congress as wholeheartedly as ever. Dewey stressed the idea of national unity—of course, under Republican leadership. Thurmond spoke in favor of states' rights. Wallace urged the voters to give up the European Recovery Program and to come to terms with Soviet Russia.

The pre-election polls all seemed to point to a sweeping Republican victory and most of the nation's newspapers took such a victory more or less for granted. But the elections, held on November 2, provided one of the biggest upsets in the nation's history. Although the popular vote was fairly close, Truman won 303 electoral votes to 189 for Dewey. Thurmond failed to carry the "solid South"; he won only four states (Alabama, Louisiana, Mississippi and South Carolina) and he received 39 electoral votes. Wallace failed to win a single electoral vote, and he polled only about 2 per cent of the popular vote.

The Democrats won control of both houses of Congress by comfortable margins. They now had a 54-to-42 majority in the Senate and a 263-to-171 majority in the House. (The House also had a single American Labor party representative.) Besides, the Democrats had a majority of the governorships—30 to 18.

In the spirit of American sportsmanship, Governor Dewey congratulated President Truman on his election. "I urge all Americans," he said, "to unite behind you in support of every effort to keep our nation strong and free and to establish peace in the world." In this he had the hearty support of all patriotic Americans; for they realized how necessary national unity would be in the trying days that lay ahead for the whole world.

President Truman returns in triumph to Washington after his successful election campaign.

ACME

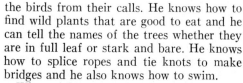

Boy Scouts of America

By ARTHUR A. SCHUCK, *Chief Scout Executive*

SCOUT training makes a boy skillful and able to take care of himself in all kinds of weather and in all kinds of country. A Boy Scout hikes over unexplored trails, knowing how to use his compass, how to follow a map or to make one for himself. With his pack on his back and brother Scouts at his side, he is ready for adventure.

He knows the animals by their tracks and the birds from their calls. He knows how to find wild plants that are good to eat and he can tell the names of the trees whether they are in full leaf or stark and bare. He knows how to splice ropes and tie knots to make bridges and he also knows how to swim.

When night comes, he sets up his tent or makes a shack of branches and grass. He builds his own fire to cook his meal or to keep warm, and he knows how to build it safely and to put it out when he should. To take care of himself and of others in case of injury, he also knows First Aid.

When a boy joins Scouting, he joins a world-wide club. The same day that he is hiking through the hills, the chances are that other Scouts in other countries are doing the same thing, for there are Scouts in almost every land in the world.

Many Scouts live in the war-torn countries, where life is still very difficult. So Cub Scouts, Boy Scouts and Senior Scouts helped them during the year, sending them gifts of money, food and uniforms through the World Friendship Fund.

Cub Scouts are boys 9, 10 and 11 years old. Boy Scouts are 12 and older. Senior Scouts are young men 15 years of age and up. Altogether, in 1948, more than a million and a half were members of the Boy Scouts of America.

Scouts belong to Scout Troops under a grown-up leader called the Scoutmaster. Five or more boys make a Scout Troop, and each Troop is made up of Patrols with boy Patrol Leaders. As few as two boys may start a Neighborhood Cub Den or a Neighborhood Patrol, or they can be Lone Scouts. Senior Scouting is for young men. They can learn about aviation in Air Scouting, advanced camping and exploration in Explorer Scout-

Food tastes good when you cook it over the blazing campfire in the lee of a shelter tent.

ing, or Seamanship in Sea Scouting. Each branch of Scouting has a uniform of its own. Cub Scouts wear blue and gold. Boy Scouts wear khaki. Senior Scouts have different uniforms according to what they are interested in.

Scouting in the United States became thirty-eight years old on February 8, 1948, and the birthday celebrations were held all week long. Another big celebration was the autumn Round-Up, when new boys were invited to join Scouting units. There were father-and-son hikes and dinners and parties. On a certain day in different communities, Scouts mobilized to hunt for a "lost" child. Of course this was not really a lost child, but the Scouts learned a lot about finding people who are lost in the woods or in the country and they had a fine time. At election time they helped to get out the vote. The climax of the Round-Up was a ceremonial for the new boys who had joined during the Round-Up.

"Camporees" and pilgrimages were made during the year to places of historic interest. One of the big ones in the East was held on October 16, when Scouts journeyed to the grave of President Theodore Roosevelt at Oyster Bay, Long Island.

Cub Scouts have three ranks—the Wolf, the Bear and the Lion. During the year three new books, named after these ranks, were published for Cub Scouts. These books, with their wonderful pictures, help them to learn many interesting things to do.

During the year, Cub Scouts learned a great deal. For instance:

1. SKILLS. Feats of skill, more difficult for each rank, such as climbing a pole, floating in the water, playing baseball, climbing a rope, jumping.

2. FLAGS. Knowing something of the history of our country's flag and how to display it correctly.

3. KEEPING STRONG. Knowing health rules and First Aid.

4. HELPING. At home, school, church or synagogue.

5. TOOLS. How to use a jackknife and make things with carpenter's tools.

6. COLLECTIONS. Rocks, maps, match covers and stamps.

7. SCRAP BOOKS. Making a neat hobby book with photographs, clippings and so forth.

8. KNOTS. How to tie several useful knots.

9. SAFETY. How to avoid accidents in the street and how to make one's home and backyard safe.

10. FAMILY FUN. Games, family walks, handicrafts and good times.

11. THE NEIGHBORHOOD. Knowing the schools, fire alarms, railroad stations, bus lines and interesting places.

12. READING. Getting to know good books and magazines, and how to take care of and repair them.

Boy Scouts of Canada

By Maj.-Gen. D. C. Spry, C.B.E., D.S.O., *Chief Executive Commissioner*

A TENT city of about 3,000 Boy Scouts will spring up near Ottawa this summer. Here, for one week, First Class Scouts from all parts of Canada, the United States and other countries of the world will meet, live together and take part in the first National Boy Scout Jamboree.

Ottawa was chosen as the site of the Jamboree to give Canadian Boy Scouts an opportunity to see their capital city, as well as to take part in the program. Small groups of Scouts from other countries have been invited to attend—including a group of fifty representing all parts of the United States.

One of the most distinguished visitors expected to be present is the Right Honorable Viscount Alexander of Tunis, governor-general of Canada and chief Scout of the Dominion.

Membership in the Boy Scouts Association reached an all-time high during the past year. There are more than 100,000 boys and leaders, plus many thousands of adults who are members of local Scout associations, committees and other auxiliary groups. The largest increases in membership were in the Wolf Cub and Boy Scout sections. Many also joined the Rover Scouts. Eight hundred

Canadian Scouts earned the coveted King's Scout Badge during the year.

A new winter uniform is in the making for Scouts. It is especially designed to meet the extreme cold weather of the Canadian winter. It is now undergoing trials in every part of Canada, under different weather conditions. The design and material to be used will not become permanent until trial reports have been studied. The uniform consists of a parka with a furred hood, a ski cap and ski-style pants. It is made of windproof and snow-resistant material in a forest-green shade, and the design is based on uniform requirements of the armed services of Can-

Neither wind nor snow nor bitter cold can penetrate the Canadian Scouts' new uniform.

ada and the United States while on duty in the Arctic.

Another new step in Canadian Scouting was taken during 1948. Scout leaders from all parts of the Dominion took part in a special training course, near Ottawa, that lasted nearly three weeks. They studied the newest methods of training others so that Canada's Scouts may benefit from new ideas. The course was directed by Ernest F. Mills, executive commissioner for training at Dominion headquarters. Instructors included government experts, Red Cross officials and a member of Canada's famed Royal Canadian Mounted Police.

The Baden-Powell Guild of Old Scouts was launched during the past year. The aims of the guild are three-fold: 1) to keep alive, among its members, the spirit of the Scout promise and law; 2) to carry that spirit into the communities in which they live and work; and, 3) to give active support to the Boy Scout movement as far as their responsibilities allow.

The Guild Was Named for the Founder of the Boy Scout Movement

The name of the guild was chosen by the International Committee on Scouting, and honors Lord Baden-Powell, the founder of Boy Scouting. In the British Empire and Commonwealth, His Royal Highness the Duke of Edinburgh, husband of Princess Elizabeth, is the patron of the guild. Similar groups are being organized in all parts of the world.

Many Canadian Scouts learned the first steps in mountain climbing when they attended the Canadian Alpine Club Camp in the Rocky Mountains. Another group of Western Scouts attended an exploration camp on the Snider Ranch, in the foothills of the Rockies. French- and English-speaking Scouts joined in another exploration in Quebec.

Honors Were Conferred on the Chief Scout of the Empire

Lord Rowallan, Chief Scout of the Empire and Commonwealth, received an honorary degree from McGill University. Prior to the convocation, he had attended the annual meeting of the Boy Scouts of America in Seattle, Washington, where he was awarded the highest honor given by the Boy Scouts of America, the Silver Buffalo.

Girl Scouts

By CONSTANCE MORGAN RITTENHOUSE
National Director

THE faces that you see on postage stamps are always those of people who have done something very important for their country—generals, presidents, scientists, explorers and the like. Only a few women have ever been honored in this way by the United States Government. For this reason, every Girl Scout can feel pride in the new postage stamp voted by Congress in 1948. It bears the picture of a pretty, dark-eyed woman named Juliette Low, the founder of the Girl Scouts in the United States.

It all began with two very simple things—a telephone call and a tea party. In the spring of 1912, Mrs. Low had just come home to Savannah, Georgia, from a visit to England. There she had talked to General Sir Robert Baden-Powell and Lady Baden-Powell, who were working out the idea of Scouting for boys and girls.

Mrs. Low was so filled with enthusiasm for this new and exciting adventure that she wanted her young friends in Savannah to be a part of it. She called one of her neigh-

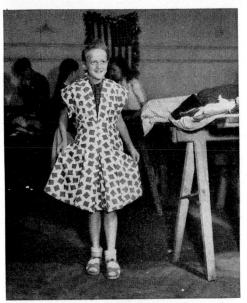

A happy little girl in Germany tries on a pretty new dress sent her by unknown friends—Camp Fire Girls of Toledo, Ohio. At the top we see the dress being made, and ready to pack.

bors and said eagerly, "Come right over. I've got something for the girls of Savannah, and all America, and all the world, and we're going to start it tonight."

The two friends sat down together and planned a tea party for the afternoon of March 12. They invited twelve girls, who listened eagerly while Mrs. Low told them what it meant to be a Girl Scout. From this meeting grew a movement which proved to be truly "something for the girls of all America." Today there are a million members in the United States alone, and additional troops as far away as Japan and Saudi Arabia, where American families have gone to live and work for a while.

At the same time the Girl Guide movement spread from England to all parts of the British Commonwealth, and many other countries also took it up. When the World Association of Girl Guides and Girl Scouts met in New York in 1948, there were people from twenty-seven countries that have their own separate kinds of Girl Scouting. The uniforms are different in different places, and so are the names. In Holland, for instance, they are called Padvinsters, in Brazil, Bandeirantes, in France, Eclaireuses, and in more than a dozen nations scattered all over the globe they are called Girl Guides. The Girl Scout Promise and Laws are the same everywhere—no matter what language you speak or what clothes you wear. For that matter, as you know, the Girl Scouts of the United States adopted a brand-new uniform in 1948, without changing any of their beliefs or the things that they do.

The real meaning of being a Girl Scout does not change with time, either. Just as Juliette Low first explained it on that spring day long ago, it is having fun and learning about the world you live in, while helping other people. Above all, it is the good feeling of belonging, whether you are a seven-year-old Brownie Scout or a seventeen-year-old Senior Service Scout and almost grown up.

A good example of how the Girl Scouts work is the "Clothes for Friendship" drive. In 1948, the Girl Scouts of this country pledged themselves to furnish complete outfits for 100,000 boys and girls in parts of Europe and Asia, where people do not have enough to eat and wear as we do here. In this way they hoped to make warm friends all over the world.

One of the first kits shipped to Europe came from a Baptist Church in Toledo, Ohio, where everyone from the smallest Brownie to the oldest troop leader helped to make new clothes, or to wash and repair old ones. Another kit was from the Shriners' Hospital for Crippled Children, in San Francisco—where Girl Scouts who could not walk forgot their own troubles in trying to solve the problems of others.

Girl Guides

By MARY F. BISHOP, *Commissioner of Publications*

EVERYONE has heard of family reunions, when many members of one family travel from far and near to get together for a few days. They meet to talk over old times and what they plan to do in the future. If you have ever been to a family reunion yourself, you know how pleasant it is to be a part of it.

Canada's Girl Guides took part in just such a gathering last summer when a very large family held its twelfth reunion—the Girl Guides and Girl Scouts of the world. There are 3,500,000 members, so, of course, they all could not crowd into the little town of Cooperstown, New York, where the meeting was held. However, they sent representatives to tell how they were getting along. The head of the family was there, too—Lady Baden-Powell, world chief Guide.

A Girl Guide is really the same as a Girl Scout. Each one promises to be loyal to God and her country and to try to be a good citizen—helping other people at all times. She may be called a Bandeirante in Brazil, a Padvindster in the Netherlands, or a Proskopine in Greece. Whatever her name or her race or religion, she makes the same Promise and follows the same rules. She learns all sorts of useful things and has an exciting time of it hiking and camping—learning how to get along in the outdoors by using woodcraft knowledge.

Sometimes a Girl Guide goes to a camp in another country and brings home interesting news. She discovers how the Guides abroad live, what they like to do and what they like to eat. This is one way in which she learns to understand and to work with others for the good of all.

At the world conference in Cooperstown,

the representatives held their meetings for ten days. There they decided to have a world-membership pin which any Girl Guide anywhere may wear. They will also exchange films from country to country so that Girl Guides may learn more about each other. In the summer of 1949 there will be many more international camps than ever before. Some of these will be especially planned for older Guides who will have a chance to make recommendations to the world association as to how it should operate.

Girls of Three Nations Enjoy the Fun of Camp Life

While the world conference was going on, a very interesting international camp was taking place right next door. Ninety girls from Brazil, Canada and the United States had come to help at the conference. They lived together in tents on a pretty hillside, enjoying all the fun of camp life when they were not busy at the conference. The Canadians and United States Girl Scouts soon learned to speak a little Portuguese (the language of Brazil), and the Brazilians improved their knowledge of English. Evenings, there were campfires, colorful national dances and songs.

One evening a world-friendship ceremony was held around a huge campfire. All were dressed in their national costumes and carried the flags of the twenty-six countries which were represented. The representatives of each country threw a bundle of sticks into the fire and made a wish for world peace, absent friends and good Guiding. Every morning when the flags were raised on the big flagstaff each one renewed her Promise.

The Girl Guides of Canada have nearly 65,000 members. They, too, are fond of camping and especially of international camping. Recently, they invited Girl Scouts from the United States to a "good neighbors" camp at Parry Sound, Ontario, and to another at Morin Heights, Quebec Province. Canadian Guides visited Girl Scout camps in Michigan and Massachusetts.

Through their contributions to their World Friendship Fund, they have sent Guide representatives to conferences in Italy, Belgium and the United States. They have sent parcels of food to Girl Guide training centers in Great Britain and to the Guides of Austria and China. A gift of camping pins was also sent to The Netherlands.

As you know, many immigrants from Europe are coming to Canada. The Canadian Guides have their leaders meet the immigrant ships docking at the great port of Halifax to welcome those who had been Guides at home. They then arrange for them to join Canadian Guide companies. There has been a serious shortage of hydroelectric power in Ontario Province. A large number of factories use electric power, and there has been a shortage of rainfall. The Ontario Girl Guides are helping the government campaign to save electricity by being careful in their own homes and by helping to inform other people of ways to save electricity.

There are Girl Guides north of the Arctic Circle in Canada—the most northerly groups in the world. There, Eskimo and Indian children are learning the same things that Guides in the rest of Canada learn. Not long ago a Guide leader went by airplane into the Arctic to help the leaders there. She took with her news of world Guiding and new ideas from outside.

Six Canadian Girl Guides were awarded medals for bravery in the past year. These were for saving lives—some for rescuing children from drowning, and one for saving a small boy from injury by a speeding automobile. Plans for the coming year in Canada include carrying on the work of welcoming new citizens from abroad, sending parcels of clothing and food to Girl Guides in Europe, and holding more international camps.

Canadian, American and Brazilian hostesses at the 1948 world conference at Cooperstown, N.Y.

YOUNG FOLKS

Camp Fire Girls

By MARTHA F. ALLEN,
National Director of the Camp Fire Girls

HAVE you ever built a "friendship bridge"?

It is amazing what long distances you can span, and how much fun you can have, when you build friendships with boys and girls around the world. Just include a warm heart and plenty of imagination in your tool kit.

For instance, it is about six thousand miles from Tulsa, Oklahoma, to Cochabamba, Bolivia. Yet Camp Fire Girls in Tulsa built a very sturdy friendship bridge last year that stretches all the way to Cochabamba. It connects the Tulsa Camp Fire Girls with the boys and girls in a Cochabamba missionary school called the Instituto Americano.

The materials these Tulsa girls used were not the kind with which engineers usually build bridges. No, indeed! The Camp Fire Girls used popcorn balls and chewing gum. They used a quiz game about the United States and a pin-the-tail-on-the-rabbit game.

They used a complete toy village and a three-ring circus cut out of cardboard!

You see, the Camp Fire Girls in Tulsa wanted the boys and girls in the Bolivian missionary school to share some of their fun. So they sent them "party kits." Each kit contained games, songs, prizes, favors, refreshments and other gay things that boys and girls in the United States enjoy at their parties. Blue Birds, the younger members of Camp Fire who are seven, eight and nine years old, prepared some of the kits. Others were sent by the Camp Fire Girls, who are ten through fourteen years old. More party kits were planned and sent by high-school Camp Fire groups of older girls, called Horizon Clubs.

However, it was not only the Camp Fire Girls of Tulsa who wanted boys and girls in other countries to share their fun. Every year the Camp Fire Girls all over the nation work on a special project. Their 1948 proj-

Blue Birds of Laramie, Wyoming, do their bit for the hospital, folding and delivering hospital bags in an ambulance made by themselves.

ect was: "Hello, World: Let's Get Together!" Camp Fire Girls everywhere sent party kits to thousands of boys and girls in dozens of faraway lands as a part of this international friendship program.

Why did they choose party kits? We are always sending shoes and shirts and food to children overseas, they thought, so let's see them have some fun once in a while, too! So party kits were used to build hundreds of friendship bridges. For instance, one stretches from Boston, Massachusetts, to London, England. Another goes from the Camp Fire Girls of Ottumwa, Iowa, to a child-welfare center in Canton, China; and another from Columbus, Ohio, to Wetzlar, Germany.

Letters and Gifts from Friends in Far-away Places

Understanding travels across all these hundreds of bridges that the Camp Fire Girls have built around the world. In return for their party kits, many Camp Fire Girls received letters and gifts from their foreign friends. The letters helped the American girls to see how boys and girls live in other lands—what kind of houses and schools they have, the kind of clothes they wear, food they eat and games they play.

Camp Fire Girls do not spend all their time getting to know boys and girls in other countries. They think it is just as important to get to know the girl next door, and to "get together" with their own families, schools, churches and towns. They know that all of us must learn to work in harmony with our neighbors.

What does American democracy mean to you?

The best way to answer that question is not by words alone, they think, but by actions as well. That is why the Camp Fire Girls have chosen the theme, "Make Mine Democracy!," for their 1949 project. They want to see, do and tell about democracy in many different ways. They want to make democracy a living thing for themselves and their neighbors.

In their own groups, Camp Fire Girls are making a special effort to see that every member shares in the work and the fun, and in reaching group decisions. They are exploring the history of their home towns and discovering that the rough trail to democracy is gradually becoming a smoothly paved highway for the progress of mankind.

Because democracy includes the idea of sharing, Camp Fire Girls are working on many service projects. For instance, they are sending gifts to American Indians on reservations, and helping newcomers to the United States to feel at home. They are giving parties for children in orphanages and hospitals.

Camp Fire Girls have always believed that helping others is an important part of being a good citizen. They also believe in having fun while they are giving service. One day the Camp Fire Girls of Detroit, Michigan, combined the two in an exciting Gypsy Day project. The girls divided into bands. They put on gay skirts and blouses and, carrying their lunches wrapped up in colorful bandanas, hiked to neighboring farms around the Camp Fire Girls camp. Then they offered their services, doing odd jobs around the farms. The busy farmers were only too glad to have these Camp Fire "gypsies" pick berries and apples, mow lawns and do other extra chores. At the end of the Gypsy Day, the tired but merry girls talked and talked about the good times they had enjoyed while helping their neighbors.

Camp Fire Girls Learn to Be Good Citizens and Good Homemakers

Besides training to be good citizens, Camp Fire Girls have fun learning things that will make them good mothers and homemakers when they grow up.

You can not eat like a bird and work like a horse, they think. They came to that conclusion when they put on a skit for their annual Better Breakfast project. They learned how important it is to start each day with a good, hearty breakfast including fruit, cereal, milk, bread and butter. They prepared "better breakfasts" for their families so that their mothers and fathers, brothers and sisters would also be healthy and strong.

Camp Fire Girls also keep busy and happy in many other ways. They build things for their own rooms, learn to care for their bicycles, and to keep budgets. They go on cookouts and camping trips, enjoy sports and games, and carry out a thousand and one other interesting activities.

Camp Fire Girls enjoy themselves while they learn to be at home with their families and friends, in their communities and with people around the world.

401

YOUNG FOLKS

Boys' Clubs of America

By DAVID W. ARMSTRONG,
Executive Director, Boys' Clubs of America

A BOYS' Club is a boy's own club. Any time he wants to go there during the week-day afternoons and evenings, whenever he has free time, he may go. He will always find boys of his own age there or fellows who are interested in doing the things he likes to do. A boy can always find companionship in his Boys' Club.

The Boys' Club has a clubhouse or quarters of its own, with game rooms, craft shops of many kinds; a gym, library, showers and often a swimming pool and an outdoor playground. In other words, it is a real clubhouse, where something is going on all the time and any boy can find something interesting to do.

Many of the clubs have summer camps. Some of them have both summer and winter camps. Several of the Boys' Clubs in California have camps high up in the mountains where, even in the summer, the boys may enjoy winter sports. A number of clubs have camps on the rooftops of the clubhouses where, overlooking the cities, the boys cook their meals over outdoor fireplaces and sleep in the open.

Every club has a wide variety of activities —from stamp collecting and holiday parties to baseball and track meets. A boy member may invite his sister and her friends to special events, such as a Hallowe'en party or a play given by the boys who like to act. For events such as an open house, a boy may invite his whole family and all of his friends for a visit. Every April, during Boys' Club Week, the entire community joins in the celebration of the week.

The director of the Boys' Club and other men who are club leaders can help a boy with personal problems. Or a leader can show a boy how to make a model jet car, play basketball, or swim the length of the pool. These men are fellows a boy considers his older friends.

Since a Boys' Club is for boys only, a member never has to stay away because the gym or woodworking shop, or whatever it may be, is being used by other people. He does not have to wait for a certain afternoon or evening to go for a swim in the pool, take a shower or read in the library.

As a member of a Boys' Club, a boy has yearly dues to pay, but they are never a strain on his pocketbook. Dues are so low that any boy at all can belong. There are no special qualities or interests that a boy must have to be a member of a Boys' Club. Just being a boy is enough. Boys from eight years up to eighteen or twenty years old are members of Boys' Clubs, although most of the members are under seventeen. There are over 275,000 boys in the United States who are Boys' Club members.

Most of the large cities have a number of Boys' Clubs. The clubhouses are near the homes of the young members, in neighborhoods where families do not have large houses or apartments. Without a clubhouse in such sections, if a boy wants to play with his friends, he has to play in the streets. In the smaller cities and towns, the Boys' Club is in a central location so that all the boys can reach it easily.

Boys' Clubs of America is the national organization of the 300 Boys' Clubs in the United States.

A 4-H CLUB MEMBER

LIVES HERE

By Ralph M. Fulghum
United States Department of Agriculture

PERHAPS you have often seen this sign in front of a farmhouse and wondered what it means. You know that if you find a four-leaf clover it is supposed to bring good luck; but the four-leaf clover on the sign means something entirely different to boys and girls who live in the country.

It shows that they are members of one of the largest boys-and-girls clubs in the world, the 4-H Club. As members they not only have good times, but also learn to become expert farmers and homemakers.

Look a little closer the next time you go to the state or county fair. Wherever you see the sign there will be something interesting. It may be a prize-winning cow or calf, or an exhibit of vegetables or of canned food. A well-trained demonstration team of teen-agers may be showing and telling us why we should eat fresh vegetables, or how to wire a farm home for electricity. You might even see a group of girls modeling or exhibiting dresses which they made as a club project.

In every state and territory you will find farm boys and girls of 4-H doing and learning all sorts of things about farming, home-making and good citizenship. Their motto is, Learn by Doing; their goal is, Make the Best Better.

Perhaps you are wondering what the four H's on the clover mean. The pledge of the club members explains the meaning best.

My *H*ead to clearer thinking
My *H*eart to greater loyalty
My *H*ands to larger service, and
My *H*ealth to better living for
My club, my community and my country.
There are from five to twenty or more members in each club. The boys and girls plan their own club projects and conduct their own meetings. Each member also carries out one or more individual projects at his own farm home during the year.

For example, during the past year they cared for more than 350,000 home gardens. They raised 8,000,000 chickens, 130,000 cows and calves, 131,000 cattle for beef and 377,000 hogs. They learned how to raise better crops at less cost. Girls planned 8,500,000 meals for their families, and in doing so learned much about vitamins, minerals and all the other things necessary for a good diet. The girls also made 1,500,000 dresses and other items of clothing for themselves, and canned 18,000,000 quarts of fruits, vegetables and meats for their families.

There is a voluntary leader for each club, who advises members about their projects.

Vernon Wolf, of Carroll County, Md., grooming his Aberdeen Angus steers for the fair.

ED HUNTON, U.S.D.A. EXTENSION SERVICE

403

This leader is usually a farmer or farm woman in the neighborhood, or an older 4-H Club member. The Federal and state governments also help through county extension agents who advise the boys and girls. These agents also help adult farmers and farm women to apply science and the results of agricultural research to farming and homemaking.

Let's pay a visit to some of the clubs and see what their members did during the year.

In New Hampshire, one girl specialized in freezing foods. She prepared 320 packages of fruits and vegetables and 102 pounds of fish chowder, lobster, broilers, venison and other meats. Because of the knowledge and experience that she gained, she has become a center of information on freezing foods in her community.

A club in Tennessee made a survey of the sanitation and public-health conditions in its farm community and won an award from the state for it. In near-by Kentucky the girls of one club used prize money to buy a sewing machine for their high school, and taught the younger girls how to sew.

The members of a club in Virginia wanted a club house. They worked and raised a fund of $125, but that was not enough. So they bought livestock with the money and each member set about raising a calf at his farm on home-grown feed. When the animals are sold, they hope to build the club house.

In the state of Massachusetts, the girls of 4-H Clubs in twelve counties go on an annual tour of the city of Boston. More than three hundred took the trip last year. Last year's trip had "careers" as a theme and included visits to hospitals, department stores, museums and historic spots. Merchants and young people of the city co-operated to make the girls' visit pleasant.

So long as the boys and girls, the future citizens of this country, try to improve themselves, their club, communities and their country; so long as they are concerned about the peace of the world, we can continue to be proud of the America in which we live.

There are expert gardeners among the 4-H Club membership. These two are dusting bean vines.

ED HUNTON, U.S.D.A. EXTENSION SERVICE

THINGS TO MAKE AND
THINGS TO DO

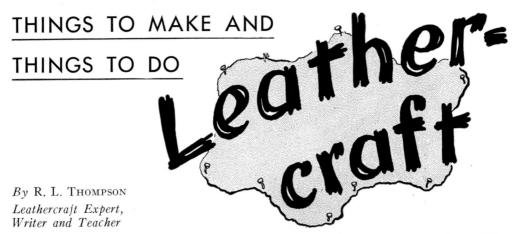

By R. L. Thompson
Leathercraft Expert,
Writer and Teacher

LEATHERCRAFT—the art of making articles of leather—is one of the most fascinating of all hobbies. There is a real thrill in seeing a piece of animal skin gradually take shape under one's fingers until it becomes at last a thing of beauty. You need not be an expert to work at this hobby. Beginners with little or no experience can turn out ornamental and useful things.

It is for such beginners that I have written this article. I shall tell you about some of the tools used in leathercraft and I shall show you how to use them. Then I shall give you three simple leather projects—a book mark, a wallet and a key case.

There are a good many different kinds of leather to choose from in starting on a project. I think, though, that it would be wise for the beginner to select the leather called tooling calfskin. This is soft and flexible and has a smooth and highly polished grain side. (The grain side is the finished side of the leather.) You may obtain tooling calfskin at most handicraft or Scout supply houses; it is usually sold in whole, half or quarter skins. It may be bought dyed in various colors.

Sometimes tooling calfskin comes cut to size for various types of projects. The chances are, however, that you will have to cut the leather yourself. For this operation you will need the following tools: (a) a cutting board (any smooth piece of board); (b) a very sharp cutting knife; (c) a steel square; (d) a template, or pattern, made of metal or cardboard.

Lay the leather on the cutting board with the flesh side down. (The flesh side is the rough or unfinished side.) Select the best part of the skin, toward the outer edges, for cutting. Very seldom, if ever, are pieces cut from the center of the skin. If patterns are used, try to place them so that there will be as little waste as possible. Using the pattern or the steel square as a guide, cut the leather to the required dimensions. Make sure that the blade of the knife is always against the edge of the steel square. Apply enough downward pressure on the knife to cut through the leather and into the wood. Be sure that your fingers are well out of the path of the cutting blade and cut the leather with one stroke. To avoid cutting the fingers when doing straight lines, it may be advisable for very young leathercraft workers to use an angle iron instead of a steel square. Figure 1 shows what an angle iron looks like and how it is used. You may cut curved pieces with scissors or shears.

After the leather has been cut to size, it may be decorated by tooling, or modeling, the grain side. Tooling consists of pressing down into leather so as to make a line in it.

Before you do any tooling, you will have to apply a design to the leather. You may create your own design; or else you may copy one from a book, magazine or other source. The beginner should select a design that is fairly simple, with large flowing curves and straight lines.

If you select a design from a book or magazine, place a sheet of tracing paper over it and trace it carefully with a well-sharpened pencil. The first step in transferring a design from tracing paper to leather is to set the leather in place, flesh side up. Dampen the entire surface evenly with a sponge dipped in cold water. Be careful not to make the leather too wet. If water oozes out when you begin to transfer the design, lay the leather aside until it is dry and then moisten it again.

As you dampen the leather, turn it over from time to time and examine the other

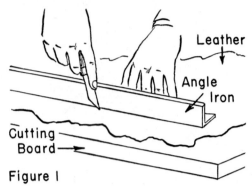

Cutting Board

Leather

Angle Iron

Figure 1

side. If dark, wet spots appear on this side, you will know that you have used too much water. After you have moistened the leather evenly, place it grain side up on a smooth surface, such as glass or hardwood. Be careful how you handle the dampened leather. It is now very soft and easily marked.

When you are ready to transfer the design to the leather, fold the edges of the design under the edges of the leather. You will then be able to hold both in place with one hand, while you trace the design with the other. A pencil makes a good tracer. Hold it in a slanting position so that it will not dig through the tracing paper and into the wet leather. When tracing, use firm and steady pressure. Never go over the same line twice.

To make sure that all the lines have been traced, slowly peel back one side of the design sheet until part of the design can be seen. If any lines have not been traced, smooth the sheet of paper back into place and continue with your tracing. When you have finished, remove the design sheet.

Tooling is generally done with a small tool called a spade or spoon and point modeling tool (Figure 2a). It has a smooth, curved point at one end; the other end is shaped somewhat like a very small spoon. Other modeling tools are the ball end tool, with a little sphere at each end (Figure 2b) and the deerfoot modeling tool, with both ends shaped somewhat like the hoofs of a deer (Figure 2c). You will need only the spoon and point tool for the projects given in this article. A good modeling tool can be made from an old nutpick by filing and polishing the point. In an emergency you can even use a nail as a modeling tool. Bend the end of the nail into a curve and polish the point.

One of the easiest methods of tooling is outline tooling. Place the leather, grain side

up, on a piece of glass or other hard surface. With the curved point of the spoon and point modeling tool press down along the lines of the design (Figure 3) into the dampened leather. Hold the tool at the same angle as you would a lead pencil. Place the rounded part of the pointed end on the line of the design. Pull the tool toward you, applying considerable downward pressure. When you round a curve, turn the leather with one hand and hold the tool steadily in the other. In making a square corner, push the tool to the corner from first one direction and then the other. Do not tip the tool too far forward or else it will dig into the dampened leather. Use a steel square and the modeling tool for all straight lines. Go over the design several times until it stands out clearly. Work carefully; a mistake can not be erased.

After you have tooled the outline, you can stipple (make dots in) the background of the design, if you wish to do so. Stippling is another form of tooling; it depresses (presses down) the background and leaves the design and border standing out in contrast. In stippling, tap the background of the design with the pointed end of the modeling tool. (See Figure 4.) There is a special stippling tool with six or seven blunt points (Figure 5); but you can stipple with any blunt-pointed tool.

Use enough pressure to depress the leather; but do not strike so hard that you will break through to the unfinished side. Be careful when you stipple near the tooled lines of the design. When you have finished stippling, it may be well to retool the design lightly. If you wish, you can reverse the stippling; that is, you can stipple the inside of the tooled design, leaving the background plain.

Another form of tooling is called flat modeling. In this the background is pressed down, while the design is left untouched. Pass the spoon end of the modeling tool over the leather with an "around and around" motion and gradually press down the background of the design. Use very little pressure

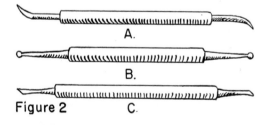

A.

B.

Figure 2   C.

on the modeling tool at the beginning. Start from the edge of the design and work away from it. Increase the pressure as the background flattens. At some parts of the design a straight movement, to and away from the design, might be better. Careful tooling will give a clear-cut edge between the design and the background. The background may be further depressed by placing several soft paper towels between the leather and the glass. The leather will be pushed into the towels.

When the flat modeling is finished and the leather has dried, the parts which have been pressed down will be darker than those which are in relief (which stand out). This will give an appearance of depth to the design. You can vary the flat modeling process by depressing the design, instead of the background.

You should always complete whatever tooling there is to do in your leather project before you do such work as lacing and attaching snap fasteners.

The edges of most leather projects are finished by lacing. This improves the appearance of the project. It protects the edges of the leather; it also serves as a means of fas-

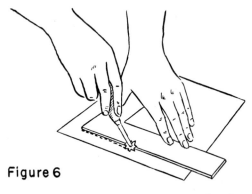

Figure 6

tening together two or more pieces. Leather lacing is usually made of goatskin or calfskin and is cut in narrow, continuous lengths. The usual width of the lace is $\frac{3}{32}''$. It may be bought by the yard in spools of from 50 to 1,000 yards.

Before you can begin to lace the edge of the leather, you must punch the holes through which the lace will pass. The holes are spaced with a tool called a space marker or spacing wheel (Figure 6). Place a steel square $\frac{3}{16}''$ from the edge of the piece of leather to be laced; then run the spacing wheel along the edge of the square. The saw-toothed wheel will mark the center of each hole to be punched. There should be five, six, or seven holes per inch. You can also space the holes by means of a pencil and ruler.

When punching lacing holes in a leather project, it is wise to assemble (put together) all the pieces and fasten them to one another temporarily with a little leather cement or tape. Punch each hole through the various pieces of leather which are to be laced together. Round holes are punched with a tubular (tube-like) punch (Figure 7a and b); slits or rectangular holes, with a thonging chisel and a mallet (Figure 7c).

There are two popular methods of stitching leather: the over-and-over, or whip, stitch and the buttonhole stitch.

For the over-and-over stitch, cut a piece of lacing long enough to go around the outer edge of the work three times. Begin the stitch at a place where there are at least two thicknesses of leather to be stitched together. First point one end of the lace with a knife (see Figure 8). Holding the work in the left hand, pull the pointed end of the lace through the first hole, until all but a half inch of the lace has been drawn through. Put leather cement on this bit of lace and tuck it

Figure 3

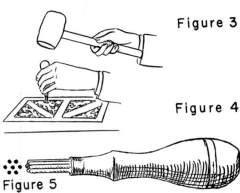

Figure 4

Figure 5

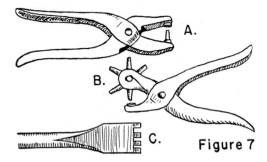

Figure 7

between the two pieces (see Figure 8a). Whip the other end of the lace over the edge of the leather and then through the next hole. When lacing the corner, go through the corner holes three times (Figure 8b). It would be well to enlarge the hole with the pointed end of the modeling tool in order to make room for the extra lacing. Finish the stitch by threading the end under several of the first stitches (Figure 8c). All sharp corners may be rounded off with shears.

The buttonhole stitch, sometimes called the single-loop stitch, really consists of a series of knots along the cut edges of a leather project. This type of stitch is strong, wears well and is very ornamental. The buttonhole stitch will take six times as much leather lacing as the length of the edges to be laced. As in the whip stitch, three stitches must be made through each corner hole.

You should start the buttonhole stitch where there is more than one thickness of leather. This will enable you to conceal the ends of the lace between the two pieces, so that these ends cannot be seen when you finish the stitch.

Point one end of the lace as before. Hold the project to be laced in the left hand with the tooled or decorated surface toward you. Start the lacing at the center of the top edge, or where there are two pieces of leather to

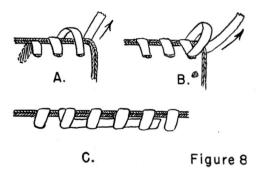

Figure 8

conceal the ends. Push the pointed end of the lace from front to back through one of the lacing holes. Draw it through in back until only several inches are left in front. Carry the rest of the lace over the top edges of the leather and insert it, from front to back, in the next lacing hole. Again draw it through from the back until there is a small loop left around the edges of the two pieces of leather (see Figure 9a).

Again carry the lace over the top edges of the leather and insert it from front to back through the loop (Figure 9b). You will notice that there are two loops. With the right hand, pull on Loop 2, as shown in Figure 9b.

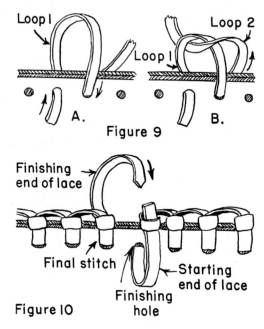

Figure 9

Figure 10

This will bring Loop 1 tightly against the edge of the leather. Then pull on the end of the lace, thus bringing Loop 2 also against the edge of the leather. One stitch is now complete. Repeat the operation until the entire project is laced.

Make sure that each knot is directly over each punched lacing hole (see Figure 10). Do not let the lacing slant. It is wise to keep the forefinger and thumb of the left hand directly under each knot when you begin to tighten it. This prevents the leather edges from being stretched or pulled out of shape by the pressure from the lace. Do not allow the lace to become twisted. Be sure that the finished side of the lace is always on top.

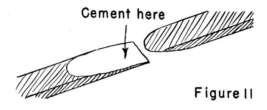

Figure 11

When the project has been entirely laced, the lacing may be joined as follows:

(a) Pull out the short end of the lace left in the first hole (see Figure 9a). Make a final stitch in this hole(Figure 10).

(b) Pull the starting end of the lace down and out of its loop (Figure 10) and push the finishing end of the lace through the same loop. Both ends of the lace will now be on the front side of the project.

(c) Draw the finishing end of the lace through the finishing hole in the front piece of leather and insert it between the two pieces; do the same with the starting end of the lace. The two ends, which should be from ½″ to ¾″ in length, should be glued down to the back piece of leather. Once this has been done, it is practically impossible to tell where the lacing was started and finished.

When lacing a large project with either the whip or buttonhole stitch, it is not very convenient to cut long pieces of lace. It is much easier to cut the lace in two or three-foot lengths and to splice them together, whenever it becomes necessary. The ends to be spliced are tapered, as shown in Figure 11. Leather cement is then applied to the cut portions and they are joined together.

When making a key case, it is necessary to fasten a key plate, either four-hook or six-hook, to the leather to hold the keys. Key plates are generally manufactured from tempered steel; you may buy them either one at a time or by the dozen. Eyelets are used to fasten key plates to leather.

Set the key plate on the leather. Mark the position of the holes and punch them. Place the eyelets through the holes in the key plate and then through the holes in the leather. Put the work on a hard surface, such as a cutting board. Insert the point of an eyelet setter (see Figure 12) into the small end of the eyelet. Tap the end of the eyelet setter with a mallet. The eyelet end will spread and the key plate will be riveted to the leather.

You will have to insert snap fasteners in such leather projects as key cases or change purses. Each snap fastener consists of four parts: the cap, the eyelet, the cage (or spring) and the post. They are shown in Figure 13. The cap is attached to one part of the leather, the cage to another part. When you wish to fasten the two parts together, you insert the cage in the cap. The cap is held in place by the eyelet; the cage, by the post. The cap is generally made of metal, covered

Figure 12

Eyelet Setter

Eyelet

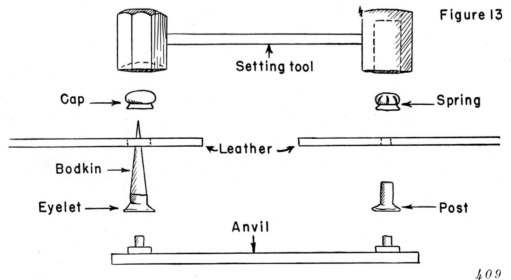

Figure 13

Setting tool

Cap — Spring

Leather

Bodkin

Eyelet — Post

Anvil

with celluloid; it is from $\frac{5}{16}''$ to $\frac{5}{8}''$ in diameter. Caps are available in almost any color.

You will need a snap fastener set to attach snap fasteners. This set consists of an anvil, a setting tool and two bodkins (Figure 13). You will also need a leather punch and a mallet.

First lay out the position of the cap and cage; remember that the cage will fit in the cap. As we have seen, the cap will be held in place by an eyelet. Punch a large hole for the eyelet and insert it in this hole. Set the cap on the small end of the eyelet. Place the large open end of the eyelet over the large anvil of the snap fastener set. Put the large end of the setting tool on top of the cap. Strike the setting tool several firm blows with a mallet. The eyelet will spread inside the celluloid cap and will rivet it to the leather.

If the punched hole is too small for the eyelet, it may be enlarged with a bodkin. This is a small, conical tool; it is also called a needle (see Figure 13). Place the bottom part of the bodkin in the top of the eyelet (Figure 13). Then put the pointed end of the bodkin in the hole which has been punched into the leather. Push the eyelet and bodkin through the hole until you have widened this enough. Then remove the bodkin and apply the cap to the eyelet.

The spring and post are assembled in much the same way as the cap and eyelet. Punch a small hole for the post. (This is really the eyelet for the spring or cage.) Insert the post in the hole and place the cage on top of the post. Put the large open end of the post on the small anvil of the snap button fastener (see Figure 13). Set the small end of the setting tool over the cage. Strike the setting tool several firm blows with a mallet. The post will spread inside the cage, riveting it to the leather.

Leather projects may be cleaned with saddle soap. Dampen a cloth and apply the soap to the leather. When the leather is completely dry, it may be polished with a soft, dry cloth. The finish can be preserved by applying a coat of paste wax. Allow the wax to dry and then polish.

Here are three simple projects with which you can begin your leathercraft career:

A LEATHER BOOKMARK

The leathercraft novice would do well to begin with this simple project.
- (a) Cut leather to size (2" x 8").
- (b) Select a design for tooling; it should not be larger than $1\frac{1}{2}''$ x $4\frac{1}{2}''$ and it should be centered on the leather.
- (c) Trace design.
- (d) Moisten leather.
- (e) Transfer design to leather.
- (f) Dampen leather for tooling.
- (g) Tool design on grain side of leather.
- (h) Stipple the background of the design.
- (i) Fringe the ends of the bookmark. Beginning $1\frac{1}{2}''$ back from each end of the leather, draw a series of lines running lengthwise and $\frac{1}{4}''$ apart. Use a pencil and ruler for this operation. Place the leather on the cutting board and with your knife and steel square cut along the lines.
- (j) Clean leather with saddle soap; polish.

A LEATHER WALLET

This project will enable you to show your skill in both decoration and stitching.

(a) Select a suitable design. This is to be tooled on the grain side of the wallet cover and should be about 3″ x 8″.

(b) Trace the design.

(c) Cut four pieces of leather to the dimensions indicated in Figure 14.

(d) Moisten the flesh side of the cover.

(e) Trace the design on the grain side.

(f) Dampen the leather for tooling and tool the design into the leather. Stipple or model the background of the design.

(g) Assemble the pieces of leather. The bottom of the inner piece should be flush with the bottom of the cover. The cover should overlap by ⅛″ on either side. This is because the cover is ¼″ longer than the inner piece, thus providing extra leather for the fold. The pockets are to fit as indicated by the dotted lines in the diagram.

Place a little leather cement on the corners (flesh side) of the inner piece and the two pockets. The flesh side of the inner piece should be cemented to the flesh side of the cover. The flesh side of the pockets should then be cemented to the grain side of the inner piece.

(h) Lay out the lacing holes with a steel square and a spacing wheel at a distance of ³⁄₁₆″ from the edges. The holes should be laid out on the grain side edges of the cover and on the top edge of the inner piece. Punch the holes with a leather punch. (The holes at the top edge of the inner piece should *not* be punched through both thicknesses of leather.) When punching the holes at the sides, the wallet should be folded to almost a closed position.

(i) Lace the pieces of leather together with the buttonhole stitch. Start the lace in the middle of one end

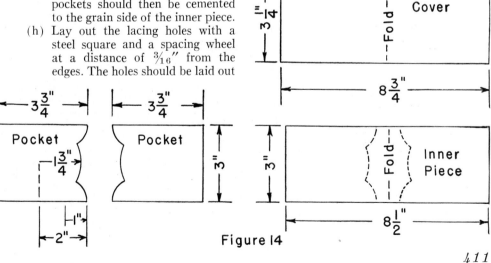

Figure 14

411

of the wallet and lace entirely around the outside edges. You will note that the inner pieces and the cover will be fastened together on three sides only. Of course the fourth side is left open so that the user can insert paper money in the wallet. Lace the top edges of the pockets to the top edge of the inner piece. You are to do this by starting the lace at the top left-hand corner of the inner piece and lacing all the way across.

(j) Lay the leather on the cutting board. Tap the lace with a mallet.

(k) Clean the leather with saddle soap, apply several coats of wax and polish.

A LEATHER KEY CASE

This key case, with its tooled design and fine stitching, will make a welcome gift.

(a) Select a suitable design. It should be about 2″ x 3½″, since it is to be tooled on the back of Section B, as shown in Figure 15.

(b) Trace the design.

(c) Cut three pieces of leather to the dimensions indicated in Figure 15.

(d) Moisten Section B of the largest piece of leather.

(e) Transfer the design to the grain side of Section B.

(f) Dampen leather for tooling.

(g) Tool the outline of the design into the leather.

(h) Lay a key frame on the top of the piece of leather cut for the frame holder, and mark the position of the eyelet holes. Punch the holes with a leather punch. Rivet the key frame to the leather.

(i) Fold Section A on fold line, flesh side to flesh side. Fold Section C on fold line, so that it will rest on Section A. The flesh side of Section C will be against the grain side of Section A. Lay out the position of the hole for the eyelet of the snap fastener on the grain side of Section C. The hole which is to be punched should be midway between the top and bottom and about ½″ in from the side edge of Section C (Fig. 16a).

Punch the hole. Insert the eyelet in the hole from the flesh side of the leather (Fig. 16b). Again fold the key case with Section C over Section A. Insert a pencil

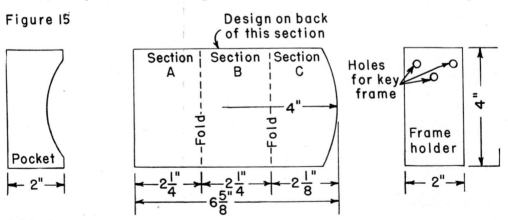

Figure 15

Design on back of this section

Section A | Section B | Section C

Fold | Fold

4″

2¼″ + 2¼″ + 2⅛″

6⅝″

Pocket

2″

Holes for key frame

Frame holder

4″

2″

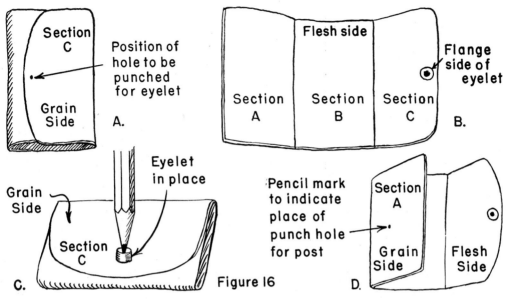

Figure 16

through the eyelet, keeping the point at the exact center of the eyelet, and make a mark on the grain side of Section A (Fig. 16c). This will mark the position of the hole which is to be punched for the post (Fig. 16d). Punch this hole. Insert the post from the flesh side of the leather.

With the snap fastener outfit fasten the cap to the eyelet and the cage to the post.

(j) Put a little leather cement on the corners of the pieces of leather cut for the pocket and the key frame holder. The cement should be applied to the flesh side.

(k) Place the pocket on Section A of the key case, and the frame holder on Section B. The leather pieces in question should now be assem-

bled flesh side to flesh side.

(l) Lay out the lacing holes on the grain side of the key case, using a steel rule and a spacing wheel. Only the outside edges should be laid out for lacing.

(m) Punch the lacing holes through all three pieces of leather.

(n) Lace the key case, using either the over-and-over stitch or the buttonhole stitch. The assembled pieces will thus be fastened together.

(o) Place the key case flat on the cutting board. Lightly tap the lace with a mallet. This will flatten the knots to about the same thickness as the key case. It will also imbed the lace permanently.

(p) Clean the leather with saddle soap and apply several coats of wax.

THE ARAB'S WILL

A DYING Arab who had three sons made a will. The oldest son was to receive one-half of his father's estate; the second son, one-third; the third son, one-ninth. The old Arab's fortune consisted of seventeen camels; and so when he died his sons were greatly puzzled, for how could they carry out the terms of the will?

They went to a wise old Arab for advice. He bent his head in thought for a moment. Then he showed them how each one could obtain even more than he was entitled to under the terms of the will. And all seventeen camels would remain intact! How was this possible? the answer is given on page 420.

A MODEL AIRPLANE

By FRANK ZAIC

Model-Airplane Pioneer and Writer on Aeronautics

THE building and flying of model airplanes will give you many hours of pleasure and will help you understand why planes fly. "But," you will say, "model building is much too hard and expensive; besides I don't have the necessary tools." Actually, it is quite easy to make a model plane, once you know how to use the various materials. And don't let the cost scare you. The prices of other things may be sky-high, but model supplies have cost the same for many years. You can make the model described in this article for something like fifty cents; half of this amount will be for the rubber motor. As for tools, all you will need will be a single-edge razor, ordinary pliers, pins, a board, a sharp knife and some sandpaper.

The model that you are now going to make is the sort of thing that the average kit would offer. If you can build it, you will be able to build almost any model that comes in a kit.

There is no better way to begin a career in aviation than to build your own model airplane.

LUNDH FROM FREDERIC LEWIS

(This statement does not apply to model planes built to use small gasoline motors.)
SUPPLIES. You will need the following items:

Balsa wood; see the specifications shown in Figure 1.

2 feet of .032 wire, for the landing gear and propeller shaft.

1 propeller block, $1\frac{3}{8}''$ x $\frac{7}{8}''$ x 8″.

6 washers, $\frac{3}{16}''$ in diameter.

2 wooden model wheels, $\frac{7}{8}''$ in diameter.

1 hardwood dowel, 1″ long and $\frac{1}{8}''$ in diameter.

8 to 12 strands of $\frac{1}{8}''$ rubber.

Several sheets of colored tissue paper to be used as covering.

1 ounce of model cement.

1 ounce of model dope.

You can buy these supplies at any airplane-model shop. If there is no such shop near you, consult a model magazine for a list of supply companies. Write to these for free catalogs, so that you may order what you want by mail.

GENERAL REMARKS. Before you start working on your model, let me give you some friendly advice. First of all, try to do your work in a place where shavings and dust will cause as little annoyance as possible to other members of the family. Of course a basement or a special workroom would be ideal. If such a place is not available, the kitchen will do very well. The floor of this room generally has a smooth surface—linoleum, or tile or paint. That means that you will be able to gather together balsa shavings and dust easily after your work is over. If you are doing a lot of carving, put a large wastepaper basket or a paper bag under your work, so that shavings will drop directly into it.

Perhaps you are permitted to build your model in your own room. If so, try not to work any place where balsa shavings or dust can lodge in curtains, bedspreads and carpets. Clean up as thoroughly as you can after you have finished working on your model.

In making your plane, it is best to work on a large board, on which you can set the plans of the model. When your working hours are over, simply put your board out of the way until the next session. In this way you will waste no time preparing the table in your kitchen or in your own room every time that you want to build. In selecting the board, keep in mind your future projects. If you intend to make big models later, get a large-size board. It should be made of soft wood, since you will have to push pins in it to hold various pieces in place. Never select composition or plywood boards.

To prevent spilling your cement and dope, use containers with wide bases, such as cans. All containers should be kept closed when not in use, to keep the liquid from evaporating and from being spoiled by too long contact with the air. You will find that a little of the liquid, which has become solid, will collect at the opening of the container. You can cut this off with a sharp razor. Since dope has a pretty strong odor, it would be well to apply it only when the family is out.

It would be a fine idea to wear an apron or smock while working on models; but I have yet to see a model-builder wearing either apron or smock. I would urge you very strongly, however, to put on old clothing when you plan to work.

The tools that we mentioned above are all you will need to construct this particular model. If you intend to do quite a lot of model-building later on, you may want to invest in a more complete outfit. Here are some useful items: a small block plane; various

After you have acquired skill in model-building, you will be able to create your own designs.

LIONEL GREEN FROM FREDERIC LEWIS

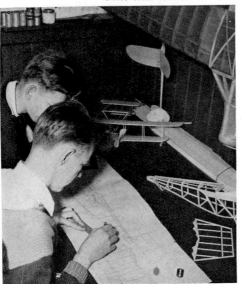

grades of sandpaper; soap or wax; a steel-edge ruler; a T square; a French curve; a compass; drawing paper and thumbtacks; good soft brushes; a hack saw; a hand drill; several files.

PLANS. We give you the complete plans of the various parts of the plane in the diagrams that accompany this article. Before you begin work on the wings, fuselage, stabilizer and rudder, you should make full-sized plans of these parts, using the dimensions as shown. If you write to the editors, enclosing twenty-five cents, they will send you a copy of the diagram on page 416, drawn fully to scale.

FUSELAGE. Most model-builders begin by making the fuselage. You should work from a full-size plan of the side view of the fuselage, as shown in Figure 1. Place the strips which are to make up the longerons, or lengthwise pieces, over the plan, holding them in place with pins. Next, make the fuselage uprights, which are the connecting pieces between the longerons; they should be the exact size shown in the plan. Then cement the uprights into place along the longerons, using plenty of cement. Note the construction at the fourth upright from the rudder. This is made up of two pieces of $\frac{3}{32}$" x $\frac{1}{4}$" balsa, cemented together so as to leave a round hole at the joining. The hardwood dowel which is to hold the rubber motor is to pass through this hole and the one on the other side of the fuselage. Figure 1 shows you what the dowel looks like and how it will fit.

When one side of the fuselage has been made, let it dry for about thirty minutes. Then remove the pins that held the longerons in place and take the completed side off the plan. Make the other side just as you did the first. The two sides are assembled into a fuselage by cementing them together with cross braces of balsa, $\frac{3}{32}$" square, as indicated in the plan. Cement the tail end together first; next, insert the cross braces at the windows. Finally, put the rest of the pieces in place. Note that the front end of the fuselage is covered at the top, bottom and sides with $\frac{1}{20}$" sheet balsa, which is cemented into position.

You are now ready to make the nose plug, which is to fit in the inside of the fuselage at the front end, as shown in Figure 1. The nose plug is built up of $\frac{1}{20}$" sheet balsa, which is cemented together in layers. A hardwood but-

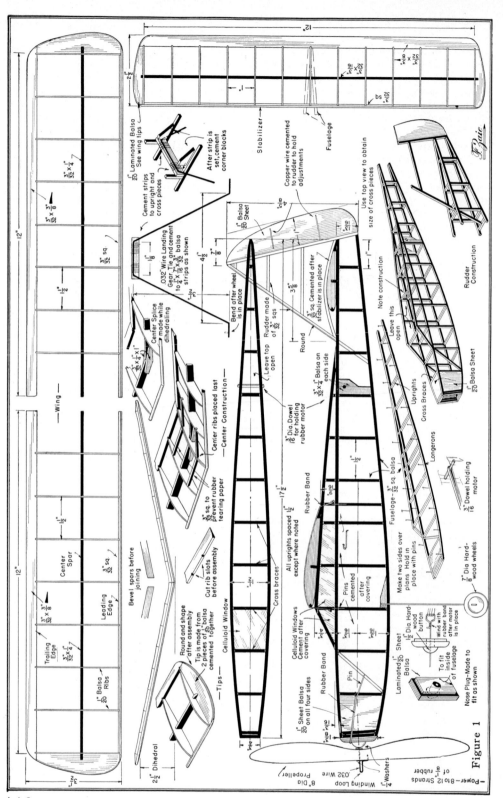

Figure 1

ton is then to be set in position, as shown. If you can not obtain one, you can cement washers on each side of the nose plug to provide bearings for the propeller shaft. The propeller shaft is to pass through the center of the nose plug assembly. Note how the plug is held in place with a rubber band.

Next, we make the landing gear. Bend the .032 wire that you use for the gear to the shape shown. Slip on the wheels, which are to be of 7/8″ diameter hardwood. Bend the ends of the landing gear upward, so as to prevent the wheels from falling off. Next, cement the top of the landing gear to a strip

size plan of each of the two halves and do each half in turn. First, set the two trailing (rear) edges upon the corresponding places on the plan, holding them in place by means of pins. Note the slots made in the trailing edge of the wing. The ribs, serving as cross pieces between the trailing and the leading (front) edges of the wings, are to fit in these slots.

Place the center spar over the drawing; keep it lined up by means of pins. Put the ribs in place, beginning at the end of the wing and working toward the center. It is not necessary to use much cement at first; but

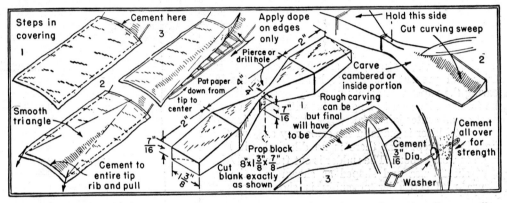

Figure 2. Important processes in making the plane—covering wings and carving the propeller.

of balsa and bind it with thread, as shown in the drawing. Cement this balsa strip to the fuselage at the point indicated in the diagram. Add two corner blocks to hold the landing gear firmly in place when the model lands.

WING AND TAIL. The hardest job in making the wing and tail is the cutting of the ribs, which have the shape known as the wing airfoil. The ribs are to be cut from 1/20″ sheet balsa. You will have to make yourself a rib pattern and then use this as a guide in cutting the ribs. Trace the full-size airfoil outline, as shown in Figure 3; paste the tracing on a piece of stiff paper, such as the covering of a notebook. Then cut the pattern. Use this to guide the razor blade as you work on the balsa sheet. (In kits the outlines of the airfoils are printed right on the balsa sheet.) The leading edge of the wing will fit in the notch at the front end of the rib; the center spar will fit through the notch (represented in black) at the center.

Before assembling the wings, make a full-

be sure to go over all the joints after the wing is taken off the plan. After all the ribs are in place, cement the leading edge. Apply cement to all notches before putting the leading edge in position. Hold it firmly against the ribs while the cement is drying, using pins.

The wing tip is made up of two pieces of 1/20″ sheet balsa, cut to shape roughly and then cemented together. When the cementing is done, place the tip under the wing end and cut it so that it will go in position. Cement the tip to the wings; you can make the exact outline afterward.

When you have finished the two halves of the wing, you are ready to put them together so as to form the dihedral angle, as shown in Figure 1. To form this angle, place one wing-half flat on the table. Prop up the other half by means of books so that the extreme tip will be five inches from the surface of the table. Bevel the ends of the center spars so that they will fit tightly. Then cement the two wing-halves together. When the cement

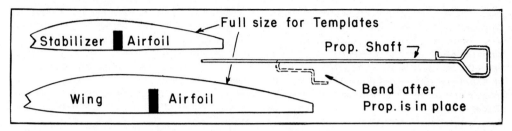

Figure 3. Full-size stabilizer, wing airfoil outlines and propeller shaft. Trace airfoil outlines; paste tracing on a piece of stiff paper. Then cut pattern and use it in working on the balsa sheet.

is dry, strengthen the center splice by adding strips of $\frac{3}{32}''$ x $\frac{1}{4}''$ x $1''$ balsa on each side. Because of these strips, you will have to make the spar slots on the center ribs larger so that they will slide over the reinforcement. After the ribs are set and the cement is holding them firmly, cut small $\frac{3}{32}''$ square slots to take the $\frac{3}{32}''$ strips, as shown. These strips will prevent the rubber band from tearing the paper when you put the wing on the fuselage. Be sure to be generous with cement on all center joints.

The stabilizer is made in the same way as the wing, except that there is no dihedral angle to worry about. The rudder is cut from $\frac{1}{20}''$ sheet balsa and shaped as shown in Figure 1. The rudder assembly is shown clearly in the diagram.

PROPELLER. In Figure 2 we give you a diagram of the propeller, as well as the method of carving. Make the blank as shown from a balsa block $8''$ x $1\frac{3}{8}''$ x $\frac{7}{8}''$ (first step). Carve the inside portion (second step); then sand it smooth before starting the outside part (third step). Apply two coats of model dope to the propeller; then sand it. Insert through the center of the propeller the straight end of the propeller shaft, which should be bent to shape as shown, to provide a winding loop and anchorage. Be sure that you have the nose plug and washers in the proper place before inserting the shaft. It is important that the washers on each side of the propeller should be well cemented in place.

COVERING. Start with the fuselage. First cut off enough tissue to cover one side of the fuselage, leaving a certain amount of surplus material at the edges. Apply dope to two uprights under the wing on each side of the fuselage, and also the parts of the longerons which are between these two. Place paper over this area and tap it against the strips so that the dope will seep through. Let the dope

dry. This will give you a firm starting place. The rest of the side is covered by raising the ends of the paper, covering two or three uprights and the longerons between them with dope and then placing paper over them. You will find that you will be able to stretch the paper a bit while you tap it down against the strips and dope. After the entire length of the fuselage is covered, trim off the surplus with a razor. Be sure to cement all loose edges to the longerons. Cover the rest of the fuselage in the same way. Cut out the paper on the top section over the dowel, as shown in Figure 1.

After you have covered the four sides of the fuselage, crumple into a ball the bits of excess tissue paper that you have cut off at the edges. Dip this ball of tissue in water, and then wet the entire surface of the fuselage with it. Apply it gently, as paper is very weak when it is wet. You will be surprised to see how tight the fuselage covering will be after it dries.

In covering the wing and tail, you are to use a special technique (see Figure 2). Cut a strip of tissue the general size and shape of half of the wing, allowing for excess material at the edges as before. First cover the top of the wing. Apply dope to the middle of the center rib and cement the tissue paper at this joint. When this is dry, coat the ends of the wing tip rib. Pull the tissue paper over the wing tip rib, smoothing the triangle formed by the middle of the center rib and the ends of the tip rib.

The part of the wing between the last vertical rib and the wing tip is covered by slitting the tissue lengthwise and working each segment in position separately. Next, cement the tissue paper to the leading and trailing edges; do *not* apply dope to any of the other ribs. Trim off the excess tissue paper. Do the other half of the wing top in the same way. Next, cover the lower halves of the wing. A dope brush, passed along the edges, will provide a smooth finish.

Wet the tissue paper as you did in the case of the fuselage covering. While it is drying, be sure that the wing is not being warped. Set one wing-half flat on the table and be sure that the extreme tip of the other wing-half is still at a distance of five inches from the surface of the table.

The next step is to give the entire model one coat of model dope. You can use rolled-up tissue for a brush. After the dope is dry, cut out the paper where the windows are and cement strips of celluloid, as shown. (You can omit this step, if you wish.) Finally cover and dope the stabilizer and the rudder.

FINAL TOUCHES. Our model is now almost done. Pins are cemented to the fuselage after covering, as shown in Figure 1. The wings are fastened to the top of the fuselage by means of a rubber band passed under the curved tops of pins. The stabilizer is cemented in place. As we have already mentioned, the nose plug assembly is held in place by means of a rubber band.

The motive power of the model is supplied by a continuous piece of $\frac{1}{8}''$ rubber, which is fastened at the ends and then looped to form from eight to twelve strands. Eight strands are enough for ordinary flying conditions; twelve are better for windy weather. These strands of rubber are to be our motor. Fasten one end of the rubber motor to the end of the propeller shaft. Tie a piece of string to the other end of the motor and drop it through the fuselage. Pull it out at the place where the top of the fuselage has been left open. Slip the dowel through the various strands of rubber and then set it in place. Untie the thread. Now put the nose plug in position, holding it fast by means of a rubber band.

FLYING. Lubricate the rubber with glycerine before you insert it in the fuselage. After the rubber is in place, you must wind it up. You can do so by holding the fuselage of the model in your left hand and by turning the propeller with the forefinger of your right hand. You can wind the propeller by hand from 80 to 150 turns (depending upon the elasticity of the rubber). You can wind it many more turns by using an ordinary hand drill, replacing the drill with a bent nail. Have a helper hold the model. Remove the rubber band from the nose block assembly. Then pull out the propeller, which is still connected to the rubber motor, and stretch the rubber to about four times its normal length. Insert the wire hook at the nose of the propeller in the hook formed by the bent nail in the hand drill. Turn the handle of the latter so that you will have from 300 to 500 turns on the motor (depending again upon the elasticity of the rubber). Holding the propeller firmly so that it will not turn, replace it in position and secure the nose block to the fuselage with the elastic band.

You should pick a grassy and open place for flying. Face the wind and launch your plane. If it dives into the ground, add a bit of modeling clay to the tail. If it points upward after launching and then drops, add clay to the front part of the fuselage. Very little clay will be needed in either case. If you move the trailing edge of the rudder to the right (looking from the rear), the model will circle to the right. It will fly much better than if it were headed in a forward direction.

This model will not have much of a glide after the motor can no longer supply power, as the propeller will act as a brake. More advanced designs have free-wheeling propellers, which make it easier to obtain smooth glides. On larger models we use propellers whose blades fold along the body during the glide. If your model is equipped in this way it will be able to make unusually long flights. Your hobby dealer may be able to show you how you can prepare such a propeller.

A SIMPLE MATCH TRICK

YOU can arrange twelve matches to form an equation in this way:

The unfortunate thing about this equation is that it is wrong; as you know six minus four does not equal nine. However you can make the equation correct by changing the position of a single match. The solution is given on page 420.

A MIND-READING TRICK

HERE is an arithmetical trick that may give you the reputation of being a mind reader. Tell one of your friends to think of a number made up of three figures, the first and last of which are not the same. Let him form a second number by reversing the figures of the first. Next, he is to subtract the smaller of these two numbers from the larger. If the answer consists of two figures, you will be able to tell him what these are. If there are three figures in the answer, let him give you the first of these and you will be able to give the other two.

For example, suppose the number that your friend chooses is 201. Reversing the figures in this number, we have 102. If we subtract 102 from 201, the answer is 99. There are two figures in the answer. When this is so, the two figures are always 99!

Let us take another example. Suppose your friend selects 237. Reversing the figures, we have 732. If we subtract 237 from 732, the answer is 495. Your friend will inform you that there are three figures in the answer. If he tells you that the first figure is 4, you will be able to give him the other two figures—9 and 5. You simply subtract the first figure from 9 and that will give you the last figure. The second figure in the answer is always 9.

Solution of the match trick on page 419

THIS is how you must arrange the matches in order to have a correct equation:

$$VI + IV = X$$

$$V + IV = IX$$

Answer to the problem on page 413

THE old Arab told the three sons to take one of his own camels and add it to their father's animals; thus there were 18 in all. The oldest son was to take one-half of these 18 camels: that is, 9. As he was only supposed to receive $8\frac{1}{4}$ camels (one-half of 17) by the terms of his father's will, he was entirely satisfied. The second son was to take one-third of the 18 camels, or 6. He, too, was content as he was supposed to receive one-third of 17 camels, or $5\frac{2}{3}$ camels by the will. The youngest son was to take one-ninth of the 18 camels, or 2. Of course he was also satisfied, since he was originally supposed to receive one-ninth of 17 camels, or $1\frac{8}{9}$.

The old man then said: "You have taken 9 plus 6 plus 2 camels; that makes 17 in all. That means that you will be able to give me back the camel that I let you have." This was possible because the father of the three young Arabs had not really left his entire fortune to his three sons, but only seventeen-eighteenths of it.

$$\frac{1}{2} + \frac{1}{3} + \frac{1}{9} = \frac{17}{18}$$

INDEX

A

A4-b, rocket, 215
ANTU, chemical, 130
Abdullah Ibn Ul-Hussein, 260, 262-64
Africa
    expedition from Nairobi, 173-78
    Union of South Africa, 377-79
    See also Middle East
Aftosa, hoof-and-mouth disease, 259
Agriculture
    helicopters used to dust crops, 66
    in Deep South, U. S., 140
    in Mexico, 258-59
    in U. S., 389-91
    soil conservation, 14-20
    terrace-farming in Peru, 295
Air Force, Royal Canadian, 85
Air Force, U. S., 387-88
Airlift, into Berlin, 62-64, 160
Airplanes, model, how to make, 414-19
    See also Aviation
Akalakuf Indians, of South America, 230
Alabama, 140-42
Alaska, 134-35
    government, 200
Alaska Highway, 87, 101-02, 136
Alberta
    Leduc oil field, 86
Alcor, star, 40-41, 45
Algol, star, 43, 46
Aluminum industry, Quebec, 231-32
Amazon River
    headwaters, in Peru, 293
Amazon Valley, 136-38
Ambrose Channel lightship, 243
American Indians
    Aymarás, 294
    folklore variations, 180-82
    Guaranis, 286-87
    Incas, 295-96
    of Northwest Territories, 100-01
    of South America, 224-30
    place names, 313
    Quechuas, 294-95
Amino-acids, 319-21
Anderson, Clinton P., 391-92
Andes Mountains, in Peru, 298
Animals
    chimpanzees learn to use "money," 265-67
    elephant-training, Congo, 177
    hoof-and-mouth disease, 259
    Lerner Marine Laboratory, 75-78
    new discoveries about, 73-74
    pets, 299-302
Antarctica
    Ronne expedition, 21-25

Apes
    chimpanzees learn to use "money," 265-67
Arabia
    oil pipe line, 307-11
Arabs
    conflict with Israel, 262-64
Arab's will, puzzle, 413
Araucanian Indians, of South America, 230
Architecture
    homes in Canada and U. S., 26-28
Arctic regions
    Canadian development, 86
    Greenland, 201-04
    Peary cache, 290-92
Argentina, 329-31
    government, 195-96
Arithmetic trick, 420
Arkansas, 140, 142
Army, Royal Canadian, 85
Army, U. S., 387-88
Art
    French tapestries, 360-63
    illustration as a career, 112-15
Arvida, Quebec, bridge, 231
Asia
    year's events, 29-36
    See also Middle East
Astronomy, 37-39
    double stars, 40-46
Atahualpas, Inca ruler, 295-96
Atherton, Gertrude (1857-1948), American novel-
    ist. An almost legendary figure in San Fran-
    cisco, her birthplace, her books had a wide
    variety of backgrounds, from ancient Greece
    to modern California. Among the most widely
    read were Black Oxen and The Conqueror.
Atlantic Union, 85
Atom-smashers, 304-06
Atomic energy
    Canadian development, 87
    for aircraft propulsion, 64
    peacetime uses, 47-50
Atomic particles
    mesons, 303-06
Aureomycin, drug, 130
Auriga, constellation, 41, 44
Australia, 51-54
Austria, 156
Automobiles
    development, 55-56
    magnetic oil clutch, 306
    trucking freight, 235
Aviation
    advances, 57-64
    Berlin Airlift, 62-64, 160
    cargo planes, 235-36
    helicopters, 65-67
    in Canada, 86, 88

421

D

G

Games
See Sports
Gandhi, Mohandas K. (1869-1948), leader of the independence movement in India for more than 20 years. It was largely through his efforts that India became a dominion in 1947, though divided. Regarded as one of the truly great men of the 20th century, he was utterly selfless and devoted to the Indian people, who called him Mahatma (Great Soul). He was assassinated by a Hindu fanatic. *See also* 30.
Gas, natural, pipe lines, 236
Gas turbine engines, 188-89
Gasoline from coal, 186-89
Generators, ultrasonic, 376
Georgetown, British Guiana, 205-06
Germany, 156, 158-61
    Berlin Airlift, 62-64, 160
Germs
    effect of ultrasonics on, 375-76
    germ-killers, 130
Girl Guides, 398-99
Girl Scouts, 397-98
Glaspell, Susan (1882-1948), American playwright and novelist. Her play Alison's House, produced in 1930, won the Pulitzer Prize; her novels included Brook Evans, Fugitive's Return, and Judd Rankin's Daughter. Founder with her husband, George Cram Cook, of the original Provincetown (Cape Cod) Playhouse, she is credited with having given Eugene O'Neill his start in the theater.
Glass fibers, 129, 367-68
Gliders, in Canada, 88
Gloucester, Mass., light, 241
Glubb Pasha, 260, 263
Gobelin tapestries, 362-63
Gold, changed into mercury, 50
Gold rush, California, 183-85
Goldfish pets, 302
Golf, 356-57
González, Juan Natalicio, 289
Goodricke, John, 44
Governments, of Western Hemisphere, 192-200
Gran Chaco, South America, 285-86, 288-89
Grass farming, 20
Great Bear Lake, 100
Great Britain
    colonies in Western Hemisphere, 198-99
    Eddystone Light, 242
    Guiana, 205-09
    Kenya territory, 173-75
    Palestine mandate, 260-61
    year's events, 157, 162
Great Lakes waterway, 91-95
Greece, 163
Greece, ancient
    North American place names from, 314-15
    Orpheus and Eurydice myth, 172-82
Greenland, 201-04
    government, 199

Griffith, David Wark (1875-1948), pioneer American movie director. His film Birth of a Nation, produced in 1915, is a landmark in the history of motion pictures. He introduced such techniques as the close-up, the cut-back (cutting back and forth between 2 scenes), using lighting to heighten dramatic value, and cutting—methods which are still used. He also made prominent such players as Mary Pickford, Dorothy and Lillian Gish, Alice Joyce and Richard Barthelmess.
Guadeloupe, 198
Guarani Indians, 286-87
Guianas, 205-09
    governments, 198-99
Guided missiles, 210-15
Guinea-pig pets, 301-02
Gunarhnesemgyet, myth of northwest Indians, 181-82

H

Harriman, W. Averell, 391
Harrison, Mary Scott Dimmick (1858-1948), widow of the 23rd president of the U. S., Benjamin Harrison. She never occupied the White House as first lady, as she was married to the former President three years after his administration. Up to her death she retained an interest in national politics.
Hatta, Mohammed, 35
Hatteras Light, N. C., 241
Hawaii
    myth of Hiku, 180
Haynes, Elwood, 56
Health
    research on disease, 72-73
Heat pumps, 190-91
Hebrews, *see* Jews
Helicopters, in Canada, 65-67
Herschel, Sir William, 41-42
Herzfeld, Ernst Emil (1880-1948), German-born archeologist and retired professor in the School of Humanistic Studies at the Institute for Advanced Study in Princeton, N. J. He was a world-famous authority on Babylonia.
Hiku, in Hawaiian myth, 180
Hobbies
    doll collecting, 146-54
Hockey, ice, 358-59
Holland, *see* Netherlands
Hollywood Bowl summer concerts, 274
Hoof-and-mouth disease, 259
Horse racing, 359
House heating
    from the earth, 190–91
Housing
    U. S. shortage, 390
Hughes, Charles Evans (1862-1948), chief justice of the U. S. Supreme Court 1930-41, Secretary of State 1920-25, governor of New York twice (earlier) and Republican candidate for president in 1916. He achieved world-wide

M

Spaatz, Carl, 388
Spain, 156, 163
    conquest of Peru, 295-96
    rule in Paraguay, 286-87
Speaks, Oley, 276
Spectroscope, astronomical instrument, 45-46
Spectroscopic double stars, 46
Spelunking, 332-34
Sports
    in Canada, 87-88
    Olympic Games, 335-39
    professional sports, 351-52
    pitching baseball, 340-42
    sailing, 343-46
    single wing or T formation, football, 347-50
    year's events, 353-59
Stars, 37-39
    double stars, 40-46
Stassen, Harold E., 392
Staten Island, N. Y.
    Billop House, 27
States' Rights Democrats, 392-93
Steam power, 233-34
Steel, ultrasonic tests for, 376
Stokowski, Olga Samaroff (1883-1948), American
    musician. She was an outstanding pianist,
    teacher of such noted performers as William
    Kapell, Eugene List and Joseph Battista, and
    music critic. Her popular Layman's Music
    Course was a regular feature at Town Hall,
    New York City.
Stories, folklore variations, 179-82
Stratosphere balloons, 58
Strip cropping, in farming, 19-20
Subsonic speed, 60-61
Summer concerts, 273-75
Supersonic speed, 60-61
Surgery
    use of ultrasonics, 376
Surinam, 205-09
    government, 199
Synchrotrons, 306
Syria, 262-63

T

T formation, football, 347-50
Taft, Robert A., 392
Taft-Hartley Act, 390-91
Tapestries, French, 360-63
Tapline, Arabian pipe line, 308-11
Taxes
    in U. S., 390
Taylor, Glen, 392
Tehuelches Indians, of South America, 230
Telephones, long distance, 364-66
Telescopes, 37-39
Television and radio, 322-25
    musical programs, 273
Tennessee, 139
Tennis, 357
    Davis Cup matches, 54
Terracing, in farming, 19

Textiles
    French tapestries, 360-63
    new chemical treatments, 128-29
    new yarns and fabrics, 367-69
Texture, in fabrics, 368-69
Theater
    ballet, 68-71
    children's theaters, 370-71
Things to make and do, 405-20
Thiophos, chemical, 130
Thurmond, J. Strom, 393
Tiahuanaco people, of Bolivia, 226
Tierra del Fuego, South America
    development of, 138
    Indians of, 230
Tillamook Rock, Oregon, 240
Tingo María Highway, 137
Tinker, Joe (1880-1948), American baseball player.
    With Johnny Evers, Tinker formed one of the
    greatest second-base combinations of all time.
    These two, with Frank Chance, gave their
    names to an expression which has become part of
    the language—"Tinker-to-Evers-to-Chance"—
    for the most famous double play in baseball
    history.
Tito, Marshal, 158
Tobin, Maurice J., 392
Toronto, Ontario, 89-90
    Opera School of Royal Conservatory of Music,
    276
Tracer atoms (isotopes), 48-50
Track and field, sports, 357-58
Trade
    Canadian, 83
    in South America, 328-29
Transistor, radio tube, 303, 306
Trans-Jordan, 260, 262-64
Transonic speed, 60-61
Transportation
    Alaska Highway, 101-02, 136
    automobile development, 55-56
    Canadian waterways, 91-96
    development in relation to industry, 231-36
    gas turbine engines, 188-89
    Tingo María Highway, 137
Tricks, 419-20
Triple Alliance, War of, 288
Truman, Harry S., 316-18, 390, 392-93
Tsimsyan Indians, folklore, 181-82
Turbojet engines, 59
Turboprop engines, 60
Turkey, 264
Tuscaloosa, Alabama, 142-43
2,4-D, chemical, 130

U

Ultrafax, communication device, 303
Ultrasonics, 372-76
Union of South Africa, 377-79
Union of Soviet Socialist Republics, 161-62
    music criticism, 275
    relations with U. S., 384, 386-87

V

W

X

Y

Z

PRINTED IN U. S. A.